MOVING IMAGES OF ETERNITY

MOVING IMAGES OF ETERNITY
George Grant's Critique of Time, Teaching, and Technology

William F. Pinar

University of Ottawa Press
2019

University of Ottawa **Press**
Les **Presses** de l'Université d'Ottawa

The University of Ottawa Press (UOP) is proud to be the oldest of the francophone university presses in Canada and the only bilingual university publisher in North America. Since 1936, UOP has been "enriching intellectual and cultural discourse" by producing peer-reviewed and award-winning books in the humanities and social sciences, in French or in English.

Library and Archives Canada Cataloguing in Publication

Title: Moving images of eternity: George Grant's critique of time, teaching, and technology / William F. Pinar.
Other titles: George Grant's critique of time, teaching, and technology
Names: Pinar, William F., author.
Description: Includes bibliographical references and index.
Identifiers: Canadiana (print) 20190079800 | Canadiana (ebook) 20190079916 | ISBN 9780776627878 (softcover) | ISBN 9780776627885 (PDF) | ISBN 9780776627892 (EPUB) | ISBN 9780776627908 (Kindle)
Subjects: LCSH: Grant, George Parkin, 1918-1988.
Classification: LCC B995.G724 P56 2019 | DDC 191—dc23

Legal Deposit: 2019
Library and Archives Canada
© University of Ottawa Press 2019

Copy editing	Robbie McCaw
Proofreading	Robert Ferguson
Typesetting	Édiscript enr.
Cover design	Édiscript enr.
Cover image	Untitled by Paul Butler, 2017, 24 × 24, collage based Diasec mounted C-print. Reproduced with kind permission from the artist.

The University of Ottawa Press gratefully acknowledges the support extended to its publishing list by Canadian Heritage through the Canada Book Fund, by the Canada Council for the Arts, by the Ontario Arts Council, by the Federation for the Humanities and Social Sciences through the Awards to Scholarly Publications Program, and by the University of Ottawa.

  Canada

u Ottawa

Table of Contents

Acknowledgements

I am grateful to Dwayne Huebner and William E. Doll Jr. for their invocations of spirituality, an intermittent interest of mine that is intermittent no longer. Thanks again to Bill Doll for his emphasis upon modernity, another topic with which George Grant was much engaged. My thanks to John Willinsky for suggesting I publish this project in Canada, and to Nicholas Ng-A-Fook, who encouraged me to pursue its publication at the University of Ottawa Press. My thanks to Samuel Rocha for suggesting Jean-Luc Marion; to Dónal O'Donoghue for recommending Williams' *Ponder These Things*; Fay Bigloo for giving me a copy of Jalal Al-i Ahmad's *Occidentosis*; and to Bruce Moghtader, who not only recommended reading Marie-José Mondzain's *Image, Icon, Economy* but who helped—along with Xinyan Fan—with permissions, no small task in a citation-centred study. Bruce also kept his editorial eye open, scanning the manuscript slowly and carefully; Bruce also helped me make adjustments in light of the anonymous reviewers' recommendations. Finally, my thanks to members of the 2017 fall term George Grant seminar, whose careful study and questioning animated mine.

Preface

Formerly famous,[1] now forgotten, George Grant (1918–1988) becomes compelling in an era eclipsed by technology—rendering reality virtual, news fake;[2] punctuated by tweets and school shootings; by stolen identities, personal data, and presidential elections; by bullying, sexting, and standardized testing—an era some characterize as "posthuman."[3] Submerged in the present, we lose the perspective the past provides. Technology dissolves time, replacing it with an endless immediacy, substituting simulation for embodied experience, ocularcentrism for orality, the cloud occluding what is concealed underneath the Internet of things. Sixty years ago, George Grant cautioned Canadians concerning the cultural consequences of unconstrained technological development.[4] That prescience is evident in his critique of time, teaching, and technology.

Technology seems salvational—medical, economic, and educational breakthroughs are among those areas depending upon its development—but fusion with it can carry unwelcome consequences: interpersonally, spiritually, intellectually.[5] Technology murders materially, and on a mass scale, as Grant knew from his own experience of the 1940 bombing of London by the Luftwaffe. Grant knew that pinning all our hopes on technology—rendering it an idol—abdicates our moral responsibility to relegate it to its proper place, a prosthetic extension of compassion, for example, another medium of justice. Time is not only money, to be compressed until it becomes a curse, it is also a gift to be lived through and reflected on, another moving image of eternity. Teaching is no conversion of objectives to outcomes, a magician's trick that can be informative even entertaining but not necessarily educational. Teaching is also not only vocational training, not even the academic kind, but, as Grant knew, a testimony to the meaning and mystery of life on earth. Curriculum is crucial, as it authorizes what students study and teachers teach. Like time and technology, teaching too can become iconographic—not idolatrous, not an end in itself—but a conveyance to transcendence. It was for George Grant.

Through the recovery of his moment, we might experience (or re-experience, for those who were alive then) the moment before we disappeared into our devices. Digging deep into the thought of one person,[6] we might glimpse what ethical engagement—with the historical moment, with the place wherein we dwell, and to what the transcendence of both—might mean for us: as educators and students, particular persons alive now.

The preservation of particularities—including the continuance of Canada itself—comprised Grant's abiding concern, worried as he was that globalization would erase local as well as national histories and cultures. Replacing these particularities would be a technological homogeneity universally enforced. Within his panoramic perception of what could come, present-day eruptions of right-wing populism—notably in the United Kingdom and the United States, but hardly only there—seem predictable, if pathetic, protests against what Grant warned.

Educationally, the universal homogenous "state" exists already. Globalization of standardized testing—the most prominent instance of which is the Program for International Student Assessment—reduces learning to standardized test scores and teaching to test preparation, threatening to restructure schools into technological sites of political socialization, conditioning children for compliance to a universal, homogeneous state of mind. For humanity's survival—political, cultural, ecological—returning education to its sacred calling was, for Grant, urgent. Despite his denials, Grant remained a progressive who, during the calamitous historical moment that was the Second World War, accepted Christianity, later juxtaposing it with Platonism, thereby crafting an apparently incompatible combination that compelled him to work through the inexorable tensions interlocking secularism, spirituality, politics, and education.

While there are superb studies of Grant as political philosopher and theologian—upon which I draw—there is no sustained study of Grant as educator, and, specifically, no study of his teaching's intertwined relation to his political philosophy and theology. No study has drawn extensively on the collected works—including his talks to teachers and his doctoral thesis—or upon his biography, the collected letters, and the considerable secondary literature, all of which are referenced here extensively. This is, then, a citation-centred study that enacts my conception of curriculum as complicated conversation, in this case among Grant, his time and place, his colleagues and students, and, most broadly, his fellow citizens of Canada.

This book is what we curriculum specialists term a "synoptic text," an overview of a subject or person; that is, the much-maligned textbook. In the past, structuring the textbook by sequence—proceeding from the simple to the complex, from the past to the present, often by topic—has served us well, but I have supplemented these time-tested forms of sequencing with the concept of juxtaposition,[7] subject matter in tension with itself, a generative tension[8] that encourages readers to proceed more slowly, encouraging contemplation, not takeaways.[9] Conceiving knowledge as palimpsest—a conception that emphasizes its embeddedness in other knowledge, including suppressed and marginalized knowledges—encourages juxtaposition, as the fissures juxtaposition etches can disclose what resides just under the surface, an excavation I enact with what might seem to be endless endnotes. Irritating for those who want to be done with it, for those who affirm academic study as a spiritual as well intellectual undertaking, interrupting the main text with constant commentary on it could be a welcomed opportunity to study slowly, to contemplate, to question.

Aside from its synoptic status—it can serve a reference book for students of Grant as well as textbook for students of education, encouraging all, I trust, to return to Grant's original texts—this volume includes (1) my interpretation of Grant's critique of time, teaching, and technology as a critique of idolatry; (2) my emphasis on his praise of Eastern Christianity's reverence for icons, associated also with his study of Simone Weil, from whose work I quote, accenting her influence on Grant; (3) my reconstruction of Grant's critique through the elaboration of concepts of attunement; and (4) my characterization of Grant as a progressive Christian Platonist, that first contradictory term an acknowledgement of his imprinting as a child and of his life-long (if inadvertent) affinities with John Dewey; and (4) my commentary on one of Grant's keywords—eternity—juxtaposed with time. My teaching of Grant emphasizes his timeliness, his timelessness, acknowledging his prescience by referencing educational issues today—especially the technologization of education—that Grant critiqued decades ago.

I was drawn to Grant's concentration upon curriculum, both as a course of study and as a live, ongoing event.[10] A student of the subjectivity[11] of educational experience, I was intrigued by a scholar who disdained the autobiographical as he blurred the lines between his lived experience and his teaching. A critic of the profession's uncritical enthusiasm for technology in education, I share Grant's skepticism concerning technology—acutely aware, as he was, of its associated military, ecological, and cultural concomitants—and his acknowledgement that it's not going anywhere. His questions are mine: How are we to live with it, within it, with it inside us? What's left of us when we separate from the device?

Then there's the spiritual issue. A secular person, I have wondered from where comes my moralism: my life-long efforts[12] at subjective and social reconstruction animated by indignation at economic inequality, political oppression, cultural genocide. Studying Grant compelled me to face my moral imperative autobiographically and theologically, accepting (not without struggle) that my secularism has its spiritual subtext.

As an American, I was forced to face my own national imprinting: political and psychic and intellectual. Completing the book after the triumph of Trump has forced me to face (yet again) my country and myself. That turning inward— "working from within" is the phrase I invoked in 1972 to name the location of academic study—remains for me the touchstone[13] of teaching, recasting the classroom as civic square *and* a room of one's own, the teacher as a private and public intellectual. Grant was both.

I address Grant's significance for us alive now in more detail in chapter 1. In chapters 2–4 I focus on Grant's critique of time, teaching, and technology; I attempt to reactivate Grant so you might hear him again, speaking to you now. These are followed by three chapters (5–7) in which I reconstruct his critique into terms of idolatry, iconography, and attunement, with an eye toward eternity. The first term names Grant's critique and our dilemma still, the second and third provide possible if elusive means to extricate ourselves from it. Eternity is an enabling abstraction, encouraging us to convert our idols into icons. The introduction outlines the book as it defines keywords; I conclude with an epilogue wherein I review the main points and show (again) Grant's profound pertinence for students and teachers today.

I intend these terms—"students" and "teachers"—in their broadest possible sense, teachers whose students include themselves, as well as the very young and the aged, those enrolled in educational institutions and those taught informally in families, among friends and fellow citizens. Grant's adult-education work expanded his sense of teaching to encompass what now is termed "public pedagogy."[14] Through his CBC (Canadian Broadcasting Corporation) broadcasts, his books, and lectures, Grant's classroom, it seems clear, was Canada itself. And, it is also clear, through his ongoing academic study he also taught himself.

Grant threaded his teaching through his academic erudition but also through himself as a human being, alive in a certain place at a certain time, faced with specific students struggling to traverse generational divides over politics, culture, and identity.[15] Intensely attentive to those in his midst, Grant taught from his head and his heart. No monolith, indeed infinitely inspired, Grant's subjective presence inspired others to become subjectively present too, comforted and challenged when realizing that Grant's struggle was also their own. A teacher disinterested in disciples, Grant enabled others—individuals and a generation—to find their own ways, and on their own terms, protesting those conditions that disabled them and others from doing the same. Is that not our obligation, too, inhabiting a planet threatened by political, economic, and ecological catastrophe? Grant sensed this state of emergency sixty years ago. By reactivating his alarm, we might re-experience a past when there seemed to be more time, time when we were less submerged in the screen. From that past we might find our way to a future unforeclosed by the present.

Notes

1. Already known for his 1959 *Philosophy in the Mass Age*, Grant was catapulted to centre stage of Canadian nationalism upon publication of his 1965 *Lament for a Nation: The Defeat of Canadian Nationalism*.

2. "The Nazis applied the term *Lügenpresse* (lying press) to the mainstream press," Sunstein (2018, June 28, 65) reminds; U.S. President Trump refers to the "FAKE

NEWS media," which, he says, "is not my enemy, it is the enemy of the American People!" The phrase is not the exclusive property of authoritarian rulers; it now depicts the "post truth" culture widely available online. One conspicuous example is Alex Jones, whose InfoWars website is viewed by millions; Jones alleges that the 2012 shooting that killed twenty first-graders and six adults at an elementary school in Newtown, Connecticut, never happened, that it was a fabrication scripted by government-backed "gun-grabbers" (quoted in E. Williamson 2018, A1). As Elizabeth Williamson reported in the *New York Times*, the families of Sandy Hook victims still suffer "daily threats" and "online abuse" (A1) from those who trust Jones' account. In 2018, in three separate lawsuits, the families of eight Sandy Hook victims and an FBI agent who responded to the shooting sought damages for defamation, alleging, in one suit, that Jones and his colleagues "persistently perpetuated a monstrous, unspeakable lie: that the Sandy Hook shooting was staged, and that the families who lost loved ones that day are actors who faked their relatives' deaths" (A16). "More broadly," Williamson suggests, "the families are seeking society's verdict on 'post-truth' culture in which widely disseminated lies damage lives and destroy reputation, yet those who spread them are seldom held accountable" (A16).

3. See, e.g., Foster 2005.

4. Grant also appreciated the reduction of toil—especially manual labour—technology engineers, although automation can also be a problem; artificial intelligence threatens to produce, if not massive unemployment, at least massive redeployment. Lohr (2017, B3) reports that in November 2017 the McKinsey Global Institute concluded that, thanks to technologization, "Up to one third of the American work force will have to switch to new occupations by 2030, in about a dozen years." Increasingly technologized and dependent upon the American economy, can the Canadian workforce be insulated?

5. "Technology is not neutral," reminded Mehran Salhami, a Stanford University computer-science professor who is helping to develop coursework on the ethics and regulation of artificial intelligence. "The choices that get made in building technology then have social ramifications." Laura Norén, a postdoctoral fellow at New York University who is teaching a new data science ethics course cautioned: "We need to at least teach people that there's a dark side to the idea that you should move fast and break things. You can patch the software, but you can't patch a person" (quoted in Singer 2018, B4). Harvard, the Massachusetts Institute of Technology, and the University of Texas at Austin are among US universities offering course on the ethics and regulation of artificial intelligence, Singer reports.

6. Like Caputo (1987, 289), "I want to dust off an old word...*per-sona, per-sonare*, the person as sounding-through, resonating." In contrast, he continues, "to the modern notion of self-identical ego or self-present consciousness, the old sense of *per-sona* speaks in terms of difference and non-identity. It recognizes the media, the per, that nothing is immediately given or present here" (289).

7. I am not alone. In her work with teachers, Teresa Strong-Wilson (2008, 63) regarded "juxtaposition of stories" as "part of the process...in 'bringing memory forward.'" She explains: "I juxtaposed a familiar with an unfamiliar story; we read the familiar one first, then the unfamiliar one. The familiar book constructed 'the Other' within a mainstream ('white') imagination; the unfamiliar book was a story written by an

'Othered author'" (63). Such juxtaposition can question both categories as it creates crevices between them, requiring reconsideration of each.

8.   Speaking of the lived space between Japanese and English (his own internally juxtaposed cultures), Aoki ([1995] 2005, 310) describes it as "a space of paradoxical ambivalence," but "a generative space of difference, an enunciatory space of becoming, a space where newness emerges."

9.   "Take-away" is a concept emphasizing action, relegating information to its utility. Ordinarily defined historically as the era after industrialism, characterized by proliferating publication made possible by computers and computer networks, *informationalism* also denotes a distancing between the subject of writing and the writing itself, resulting in what Grant decried as objectification (see ch. 5). While I write *about* Grant—at a distance—I also worked to write *within* his lingering subjective presence (embedded in his writing), as if sitting in his seminar while alone in my study, attempting to bridge his time, his thought, his teaching, and mine.

10.   What Aoki theorized as the "curriculum-as-planned and the curriculum-as-lived;" see Aoki (1986/1991) 2005, 159.

11.   Subjectivity is what technology eviscerates, evident in the effects of what Jalal Al-i Ahmad (1984, 135), referencing Camus' *The Plague*, termed "occidentosis"—Iran's cultural colonization by the West. Colonization resembles, he thought, an "infestation of weevils. Have you seen how they attack wheat? From the inside. The bran remains intact, but it is just a shell, like a cocoon left behind on a tree" (27). The colonization Al-i Ahmad condemns is, above all, technologization. "We," referencing his fellow Iranians, "have been unable to take a considered stand in the face of this contemporary monster" (31; privately published, serialized in a censored format in 1962, then banned, the uncensored book was published in Tehran in 1978, following the revolution). Have "we" in the West? That is what Grant's critique encourages "us" to do.

12.   These were intertwined with sexual and other experiments, what, during disco days, we termed "divine decadence."

13.   "The tenacity of touchstones," Strong-Wilson (2008, 105) suggests, "would seem to lie in large part to a pronounced attachment to particular experiences."

14.   For one chilling and inspiring example, see Salvio 2017.

15.   Such divides can be—no doubt were—lacerating, but they can also, like those crevices created by juxtaposition, encourage subjective and social reconstruction, a political possibility African-American philosopher Alain Locke realized in his theorization of a black renaissance in 1920s America. For Locke, Stewart (2018, 821) points out, "culture was always a choice, and aesthetics was not just transcendence of a colonial mentality, but a way to reconstruct one's identity in ways that eluded the erosions of racism." Grant too affirmed culture as a means of eluding the erosions continentalism—Americanization—effected.

Introduction

> Education is itself the purpose of our existence.[1]
>
> George Grant

"A good society," Grant remembers, "was one in which as many people as possible came to that liberation of the soul. Society existed to promote the education of persons, not vice versa."[2] Such education was "often confined to a pitiably few," but, at least in theoretical terms, one "knew what the real point [was] in educating people."[3] The question we face now, Grant argued, was the provision of education in its "broadest sense," to counter the "new boredom of passive acquiescence in pleasures arranged by others."[4] In "rightfully cultivating the fullest equality," he cautioned, can we manage to avoid producing "a society of mediocrity and sameness rather than of quality and individuality?"[5] Not education for endless freedom[6]—a concept confined to consumer choice and profit-seeking in an economistic era[7]—but for "order and self-discipline," a "society which restrains the selfish and the greedy without becoming so authoritarian that individual initiative is crushed."[8]

Faced with such a challenge, at such a historical conjuncture, what action can the educator possibly take, except, as Grant ruefully suggested, "play the role of flatterers to a disappearing democracy."[9] While he will return to the past in his efforts to supersede this nightmarish moment, Grant remains firmly planted in the historical present:

> To meet such a situation, our democracy must consciously stimulate the equality of participation in mind, in ways that it has never dreamed of in the past.... To overcome the impersonality of the mass society, new relationships in work

1

and leisure must be developed and lived out; indeed new relationships at every level of existence—in art, in sex, and in religion.[10]

Trying to think the whole from within the world, that was the scale of Grant's aspiration.[11]

One aspires to understand the whole while splintered into parts, too many of us struggling to survive physically, suffering extreme poverty in the midst of outrageous wealth. Grant knew that in a society like ours—"where wealth and power and comfort and success are more and more exalted as the ends for which life should be lived"—education is reduced to a "useful means to achieve these other ends."[12] In such a society, Grant knew, "there can be no possibility that that the teaching profession will be considered seriously," why in Canada, he thought, "despite a lot of pious platitudes to the contrary," the "teaching profession is not considered of great importance."[13] Prosperity does not require education, Grant pointed out, and, he continued, success might even come more easily to those who know less: less about ethics and spirituality, that is, less about the history of economic inequality and social injustice.

The relegation of education to means, not ends—indeed the "transformation of the *homo sapiens* into the *homo economicus*"[14]—is evident in the "half-truth" that "education is everybody's business."[15] While Grant acknowledges the half that is truthful—it *is* everyone's obligation to ensure that all children are well educated—he focuses on the half that is false: that education is a business. The person[16] who studies the humanities, especially philosophy, "will know," Grant courageously asserts, "what these subjects do for the human soul in a way that the parent who is a salesman or an engineer just cannot know."[17] But in a society where the economy defines everything, he laments[18] that "everybody thinks they know automatically what is good—power, success, and wealth—and as I have said, all else is seen as subsidiary to those ends."[19] The teaching profession, he concludes, "can only become what it should be if the spiritual end of education is consciously known and held."[20]

"Known" and "held" imply remembrance and memory. But "in very fast-moving technical societies," Grant knew, "memory goes."[21] Distraction, demands, self-dissolution—one runs fast to remain in place, updating to stay the same.[22] "If memory goes," Grant cautioned, "men and women cease to be men and women because memory is one of the most prodigious observers of good in the world. You can memorize bad things and can be terrible, but without it one is lost."[23] When information is available online, why remember anything?

It was 2017 when I began composing this introduction—the year of Canada's sesquicentenary—I was nearing what I suspected might be the midpoint of the book.[24] That spring term I offered a course on Grant, in the announcement reminding students of Grant's centrality to Anglo-Canadian nationalism and to the disciplinary establishment of Canadian studies. There were, alas, only six takers. With budget constraints in place, the course was cancelled, rescheduled for the summer, when schoolteachers often come to campus for coursework. By mid-June the enrolment figure had not increased, and so the Grant course was rescheduled for the fall.

There are reasons why George Grant's Critique of Education (the course title) might not be a compelling topic for students of education. One is that the field has been dominated by technique—as Grant knew, the "central revolution of our era" is the "technological revolution"[25]—so that students may well have been scanning offerings for courses that could prove useful in their teaching. Practicality[26] has proven powerful in the academic field of education, perhaps less so in Canada[27] than in the United States, and on that topic, as well as on technique, Grant has many comments to make.[28] He told David Cayley:

> Well, I think first of all that whatever the relation between the theoretical and the practical life there is bound to be some division, and so there is something nonsensical about giving immediate advice to people who have to carry it out practically. I think there is something impudent about that…. Secondly, I would say that anybody who carries theories so far that he says that it doesn't matter what happens is just an ass. What everybody does finally matters— whether they are theoretical or practical people.[29]

In curriculum studies—the field of my specialization and a subject on which Grant had strong convictions[30]—more specific and political reasons could have been in play why the course was passed by.

In curriculum studies the political has come to predominate, replacing the canonical curriculum question What knowledge is of most worth?[31] with *Whose* knowledge is of most worth? After the 1960s, neo-Marxism animated a politicized curriculum studies field in the United States, but by the turn of the century *class* had splintered into *identity*: gender had been first to the forefront, quickly followed by race. In Canada, gender was also first, but truth and reconciliation with Indigenous peoples has come to occupy centre stage today. Accompanying these developments have been eddies of emotion that, while understandable, threaten to swallow the histories that made these political movements necessary. I decode this emotion as indignation over an unjust past and its inadequate representation in the school curriculum and in the academic field devoted to curriculum. Self-appointed representatives of those who have suffered—who suffer still—sometimes assume a moral superiority to those whose ancestors may have participated in (or at least acquiesced to) the injustices whose consequences reverberate so strongly today. Because the past was unjust it seems to many righteous to dismiss it.

Judging actors from earlier eras in terms current today seems irresistible, despite long-standing historiographical cautions and principles. Doing so makes easy discarding a past that does not serve present preoccupations. But then how would one know what might serve the present unless one has studied the past?

Samuel Rocha critiques "this notion of identity as a false representation of vitality," adding that "there is a sense that we live through representation and a corresponding fear that, in the absence of recognition, we will die."[32] He concludes: "Not only are these beliefs ungrounded in reality, they also overlook the importance of 'being there,'" a fact that "lends importance to recognition and representation in the first place," concluding that being present "will not stand reduction to identity."[33] In such a politically polarized milieu, George Grant's critique of education might seem irrelevant (at best), a provocation (at worst). A member of an august Ontario family,[34] educated at Queen's and Oxford Universities, remembered most for his role in mid-twentieth-century Anglo-Canadian nationalism, Grant could be ignored by students shopping for courses within the identitarian currents we swim today.

That would be a mistake. There is much in Grant's teaching that supports the current concern for truth and reconciliation, terms to which Grant would accord spiritual as well as economic and political meaning. He thought that only recollecting[35] the past—"archaic eddies of being"[36]—might we find our way out of a suffocating present that portends an intolerable future. The prospect of such a future—one of stultifying standardization—moved Grant to embrace particularity.[37] Canada itself, he feared, was an endangered series of particularities. Like his expansive sense of culture, Grant called for an Indigenous philosophy, theology, and, implicitly I suggest, an Indigenous education—knowledge inspired by but not confined to the love of one's own,[38] a love of knowledge (and vice versa) he exemplified by "being there"—in my terms subjectively present—during his lifetime of teaching.

Except for Quebec, Grant does not emphasize the concerns so central today.[39] He acknowledged that "we do have a large population that was brought unjustly to North America as slaves"[40] but I found no explicit reference to slavery in Canada,[41] or to the Jamaican Maroons in Nova Scotia.[42] In that he reflects but does not supersede his era.[43] In a 1938 letter to his mother he even describes his fellow undergraduates as "full of fun and work like niggers, yet never let it get the better of them,"[44] unforgiveable today,[45] but no explicit expression of racial prejudice as indicated by the term's association with fellow (Anglo-Canadian) undergraduates.

Two years later, Grant wrote to his mother—he wrote her regularly, often weekly—that he has purchased a recording of Marian Anderson, the African-American contralto, effusing that "she is Ceres and Aphrodite rolled into one, that glorious liquid passionate confident voice moves me as no other singer does."[46] Periodically he acknowledges racial realities in the United States—on one occasion lynching specifically[47]—and the problem of racial prejudice generally.[48] "Freeing one's mind" from such prejudice—he writes in a piece about adult education—should be considered "equally education."[49] Complaining about the "increasingly dog-eat-dog quality" of the "contractualized" world, wherein industry requires "new waves of immigrants to do the dirty work," he concludes that contemporary society has the quality of "increasing racial disparity."[50] Here Grant associates racism with colonialism, cooptation, and exploitation generally.

Was gender in play for Grant? At one point he asks women in his class to comment on Nietzsche's writing about women, acknowledging that there were very "fine" women in the class, quite capable of confronting the great philosopher.[51] Certainly sex was in play, and perhaps more and differently than one might assume, as the happily married man and father of six children records in his (premarital) diary that he had turned away from homosexuality.[52] "Decades later he tells students it is a "bisexual world."[53] In one sentence sex becomes sacred: "We cannot doubt," he said, "that sexuality is the core of human beings in the sense that it is there that flesh and spirit most concretely are at one."[54] Certainly human life was: the former pacifist opposed any form of violence against humanity, including abortion.[55] In the United States, *Roe v. Wade* legalized abortion on demand, which he opposed.[56] "I think the feminist cause was an excellent thing," he told Cayley, "largely right, but I cannot see it condoning the mass slaughter of fetuses."[57] His opposition to abortion on demand was based on his affirmation of human life, fuelled by his fear that it would lead to the extermination of others who may also become inconvenient: the disabled, the elderly, the seriously ill. He asks: "If the fetuses are accidental blobs of matter, aren't we also?"[58] His anti-abortion activism—conducted with his wife, Sheila[59]—contradicts the more situated ethics he endorses on other occasions. But he had his limits: in a letter to the Coalition for the Protection of Human Life he objects to its association of abortion and homosexuality.[60] Limits[61] were important to Grant, as was moderation,[62] although on abortion he seemed to slide toward extremism.

"The central truth of Western ethical teaching," Grant asserted, "has been that no human being should be treated simply as a means—but also as an end."[63] Machines are never ends but always means, he emphasized; when humanity is reduced to machines—when they are exploited or objectified—the "central truth" of Western ethics has been violated. How can that truth be known? Because philosophy could lead to "understanding of the whole," Grant surmised that philosophy could also steer us toward "the good."[64] For Grant "philosophy was the heart of education," reminding us that philosophy is defined by "the love of wisdom," calling us to want "to be wise," requiring each of us to "pursue philosophy" as much one's "talents and circumstances" allow.[65]

This eternal ethical obligation becomes historicized—"circumstances" in the quoted passage above implies historical time—and thereby particularized, even politicized. Marx declares the point of philosophy not to understand but to change what is.[66] "Marxism claims to be historical prophecy," Grant writes, "which is itself the instrument for the overcoming of the evils which stand in the way of its own vision—evils which Marx so passionately and concretely describes."[67] But, he continued, "by insisting that history is the central category of modern thought Marx shows how an end has come to the old idea of an independent nature without human significance. As God has become man, so man has become the creator of nature and makes it the servant of his freedom."[68] Wisdom is replaced by being smart and strategic; reality becomes pervasively political.

Grant appreciated that the politics of his era revolved around two questions.[69] The first concerned maintaining "some independence"[70] from an imperialist United States.[71] Regarding the "great Colossus to the south,"[72] Grant conceded that America was "much more advanced" than Canada, but, he added, "I don't use 'advanced' as meaning good," but only as "farther along in the way of what a liberal society becomes," thereby (he hoped) giving "Canadians pause," so that Canada does not follow the same path.[73] The "Great Republic"[74] had become a "monolithic tyranny" characterized by "sophisticated vulgarity."[75] Canadians ought not be surprised; after all, Grant asserted, America's "basic moral teachers" had been—were—"morally shallow."[76] Any society, Grant insisted, making his main point, "that puts its trust in affluence and technology results in using any means necessary to force others to conform to its banal will."[77] Despite similarities, Canada, Grant declared, is no "pale imitation" of America but "something richer," in part because Canadians appreciate "better the dependence of freedom upon law."[78] He continued: "If we in Canada want to be a country, we have to stand on some principle which preserves some communal individuality in the face of the persuasive power of American homogenization."[79] While he was accused of pessimism (which he denied[80]), he expressed satisfaction in Canada's "new nationalism."[81]

The second political question Grant identified is the negotiation of "workable relations"[82] between French- and English-speaking communities, a "contract with Quebec in which what both parties' needs can be put together."[83] What such negotiation required, Grant emphasized, was "moderation," by which he meant not "weakness," in fact "clear firmness," the "opposite of intemperance and confrontation."[84] Moderation had not characterized the history between English- and French-speaking peoples in Canada, Grant knew, as, for example, military conscription had been "enforced" in 1917 "against the will of Quebec," thereby sowing "the seeds of an extreme French-Canadian nationalism."[85] In failing to recognize what was at stake for Quebec[86] in the struggle to preserve language and culture, English-speaking Canadians, Grant concluded, "show that they are not sufficiently alive to the facts of their own destiny."[87] Margaret Atwood makes a similar point when she observes that cultural survival has remained the main motive, adding: "And in English Canada now while the Americans are taking over it is acquiring a similar meaning."[88] Evidently Atwood, as well as Grant, knew that Canada had been intended to be a society more "ordered" and "caring," decidedly "less violent"[89] than its neighbour to the south.

Given the sea of English-speaking peoples surrounding it, Grant was skeptical that preserving the primacy of the French language would by itself ensure Quebec's particularity; he thought the preservation of culture—including religion,[90] specifically Catholicism[91]—would also be needed.[92] There could be no guarantees of course, and the "central" question that faced English-speaking Canada would continue to challenge Quebec:

> That fact is how can a French society continue to survive on this continent in the face of the homogenizing power of the North American technological empire—particularly when this capitalist empire is English-speaking?[93]

Technology enables communication through standardization,[94] and Quebec faces not only that force of standardization, but one that speaks English. Grant was unclear by what political means Quebec could survive.[95]

Each of these two political questions—Canada's relationship with the United States and the relationship between English- and French-speaking peoples within Canada—is complex in its own right, but each can only be addressed, Grant suggested, together. For Grant, "[w]hat unites Canadians, whether French or English," Neil Robertson points out, "is an attachment to the universality of the pre-modern tradition that is instantiated in differing forms in Quebec and in English Canada—a shared standpoint deeper than the differences of culture and equally opposed to American modernity."[96]

Given Grant's affirmation of pre-modernity and particularity, had he lived longer[97] I suspect he would have revised that list to include a third: the question of the Aboriginal peoples.[98] The tyranny of modernity—for Grant it was the obliteration of particularity[99] and eternality—he protested by teaching "ancient religions and philosophy at university," but he recognized that it could also be subverted by "working with the Métis," by Indigenous cultures.[100] He told David Cayley:

> I take for granted that Canada is an entity that will go on; I hope it is able to maintain an Indigenous culture; I hope above all French Canada can have a culture that is somehow different from the rest of North America. And I mean by culture quite a big thing—I don't mean only art galleries and rock concerts, I mean the way in which people live in all sorts of towns and all sorts of situations.[101]

How? While the question of political means remains, Grant's answer is expressed on the scale not of a nation but of life within it: "[A]bout all I can do is carry out my private duties and think my private thoughts. There is not much that anybody can do to stop this tyranny from being; one simply has to live through it."[102] Private duties and private life: these two might be thought "together," as the reasoned enactment of obligations to others seem dependent upon the revelations of the inner life.[103] Survival—"living through it," in Grant's phrase—is, as Atwood famously suggested, the challenge Canadians have faced, face now. Certainly it was the challenge George Grant faced.

And what about the "tyranny" in the face of which Grant retreats into private thoughts and duties? How will we—living in advanced democratic societies—know when it comes? No brown shirts this time, Grant knew, but businessmen with smiles, coaxing us to come along. "If tyranny is to come in North America," Grant predicted, "it will come cosily and on cat's feet."[104] Its ugly side will surface, he thought, through the technological enforcement of cosiness, comfort and convenience. With what is inconvenient or uncomfortable we can dispense, by abortion and euthanasia or other forms of disposal, each foreshadowing, Grant worried, the eventual extermination of all those "who cannot defend themselves" when subjected to the "cost-benefit analysis of human life."[105] Like those progressive predecessors he disclaimed, Grant decried tyranny, however alluring its pillow talk. Perhaps because he worked from within—honouring his private duties, working through his private thoughts—Grant could be the courageous intellectual activist he became. However stacked the deck against him—against all educators in a technological era, as he emphasized over and over again—Grant persevered. Seeking truth in hopes—but without expectations—of reconciliation: such resolve and aspiration could be said to structure Grant's teaching and study.[106] Teaching and study were his forms of political and spiritual engagement in a time of tyranny. In 1981 he wrote William Christian that "it is imperative that we think about what our societies have become, as it is necessary in that thought to have everything broken for one, so that one opts in action for such terrible extremities, or else is one just moved into impotence outside the world?"[107] It seems to me that Grant did both: thinking[108] through the historical moment[109] prompted protest against injustice[110] and propelled him outside the maelstrom of modernity.

Maybe. E. Joan O'Donovan wonders if Grant's conception of modernity as a "unified fate" does not undermine his hope that the unfolding presence of "the whole" can become accessible to human awareness and thought.[111] "So total is the bondage of our desiring and thinking to technological necessity," she reasons (quoting Grant), that even "loving" and "thinking" are contingent on "recollection," which is a "chance event."[112] Our subjection to technological necessity would seem to leave us as cogs in the machine, ourselves like moving parts we keep functioning efficiently, increasing productivity, calculating creative destruction of what is, the human will now materialized, (de)vices ensnaring us in convenience, connectivity, calculation. For those whose souls have not (yet) been extinguished, one can sense Grant's presence[113] in his insistence that it always matters what one does, and that what one does depends in part on one's capacity for contemplation,[114] as attunement to eternity reveals what ethical action to take in this world, now.[115] That, in Jean-Luc Marion's phrase, is the "urgency of contemplation."[116] Arthur Davis and Henry Roper summarize:

> George Grant was fearless in his willingness to question the intellectual and spiritual foundations of modernity, as well as subject his own ideas to revision. He believed that the purpose of thinking was to uncover what humans are and how they should live. For Grant the life of the mind meant engagement with the most immediate problems of existence in the world, and in

this engagement he was as critical of corporate capitalism as he was of communism. Although given to moments of despondency, he never lost his conviction that life is not a "tale told by an idiot," in the despairing words of Macbeth, but has meaning and purpose.[117]

Activism and quietude, alternating, imbricated, melding him together and pulling him apart: George Grant embodied[118] his era as he sought to supersede it.[119]

A Progressive Christian Platonist

> Modern science and thought—or modern truth-seeking—has shown us that life is without purpose.[120]
>
> George Grant

To think through one's era as an ethical obligation positioned Grant paradoxically.[121] His "genius," Ted Heaven suggests, was that "throughout his intellectual life, Grant's mind was simultaneously operating on two levels,"[122] revelation and reason, philosophy and Christianity.[123] He was, Harris Athanasiadis observes, "especially conscious of historical time and place," and his "struggle in thought and practice was very contextual."[124] A. James Reimer notes that "there continues to be a strong residue of his early liberalism in his later thought."[125] Ian Angus appreciates that a "critical historical understanding underlies Grant's non-progressive and anti-technological Christianity."[126] Davis registers this sequence: "Grant was raised a progressive and became a Christian Platonist."[127] O'Donovan also acknowledges that Grant began as a "progressive conservative, that is, a well-tempered liberal," in the "late forties and fifties...cautiously" accepting the "mood of expansion and reconstruction."[128] But the sixties were "sobering," she continues, supporting a "change of heart,"[129] specifically after the move to southern Ontario, followed by the defeat of the Progressive Conservative Party in the 1963 federal election, surrounded by America's involvement in Vietnam's civil war.

Athanasiadis suggests less a shift than a sharp break in Grant's thought during the 1960s, asserting that he "fully shed the modern world-view from his thinking and conceived of a different way of being and loving in the world."[130] Shed one's childhood formation few of us can do, but reconstruct it we can and sometimes do. While accepting that there were shifts in Grant's emphasis, I do not believe he disavowed altogether the self his childhood had formed. Grant incorporated both his childhood and his adult experience into a layered if shifting sense of thought and identity. He acknowledged his imprinting as a child—his progressivism—as the ongoing basis of who and what he became. It seems to me that Grant reconstructed his childhood formation as a progressive by embracing Christianity and Platonism, the two tensioned traditions threaded together through his study of the work of Leo Strauss[131] and Simone Weil.[132] However paradoxical (indeed logically impossible) the phrase is, I characterize Grant as a progressive Christian Platonist.[133]

His resolve to redo himself is evident, as Athanasiadis points out, in that Grant had "little positive to say about his early years or his roots,"[134] but his letters[135] confirm his continuing loyalty to his friends and family, especially to his mother, Maude Erskine Parkin,[136] whom Athanasiadis oddly omits in listing the "three key figures"[137] in Grant's life.[138] Maybe half of his letters are addressed to his mother.[139] Like the three key men, Grant's mother was too a "Protestant educator, believer in historical progress, and promoter of imperial federation. All three were also believers in their divine vocation to work in cooperation with divine providence toward the realization of universal freedom and justice (the kingdom of God) in the world."[140] Like the music he so admired, Grant's teaching testifies to transcendence, but from within the worldly ideas and practices he had internalized as a child and learned as a young man. No revolutionary, Grant worked within the world he had been bequeathed, protesting and praying for another world to come.

Given this paradoxical complexity within Grant's life and thought it is unsurprising that Athanasiadis asks: "But was there a center to Grant's thought?"[141] For Athanasiadis the answer is Martin Luther's theology of the cross. Athanasiadis's argument for—and Sheila Grant's affirmation of—this answer is persuasive but (to my mind) does not exclude others. "Grant's thinking always turned to the mystery at the heart of things," Dart suggests, "the God of Love whom we could sense but never full know."[142] In characterizing her project O'Donovan suggests that centre of Grant's thought is not eternity but its moving image: modernity.[143] She writes:

> Our primary task, then, is to understand the unity and the movement of Grant's thought in terms of his abiding concern to interpret the modern conception of "history," a concern arising out of his initial struggle to comprehend the break with the tradition of our (Western) past that modern thought and action represents.[144]

Suffering and history—these are intertwined concepts, each contributing to, even comprising, the unity, the centre, of Grant's thought.[145]

Grant's thought can come into even sharper focus by emphasizing his life-long commitment to education: teaching as testimony to affliction[146] animated by love.[147] Academic study and teaching as simultaneously self-referential—to Grant and the moment and situation in which he is teaching—but also pointing to what lies beyond these, beyond in both historical time and metaphysical space. I am thinking here of Weil's concept of *metaxu*, those spaces of mediation between here and eternity: between Grant's persisting progressivism and his Christian Platonism, between Socrates[148] and Jesus.[149] Even the cross, the very concept of incarnation and the sign of suffering, inhabits space in between the transcendent and the mundane.[150] Both domains—and their finally inscrutable relation to each other—comprise the world we inhabit. For Grant, Athanasiadis knows: "The critical task of thought requires naming reality or the world as it is."[151] Rendering the world intelligible to himself and others—study and teaching as forms and spaces of mediation—is the calling educators enact.[152]

Grant became compelling to me as a curriculum-studies scholar due to his enactment of the curriculum. Note here too the term (enactment) moves our attention slightly off-centre, because the curriculum is a complicated conversation, and not only with students (and indirectly with those who have influenced them, and who speak through them now) but also with colleagues (fellow participants, living and dead, in the field in which one works), and with circumstances (disciplinary, institutional, regional, national, and, increasingly, international).[153] Enactment emphasizes behaviour and, for me, the person[154] performing and those participating in that complicated conversation that is the curriculum. Enactment occurs in place and time, incorporating—reconstructing, as progressives urged—what was occurring in that place at that time. From his pedagogical to political to philosophical interventions, George Grant incorporated, and reconstructed what he found, what he experienced, what was underway in society.

No one can copy Grant.[155] One can aspire to thread one's own needle[156] as he did his, but circumstances—the institutional curriculum itself—shifts, and so the complicated conversation in which one is participating is not only different, one's participation in it differs according to time, place, circumstance, and one's judgments concerning these.[157] Despite the cumbersome structure of that sentence, there is no formula here: teaching is, as Ted Aoki knew, improvisation.[158] Even that non-formula is false—on occasion one does not improvise. The searing specificity of the historical moment, of the individual life, of one's students, and of the teaching is precisely what distinguishes and—given its content—what consecrates George Grant's critique of technology, time, and teaching.[159]

Subjective Presence

> To be present to one another is not a matter of recognition of each other's qualities, qualifications, talents, and shortcomings, which we may display or hide; it is a matter of revelation of a "who" which is implicit in everything one says or does in that moment.[160]
>
> Anne Phelan

George Grant reconstructed his upbringing by becoming historical—insisting, that "we must recognize that we are at a bad time in human history"[161]—while reaffirming time as a moving image of eternity.[162] The sincerity of his Christian conversion and his association of it with Platonism I do not doubt. That conversion was a repudiation of calculation, his acceptance of Christ a denunciation of materialism, his absorption in Platonism a self-extrication from the present into an ancient past from which he could then see through the present.[163] These diverse and interrelated movements—of "enucleation,"[164] to invoke his term—Grant undertook as a progressive committed to progress, correcting the mistakes his ancestors had made, rerouting the technological direction of the history in which he found himself embedded, a history also embedded in him.

That sincerity—replaced now by authenticity, as Lionel Trilling has shown[165]—constituted a rejection of conformity. Truthfulness is a precondition of seeking truth. No free-floating quality, sincerity is a state of mind one cultivates from within, with oneself and those one encounters. Working within takes courage, and caution. Moreover, the cultivation of sincerity can be undermined by oneself (as Freud established) and by others (who can snicker at its straightforward expression). Not reducible to a set of behaviours, sincerity is conveyed through one's person, if differently according to circumstance. Such a characterization of George Grant is confirmed by his person, his subjective presence.[166]

While physical presence[167] is preferable, one can sense Grant's subjective presence—his struggle with the world, with himself—in his words.[168] Not in every word, but Grant's communicative undertakings overall—from diary entries to letters, essays and books, from lectures to interviews—show sharp sensitivity to the situation, especially to those physically or virtually present (through print), conveyed by his subjective presence, his being present there, with others.[169] Consider his correspondence. Those who read it will agree with William Christian that he was a "remarkable correspondent."[170] What Christian says of Grant's letters, I suspect, is also the case with Grant's teaching: "His letters are direct, intensely personal communications with the individual to whom he wrote. Whether they were to a close friend, or to someone who had written him an interesting letter, if they deserved his full attention, they usually got it."[171] Like his journal entries, these letters may not have been intended to be published, a point Christian implies when he acknowledges the "freshness and the candour, the flashes of insight and the intellectual daring," all present in "full force."[172] As I read them I was struck by the sense of immediacy and detail, intertwined with his erudition, his dwelling in the moment, his attentiveness—at times associated with attunement to the transcendent—his "being there."[173] Not "there" inside the screen, but "there" as in "here," in this world, attuned too to what lies beyond. Subjective presence is not only *self*-expressive but also, in Grant's case, expressive of the situation, as if he were a medium of metaphysical realities.[174] The "full attention" Christian cites above hints at the singular, sometimes searing, subjective presence of George Grant.[175]

Like "enactment," the term "subjective presence" may be misleading, as it can also imply a mobilization, a term with military connotations. I have invoked it to suggest what teachers might undertake as they face scapegoating by (especially US) politicians and businessmen.[176] Less militarily, mobilization implies the actor's summoning of him- or herself to enact the script, surely an element of effective acting and possibly of teaching, two occasions when one can become present through the texts of others. Perhaps self-summoning is preferable to mobilization, but in any case, in Grant's case, it would not be "personal presence without principle."[177] Principle provided the structure to the presence Grant embodied and enacted.

Certainly Grant summoned himself. Pummelled by two world wars, Grant testified to the complicated crosscurrents of his lived experience, "being there," especially it seemed, in his writing and teaching, intertwined endeavours to be sure. What were those currents? Certainly what surrounded him—his family, their history, their circumstances and their expectations for him—constituted the first circle of currents, a circle to which he remained loyal, despite his intellectual explorations far from home, often undertaken (it seems to me) to extricate himself from his inheritances. Love of one's own[178] seemed the centrepiece of his conception of charity[179] that extended beyond his family to humanity.[180] Wider circles of influence included his teachers (R. A Trotter, A. D. Lindsay, among others), fellow students, friends he made where he studied (Derek Bedson, Peter Clarke, Peter Self), and his colleagues, not only in Canada (William Christian, James Doull, Fulton Anderson, C. N. Cochrane, E. P. Sanders, Leo Strauss) but including those he never met but whose past presence in the world very much influenced his (Weil, philosophers from Plato to Heidegger). Phenomena—from politics (Diefenbaker, anti–Vietnam War protests, the formation of the New Democratic Party, Pierre Elliott Trudeau) to teaching positions (Dalhousie, York, McMaster Universities) to technology (the car, computer, refrigerator)—were primary, as I acknowledge in the chapters to follow. My point here is to emphasize Grant's embeddedness in relationships intimate and formal, abstract and concrete, his immersion in events and circumstances private and public, his ongoing intellectual efforts to understand what he saw and felt and suffered, yes for his sake but also for others, all communicated in letters (personal, attentive, solicitous), in books (and essays, articles, book reviews), and talks—on radio, in churches, in classrooms. George Grant studied what he underwent as a human being, as a man, as a Canadian, a person standing solitary in the midst of, supported by, others (alive and dead), events as concrete as the deadly 1940 blitz of London[181] and as abstract as modernity itself.[182]

This Book

> Film represents an indelible past that produces a highly cathected experience of presence. The inflated rhetoric of movement, life, and death that accompanied the emergence of cinema confirms the cinematic debt to a dream of revivification and "presencing."[183]
>
> Mary Ann Doane

No movie, this book[184] communicates, I trust, "a highly cathected experience of presence." The images it provides of George Grant are not visual but auditory, words he wrote and spoke, words that can revivify not only the moment in which he dwelled, but also your moment, now. Academic study engages emotions as well as mind, intertwined as these can be, and one replies to each—feeling, thoughts—by taking notes, mental if not written. There is a conversation that can occur, yes between you and yourself, you and Grant, maybe you with me, a conversation that extends to those who knew and studied Grant before you, a conversation past and present in which you can now participate.

The field in which I work—curriculum studies—has a tradition of what we call the synoptic text, a commitment to review whatever is relevant to teach a topic. The short of it is, we take the textbook seriously. Whatever is relevant once seemed a scale on which one could work, but for decades now clearly it is not. While I failed to include here all that is relevant to the study of George Grant, I did manage to work through the collected works and many of the commentaries and critiques of Grant's work. In teaching Grant I have emphasized certain aspects—evident in the subtitle—and deemphasized others, often associating his work with mine.[185] No fused identity, but an instance, I hope, of fidelity to his teaching: being present within the subject matter—that last term in the double sense of what one studies and who is studying—attuned to what might be beyond both. "But above all," Grant wrote, "it must be insisted that the purpose of a commentary does not lie in itself, but in aiding that fuller reading of that which is commented upon."[186] I want to return the reader to Grant's writings, in part by emphasizing what has not been emphasized before—namely his critique of teaching, intertwined as that was with his critique of time and technology.[187]

Not only what I emphasize distinguishes this book from others[188] but also how I emphasize it: through what might seem like endless citation.[189] For me these quoted passages[190] not only document Grant's teaching, they re-enact the complicated conversation in which Grant participated and that he has bequeathed us, in which we—as students and teachers—try to participate now. "In order to understand the movement of Grant's thought," O'Donovan appreciates,

> we must in the first place pay attention to his intellectual conversation with the "great thinkers," those enduring influences on his thought. Moreover, we must also attend to the particular details of Grant's life, to his practical, existential involvements as shaped by his personal inheritance. For it is somewhere between the urgent demands of the practical life and the compelling challenge of intellectual and spiritual mentors that Grant's thought takes seed, germinates, and comes to fruition.[191]

Like R. G. Collingwood, "My inclinations have always led me rather toward detail than towards generalization."[192] Even so, listening to Grant teach through studying the texts he composed—his conversation with "great thinkers"[193] and with those in his midst—summons his subjective presence, requiring reactivation of the past that inhabits us, providing an opportunity for subjective reconstruction, perhaps even a portal to transcendence.[194]

"Living thoughts are sensitive surfaces," Cusset suggest, "skins lightly touched, dark folds—less a body of thought, compact and muscular, than a zone of contact between eroded borders. A single citation may be enough to communicate them."[195] No single citation here as you can see, almost a cacophony of them, a complicated conversation in which Grant is the primary teacher, his subjective presence audible in citation. Citation can be an effort to enact orality, sound as a "zone of contact between eroded borders" (as Cusset says), sound entering us even against our wills. "Sound is essentially immediate and evanescent," Ian Angus points out, adding: "Oral society is based upon the notion of speech as action, rather than language as description, and has evolved many strategies for overcoming the tendency of spoken words to be forgotten. Stories, rituals and so forth are building upon formulas and mnemonics."[196] Discussing Grant's conclusion to his "In Defence of North America," the poet Dennis Lee draws our attention to this "zone of contact" when he asks us to: "Listen to how the symphonic cadences of witnessing lengthen our attention, slow down our agitated response, to the point where we are able to gaze into hard and terrible truths without just running out and *doing* something, anything, to make them disappear."[197] Like the music of Mozart[198] Grant so loved, Grant's prose represents an arrangement of instruments or ideas, tones and narratives, eddies and currents, that can carry us away, to another time and place, extricating us from this one.

An oral society, Angus points out, "orients much of its energy towards not forgetting, towards continuously re-enacting the past in the present," adding that the "oral mind is oriented towards narrative accounts, stories rather than lists."[199] Moreover, Angus continues, "orality is participatory and inclusive, not distant. It acts over small spaces and unites people in face-to-face encounters."[200] Even when our "face-to-face encounters" occur during study of a text composed by a person long gone.

Discussing another great Canadian scholar, Harold Innis, Judith Stamps suggested that "the oral tradition is also important because of the level of mimetic identification that it encourages between speakers and listeners."[201] Identification with Grant—the reader's intimacy with the writer is also implied in the Cusset-quoted passage above—could encourage you to teach yourself as Grant taught others: study as an iconographic space that intensifies the experience of its temporal singularity while enabling attunement to what is immemorial.

My citation of Grant follows no chronological order because I am trying to teach its dynamic totality—implied by the concept of subjective presence—always inviting students to return to the original.[202] I attempt to invoke the man[203] and the world he inhabited. But the steady stream of citation is not only reactivation of Grant's subjective presence and its emplacement in the historical world, it is an assertion of academic study, supporting a "slow"[204] student in search of knowledge that can enrich one's experience (not only information one can use to get ahead). Extensive citation—in the endnotes as well as the main text—could encourage such slow study, as one's reading is interrupted and extended by end-notes.[205] I think of endnotes as sometimes long eddies of experience and thought, showing how the steady stream of Grant's thought and life is itself flowing along-side of and into other streams, sometimes subterranean to the surface.[206]

Sometimes exclusively associated with Aboriginal peoples, the oral tradi-tion is also European. In the "medieval semi-oral mode of education," Stamps reminds, educational institutions held "public dispositions" organized around the pressing philosophical issues of the day.[207] "Questions could be posed by lis-teners," she adds, and "such general interaction was thought to advance and dis-seminate knowledge throughout the Western world...a conscious continuation of a dialogue that had begun with the dawn of philosophy in the West."[208] Stamps attributes to Marshall McLuhan and Harold Innis "a new kind of orality—a liter-ary anticipation of the community of speakers in a world beyond modernity."[209] George Grant too thought about, prayed for, taught toward a world beyond modernity, but it was a world that was not new but old, in fact timeless.[210]

What qualifies me to undertake this task? Not generational empathy, as the dates of Grant's birth and death (1918–1988) almost coincide with my father's. There is second difference between us: sexuality. While I grew up "straight" I am now married to a man, still grateful for the son (and his wife and their three chil-dren) that my youth brought. Third is national difference—I am an American liv-ing in the United States. Grant comments regularly about the United States—you note a few in this introduction and you will find more scattered throughout the book—and I have welcomed these as reminders how national culture and history becomes intellectually and subjectively embedded within the singular experience of one person. Fourth, while secularist[211] during my adult life, studying Grant has provoked me to rethink religion, not its relation to the state (where my sympa-thies remain with secularism, if only for the protection of religion), but within my subjective life. Perhaps, Terence Penelhum is right: "[I]t is misleading to oppose faith and secularity in a manner that implies a given person must be an example of the one or of the other, but cannot show traces of both."[212] Certainly humanity claims to have experienced "something" beyond the everyday and the empirical, but I am "historicist" enough to insist that testimonies to such experience cannot escape being "dated" by time and place. I wonder if the fantasy of transcending time entirely can be true to its aspiration, as it surely seems that aspiration itself is trapped in time.[213] As the icon invites infinity—Mondzain coins the icon "a structural relay"[214]—could not being "dated" also be a passage to eternity, insofar as one can imagine it as a "moving image" of timelessness? So my fifth differ-ence with Grant is historicism. Not that I embrace a simplistic sense of history as totalizing and definitive, but in the time of Trump, a time of historical amnesia,[215] becoming historical seems ethically urgent. In the service of remembrance of the past I suggest its reactivation, a re-experiencing of certain moments—awful and awesome, the two ends of the spectrum sometimes intertwined—in order to "reset" the course of present events.[216] There is no cause-and-effect possible here, but I want to invoke a moment before we disappeared into the device.[217] When (and where) that moment was is endlessly arguable, but I am inviting you to study Grant as if he inhabited it.

Reactivation

> Fifty years ago the important frontier of this continent was physical; today the more important frontier is spiritual.[218]
>
> George Grant

What knowledge is of most worth? Grant asked and answered time and again as he struggled to decipher the meaning of "what this is that we are."[219] Spurred to sustained study, he worked his way through several academic disciplines—history, law, theology, philosophy—while remaining alert to art, culture, and politics. Like Martin Luther, he was determined to see things as they were. Also like Luther, Grant was determined that things be different than they are.[220] "How does one then ever move out of the circle of our present destiny?"[221] he asked, answering: "It is by looking at modernity in its greatest power that one is perhaps able even slightly to escape its power."[222] Central is non-coincidence with what is—not looking the other way and staying distracted, but by staring straight into its mesmerizing eyes, steadied by knowledge, in Grant's case, philosophical knowledge.

> As a regenerate Platonist I would affirm that philosophy stands or falls with its ability to transcend history…. Indeed in speaking about perspectives for philosophy I would say that in homogenized societies of the future, the hope of philosophy will be with those who understand that thought can partake in that which is not dependent on any dynamic context. It will lie with those who can rise above the historicism which has permeated Western thought since Nietzsche…. The possibility of standing above "history" must depend on having lived through the awful responsibilities of time.[223]

Transcendence can occur by the living through of what is, Grant is suggesting: immersion in the moment but attuned to the eternal.[224]This conclusion I reach by focusing on his use of the verb "partake" in the second sentence of the above-quoted passage, and the linking of transcendence ("standing above history") with living through the "awful responsibilities of time" in that last sentence.

Partake means to enter into, and studying Grant affords one the experience of sharing something of the moment in which he was embedded, the moment from which he worked to extricate himself through academic study and teaching. Studying Grant enables one to share something of these efforts by partaking of the past.[225] Partake implies sharing with others, communicating what one is undergoing but also listening to others, even joining others in undertaking together what must be done, the awful responsibilities of one's time.[226] Partake also means to take part *in* something, suggesting that one takes on some of the qualities *of* that something. In other definitions of partake the ingestion of food or drink is mentioned, as if that "something" is now inside one, altering one's psychic chemistry as it were.[227] In sharing something—entering into it, and being entered—one exceeds oneself.[228]

Grant exceeded himself through study of the teachings of Christ and Socrates. Studying each—ingesting the words, experiencing something of what each thought and might have undergone—enabled erudition but subjective reconstruction as well. Grant was (one can be) changed by such emotional intellectual even mystical immersion and, like a baptism or conversion, one emerges altered. When not working with others, study requires quietude,[229] encouraging contemplation, of whom and what one is studying and of the person studying. However intensely one might re-experience something of ancient Athens or Jerusalem, one returns right here, right now, and that is the second point about Grant's insight—in the quoted passage above—I want to underline.

Extricating oneself from the present moment can occur not by planning the future—addressing the crises technology has created requires more technology—but by reactivating the past. Like the term "transcendence," "standing above" history is a spatial, not necessarily a temporal, position. It implies the detachment contemplation encourages. But "standing above" is not split off from the present; indeed for Grant it *depends* "on having lived through the awful responsibilities of time," an adjective suggesting survival through suffering, a noun honouring the obligations being embedded in historical time incur. Each of these terms structure Grant's thought. In my terms, transcendence and worldliness are not opposed but reciprocally related, implied in O'Donovan's reminder that, for Grant, "*recollecting* the good and *thinking* our deprival are one."[230] Juxtaposing the modern and the classical, and "in the same thought," Dennis Lee writes, Grant tried to hold together "the good and technology; sacramental meaning and the fact/value distinction; natural law and freedom to invent the world; reverence and mastery."[231] Attunement to the eternal occurs within time.

The concept of praxis—simplified as theory and practice, thought and action[232]—has structured curriculum theory for decades. Notice that Grant's insight revises the concept considerably, altering both the "thought" and "action" that comprises it. Study requires thought, not only thought about but also a certain immersion in the past. In studying Grant, in becoming his student, one *partakes* of the past, ingesting it, allowing it to alter one's composition, one's constitution, one's character.[233] Such study requires receptivity, even reverence, but also judgment, even wisdom: after all, one doesn't want to partake of (even if one is obligated to know about) the evils of ancient Athens and Jerusalem. Partaking reactivates the past within oneself, altering one's subjectivity, and not only with facts and ideas, as central as these are, but with an altered inner structure. One becomes temporally restructured, as the past inhabits the present that in our time is so often focused on the future even as it fused with the present. Structured so, and with facts and ideas (principles Grant might prefer), one declines to coincide with the present moment. One lives through it, attuned always to what is revealed during study, what was learned during living: revelation and reason not opposed but reciprocally related.

What reason reveals, Grant suggests, is that living means honouring one's obligations. The present is not only space—empty, endless opportunity, absolute freedom—it is place. And place is not only physical but cultural, often spiritual, and certainly historical, haunted by what has happened (t)here, threatened by what may. It is no environment, in the sense of a clean slate, but a situation, already structured, in process, well underway, and within which one has perhaps unchosen obligations. Learning what those are and how one might honour them is surely central to and enabled by study; it derives from that non-coincidence with the present that study allows. Obligation requires action; it invokes duty. One is free to ignore all—go shopping or surfing on the Internet instead—but Grant is calling us home, to our senses, to our time, to the world: each a moving image of eternity.

Notes

1. Davis 2002b, 437; see also 183.
2. Davis 2002b, 183.
3. "The very word education," Grant reminded, "comes, as you know, from an allegory of Plato's. He describes human beings as chained in a dark cave, and their lives as the struggle to free themselves by knowing from the chains of ignorance which bind them, and to struggle up out of the cave into the sunlight of knowledge which is the radiance of God. *Educo*—to lead out. As Jesus put it brilliantly, 'the truth shall make you free.' Now this was the traditional idea of education in the Western world at its best. Education was the end for which free rational men existed" (Davis 2002b, 183).
4. Davis and Roper 2005b, 32.
5. Davis and Roper 2005b, 32. Political and economic efforts to redress inequality follow from historical injustice and injury, but also, as (Athanasiadis 2001, 109) acknowledges, from the "inequality of talents." But "above" such inequality "lies an essential equality of personhood. Such an equality is rooted in the Christian mystery of every human being as equally the object of divine love" (109). Grant embraced the latter equality, while endorsing political and economic efforts to redress injustice. The equality he criticized was the one that translated into cultural homogeneity and the suppression of difference: equality as sameness.
6. Rocha (2017, 21) warns that "freedom can serve as an intoxicating sedative that stifles human flourishing; I suggested that it is the real opiate of the masses whether peddled by Church or State," adding that "liberty can work like the water that boils the unsuspecting frog to death slowly."
7. "How can we cultivate freedom for the individual," Grant asked, "without having it become identified (as it now is) with ruthless self-interest and the grasping of more

than a fair share?" (Davis and Roper 2005b, 32). "If "freedom" is accorded "priority,"
Ajzenstat (1992, 87) affirms, freedom-based "rights have no inherent limits," and the
first casualties will be "the weak."

8. Davis and Roper 2005b, 32. "The promise of modernity is the idea of freedom,"
Sibley (2008, 208) notes, "but freedom in the modern world seems to entail a high
degree of interdependence." For Grant that interdependence is not only social but
also spiritual.

9. Davis and Roper 2005b, 37. Democracy devours itself, as it requires an educated
citizenry—spiritually attuned, ethically engaged—that its populist profit-seeking
undermines. Athanasiadis (2001, 109) summarizes: "Yet democracy also undermines true education. In Plato's *Republic*, democratic society is viewed so negatively
because the rule of the masses also means the rule of the lowest common denominator of the appetites. Reason, which may be inspired by love but not equally open to
all in talent and ability, is dethroned from its rightful place of leadership. The present
transformation of schools and universities into technical colleges aimed at serving
the degraded ends dictated by society is the result of democracy."

10. Davis and Roper 2005b, 47. The scale and structure of Grant's aspiration are similar
to that of the great post–Second World War poet, novelist, filmmaker, and public
intellectual Pier Paolo Pasolini, as implied in Noa Steimatsky's (2008, 138) depiction
of "Pasolini's archaistic imagination aspires to a primal sense of the cinematic image
as reality's direct emanation—one that carries the evidentiary force of an imprint but
also the magical resonance of a temporal bridge to the past, as to an altered state: a
simultaneity of different temporalities, different orders of being." Referencing his
1964 film *The Gospel According to Matthew*, she adds: "In the context of an adap-
tion of the Gospel, this confronts us with the doctrine of the Incarnation and, more
specifically, with the theology of the icon. Pasolini's aesthetic system draws on the
potency of the devotional image, whose reverential archaism also carries a realist
claim" (138). Devotion, reverence, and the icon threaded through the archaic past
typify the teaching of Grant as well, as my study I trust testifies. "I am not interested
in deconsecrating," Pasolini explained, "this is a fashion I hate, it is petit bourgeois.
I want to re-consecrate things as much as possible, I want to re-mythicize them"
(quoted in Steimatsky 2008, 137). Despite the differences between these two men,
their commitment to consecration was shared.

11. "Now to return to this course," Grant told one group of students, "let me say there
have been three central questions this year: (a) what is modern technique? (b) what
are its historical origins? And (c) how should we live amongst it?" (Davis and Roper
2005b, 680). To ask these questions—what is the historical present, how did it become
what it is, and how might we survive it ethically—implies the whole (a phrase Grant
invoked often, one we will survey in more detail in ch. 1) of human history, but
such a sweep requires one stand outside it, attuned to a "whole" outside human
history. To think the whole from within its part—to think time as a moving image of
eternity—summarizes the scale of Grant's intellectual and spiritual aspiration. It is
aspiration he will enact, I suggest, through academic study and teaching.

12. Davis 2002b, 185.

13. Davis 2002b, 185. Surely the situation is worse in the United States, where, Bruni
(2015, A17) reported, "more than 40 percent of those who become teachers exit the
profession within five years, in part due to scapegoating by politicians and those in

public who believe them, leaving "many teachers feeling like pawns and punching bags."

14. Rocha 2017, 33.

15. Davis 2002b, 186.

16. Discredited (presumably) by post-humanism and the new materialism, the concept of person seems appropriate to this study of Grant, derived as it seems it was (at least in part) from Augustine, whose work Grant studied. "Personhood emerges as the historical self-enactment of will," Scanlon (2005, 161) points out, "and it is personhood in this sense that Augustine explores with this understanding of the 'soul'... [neither] Aristotelian 'substance'—nor...the Cartesian 'ghost in the machine,' [but] what is referred to today as the 'subject,' but the subject as derived from and dependent upon the God of the Bible." Laying bare its sacred subtext, Scanlon (2005, 162) reminds us that "[h]uman personhood is discovered as the anthropological correlate to the revelation of a Personal God." See Sibley 2008, 192–6.

17. Davis 2002b, 186.. Such study could also clear one's head, as Grant told his 1975–76 graduate seminar at McMaster University: "This is what philosophic education is. By concentrating on what a great thinker asserts elementally one clears one's own mind" (Davis and Roper 2009b, 824)

18. Lament, Hall (1978, 124) suggests, is "present" in all Grant's works.

19. Lament, Hall 1978, 124.

20. Davis 2002b, 187.

21. Davis and Roper 2009b, 172. Recollection becomes a key concept for Grant, one I modify with reactivation, to accent the immediacy of the past in the present. For Grant memory provided the path to the transcendent, an idea he may have derived (or had confirmed by) Augustine. "For Augustine," Capelle (2005, 120) points out, "it is memory, exceeding the limits of the human mind, that is open to presence, in each person, of the interior Word."

22. "The liberal notion of the self," Dart notes, "tends to lack a certain depth and inner structure" (Dart and Jersak 2011, 63).

23. Dart and Jersak 2011, 63.

24. I had hoped to have the book out in time for Grant's 100th birthday, but I didn't want a date to dictate how fast I would proceed. In declining the possibility of a chair in Canadian studies, Grant wrote William Christian (1996d, 278) that "I have spent a great deal of my life organizing things and don't regret it, but I have come now to the point where I want to write one thing out as well as I can" (278). Exactly how I feel about studying your work, Professor Grant. I regret missing your birthday, still.

25. Davis and Roper 2009b, 81.

26. Grant wondered "Is it true that our practical spirit, as it achieves its immediate ends, must produce a society in which the human spirit cannot flourish?" (Davis 2002b, 253).

27. "The big picture," Adams (2009, 78) cautions, "no matter how legitimate or by and large true, is almost never the whole story. This is particularly so in North America, whose population is so diverse and whose regions are so large and distinct that the big picture almost always demands some qualification."

28. As early as 1943 Grant is complaining that "[u]niversities have served to produce techniques and technicians rather than sane ideas and thinking citizens" (Davis and Emberley 2000b, 92).

29.   Cayley 1995, 169.

30.   "The heart of any university or department is its curriculum," Grant knew (Davis and Roper 2005b, 651).

31.   Herbert Spencer asked this question in 1859, but its posing precedes modernity by millennia. "What must be a person know to be educated?," Grant asked. He knew that "this raises the question what is really worth knowing" (Davis and Roper 2009b, 103).

32.   Rocha 2017, 178.

33.   Ibid.

34.   O'Donovan (1984, 12) calls him a "scion of one of Canada's oldest most distinguished, and most influential families, connected with wealth, prestige, and political power."

35.   Christian (1990, 194–5) points out that "Grant drew on the Platonic theory of knowledge as recollection," of "what has once been known and then subsequently forgotten."

36.   Lee 1983, 3.

37.   Like Ian Angus, I prefer *particularity*, a concept from Grant's oeuvre. For Angus (1997, 8) the term "provides a sounder philosophical basis for the rethinking of the relation between specific identities and human universality than the concept of difference, which tends towards a blindness to, or even outright rejection of, the notion of universality altogether."

38.   Angus (1997, 155) suggest that "George Grant introduced the term 'one's own,' or 'particularity,' in order to defend the existence of Canada against its incorporation into the U.S." No nationalism unhinged, one's own or particularity is a protective, defensive term, as Angus (157) explains: "The concept of particularity is used by Grant, I believe without exception, in order to defend a particular allegiance at a moment in which it is perceived as threatened." Grant may also derived the phrase—love of one's own—from his study of Augustine. Elshtain (2005, 249) points out that "love of friendship that lies at the root of what might be called Augustine's 'practical philosophy,' his history, ethics, social and political philosophy," emphasizing that "[f]or Augustine, neighbourliness and reciprocity emerge from ties that bind, beginning with familial bonds and extending from these particular relations outward."

39.   Nor could I find in Grant's collected works any acknowledgement of—referencing Fierlbeck's (2006, 63) list—the "onerous restrictions against Chinese immigrant labourers (including the notorious head tax), the lukewarm response to Jewish refugees, the internment of Japanese-Canada citizens, Quebec's Padlock Act against communists, and various legislation vis-à-vis Aboriginal groups are concrete instances of less than tolerant social attitudes." No doubt there are others to add to the list, among them the notorious residential schools for Indigenous youth and the federal government purge of homosexuals, for which Prime Minister Justin Trudeau recently apologized: https://www.nytimes.com/2017/11/28/world/canada/canada-apology-gay-purge-compensation.html.

40.   Cayley 1995, 106–7.

41.   See, for instance, Trudel 2013, A. Cooper 2006.

42.   See J. N. Grant 2002. Nor did Grant ever mention the fate that befell black and Indigenous people after the 1917 explosion in Halifax harbour that killed 2,000 people, injured some 10,000 others, blinding nearly 600). Austen (2017, A6) reports that

Halifax had at that time a large number of black residents who, during the rebuilding of Halifax, were given substantially less compensation for rebuilding than whites. At nearby Tufts Cove, a Mi'kmaw community of about two-dozen families was "hit by the explosion and the tidal wave it created. Not long before the blast, their land had been expropriated and they were preparing for a forced relocation." For Catherine Martin, a descendent of the Mi'kmaw survivors, "it's all sacred land," adding: "After the explosion, the Mi'kmaw were left to fend for themselves" (quoted in Austen 2017, A6).

43.   Fierlbeck (2006, 113) confirms that "the issue of race in political thought became prominent only when intellectuals outside western democracies began to examine the legacy of colonialism. The dearth of theoretical literature did not mean that the politics of race was either unimportant or non-existent in Canada. First Nations groups, in particular, gained a much higher profile in Canada than in the U.S." Again, that "profile" was gained after Grant's death. Even then, Fierlbeck notes that "much of the *contemporary* philosophical debate over the place of First Nations is subsumed within the debate over minority rights" (9).

44.   Christian 1996d, 32.

45.   Fierlbeck (2006, 17) makes the more general historiographical point: "It is also scoring cheap points to judge early thinkers by their failure to address what are by today's standards clear moral deficiencies in their social values." Does, then, Grant deserve a pass for his failure to address Indigenous and racial issues? Not completely, given his skepticism toward historicism, embedded as that is in Fierlbeck's point. "According to nihilistic historicism," O'Donovan (1984, 53) writes (in accord with Grant, presumably), "all past thinkers were bound absolutely by the limitations (that is, the prejudices and ignorance) of their age." Except ourselves, of course; perhaps the issue is not entirely historiographical, but also ethical. So the points are cheap, but they are points.

46.   Christian 1996d, 71.

47.   Davis 2002b, 457.

48.   See Davis and Emberley 2000b, 130, 348, 452; Davis 2002b, 69, 254; Davis and Roper 2009b, 747; 2005b, 213, 238; Davis 2002b, 254; Cayley 1995, 146.

49.   Davis 2002b, 69.

50.   Davis and Roper 2009b, 491.

51.   Davis and Roper 2009b, 989. Often Grant employs the genderless terms "man" or "men," common to English usage in his era.

52.   Davis and Roper 2009b, 316.

53.   Davis and Roper 2009b, 988.

54.   Davis and Roper 2005b, 265–6.

55.   Although his anti-abortion stance linked him with the New Right during the seventies and eighties, that link, Greenspan (1990, 3) suggests, was "not as intense as his relationship to the Left in the sixties." Greenspan contends that the difference between the conservatism that Grant represented with "its emphasis on the organic, interdependent societies as opposed to the ultra-individualism of Reagan's (or even Thatcher's) conservatism has been noted many times. It should also be noted American conservatism's euphoric scenario concerning technology, whose expansion will lead to the reinstatement of homey values of family and religion, is the most vivid antithesis of Grant's doctrines that could be imagined" (3).

56.   Cayley 1995, 152–3. "Grant is undeniably correct," Bradshaw (1996, 221) "in his claim that *Roe v. Wade* provided beyond a doubt that the right takes priority over the good in contractually based liberal societies. Grant sees that this is the inevitable consequence of the logic of liberalism. The United States Constitution is based on the idea that there is moral pluralism in society, and that this pluralism is justified because liberal societies must remain neutral on the question of what is a good."

57.   Cayley 1995, 153.

58.   Davis and Roper 2009b, 494.

59.   "Two emotional absolutists," he admitted (Christian 1996d, 313). Christian ([1995] 2001, xxi) seems to suggest Grant's engagement in the anti-abortion followed from his wife's, noting that Sheila had been "active" in the right-to-life movement, and that her "concern about the implications of *Roe v. Wade* brought Grant into the controversy." That legal judgment, with its denial of rights to fetuses, represented for Grant the "theoretical and practical confusion" that accompanied the "modern doctrine of rationality" (xxi). That doctrine, Bradshaw (1996, 221) points out, asserts "rights" over "the good," presumably in service of "moral pluralism," an idea that requires the state to remain neutral on the question of the good. Without the religious conviction that all human beings are endowed by their creator with certain inalienable rights, states decide whose rights are recognized. The political prevails over the ethical. With power primary, Grant worried that only the strong will survive. In time not only fetuses will lose their right to life, so will, he thought, the "aged, the infirm and the socially deviant" (Bradshaw 1996, 223). Bradshaw finds "Grant's 'slippery slope' argument is misplaced. Abortion is not the first step on the path that leads toward slaughtering the infirm, the aged, and the deviant" (230).

60.   Christian 1996d, 348.

61.   "Grant's real theme is the collapse of limits," Minogue (1990, 170) suggests.

62.   For Grant, Athanasiadis (2001, 215) reminds, "moderation was not weakness. It was the opposite of intemperance and confrontation. But Grant also realized that moderation was incredibly difficult in a highly immoderate era." Craiutu (2017, 238) also appreciates that "political moderation is particularly relevant and important in a post-ideological age such as ours, when old political doctrines and ideas have lost their sharp contours and new forms of extremism are on the rise." While "moderation has many related faces—personal, ethical, institutional, constitutional, and political" (229), "as a certain form of sensibility or disposition, moderation is a cardinal virtue related to civility, self-control, equipoise, temperance, and prudence" (229). No "panacea," (233) Craiutu cautions, "moderation...also demands a combination of intuition, foresight, and flexibility, complemented by good luck" (243).

63.   Davis and Roper 2005b, 128.

64.   Davis and Roper 2005b, 68. "For Grant," Planinc (1992, 34) points out, "the good itself transcends being; it is another name for God." True, but that hardly settles the matter. Like the colour green, goodness escapes exact definition, "but you know it when you see it" (see Andrew and Planinc 1990, 180). As to its contrary, Athanasiadis (2001, 223) writes, "Evil has no independent existence," adding: "It exists as a negation of the goodness of created things." Admittedly maddening for the empiricist, but for the spiritually attuned this makes sense.

65.   Athanasiadis 2001, 223. "Throughout his corpus," McCarroll (2006, 271) notes, "Grant regularly contemplates the relationship between knowing and love."

66. From his *Theses on Feuerbach* and inscribed on his gravestone, the actual line is: "The philosophers have only interpreted the world, in various ways. The point, however, is to change it."

67. Davis 2002b, 227.

68. Davis 2002b, 231.

69. On another occasions—as in the following sentence—economics plays a more prominent role, but I suspect it is the United States not Canada he has in mind in this invocation of ancient Rome: "We don't live in a democratic society; we live in a mass, bureaucratized capitalism—the nearest parallel to which is the Roman Empire at its height" (Davis and Roper 2005b, 210).

70. Schmidt 1978a, 17.

71. Davis and Roper 2009b, 330; Heyking and A. Cooper 2006, 177. America's imperialism, Grant suggested, developed after the conclusion of the Second World War and before the onset of the Vietnam War (Heyking and Cooper 2006, 178), although during the 1950s Grant could still write that "for the ordinary person," America "combines openness and kindness as no other" (Davis 2002b, 255). Heyking and Cooper (2006, 178) suggest that "Grant's critique of the U.S. was fairly consistent throughout his career." Grant himself regarded his antipathy to the United States as "deep" and "ancestral antipathy," given that his ancestors had fled the American Revolution (Davis and Roper 2009b, 85).

72. Davis and Roper 2005b, 436.

73. Davis and Roper 2005b, 452. In Grant's term, Gillespie (1990, 128) explains, "Liberalism...is an essentially hedonistic doctrine that aims not at virtue or goodness but at preservation, a liberation of the passions, and a pleasurable life." Why are these mutually exclusive?

74. Schmidt 1978a, 63. Grant may have uttered the phrase sneeringly; Warren (1990, 63), among others, has noted "Grant's anti-Americanism." (The negative nature of Canadian identity I reference in Pinar 2011c.) "Anti-Americanism has always been an aspect of Canadian political culture," Fierlbeck (2006, 53–4) explains, "but it was only in the twentieth century that the expression of anti-Americanism became a clear response to a society built upon the exaltation of individualism, the use of technology, and the force of consumerism. In Canada's geographical and economic vulnerability, Canadians quite quickly became aware of the consequences of this web of modernity."

75. Davis and Roper 2005b, 421. What would Grant say now, in this time of Trump? Vulgarity remains prominent but just the start of what one must say has become of the land of the free and the brave.

76. Davis and Roper 2005b, 467. Those teachers included John Locke, Benjamin Franklin, Thomas Jefferson, and John Dewey.

77. Davis and Roper 2005b, 468. Despite their "morally shallow" tradition and present degradation, Grant allowed that there are "many Americans [who] have seen with clarity the nature of that which chokes them and seek for ways to live beyond it" (468). Despite our disagreements over abortion, euthanasia, sexuality, and religion, I believe Grant would concede that I belong in this category.

78. Davis and Roper 2009b, 405. "Thus," Meynell (2011, 52) writes, "not until freedom has content is it real or rational."

79. Davis and Roper 2009b, 416.

80. In a 1965 letter Grant wrote: "I do not think I lack hope, because in the Christian sense I interpret hope as a supernatural virtue, and courage is what is necessary in the world" (Christian 1996d, 229).

81. "I think it's great that there's new nationalism in Canada; I think it's great that there has been new nationalism of an authentic kind in Quebec" (Cayley 1995, 107).

82. Davis and Roper 2009b, 335.

83. Davis and Roper 2009b, 337. Even while defending Prime Minister John Diefenbaker against those favouring continental integration, Grant criticized him for failing to recognize the centrality of Quebec to Canada (see Davis and Roper 2009b, 403). Writing Diefenbaker two years after the Tory leader had been forced out of office, Grant testified that "Canada cannot do without Quebec; Quebec cannot do without Canada.... Yes, the Conservative party says one Canada; but one Canada which rejoices in its diversity" (Christian 1996d, 235). Grant was also critical of Liberal Prime Minister Pierre Elliott Trudeau over the issue of Quebec, in part because Trudeau was, he thought, a centralist and a continentalist (Davis and Roper 2009b, 410). That point I'll reference again in ch. 1.

84. Davis and Roper 2009b, 337. "Moderation is not only needed from our political leaders," Grant emphasized, "but from the rest of us" (337).

85. Davis 2002b, 150. Anti-conscription and anti-English riots occurred in Quebec, Grant reminded (151).

86. Grant's understanding of French-Canadian nationalism is, Parel (1992, 144) judges, "remarkable for its insight into the influence of Catholicism on the formation of French-Canadian identity. What brought forth a nation in Quebec were its language, its geography, and its Catholicism. It lived by a public philosophy that viewed virtue as being prior to freedom, and the common good as being the conditioning norm of private good."

87. Davis and Roper 2009b, 416. In 1979 Grant was awarded an honorary degree from the University of Toronto, in 1980 another one by the University of Guelph; on both occasions he spoke on the same subject: Canada and Quebec (see 415).

88. Atwood (1972) 2012, 9. See also Chambers 1999.

89. Emberley ([1994] 2005, lxxx).

90. "It is implicit in Grant's thought," Parel (1992, 149) writes, "that religion is the single most powerful force that can counteract the baleful effects of modernity." That almost seems a progressive argument for accepting religion "as if" it were true, a strategic justification. There are also epistemological ones as well, as I shall discuss later.

91. Not that Grant viewed Quebec—and Catholicism—without ambivalence: writing his mother in June 1953 he complained that Quebec is a "mixture of ugly and dogmatic Catholicism mixed with the industrial society, but then French Canada is not my responsibility the way that English-speaking Canada is" (Christian 1996d, 180).

92. See Davis and Roper 2009b, 746. Including education, one key transmitter of culture; on that front, one observer was not optimistic. From a "Grantian perspective on Quebec," Caldwell (2006, 34) "lamented" the surrender of the province to technique, an allegation he illustrated by referencing the mid-1990s shift in teacher education: teachers no longer were required to have a specialized degree in an academic field; worse, they must then suffer through a four-year "socialization" by an education faculty, and would no longer "require the approbation of teachers in a school before

receiving life-long teaching certification.... This change constitutes the victory of technique over substance and virtue."

93. Davis and Roper 2009b, 416.

94. Grant's support of French culture in Canada derives also from his critique of technology as centralized and standardized: "[T]he more division there is, the better; this is why I'm for Quebec" (Davis and Roper 2009b, 579).

95. Writing Hugh MacLennan, Grant expressed his "hope" that "the French in Quebec keep their determination not to be slowly smoothed out of existence, but not knowing the province I do not know what should be their political instrument for achievement this end" (Christian 1996d, 250).

96. Robertson 2006, 160. For Peukert (1992, 81–2), "modernity" refers "to the form of fully fledged industrialized society that has been with us from the turn of the century until the present day. In an economic sense, modernity is characterized by highly rationalized industrial production, complex technological infrastructures and a substantial degree of bureaucratized administrative and service activity; food production is carried out by an increasingly small but productive, agricultural sector. Socially speaking, its typical features include the division of labour, wage and salary discipline, an urbanized environment, extensive educational opportunities and a demand for skills and training. As far as culture is concerned, media products dominate; continuity with traditional aesthetic principles and practices in architecture and the visual and other creative arts is broken, and is replaced by unrestricted formal experimentation. In intellectual terms, modernity marks the triumph of western rationality, whether in social planning, the expansion of the sciences or the self-replicating dynamism of technology, although this optimism is accompanied by skeptical doubts from social thinkers and cultural critics."

97. "In Grant's view," Sibley (2008, 276) notes, "the fundamental purpose of Canada is the maintenance of its French- and English-speaking partnership." Recall that Grant died in 1988; Indigenous peoples, Fierlbeck (2006, 37) notes, "became more politically active in the 1990s." Atwood ([1972] 2012, 83; see also xiii) confirms that "[u]ntil very recently, Indians and Eskimos made their only appearances in Canadian literature in books written by white writers." Had Grant lived even longer, no doubt he would have attended to the integration of new immigrants too; as Barry Cooper (1992, 161) notes: "The number of Canadians who meant Britain when they spoke of home grew exponentially smaller with each generation. The substance of Grant's meditation, therefore, was an *evocative vision* of Canada, not an *empirical description*."

98. Rigelhof (2001, 146–7) acknowledges that Grant "draws less attention to the Indigenous and Asian presences in Canada than the twenty-first century requires." That is indisputable. "When we go into the Rockies," Grant wrote, "we may have the sense that gods are there. But if so, they cannot manifest themselves to us as ours. They are the gods of another race, and we cannot know them because of what we are, and what we did." At first I decoded these sentences as suggesting pantheism, but Margaret Atwood (who quotes them) associates them with Indigenous peoples (see Atwood [1972] 2012, 82). If so, here is Grant's acknowledgement of both cultural incommensurability and cultural genocide.

99. "Our failure to think through the claims of "particularity" is evident," Angus (1997, 76) argues, "in the exclusion of Indigenous people as founders, the trivialization of ethnicity, and our inability politically to represent regionalism."

100. Christian and Grant 1998b, 101. "Although he [Grant] saw no way for the demise of local Indigenous cultures to be avoided," Caldwell (2006, 29) notes, "he very much admired those who resisted."

101. Cayley 1995, 109. Caldwell (2006, 29) adds: "Grant was convinced that the geopolitical instrument of this process was the American empire, and the local Indigenous cultures with which he was most concerned were, of course, those of his own Canadian society, constituted mainly of British and French cultural traditions."

102. Christian and Grant 1998b, 101.

103. These phrases may represent traces of Augustine's influence on Grant's thinking. Scanlon (2005, 100) suggests that "Augustine's discovery of the 'inward life,' focused on the will, was the beginning of a new era in the history of thought." That era superseded the ancient view, wherein, Angus (1997, 77) reminds: "The private realm (*idiom*), which was understood in classical philosophy as merely a prerequisite for universal political life, has been *submerged* by modern technology. It thus needs to be rediscovered and reformulated in a radical manner not necessary previously."

104. Davis and Roper 2009b, 495.

105. Davis and Roper 2009b, 495.

106. in speaking of a scholar he very admired, Grant shows that study is subjectively self-sustained, an ongoing and embodied (if elusive) admixture of subjective specificity and academic erudition: "[C. N.] Cochrane was not first and foremost a specialist; he was first an educated man who looked at the ancient world from out of his long life of sustained self-education" (Davis and Roper 2009b, 423). He wrote his mother in 1948 that "Charles Cochrane's description of St. Augustine's attitude to the world is still the most pertinent writing on the modern world I have ever read" (quoted in Jersak 2012, 184).

107. Christian 1996d, 313.

108. Grant knew that "anybody who has time to think has been given a great privilege by society" (Cayley 1995, 170).

109. Grant's attunement to the historical moment is almost everywhere evident. In a 1948 letter to his mother, for instance, he wrote that "most people still teach philosophy as if there were still a civilization in North America, instead of teaching it as if the old traditions were completely finished and we had to build new ones" (Christian 1996d, 155). Grant knew what time it was.

110. "[W]e have lost our way," Grant lamented, "in thinking what anything is fitted for" (Davis and Roper 2005b, 623).

111. O'Donovan 1984, 105. For Grant, the "presence" which is "modern technological society" is "in us," O'Donovan (109) points out, requiring (I would suggest) cultivation of subjective non-coincidence with even internalized states. For Grant such non-coincidence is intellectual and temporal, e.g., Christian Platonism and recollection of its past presence, a time before its secularization into science and technology.

112. O'Donovan 1984, 105.

113. In the *Phaedrus*, Planinc (1992, 41) reminds, "Socrates says the discourse of a written text is nothing in comparison to the discourse within the soul of its author expressed in the text." Grant's writing is in this sense soulful.

114. "Contemplation is related to charity," Athanasiadis (2001, 167) explains, an "openness to the other. Contemplation stands over against mastery, and seeks to understand in order to admire and wonder rather than to control."

115. Emphasizing questions of right conduct, ethics is conspicuously absent in modernity, Grant laments: "Modern thought at its height is led to be able to say nothing about how it is best for man to be together…what is the best life for man?" (Davis and Roper 2009b, 1077).

116. Marion 2012, 178

117. Davis and Roper 2009a, xxv–xxvi.

118. Grant embodied as he articulated, in Trilling's words (1972, 157) "the momentous claim which life makes upon us, by very reason, it seems, of is hardness, intractability, and irrationality."

119. "More and more," Reimer (1978, 53) writes of Grant, "he sees the task facing the modern world not as the war on poverty or the creation of an organic society, but rather resistance to the technological monolith."

120. Davis and Roper 2009b, 968. Grant credits Nietzsche for making this plain. In cosmological terms, I accept that life is without purpose—except, at some instinctual level, survival—but I cannot rule out that Grant knew otherwise. Without cosmological purpose, one accords meaning to one's life oneself, as Sartre (whom Grant first admires, then comes to loathe) has Roquentin realize in *Nausea*. One's seemingly self-conferred project substitutes for cosmological structure as it informs, even propels, one daily life, and in doing so, affords meaning, not only instrumentally rationalized but also intrinsically (or so it seems to me) satisfying. But studying Grant has encouraged me to think "as if" Grant did indeed know otherwise. In short, I study George Grant for the same reason he studied Simone Weil: "The reason why I study the writings of Simone Weil is that I learn from them" (Davis and Roper 2009b, 808).

121. I am reminded of Alain Locke, the self-described "philosophical mid-wife" (quoted in Posnock 1998, 184) to the Harlem Renaissance, who, in a late-in-life reflection, depicted himself as having lived in "paradox" (185). Adamantly anti-imperialist, universalist, and internationalist, Locke had been "forced by a sense of simple justice to approve" of "militant counter-nationalism" in Turkey, Palestine, India, but whose cosmopolitanism had not discouraged him from advocating "cultural racialism," if as a "defense counter-move for the American Negro" (185). Locke's attentiveness to circumstances recalls for Posnock "Du Bois[,] and suggests the capaciousness their shared pragmatism encouraged" (185). Double consciousness demands dexterity.

122. Heaven 2006, 317.

123. Heaven (2006, 317–8) continues: "I personally have been reflecting on these contraries for the forty years since I first encountered Grant's thought. I studied under him at McMaster, taught with him in the same department, and cherished a distant relationship with him until his death. As an ordained minister and a teacher of philosophy, I have lived the conflict of which I have written here."

124. Athanasiadis 2001, 250.

125. Heaven 1990, 109.

126. Angus 2006, 358.

127. Davis 2006, 63. Michael Ignatieff (2010, 137) characterizes Grant—his uncle (an irony made great when Ignatieff became the federal Liberal Party leader, in 2009)—as a "Christian conservative philosopher," making no reference to either progressivism or Platonism.

128. O'Donovan 1984, 47.

129. O'Donovan 1984, 47.

130. Athanasiadis 2001, 31. He does acknowledge Grant's "struggle with his own forma-tive influences" (32), writing: "As a Platonist and conservative, Grant recognizes the truth of a hierarchy of talents. But he also believes that any recognition of inequality must be subsumed within a greater recognition of equality" (108). That last phrase implies that Grant remained a progressive as well, if secondarily. As Athanasiadis acknowledges: "While he [Grant] values deeply the moral and spiritual traditions of his progenitors, the experience of war and conversion distances him from them as well" (21).

131. Strauss's significance for Grant, O'Donovan (1984, 50) suggests, concerned their shared commitment "to recover the truth of our classical past." (She contrasts Grant's Hegelianism in *Philosophy in the Mass Age* with Strauss's rigid rejection of any historicism in favour of eternity; 50.) Havers (2006, 124) suggests a progressive subtext to Strauss's significance: "Grant especially embraced Strauss's call to return to the great pre-modern texts to comprehend and overcome the most pernicious effects of modernity." Whatever his motive, Grant's debt to Strauss was, in Heaven's (2006, 301) view, "immense." For Duff (2006, 108), however, "Grant's thought is less indebted to Strauss than challenged by it," as Grant confers authority on the Christian Bible (117), from which philosophy follows, a "tension" between religion and philosophy Athanasiadis (2001, 132) and Heaven (2006, 302) also acknowledge. Heaven distinguishes between Strauss's construal of Greek philosophy as the quest for *knowledge* of the Good (an essentially Aristotelian project) and Grant's affirma-tion of Plato's affirmation "*love* of the Good," which for Grant "is at the heart and center of philosophy" (303).

132. "What Grant learned from Weil," Sibley (2008, 132) asserts, "can be boiled down to a single core idea—the idea of a limit to human freedom, individuality, and willing," adding that this idea of "limit" is akin to "the idea of God, and with it the notion that there are things that humans are not free to will and cannot know, especially the essential inscrutability of providence" (132). To issues of freedom and obedience, of inscrutability and intelligibility we turn in ch. 5 and 6. "Grant made no comprehen-sive statement on Weil," Kirby and Greenspan (1990, 154) note, "and the exact nature of her influence on him is difficult to discern." Surely it was spiritual but it may also have been pedagogical: among Weil's undertakings in her short life was secondary-school teaching (Thibon [1947] 2002, xvi). In a 1951 letter to his mother, Grant men-tions reading Weil's *Waiting on God*, judging it "magnificent" (Jersak 2012, 153).

133. "While his many commentators are correct to emphasize the importance of Christianity for Grant," Meynell (2011, 159–160) writes, "I contend that in its ideo-logical form as opposed to its experiential form, his Christianity is strongly informed by Hegelian idealism. Those who claim that his Hegelianism is merely a passing phase are missing a crucial dimension of Grant's thought. He is indeed a Christian Platonist, but a Christian Platonist who understands that identity in Hegelian terms." Sibley (2008, 113) argues that "despite Grant's disavowal, Hegel continued to have an abiding influence on his thought," indicated, he suggests, in Grant affirmation of the "unity of the whole, the idea that all entities are merely differentiated aspects of one systematic and rationally ordered whole" (46). Recall that Dewey—the quintes-sential American progressive, whom Grant disdained—acknowledged the so-called Hegelian deposit in his own thinking. The progressivism from which Grant fled was

informed by the Hegelianism Meynell and Sibley reference: "[T]he foundation for his arguments from the beginning of his career to its completion" (Meynell 2011, 105).

134. Athanasiadis 2001, 7.

135. Citation of his letters accents the immediacy of Grant's experience as he was living it, rendering that past moment present. Immediacy was a stylistic concern for Pasolini. Steimatsky (2008, 155) suggests that "[a] 'casual' effect of immediacy that Pasolini described as borrowed from sports or news reportage results, paradoxically, in an icon-like presentness of the image." Such "presentness" echoes, I hope, Grant's subjective presence as an educator. To questions of icons and images I turn in ch. 5.

136. Taylor ([1982] 2006, 136) seems sure that "the dominant influence" on Grant was "his mother," among the first female graduates of McGill and later head of its Royal Victoria College. "Maude Parkin was formidable. "It was hard to be her son" (136), Taylor reports Grant saying.

137. Athanasiadis 2001, 7.

138. George Parkin, George Monro Grant, and William Grant. I suggest there were five—the three men Athanasiadis lists plus his mother and his wife.

139. Grant described himself as having an "Oedipus complex the size of a house" (quoted in Christian 1996c, vii–viii). From the time he left for Queen's University in 1936 until she became too senile to make any sense of his letters, Grant wrote his mother almost weekly. "Dearest Ould," he wrote in 1948, using his pet name for her, "Why does life keep us apart? There are so few people that one longs for" (Christian 1996d, 154–5). Maude Grant saved her son's letters, as she did other family correspondence. Grant characterized his family as a "gynarchy," but the more common term, Christian (1996c, vii) points out, is "matriarchy. The core of the family was Grant's mother and her sister Alice."

140. Athanasiadis 2001, 7.

141. Athanasiadis 2001, 4.

142. Dart 2006, 24.

143. If modernity is an extension—a creation—of humanity, then is it an image of the Good? "Throughout the twentieth century," Mondzain (2005, xii–xiii) observes, "the image has been at the heart of our concern for the safeguarding of liberty and thought. However, since a visual and audio-visual imperialism has invaded the planet and reduced all critical reflection and discussion to a state of servile stupor and acephalic fascination, it has become incumbent on us to attempt to understand the elements of a genealogy whose ultimate offspring is the carrier of the best as well as the worst of things. Perhaps no great disaster is brewing other than the always threatening one of the abdication of thought, but the image is not responsible for that. Rather, it awaits consideration in terms of both its present crushing vitality and its history." Mondzain writes these words introducing her study of the Iconoclastic Controversy during the eighth and ninth century in the Byzantine Empire over the use of religious images. Icons and idols are the subject of ch. 5—central, I suggest, to understanding Grant's critique of technology, time, and teaching—and there too I again reference Mondzain. I quote her here to introduce the centrality of image to Western culture and its virtualization in contemporary technology.

144. O'Donovan 1984, 5.

145. Suffering and history are evident in Heaven's (2006, 310–11) assertion that "[f]or Grant," the "cross of Christ is the supreme image of the ways things are for humans,

bound up as they are within the desire for good and simultaneously crushed by necessity." In different language with similar meaning Ward (1990, 101) writes, "According to Grant, a true theodicy requires the simultaneous affirmation of the perfection of God and of concern for human affliction; the two must be held together in a way that does not exclude either pole of the contradiction." I return to the question of the unity of Grant's thought in the epilogue.

146. "Everyone," Athanasiadis (2001, 65) writes, has a limit beyond which they break. Affliction is a point beyond this limit and involves the total loss of dignity."

147. "The idea of love based in pedagogy may seem quaint to some modern readers and repellent to others," Trilling (1972, 82) acknowledges, "but unquestionably it plays a decisive part in the power and charm of Jane Austen's art. And if we attempt to explain the power and charm that the genre of the novel exercised in the nineteenth century, we must take full account of its pedagogic intention and of such love as a reader might feel was being directed towards him in the solicitude of the novel for his moral well-being, in its concern for the right course of his development." For Grant, charity informs the love (a concern for the "right course of development") expressed through his subjective presence in print and in person.

148. "Justice and love," Heaven (2006, 307) suggests, "are intimately bound up in the life and teaching of Socrates." Discussing Jesus and the concept of divine commands, Penelhum (1983, 96) writes: "There are general guidelines (something, incidentally, that even Socrates sometimes agreed were necessary for enlightened conduct), but they are not to be applied uncritically." I focus on obedience and freedom in ch. 6.

149. "Jesus" is my word choice. Heaven (2006, 310) points out that "[i]t is the Christ of the Gospels that is the revelation of perfection, not the Jesus of history. Grant rarely, if ever, speaks or writes of Jesus." There is too, perhaps most prominently, Grant's juxtaposition of the two. "Reflecting on the correlations of contraries was a central preoccupation of George Grant's philosophic life," (300) Heaven affirms. "The primary contrary in Grant's comprehensive vision," he continues, "is that between Socrates and Christ (rather than Athens and Jerusalem of Leo Strauss), and the link between the two is at a level at which they must be held together even though they cannot be thought together" (300). One link is the death of the two figures. "The primacy of Christ's death over Socrates' death," Kaethler (2009, 9) concludes, "is a theme that flows through all of Grant's writings."

150. What Trilling (1972, 96) writes of the contemporary artist one might observe of Grant the educator: "The artist—as he comes to be called—ceases to be the craftsman or the performer, dependent upon the approval of the audience. His reference is to himself only, or to some transcendent power which—or who—has decreed his enterprise and alone is worthy to judge it." In Grant's case, I would substitute "both" for "or" in that sentence.

151. Athanasiadis 2001, 6.

152. "Enact" is not exactly the word I want as it connotes behaviour. Not that I ignore behaviour—as Grant himself insisted, it matters very much what one does—but in the research on teaching there is an excessive interest in behaviour, an insufficient attention to what precedes, accompanies, and follows behaviour. What cannot be observed or measured is a part, often the major part, of what happens. Efforts to understand reality must attend to both the mundane and the transcendent, testifying to their elusive relation.

153. "Regional diversity has not yet succumbed to the federalist view of Canada," Angus (1997, 76) writes, adding that "these threads in the fabric of Canadian society have not been strong enough to withstand the homogenizing influence of advancing technology." Regionalism may, then, disappear into the national, and the national into the global: Grant's fear of a universal homogenous society seems embedded in Angus's sentence.

154. "The human person," Rocha (2017, 18) reminds, is that "referential being that exists only insofar as it is loved.... The order of love is the center of a true politics for the person. It is the alternative to the nihilism of liberal individualism."

155. Grant's teaching, I suggest, was iconographic, a topic to which I return in ch. 5. "Iconography," Ouspensky (1982, 43) explains, "is not copying. It is far from being impersonal, for to follow Tradition never shackles the creative powers of the iconographer, whose individuality expresses itself in the composition as well as in the colour and line. But the personal is here much more subtle than in other arts and so often escapes superficial observation."

156. To change images, one might say, as Dewey (1922, 182) did, that "the path of truth is narrow and straitened."

157. Grant's subjective presence structured his conversation, especially privately it seems: "Those familiar with him know that his conversation was like a spaniel exploring a field, setting off in one direction, then veering in another. It would be impossible to convey the sense of being in the presence of pure thought itself that this conveyed" (Davis and Roper 2009b, 736). Like a religious icon, Grant's presence was not static but ecstatic or *ekstasis*; from the Ancient Greek ἔκστασις, "to be or stand outside oneself, a removal to elsewhere" from *ek-* "out," and *stasis* "a stand, or a standoff of forces."

158. Aoki (1990) 2005, 368.

159. Grant's critique of technology, time, and teaching can be summarized as a critique of our idolatry of these; in contrast to idols, icons create a space which affirm both the particularity of everyday existence and the universality of spiritual life. "The icon sets the visible and the invisible into a relation with each other without any concession to realism," Mondzain (2005, 85) explains, "yet without contempt for matter." To these topics I devote ch. 5.

160. Phelan 2015, 3. "The economic questions of teacher pay and unions are mostly distractions," Rocha (2017, 79) writes, "obscuring the difficult truth that the ontological status of the teacher is the real stake in today's game."

161. Davis 2002b, 187.

162. Referencing Plato, Grant reminds that this idea declares that not only time but the world itself "points to its perfection beyond it. That is, this world is an image of the eternal world" (Davis and Roper 2005b, 704–5).

163. "[W]e must detach ourselves from the Greeks while simultaneously 'turning' toward them," James Magrini (2017, 5–6) advises, "recognizing the chasm that separates us historically, temporally, and linguistically; otherwise the possibility exists for misinterpretation."

164. The term shows up regularly in Grant's work. For instance: "This English-speaking modernity began that public enucleation of the modern with its exaltation of motion over rest, of potentiality over actuality, of interest as detached from virtue" (Davis and Roper 2009b, 84).

165. "If sincerity has lost its former status," Trilling (1972, 9) suggests, "if the word itself has for us a hollow sound and seems almost to negate its meaning, that is because it does not propose being true to one's self as an end but only as a means." Authenticity, Trilling writes, implies "a more strenuous moral experience than 'sincerity' does, a more exigent conception of the self and of what being true to it consists in, a wider reference to the universe and man's place in it, and a less acceptant and genial view of the social circumstances of life" (11). Was Grant's sincerity—being true to himself and others by decrying deprival—a progressive regression to a past when being true to oneself implied ethical fidelity to others?

166. Ignatieff (2010, 120) characterizes his uncle as "all passionate conviction, consequences be damned." Grant was a "huge presence in my childhood," Ignatieff acknowledges, "gigantic, shambling, dishevelled, smoking cigarette after cigarette, but so engrossed in his talk that he would not notice as the ash fell upon the lapels of his jacket…. It was not hard to be entranced by someone who sang out loud to operas on the stereo and, after motioning for reverent silence whenever the quintet in Mozart's *Cosi fan tutti* was sung, bent his head and listened in tears" (25). Presence implies its contrary, and I am working from a sense of absence—not being here, now—in my recognition of Grant's insistence on being present in the numbing, sincerity-silencing maelstrom of modernity. Comparing the two societies, Trilling (1972, 113) observes: "And in this respect the American self can be taken to be a microcosm of American society, which has notably lacked the solidity and intractability of English society; it is little less likely to be felt by its members as being palpably *there*." In the swirl of modernity—intensified in late or postmodernity with the prevalence of virtual reality—nothing can seem "palpably there," even the person next to me, indeed, not even "me."

167. Describing his "five tumultuous hours" interviewing Grant, journalist Charles Taylor ([1982] 2006, 129–30) wrote: "Sheila Grant—a statuesque, white-haired women with a regal bearing and a ready wit—sat in one of the arm chairs. There was nothing regal about George as he presided from the *chaise-longue*, although he was even more monumental. Grant is a burly man with an impressive corporation, but what you really notice is the massive head and shaggy bear. (He'd be splendid in a toga.) For a man in his sixties, his face is youthful—lined but not wrinkled. His full head of brown hair is brushed and parted, although not quite tidy. Even in a suit, Grant appears rumpled and dishevelled. All in all, he often suggests an overgrown schoolboy trying to be proper, but not fully succeeding. His voice has traces of an English accent: neither very loud nor very deep, it *feels* both loud and deep, something like an organ."

168. That is, if one studies not scans Grant's words, thereby partaking of the moment during which they written. A true teacher, Aoki (1986/1991) 2005, 159) suggests, becomes revealed "by her mere presence in the classroom as teacher…. [She] initiates a transformation of a sociocultural and physical environment into something different…. The environment ceases to be environment, and in its place comes into being a pedagogical situation, a lived situation pregnantly alive in the presence of people." Culturally compacted, historically layered, biographically imbricated, the situation calls for deciphering what is in between the lines participants in this complicated conversation speak.

169. Weil's prose, Thibon ([1947] 2002, xix) writes, are "bare" and "simple," as was, he suggests, her "inner" life. Grant's texts are anything but bare and simple; they

convey his expansive incorporation and animated articulation of time, place, and circumstance in the presence of other persons.

170. Christian 1996c, vii.

171. Christian 1996c, vii.

172. Christian 1996c, xi.

173. Grant appreciated the significance of being subjectively present in others too. Discussing Céline, Grant praises the artist's capacity to create the sense of "being directly present in the midst of events," of "being there" (Davis and Roper 2009b, 464). One feels "there" with Grant as well.

174. For Weil, Thibon ([1947] 2002, xi) tell us, what mattered was writing "stripped" of any "adornment," style expressive of the "soul," as explained in her note to Thibon: "The effort of expression has a bearing not only on the form but on the thought and on the whole inner being" (xi). Subjective presence signals such "effort of expression."

175. Like "authorship," as Annovi (2017, 9) writes, subjective presence is a "transdisciplinary concept," one that acknowledges that "the author is not simply in the *text*, a la Barthes, but in the interwoven and inextricable *texture* of his interdisciplinary body of the work. He is the matrix of the work." In this sense, Annovi adds, "the author, in short, is a countercultural figure, characterized by his profound difference to the social body. In short, the author is the other, the antibody" (9) Grant was, in this sense, an author; he was the "matrix" of his wide-ranging work and his presence provided a powerful "antibody" to technological society.

176. In a 1948 letter to his mother, Grant was less subtle: "No wonder the businessmen walk over teachers. Most of them are such ninnies" (Christian 1996d, 154).

177. Davis and Roper 2005b, 61.

178. "The term 'one's own' was used by Grant mainly to justify Canadian sovereignty," Angus (1997, 173) explains, "but also as the philosophical concept of particularity that theorizes local attachments in the midst of the drive to universality and homogeneity characteristic of modern technological empires." I am reminded of Madeleine Grumet's (1988, 181) emphasis upon attachment; at one point she noted that "[i]n schools we become civilized by denying attachment."

179. "[F]or the enlightened exercise of charity and the administration of alms," Mondzain (2005, 62) explains, "is similar to the administering of medicine or the teaching of truth."

180. For Grant, Athanasiadis (2001, 165) clarifies, "love of one's own, be it a person, tradition, or nation, is a means to love of the good. But the two loves must be separated; otherwise, love of one's own can become absolute and, therefore, idolatrous." Athanasiadis emphasizes that "although no tradition can incarnate the universal good adequately, one can only access the universal good through some particular tradition or roots' which serve as an image or gateway. Here again, we detect the influence of Weil's understanding of the importance of human roots and *metaxu*" (165).

181. While volunteering there in 1941, Grant wrote his mother that the bombs "descend &, in the space of a second destroy even the most intricate, delicately balanced human personality. Not only is the beautiful mechanism of the body torn, ripped, masticated by the tiger-like violence of the high explosive, but the existence of the person knitted with his thoughts, passions, ambitions, inhibitions is destroyed" (Christian 1996d, 75). The bombs nearly destroyed him, psychically and physically.

182. As noted earlier, above all modernity designated the obliteration of particularity and the triumph of homogeneity. We return to the term—and Grant's grappling with it—in ch. 3, but for now a 1945 letter enables us to gain an incipient sense of what is at stake, including humanity's capacity to supersede what has befallen it. In this passage industrialism is his moniker for modernity. "Historically, that is looking at what has been, to try and determine what should be, I have a feeling that man, faced suddenly with the problems of industrialism and all that it entails—urbanism, new forms of work, leisure, tremendous power of nature—has started (as is quite natural) badly; and, as he does it and makes these mistakes, he starts naturally to look for blame, and will probably blame the wrong things & then will eventually say & do: We must have a saviour to pull us through this.... Of course, historically, there is proof that there is something special in mankind, supra animal, more than material, that will make him eventually pull up his socks and be on the way up again; but at the moment, this colossal, material change of industrialism has been too much for our great tradition (really a remarkably thin veneer) of personal responsibility, the dignity of the individual" (Christian 1996d, 114). Faith in human nature—how I wished I shared it—steadied him in face of calamity, faith itself founded in Christian Platonism.

183. Doane 2002, 220.

184. I am conscious, as Benedetti (2005, 115) points out, that "the late-modern writer is continually struggling against the incumbent conventionality of whatever stylistic and formal choice he or she makes." Is the late-modern compulsion to innovate—a contradiction in terms as Benedetti makes clear—another, if contemporary, instance of Nietzsche's eternal return?

185. Combs (1983a, vii; emphasis added) introduces *Modernity and Responsibility*—a collection of essays presented to Grant on the occasion of his sixtieth birthday, in 1978— as I might introduce this one: "The book is not directly *about* Grant, his life and thought, and it is indirectly about him in that it explores matter that have interested him and held his attention throughout his life. The volume is about matters that matter and so tries to honour and represent George Grant's thought." That last sentence speaks directly to the final three chapters of this book, topics about which he wrote little directly—he references eternity frequently but writes in detail about it little— but topics about which I think he might have taken an interest.

186. Davis and Roper 2009b, 810.

187. In so wanting, am I affirming, as students suspected from the start, that this book is, despite its enactment of complicated conversation in an era of tweets, an old-fashioned form? "To innovate means to keep an eye on what is old," Benedetti (2005, 115) points out, "to perceive the process of exhaustion or of conventionalization that invests literary forms. This presupposes a great capacity, analogous and parallel to the one that readers have developed, to perceive the first signs of convention, to sniff out even its faintest whiff." Not so faint, is it? Not only do I affirm the convention of the book, but of the textbook, too. In an era of PowerPoint (and its bullets), tweets, and other such utterances, a sustained contemplation of one person—in this instance a great man (with our knee-jerk dismissal of the very idea)—seems especially (un) timely, e.g., progressive.

188. Not so fast, Benedetti (2005, 195) would interrupt, asserting that "the writer is no longer someone who generates or increases, but merely a *scriptor*: a scribe, a scrivener,

a copyist, a craftsman, a collector of pre-existing writings, a librarian, a *bricoleur*, a prop-man for the literary bazaar." The labour of a scribe was once sacred, I might reply, but my anxiety is that Grantians will cry foul, that I have corrupted the great man. My steadying sense is that I am teacher, working to render accessible in today's Age of Ignorance the work of this great educator, this great Canadian.

189. There are of course precedents to employing citations to enact a complicated conversation, among them Marshall McLuhan, who evidently organized *The Gutenberg Galaxy* as, in Stamps (1995, 135) words, "almost entirely a collection of voices," taking, she adds, "the forms of quotations from literature and scholarly sources juxtaposed with McLuhan's own 'voice-over'-style glasses and commentary." Less a "voice-over" than dialogical encounter, my engagement with Grant enacts aspects of the complicated conversation that is the curriculum as taught and as studied.

190. Derrida asserts that "quoting is not an innocent operation; it is really violent, a violent appropriation" (Kearney 2005a, 30), but I suggest that is an overstatement. Removing a sentence—or a paragraph—from its place in the original text *is* violent, but not necessarily deadly, as it allows that sentence or paragraph to breathe different air in a temporal location the writer might not have imagined. Grant himself quoted others of course; referencing Sheila Grant, Kaethler (2009, 94) reports that "Grant was never confined by context and would take thoughts and quotes from other thinkers making them his own." See Kaethler 2009, 94n345.

191. O'Donovan 1984, 11.

192. Collingwood 2002, 74. Collingwood felt sure that "you cannot find out what a man means by simply studying his spoken or written statements, even though he has spoken or written with perfect command of language and perfectly truthful intention. In order to find out his meaning you must also know what the question was (a question in his own mind, and presumed by him to be in yours) to which the thing he has said or written was meant as an answer" (31). While that seems too simple—never mind its contradiction of his disavowal of generalization—were I to name Grant's question, it would be the one I chose to title ch. 1.

193. Rigelhof (2001, 123) points out that "[g]reat thinkers and artists and poets and saints, most of all, can show us the way back to a living, vital relationship to the past. Through them, we begin to once again know that changes in the world can be judged by some other standard than their newness."

194. "However," Mondzain (2005, 91) points out, "the presence of the iconic gaze cannot be described as a real presence. In the artificial image, it is the pressure of absence that bears all the weight of authority." Likewise, the trace of this man in his text is likewise "the presence of an absence" that those of us who never met George Grant can only glimpse through the "weight of authority" his text conveys.

195. Cusset 2008, 337.

196. Angus 1997, 64.

197. Lee 1990, 22.

198. For a while Bach and Beethoven were his favourite composers; see Jersak 2012, 184.

199. Angus 1997, 64.

200. Angus 1997, 65. Angus cautions that "orality is just as partial as any other medium of communication" (67).

201. Stamps 1995, 83. Speakers and listeners included for Grant all of humanity, especially those unable to speak or listen. Ajzenstat (1992, 86) reminds us that Grant

never abandons "his conviction that a still, small voice speaks to us through the weakest members of society."

202. For me original sources are themselves "secondary"; they comment on conversations occurring in the past, to which one has perhaps come too late. On occasion one starts a conversation I suppose, but even then the echoes of conversation past reverberate in whatever one offers to others. Of course to make claims about Grant one must examine the textual evidence that supports them: returning to the original is a prerequisite. But the original is no origin but more like, as Sikka (1997, 265) noted about "Heidegger's thought," no "mere copying of the past but a transformative appropriation." Benedetti (2005, 98) might retort that my "postmodern renunciation of originality...is only a denial, not an abandonment[,] of originality." Of course.

203. Referencing Weil, Grant noted that "always we must try and reach what she is saying" (Davis and Roper 2009b, 838), an effort I also made with Grant, the second verb implying a shift in one's subject position.

204. Akin to the slow professor; see Berg and Seeber 2016. And to slow art; see Reed 2017.

205. I describe my effort as Reed (2017, 15) describes his. "This book," he writes, "doesn't simply *describe* slow art; reading it in some measure *performs* slowness against the backdrop of our warp-speed present."

206. The psychoanalytic subtext of the idea of reactivation is not the only archaeological substratum of the idea; in a temporally empty present it is a progressive gesture toward becoming historical. Like Romanticism—on which Benedetti's (2005, 108) comment is focused—Grant's thought also exhibits a "tendency...toward using the ancients in order to estrange the present." There must be some way out of here.

207. Stamps 1995, 137.

208. Stamps 1995, 137.

209. Stamps 1995, 137.

210. There is comparison of Grant with Innis and McLuhan—see Kroker 1984—but here I want to emphasize Grant's skepticism concerning technology (not unshared by McLuhan and Innis of course). Grant knew that "most of our thinking about technology becomes a simple surrender to it" (Davis and Roper 2009b, 134); he might retreat (into quietude) but surrender he never did.

211. Evidently an agonistic, the journalist Charles Taylor ([1982] 2006, 138–139) registers his difference with Grant on the matter of religion: "Unlike Grant, however, I had not discovered God in the course of my travels.... By the time I came to tackle Grant, I knew that a conservative *must* finally acknowledge the existence of some such order... In my case, however, this belief was the product of mere mind: I had never had a mystical experience of the Deity, or whatever term might best define that higher intelligence. I knew it was there, but I hadn't felt it. Clearly this would limit my ability to fathom Grant, although it did not inhibit me from plunging into the more political aspects of his thought." I am not entirely sure "higher intelligence" is "there," although in studying Grant I have tried to act "as if" it might be. Politically, I've been no conservative—certainly in no sense the term has political currency in the contemporary United States—but here too Grant's rather different sense of the appellation I found appealing, so much so that I suggest that being "progressive" today may mean becoming "conservative" as Grant defines. In any case, like Taylor, these differences have not prevented me from plunging into Grant's thought.

212. Penelhum 1983, 94.
213. The paradox is indicated, it seems to me, when Grant (almost offhand) says: "Indeed it is only perhaps 'history' or the attempt to overcome that concept which can excuse the words of autobiography which follow" (Davis and Roper 2009b, 507). Autobiography acknowledges time in its effort to supersede it, as re-entering the past and imagining the future enables one to move through and beyond what occurred in time. Admittedly I am speaking here of the "immanent" and not the "transcendent" (in Grant's sense), but the more modest movement autobiography encourages can complement, perhaps even initiate, the more unworldly movement of the latter.
214. Mondzain 2005, 22.
215. Decades before Trump of course, as Trilling (1972, 137) reminds us of J. H. Plumb's view "that the past itself is on the point of being extirpated from the consciousness of modern man."
216. "History did not mean knowing what events followed what," Collingwood (2002, 58) asserted, "it meant getting inside other people's heads, looking at their situation through their eyes, and thinking for yourself whether the way in which they tackled it was the right way." Jay (2005, 236) notes that Collingwood "shared with his German predecessor [Wilhelm Dilthey] a belief that some sort of re-experiencing of the past was essential to historical knowledge." Collingwood distanced himself from Dilthey, Jay continues, in part by arguing "for 're-enactment' rather than 're-experiencing,' a distinction that emphasized the importance of actions in the past as the target of historical inquiry" (236–7). Reactivation incorporates both of these concepts in its effort to reconstruct the present. What I mean here might become clearer considering Mondzain's (2005, 72) conclusion that "the only *mimésis* (we should not translate this too hastily as imitation, but rather as an act that aims to make present, to make *manifest*) 'in truth and spirit' will be the cross, the eucharist, the virtuous life, and good government." For me, living in the time of Trump, the Weimar Republic becomes knowledge of most worth, but the educational point of reactivation—"to make present" is clear.
217. The typical iPhone owner, Carr (2017, C1) reports, uses it "some 80 times a day," some 30,000 times during the year, concluding that the device has become a "repository" of our experience, even defining "who we are." Carr concludes: "When we constrict our capacity for reasoning and recall or transfer those skills to a gadget, we sacrifice our ability to turn information into knowledge. We get the data but lose the meaning" (C1). In the interest of meaning, like Grant—and Pasolini—I suggest reactivating the past. "In the fabric of his own cinema," Steimatsky (2008, 162) points out, "Pasolini sought instead, and with remarkable consistency throughout his work, to explore potent continuities in the embrace of a disappearing but still vital archaic domain, and the modernism of a social and political, indeed, revolutionary possibility." Less revolution than recovery of what has been lost, Grant's invocation of ancient Athens and Jerusalem and his incorporation of these in addressing the issues of his moment testify to his "embrace of a disappearing but still vital archaic domain."
218. Davis 2002b, 94.
219. Davis and Roper 2009b, 133.
220. Unlike Luther, Grant was not anti-Semitic.

221. Schmidt 1978a, 67.
222. Schmidt 1978a, 67. "Staring" at our situation is not what our times encourage, rather distraction through stimulation, likely in increasing doses. When Grant made this point the "strongest stimulations" were receivable "on pay television" (Davis and Roper 2009b, 492), but by making that observation it is as if he knew the "smartphone" was coming.
223. Davis and Roper 2009b, 679–80n69.
224. "In Ruskin's view," Dinshaw (2012, 70) suggests, "Longfellow's is a complex form of time-consciousness in which perceptual attention in the present day allows for a sharper perception of another time." I quote this passage (despite its alluring reference to Ruskin and Longfellow; for that read Dinshaw) to emphasize the idea that immersion in the moment can also allow attunement to lie beyond it.
225. For Grant, O'Donovan (1984, 128) points out, "remembering...is the way of making present that truth which is absent from our daily living in the technological 'dynamo.'"
226. Grant reminds us that "religion," derived from the original Latin verb *religere*, means "to find together" (quoted in O'Donovan 1984, 62).
227. "We know we have psyches," Trilling (1972, 55) quips, "because they make trouble for us—our most constant and reliable awareness of selfhood derives from the experience of that trouble." And of satisfaction, joy, peacefulness.
228. Finally, there is an association of partaking with iconography—think of the Eucharist—as Steimatsky (1998, 246; emphasis added) suggests: "Incarnation, the possibility of God's materialization in Jesus, defines Christianity and its promise of redemption vis-à-vis Judaism, for example. The icon repeats at a secondary level this anthropomorphic incarnation, celebrating the divine descent into form and flesh. The icon, like the relic, is a memento left by Christ as a promise of the vision of God in eternity; it is seen to provide visual evidence for the incarnation of the sacred in the world. The iconic image is not simply 'symbolic' or 'allegorical' in relation to meaning, as it would be in a Protestant system that severs the manifest and the hidden, the flesh and the spirit. Rather, it is grasped as participating in what it represents: it is an index of Christ's humanity; in *partaking* of his body it incarnates God."
229. An inner state I contrast with quietism (specifically political acquiescence), although historically the two terms intersect, both privileging contemplation, even in the midst of action.
230. O'Donovan 1984, 129. In Angus (1997, 96) terms, "Escaping the technological empire requires, in the first place, understanding how deeply we are each caught up in it."
231. Lee 1990, 19. "Natural law," Kirby and Greenspan (1990, 159) conclude (summarizing conference presentations), was a "looming presence in Grant's writings rather than a doctrine. It coexisted with other presences that sometimes seemed contradictory."
232. Jennifer Summit and Blakey Vermeule (2018, 31) decry their polarization and endorse their interrelation and interdependence (141); Grumet and I ([1981] 1988) argue for sharp separation, etching a space in between where educational experience can occur.
233. "This process of Socratic learning, or *Being-educated*," Magrini (2017, 104) suggests, "is ethically '*kathartic*' and transforms the disposition (*hexis*) comprising one's character." Grant had character; in a previous era he would be termed a man of substance. As O'Donovan (1990, 141) explains: "For 'substance' denotes the inner, active

unity of the individual which integrates the composite structures and processes entailed in its being." Despite the range of topics he taught and on which he wrote, there remains a strong sense that Grant's "inner, active unity" is a coherent and often commanding subjective presence.

CHAPTER 1

Why?

We move into the tightening circle in which more technological science is called for to meet the problems which technological science has produced. In that tightening circle, the overcoming of chance is less and less something outside us, but becomes more and more the overcoming of chance in our own species, in our own very selves.

George Grant[1]

Such a question—why?—could convey an effort to persuade reluctant readers to keep reading. While I hope the chapter does convince readers that studying Grant—reading him in the original as well as my reactivation of him here—is worth their time, with this question I am thinking of Sonya Sikka's association of the question "why" with humanity's historic preoccupation with transcendence, for Heidegger[2] a question that is "ultimately grounded in *Dasein*."[3] During his lectures (1972–73) on Heidegger's thought, Grant acknowledged that "at that center is *Dasein*," which he defined: "Literally, to be there—man." To be there— here—denotes subjective as well as physical presence. So present, Grant represents a living protest of modernity, lamenting the loss of the question "why?" now supplanted with "how?"[4] The former question also recalls Augustine, with whose work Grant grappled. As Jean Bethe Elshtain explains, for Augustine,

the mind can never be transparent to itself; we are never wholly in control of our thoughts; our bodies are essential, not contingent, to who we are and how we think; and we know that we exist, not because "I think, therefore I am," but rather, "I doubt, therefore I know I exist." Only a subject who is a self that can reflect on itself can doubt. His *Confessions* is a story of a human being who has become a question to himself.[5]

Grant made a question of himself as well, a question refracted through the wide range of impressions he left on others, others who described their impressions of him in the following terms.

Perhaps most prominently, Grant has been deemed a political philosopher, nationalist, theologian, witness, and prophet, that last designation conferred by both William Christian[6] and Mel Hurtig.[7] On another occasion Christian extolled Grant as a "singer of enchanted songs...that scare away...the frightful apparitions that flit about in the darkness, particularly that night which envelops our civilization."[8] In an editorial note to Grant's letters, Christian—also his biographer—names him "the most famous philosopher in Canada and one of the country's best teachers."[9] That judgment is one Larry Schmidt shared.[10]

That assessment, that Grant was one of the country's best teachers, a "real professor,"[11] Alex Colville felt, seems shared by the political philosopher Tom Darby, who likened him to Socrates, suggesting that "Grant's rootedness in, but criticism of, his own society recalls Socrates' similar relation to his city."[12] Darby also likened Grant to the biblical Jeremiah,[13] a preaching prophet[14] who condemned idolatry.[15] "Prophets are often marginalized when alive," Dart reminds, acknowledging that "Grant faced his share."[16] Also emphasizing biblical associations, Dennis Lee depicted him as a witness.[17] The journalist Charles Taylor terms him an a "trenchant moralist" very much needed "to arouse our apprehensions."[18]

For Schmidt, Grant was also Canada's "foremost political philosopher."[19] Graeme Nicholson termed him a "public philosopher...very much an academic, but one with a public, a readership."[20] "Some say he was the foremost indigenous philosopher Canada has produced," Athanasiadis acknowledges, enjoying "popular appeal" and demonstrating "deep wisdom and originality."[21] Hugh Donald Forbes regarded Grant as more a theologian than political philosopher[22]—Andrew Kaethler calls him a philosopher *and* a theologian[23]—but Robert Meynell appears to disagree with both, listing Grant alongside C. B. Macpherson and (the philosopher) Charles Taylor as one of the "three leading Canadian political philosophers."[24] Meynell is in good company, as Arthur Davis and Henry Roper also acknowledge Grant as "one of Canada's leading political philosophers."[25] Davis adds that while on occasion Grant regarded himself as a moral and political philosopher, "he was reluctant to call himself a theologian."[26] A "political philosopher," Andrew Potter writes, Grant is also remembered as the "father"[27] of English-speaking Canadian nationalism.[28]

Grant later devalued the significance of political philosophy[29] and was reluctant to claim the title of philosopher. "What I dare not do," Grant once remarked, "is to make the claim that I am a philosopher."[30] Grant said the same to David Cayley: "I wouldn't for a moment call myself a philosopher," adding that

"I would call myself a really quite competent teacher of philosophy and quite competent student of it."[31] Robin Lathangue cast Grant in broader terms still, as a "public intellectual,"[32] as does Nicholson, who affirmed that "George Grant was *Canada's* most significant public philosopher, meaning that his public was Canadian."[33] Ramsay Cook, Sibley reports, regarded George Grant and Pierre Elliott Trudeau as "the two most important Canadian intellectuals of the past twenty years."[34] Greenspan also emphasizes that

> Grant steadfastly addressed the public realm. The simplicity of his prose and the eloquence of its rhythms presupposed a public agora, an assembly where all citizens listened and spoke on the momentous issues of the day. He rarely chose academic journals as his forum. He preferred magazines and publishers devoted to public affairs, as well as the C.B.C [Canadian Broadcasting Corporation]. In response, the Canadian public or at least a large segment of it, looked upon George as its philosopher.[35]

As a "public man," E. Joan O'Donovan confirms, "Grant has continually engaged the traditions of his society in a self-consciously questioning way."[36] Invoking an even broader term, Barry Cooper accords him the status of, simply, a "thinker."[37] Grant viewed his own fate to be that of "a lesser thinker," too humble a self-estimation in my judgment, but consistent with his humility.[38] That virtue maybe political as well as personal, as Craiutu points out that political moderation "is sustained by a sense of humility, the rejection of self-righteousness, and a profound mindfulness of one's limited knowledge and potential for error and violence."[39]

"So what was he?"[40] Rigelhof asks. He quotes University of Toronto philosophers Francis Sparshott—"George Grant was a visionary cultural critic who had a dream of what philosophy might be"—and Mark Kingwell—"George Grant was a towering force in the intellectual life of this country, perhaps the first truly public intellectual Canada has produced," and adds, "Irascible, opinionated and arrogant, he attacked enemies of wisdom with verve, charm and tenacity."[41] As for Rigelhof himself? "Grant was a brilliant talker—as his [published] conversations with [journalist] Charles Taylor and David Cayley make abundantly clear. He was also a remarkable listener, especially when he went head-to-head with one other person."[42] Perhaps the phrase "larger than life" must be included in any description of George Grant.

While his political sympathies were often on the left, Umar notes, Grant was no "left-wing intellectual."[43] Indeed, to the American sociologist Seymour Martin Lipset, Grant was "Canada's most distinguished conservative intellectual."[44] That adjective, "conservative," requires clarification, as the term connotes for Grant a different set of political preoccupations than it does in the United States,[45] where it signifies, Grant noted, "those who exalt the rights of private property so that they can do what they want at whatever expense to the common good."[46]

Neither "reactionary" nor "revisionist," Grant's conservatism, Sibley suggests, is "grounded in the assumption of an overarching good—in this case, the good of Canada as a sovereign nation-state able to exist as long as it holds to the intentions for which it was founded."[47] That view resonates with Grant's assertion that the "truth" of conservatism is that of "order and limit" in "social" and "personal" life.[48] In an April 1959 letter[49] Grant wrote: "If ever there was a need of spiritual conservatism (I do not mean economic) it is now."[50] For Grant, "to be a Canadian," Muggeridge concludes, "is to be *per se* a conservative."[51]

Lamenting the loss of Canada—as Grant famously did in his 1965 book[52]— was lamenting not only the loss of Canada[53] but of its founding conservative idea.[54] Lament, Reimer suggests, is "the re-collection of a past good, of 'one's own,' of tradition, of time before the triumph of the modern age…a much more distant past—the truths of Athens and Jerusalem."[55] Greenspan suggests that the book "elevated" Canadian anxiety over its neighbour into a "cohesive philosophy of history exposing the breakdown of that tradition that had founded Canada as a sanctuary of pre-modern reverence for the transcendent order."[56] Not stuck in sadness[57] (he was often accused of pessimism,[58] which he denied), Grant appreciated keenly conservatism's appropriation: "Yet to express conservatism in Canada means de facto to justify the continuing rule of the businessman and the right of the greedy to turn all activities into sources of personal gain."[59] In contrast, Ian Angus suggests, "Grant's conservatism was more like the conservationism of the ecology movement than [of Canada's] Conservative Party."[60] In this regard, "Grant identifies himself with a much more radical form of conservatism," Reimer clarifies, "an ancient non-historicist type of conservatism."[61] Such conservatism could not be more different from the revolutionary "conservatism" of the radical Right in the United States today.

Each of these callings was undertaken, I would say realized, through George Grant's teaching. An "intense and gifted teacher," Cayley appreciated, "Grant was unusually open to dialogue with his students."[62] Cayley quotes Louis Greenspan, who remembers that the Grants regularly shared their Halifax home—already filled with six children—with students, creating (quoting Greenspan) "a kind of salon for philosophy students."[63] When the novelist Matt Cohen met Grant during the 1960s, Cayley reports (quoting Cohen):

> [I] was very impressed by his willingness or even eagerness to take what I said seriously…. His whole method of teaching and of discourse was not to say what was right and what was wrong, although he certainly had his own thoughts on these questions, but it was much more of…a Greek approach to things, where he believed that people should lead themselves…because he believed that what was right and wrong was within people [we share that], within every person…. To him the business of living and the business of philosophy were the same thing.[64]

Cohen's reference to the ancient Greeks[65] is surely appropriate, but, as we will see, not only the ancients are reactivated in Grant's linking of life with learning.

A "born teacher," Kenneth Minogue suggests, Grant was "almost too involved in his own time to be a pure philosopher. His was a complex achievement—philosophy, prophecy, political argument, and social criticism."[66] While the topics were many, each was studied and taught, and to just as varied a set of students: those enrolled in university, those listening over the radio, concerned citizens reading his texts. Over the course of his lifetime, George Grant was engaged in various forms of public education (that is, educating the public[67]), first through his Second World War work with the Canadian Adult Education Association (CAAE), then teaching philosophy at Dalhousie and McMaster Universities, during his brief relationship with the *Encyclopedia Britannica*, through his lectures on the CBC[68] and at public events, from teacher meetings in Halifax to teach-ins in Toronto. And certainly Grant was teaching when he wrote. Grant was not "confined by the university," as David Cayley notes, acknowledging during their interview that "you've been a public person…widely read and consulted on the questions of the day."[69] Barry Cooper also emphasized that Grant addressed a general public, often writing in popular periodicals, positioning his listeners and readers as "equals," as "fellow citizens concerned about right and wrong in the world."[70] O'Donovan acknowledged Grant's "distinguished career as a public educator," adding that "throughout his life Grant's primary *political* activity is that of educating."[71] For Whillier, "Grant proved himself a philosopher, at least as great teacher."[72] As we see, then, the centrality of teaching to the realization of Grant's various callings has been already acknowledged.[73]

"George Grant's work," Cayley summarizes, "revolved around the question of whether human beings can have confident knowledge of a truth outside time and space, or whether all is knowledge is finally conditioned by our circumstances."[74] From here to eternity sketches the arc of his teaching and study, "Grant's search for the truth about existence," a search that, as Davis and Emberley appreciate, "was always under way."[75] Studying George Grant invites us to join in that search for a way out of this present moment in which we are imprisoned, that "tightening circle" that Grant depicts in the chapter epigraph, "a rather dead era."[76] Despite the spatial imagery in the epigraph, I emphasize movement through time, as the future is not in front of us, but in back.

In this textbook for teachers and scholars, broadly conceived as those three terms can be, I reactivate George Grant's critique of time, technology, and teaching.[77] That verb implies a regression—think psychoanalysis for the moment—in which one re-experiences elements of the past[78] in the service of insight into the present.[79] My motive is not narrowly instrumental—not, as Grant notes in the epigraph, an effort to overcome chance[80]—but educational, as I attempt to learn from my experience of studying Grant, inviting you to learn from yours. The consequences[81] of such study could be the expansion, even perforation, of that tightening circle Grant describes.

In the first section, chapters 2–4, through copious citations of Grant's writings and aided (and not hindered, I hope) by my engagement[82] with them, you can re-experience something of the past, in this instance through Grant's subjective presence in his teaching. Steimatsky's depiction of Pasolini's cinematic style may specify how Grant's presence remains audible in its reactivation:

> [T]he frontal assault of his camera endows its objects—figures, landscapes— with a corporeal, incarnationist presence projecting forth, imprinted, onto the screen. It yields a sense of the material world as itself already a pictorial surface, not inconsistent with Pasolini's theoretical conception of reality as already inherently articulate, semiotic, cinematic.[83]

Substitute *textual* for "pictorial," and *auditory* for "semiotic" (although those terms are not mutually exclusive), the latter enacted textually through constant *citation*, and one can almost hear the cries and whispers of spirits past. Embedded in as it transcends his historical moment, expressive of his lived immediacy,[84] even urgency,[85] attuned to eternity, Grant's teaching can change how we live now.[86] Grant's prescience[87] provides one answer to the question posed in this chapter's title.

Reactivation

> Consciousness always includes within itself "it was."[88]
>
> George Grant

Reactivation is a reformulation of the regressive phase of *currere*, a method[89] of studying one's lived experience of curriculum that encourages not only the remembrance of things past from points of view in the present, but also a re-experiencing of their immediacy there, a temporal regression in the educational service of reconstructing one's subjective[90] experience of the present.[91] Why is reactivation[92] the prerequisite to reconstruction? It is, Grant tells David Cayley, "very important to try and say what the present is as clearly as one can, because it isn't as if it were obvious what the present is."[93] But proceed we must, as the "only time any of us has to live is now," Grant stressed, and "it's for this reason that I have stressed remembering."[94]

Now is a time of intensifying technology,[95] in which memory—including political memory—is effaced.[96] "What happened ten years ago is ancient history,"[97] Grant quips.[98] In such a "darkened glass," for Grant to "remember"[99] becomes sacred.[100] The point, Grant explained to students one day, is that the past—he was referencing specifically the ancient Greek philosophers—"teach us something real and important about the here and now."[101] Through "so remembering we can get to know," Grant suggested, "divine life itself."[102]

How to get there from here? In Joseph Power's view, Grant fails "to formulate a credible language capable of spanning the gap between what is given us to think in the modern experience and what we are able to remember of a good that is not of our making."[103] Fair enough, but Grant does point where such formulation may be undertaken: "In the losers of history," O'Donovan explains, "we encounter the claim of what is 'not our own,' which opens us to those universal standards by which to judge 'our own.' This is why historical recollection is for Grant a way to knowledge of the eternal and unchanging good."[104] From the past in this world—and specifically the study of its victims—one might find one's way out of here.

Finding a path ahead, then, as Douglas John Hall appreciates, demands "a disciplined return to the roots of our civilization, for even if remembrance and hope" are not equivalent, for Grant "there can be no authentic hope which is not first a remembering."[105] Schmidt emphasizes that "remembering is the only way out of the wasteland of the present."[106] Indeed, it is the present moment—specifically the deprival we experience within it[107]—that provokes Grant to recollection,[108] "not in any practical hope of deriving from them [ancient philosophers] some kind of 'ethics' in terms of which to adapt to technique, but rather in the light of their [the ancients'] reflection about what is, to find means of understanding this remarkable civilization in which we are engrossed."[109] Recollection—I invoke reactivation to stress experiencing the lived immediacy of the past when studying it—creates a space of non-coincidence with what is.[110] From the re-experienced past to the reconstructed present, from the contingent to the transcendent, from time to eternity, for Grant, O'Donovan explains, "historical totality is an image of eternity, even if an inverted image," as "the present darkness is meaningful as darkness."[111] Lisbeth Lipari reminds:

> We typically think of time as an indistinct but insistent river flowing eternally from past to present to future. But this view obscures the many ways the lives of our minds are a tangle of braided streams, currents, shallows, eddies, and swamps of memory and anticipation, sparkling with an occasional visit to the present moment. It also obscures the rich dialogicality of every moment, echoing eternally with words from the past, often below the surface of awareness.[112]

Reactivating the past may enable us to re-experience such "eddies "and "braids" before they were woven into "cloth" or disappeared into "swamps." Such regression supports not only the revelation[113] temporal relocation allows—adding missing pieces of the conceptual puzzle that is the present—it precipitates reconstruction of the present moment, altering the table (as it were) on which the puzzle rests. This reciprocity—between knowledge and memory, experience and subjectivity—is evident in Fishbane's faith that "the old words of scripture are spaces for ever-new moments of spiritual consciousness and self-transformation."[114] Perhaps such spaces can become available to those of us imprisoned in the present when we reactivate the "old words" of George Grant.[115]

Reconstruction

> We make ourselves as we go along.[116]
>
> George Grant

Reconstruction[117] is a reformulation of the analytic phase of the method of *currere*, wherein one attempts to learn from what reactivation of the past has disclosed, incorporating the knowledge[118] revelation[119] presents into a reconstructed understanding of who one was made to be, of what is at stake in the present moment, understanding that is now informed—experientially and intellectually—by George Grant's critique of time, technology, and teaching. Such a subjective synthesis produces what seems like slippage[120] between Grant's critique and one's own understanding, but slippage denotes the "contaminated"[121] character of reconstruction.

Certainly there is slippage within one's own life, between then and now—as the quoted Lipari passage above registers—between what might have been, could be and is now, slippage that can be separated by regression. Grant acknowledged his own subjective synthesis, writing in a 1972 letter that "[I] am a person who, because of the first decades of my life, has had to put himself together late in life, and that is never an achieved process."[122] At that time in his life self-trust was evidently at issue, his relative resolution of which he attributes to studying Plato and Jesus. From within this synthesis he addressed present concerns—trust among his colleagues at McMaster seemed at stake—not applying commandments mind you, but threading those "braids" at which Lipari looked, weaving a psychic "cloth" constituting subjective and social reconstruction.

"Because of my unsettled and wild being," Grant wrote to his colleague, "we must always be careful that we communicate with each other and say, in the best moments, exactly what we think about matters in which we both have interests and differing thoughts."[123] "Precision and soul" was Robert Musil's phrase—*parrhesia*[124] for the ancient Greeks—for expressing "exactly what we think" and feel, and in ways that encourage others to speak "exactly" from their own unique lived locations. As in psychoanalysis, the articulation of revealed experience can be the dynamic by which reality becomes reconstructed, in this instance inspired by Grant's hope to convert the "battlefields of McMaster"[125] into sites of dialogue, even friendship, thereby linking his affirmation of careful communication with a specific situation: "To build a good department of religion in the midst of this very strange modern world will require that kind of adult friendship,"[126] an acknowledgement of the significance of relationship[127] in professional conduct, not only among colleagues but with students as well.

The present study is, then, an exercise in reactivation and reconstruction. I labour to re-experience Grant's critique of time, technology, and teaching so that I might reconstruct his—and my—understanding[128] of what is at stake in the future we face now. It is an educational exercise, as I aspire to learn from that experience, to reconstruct myself—intellectually, experientially—by study that is simultaneously academic and subjective, dialogic and solitary.[129]

While there are significant studies devoted to Grant's political philosophy, to his theology, and to his significance to especially English-speaking Canada, there is no book dedicated to Grant as teacher, to his life's work as a teaching. "I mean by a teaching," Grant wrote, "a Way as well as a Truth."[130] The aforementioned phrase "public intellectual"[131] has (or had) more currency academically than "teacher," but the former term doesn't quite capture Grant's commitment to the specific subjects of curriculum ("a Truth") and pedagogy ("a Way")[132] as both professional and public (as well as private) concerns. While distinctive, these concerns—curriculum and pedagogy, professional and public (and private)—blur in the debates in which Grant became embroiled at McMaster University, controversies that became public, as we will see in chapter 5.

Curiously, Grant's teaching often contradicted his adamantly anti-progressive assertions. After depicting him as an "accessible public philosopher," Cayley notes that Grant was "easily read and easily met with during his years as a teacher, lecturer, and writer."[133] As progressive educators[134] (an association Grant would have eschewed[135]) have emphasized, accessibility is a prerequisite to classroom communication. But Cayley is noting more than Grant's capacity to make "content" accessible. Grant was often open to others—psychologically it seems, as well as intellectually—often easy to engage in conversation, often inviting others into his subjective presence.[136] In the conversation with Cayley,[137] "Grant [Cayley tells us] can be met with again, doing what he did while he lived: teaching philosophy."[138] Grant taught philosophy all right, as an academic discipline but also as a medium through one might engage one's fellow citizens, one's fellow human beings, including one's own self, asking the fundamental questions of human existence.[139] One hundred years after his birth, thirty years after his death, it is time for teachers to meet George Grant again.

Moving Images

> For Plato, in his famous phrase, time was the moving image of eternity; that is, the eternal was primary and changes in the world took their meaning from their relationship to that which did not change.[140]
> William Christian

Grant's efforts to educate the public were historically prompted, spiritually attuned, and pedagogically precise: in Grant the three are interrelated. "Grant reminded people of something lost," Cayley observed, "but at the same time gave them hope—both in his person and in his writings—that it might be recovered."[141] While I am no fan of hope—and on at least one occasion neither was Grant[142]—his wife, Sheila Veronica Mary Grant (née Allen),[143] and his biographer, William Christian, reference Grant's "almost unlimited hope as to what might be achieved through genuine education."[144] Through such education students could become "open to the whole,"[145] and discover their capacities for "careful thought."[146] Those capacities for careful thought could open one to "the whole."[147]

In an era when capacity (or potential[148]) is conflated with its possible economic outcomes[149] and almost all systematic thought is imprinted by science, Grant's phrase can seem enigmatic. When science is seen as a secular[150] form of religion[151] ("science becomes the central means of bringing in that hope...the meaning of redemption,"[152] as Grant explains), then its metaphysical substratum is revealed. And if associated with attunement—attentiveness to that which is not only observable, measurable, or logical, to what is beyond scientific rationality—"the whole"[153] becomes reciprocally related (however mysteriously) with everyday life, a relation (however shifting and situational) to be cultivated through study,[154] including academic study.[155] Not necessarily cramming for a test or completing homework assignments, study becomes an interrelated spiritual and intellectual undertaking guided by one's curiosity, imagination, instinct, and, when one is fortunate, by engaging teachers and timely texts.[156] Its site is subjectivity[157] as one attunes oneself to what one is experiencing, yes to its immediacy and specificity but also to its situatedness, relatedness, including to what lies beyond it and not only spatially but temporally. "[I]n our intellectual life, our life of study," Grant appreciated, "we have to ask as much as in any other part of our life, what is worth doing. That depends for me on the primal question: what kind of a world is it?"[158] The inability of the world to stay static affirms its immanence[159] or transcendence, that is to say, what is more[160] than itself. "One thing is clear," Grant appreciated: "[T]o be a good teacher one must have a private life of study and thought of one's own. Otherwise we are simply pulled into the mediocrity we are trying to change."[161] That mediocrity is, in a word, modernity.[162] Modernity, for Grant, is a time[163] in which technology has triumphed.[164]

If time, technology and teaching are moving images of eternity,[165] curriculum and pedagogy[166] are also, both "moving" and "images," but no explicit, empirical, or exact representation of eternity.[167] Attunement to the timeless—to what Grant termed "the Good"[168]—can be ongoing, steadied by ritual,[169] structured by study. Associating eternity with certain academic subjects[170] to study, subjects with presumably unchanging or intrinsically important content, subjects that supposedly mirror the "original," reifies the original it seems to me, rendering an icon an idol.[171] I suggest Grant himself constructed his curriculum not only as mirrored images of eternity, but also as ethical and political replies to his historical moment: modernity characterized by pervasive technological violence that he himself had experienced firsthand. If reality is an endless series of "moving images," the canonical curriculum question—What knowledge is of most worth?[172]—cannot be settled for all time by declaring one set of subjects eternally important.[173]

Just as history can be conceived as a moving image of eternity, so can be academic knowledge generally, including its representation in the curriculum, a complicated conversation that studies knowledge through dialogical encounter[174] that is not only place-sensitive (perhaps classroom-centred) but also within one-self. Eternity here is less a conceptualization of time as it is an acknowledgement of timeless human aspiration—"human excellence,"[175] as Grant affirmed it. To substitute a specific subject or predetermined outcomes—test scores, vocational eligibility, or even the end of racism—risks committing academic idolatry; for example, mistaking the material item for its educational capacity to become a portal for the student and teacher to experience subjective, social, spiritual rev-elation.[176] Like religious icons, academic subjects can provide passage to realities beyond the empirical present, realities past and future,[177] encountered in a present now expanded to include intimations of each. In secular terms, the educational significance of subject matter is that it enables the student to learn from actual embodied experience, an outcome that cannot always be engineered.[178]

Modernity[179]—suspend for the moment the matter of postmodernity[180]—is typified, in part, by its tendency to temporalize immanence: creative destruction and disruption becomes valorized positively, despite the cultural and psychologi-cal havoc constant change leaves in its wake. Sans eternity, there are *only* "moving images," the material world about us, awaiting our intervention. As endless time or as timelessness, eternity is nothing we—as embodied human beings destined to die—can know, except perhaps psychologically, as momentary experiences of apparently immeasurable time. I am thinking more of that sense of timelessness more associated now with the cellphone or computer screen than with an embod-ied experience of a lived present that stretches from the past into the future, a sense of subjective continuity, "that very unity which we call the self,"[181] as Grant phrased it. In modernity one can become enraptured with, submerged in, the temporally empty[182] present, no longer a moment *in* but a suspension *of* time, absorbed by—fused with—the images in front of our face, oblivious to what might be beyond them.

Because technology takes us from time, even time deemed as only histori-cal, education, I suggest, becomes a passage from the present into a future not in front of but behind us, for Grant, in ancient Athens and Jerusalem. Because his-tory is, in modernity, something we make—the capital "H" replaced with "h" to indicate this is a narrative we are composing—we are left calculating how to get there (the future) from here, a present preoccupied with the screen in front of us. To extricate oneself from this technological present, I recommend reactivation of the past. Making history a distant and foreign land—an object[183] of research[184]— sucks the life not only out of the past but also, Grant seemed to suggest, out of us.

William Christian and Sheila Grant remind us that Grant "did not want to go back to Plato like visiting a museum,"[185] but rather he "strove to think Plato's certainties in the world as it has now become." They continue: "That was Grant's approach to all the thinkers with whose thought he wrestled and it is why we call this section 'Thinking Their Thoughts.'"[186] The point they make echoes Grant's idea for the Department of Religion at McMaster University, hiring faculty who could teach from within their specializations and religions.[187]

For Grant, the educational point was not to conduct research *about* the past or the future, but to attune ourselves to each, as much as one's modernistic apparatus of apprehension allows. Careful sustained thought can help. Not about anything, but about what matters, and knowledge that matters, for Grant, becomes present in the past. Perhaps William Christian and Sheila Grant used the verb "strove" in the above-quoted passage as Grant was, as are we, positioned to apprehend the past in terms of the present, where we are located and which, maybe against our will, locates us. I invoke the term "reactivate"[188] to specify the effort, through study, to think even experience the thoughts of those who lived elsewhere and in another time. To return to the past is of course empirically impossible, but one can attempt to attune oneself to it. Through study—and the "careful thought" that accompanies it—one can allow oneself to experience, as much as one can, what was present there. As in psychoanalytic theory,[189] reactivating the past enables re-experiencing the present. One can learn from it, undertaking what can become educational experience.

Such experience—openness[190] to alterity[191] or to "the whole" in Grant's phrase[192]—enables one to reconstruct not only what one knows and can think but also how one is. Not necessarily dramatically, as learning from experience often occurs incrementally and according to circumstances, restructured as these can be by one's ongoing self-relationship, while engaged in conversation with teachers and students and parents too. In a historical moment when many seem submerged in social media,[193] time seems to stand still, screen time occurring in an apparently endless present too often punctured by violence: bullying, surveillance, theft.

What should one study in a time like ours? One answer is George Grant's critique of time, technology, and education. I use the singular because I think his critique of the three topics is intertwined. Time as only history[194]—technology as "enframing"[195]—education as objectifying:[196] these specify Grant's indignation over a totalizing civilizational idolatry, his lifelong protest against substituting[197] inappropriate objects for what they represent. Grant implies that appropriate objects—like religious icons—can become subjects that serve the sacred. It is "as if"[198] there could also be academic icons that remind us of what lies beyond them.[199] The study of art and the humanities—but maybe not STEM[200]—could encourage attunement to "eternity," could communicate a timeless sense of what is at stake in everyday life. "In every situation in human life," Grant knew, "it always matters what you do and this is a situation where protest must go on."[201] For me, what matters and what you do are not self-evidently linked; as Benedetti observes, in our time "no matter what you do, you are prisoner to the already-given. This is the way late-modern learning is: modernity sees itself in the mirror and is paralyzed by its own gaze."[202] For Grant it always matters what you do, not only because it might move one away from the gaze, but because it is right.

Teaching

Teaching is a fundamental mode of being.[203]

Ted Aoki

The juxtaposition of immediacy and eternity animated Grant's teaching—a term referencing both his conduct in (and out of) classrooms *and* the content of the curriculum he felt committed to teach, often a merged "lesson," teaching as testimony to ongoing study. Like study, teaching becomes a dialogical encounter with whom and with what one does not know and aspires to understand.[204] As ongoing ethical engagement[205] with alterity—including "the alterity within me, which is not me"[206]—teaching, like study, becomes a spiritual[207] as well as intellectual and ethical undertaking to decipher words on a page or uttered in a classroom. While doing so one can attune oneself to the spirit beyond the print on the page or screen, "text"—written and spoken—as a moving image of eternity.[208] Conceived as iconographic rather than idolatrous, teaching and study can be converted[209] to sacred callings[210] as well as professions, labour in the service of attunement to alterity.

In this tribute to George Grant my teaching and study start with what is written, often in the form of citation. The citations, and my commentaries on and reconstructions of them, create a constellation[211] that is itself of the present, occurring during the second decade of the new millennium. On September 23, 2018, it had been thirty years since Grant died, but for me he—still alive in his writing—sits across from me now. Attunement to George Grant means re-experiencing, as best I can, his subjective presence. It requires regression from my present into his past. Such embodied[212] study—"To a remarkable degree," Warren writes, "this man thought with his whole body and being, and suffered the pragmatism that is the sophistry of our age with a species of physical pain"[213]—reveals him as both dated[214] and eternal.[215]

Study and teaching become, then, intertwined, efforts to understand one's subjects in a doubled sense, as academic knowledge and as human persons[216] in time[217] and place.[218] Taking teaching as testifying to study repositions the teacher from entertainer or engineer to contributor to a complicated conversation that precedes one's participation in it, prompting acknowledgement of one's contingency, but also one's capacity to converse across time and space, an acknowledgement of eternity. In teaching George Grant's critique of time, technology, and teaching I reiterate the details of that critique. In doing so, I aspire to reactivate its existential immediacy in our present moment. Becoming attuned to the historical moment invites readers to re-experience what is lost.[219]

Such a sense of teaching as testimony to study, as attempting to contribute to conversation that occurred before and can continue after one's own time, perhaps into time immemorial, accents the humility[220] of the teacher. Cayley observes that Grant had a "quite sincere sense...of his own intellectual limitations"[221] (as, allow me to say, do I). No philosopher, I am—aspire to be—an educator, teaching others' work, contributing my own commentary as curriculum for prospective and practicing teachers—students all—to study facts and ideas they may reconstruct for their own classrooms. This textbook testifies to my ongoing study as it invites students to renew their own: working together, separately. Grant emphasized the significance of solitary study, not to "deny…community—but if the community is to be more than a beehive it must be made up of individuals who are in themselves something."[222] In fact, "as teachers we must cultivate our aloneness so that when we come to a group, we come as somebody."[223] Study[224] invites subjective reconstruction.[225]

The subjective significance of study for Grant is acknowledged in a November 1974 letter[226] he wrote to Patrick Atherton,[227] wherein he reports that he has become "solitary," focused on what "really interests" him.[228] Aside from his "family," he explains, what interests him is "teaching the young," explaining to those around him the relation between "technique" and "Christianity."[229] Those phrases pinpoint the range and complexity of Grant's critique. In emphasizing his family[230] he is expressing love of one's own,[231] a famous phrase of Grant's that expresses his conviction that knowledge is illumined by love[232] (an insight he attributed to Simone Weil[233]), that cosmopolitanism[234] commences within intimacy and fidelity, not in free-floating ideals[235] one espouses and can engineer. "If you're teaching the young," Grant insisted, "in all their variety and all their difference, one must love them, or else what the hell? Why do it?"[236] That love was less explicitly affective, certainly not expressed through technique (what today is commonly characterized as "best practices"), but through academic knowledge threaded through his subjective presence, knowledge Grant deemed of most worth.

"There must always be something unsatisfactory in writing or speaking about the productions of the great," Grant wrote about his effort to describe the work of Weil.[237] I feel something of the same writing about George Grant. He was no saint: that was part of the problem Grant felt he faced writing about Weil. In the "presence of the highest," he suggested, one must "listen, be silent, pay attention, study,"[238] a version perhaps of attunement, of what Grant termed "obedience."[239] Vis-à-vis Grant, silence is not an option for me, as he incites me to speech, just as those he studied sparked him. Engaging him here is my articulation of attunement to his teaching.

I feel about my writing in relation to Grant's as he felt about his in relation to Weil: "My muddy and confused words seem so tedious compared with the cutting clarity of her language."[240] With these impediments laid bare, Grant proceeds, and so do I, as it is not only to the young that the educator of the public "must do a medium amount of talking so that they do not miss their encounters with the great—those sudden encounters which are the joy of education—and this talking has a particular use in a society in which the tawdry is all around them."[241] I compensate for my "talking" by quoting Grant as often as copyright considerations and narrative continuity allow. Overlooking his inadvertent use of "use" (and the implied utilitarianism he abhors), I will draw your attention to "tawdry" in the above-quoted sentence, a timeless feature of human society (yes "gaudy, shoddy, and cheap" but also as distraction[242] from what is, and could be), and to his use of "great," implying not only size (as in greater magnitude of mind) but also of "superior quality," a judgment implied in the canonical curriculum question: what knowledge is of most worth? Surely Grant is right in character-izing "encounters with the great" as "the joy of education," even if he and I might disagree over which instances of "the great" are appropriate when and where and for whom.

Becoming Historical

> Becoming historical involved a histori-cal reconstruction of the current forms of self-identification...as a specific product of human practices in time.[243]
>
> John Toews

We would not disagree, I think, over acknowledging that curriculum questions are questions in contexts, disciplinary but also historical (despite his insistence on timelessness) and often political. His assertions while heading the Department of Religion at McMaster University—affirming that the curriculum is appropriately articulated by those working from within the various faiths[244]—were all three. They addressed non-curricular concerns, such as shifts in university funding from teaching to research, and his positions were on the losing side, but his respon-siveness to the historical moment was unmistakable. Hiring faculty from within their faiths was not only necessary because "knowledge is illuminated by love" but also because he was—we are—living in a time of technologization, in which academic subjects have become objects of research rather than living traditions.[245] It was the political ascendency of research—in forms mirroring natural science, forms restructuring even the humanities[246]—that prompted his going public over his resignation. He complained in the *Globe and Mail* that McMaster University was betraying students[247]—its primary responsibility he was sure—for the sake of "research," an objectification of nature (including human nature) for the sake of "mastery." While in that newspaper article he does not define teaching, implied is its contradiction of objectification, also implied in the earlier quoted passage. There, as you note, he registered the "joy" of education through "encounters"— "sudden" he emphasizes (perhaps acknowledging his own dramatic presence[248] as a pedagogue) encounters with "the greatest," with persons and knowledge that exceed the scale of everyday life, that encourage students' attunement to "the whole," to the "good" that transcends the confines of contingency. Attunement and transcendence play prominently in my reconstruction of Grant's critique, as you will see in chapter 6.

Acknowledging that the work of Simone Weil remains unknown by many, Grant cites the historical moment, noting that the years since her death in 1943 have been "wordy and noisy ones,"[249] especially in North America. "Ours is not an era," he writes, "in which the note of genius is heard through the avalanches of print, and this applies particularity to the genius of sanctity."[250] He concludes: "There is, therefore, perhaps some purpose served in speaking of Simone Weil."[251] It seems a simultaneously historical, political, religious, and pedagogical purpose. Engaged in the present moment, inspired by the past, in terms that attempt to bridge the two, Grant's teaching was addressed to the dead as well as the living, the timeless and the timely. Grant's teaching draws attention to by drawing it away from the distractions of the everyday; they can become, as I suggest in chapters 5–7, portals to timeless truths. Grant's teaching also points to "her genius," to "persuade you to read her works...not to interpret her thought for you,"[252] as do I here. Rather than representing her thought, Grant aspires to provide an "introduction"[253] to Weil. My effort is less an introduction to Grant's thought (there are excellent instances of that) than it is a reactivation of his thought, an effort to encourage you to read or reread Grant's works, to address in your individual ways Grant's critique of time, teaching, and technology. It seems to me Grant aspired to the same in his writing: teaching to the particular toward the universal.

Progressivism

> In effect, progressive education began as Progressivism in education: a many-sided effort to use the schools to improve the lives of individuals.[254]
>
> Lawrence A. Cremin

One of the lasting lessons of US progressivism is to meet the students where they are. During that great progressive experiment of the 1930s—known as the Eight-Year Study,[255] in which teachers were free to construct curriculum as they saw fit, freed from college-entrance requirements—there was even attention to the home situations of students. At the minimum, requiring subjects such as Latin, a lightening-rod curricular issue between "progressives" and "traditionalists," seemed questionable.[256] What was not questionable was lecturing, as "discussion" was contested as educationally valuable, at least at the University of Chicago of the 1940s.[257] Even when speaking, teachers were admonished to attend to "where the students were," a catchall phrase that included attentiveness to intellectual, social, and emotional maturities, to engage in what decades later would be reduced to "developmentally appropriate practices." During an interview at the University of Toronto George Grant said the same: "At all times and places human beings have had to talk at different levels of intelligible discourse, not only because of the difference of the people they are talking with, but also because of the strange situation of knowing and not knowing."[258] Grant is not speaking of schools or of teachers specifically here, but he is acknowledging a fundamental fact of communication, namely that one's capacity for comprehension differs from others', even from one's own at certain ages and, as any classroom teacher knows, even on certain mornings.[259] One is forever altering—that phrase overstates how self-conscious the process is and detaches it from the relationships one has formed with one's students and/or other interlocutors, even from the ambience of the setting—what and how one says, mindful of one's obligation to the task at hand, in light of one's knowledge of the subject.

Another lasting lesson of US progressivism is the association, often unstable and indirect, between what is taught in schools and what is occurring in society.[260] It was an idea John Dewey[261] had helped encourage with his assertion of the school classroom as a laboratory for democracy.[262] While Dewey had abandoned that idea—no one institutional site could play such a grand and causative role in the formation of civil society[263]—by the end of the First World War, the idea was taken up by progressives like George Counts,[264] politicized by the traumatic experience of the Great Depression. The idea remains in play today, with progressives in the United States and Canada resolved to make reparations for past injustices through the curriculum, and today's "social efficiency" enthusiasts—the third wing of US progressivism in Ravitch's scheme, devoted to preparing children for success—demanding and predicting closer association between the school curriculum and the technological industries.[265]

Time and again Grant repudiates progressives, especially US ones but Canadian liberals too, but he ignored the divisions within progressivism as he decried the tendency to ally schooling with technological society.[266] In his assertions of associations between curriculum and society—for instance during the McMaster controversy—and through organizing his university coursework around topics he took to be both timely and timeless, Grant could be considered a progressive, not the social-efficiency kind, but those called child-centred and social reconstructionist. Grant would dispute me no doubt, but by addressing what he took to be the greatest "needs" of his students, namely their spiritual impoverishment in a soulless era, Grant was simultaneously focused on the existential situations of students and the society wherein they studied. He situated the study of Plato, Kant, and Nietzsche—later Heidegger—within an academy increasingly structured by scientific research, itself located within a society devoured by consumer capitalism. In the face of these historical tendencies, Grant's intellectual courage is admirable and, in the specific sense, Cayley suggests, "something that strikes the soul with great force,"[267] and thus humbling; my appreciation for it has only increased as I contemplate how self-consciously he proceeded as an educator of the public, by becoming historical, attuned to the present moment, and addressing that moment through his teaching.[268]

It is this specific sense of "becoming historical"[269] that I reactivate George Grant and his critique of time, technology, and teaching. In doing so I ask progressives to reconsider what "progressivism" means today, a time when even demands for reparation—sometimes shrilly and self-servingly expressed in identity politics[270]—dissolve those social bonds prerequisite to collective action. Justice[271] for the deceased and living becomes less likely when political polarization tempts retreat from the past and its progeny, the present, into private worlds of entertainment and fantasy associated with the cellphone and other virtual escapes. Re-experiencing Grant's presence reminds us of an era before technology triumphed, when many students listened to their teachers, not scrolled on their cellphones; when the meaning of life was not obsessing over the salary that graduation from the university students attend promises. Spiritualization[272] not technologization is, I suggest, a progressive agenda for such a time.[273]

Conclusion

> [W]e must think about what is going on.[274]
>
> George Grant

Studying George Grant opens (yet) another window on the sixties. It is a somewhat specific window through which Americans of my generation have rarely looked, given that he was located in Canada and had been designated a "Red Tory,"[275] a mix of Canadian conservatism and socialism.[276] It was a political category Grant himself resisted and one which is not quickly comprehended in the United States.[277] Like others of his generation in the United States, Grant had sympathy for the anti–Vietnam War protestors[278]—he even seemed to share in what Charles Reich would a few years later proclaim as a "greening of America" (for Grant a new dawning of reason[279]), before becoming ensnared (some would say, although he had denied "pessimism") in disappointment and prophecy.

Despite our differences—generational and national among others—Grant's work has been a great gift to me, requiring me to grapple with a number of issues secularism had seemingly settled. "In the context of learning," William Christian and Sheila Grant write, affirming Grant's positioning of philosophy as central to education, "knowledge must be related to its proper place in the whole."[280] Knowing such "proper place," from my point of view, must be impossible in principle, as "the whole" is a term that only omniscience allows.[281] The "moving images" of "eternity"—each term a human construct—is what we have, who we are, how we live. Through time and space we move, itself an assertion embedded in language, not free from experience. Even if experience of what Grant terms "Goodness" or "God" (or simply the supernatural) redirects one's motion or shifts its speed (as it did for George Grant), it remains enfolded in human experience, itself a refracted image of that "whole" the existence of which Grant apparently apprehended. The quote marks show my hand—I remain skeptical that such a scale of "reality" can become intelligible for us, although it may well exist for other creatures whose "existence" we can only imagine. (Of course science fiction itself derives from human language and lived experience). Surely there are realities beyond what I experience and can know, and there are many reports—Grant's among them—to confirm that speculation.[282] That word "beyond" human experience is itself a concession studying Grant secured from me, as before I have insisted that immanence not transcendence is the best one can do.

Academic study, then, can become a portal to spiritual realization. Even for the strictly secular, study can expand what it is possible to think and feel, enabling us to experience what thought and feeling had before obscured. Scholars have known this extra-academic benefit for centuries; speaking to students as he introduces Nietzsche, Grant says it succinctly: "As I have often said it seems to me we are trying to learn from a great thinker who sees many things with great clarity and depth and there is much to be learnt from him and what we do is to learn it from within our perspectives and so hope to broaden our perspectives."[283] For me, and for you who choose to study this book, Grant, not Nietzsche, is our "great thinker" from whom there is much to learn. "Our perspectives"—and Grant means ours, not his[284]—may not broaden so as to apprehend "the whole," but any such subjective expansion in this technological era of subjective evaporation is welcome.

Like David Cayley, "I hope this book will provide Grant's old friends with the pleasure of hearing his resonant voice once again, and that it will make new friends for a body of work that I think remains vital even in changed circumstances."[285] Indeed, Grant resounds in the present moment, wherein so many of his fears have been realized, and new horrors visited upon us he might have imagined. With William Christian, "I take him to be uttering a prophecy which he hopes is self-defeating."[286] That time will tell. What time has told us is that once there was among us a prophet who cautioned us about what was to come, what we live now. Cayley quotes a colleague of Grant's at McMaster University, Louis Greenspan, who gives us a glimpse of him: "I still remember his first entrance into class. He came walking in with a rather dishevelled outfit. But then when he turned to the class he spoke with tremendous clarity, dignity, almost defiance.... I...thought of him as a member of an aristocracy, most of whose members had been recently guillotined. He was the remnant."[287] A remnant and, I suggest, an icon, a "mediator between humans and God."[288] As Steimatsky explains: "The icon has, by implication, the properties of what it represents: hence, it is venerated, it participates in processions, and it is expected to heal and to perform miracles. In this way, it inherits the functions of a relic."[289] Quoting Matt Cohen, Rigelhof casts Grant as "a walking fragment of the country."[290] From this subjectively present trace of what was[291] we might find our way through what the past has become.

Notes

1. Davis and Roper 2009b, 295.
2. Heidegger is "certainly the greatest philosopher of the modern era," Grant writes in a 1987 letter to his old friend Peter Self (Christian 1996d, 365).
3. Sikka 1997, 145.
4. Kaethler (2009, 37) comments: "The nature of thought that produced science only asks, 'Can we?' The question 'Ought we?' belongs to a time in which classical thought flourished." Socrates, Magrini (2017, 182) suggests, "courageously finds within such a form of knowing yet another powerful manifestation or *presence* of all that is difficult and all that must remain *question-worthy* in our lives." Presence is what technology simulates and thereby erases. Why?
5. Elshtain 2005, 246.
6. Christian 1996c, xiii.
7. Hurtig 1990, 56; see also B. Cooper 1978, 22.
8. Christian 1990, 19.
9. Christian 1996d, 147.
10. Schmidt 1978a ix.
11. A painter, Colville (1990, 4) considered his "reaction" to Grant "rather child-like." Like a religious icon, a "real professor" might well have such an effect.
12. Andrew and Planinc 1990, 186. Grant may recall Socrates but need not necessarily imitate him, as Magrini reminds (2017, 71).
13. Andrew and Planinc 1990, 187.
14. "[T]here can be no question," Hurtig (1990, 56) concludes, "that George Grant was a prophet."
15. Jeremiah 3:12–23; 1:1–4. "Economic expansion through the control of nature has become the chief purpose of our existence," Grant explained, that "to which every-thing else must be subordinated, the God we worship" (Davis 2002b, 158).
16. Dart and Jersak 2011, 5.
17. Lee 1990, 20. "His primary vocation in writing," Lee writes, "was to suffer with all his mind, and all his body, heart and soul, the emergence of the nihilism which had been unfolding over the past centuries from within the project of modernity. This nihilism seemed from the increasing difficulty of discerning any sense in which we are subject to the claim of the good; indeed, any sense in which 'claim' or 'good' have substantial meaning at all. It fell to Grant to give witness to this civilizational end-game" (20). Lee adds: "That's not a vocation any sane person would choose: to bear witness to the closing down of articulate meaning in one's civilization" (20).
18. Taylor (1982) 2006, 156.
19. Schmidt 1978a, ix. The "cornerstone of Grant's political thought," Caldwell (2006, 29) summarized, was "the dehumanization occasioned by the new world order being ushered in by bureaucratic state capitalism."
20. Nicholson 2006, 323.
21. Athanasiadis 2001, 3.
22. Forbes 2007, 175.
23. Kaethler 2009, 3. "It is only with the combination of these two disciplines," Kaethler adds, "that Grant believes one can come to understand the whole" (3).
24. Meynell 2011, 3.

25.   Davis and Roper 2009a, ix. It bears noting, as Cayley (1995, 14) does, that "premodern philosophers saw virtue as the end of political life, and defined the best regime as an order likely to produce such excellence." Virtue, not power, preoccupied Grant as well, lending support to his characterization as theologian *and* political philosopher (the latter in its ancient not modern sense).

26.   Davis 2006, 78n10. "After 1947," O'Donovan (1984, 20) asserts, Grant never made Christian theology the subject of an essay, writing instead "as a philosopher about philosophy"; she notes that on occasion "philosophy and theology appear indistinguishable in Grant's thought."

27.   Potter 2005, ix.

28.   In acknowledgement, one supposes, Grant was invited to consider a chair in Canadian studies. In an October 1974 letter to William Christian (1996d, 278)—the future biographer of Grant was here on formal terms with him—Grant declined, writing that "I would have to keep abreast of recent things in Canada and so much of it I don't understand. Also, I would have to pull together what I think a Canadian Studies program should be and I have done that kind of thing three times in my life and don't feel now I can do it again." Grant's humility and devotion to his calling are discernible: "I have come now to the point where I want to write one thing out as well as I can" (278).

29.   Whillier 1990b, 64. See ch. 6 in this volume.

30.   Davis and Roper 2009b, 320.

31.   Cayley 1995, 80. Such teaching required attunement to transcendence *and* to historical contingency, a complexity constant clarification might unravel, as Cayley implies: "Under these circumstances, Grant thought, the public role of the philosopher is to attempt a systematic clarification" (41).

32.   Lathangue 1998, vii.

33.   Sibley 2006, 323.

34.   Sibley 2008, 159. Commenting in the 1970s, Cook contrasted the two in this way: "Trudeau, the liberal, believes that technology can be controlled for man's benefit; Grant, the conservative, believes that technique already controls man" (160). Sibley notes that "Grant never did a theoretical analysis of Trudeau's thought as a whole, but his writings contain scattered critiques of Trudeau, both as a politician and as a political thinker" (162). Sibley reports that Grant saw Trudeau as "an unwitting agent" (165) of universalization and homogenization.

35.   Greenspan 1990, 1. Greenspan adds that Grant was—will remain—"a symbol of resistance to the domination of America" (2).

36.   O'Donovan 1984, 4.

37.   B. Cooper 1990, 103.

38.   Grant admitted to Cayley (1995, 75): "A lot of the great questions are quite frankly just beyond me." During his lectures on Aristotle to a graduate class in 1970, Grant offered: "[A] person of my abilities can only scratch the surface" (Davis and Roper 2009b, 1079). "Please be aware of my limitations here," he reminded students on another occasion; there are "questions where I am much clearer than I am about others" (1033). "Grant had a quite sincere sense," Cayley (1995, 18) concluded, "of his own intellectual limitations." Weil ([1947] 2002, 40) regarded "humility" the "queen" of "virtues." And another of Grant's teachers—Socrates—"is legitimately embracing and acknowledging the limits of his own knowledge, his professed or learned ignorance,'" as Magrini (2017, 142) reminds.

39.   Craiutu 2017, 103.

40.   Craiutu 2017 , 137. I am reminded of Grant's pacifism when Craiutu notes "the relationship between meekness and nonviolence" (142).

41.   Quoted in Rigelhof 2001, 137–8.

42.   Rigelhof 2001, 143.

43.   Umar 1992, 15.

44.   Lipset 1990, 36. In the United States, Rocha (2017, 15) observers, "The problem is that both major…political parties are decidedly committed to liberalism…. *There are no conservatives out there today*." Rocha explains: "Liberal articles of faith come in the form of two myths: (1) secularism, or the notion that the state should be neutral in matters of faith; and (2) the notion that the autonomous individual represents the basic unity of value in the body politic" (p. 16). Rocha emphasizes that "[c]*onservatism* is not the mere converse of this view. It is not pure resistance to change. Instead, it articulates two independent views of its own: (1) the existence of a divine will or natural law—some ontic primordiality—as the ineluctable, fundamental source of any authority; and (2) the notion that the person cannot be reduced to anything but personhood; the whole cannot be reduced to its parts" (p. 16). Rocha's conception of conservatism aligns with Grant's.

45.   In a September 1986 letter Grant learns about the Southern Agrarians, offering that "knowing so little of the U.S.A. I had taken 'conservatism' in the U.S.A. as simply a debate about the relation between private business and the government and had known nothing of this [John Crowe Ransom, Allen Tate, and others] tradition, of the hope of the continuities and the belief that life was more than expansion" (Christian 1996d, 358). But in a letter written twenty-two years earlier, Grant wrote as if he knew more than a "little," comparing Conservatives in Canada to the Republicans in the United States—characterizing the former as a "pleasant wing" of the latter—even suggesting that if he lived in the United States he might vote Republican, writing that "[t]he last four years have cleared my head greatly and I am now an unequivocal anti-progressive" (223). In a letter composed a year later he qualifies his preference, writing that "I would not have found it impossible as an American to have voted for Senator Goldwater on domestic, but not on international issues. I unequivocally would have voted for General Eisenhower in both elections. Yet again, as a Canadian, I would have in the past believed in a strong federal government to maintain our independence" (227). (Regarding Eisenhower, Grant had evidently changed his mind: in a November 2, 1956, letter to his mother he wrote that "I hope against hope that Stevenson will beat him on Tuesday. Above all I dislike the way Eisenhower has sold himself to the public relations boys and the general platitude gang" (189). Twenty-five years later, Grant shifts again, wishing that Canadian leaders would, like Republican US Senator Jesse Helms, stand against abortion (319). In that 1986 letter, he wrote that "my sense of the greatness of the U.S.A. has been greatly raised by the presence of the anti-abortion movement" (359). Dart's (2006, 24) assertion—that "Grant, in short, deftly eludes the ethical tribalism that so dominates the landscape of the political right and left and points to a third way that cannot be easily appropriated by political ideologues"—seems to me not inaccurate but over-summarizes the movement of Grant's political thought.

46.   Davis and Roper 2005b, 602.

47.   Sibley 2008, 118.

48.   Grant (1959) 1966, 108. Dart (2006, 16) appreciates that, in Canada, "conservatism has never been as opposed to the use of the federal state to create and bring into being the common good as has American conservatism."

49.   I shall quote from Grant's letters as much as I can as they affirm the immediacy of his mind, its weddedness to relationship—most enduringly with his mother—and, as Christian (1996c, xiii) notes, "much daring speculation that he was reticent to include in his published work."

50.   Christian 1996d, 195.

51.   Muggeridge 1978, 44; see also B. Cooper 1992, 153. Muggeridge adds: "Loyalists hold fast to that which seems good; modernists, to that which seems expedient" (44). That said, Grant knew that many of his fellow Canadians had become modernists. In his interview with Charles Taylor ([1982] 2006, 131) Grant was quite clear, even indignant:"'You'd be wrong to think that Canadians have no passion. They have a huge passion....' He raises his arms, opening them wide, 'to make money. MONEY!' he roars. 'They stop at nothing. Families break up. Children are neglected. For the sake of more money. I find it...awesome. But it's there...a huge, cold, intense passion.'"

52.   A "political masterpiece and a missive of prophetic vigour and depth" (Dart and Jersak 2011, 24), *Lament for a Nation* was prompted by what Cayley (1995, 1) calls the "defence crisis of 1963," a crisis that occurred when the Diefenbaker government declined to comply with the US government's demand that Canada arm missiles with nuclear warheads, missiles it had acquired from the United State. Sensing vulnerability—I am following Cayley's account—the Liberal Party reversed its opposition to nuclear weapons deployed on Canadian soil. At a press conference in Ottawa, an American general challenged the good faith of the Canadian government. Diefenbaker's defence minister, Douglas Harkness, resigned, and the NDP joined with the Liberals, bringing down Prime Minister Diefenbaker (1–2). "But what was so strikingly different about Grant's book," Cayley comments, "was that he treated Diefenbaker's flaws as tragic, not comic...in what others had derisively dismissed as good riddance, Grant discovered the symbolic moment at which Canada had ceased to be a distinct society. Canada, Grant argued, had been founded on its difference from the United States.... Diefenbaker's confused and incoherent resistance to American bullying in 1963 was the last doomed gasp of our independence" (2–3). Davidson (1992, 132) notes that the federal election of 1963 was "the only election in modern Canadian history in which the U.S. intervened directly and against the government," adding that "the continentalist pull into the U.S. defense orbit had been aided and abetted by Canadians themselves." Confirming Grant's *Lament for a Nation*, Davidson suggests that "military arrangements tend to precede other aspects of integration" (123). Muggeridge (1978, 44) offers that "in Diefenbaker, Grant hears the last strangled voice of his pre-modernist Loyalist ancestors. Diefenbaker stood for something beyond efficiency. His very absurdity is an unprogressivist mark in his favour." Grant tells Cayley (1995, 98): "I may have been too taken up with political ire in my love of Diefenbaker," as "he often did very silly things in power" (99), "but I admired him in his fall and saw a lot of him afterwards. He asked me to write his life, but I couldn't. It would have taken years, and I couldn't just drop my work. I like both, but philosophy is incomparably more important to me than politics" (100). To that last comment I will return.

53. In September 1965 letter to Diefenbaker, Grant wrote: "The Conservative party has always been the instrument for the building of a united Canadian nation…. The party of Macdonald and Cartier did not think that in such a nation all regions, all peoples, all cultures should be the same. They knew that one great purpose of Confederation was to preserve and maintain French culture on this continent…. Today, just as much as a hundred years ago, Canada cannot do without Quebec; Quebec cannot do without Canada…. In the prairies and in the large cities of Ontario, to be Canadian does not mean to give up your own traditions. It means to bring that heritage into a common loyalty, the loyalty to Canada as a nation…. Yes, the Conservative party says one Canada; but one Canada which rejoices in its diversity" (Christian 1996d, 234–5).

54. Conservatism becomes impossible in our time, Charles Taylor ([1982] 2006, 147) agrees: "Because technology and science produce such a dynamic society, nothing can be preserved for long: all institutions and standards are constantly changing." And constant change becomes permanent, dissolving change. "Late-modernity's bereavement," Benedetti (2005, 202) suggests, "is over the impossibility to create; it perceives itself as a terminal culture." Lament all round.

55. Reimer 1978, 56. "I prefer Christ and Socrates to Athens and Jerusalem," Grant wrote E. Joan O'Donovan in 1982 (Christian 1996d, 323). Scanlon (2005, 160) suggests that "if Athens discovered the mind, Jerusalem discovered the will." For Grant, "careful, coherent thought is what I mean by the word *Athens*" (Cayley 1995, 59); revelation was represented by Jerusalem. Maybe Grant lamented the often inscrutable relation between the two, what he called the "great question is the relation of philosophy to revelation, or as it has been put, what has Athens to do with Jerusalem?" That question reverberates for Grant; we will ask it again in the final four chapters.

56. Greenspan 1990, 2.

57. "Grant's longing for the ancient past is not simply remembering," Reimer (1978, 56) explains, "It is an affirmation that there in fact exists an eternal realm, which the ancients recognized and which we have lost…. This realization drives Grant beyond a pure fatalism, pessimism, or even despair." Indeed, Reimer continues, "Grant's conclusion is a hopeful one: that nature itself will revolt, that the noble, the great, and the good will ultimately triumph. But this victory will not be brought about by political activity as it is perceived in the modern world." That realization, I suggest in ch. 6, leads Grant to consider quietude.

58. "If there is one word which seems to characterize George Grant's thought," Taylor ([1982] 2006, 153) concluded, "that word is pessimism." Taylor adds: "Somber and gloomy, Grant's perceptions have brought him close to personal despair" (154). But, he continues, "this is not the message which I derive from Grant. Instead of gloom, somehow he induces hope…. For me, Grant is always exhilarating, despite his direst warnings. Judging from the growing number of younger writers and academics who wrestle with his writings, my reaction is far from singular. Now I was finally starting to understand the process. In predicting the worst, Grant also reminds us of the best—especially those classical standards of justice and freedom by which he judges our modern era and finds it wanting. He arouses not only our apprehension of man's propensities to evil, but also our awareness of man's timeless quest for the good. He seems to challenge us to prove him wrong" (154–5). Michael Ignatieff tells us he "rebelled" against his uncle's "pessimism" (2018, 28). "But George Grant's pessimism lays down the gauntlet," he acknowledges (142).

59.   Grant (1959) 1966, 109.

60.   Angus 1997, 231; see also 175.

61.   Reimer 1978, 54. It must be said that Grant's conservatism changes over time. In a 1964, for instance, he endorses "unequivocal identification of the Conservative tradition with God" (Christian 1996d, 227). For Grant that term can be blurry, too, often identified with "the Good."

62.   Cayley 1995, 22.

63.   Cayley 1995, 22. See also Davis 2002a, xix.

64.   Cayley 1995, 22.

65.   Duff (2006, 112) summarizes these ancient principles: humanity's "highest good or happiness is wisdom, that even its pursuit, let alone its realization, is available only to the few; and that the actualization of the accordingly best regime is dependent on chance." Within that view, modernity's aspiration for the "universal and homogenous state"—*e pluribus unum*—"is a tyranny" (112).

66.   Minogue 1990, 161. Minogue is not the only one, of course. On the inside flap of the paperback copy of the David Cayley interview with Grant that I bought (used—it must be out of print) there is a handwritten note from a father to his son, to whom the book is presented: "To Brad / From Dad / George Grant taught me Ethics at Dalhousie in 1959, and he changed my life. It won't be light reading—but enjoy / With all my love." What Brad thought one can't know, but to record such praise within the intimacy and complexity of a father-son relationship testifies to Grant's enduring private as well as public importance.

67.   "It seems to me," Cayley (1995, 122) tells Grant, "that trying to reveal what is within common words is one of the main ways in which you teach."

68.   In a January 1949 letter, Grant wrote to his mother announcing he would be "on the radio this Tuesday 11 January. I am not quite sure when—afternoon or evening— on a CBC program called *Points of View*. The question "On Human Happiness"… [an occasion] where one can say something that one believes to be true" (Christian 1996d, 158). His "lifelong association" with the CBC, Cayley (1996, vii) tells us, began as an "organizer" for CBC Radio's *Citizens' Forum*, in 1943, to which he contributed reviews and "talks," as Cayley reminds were then called, throughout the 1950s. In 1958 Grant inaugurated *University of the Air*, Cayley continues, a program that became *Ideas*; his lectures there published in 1959 as *Philosophy in the Mass Age* (vii). He continued to be broadcast on both radio and television during the 1960s; in 1969 he recorded the CBC Massey Lectures, which appeared in book form as *Time as History*. "Altogether," Cayley summarizes, "his contributions to the CBC probably exceeded those of any other Canadian thinker of his generation, except perhaps Northrop Frye" (viii). Cayley himself "had the honour of making the last major presentation of Grant's ideas on CBC radio: a three-hour series called 'The Moving Image of Eternity,' broadcast on *Ideas* beginning in January of 1986, less than three years before his death" (viii). Grant was so loyal to the CBC—to its concept one supposes—that once he even considered voting for the Liberals, as the Tories were threatening to cut the budget of the public broadcaster (see Christian 1996d, 180).

69.   Cayley 1995, 69.

70.   B. Cooper 1978, 23.

71.   O'Donovan 1984, 106.

72.   Whillier 1990b, 63.

73. See also Heaven and Heaven 1978, 77; Dart 2006, 7.

74. Cayley 1995, 43.

75. Davis and Emberley 2000a, xv.

76. Grant in his interview with Cayley 1995, 79.

77. "The critique of technology," Angus (2006, 357) reminds, "implies a conception of a Good that is not of our own making." Even when not equivalent to God—as the Good could be for Grant—it can predicate ethical life, as I suggest in ch. 6.

78. Writing his mother in 1940—he was just twenty-two years old—Grant wrote: "The memory of things past remains as the nicest of all gifts" (Christian 1996d, 58). Simone Weil ([1947] 2002, 175) thought while the past was "something real" and "beyond our reach," we can even so turn toward it so that an "emanation from it may come." In that sense the past, she continues, constitutes the "most perfect image of eternal, supernatural reality" (175). In this view, reactivation of the past provides a portal to transcendence, becoming, in effect, a form of attunement, topics I discuss in ch. 6.

79. The reactivation of the past and its incorporation into the present—retaining the distinctiveness of each in the immediacy of their juxtaposition—achieves a restructuring of the present, not unlike, as Steimatsky (2008, 132) notes, "Pasolini's conscious confrontation of the archaic and the modern—at the two ends of the historical process—simultaneously imagined, animating each other."

80. "In evolutionary theory," Doane (2003, 86) reminds, "chance becomes determinant, the basis of law." Grant asked: "Does not the conquest of chance consist of a eugenics program undertaken from beyond good and evil" (Davis and Roper 2009b, 1004)? "[R]edemption," Grant added, "consists in…the affirmation of chance" (1005).

81. But not only consequences: "As far as the management of the iconic economy is concerned," Mondzain (2005, 64) explains, "we will see that only purity of intentions will serve as a guarantee of the good use of our carnal pleasures at the heart of the visible world."

82. In Nagatomo's (1992, 189) theory of attunement, "engagement is the most fundamental designation for a structural relationship obtaining between the personal body and his/her living ambiance." It may be the most fundamental but it does not neutralize the risk of appropriation. Thibon ([1947] 2002, xix) cautions that Weil's work can only be "weakened" by commentary. Not necessarily. I found Weil's writing illumined, not obscured, by Thibon's commentaries, an effect I aspire to replicate here.

83. Steimatsky 2008, 142.

84. By constantly quoting Grant (and those who have studied him), I aspire, quoting Cayley (1995, ix) now, to "preserve the vividness of spontaneous talk" (also making a theoretical point that orality can be enacted textually). Not that, in Cayley, Grant endorsed "unlimited human self-assertion" as "the highest good" (43). Indeed, it is within the restraint the subjective presence of others installs that spontaneity surfaces. What Cayley appreciated in Grant was "the way he brings the most important questions before us, and the poetical, deeply suffered clarity with which he expresses them" (44). One of those questions was the matter of restraint or limits. "Only within limits," Cayley writes, "is there any hope of shoring up memory and finding a way out of the labyrinth of endless overcoming, back to what every civilization, including our own, once recognized as the human condition" (44). Whillier (1990a, vi) suggests that for Grant "the idea of limit is the idea of God," an idea I confess I find idolatrous. Isn't "God" limitless?

85. "It seems to me there are moments in human life," Grant told Cayley (1995, 58) "moments of very great intensity and probably to do with action in regards to other people—that is, with morality—where one asks more than a fine question. One asks, What is it all about?"

86. "[W]e comprehend technology in [the] act of living in it," Grant knew (Davis and Roper 2009b, 129). If we juxtapose that existential fact with sustained academic study, we might expand the space of non-coincidence with technology, a space of subjective freedom wherein we might engage in subjective and social reconstruction. Writing about Torah study, the distinguished Jewish theologian Michael Fishbane (2008, 147) makes my point (if differently): "Through recitation and assimilation of the words of the past," "the oral tradition becomes alive in one's mouth." While working in a different tradition, Pérez-Gómez (2016, 171) writes that "reading a text oralizes it," even insisting that "real, effective understanding depends on a reader's dialogue with an absent author," reminding us that "even within the European tradition, reading was always enacted as vocalized utterance; reading aloud was the norm well into the eighteenth century." I am not recommending reading aloud as much as reading as if prose could also be poetry, focused on the subjective presence within the patterns prose as well as poetry presumes.

87. In addition to the effacing of civil society and human subjectivity that the triumph of technology would bring, Grant knew decades ago that income inequality and political polarization would intensify. In 1976 he wrote: "I think that on the whole, there is going to be less to go around in the North American economy, making it tougher to divide the pie than in the past. I regret it, but I think there is going to be an increase in class struggle. I am not a Marxist and I regret that tougher actions will result from the divisions in the economy. When there are tough actions, the weak suffer (Davis and Roper 2009b, 299)." It is as if Grant saw the 2016 US presidential election coming when he warned us against "falling for the politics of theater and confrontation" (417).

88. Grant (1969) 2001, 53.

89. The Latin infinitive of curriculum, I invoked *currere* in 1974 to emphasize the experience of curriculum, experience that was structured by the past if focused on the future. In the regressive phase one returns to the past (or aspects of it; for instance, one's school's experience, the experience of an influential teacher or text, one's ongoing relationship with an academic discipline), imagines the future (personal, social, political, ecological), then analyzes these texts and the experiences they register to understand what before had been obscured in one's work at present, encouraging a synthesis of lived and comprehended experience that perhaps alters how one is in not only the classroom but perhaps in the world. For the original formulation see Pinar and Grumet ([1976] 2015; for other formulations, see Pinar 2004, 2012, 2015a, and https://www.www.currereexchange.weebly.com). As the co-authored text makes explicit, Madeleine R. Grumet and I worked closely together. While she was at that time enrolled as a doctoral student under my supervision, the truth was that I was hers.

90. "And the more we think about subjectivity," Grant mused, "the more mysterious it becomes. On the one hand, it is always there, we cannot escape ourselves. On the other hand, though we can never escape ourselves, we can never find ourselves (Davis 2002b, 125)." I suggest we can find ourselves—at least those dimensions pertinent to the present—in the past.

91.   "This objective spirit of the European and North American middle classes has been a remarkable phenomenon," Grant acknowledged. "Nobody should fall into the trap of despising it lightly. It did much to reform and transform the external world. It had, however, a deadly weakness; it came more and more to deny human freedom and subjectivity in both its thought and practice" (Davis 2002b, 126). "In spite of this sober estimate," Badertscher (1978, 87) explains, "Grant sees resources in the human situation from which a response to the problem of freedom can be fashioned. We can yet nurture other human possibilities—the power of recollection or participation in a living tradition, desiring or loving, and thinking. Taken together, these powers ground the possibility of reverence." And "reverence or piety," Grant reminded, "is unequivocally said to be part of the full life for man" (Davis and Roper 2005b, 739).

92.   O'Donovan (1984, 73) notes that "Grant entertains the restoration of past thought as a theoretical possibility."

93.   Cayley 1995, 170. Grant confessed that he found it a "mystery" that "someone else's account should sometimes be able to restore one to reality more completely than one's own experience" (Davis and Roper 2009b, 432). Does it not have to do with the mystery of the icon, an "account" that traverses time and place, embodies contingency and transcendence, that refracts what is beyond as it invites the viewer—the student—to reflect on oneself?

94.   Cayley 1995, 137–8. Reactivation of the past in service to subjective reconstruction in the present is implied in Kaethler's (2009, 54) observation that the understanding of modernity that Nietzsche and Heidegger brought to Grant "forced [him] to dig deep into his roots (Platonism and Christianity) in order to rid himself of modernity's stronghold." His roots, be reminded, were progressive: Platonism and Christianity enabled him to pull himself up, reconstructing himself as a (progressive) Christian Platonist.

95.   Technology and humanity have been intertwined since pre-history, of course, and even technology's association with modernity was centuries in the making, as Al-i Ahmad (1984, 59) complains: "[T]he god technology had for years exercised absolute rule over Europe mounted on the throne of its banks and stock exchanges, and it no longer tolerated any other god, laughing in the face of every tradition and ideology."

96.   Once technology is internalized, Cayley (1995, 27) summarizes (during his interview with Grant) our memory goes blank (like the screen in front of us): "[H]ow can we know what we have lost, or even that we have lost anything?" Not only memory goes, any non-coincidence with what is shrinks. As Hall (1978, 125) appreciates: "The consequences of the technocratic captivity of the soul is that we have lost any vantage-point from which to make a discerning assessment of what is happening to us."

97.   Davis and Roper 2009b, 817.

98.   R. G. Collingwood (2002, 88) thought "we might very well be standing on the threshold of an age in which history would be as important for the world as natural science had been between 1600 and 1900." While Collingwood and Grant are very different thinkers, they intersect slightly when Grant invokes recollection and Collingwood suggests re-enactment in their respective reactivations of the past. "For Collingwood," Hutt (2013, 68) explains, "it was only through the 'practicing of historical thought'—that is, rethinking the way different witnesses once thought—that

knowledge of the past could be attained. This was done by asking 'why' past others—like Plato or Caesar—behaved in the way that they had. Collingwood was after the 'inner' intentions and motives of his sources." In reactivating history I am interested in the educational significance of the past, how re-experiencing the past—mediated as that necessarily is by the present—can reinstate temporality, even acting as a cohesive, as when "the 'memory image' of an event or a person...binds a tradition together" (72).

99. Davis and Roper 2005b, 9.

100. Athanasiadis (2006, 256) defines the sacred as "something that is known as other than us while at the same time penetrating us. We encounter the sacred within us but the sacred we encounter within us is greater than us, transcending us and opening us to otherness as that which is beautiful and good." Spirituality is, then, the experience of the sacred (256). "In postmodern political vocabularies," Ziarek (2001, 5) points out, "the category of the Other, most frequently associated with women and people of color, is synonymous with objectification, exclusion, and domination. It is either a negative foil for the identity of those who count as political subjects or a fetishistic screen for the projection of social antagonisms." Athanasiadisis invoking the term in its spiritual sense.

101. Davis and Roper 2005b, 727.

102. Davis and Roper 2005b, 727.

103. Power 1978, 97. The spiritual and personal converge on occasion. In a January 1976 letter, Grant writes that "I hate living with the nearly complete break with one's past—but that seems the way of the world now" (Christian 1996d, 290). They converged on occasion in his classroom teaching too, as he explains an autobiographical moment by saying: "[T]he point of teaching is not in any sense to try to teach [you] to parrot the propositions by which I live—but to try to persuade some of you to go back to the roots for yourselves.... None of you in this class should feel that to do well you have to agree or indeed to disagree with anything I say; how I will judge you is how much by reading the books I suggest you are able to go back to the roots" (Davis and Roper 2005b, 726).

104. O'Donovan 1984, 103. "Recollecting means returning to the beginnings where the truth of the tradition makes its appearance," O'Donovan adds, a truth that enables us to "think the present in terms of the supremacy of willing, the rule of 'technique'" (115).

105. Hall 1978, 124. "On the other hand," Hall adds, "there can be no thought of a simple return for those who have gone as far as we along the road of modernity" (124). Reactivation requires reconstruction; the curriculum juxtaposes the two.

106. Schmidt 1978b, 130.

107. Athanasiadis (2001, 178) suggests that the "task of listening and waiting for intimations of the good of which we are deprived is, therefore, to discover how technological society deprives us of it." Thinking our deprival and recollecting the Good are therefore associated undertakings. For Grant, O'Donovan (1984, 129) specifies, it is "Plato and the Gospels we must recollect" (130).

108. For Grant, Christian (1990, 194–5) clarifies, recollection is not psychoanalytic (as it is for me, hence the term "reactivation"), but Platonic, recalling the ancient myth that "all souls, before they were embodied, had knowledge of the eternal and transcendent reality, but just prior to embodiment they were washed in the river Lethe,

or Forgetfulness. The knowledge which they enjoy in this world, then, is the consequence of recollecting what has once been known and then subsequently forgotten."

109.   Davis and Roper 2009b, 136.

110.   Discussing Hegel, Grant tells Cayley (1995, 87) that a "subject is never identical with itself"—except when someone is crushed, I'd add—but Grant's point is that that fact morphed into modernity's emphasis upon "objectivity," which, he notes, "comes from the Latin for something to be thrown away from us." He adds: "When you see something objectively, you hold it from you. It is not something you can love" (87). That positioning—and absence of love—becomes crucial in Grant's curriculum theory, as we see in ch. 5. In modernity's bifurcation, not only the object suffers, so the subject, as it means, Grant suggests, "thrown under" (88), as in being subject to authoritarian rule. But Grant is thinking here in metaphysical as well as worldly terms, as he tells Cayley that "this property of being as 'identical with itself,' it seems to me, is something that Hegel is getting rid of, in talking about God as subjectivity" (88). Subjectivity exists in the space of non-coincidence.

111.   O'Donovan 1984, 167.

112.   Lipari 2014, 141.

113.   For Marion (2001, 157), "Revelation communicates the very intimacy of God—distance itself." In secular terms, can we say that in the distance between now and then is located an experience of intimacy with our predecessors?

114.   Fishbane 2008, xiv. "How we collect such events in our personal lives," Fishbane adds, "and how we keep them alive, determines the nature of our character; and how a culture does this through education and the selection of events for public recollection affects the moral shape of society" (21). Referencing Herbert Marcuse, Trilling (1972, 166) notes that "he *likes* people to have 'character,' cost what it may in frustration. He holds fast to the belief that the right quality of human life, its intensity, its creativity, its felt actuality, its weightiness, requires the stimulus of existence." Such stimulus—or abrasiveness—of embodied experience, rarely "right" one needs to remind oneself, is surely the stuff of memory and education.

115.   McDaniel (2016, 263) describes "eternalism," a view in which "there is no change in time, and location of time is analogous to location in space: just as Syracuse, New York, is real although it is not here, so too Julius Caesar is real even though he is not now." For me, the past remains "real" even if it is not "now."

116.   Grant (1969) 2001, 41.

117.   "To remake ourselves," Grant wrote, "as individual persons and as a society, the most radical investigation of our first principles becomes necessary" (Davis 2002b, 114). Academic study—and one's lived experience of it—can be key; in this larger passage from which Grant is quoted he recommends Cochrane. I'm recommending Grant.

118.   Like Grant, "I do not use the word knowledge, as is generally done in our pragmatic age, to mean understanding's manipulation of the world for its own purposes. I use it rather as any means that brings the human spirit to self-consciousness" (Davis 2002b, 68).

119.   "Revelation which is rooted in trust," Whillier (1990b, 67) notes, "stands in position to philosophy which is rooted in doubt." Trust and doubt I treat in ch. 6.

120.   My thanks to UBC Professor Steven Taubeneck for raising this issue. Worried about his writing on Simone Weil, Grant too appreciated this problem: "Many

commentaries turn out to be inadequate synopses and are often chiefly concerned with what the commentator thinks important rather than with the work of genius" (Davis and Roper 2009b, 806–7). In this volume, in the chapters of reactivation, ch. 2–4, Grant's critique rings loud and clear (I trust); in those of reconstruction, ch. 5–7, Grant's voice remains audible, my analysis and synthesis predominate. With my reconstructing Grant, some slippage is inevitable; it's appropriation about which I worry, e.g., citing Grant's work for my own purposes, something Dalton Kingsley Camp (1920–2002; see Davis and Roper 2009b, 407n7), was evidently accused of; see Planinc 1992, 23.

121. The term is Pasolini's; it involves, a "recuperation of the past," as Rumble (1994, 225) notes, in Pasolini's effort to "evoke a cultural memory in the spectator, to force a conflict between memory and perception, and to thus raise him or her to a position from which to critically judge the present." For Rohdie (1995, 123), contamination was less temporal than "formal-linguistic…contaminations formed by often surprising juxtapositions of high art and low life, the sacred and the terrestrial, literary speech and gutter slang, was a means for bringing together formal structures and representation, form and substance. The elements in these monstrous hybrids made differences felt in the grating and similarities seen in the reflections. It could create considerable formal beauty even when the content of the representation was vulgar or even repulsive."

122. Christian 1996d, 258.

123. Christian 1996d, 258.

124. The standard Greek word for freedom of speech (see Pagels 1989, 171n97), *parrhesia* here emphasizes "frank" or even "fearless speech," a key concept from Michel Foucault's unpublished lectures on ancient ethical practices as these are discussed by political theorist Nancy Luxon (2013, 2), who juxtaposes such speech to the candour of psychoanalytic encounter in order to think through conflated issues of authority and relationship, personal and political.

125. Christian 1996d, 220.

126. Christian 1996d, 258.

127. As I too have suggested; Pinar 2017a.

128. It is a multi-dimensional sensed understanding, informed by academic study of course, but also by attunement to the Good. However tentative and provisional, such understanding could be associated with the two men Grant studies most of all: Jesus and Socrates. Regarding the latter—and concerning the matter of "understanding"—Magrini (2017, 11) points out that "Socrates is aware that this understanding will always fall short of either propositional or axiomatic certainty."

129. That last term has always seemed central to me. In a 1974 letter to former Dalhousie classics colleague Patrick Atherton, Grant wrote, "I have become a solitary in the sense that the only things that really interest me (other than my family) are teaching the young and trying to write down what I am thinking about technique and Christianity. I am not solitary vis-à-vis students or necessary details of organization, but I am solitary insofar as not allowing anything to stand in the way of my thinking" (Christian 1996d, 279–80). Sustained study is one site of solitary thinking.

130. Davis and Roper 2005b, 674.

131. George Grant was an "unusual combination of public intellectual and cloistered scholar," Forbes (2007, 3) notes. Given his containment within Canada, Grant might

not be accorded "public" status by non-Canadians. I want to suggest that in this moment of technological hegemony Grant speaks to "us"—maybe "everyone"—now that there is the suggestion that soon "we will all be connected directly to the Internet via a neural implant" (Halpern 2011, 33).

132. While pedagogy and study become subsumed in my expansive conception of curriculum as "complicated conversation" (Pinar 2015a, 109), distinguishing among them remains clarifying, especially given Grant's phrasing above.

133. Cayley 1995, x.

134. The progressive movement in education emerged in the 1890s, Ravitch (at the time of this writing adamantly anti-progressive herself; regarding her shift, see Pinar 2012, 198ff.) notes, about the same time as the larger progressive movement intensified in US politics. Progressives advocated an array of reforms, among them expanded participation in the political process, the regulation of monopolies, the improvement of living conditions of the urban poor, equitable taxation, and the reform of municipal politics. Progressives, she adds, were also associated with anti-immigrant causes such as nativism, immigration restriction, and eugenics; many, however, were ambivalent over women's suffrage (see Ravitch 2000, 53). In education, Ravitch continues, progressivism's "primary purpose, as defined by its leading spokesman, John Dewey, was to make the schools an instrument for social reform" (57). While inspired by but not always loyal to Dewey's vision, Ravitch explains that in private "progressive schools, which enrolled the children of well-to-do families, the 'new education' was child-centered, meaning that children's interests and activities were the basis of the curriculum. In big public school systems, however, the 'new education' meant vocational and industrial education to train the children of the masses for work in farms, shops, factories, and homes. Such curriculum changes appeared to be socially efficient" (59). For other histories of educational progressivism, see Cremin 1961; Spring 1972, 1976.

135. See, e.g., Davis and Emberley 2000b, 133; Davis and Roper 2009b, 751; Davis 2002b, 197. "Grant was raised a progressive," Davis (2006, 63) reminds, "and became a Christian Platonist." ("But in the end," Cayley [1995, 28] comments, "Grant seems to me much closer to Christian mysticism." Athanasiadis [2001, 229] suggests that Grant felt that "mysticism was better able to convey the experience of God than philosophy.) When Grant read the American pragmatist philosopher William James, Christian (1996a, 61–2) reports, he was "impressed, writing his mother that it was "absolutely fascinating stuff, not very clear but [full] of brilliance." Even in his maturity, Davis (2006, 68) believes, "Grant did side with the modern idea of changing the world to make it a more just place for the many." Koopman (2009, 164) argues that pragmatism shares several "central assumptions" made by conservatives: "Against the ahistoricism of both the rationalists and irrationalists, pragmatists tend to side with those conservatives who articulate evolutionary, developmental, and situated conceptions of political practice." When Grant noticed that the wealthy were in praise of Nilda Neatby's (1953) *So Little for the Mind*—a book of which Grant first approved (see Davis 2002b, 161), and with the author of which he corresponded—he admitted "I suddenly realized I had more in common with the goodhearted enthusiasm of progressive education—because however vacuous and foolish progressive education is the motive of egalitarian kindness behind it gives it at least more of the spirit than does middle-class success-seeking" (103).

136. I add the modifier to emphasize that Grant's invitation was not only physical prox-imity but into his "home," where he "lived," his interiority or subjectivity, where he would often reference his own situation as he sought to understand those with whom he was engaged. For Ian Angus (1997, 232), Grant's "presence was always unsettling." Angus draws a distinction between Grant's writing and speaking: "Unlike his writing, which begins with a sure and clear statement of an issue, his speaking voice began slowly, tentatively, clearing a common ground" (232). I am reminded of homiletics and the concept of "blended force," in which one's witness-ing "arises from a communal experience of time and place, experience animated by both the human and the divine" (Pinar 1988, 271).

137. While I very much appreciate Larry Schmidt's (1978a) conversation with Grant, and Charles Taylor's ([1982] 2006) account of his time with Grant (intriguingly, Taylor concluded that "a conversation with Grant is like being attacked by a renegade steam roller—one is finally pulverized" [208]), Cayley's (1995) was for me the most pleas-ing of Grant's interviews, partly because Cayley has done his homework (so had Taylor and Schmidt) but also because Cayley's questions and comments often point to matters of public concern as well as to Grant himself. In a letter dated February 12, 1986, Grant himself conveyed his appreciation to Cayley for his earlier radio interview (as part of "The Moving Image of Eternity" on *Ideas*), upon which the book was predicated, as well as for his at-home interview in Halifax: "Dear David, This is to say thank you for the care and lucidity with which you enucleated my thoughts on the radio.... [W]hen you were here you gave me such confidence by the careful questions you asked" (see Christian 1996d, 355).

138. Cayley 1995, x. "Philosophy," Grant tells Cayley, "is the extreme human presump-tion of claiming to be open to the whole, isn't it?" (54)

139. In a 1952 letter to his mother, Grant complains about university philosophy depart-ments having "surrendered their true task. They turned philosophy into technical work for the few rather than a way of life open to all" (Christian 1996d, 175). For Grant, Whillier (1990a, vi) suggests, "the fundamental fact of human existence is existence itself as more than mere chance," adding: "Existence is a fundamental goodness."

140. Christian 1996a, 282. "Now Nietzsche said," Christian continues, "and men believed him, that time was history—and nothing more. Mankind was like a mariner, alone on the sea under an overcast sky, without charts or compass. Some would drift as the cur-rent took them, but others might choose a course and strike out boldly, willing their fate—whatever it might be. For those latter, Nietzsche taught, the situation was not a disaster, but an opportunity, the greatest ever offered to mankind, the life of absolute freedom" (282). Christian commented: "The conception of time as history was not, George affirmed, one in which it was possible to live a fully human life" (282).

141. Cayley 1995, 6. For example, Cayley writes, "*Lament for a Nation*...produced an effect of exhilaration in its readers, even as it apparently left them standing in midair. It was an elegy that induced hope, an evocation of a vanished good that still seemed pregnant with some new possibility" (5). Charles Taylor ([1982] 2006, 148) remem-bers: "Yet *Lament* did not make me despondent: just the opposite, since I found it exhilarating. This paradox was difficult to explain, but it seemed that others had a similar reaction. According to the socialist Jim Laxer: 'It's the most important book I ever read in my life. Here was a crazy old philosopher of religion at McMaster and

he woke up half our generation. He was saying Canada is dead, and by saying it he was creating a country.'"

142. Speaking about 1960s student protestors, Grant admitted that "their politics of hope and Utopia—indeed with some of them another outbreak of the traditional form of the politics of the apocalypse—seems to me a kind of dream from which analysis should awaken them. They seem to think that these massive institutions which stifle humane excellence can be overcome, and I think this arises from a profound misinterpretation of modern thinking" (Christian and Grant 1998b, 86). "Hope is a great virtue, Grant wrote, "but I do not think it should be concentrated on the events of this world but on the eternal order" (Christian 1996d, 160). Without hope, I focus on "resolve" (Pinar 2015a, 180).

143. "Grant found the Christian intellect after which he sought," O'Donovan (1984, 14) tells us, in Sheila (and the philosopher and biblical scholar Austin Farrer, under whom he studied). Along with James Doull (his colleague at Dalhousie who taught Hegel, including to Grant, and whom he also first met at Oxford), Sheila Grant was the other person who affected Grant's life most (see Schmidt 1978a, 64). The mother of their six children, she would also, Davis (2002a, xviii) tells us, serve as "his lifelong intellectual companion and editor-collaborator, whose impact on his thought cannot be overstated." The two discussed his lectures; on occasion she attended his graduate seminars (which were, Davis continues, sometimes held at their home in the early 1950s) and serve as an editor, reviewing his writings "line by line" (xviii). And too his teaching, implied in his introduction of her to students: "My wife [is] here because I have to justify to her the teaching of Nietzsche" (Davis and Roper 2009b, 1002).

144. Christian and Grant 1998a, 11.

145. Grant started to invoke this phrase in the late 1950s, McCarroll (2006, 270) reports. "According to Grant," she continues, "the Whole includes all of reality—the universe, human and non-human being, and God. The essence of the Whole, however, is love. In a more precise sense, then, the Whole is the vast and intricate network of relationships within the universe and between human and non-human being and God. This network of the Whole is held together by love, visible and invisible" (270). Its contemplation is ancient, Grant reminds (Davis and Roper 2005b, 67). As well as the totality of reality, "the whole" also seems to denote the "unity" within it: "[P]hilosophy seeks to know that principle of unity upon which all depends: that is the highest object of knowledge" (690). That "ultimate unity" is for Grant "the Good—the One" (67). In his 1988 addendum to the 1953 essay "Two Theological Languages," Grant registers "how fragile is the attempt to have knowledge of the whole" (Davis 2002b, 59).

146. Christian and Grant 1998a, 13.

147. In his 1975–76 graduate seminar in the Religion Department at McMaster University, Grant admitted to students that "the whole presents itself to us as staggeringly ambiguous" (Davis and Roper 2009b, 830). "If 'the whole' is seen as 'confused' rather than orderly and rational," Lionel Trilling (1972, 121) points out, "the human relation to it need not be fixed and categorical; it can be mercurial and improvisational." For Dewey (1922, 203), "consciousness of the whole has been connected with reverences, affections, and loyalties which are communal." I wrestle with one's relation to "the whole" in ch. 5–7.

148. See Lewis 2013.

149. "Since Machiavelli," Knopff (1992, 71) observes, "this rank ordering [of the ancients] has been reversed: results have been preferred to acting well; or rather, acting well has been defined in terms of the achievement of desired results." Rocha (2017, 70) rues: "After the secular dethroned the sacred, claiming to act in the name of reason, economics dethroned reason by proclaiming itself the end of reason. The distance from the sacred, if anything, increased. As of this writing, we are two gods removed from God."

150. For Grant, secularization meant "making Christianity worldly...time is all—oblivion of the opposite of time, which is eternity—expressed vaguely as timelessness" (Davis and Roper 2009b, 934–5). For Kevin Burke and Avner Segall (2017), secularization—at least in the United States—is Christian. "[S]ecularization is not quite the same as religious scepticism," Penelhum (1983, 93) suggests, "though of course they are closely connected."

151. "Religion means to me above all adoration," Grant explained (Davis and Roper 2009b, 1061), but in a conversation with William Christian two months before his death, Grant sounds unsure: "I am never sure what people mean by religion. I know what are particular religions like Hinduism, Buddhism, Christianity. But religion is a strange, unknown [thing]" (Davis and Roper 2009b, 737). Perhaps the origin of the term provides a clue: in Latin it was, Grant notes, "what binds together" (946).

152. Davis 2002b, 231. Anticipating ch. 5, Grant also warns that "the idea of the progress of science becomes a Moloch to which anything can be sacrificed" (256).

153. "The meaning of the whole," Grant emphasized in a 1965 letter, "cannot easily be put aside either existentially or scientifically" (Christian 1996d, 231).

154. To "become an educated human being through a sustained life of study" was the traditional understanding, Grant noted (Davis and Roper 2009b, 423), but, as he complained, now scholarly "production"—co-authored articles, collaborative projects, conferences, constant presentations—substitutes for solitary study. Never mind email (which Grant was spared).

155. Pinar 2015a, 11; 2017b. Understood as ongoing engagement with alterity, study is not necessarily academic of course, as Grant made plain: "You cannot have a free and vibrant society unless there are free and vibrant people in it. Obviously there are large numbers of free people in Canada who have no touch with higher education. Their freedom has other sources. Nevertheless, it is important for the health of any society that there are people in it whose sense of freedom is sustained by having thought in a disciplined way about the supreme questions of human life" (Davis and Roper 2009b, 424). "[W]hat acts as a consistent motif in a great deal of Canadian political thought," Fierlbeck (2006, 154) suggests, "is the belief that 'freedom' must be understood as something beyond the liberal manifestation of negative individual liberty." Grant criticizes negative liberty as ethically empty, and, in Meynell's (2011, 115) view, "follows Hegel in making the case for giving freedom content and concrete purpose," adding that "[f]reedom is not unlimited licence; it is realized when we understand our place in the larger order and work toward our proper end." Such understanding is the aspiration of sustained study.

156. "Textual study thus becomes a discipline of ethical and spiritual self-cultivation," Fishbane (2008, xii) writes, "and scripture is transformed thereby from an authoritative corpus of received laws, beliefs, and memories into an authorizing matrix of ongoing meditative reflection and reflective action." While I would expand

"scripture" to include secular texts—those by and about George Grant in the present study—Fishbane's sense of study is one I share.

157. "[S]ubjectivity begins, is born, in the encounter with another," Lipari (2014, 190) notes (citing Buber). That first "other" may be the mother or primary caregiver, if the psychoanalytic (object-relations) theory of the splitting of the fused identity between mother and infant is at all accurate (see Chodorow 1978 for a summary). Within that realized non-coincidence with the maternal body, subjectivity—including that sense of solitude wherein one's subjectivity becomes predominant—starts, perhaps. Like attachment, solitude can be sacred too: in his DPhil thesis, Grant wrote: "The decisive meetings between man and God are only possible in our aloneness" (Davis and Emberley 2000b, 326).

158. Davis and Roper 2005b, 658.

159. Grant himself railed against immanence in defence of transcendence. On this point—without the Christian faith he felt so strongly—we part company (and not for the only time); Pinar 2009, 146.

160. "This going beyond," Huebner (1999, 344) explains, "this 'moreness' of life, this transcendent dimension is the usual meaning of 'spirit' and 'spiritual.'"

161. Davis 2002b, 178. Grant associates love of one's own with love of "the good," warning that those who are "deracinated" may have "nothing which is really their own" and thus can "rarely can move to the good" (Schmidt 1978a, 21). That relation between reason and attunement I reference in ch. 6; the relation between the particular and the universal I explore in ch. 5 and 7.

162. It occurred to Grant "that perhaps the Western experiment, the experiment that had gone on since the seventeenth century in both natural science and political science, had been a mistake" (Cayley 1995, 74). That seems to me a curiously "modernist" judgment to make, unless one is assuming a God-like point of view, above, and capable of changing, the direction of human history.

163. Now, postmodernity or late modernity are the terms of choice, implying modernity has dissolved but not disappeared, evident in Kittler's (2013, 206) terminology: "And so, the self-guided weaponry of the Second World War did away with the two fundamental concepts of modernity—causality and subjectivity—and inaugurated the present as the age of technical systems," systems, he adds, "whether they are digital or analog…are always self-guided." The Enlightenment concept of the human subject—emphasizing the capacity to think and act "independently"—has "disappeared," he continues," along with the fifty-five million human beings who died in the world war" (206). For Grant the Second World War was also self-defining: "The great public event which shaped me was the great war of 1939 to 1945 and what it did was to drive me out of the bourgeois atheistic liberalism in which I had been raised because of the enormous, almost limitless repugnance I felt toward the modernity which had manifested itself in what I had seen in the war. This led me to think about and live in the world in terms of Christianity expressed philosophically in Platonic terms" (Davis and Roper 2009b, 1009).

164. "The modernist faith—in the domination of nature, in history-making, in optimism about the possibilities of worldly life—has formed our institutions and patterns of life more completely than in any other society," Grant knew (Davis 2002b, 240). The "modern," he writes in another place, "has in fact cut most of us off from apprehending the eternal" (Davis and Roper 2009b, 957). Presumably modernity and

secularism—making Christianity "worldly," Grant asserts—are reciprocally related, but by making it (in the first phrase quoted above) a modifier of faith, Grant implies they are both "religious" (934).

165. This conception of Plato's Wilberding (2016, 30) characterizes as "enigmatic," but only, he suggests, if eternity means timelessness. Wilberding suggests that for Plato both eternity and time "involve duration" (30), as eternity means not only durational extension but a sense of completion as well (31). For me, that latter sense seems hinted in Augustine's sense of eternity as "the whole being always in the present without change" (45). "The whole" becomes an important marker for Grant, implying transcendence of the particular and the temporal. If time is a moving image of eternity, it seems to me the contingent world becomes spatially and visually defined, as motion and appearance become refractions of what is visually absent—for Grant "the Good" or God —from the everyday. Whether [in] those refractions of what is absent we see functions as icons or idols is a question I explore in ch. 5.

166. Pedagogy—and study—are for me subsumed in my conception of curriculum conceived as complicated conversation (Pinar 2015a, 109).

167. In his discussion of *imago Dei* (Gen. 1:26–7), Richard Lints (2015, 29) insists that "[t]he language of 'image' argues for a dependence upon an 'original.'" In this instance, as in that of "eternity," the "original"—absolute alterity—is beyond comprehension, perhaps beyond apprehension, an issue (inspired by Weil) on which Grant comments, as I note in ch. 5–7.

168. In the interview with Cayley (1995, 175), Grant, referencing Weil and Plato, associates (as noted earlier) "God" with "the Good." Power (1978, 94) reminds that for Grant "values" are not the equivalent to "the Good"; Grant notes that "the modern view of goodness is that which is advantageous to our creating richness of life (or, if you like, the popular modern propagandists' 'quality of life')" (Davis and Roper 2009b, 292). In a graduate seminar Grant defined "good is what we are fitted for" (819; see also 933). Dart (2006, 25) suggests that Grant "equated" God with "the Good," but, as just noted, there are occasions when he associated the good with "what we are fitted for, what we aspire to" (Davis and Roper 2009b, 304). Are the two interrelated, something revealed through attunement to the transcendent?

169. For Ellul—whose work influenced thinkers as different as Grant and Pasolini—the pre-modern mind inhabited an eternal mythical present periodically affirmed by means of rites (see Maggi 2009, 6).

170. "[I]n the process of study, Fishbane (2008, 3) acknowledges, "one may integrate some topics and terms while casting others aside."

171. Grant affirmed education as an "end in itself"(Davis 2002b, 432), a view I share. That education is intrinsically important does not mean specific school subjects are, even if Grant's complaint seemed not specific to content but to difficulty: "[T]he problem of curriculum, for instance, in which the progressive educators are substituting for the ancient and difficult studies a lot of easy new ones designed to help children conform comfortably to society but not to make them intellectually alive and morally independent" (435). Nor did subject specificity seem to preoccupy Joseph J. Schwab (1983, 250), the distinguished curriculum theorist who wrote that maybe the most "durable, widespread" and "self-destructive fallacy" of American education is that "belief" that there is an "eternally true, ineluctable content" of the school subjects. When following this unshaken faith, he continues, teaching becomes "telling," with

inadequate attention to "argument" and "evidence," to critique and the posing of alternatives. Mistaking the "habitually taught" for the "durable truth," Schwab concludes, represents "one of the great barriers to any curricular change and as the greatest barriers of change which will not, in its turn, become virtually religious dogmas" (250). In this passage Schwab starts questioning the curricular subjects as idols, but then switches to how they are taught (e.g., "telling"). This sharp distinction, I suggest, becomes part of the problem modernity poses; e.g., the instrumentalization of means, which then become substitutes for ends. In the quoted passage above, even Grant seems to succumb.

172.   As early as 1943, Grant is asking this canonical curriculum question: "However much we busy ourselves with techniques for getting ideas across to the community we serve, what ideas we intend to get across will continue to be the more vital question to interest us" (Davis and Emberley 2000b, 91). Later, Grant describes education as learning "what was truly worth desiring" (Davis 2002a, xxi). As Grant put the matter: "For what men believe to be ultimately true is what makes them what they are and through them their society" (Davis 2002b, 163).

173.   Some subjects seem to me especially important now—history for one—but when and how history is to be studied in K–12 or university curriculum must be an ongoing and open question. In an era very different from ours, one submerged in history, in which the past has become an idol, it is imaginable that history should be deemphasized, its study even suspended. Given our presentism, reactivating the past becomes precious.

174.   Associated with the pedagogical theory of Paulo Freire (1970), dialogical encounter requires a technology-poor curriculum (Pinar and Grumet [1976] 2015), as, Kittler (2013, 154) observes, the "technology of transmission" has been taken "from people"—once "interfaces of traditional literature" (reading as embodied encounter)—"and installed in machines." Indeed, one becomes a machine, as Grant complained in a 1948 letter to his mother: "One is simply a lecture machine and not a very good machine at that" (Christian 1996d, 152). To my mind, that failure (to be "a very good machine") constitutes a success.

175.   "Society as a natural entity has its highest end," Grant insisted, "the education of its members, adding that "economic competition or even survival are not in themselves ends which realize human excellence" (Davis and Roper 2005b, 240). Human excellence for Grant, I suggest, required attunement to the transcendent, a state of being what one is fitted for, e.g., justice, itself predicated on material well-being, cultural recognition, and social ethics.

176.   This is not a matter of either/or but, as Aoki ([1993] 2005b, 295) would have it, "both...and." A calling can be—most often is—secular of course, if with a spiritual subtext: "The artist, scientist, citizens, parent," Dewey ([1934] 1962, 23) suggested, "as far as they are actuated by the spirit of their callings, are controlled by the unseen." Attunement to the transcendent, as Grant knew, can be threaded through the material, e.g., the curriculum as iconographic (see ch. 5).

177.   Mondzain (2005, 89) explains that "the anagogical property of the icon leads us through a site of which it is the itinerary, the path. The limit of iconic vision is the gaze of the icon in the uninterrupted volt of the face-to-face encounter." In the epilogue we will hear Grant advising prospective teachers to allow what is "really grasping you"—"the gaze of the icon"—to lead the way.

178. Curriculum design may not be intrinsically impossible (as I once argued); see Grimmett and Halvorson 2010. But the project of the so-called learning sciences seems overreach; see Taubman 2009. When human conduct can be predicted and controlled, Bauman (1978) cautioned, transcendence is absent.

179. While the term implies schisms in time and outlook, Robinson (2010, 74) points out that "little that is modern departs as cleanly from its precursors as myth would have us believe," save one that is: "Our conception of the significance of humankind and for the universe has shrunk to the point that the very idea we ever imagined we might be significant on this scale now seems preposterous. These assumptions about what we are and are not preclude not only religion but also the whole enterprise of metaphysical thought." Surely it is this shrinking of significance that characterizes the ethical crisis of modernity, the crisis to which Grant's teaching replies.

180. For Benedetti (2005, 22) "The postmodern does not therefore represent a true leap forward with respect to what it claims to have left behind, but rather a reaction (and, as we shall see, a pathological one) to the malaise of modernity." Planinc (1992, 42) quips that "post-modernity is really just modernity with a touch of amnesia." Twenty-five years ago the "post-modern" seemed another opportunity to reinvent the progressive agenda in education, as William E. Doll Jr. (1993) made clear (hyphenating the term to emphasize its proximity to modernity). Now not so much—Doll moved on to complexity theory; see Trueit 2012. Contemplating the difficulty of "doing" Jewish theology now, Fishbane (2008, 9) points to the "felt absence in our times of one coherent or compelling worldview. A dizzying swirl of methods populate the landscape of modernity, and variously claim to be the most suitable cognitive matrix for perceiving or assessing reality." Without memory, the postmodern possibility devolves into consumer choice, choice eviscerated by suspicion. Discussing Grant's close colleague at Dalhousie, James Doull, Robertson (2006, 151) depicts postmodernity as an "all-dissolving scepticism."

181. Davis 2002b, 41.

182. "Our notions of *being* are changing as we spend more time online," Petitfils (2015, 7) appreciates, adding: "With this in mind, we must ask ourselves, are we also beginning to see a new possibility emerge: that of the *atemporalization* of man?"

183. "Object means literally some thing that we have thrown against us," Grant emphasized, the "summoning of something before us and the putting of questions to it, so that it is forced to give us its reasons for being the way it is as an object," requiring "well defined procedures...what we call in English 'research'" (Davis and Roper 2009b, 390). Minogue (1990, 165) finds Grant's view "melodramatic."

184. In which "the past is summoned before us as object to be put to the question," Grant observed (Davis and Roper 2009b, 391), the contrary relation to reactivation. The past is no object of course, but an ongoing if elusive presence; it becomes an object, Grant specified, when it is "placed in a certain relation to us—that of being at our disposal" (393).

185. Christian and Grant 1998a, 20. Discussing multicultural curriculum, Aoki ([1986/1991] 2005, 380–1) also cautioned against "the museum approach," which "assumes the structure of the viewer-viewed, of subject-object separation. As such, it is reductive—reducing others to objects, allowing a study about. And we know that the preposition 'about' calls for 'objects.'"

186. Christian and Grant 1998a, 20.

187. At McMaster, Grant's curriculum theory becomes clear. In a word, it is iconographic (a concept to which I attend in ch. 5); locating curriculum as theology is for Fishbane (2008, 34) "situated at the border of the known and unknown, of the manifest and the concealed."

188. Reactivation in this sense is a form of attunement (the subject of ch. 6). Løvlie (2003, 158) reminds us that Von Humboldt recommended that students "translate classical texts into German, not for discipline, but because it helped to 'attune the spirit of the reader with that of the original author.' His idea of *Bildung* was thus one of aesthetic attunement rather than of grammatical and textual knowledge." While I do not share his enthusiasm for this specific exercise—nor do I see "attunement" and "textual knowledge" as necessarily in tension—the point of re-experiencing the past (to the extent one can extricate oneself from the present) resonates with my conception of "reactivation." I return to this idea—referencing Collingwood—over and over again, as it seems to me it offers our only chance to evacuate the present.

189. "I entirely accept the lesson of the psychoanalytic tradition," Grant writes, "which is that you have to overcome the useless torture and the crazy repression of our human instincts. On the other hand, I'm also held by the ancient tradition that human greatness and nobility are not possible without the virtues of moderation and courage. And this in some sense must mean the overcoming of passion" (Davis and Roper 2005b, 598–9). On the topic of abortion Grant could succumb to passion: "I am not very right-wing. I have come to be friends with many right-wing people and many left-wing people over abortion. Murder surely transcends these kinds of passing American categories" (Davis and Roper 2009b, 571). If "just war" can be Christian (see 566), cannot abortion—and euthanasia (another topic about which Grant felt passionately; see Cayley 1995, 159)—be sometimes justified? Grant's moral concern was "for the rights of those people who cannot speak for themselves, the unborn and the just born, the old, and the poor" (Cayley 1995, 160), obligations to whom seemed to Grant to continue to weaken in secular modernity. Were these obligations actually stronger in pre-modernity?

190. "Levinas," Marion (2001, 217) reminds, "sometimes names that openness, precisely, distance." Fusion is closure, even for the infant who is (according to object-relations theory; see Chodorow 1978) born symbiotically identified with the maternal body.

191. Davis and Roper (2009b, 848n35) reference Weil's "Reflection on the Right Use of School Studies," where she writes: "Attention consists of suspending our thought, leaving it detached, empty and ready to be penetrated by the object; it means holding in our minds, within reach of this thought, but on a lower level and not in contact with it, the diverse knowledge we have acquired which we are forced to make use of." In this passage we can read "openness to alterity" as well as working with the experience we have undergone, e.g., educational experience as lived.

192. At one point Grant defines "religion in terms of otherness, not in terms of the subject" (Davis and Roper 2005b, 659).

193. Kittler (2013, 143) is succinct: "MEDIA exist to calculate, store, and transmit numbers." Not to understand but to calculate, that is the question of our time. G. K. Beale (2008, 298) terms the media an "idol," a concept central, I suggest in ch. 5, to Grant's critique. "The media's worldview," Beale notes, "has subtly become an idol we easily reflect" (299). God may not exist, but handheld devices do, and those we can hold as we stare, transfixed by the images we behold.

194.   The phrase summarizes "historicism," what Grant explained as "the teaching that all thought is determined by belonging to a concrete dynamic context" (Davis and Roper 2009b, 342). Grant associates historicism and yearning for technology, i.e., the belief in progress, which ironically ends history, as fusion with the present, and fantasies of the future replace consciousness of the past (see 505). I do not accept there is *nothing* but history: there is the human capability of non-coincidence with it, which allows historical consciousness to occur. But without "becoming historical"—discerning the meaning of the mutating present—I do not see how one can transcend time. Without time and transcendence "eternity" dissolves into an endless temporally meaningless now.

195.   "Only the modern age," Jay (1993, 272) notes, "had allowed what Heidegger called Enframing (*Ge-stell*) to gain full sway, turning the world into a 'standing reserve' for arrogant human domination." For Heidegger, technology is, Krauss (2007, 30) says, "a kind of challenging-forth that is also a storing-up, and in the way the dam on the river makes it possible to store-up energy in order to call upon it later. Such storing-up Heidegger will calling standing-reserve, or *Bestand*, the transformatory potential of which will turn everything within its purview into a stock-art, a cog in the machine of standing-reserve." Not only is nature reified, so is humanity. Moreover, she adds, "since *Bestand* implies orderability and substitutability, objects will necessarily lose their autonomy" (30). "[T]he enframing operations of *Gestell* represent a challenging forth, which falls upon and insults objects" (31). Grant "follows Heidegger," Potter (2005, xliii–xliv) points out, in regarding technology not as a "set of neutral instruments but as an entire 'ontology,'...a way of apprehending the world, it is a mode of existence that transforms the way we know, think, and will." As Feenberg (2010, 25) suggests, "power plants are the cathedrals of our time." In contrast to an ancient Greek understanding, technology in modernity, Feenberg continues, "does not reveal things in their essential nature. Instead what is revealed is a world of resources and components. The meaning of modern artifacts is simply their functional connection to other artifacts in a system of production and consumption" (192), e.g., enframing. See too Aoki (1987) 2005, 153; (1992) 2005, 187; Angus 1997, 92; Sikka 1997, 260–3.

196.   Grant (1969, 142) descries modernity as an "objectified world inhabited by increasingly objectifiable beings." In ch. 4 and 5 we glimpse Grant's efforts to ensure that the curriculum of McMaster's Department of Religion did not succumb to these tendencies by hiring faculty who could teach *from* their faith, rather than *about* faith, preserving the distinctiveness of the various religions and those who live within them. "Understanding," Kögler (1999, 109) emphasizes, "involves individualizing rather than normalizing, interpreting rather than objectifying, pluralizing rather than encompassing—in short, radically dialogic processes." Huebner (1999, 6) knew that "awe and wonder" requires "going beyond our abstraction of the phenomena and our objectification of it, to an awareness of its individuality—its subjectivity its existence, and consequently our existence." Individuality is lost, as Dewey knew; Donald Levine (2007, 83) reminds: "Dewey also stressed that no two students are identical.... It [education] cannot rely on standardized inputs that are applied mechanically to an entire cohort. It cannot set up objectified goals." Had Grant lived into late modernity, he might have extended objectification to include simulation, appreciating, as does Autio (2006, 97–8), that "our postmodern scene where[in]

sheer performativity may have supplanted even instrumental rationality in the form of simulation." Mondzain (2005, 223) asks: "In a world of simulation, what does our flesh become? What can we resemble?" Nusselder (2009, 102) knows: "Information technologies thus affect the (normal, social, moral) relationship between self and other by objectifying defenses: war becomes fun, as the pleasure principle triumphs, and the screen of fantasy becomes impenetrable armour."

197. "The fact that metonymic representations of God are permitted," Halbertal and Margalit (1992, 48) suggest, "supports our contention that the basis for the prohibition against images and pictures is not the fear of substitution but the struggle against mistaken or inappropriate representations."

198. "If one sees that historicism is true but that it is deadly to the soul," Grant mused, "then one way of opting out of the deadliness of the situation is to go in for mythmaking" (Davis and Roper 2009b, 313). For me, allegory is a form of mythmaking that emphasizes the ethical meaning of what happens in the world. If my invocation of "as if" amounts to a "secularized faith," Penelhum (1983, 105) judges it "literally unthinkable." Logically, yes, but imaginatively too?

199. Conservative Christians contest this suggestion. Beale (2008, 311), for instance, declares that "created objects do not contain God's living Spirit, and to the degree that people revere them, they will become devoid of the spirit—unspiritual."

200. Science, technology, engineering, mathematics. Grant was skeptical that science, however admirable its advances, could communicate spirituality; see Emberley (1994) 2005, lxxxi. At least in principle STEM could point beyond itself, if contextualized in history and society, sensitive to politics, gender, and race. But to make science spiritual seems a contradiction in terms. So to render STEM iconographic might involve laying bare its metaphysical substratum, but often the sciences are taught as self-enclosed bodies of knowledge, causing Grant to lament to Cayley (1995, 139) that "science has never been more dominating than in North American education," a fact that has only intensified in the decades since his death.

201. Christian and Grant 1998b, 93.

202. Benedetti 2005, 210.

203. Aoki (1986/1991) 2005, 160.

204. "The desire to understand the world can," Grant cautioned, "easily pass over into an acceptance of it" (Davis and Roper 2005b, 419).

205. With its Sartrean rings, engagement can also be associated with the concept of relationship, implying that it invites many modes of encounter, among them love (that Grant emphasized), recognition (associated with Grant's definition of love), critique, reconstruction, comprehension of course. My thanks to Professor Steven Taubeneck for bringing to my attention the ambiguity of the term, an ambiguity I wish to respect.

206. Derrida in Kearney 2005a, 45.

207. While I use the term "spiritual" throughout this text, there are of course critics, among them Philip Wexler (2013, 15) who writes: "The expression of individual inward experience as spirituality is different than in classical mysticism…. This life may be seen…as another form of consumerism. In either case, spirituality differs from institutional religion, but also from mysticism." Dart (2006, 24) too cautions against splitting spirituality from the church, worry that spirituality then "becomes thinned out, reductionistic, and somewhat narcissistic." For him "Grant is best understood" as living "within tradition yet critical of it" (24).

208. "Ever since the Greeks invented an alphabet with vowels that also served the purpose of musical notation," Kittler (2013, 170) reminds, "voice" and "writing" have been interconnected, potentially at least, in print that relies on as it evokes sound as well as sight. And points to a "beyond," if not God at least a muse, as Kittler notes: "The word 'music' derives from *muse*, even in Arabic" (260).

209. While now a word with almost exclusively religious connotations, Grant—teaching Plato's allegory of the cave—reminded students that "the word education…(*e*—out, *duco*—lead)…means to be led out of the cave. Also the word conversation comes from this image, *con-vertere*. To be converted is to be turned around" (Davis and Roper 2009b, 937).

210. Relatedly, Lipari (2014, 199) reminds that "vocation" derives from the Latin *vocare* (to call), related to the Latin *vox* (voice), which she associates with ethics, surely central to teaching as a sacred calling. Invoking Levinas' emphasis upon the face, Lipari suggests that "while the voice and face are both elements of the human body that can signify and express, the voice brings the *temporal* embodiment of human *being* into sharper relief" (193).

211. Quoting Adorno, Judith Stamps (1995, 32) depicts constellation as an "anti-system," a "dialectic suspicious of all identity," and a means of promoting "open thought." As a "practice," she comments, "it was an ensemble of conceptual models, which, like the conversants in a negative dialogue, 'gathered about' their objects of study in order to unlock the processes stored within them" (33). Clarke and Phelan (2017) invoke negation to think through the deprival of preparing teachers in late modernity.

212. "We humans are embodied beings," Lipari (2014, 30) reminds, "we live in and with and from our bodies." In fact, Lipari asserts that "we are all ears," the body "is one giant listening organ, one great resonating chamber" (30), an idea not very far from a conception of embodiment as the medium of attunement. Technology changes everything, as sound fills the room and our attention, altering the status of the auditory from icon to idol.

213. Warren 1990, 59. He adds: "I should make clear my qualifications and disqualifications for speaking about George Grant…. I have read Grant carefully, not with perfect understanding, but often in nearly perfect sympathy. Late in his life I went to Halifax to meet him, and spoke with him through the mornings of a vividly remembered week; and I loved the man, as many others have done, as a teacher and as a kind of father and as an exemplar of dignity, wisdom, and moral beauty. I think he is among that small number—Leacock and Emily Carr come to mind—who had something to say to the whole world that could only be said by a Canadian" (59).

214. "To read Grant now," Minogue (1990, 164) notes, "is to be reminded that he was, in many respects, a man of his time." Does that imply Grant is now out of date? Writing upon the death of John G. Diefenbaker, Grant notes that one criticism of the former prime minister was that he was out of date. What can the phrase mean, he asks, answering: "It is the language of those who think that our humanity can be made totally intelligible in terms of such concepts as 'progress,' 'history,' 'evolution.' What such words generally come down to in practice is that anything that is technologically and administratively necessary is also good. This expresses that oblivion of eternity which now defines the West" (Davis and Roper 2009b, 406).

215. "It is, of course, foolish," Grant writes, "to use the phrase 'out of date' about writers such as Plato or Tolstoy, who are telling us what is true of all times and places"

(Davis and Roper 2009b, 916). If objects and images can become like religious icons, would not "eternity" also be embedded in passing moments? After all, these are, presumably, "moving images of eternity."

216. The concept of "person" has been contested—some would say discredited—in recent years, but to my mind Grant's November 6, 1942, journal entry conveys at least the location of the concept: "Art is wonderful—it is part of all—it is the beauty that gets us nearer to the final and ultimate reality, but the reality of living is greater, nobler than the art itself. The depth of one's own feeling is deeper than any art one could produce…. It is because the medium, however well it is used…still it is a medium—& not the person" (Christian 1996d, 105). The entry is interesting also in light of his reflections on art, beauty, and spiritual knowledge.

217. An "enactment of double vision, a temporal copresence," as Dinshaw (2012, 64) describes Henry Wadsworth Longfellow's interest in medievalism.

218. "Place refers to the qualitative, embodied experience filled with meaningful things," Angus (1997, 102) explains, "whereas space denotes the empty, quantitative, and homogeneous space."

219. For Grant, Athanasiadis (2001, 174) emphasizes, "any knowledge of the good that is outside technological society must come by intimation of the deprival—that is, negatively."

220. There are examples of Grant's humility throughout the collected works. On one occasion—during a course on Plato—Grant admitted that "there are large parts of it [the *Symposium*] I do not understand" (Davis and Roper 2005b, 700). "Humility" is also a concept that surfaces in curriculum theory; Ted Aoki ([1993] 2005, 213) notes that "human, humility, humus, and humour [are] all etymologically related." He envisions a "lived space where people dwell communally, where dwelling is a dwelling with others on earth under the sky, where we find *humus* that nurtures *humans*, where *humans* caught up in binds sometimes chuckle, where we can hear laughter at the thought of humans thinking they can master the world" (300). Certainly that last thought resonates with Grant's critique. Davis (2002a, xx–xxi) reports that Grant told David Cayley—and earlier his students at McMaster (see Davis and Roper 2009b, 832)—"[Leo] Strauss once said, and I think it is the best thing I've ever known about teaching, every heard about teaching—he said, never go into a class without thinking that there is somebody in the classroom who has a greater intelligence and a nobler heart than yourself. That remark is so good, that it just reduced me [to tears]."

221. Cayley 1995, 18. On one occasion he confessed to "a sense of failure as a teacher" (Davis and Roper 2009b, 423).

222. Davis 2002b, 180.

223. Davis 2002b, 180.

224. In that solitude one attends to alterity, including within oneself. Listening, Lipari (2014, 187) appreciates, "also calls one to give attention to oneself, to heed the tumult of contradictory voices demanding to be heard, aware that our listening is itself a kind of speaking. Listening otherwise thus requires a kind of inner strength," so that we "can pay attention and tolerate our own contradictory intensions and conviction…to listen with all the presence of our being." In that presence Grant taught.

225. To which Grant was evidently committed (if by other names), implied when he writes: "It has taken me a whole life time to begin to free myself from the language of modernity" (Davis 2002b, 61). Because he was brought up to be—as he admits—a

progressive, his subjective reconstruction of his imprinting requires his dismissal of progressivism, why (I speculate) he overstates the utilitarian elements of progressive education. Grant was right, however, when he asserted that "the whole tone of his thought is unthinkable outside a secularized Biblical moralism" (262).

226. Christian 1996d, 279.

227. Christian 1996d, 280n1. Atherton was a friend and classics professor at Dalhousie University; Grant is writing during his decade at McMaster University.

228. Quoted in Christian 1996d, 279.

229. Christian 1996d, 279. Grant wrote sparingly of this faith (see Davis 2000, xxiii), perhaps in part because, as Davis and Emberley (2000b, 164) explain, Grant emphasized "that God's providence must be, for us, an ambiguous mystery, not a truth we possess and can define. The good is often not visible to us, and God's providence is inscrutable." In his DPhil thesis he had written that "truth is not reached by eclecticism, but by following our highest insights to their final conclusion, even if that means discarding much that would seem to be the essence of the biblical tradition" (325). Later he wrote that humanity "should recognize the Bible as simply one tool which reason and faith and desire must use in finding ethical and religious principles" (Davis 2002b, 217). Speaking with students, Grant suggested that even the divinity of Christ should be "an open question" (Davis and Roper 2009b, 99). On another occasion, however, Grant minced no words: "Christianity is more than myth; it is the truth" (Davis and Roper 2005b, 230).

230. Grant's family could easily become the subject of a separate monograph. Suffice to say here that Grant's mother felt sure her son was "destined" to continue in his grandfather Parkin's educational footsteps (Christian 1996d, 62). Follow—and rebel—George Grant did, never severing his bond with ancestry, especially with his mother.

231. "The term 'one's own' is," Angus (1997, 76) points out, "an excellent English rendering of Heidegger's concept of *Eigentlich*, which is conventionally translated as 'authenticity.'" Grant tells Cayley (1995, 103): "[J]ustice appears for people first in their own." It does not end there: "But people who don't pass beyond that to love of something that is of more universal significance are hardly anything," Grant adds (102). On another occasion Grant affirms that "love of one's own must ultimately be a means to love of the good" (Schmidt 1978a, 21), the particular as a portal to the universal. Interestingly, Harold Innis too "never lost his feeling of being indebted to his roots, of loving 'his own,'" Watson (2007, 426) suggests.

232. Intelligence is likewise "enlightened" by love (Davis and Roper 2009b, 386). And love is "attention to otherness, receptivity of otherness, consent to otherness" (387).

233. Grant's "greatest Christian teacher," Schmidt reminds (Davis and Roper 2009b, 771; see also 808; 2005b, 672; Schmidt 1978a, 65; Christian 1996d, 380; Taylor [1982] 2006, 132), having "a much greater authority for me than [Leo] Strauss," he wrote Joan O'Donovan in 1981 (Christian 1996d, 312). Weil provided Grant, as Davis and Roper (2009b, 774) tell us, a "Christian alternative to the liberal Protestantism within which Grant had grown up and from which he had been wrenched by his conversion experience in 1941." Grant's early writings on Weil were as much about him as they were about Weil, they suggest, but he came to call her a saint, "possessed of the 'genius of sanctity'…able to give herself away not only in body and spirit but also intellectually" (772–3). Grant corresponded with her brother André (Christian 1996d, 216), a

distinguished mathematician, and her mother (whom he met in Paris). Grant was also in correspondence with Weil's biographer Simone Pétrement (Christian 1996d, 282). O'Donovan (1990, 137) judges Grant's articulation of key concepts such as love, knowledge, justice, and goodness as "insufficiently—or questionably—developed from a theological standpoint, in part because of Grant's continuing dependence on the Christian Gnosticism of Simone Weil." Later O'Donovan concludes: "It is difficult to know how much of Weil's theological mediation of Plato and the Gospels Grant accepts, since she is very much a silent partner in his writings" (176).

234.   A term Grant disparages on several occasions, associating it with Pierre Elliott Trudeau and "Americanism" (Davis and Roper 2009b, 411), on one occasion (the interview with Schmidt [1978a, 20]) calling it a "mask for a particular imperialism." I do not doubt Trudeau (and his son Justin, the current Canadian prime minister) can be considered cosmopolitan; for me it is not a slur. But "Americanism"—to the extent it is characterized as a homogenizing, hence narrow nationalism—cannot be a cosmopolitanism. While two of three personifications of cosmopolitanism I chose to study were Americans (Jane Addams and Laura Bragg), the third (Pier Paolo Pasolini) was Italian (see Pinar 2009). For an analysis of cosmopolitanism as only malevolent, see Popkewitz 2008.

235.   Grant tells Cayley that "the ancients had no word for *ideal*. The notion of the ideal as opposed to the real comes essentially from Hegel's great precursor Kant" (Cayley 1995, 79).

236.   Grant was being interviewed by Cayley for *Ideas*; quoted in Davis 2002a, xx. Grant spoke on radio regularly, judged by one observer to have a "marvellous radio personality," whose "talks…were…clear, original but persuasive, highly personal but intensely communicative" (quoted in Davis 2000, xxvi). The same could be said, it seems to me, of his teaching.

237.   Christian and Grant 1998b, 238.

238.   Christian and Grant 1998b, 238.

239.   See, e.g., Davis and Roper 2005b, 423; 2009b, 304–5, 307, 309; Cayley 1995, 8.

240.   Christian and Grant 1998b, 238.

241.   Christian and Grant 1998b, 238.

242.   See Smith 2014.

243.   Toews 2004, 438. Discussing Kierkegaard and Marx, Toews concludes that "the goal was to experience the self that was simply given as a self that was historically particular and contingent. Implicit in this reconstructive activity was a conception of the self as not only product but also producer" (438). He emphasizes: "Experiencing one's own individual identity as a historical product implied an act, or series of acts, that brought this existing self into being" (438). Such experience is structured in part by habit (as I note in Pinar and Grumet [1976] 2015), for Kierkegaard by "repetition," the "centerpiece," Caputo (1987, 29) notes, of Kierkegaard's "existential theory of self," adding that "repetition on the ethical level is the constancy and continuity of choice by which the self constitutes itself as a self, by which it returns again and again to its own innermost resolution and establishes its moral identity" (30). It is "ethical repetition," Caputo continues, that "presses forward resolutely, makes progress, effects transcendence" (31).

244.   "When I talk of faith, I do not mean a blind act of will," but of the "experience that the intellect is illuminated by love. And that means that love will teach you about

things in a way that control won't" (Davis and Roper 2009b, 576). Grant's concern over the primacy of the will in modernity was supported, perhaps informed, by Weil, who, Athanasiadis (2001, 168–9) explains, insisted that "faith in God is a matter of knowing and not of willing. It is a matter of attention and open receptivity in thought before the truth, rather than an act of human will or choice. One cannot simply choose to have faith. Such a faith is an illusion and a human construct. The afflictions of the world taught Weil that only the certainty of divine grace and a knowledge based on divine revelation could suffice." In ch. 6, I concur that the will might be dethroned but I hope not destroyed, as it is indispensable following what faith—in Grant's terms knowledge informed by love—implies. Referencing Nietzsche, Beiner (1996, 129) makes my point: "[O]ne must embrace modern voluntarism in its most radical aspect in order to will something radically antimodern."

245. "Tradition," Lossky (1982, 11) observes, "is one of those terms which, through being too rich in meanings, runs the risks of finally having none." One is reminded of Trilling's (1972, 120) similar comment about "love" (and "irony"). Despite these difficulties, it's time to talk of "tradition" again, even if only modernity has rendered it ridiculous, as "convention," as Benedetti (2005, 113) notes—"the emblem of modernity: the critique of conventionality, the idea that convention is something ridiculous."

246. "[E]very standpoint is deemed a relative one or the expression of some will to power," Fishbane (2008, 10) laments, and the "humanities provide little guidance in these matters" (9). In my terms, as politics predominate, ethics recede. "Our moral character is stripped away," Fishbane appreciates, "and we become congeries of ideologies among other similar human types, whom we may join for certain utilitarian benefits or ideological ends; or else we simply live (and let others live) with different matrices of thought for different purposes. But surely none of this is conductive to grounding our lives" (10).

247. Grant's "commitment to teaching," Christian (1996d, 309) comments, was "evident in his resignation controversy from McMaster."

248. Not only pedagogically, as Grant once described himself and his wife, Sheila, as "two emotional absolutists" (Christian 1996d, 313). For another—and contemporary—acknowledgement of the educational significance of presence, see, for instance, Walsh, Bickel, and Leggo 2014.

249. Christian and Grant 1998b, 238.

250. Christian and Grant 1998b, 238.

251. Christian and Grant 1998b, 238.

252. Christian and Grant 1998b, 238.

253. Christian and Grant 1998b, 238.

254. Cremin 1961, viii.

255. Pinar 2010b. While working at the CAAE, Grant acknowledged "a need for experimentation in subject matter" and even in "our techniques" (Davis and Emberley 2000b, 69), asking an assessment question that could well have come from the Eight-Year Study: "Have we written study material that will help people to think for themselves and strengthen their own minds? Only in this way will be doing our job" (70). Like many progressive educators, Grant (in 1945) suggested that "all topics should be as close to the people's everyday lives as possible" (71), a curricular arrangement in the service of what today might be termed social justice, evident when he

wonders: "Can English-and French-speaking citizens work together better than in the past? Can we eliminate racial prejudice?" (Davis and Emberley 2000b, 71).

256. Latin has enjoyed centuries of curricular influence; during the Renaissance, as Ong (1971, 113) reminds, it functioned as a "puberty rite." In Canada, Tomkins (1986, 12) recounts, the first organized schools were elementary ones, the basic curriculum of which consisted of "the catechism and the three Rs, supplemented for the more gifted students by the rudiments of Latin as a preparation for secondary studies." By the late nineteenth century, new subjects—from mathematics to English literature as well as Canadian history and French—appeared (82, 84). At a 1901 Queen's University conference on the "purposes" of the high school, debate centred on the prominence of Latin (134), in which most Grade 12 students remained enrolled by the start of the Second World War (135). In the United States, Latin also been a mainstay of the classical curriculum, as Ravitch (2000, 26; see also 62) notes, but by the end of the First World War and the ascendency of the progressives—who complained that Latin served no educational purpose, that its justification as a "mental discipline" was illusory (see also Hirsch 1999, 114; Levine 2007, 182)—it began its curricular decline. Despite the "lag" between the curriculum and "the dynamic content of American life" (Rugg 1926, 3), Latin hung on, even in those "progressive" schools participating in the Eight-Year Study (see Thirty Schools 1943, 341), although other progressives argued against the subject's practical utility (for instance, see Bobbitt 1918, 272, 274). In our era, even cognitive scientists take time to question its educational point: "Music doesn't make you better at math, conjugating Latin doesn't make you more logical, brain-training games don't make you smarter," Steven Pinker (2010, A27) proclaimed, insisting that "the effects of experience are highly specific to the experience themselves."

257. "During the latter part of the Hutchins era," Levine (2007, 64) reports, "the College faculty experimented with a technique of instruction that differed from the lecture format which had dominated course work during the 1930s. They called this new technique the method of 'structured discussion' to distinguish it not only from 'shooting the breeze' but also from discussions in which students merely ask questions to clarify or to challenge something an instructor has said." Later, one of the University of Chicago's great pedagogues—Joseph Schwab—would on occasion lecture but embodied, according to Lee Shulman, the Socratic method (Levine 2007, 129–30).

258. Schmidt 1978a, 101–2.

259. In Aoki's terms (see, e.g., Aoki [1986/1991] 2005, 159) the teacher is inhabiting the space between the "curriculum-as-plan" and the "curriculum-as-lived." Grant's phrase "intelligible discourse" is itself is almost infinite, requiring one to consider, however situationally, what knowledge is of most worth?

260. "But what else is Dewey's view of education," Grant asks, "but a justification of the expanding economy and the secular society and an attack on the old traditions of education which made the end of education spiritual? What Dewey is largely interested in is turning men away from any transcendental spiritual end and making the careful adjustment of people to successful economic, sexual, and social life in society, that is, to make men healthy animals" (Davis 2002b, 185; see also 431). Dewey was no transcendentalist—although Kestenbaum (2002) casts doubt on how complete Dewey's rejection of transcendentalism was—but he was not complicit with capitalism.

261.   At this mention of Dewey I must acknowledge that Grant's criticism of Dewey went beyond critique to a generalized antipathy, quite the turnaround from his first attitude, expressed in a November 1941 letter to his mother, where he describes reading *My Pedagogic Creed* and exclaiming that "my favourite philosophers are William James and John Dewey," adding, "I hope that I survive the war to be able to contribute to that tradition & bring Canada into line with it" (Christian 1996d, 89). Years later Grant defames Dewey as "morally shallow" (Davis and Roper 2005b, 467). Despite noting the centenary of his birth, 1959, and that it "is always instructive to follow the discussion of a philosopher by those whose tradition is very different" (91), Grant seems to have read only one other book of Dewey's—*Human Nature and Conduct*—or so one might conclude from the absence of any references to others. And that one he does not seem to have read very closely, as Grant tells students: "Those, like John Dewey, who ask us not to quibble over the meaning of words like freedom do so only because the life and death issues involved in that word are not real to them. They can get on with the job without attempting to solve them" (Davis 2002b, 449). More than "quibble" over the concept Dewey (1922, 188) does in fact do, and not only in *Human Nature and Conduct*, offering a criticism Grant himself might have shared: "Glorification of freedom in general at the expense of positive abilities in particular has often characterized the official creed of historic liberalism." To make my point I shall quote liberally from *Human Nature and Conduct* in this study. Grant's failings were few, but his misunderstanding of Dewey must count as one of them.

262.   Dewey tested the idea, Levine (2007, 79) suggests: "The Chicago Laboratory School formed a principal outlet for this synthesis, embodying Dewey's view that student learning, institutional reconstruction, and civic democracy are mutually constitutive." Levine adds: "The capacity to solve social problems required intellectual habits needed to perceive problems, identify their features, and entertain in imagination diverse options for their solution. In order to promote such habits at all levels of learning, Dewey maintained that new forms of teaching were needed, forms in which curiosity and imagination were awakened through direct encounter with puzzling experiences" (80). If not only cognitive, those "puzzling experiences"—as "alterity"—could serve as portals to transcendence. "Democracy" itself is sometimes regarded as a Jewish and Christian concept. In his discussion of humanity as created in the image of God, Lints (2015, 72n43) affirms the "democratizing tendencies inherent in Gen. 1" as present in everyone, both "male and female (v.27)" (and, I should think, the transgendered as well).

263.   Westbrook 1991, 192.

264.   Perlstein 2000.

265.   For a powerful—for me chilling—theoretical formulation of this convergence between technology and social (now almost exclusively economic) efficiency, see B. Williamson 2013. In the United States, public schools (e.g., as laboratories for democracy) are being replaced by technical schools that simulate workplaces. In the state of West Virginia, Goldstein (2017, A1) reports: "Students punch a time clock, are assigned professional roles like foreman or safety supervisor, and are even offered several vacation days of their choice in addition to regular school breaks" (A1, A14). "Vocational training is a great thing," President Trump had proclaimed a week before Election Day 2016. "We're going to start it up big league" (A14). In June, Trump signed an executive order that redirected federal job-training funds toward

apprenticeships, in which students learn skills at actual work sites, but, as Goldstein also reports, the Trump's budget cuts $166 million from Perkins Act grants to the states, the primary source of funding for technical education (A14).

266. Davis (2006, 73) points out that Grant's "animus against progressives does not make him an enemy of egalitarian politics. Rather, his attack on them was part of his critique of triumphal technology, which in turn was rooted, as he said, in triumphal Western Christianity."

267. Cayley 1995, 56. Grant and Cayley are discussing philosophy; Grant asserts that it begins less in wonder than in astonishment, a distinction Cayley articulates precisely.

268. Teaching about "the Good," Grant acknowledged: "Now clearly what we are fitted for depends on the way things are" (Davis and Roper 2009b, 933). On another occasion, this one teaching Kant, Grant told students: "What I am concerned with is that I see the political and religious basis of Western civilization lying in ruins—and I am particularly concerned with these ruins in the English-speaking world and with the question of how it is best to live and what concerns us most to think about as we live as part of that ruin. Now this very much affects how I teach Kant and particularly the words I say about him" (1051). Grant may not have chosen to teach Kant only in order to address the present historical moment, but he is not hesitant to admit that it "affects" his discussion of him. If time is a moving image of eternity, surely teaching is too. As I suggest later, teaching can become a passage between the two, inviting transcendence through attunement.

269. The phrase is Toews's (2004, xix): "To become historical in the sense of recognizing that personal and communal identity were historically constituted was also to take upon oneself the obligation of constituting oneself, personally and collectively, in historical action." For Grant, historicity (summarized in the phrase "time as history") represented the oblivion of eternity"—Beiner (1996, 131n9) points out—not its reactivation. That development (time reduced to history) was itself a historical event. Certainly Grant taught with one eye on history, admitting to students on one occasion (during the 1960s) that "I find it well nigh impossible these day to think of Greek religion and philosophy in the light of the events of Vietnam.... In the light of this catastrophe [it is] very difficult to conceive of turning one's mind to these ultimate issues. Yet we must. Indeed, just because of it, we must" (Davis and Roper 2005b, 696–7).

270. As I have complained (Pinar 2009, 22). Grant's interest in politics—preserving the public sphere as inclusive, structured by justice—was, Christian (1996c, xiii) reminds, "lifelong, and his brilliant observations on Canadian and world affairs span more than half a century." While no "ultimate" interest, politics for Grant was an enduring one; see, e.g., Christian 1996d, 58, 152.

271. "My concentration on justice as against epistemology and metaphysics," Grant knew, "is difficult for it meets people who live in an imperial age when ethics is almost out of the question (particularly ethics as politics). Therefore this is one reason why academics return to epistemology and metaphysics—as harmless but understandable problems" (Davis and Roper 2009b, 315). Emberley (1990, xxii) notes that justice was "Grant's abiding theoretical and practical concern."

272. Philip Wexler has schematized what is at stake; see Wexler 1996, 2013; Wexler and Hotam 2015.

273. "To understand our ability and responsibility to make moral advances," Meynell (2011, 120) remarks, "we must be aware of the spirit of history." My sense of

"advance" seems against "the spirit of history," reactivating the past to focus on the future; e.g., an emphasis upon the untimely.

274. Davis and Roper 2009b, 459.

275. "Not a term I like very much," Grant tells us Cayley (1995, 103), adding that "I think what the term points to about me is my great resentment of the identification of the word *conservative* with the right of individuals, of private individuals, to make money any way they want." Roy (2006, 209) suggests that "the kind of Red Toryism embodied by George Grant...can be traced back to Disraeli, Shaftesbury, and beyond." Indeed; the term "Tory," Fierlbeck (2006, 45) explains, derives from the Irish *tóraidhe* (outlaw), "originally used as a derisive epithet in the seventeenth century, and, by the eighteenth century, it was a marker for those who supports the rights and privileges of the Crown in opposition to those who favoured expanding the powers of Parliament. In pre-Confederation Canada, the term was used loosely to denote those who supported the monarchy (and thus British rule of Canada) in contrast to those who sympathized with the principles of American republicanism. Later, prominent central Canadian business elites became labelled 'Blue Tories,' while those who held conservative beliefs but chafed under the political and economic control of central Canada became known as 'Red Tories.'" By Grant's time, she continues, "the term 'Red Tory' became what 'Tory' itself had originally meant: the belief that the common good was more important than individual rights, that a set of traditional (generally Christian) values were the proper foundation of a moral life, and that traditional customs and beliefs were superior to rationalist principles as a basis for social and political institutions." For Fierlbeck, "Grant was perhaps the preeminent Tory of the twentieth century, but he was also...the most anguished one" (55).

276. See Davis and Roper 2005a, xviii. Because technology became the umbrella term through which critiques of modernization, industrial society, and liberal individualism were focused, Ian Angus (1997, 5) explains, "there came into being one of the decisive features of the English-Canadian landscape: the close connection between the conservative critique of modernity and the left-nationalist critique of capitalism." Angus adds: "One might say that the main rhetorical form of left-nationalism is a lament for the failure adequately to preserve the past and an argument that such preservation requires a radical reorientation in the future. It is a vision of a Loyalist, Tory past and a socialist future" (32). Despite the use of "lament" in that sentence, Angus tells us left nationalism "rejected, in the final analysis, the standpoint of lament" (31). Warren (1990, 69) contests any characterization of Grant as a socialist: "For Grant socialism meant a railway to the Pacific, a power grid in Ontario, and the CBC— things which fall some miles short of socialism." And, adds Warren, Grant was no "Red" (69). For Grant, "even socialism could not save Canada," Sibley (2008, 124) notes, "since it shared the progressivist, pro-technological assumptions of liberalism."

277. "Toryism," Warren (1990, 69) explains, humorously but helpfully, "is the political expression of a religious view of life," and "conservatism is an attempt to maintain Toryism after you have lost your faith." And "progressive conservatism," he quips, "is an attempt to maintain conservatism after you have lost your memory, too" (69).

278. "For example in the 1960s I had great sympathy for young people who sought the immediate—I was sympathetic because technological society, because of its very definition of rationality, kills the immediate. Therefore people had a great yearning for the immediacy. But in that yearning they often confused the immediate with the

ontically more important" (Davis and Roper 2009b, 977). Notice that he was not only sympathetic, as he felt many may have idolatrized the immediate. Notice too that the judgment is historically situated, another example of Grant's historical consciousness.

279. Grant was never as swayed by events as Reich, and in fact, as (Davis 2000, xxxii) notes, for Grant reason was not the modern conception of it as an instrument through we obtain from the world what we want, but, rather, an expression of "both the nature that surrounds us and the nature that makes us what we are." Reason can become, I suggest in ch. 6, a medium of attunement.

280. Christian and Grant 1998a, 10.

281. There are, of course, secular versions of Grant's metaphysical view, including in education. "The meaningfulness of one understanding," Aoki ([1981] 2005, 228) reminded, "comes into view illuminated by the whole context; and the meaningful of the whole comes into view illuminated by a part." This reciprocity of the particular and the universal echoes the conjunction of spiritual and material in iconography. For Dewey ([1934] 1962, 26), "Understanding and knowledge also enter into a perspective that is religious in quality. Faith in the continued disclosing of truth through directed cooperative human endeavour is more religious in quality than is any faith in a completed revelation." Living in an era of compulsory collaboration, I share the insight in the first but not the second sentence of the Dewey passage.

282. See, e.g., Garb 2011.

283. Davis and Roper 2009b, 972.

284. "I do not much care that you have the same perspective as myself (that would for all of us anyway to be impossible)," Grant told students, "but that rather you come to define your own perspectives and in terms of it what questions you put to Nietzsche and how clearly you see the answers you get back from Nietzsche concerning those questions" (Davis and Roper 2009b, 972). His apparent acknowledgement of the irreducibility of individuality and his encouragement of following one's own path, cultivating one's own point of view, defines Grant as a progressive educator.

285. Cayley 1995, x–xi.

286. Christian 1978, 178.

287. Quoted in Cayley 1995, 6. "[I]t was extraordinarily astonishing for me to see," Grant tells Cayley, "after 1945, that my class was disappearing in Canada…. You see, my family were the lower reaches of the old mercantile elite, the people who really worked for them [the commercial elite]…. I'm saying that a new form of capitalism arose: industrial capitalism—continental industrial capitalism—came up in 1945, and was a quite new class, wasn't it?… Anybody who thinks…of technology as something outside themselves, doesn't know what they are talking about" (55). Was 1945 (or so) the time when technology moved inside one's skin?

288. For Weil, Kaethler (2009, 82) suggests, a "perfectly just" person would be a "mediator between humans and God."

289. Steimatsky 2003, 255.

290. Rigelhof 2001, 144–5.

291. "There is another use of the word as well," Atwood ([1972] 2012, 9) reminds, as "a survival can be a vestige of a vanished order which has managed to persist after its time is pasts, like a primitive reptile. This version crops up in Canadian thinking too, usually among those who believe that Canada is obsolete." Whether a fragment, remnant, relic, or reptile, in textual form Grant remains among us, asking "why"?

CHAPTER 2

Technology

The first task of thought in our era is to
think what technology is.[1]

George Grant

[In] "the union of art and science,"[2] Grant explained, "technology is the metaphysics of our age."[3] In modernity, O'Donovan understands, technology became "an ever-expanding and ever-intensifying web of necessity in which nature, including human nature, is absorbed."[4] That "web," she continues, "is at once an external and internal necessity: it is a law of relation between thought and action and between desire and thought,"[5] for Grant's Dalhousie colleague James Doull, "endless, insatiable technology."[6] Athanasiadis appreciates that "While in the past it was natural necessity that enslaved human beings, today it is technological necessity."[7] Lee summarizes:

> Broadly put, then, the impasse is that any would-be critical thought about technology is bound to reproduce that technology in the methods and assumptions of our thinking. We can't abide the nihilism we're enmeshed in; yet we can't think our way out of it, because we can't stop recreating it in the very fabric of our thought.[8]

For Grant, the meaning of modernity is "unique...connected with the truth of our 'primals,' our beginnings."[9] Its transcendence requires not engineering but recollection.[10] Let us start by recollecting George Grant.

Grant was born on November 13, 1918, two days after the armistice. His father, William, had volunteered for active service and had been seriously injured in France.[11] "My father," George Grant would write, was a Nova Scotian, who had grown up in Kingston, Ontario, and was essentially a very gentle, strong scholar, who I think, above all, was ruined by the First World War.[12] He was ruined physically; he was terribly wounded.[13] For these people, who had grown up in the great era of progress,[14] to meet the holocaust of the trenches was terrible.[15]

William Grant became embittered[16] over the pointless slaughter of the First World War, the first war structured by technology.[17]

Like his father, George Grant studied history. He won a history medal at Queen's University, where his grandfather had served as principal.[18] At Queen's, William Christian tells us, "he was drawn to grand themes, rather than to the minutiae of historical research."[19] That same disposition surfaced later at Oxford,[20] where he'd gone on a Rhodes scholarship to study law. While at first he welcomed the intellectual discipline this new subject demanded, soon enough Grant judged law "tiresome" due to its focus on "detail" and "its indifference to broader questions."[21]

After service as an Air Raid Precautions warden during the German bombing of London,[22] followed by a conversion experience in the English countryside,[23] Grant returned to Canada in February 1942 suffering from a nervous breakdown and tuberculosis. Much of the next year he spent in recovery. In 1943 he published a pamphlet, *Canada—An Introduction to a Nation*, and in 1945 *The Empire, Yes or No?* Returning to Oxford after the war, he left law to study theology,[24] earning extra money by writing historical articles on Canada for *Chambers' Encyclopaedia*. "Before I became a philosopher," he reflected years later, "I studied history and still think very much as an historian."[25] The history to which Grant was increasingly drawn, Christian clarifies, "reflected his early predispositions to the philosophy of history."[26] That subject became personified in his doctoral dissertation, a study of the Scottish Presbyterian theologian John Oman.[27]

While attending meetings of C. S. Lewis's Socratic Club, Grant met Sheila Allen,[28] an English student and fellow pacifist, whom he married in the spring of 1947. That year the two returned to Canada, where Grant had accepted a position teaching philosophy at Dalhousie University, in Halifax, Nova Scotia.[29] He spent the next thirteen years there, on Canada's Atlantic coast, during which time the Grants had six children. Grant found Dalhousie a "congenial place,"[30] Potter reports, but he felt he was there on the periphery of North American life.[31] In 1961 he accepted a professorship in the department of religion at McMaster University, in Hamilton, Ontario, returning to Halifax for his final years.[32]

During the 1950s Grant was studying philosophy and history, first Nietzsche, then Sartre, then Heidegger.[33] He had also undertaken study of Freud[34] and Weber.[35] By 1962,[36] Christian[37] reports, when Grant delivered a CBC Radio lecture on Jung,[38] he had begun to refocus on Nietzsche.[39] Grant's central insight between the time he wrote *Philosophy in the Mass Age* in 1959 and *Time as History* a decade later was that the contemporary conception of time was very different from the ancient one, wherein time had been regarded as the "moving image of eternity."[40] Now time was *only* history, and history had become a totalizing process within which all events are subsumed.[41] The world, in David D. Roberts' phrase, is "nothing but history."[42] Even historicists like Marx and Hegel had imagined some progressive end toward which history was moving, and in so doing had conferred a broader significance upon individual events.[43] But now the utter contingency[44] of history had stripped particularity of any general (mythic or religious) importance, as history had become "nothing but this freakish concatenation of lies, errors, and self-serving actions."[45] Roberts' descriptors could have well been Grant's, as Grant inveighed against the contemporary faith that progress meant the economic and political integration of the North American continent, a development threatening Canada's political autonomy.[46]

In its political contingency, that threatening event[47] involved the United States, but, more generally, in Canada's capitulation Grant saw, in the words of his Dalhousie colleague Doull, another "realization" of the "technological dream" (e.g., "universalization" and "homogenization"[48]) toward the "devastating uniformity of technological society."[49] Associated with modernity itself, and with the United States[50] specifically as modernity's most "expressive manifestation,"[51] technology had become not just one optional *mode d'être*—but the only way of life on earth.[52] "The mode of being of the present epoch," Sikka affirms, "is 'enframing,' and enframing is the culmination and exhaustion of that projection of being which has reigned over the first history of the West."[53] Indeed, "the essence of technology [is] enframing."[54] In Emberley's succinct summary of Grant's understanding of the term, technology had become internalized as instrumental rationality, a "domination" of nature, an "imperial, bureaucratic" politics of government, a cult of "efficiency," and a sociology of "adjustment" and "equilibrium."[55] Canada's "collapse," Grant asserted, "stems from the very character of the modern era."[56] That era, the so-called age of progress, contiguous with the rise of capitalism,[57] science,[58] and the "conquest of nature,"[59] contrasted sharply with ancient Greece, Grant emphasized. Ancient Greece and Jerusalem became the contrast to which Grant juxtaposed the present. As science achieved hegemony, Grant felt sure, "there is no place for local cultures."[60]

How could this happen? How could the local become subsumed in the global, and how had the global become technological?[61] In the West, Grant answered, there had been a "close relation" between technology and political liberalism—"another homogenizing force"[62]—by which he meant the "belief that man's essence is his freedom."[63] Such belief in a "truly liberal society," Grant observed, has been linked historically to the progress of science.[64] In something like a sleight of hand, political liberalism installed legal and social homogeneity[65] in order to guarantee individual equality—"the central political idea of the modern West"[66]—now something primarily private and psychological, and expressed through the consumption of goods.[67] In such a "universal and homogenous state," as Grant puts the matter, humanity presumably becomes "free" and "equal," and "increasingly able to realize[its] concrete individuality."[68] Significantly, and this is the crucial difference Grant draws between the ancient (Greek) world and the contemporary secular world, is that the realization of individuality is not spiritual[69] or moral or intellectual but psychological, and it is fused with technological development. As we press toward the end, "we envisage," Grant cautioned, our dependence upon technology for its "realization" becomes ever more urgent.[70] In US school reform[71] this translated into the deafening demand for "what works" in classrooms, a restated behaviourism quantified in students' standardized test scores.[72] "[W]hat is wrong with technology," Fierlbeck explains,

> is not what it produces but what it leaves out…. Qualities that cannot be measured, classified, and quantified are given little attention or credence…. Thus, what we are left with—and what is exemplified best in American culture and politics—is the glorification of not only technology but also freedom, with little understanding or concern about how best to use it.[73]

Just as education disappears into numbers on tests, moral striving is recast as increases in productivity that are dependent upon technological advancement.[74] No longer conceived as laboratories for democracy, in the United States schools have been dismissed as antiquated "bricks-and-mortar" institutions, now to be privatized, then virtualized, as increasingly the curriculum is moved online.[75]

Problem solving[76] is no longer construed as a moral imperative—as the intellectual labour of judgment informed by knowledge[77] and wisdom[78]—but, rather, applying relevant information,[79] devising a technological fix.[80] No longer public, let alone sacred, morality becomes a matter of privately held[81] values,[82] sometimes monetized as commodities, statements of personal preference, often ornamental, sometimes self-servingly instrumental.[83] Whatever their function, values[84] were to be confined to the private sphere,[85] where one was free to do what one wanted. The public sphere[86] was no longer the civic square but, rather, the marketplace, the site where one purchased whatever one valued. Such choice monetized and privatized "pluralism," Grant notes, as "differences in the technological state are able to exist only in private activities," among them food, religious, and sexual preferences.[87] From Grant's perspective, the insistence on "gay rights"—especially the right to public affirmations of private commitments, as in gay marriage[88]—risks the relegation of homosexual desire to the status of yet another option of lifestyle, another consumer choice.[89] In so doing, recognition normalizes desire. Difference becomes another potentially entertaining instance of the same.[90]

The division between private and public was first blurred then erased by technology. There remains among some a lament for the loss of privacy, under stress for centuries given the emphasis upon confession in Christianity, a compulsion for self-disclosure secularized in psychoanalysis, and popularized in less time-consuming psychotherapies and self-help options. The confessions that had before been private—confined to priests, psychotherapists, or trustworthy friends—are now exhibited openly online, risking not only reputations (also an increasingly antiquated concept) but the infinity of subjectivity as well, as now the inner life has a point only inasmuch as it can be posted in public. The technological opportunity for exhibitionism[91] and surveillance[92] coupled with an uneasiness over privacy[93] threatens the disappearance of private life. While it may not be the cause, technology could be a consequence of what Heidegger called *das Man*, the public man in conformity with his or her fellows.[94] That dispersion of an individuated subjectivity—leaving what Lasch[95] termed a "minimal self"— becomes reassembled as *das Man*, even when we are women or transgender and keep secrets. As Kleinberg notes (in a different but related context): "In the interest of uniformity and complete systematic understanding, publicness invents responses that make all cases conform to one rule, one logic, and thus removes all differentiation."[96] This obliteration of internal differentiation and external distinctiveness accompanies globalization, a phenomenon materialized through technological innovation.

As technology ensures social conformity, it dissolves individuality. Avatars substitute for selves. Without internal subjective complexity, external multiplicity fades as material fact and moral challenge. Presumably the site of freedom, the Internet and those devices that access it present new opportunities for violence, surveillance, and control.[97] Technological innovations such as the Internet[98] fly under the "banner" of "freedom" and a "liberating modernization," and, as Grant points out, this new-style "imperialism" is justified to the public.[99] This "expansionist practicality"[100] had become a common faith, and not only in America, so that to "think outside this faith is to make oneself a stranger."[101] The technological era is a time, Grant charges, during which "nobility" and "wisdom" have been "exchanged" for a "pale" confidence in progress.[102]

"Pale" here is probably not a play on racialization, although to non-European listeners, especially to the descendants of the victims of imperialism, it might seem so. Rather, the word conveys the denuded (as in "vulgar" and "brutal": Grant's words) "drive" toward a limitless "technological future," when only "technical reason" is relevant, rendering antiquated "openness" and "awe," even "questioning" and "listening."[103] These prerequisites and processes of education, of curriculum as complicated conversation, depend upon the cultivation of noncoincidence.[104] In an era of narcissism, boundaries blur, and not only between self and other but among social and political phenomena as well.[105] Technology restructures political liberalism so that it conflates instrumentalism with action, exhibitionism with communication, image with reality.[106] How can I use technology as the subject of a sentence? To do so acknowledges, in Nusselder's phrasing, "technology as *volition*."[107] In Grant's terms, technology materializes the human will to power, precipitating the "violence of an undirected willing of novelty."[108] Such commitment to "continual change," Grant appreciated, rests on "freedom" as the "first political principle," specifically the freedom to dispense with any obstacle to "technological advance," including any "conception of an eternal order."[109] When transcendence is recast as the production of novelty—new products, new ideas, always the "new"—the future becomes foreclosed.

Our Civilizational Destiny

> Surely the deepest alienation must be when the civilization one inhabits no longer claims one's loyalty.[110]
>
> George Grant

Not in the remembrance of things past or as risks taken in the name of the future, social action is replaced by proceduralism in the field of curriculum studies conveyed simplistically in the so-called Tyler rationale,[111] wherein the implementation of objectives is constantly evaluated, creating a self-referential set of cul-de-sacs reiterating what is already. Because proceduralism leads nowhere but where one began, the objectives-evaluation axis tends toward intensification, creating, in Raymond Callahan's famous phrase, a "cult of efficiency."[112] A technological society, Potter summarizes, is one that pursues the systematic application of reason to the invention of tools and methods for enhancing freedom by making all activity more efficient.[113] "Freedom's great achievement was that it allowed modern technology to appear," Grant acknowledged, and "technology's great achievement was that it allowed freedom to flourish."[114] In the private sphere, however, freedom is recast as choice of consumer goods; in the public sphere it converts to control, the demand that freedom flourish so that whatever is profitable can be pursued. In new products and increased productivity technology and capitalism conflate.[115] At the same time, in its tendency toward intensification, technology undermines freedom and efficiency, submerging us in minutiae, tying us to the present moment, an interminable atemporal present in which we become preoccupied with the next sensation, the next "bit" of communication or information,[116] focused on the expectation that momentarily "something" will happen, a new website will stimulate.

Technology is, then, no set of tools supplementary to our way of life. For Grant, Potter explains, technology not only structures how we apprehend the world, it becomes a "mode" of being that "transforms" how "we know, think, and will."[117] Nature becomes, in Heidegger's famous phrase, a "standing reserve" (or *Bestand*), a source of energy or resources[118] for future use. As Krauss points out, "*Bestand* implies orderability and substitutability; objects will necessarily lose their autonomy."[119] The system or way of thinking that enframes the world as standing reserve Heidegger calls *Gestell*; this is, Grant was sure, our "civilizational destiny."[120] It is not only nature that is wasted in this technology of thinking, it is human nature[121] itself. "Powerful" and "value-laden," Potter states, summarizing Grant's view, technology "enslaves" in the name of liberation, leaving us "heavily dependent" upon impersonal "institutions."[122] No one who lived through the Great Recession of 2008 or the European migrant crisis of 2015 can doubt our dependency on "impersonal institutions." Significantly, one response to the former was an improvisational, anti-institutional Occupy movement, as in Occupy Wall Street, a reference one supposes less to previous occupations (of the Rhineland after the First World War, for instance) than to the "impersonal" (as in "having no personal reference or connection"[123]) character of the financial system.[124]

Minus a subjectively coherent civic subject[125]—the consumer is dispersed along fused planes of desire, acquisition, possession—resistance becomes quixotic. Given our subsumption in the "technological sensorium,"[126] resistance (with its implication of a force separate from "us" that can in fact be "resisted") dissipates as a concept and social practice. Instead we have anther "reality" TV show. Referencing Marshall McLuhan,[127] Arthur Kroker points out:

> If, indeed, we are now "looking out" from inside the technological sensorium; and if, in fact, in the merger of biology and technology which is the locus of the electronic age, "we" have become the vanishing points of technique, then a way had to be discovered for breaching the "invisible environment" within which we are now enclosed.[128]

Kroker's choice of "breaching" seems especially apt, as it specifies not "push back," as "resistance" implies, but non-coincidence,[129] however internalized that "environment" has become within subjectivity.[130]

As would Aoki[131] decades later, Grant (Emberley points out) did not overlook the "moral promise and concrete achievements of modern technology."[132] Many of these are familiar—increased food production, advances in medicine, convenience of communication—if with consequences, including poisoning by pesticides, preservatives, and genetic modification; pills and practices that kill as they cure; and connectivity condensed to the constancy of information transmission as we stare at screens, not at each other, not at the world from which, evidently, we are now disembedded.[133] "Canadians in particular," Grant wrote, "felt the blessing of technology in an environment so hard that to master it needed courage. But conservatism must languish as technology increases."[134] As we saw in chapter 1, by "conservatism" Grant meant not the "defense of property rights and chauvinism"[135] but the "right of the community to restrain freedom in the name of the common good."[136] Climate change and the environmental catastrophes it promises provide one obvious example.

Technological achievements imply, Emberley notes, increasing the individual's freedom.[137] In its everyday practical sense, Grant thought of his wife's housekeeping chores, in Christian's description, her "relationship" with the "wonderful American machines that relieved her of drudgery."[138] While machines have been employed for millennia, what is different now—and this was reflected in Grant's thinking (at least in the 1970s)—was that "human beings defined and understood themselves primarily as free," a fact, Grant judged, that was a "genuine good."[139] But not only, as Grant was clear that freedom represents danger as well as opportunity.[140]

Grant was quite clear that the freedom technology affords is also the opportunity to do what is morally wrong. Of course machines make for "convenience," and yes they free people to do other things,[141] but do they render us *more* free? Does not "freedom" depend upon subjective non-coincidence with what is and the self-conscious cultivation of the capacity to critique, to reflect, to act independently of what is? Convenience comes with consequences, Grant knew.

Open access—made possible by those information technologies devised and disseminated after Grant's death—would seem to represent an instance of "non-coincidence" and an increased capacity for critique and insight. The case for open access has been made nowhere more succinctly than by John Willinsky, who links the development with its institutional antecedents:

> The public library has long been a beacon of self-directed and deeply motivated learning on the part of common readers. It is not only a vital cornerstone of democracy, but a public site of quiet solace, intellectual inquiry, and literary pleasures. To increase public access to online research and scholarship would add a great deal to what has emerged over the last decade on the Internet as a wired and virtual public library, providing people with an opportunity to explore a new world of ideas that they may have only suspected existed.[142]

Opportunity yes, but one, it bears repeating, that depends upon the curiosity and capacity of the person, assuming online access is available.

Let us consider another apparently progressive[143]—again referencing Grant's association of technology with the extension of freedom—consequence of online access. The Arab Spring of 2011[144]—more than thirty years after Grant noted "our dependence on oil and the Arab awakening"[145]—was enabled, many thought, by information technologies and social media. Research by Navid Hassanpour questioned that assumption. "Full connectivity in a social network sometimes can hinder collective action," Hassanpour concluded.[146] While Twitter posting, texting, and Facebook wall-posting may have disseminated calls to protest and facilitated the actual organization of protest events, it also communicated caution, delay, and confusion, as in, "I don't have time for all this politics, did you see what Lady Gaga is wearing?"[147] Specifically, after Egyptian President Hosni Mubarak shut down Internet and cellphone service on January 28, 2011, Hassanpour found that protests *increased*, not only in Cairo but throughout Egypt. The number of actual protestors participating had not increased, but the number of protest events had. Hassanpour terms this phenomenon a "localization process." He explains:

> The disruption of cellphone coverage and the Internet on the 28th exacerbated the unrest in at least three major ways. It implicated many apolitical citizens

unaware of or uninterested in the unrest; it forced more face-to-face commu-nication, i.e., more physical presence in the streets; and finally it effectively decentralized the rebellion on the 28th through new hybrid communication tactics, producing a quagmire much harder to control and repress than one massive gathering in Tahrir [Square].[148]

I am reminded of Harold Innis's insistence on orality as central not only to cre-ative culture but to civilization itself.[149] While orality can occur online, it is made more difficult without physical presence and non-verbal communication that can accompany it. Hassanpour is thinking of the "normalization" effect of being "connected." In an interview he suggested that "we become more normal when we actually know what is going on—we are more unpredictable when we don't—on a mass scale and that has interesting implications."[150]

Almost a decade later, contrary to facts, the fantasy that the Arab Spring "blossomed"[151] thanks to social media remains. Now, however, it is clear that the fantasy is part of a self-promotional tale the tech industry itself tells; namely, that it is a force of "freedom" and "enlightenment."[152] In his 2012 statement to inves-tors, Mark Zuckerberg, the Facebook founder, proclaimed that the corporation would create "a more honest and transparent dialogue around government," adding that the outcome would be "better solutions to some of the biggest prob-lems of our time."[153] Five years later, as Streitfeld reports, the tech industry is "under attack for causing problems rather than solving them,"[154] among them enabling Russian interference in the 2016 US presidential election. Streitfeld concludes:

> Social media might have originally promised liberation, but it proved an even more useful tool for stoking anger. The manipulation was so efficient and so lacking in transparency that the companies themselves barely noticed it was happening.[155]

But then tech companies are evidently not very interested in knowing what is "happening," despite proclamations to the contrary. By definition, companies pursue profit.[156]

Canadians' commitment to technology was not initially, Grant suggests, an expression of the will to power, the insistence on clearing any obstacles to eco-nomic development. Instead, as Margaret Atwood has also argued, Canadians' commitment to technology was associated with survival in a harsh land. But what permitted physical survival, Grant warned, threatened cultural survival. In particular, the conservation of tradition is threatened by technology's limitless expansiveness. Grant points to the particularities of one's homeland to which citizens have loyalty and in which they take pride. Such particularities come to cultural distinctive forms through time, but history—traditional education is predicated on the preservation of culture—becomes dissolved by the presentism[157] technology installs and is codified in the "new social sciences."[158] Nowhere is that more evident than in quantified educational research in the United States.[159]

School reform in the United States—always promoting technology in the classroom, now less a form of pedagogy than profiteering[160]—has been rationalized in recent years as reparation. It was especially impoverished US schools that were alleged to be failing, and it was, presumably, in the service of leaving "no child behind" that George W. Bush installed accountability schemes that deformed educational institutions into businesses.[161] Recalling our long-standing faith[162] in technological development to address hunger, ease labour, and create wealth, Grant admonishes: "One must never think about technological destiny without looking squarely at the justice in those hopes."[163] Now that faith in technology as the driver of justice is no longer so simple or strong, as we are faced—Grant was writing in the mid-1980s here—with technologically produced and interrelated crises of overpopulation, life-threatening pollution, and the catastrophes of climate change. Documenting the "determining power of our technological representation of reality," Grant notes, the political response to these developments has been a call for an "even greater mobilization of technology," rendered urgent by those "emergencies which technology has produced."[164] This paradox was evident to the influential right-wing German intellectual Ernst Jünger, who, in 1931, observed: "The history of inventions also raises ever more clearly the question of whether a space of absolute comfort or a space of absolute danger is the final aim concealed in technology."[165] Technology enables the extension of individual life as it threatens the extinguishing of the species.

"Much of the new technology upon which we are going to depend to meet these crises," Grant predicted, "is technology turned towards human beings," requiring the "proliferation of new arts and sciences directed towards human control."[166] The neurosciences might qualify as one instance, the information technologies provide another, as they create the illusion of "connectivity" while often increasing isolation[167] as they constrain one to the social networks to which, within which, one is "connected." The constancy of being connected reorganizes time around disclosure—of one's whereabouts, what one's feeling, "news" now as minutiae—and the presentism[168] of a narcissistic age is being sounded by cellphones demanding to be answered. Never mind the effects of being constantly connected to employers.[169]

Grant's example is not cellphones—he died before they metastasized—but the medical profession, whose "proliferating power," he asserted, functions to tighten "social control."[170] Sounding like Foucault, he points to the profession's alignment with law enforcement and government in addressing the problems of the "psyche," increasingly, he notes, focused on physiology as well as behaviour. The aggressive prescription of pharmaceuticals for complaints mild and severe proves the prescience[171] of the philosophy professor from Halifax. Technology, he pronounced, is "the pervasive mode of being in our political and social lives."[172]

Now humanity stares at screens. The sleight-of-hand achieved in Grant's analysis is that he—we—could somehow stand outside technology. Rather, we abstract the term "technology" from the totality as an analytic device to enable us to speak about a totality from which we cannot actually separate but with which we can choose not to coincide completely. Grant's strategy seems to be one of mobility, as he moves from one to another instance of technology's pervasiveness, as if he were skipping like a stone on the surface of the pond, knowing he would sink should he stop. Movement is propelled by thinking, including out loud; "bearing witness," one might say.[173] "If protest cannot go further than witnessing," Paras suggests (in a different but related context), "it is because the twentieth century has revealed the dangers of theorizing solutions."[174]

The instrumentalism of technology is not confined to the manufacture of "external objects"—like the computer,[175] of which (anticipating C. A. Bowers[176]) Grant is wary—as it simultaneously structures those "systems" of "organization" and "communication" as "factories."[177] I am reminded of Maxine Greene[178] when Grant writes that "to be awake in any part of our educational system is to know that the desire for these machines shapes those institutions at their heart in their curriculum, in what the young are encouraged to know and to do."[179] Not only the means of curriculum delivery (as it was phrased) then, positioning the computer as central to learning smuggles in, Grant knew, "massive assumptions about knowing and being and making," assumptions "not directed towards a "leading out"—transcendence[180]—"but towards organizing within,"[181] an evisceration of subjectivity as spiritual, among the "ravages technology wreaks on human subjectivity."[182] Subjectively contracted, we come to resemble the machines that surround us—"the computer's way is to homogenize"[183]—a symbiosis Jünger embraced.[184] As it was in the Weimar Republic, so too it seems now. As Grant appreciated: this technologization—and the desubjectification it enforces—"entails that the majority of those who rule any modern society will take the purposes of ruling increasingly to be congruent with this account of knowing."[185] Grant summarizes:

> In short, the requirements for the existence of computers is but part of the total historical situation...which is given us as modern human beings. And the conditions of that situation are never to be conceived as static determinants, but as a dynamic interrelation of tightening determinations.[186]

What is sold—including to young children, well below the age of consent—for the sake of freedom and learning threatens to freeze both in its Medusa-like stare of the screen.

Frozen is not motionless, however, as it seems we move in ever more frenzied fashion, at least with our fingers and eyes. Efficiency and rationalization accomplish homogeneity as time accelerates, flattening its own structures—past, present, future—into an apparently eternal now, yet always almost new, "marking, among other things, the priority of the values of disruption and interference over those historically establishing continuity."[187] Grant wonders how long humanity can maintain its "divided state" wherein a "hectic subjectivity" is "lived out" in an world in which humanity itself is "increasingly" objectified; what will enable us to "rage against such division," including against the onerous obligation to create oneself, one among other "objectifications" of what is still called freedom?[188] I am reminded of the likewise resounding question Alice Miller asked about child abuse.[189] How can the abused survive when love and violence become fused?

Conclusion

> What is worth doing in the midst of this barren twilight is the incredibly difficult question.
>
> George Grant[190]

While no technophobe,[191] Grant understood that technological progress transforms the human spirit as it severs social control from "traditional" morality and politics.[192] Because it is simultaneously universalizing and homogenizing, technology's intensification of immediacy and efficiency erases heterogeneity: cultural, political, subjective.[193] Whatever "difference" remains becomes commodified, incorporated into a system of exchange recalculating its value as eccentricity or pathology or sentimentality. Whatever the economic benefits (and, as the Great Recession of 2008 reminded, they are hardly uniform or predictable), technology, Grant argued, is a universal tyranny, destined to eradicate the historic aspirations of the Western world and particularly its North American experiments.[194] Contemporary society, Grant reminded, has come at the cost "all older standards of human excellence," replacing those with technological problem-solving.[195] Intensifying this "drive to technology," Grant added, was that it is conducted by those who imagine their activity as supporting human "liberation."[196]

It is as if George Grant knew that submergence in the technological present requires not resistance but reconstruction, and in its historical sense. Such reconstruction requires becoming aware, as Emberley succinctly summarizes, of "traces of practices, understandings, ways of life, and lived-experience which are pre-technological in our cultural and political legacy."[197] Grant knew that one could not escape technology, but one could, again in Emberley's words, find one's way "between local parochialism on the one hand and the deracinated life of the modern universal and homogenous state on the other."[198] As in Weimar Germany—whose dissolution was followed by arguably the first version of a "modern universal and homogenous state"—finding passage between provincialism and an incapacitating deracination, demands, as Emberley notes, "attentiveness and courage."[199] After all, "in no society," as Grant was keenly aware, "is it possible for many men to live outside the dominant assumptions of their world for very long."[200] We cannot live outside them, but, like Grant, we can decline to coincide with them.

"We thought we could pick and choose, as in a supermarket," Christian reminds, restating Grant's dismissal of the technology-is-neutral argument, that it is only a tool we can use (or not) according to our convenience.[201] That thought[202] is itself technological, affirming, however inadvertently, our demotion to "standing reserve," Heidegger's concept.[203] At first we thought "only nature would be subject to human will," but "ourselves not."[204] We are not exempt from our prostheses' power over us, Grant knew, as we have "bought a package deal of far more fundamental novelness than simply a set of instruments under our control. It is a destiny which enfolds us in its own conception of instrumentality, neutrality and purposiveness."[205] As we disappear into the technoculture we created and which now recreates us as its subjects, technology surpasses our capacity to grasp it. "We apprehend our destiny by forms of thought which are themselves the very core of that destiny," Grant understood.[206] As if conscious of the idolatry[207] technology insinuates, Grant challenged us to "understand our technological destiny from principles more comprehensive than its own."[208] For Grant, "thought is steadfast attention to the whole."[209]

Grant did not imagine that "the whole" could be grasped, intellectually or otherwise. It was one's relationship to that which exceeds understanding that absorbed Grant's attention during his final years. He reaffirmed his Christian faith as he confirmed his contempt for the cult of convenience, whether exercised in academics or abortion.[210] Could it be his anti-abortion arguments[211] and his fascination with that "darling bastard"[212] anti-Semite Céline,[213] who, Grant judged, left us "the supreme account of the truth about technological warfare,"[214] that have led to his disappearance today? Whatever the reason, Grant's courage remains, expressed through his insightful critique and searing lament. Grant formulated and followed his convictions, always engaged with his countrymen and the historical moment, seeking the timeless truth he discerned as lodged within the particularities of each. He followed his thought, his attention to the whole, wherever it led him, at whatever cost to his worldly status. He lamented the state of his nation[215] and he took on technology, not due to personal quirkiness—although there was that[216]—but in fidelity to an ancient conception of justice and truth.

"To put the matter in a popular way," Grant wrote, "justice is an unchanging measure of all our times and places, and our love of it defines us."[217] It was the love[218] of justice—no contract,[219] as his critique of John Rawls underscores—that attunes us to "the whole," that demands attention and duty. It is our love of justice, Grant insisted, that inspires us to exceed what technology has made of us. It is in fact our calling to "understand our technological destiny from principles more comprehensive than its own."[220] What principles could be "more comprehensive" than *those* principles—calculation, instrumentality, obsession—that the technological imperative installs? By the end of his life, Grant felt he had found it. The primary principle was love, which Grant conceived as "consent to the fact that there is authentic otherness."[221] He seemed to know, as if anticipating Jean-Luc Marion, that "love (like Goodness) requires distance (as unthinkable), in order that participation be fortified in, and reinforce, the mystery of alterity."[222] On the twenty-seventh of September, 1988, George Grant died. "With his death," Angus suggested,

> there will come pressure for canonization. He will be respected and quoted, probably at the cost of being read and criticized, which is what every philosopher wants. Let us not forget that George Grant was able only to begin to formulate Canadian philosophy by going outside the canons, by disturbing the boundaries between disciplines and between thought and life…. The future will memorialize him; the past has ignored him; the present needs to continue the dialogue with him.[223]

It is just such a dialogue to which I hope this study contributes.

Gone now thirty years, Grant's critique of technology remains with us, a testimony to the capacity of thought to exceed what is, including those idols whose vassals[224] Grant worried we had become. Once Grant used even stronger terms, asking at one—early, more hopeful—point: "[A]re we going to master technology and make it a means to a free life or are we going to become robots and slaves."[225] For those of us alive today, none of these terms turns out to be strong enough, as they point to political subservience not ontological[226] erasure, the latter implied in Kittler's analysis that the interface today is not humanity-machine but machine-machine:

> Causes no longer precede effects in time…physics [is stripped] of its Kantian conception of objects and reduces them to mathematic designs…[and] cybernetics, logistics, and data processing are no longer sciences performed by human beings, as was the case in late Greek culture, but rather are implemented as high technologies. They operate (if it is still possible even to say as much) as things among things.[227]

One set of machines, Grant asserts at a later, not-so-hopeful point, is ourselves. "The basic error," he suggests, is we think of technology as simply a "continuance" of humanity's engagement with "practical exigencies throughout history," that it is another "external of 'material' environment and as not touching the essence of the human condition."[228] But touch the essence it does. The "spirit," Weil knew, when "overcome" with the "weight" of "quantity," can know no other measure but "efficiency."[229] Crushed by quantification, efficiency can become genocide.[230]

Notes

1. Grant (1974) 1998, 1. Andrew and Planinc (1990, 178) suggest that Grant suffers an "impasse" in his thinking due to asking this question, which implies an ontology of technology (which Planinc denies). Andrew and Planinc continue: "Grant finds it necessary to allow himself to be seduced by modernity's magical extreme for two reasons: to preserve common sense itself; and to live through the experience in order to become a philosopher. The seduction itself, therefore, produces only an apparent impasse. Grant's true impasse originates in his Gnosticism" (179). What might seem like an impasse in Grant's thinking is for me its sheer expansiveness, its capacity to hold together contraries (among them progressivism, Platonism, Christianity). Whether technology has an "ontological" status, certainly it "is." What is it? I suggest that technology is the inhuman in us externalized, materialized, summoning us to fuse with its machinic surface.

2. Davis and Roper 2009b, 539.

3. Davis and Roper 2005b, 596.

4. O'Donovan 1984, 90. "For Grant," Reimer (1990, 106) writes, "modernity describes the post-Enlightenment age and the triumph of scientific and instrumental reason which lies at the heart of today's technological monolith. Moderns are those who have accepted the liberal assumptions of freedom behind the rise of modern technology." For Grant, Sibley (2008, 282) suggests, "technology is transforming human nature."

5. O'Donovan 1984, 86.

6. Doull 1983, 41.

7. Athanasiadis 2001, 124.

8. Lee 1990, 25. A "permanent double-bind"—the impasse he cites at the start of the quoted passage—is no "'private muddle that George Grant got himself into,' but rather 'a civilizational quandary that George Grant charted'" (24).

9. O'Donovan 1984, 105. Referencing Eric Voegelin, Rotstein (1983, 106) reminds that "Western society is not all modern but that modernity is a growth within it, in opposition to the classic and Christian tradition." Reactivation of suppressed archaic elements may then be possible. Not without risk, but desperation may make the wager worth making.

10. O'Donovan (1984, 105) asks: "But why does our transcendence of technological necessity, our original possession of the good, take the form of recollection?" She answers: "Recollection has this place in Grant's later writings because of the continuing importance of tradition as a vehicle of transcendent truth."

11. Trained in history at Queen's University, William Lawson Grant (1872–1935) lectured in colonial history at Oxford from 1906 until 1910; he then returned to teach history at Queen's. Among his publications were a biography of his father (1905), a controversial history of Canada for use in Ontario high schools (1914), and *The Tribune of Nova Scotia: A Chronicle of Joseph Howe* (1915; see Christian [1995] 2001, viii; Davis and Roper 2009b,105n2).

12. "The War was an unprecedented triumph for natural science," Collingwood (2002, 90) observed, adding: "Bacon had promised that knowledge would be power, and power it was: power to destroy the bodies and souls of men more rapidly than had ever been done by human agency before. This triumph paved the way to other

triumphs: improvements in transport, in sanitation, in surgery, medicine, and psychiatry, in commerce and industry, and, above all, in preparations for the next war." Grant knew: "In our era war has been particularly prevalent because of technology, and has taken new forms because of technology" (Davis and Roper 2009b, 476).

13.   "Grant inherited his father's passion for pacifism," Athanasiadis (2001, 11–2) "and international issues." And for history too, as well as for music and his support for Quebec; see Rigelhof 2001, 28.

14.   "Ruin" seems to have taken a compensatory route, that of reform, as Grant tells Cayley (1995, 46): "The war led my father into a lot of reform, and into an optimism about reform that would have been part of his liberalism in any case, but became more intense because of the war. Of course, he didn't live so very long after the war, because he'd been badly hurt." Cayley follows by asking: "What do you mean by his liberalism?" to which Grant replies: "Well, I mean by a liberal somebody who believes man's essence is his freedom.... It is so deeply part of the English-speaking world, to which Canada belongs, that people just take it for granted, in a certain sense, that man is free and is going to make the world as he wills" (47). Not God's will but humanity's became the marker of modernity progressively defined, but its religious subtext was nonetheless audible. "The age of progress," Muggeridge (1978, 40) notes, "far from being a departure from the age of faith, is a logical outcome of it." In Sibley's (2008, 139) summary: "Luther's rejection of 'finite images' standing between man and God is, dialectically, an assertion of unlimited freedom.... Indeed, according to Grant, Luther's theology of the Cross was transformed into the secular theology of glory that we refer to as technology."

15.   Quoted in Christian ([1995] 2001, viii–ix). "My father was a school principal," Grant told a 1955 audience assembled to honour J. W. Ansley (a school principal), "and I learned early from him that there is no more honourable or skilled profession, nor any more open to temptation in a society such as ours which does not see clearly the true purpose of education" (Davis 2002b, 166).

16.   "The horror of the Western Front deeply affected William's life," Christian (1996a, 5) comments, "and, through him, his son's."

17.   "The great dividing line of the modern era is 1914," Grant wrote, "when the Western Europeans, in largely Protestant societies, started slaughtering each other in a massive way" (Davis and Roper 2009b, 575). "To put the matter historically," Grant wrote, "Since 1914 it has surely become obvious that the truth of the assumptions of modernity cannot be taken with quite the uncritical certitude that they were previously" (Davis and Roper 2005b, 170). Harold Innis's biographer, Alexander John Watson (2007, 426), positions Grant in a generational cohort of "profound figures... whose gestation period was between the end of the First and Second World Wars." In addition to Innis and Grant, Watson adds Innis's political-economist colleague C. B. Macpherson, classics scholar A. E. Havelock, Northrop Frye, and Marshall McLuhan. "The world war is a bitter commentary on the nineteenth century misconception of moral achievement," Dewey (1922, 177) wrote, "a misconception however it only inherited from the traditional theory of fixed ends, attempting to bolster up that doctrine with aid from the 'scientific' theory of evolution. The doctrine of progress is not yet bankrupt."

18.   "[M]y grandfather," Grant told Cayley (1995, 161), "was one of these secularized Protestants. I don't think he entirely admitted he was, but he was one of the supreme

believers in progress and he took over a curriculum that would have been taken for granted." Sibley (2008, 121) is sure that "the sentiments of the elder Grant certainly find an echo in his grandson's thought," especially the grandfather's Hegelianism. Fierlbeck (2006, 53) links Grant's *Lament for a Nation* with his grandfather's 1888 "equally outraged response to Goldwin Smith's proposal for greater economic integration with the U.S." Grant's mother—"through Maude," Christian (1996a, 38) tells us, "Grandfather Parkin was [also] a living presence in George's life"—"believed her son was destined to carry on his grandfather Parkin's educational work" (Christian 1996d, 6n2). In what capacity? His mother thought he should become either prime minister of Canada or a professor at the University of Toronto (Christian 1992, 52). Educational work he definitely did but in neither capacity his mother had imagined. And the work he did do was, in part, questioning what his grandfather had believed. Emphasizing the dependent clause, Meynell (2011, 107) might be right: "In many ways, George Parkin Grant carried on the work of his grandfathers."

19.   Christian (1995) 2001, ix. He was also drawn to his teachers, especially R. A. Trotter (1888–1951, a professor of history at Queen's 1924–1950), writing his mother in March 1938 that "I just sit and worship Dr. Trotter in class because he is so magnificent" (Christian 1996d, 26). The fascination with Trotter continues after Grant graduates; see Christian 1996a, 44; 1996d, 64, 103.

20.   Rigelhof (2001, 41) reports that Balliol College, where he had been accepted, was the same college his father had attended. There, Rigelhof continues, Grant "met the brightest and most idealistic people he'd ever encountered. He fell in love with them and their ideas. People like Peter Self and Peter Clarke—his closest friends…. For them, the pursuit of beauty, truth, and goodness through art, music, literature, philosophy, and religion was far more important than financial or social success" (42). In his interview with David Cayley (1995, 52), however, Grant says only that Oxford was "very good, I was allowed to study."

21.   Christian (1995) 2001, ix. He belonged to a "class of ministers, professors, schoolteachers, lawyers, and doctors," Grant told Schmidt (1978a, 63), that was "disappearing," adding (perhaps with a sly smile), "Nothing so much can drive one to philosophy as being part of a class which is disappearing." I understand.

22.   "Without a doubt," Athanasiadis (2001, 13) concludes, "the Second World War was a primal event which would shape fundamentally the direction of Grant's thought."

23.   I pass over these events swiftly, but they were, for Grant, imprinting, telling students that the conversion was "the great event of my life" (Davis and Roper 2009b, 967; Athanasiadis 2001, 17; Jersak 2012, 83). For details concerning the bombing, see Christian 1996a, 70; 1996d, 70; for the conversion—his recognition, he told Schmidt (1978a, 63), that "I am not my own," and, as he told Cayley (1995, 49), "that beyond time and space there is order"—see Christian 1996a, 85–6; 1996d, 92; Cayley 1995, 48). Davis (2000, xxii) tells us "Both took place when he said he was 'living poetically': responding to events immediately and passionately rather than deliberately and thoughtfully" (see too Cayley 1995, 50). To my mind Grant never stopped living "immediately" and "passionately," but he did so "deliberately" and "thoughtfully," reminding me of Musil's association of precision and soul, writing in 1912 that "soul is a complex interpenetration of feeling and intellect" (Musil 1990, 10).

24.   In a 1943 letter Grant seems to attribute the shift in scholarly subject to the war and "the situation in Canada" (Christian 1996d, 108). While these are left unspecified,

they do point to the worldly impetus for the shift. Writing another letter, in 1945, Grant wrote that post-war Oxford "is still not terribly pleasant, the one thing that makes it really worthwhile is theology. It is just my subject. Never have I really felt so completely alive in anything. After the years in Canada when I had ceased to write I am now writing again, and which is better than writing it is giving me the power to make myself a better and more effective person" (124). Surely such subjective reconstruction registers the right subject, even if theology, O'Donovan (1984, 14) reports, "offended the 'secular liberal' sensibilities of his family." His study, she adds, became a "spiritual quest" (14).

25.   Davis and Roper 2009b, 97; quoted in Christian (1995) 2001, x.

26.   Christian (1995) 2001, x.

27.   A. D. Lindsay, Grant's "greatest teacher" (Cayley 1995, 52) at Oxford, suggested that Grant study John Oman for this thesis (Christian 1996a, 114). Oman (1860–1939) was considered by his contemporaries as among the "most powerful and original religious thinkers of his day…. Oman's theology stressed the freedom, worth, and dignity of the human personality, qualities which were endowed by God. He was regarded…as a man of high moral purpose and personal integrity, as well as a man of commanding physical presence" (Christian 1996d, 123n10). "Oman's faith and thought," Athanasiadis (2001, 31) suggests, "represented that of Grant's progenitors." Through him, Grant discovered the "theology of the cross" (29). Grant's thesis focused on Oman's "most admired work," *The Natural and The Supernatural* (1931), where he asserted that nature is "a realm through which God speaks to His children and through which they do his will." Grant argued that sixteenth- and seventeenth-century scientists tended to equate knowledge of nature with control over it, meaning that many "became blinded to the witness of nature in feelings, which is the foundation of all other relations to nature" (quoted passages in Christian 1996a, 147). This symbiotic (and for Grant divine) relation between humanity and nature was one of the "four broad themes" Christian identifies in Grant's thesis: (1) that science had "cut us off from nature," and in doing so that foreclosed any "possibility of approaching the divine through nature"; (2) the "success" of contemporary science is associated with "Calvinism and its emphasis on will"; (3) positing the "will" as the "fundamental" feature of humanity has undermined the "grounding for human moral equality, which depends on man's relationship to God"; and (4) the "true test" of any theology is its "capacity to give moral guidance during a crisis" (149). It was the failure of Oman's theology to provide moral guidance during the First World War that disappointed Grant most, writing (in a 1987 letter to his old friend Peter Self), that "I always refused to turn my thesis on a great liberal theologian [Oman] into a book because I did not want to produce a book which patronized a tradition which is admirable but fundamentally failing, because it did not face the profound division between Christianity & progressivism (in its best, its liberal form)" (Christian 1996d, 373). Grant faced it but, as I suggest in the introduction, he did not shed it entirely.

28.   Born in England and brought up as a Roman Catholic, Sheila Allen attended the Covenant of the Holy Child, a Roman Catholic private boarding school before studying at St. Anne's College, Oxford, where she met Grant. Attending for a time the United Church of Canada, Grant and his wife became confirmed as Anglicans in 1956 (Davis and Roper 2009b, 71n11). A decade later, the possible unification of the

Anglican and United Churches led Grant to write his friend Derek Bedson that that "would almost certainly lead me to seek admission in the Roman Catholic Church and I would deeply regret that. But I know what the United Church is too well (it is essential immanentism) to be able to sit in it. There is much in the Roman Church which appears to me totalitarian but it does not fail in guarding the pearl of great price" (Christian 1996d, 229).

29.   During Grant's time there, Davis (2002b, 443) points out, Dalhousie enrolled approximately 1,500 students. When he joined the Philosophy Department there was only one full-time appointment in addition to his, and when he left there were only three. Along with his close colleague James Doull, Grant became, Davis records, an intellectual leader to many: his classes were "exciting and controversial," as "his presence in the classroom and his sense of drama brought philosophy to life or his students.... Grant was particularly attentive to students, responding to their intellectual needs and also relating academic study to their lived experience" (443–4). Sounding here like the quintessential progressive educator, Grant enacted—through his subjective presence in the subject matter—what one could call the iconographic capacity of the curriculum. Chapter 4 is devoted to Grant's teaching.

30.   Potter 2005, xxx. Even upon his return Grant appreciated Dalhousie, at least at first, writing to William Christian (1996d, 319) in September 1981 that "Dalhousie is a vague, chaotic university compared to McMaster, but that has its advantages" (see also 311, where the characterization of "chaos" is repeated). Overall, however, Dalhousie the second time around represented, in Christian's phrase, an "unhappy return" (311).

31.   Evidently Grant approved of Halifax's provincialism, at least at first, as Christian (1996a, 164) suggests that "Nova Scotia's advantage" was that it was no "mass society," at least not yet, that there it was "still possible" to avoid being "swept away by the new worship of technique and self-expression, prosperity and power, which exalted usefulness above truth, and convenience and worldly success above knowledge."

32.   The decision to leave McMaster was difficult; I return to it in ch. 4 and 5. Returning to Halifax was welcome, to Dalhousie not so much; in a January 1981 letter to William Christian (1996d, 313), Grant expresses that "[i]t is good to be back in Halifax, less good at Dalhousie."

33.   Evidently Heidegger had become important to Grant in the late 1950s; Christian (1996a, 194) reports that he told his senior philosophy class at Dalhousie in 1959 that he found Heidegger "so important because his late works give us insight into how the particular world we inhabit came into existence." Around 1967, Christian continues, at McMaster University (where Grant had by then moved), a colleague had translated Heidegger's *The Question Concerning Technology*; Grant's graduate seminar devoted the entire year "studying the mimeographed pages" (268). After reading Heidegger's Nietzsche lectures, Grant came to conclude, again in Christian's words, that the "very process that brought technological civilization into being simultaneously eroded the validity of all perspectives other than its own" (294). Later, Grant would judge Heidegger's philosophy a failure because it did not "understand the happiness that arises from the hunger and thirst for justice" (354). Heidegger's "intellectual importance" to Grant, Christian concludes, can be "Inferred" from the presence of "nineteen works by the German philosopher in his library" (428n23).

34.   In a December 1985 letter he writes, "less held by Freud than I once was" (Christian 1996d, 354).

35.   At the 1964 Canadian Conference on Social Welfare, in a paper titled "Value and Technology," Grant told attendees—in Christian's (1996a, 218) summary—that "social work, to be effective, relied on social science and, once the writings of Max Weber took hold in North America, social science accepted the ideal that interpretation should be value-free, and hence it became, in George's view, rudderless." The emphasis must be on "took hold" as Weber's legacy is much more multi-faceted than that sentence implies.

36.   The "important discovery" of 1962, Christian (1996a, 165) reports, was Mozart. "His [Mozart's] music," Grant thought, "is like partaking in eternity" (quoted in Christian 1996a, 165). To "eternity" we return in ch. 7.

37.   Christian ([1995] 2001, xiii).

38.   "Like Pasolini," Viano (1993, 12) points out, "Jung never severed his ties with Christianity and always maintained that we need to distinguish between religiousness and organized religion. He was also at some point convinced that the only truly realist perspective is the one afforded by mythology, and he did not regard Thanatos as the perennial opponent of Eros but as the first and last metaphor, the most powerful mythical presence in the psychic underworld. Furthermore, the Jungian theory of *anima* as feminine component in every man's soul well suited an individual who felt guilty about not living up to masculinity's requirements." For Grant, the first two points are obviously relevant.

39.   The study of Nietzsche, Grant reports, was "always...a great intensity," in part because "clearly Nietzsche understands technology, that mastery of the earth which so contemporaneously worked against loyalty to the earth, to be the highest and greatest product of Christianity—as it has become secularized." Am I "too botched and bungled," Grant asks, to be "loyal to the earth?" To think "the whole" is, Grant confesses, a "very taxing task" (quoted passages in Davis and Roper 2009b, 967). "Nietzsche's immense contribution as a thinker, for Grant," Athanasiadis (2001, 188) summarizes, "is to bring to light the essence of modernity—namely, the historical way of thinking and existing—with brilliant clarity."

40.   Christian (1995) 2001, xiv. In the interview with Cayley (1995, 64), Grant describes one of these "moving images" at this time: "And then one has one's immediate experience. We were having lots of children then, and I was seeing who ran Dalhousie, how it was run, what it represented in Nova Scotian life, the relation of Nova Scotian life to Toronto and Ottawa life; that was living. At the same time what was basically happening to me was thinking about how Western Europe had been dominated by the idea of history, and history was most consummately thought in a modern way by Hegel. Our lives were not split up, and these two things were going on for me at once." Notice that there here are the two sides of study: the immediacy of experience (both personal and historical, located in but not coinciding with time and place) and sustained slow reflection upon this lived experience, informed as such reflection is by what one is thinking and reading and studying. Grant's remarks also restate the progressivism's emphasis on experience as education and learning through living.

41.   "Our interest in history as a study is directly related to our belief that we are historical beings," Grant ([1969] 2001, 10) argued: "Indeed, in modern thought the idea of

history is everywhere.... Even reason, which was traditionally conceived as transcending all development, has been given its history."

42.   Roberts 1995, 60. Historicism was a central concern of Grant's, one over which he disagreed with the man whom Grant credits with teaching him Hegel, James Doull (see Robertson 2006, 137). In a 1978 conversation with E. Joan O'Donovan, Grant confessed that "he never won an argument with Doull, but was always forced to concede to the superior strength of his friend's mind" (O'Donovan 1984, 28n1). Be that as it may, Grant refused to confer upon history ontological status. As Athanasiadis (2001, 202) reminds, for Grant "technology has become the ontology of our age."

43.   "Grant also accepts Marxism's core tenet," Meynell (2011, 121) asserts, "that overcoming evil requires an acknowledgement that no one is freed unless all are free." Grant repudiated the Hegelian elements of *Philosophy in the Mass Age* in the introduction to the second edition. Recall from the introduction here Sibley's insistence that, despite that repudiation, Hegel remained an influence, even suggesting that "in arguing that we can only fully comprehend modernity by thinking reason and revelation, Plato and Christ, together, Grant still asserts the overarching motive of the Hegelian project. That Grant came to see such a reconciliation to be impossible does not take way from the fact that it reflects his deepest spiritual and intellectual longing" (Sibley 2008, 275). Substitute progressivism for Hegelianism (they are not entirely distinguishable; some would say the former inverts the latter) and I suppose I am close to Sibley, except that I do not accord progressivism (as Sibley does Hegelianism) the status of Grant's "deepest spiritual and intellectual longing" but, instead, the imprinting of his childhood and youth.

44.   In her discussion of cinema, Doane (2003, 88) provides a contrary capacity of contingency: "As the negation of impossibility, contingency is a witness against technology as inexorability, a witness that it could have been otherwise. Through the tensions internal to its own definition, contingency might take up a double function—allowing us to derive what is positive, even utopian, from the cinema while not losing sight of what links it to future technologies and the continuing structuring/systematization of chance."

45.   Roberts 1995, 60. While no key category for Grant, allegory could be said to structure Grant's oeuvre, as he grapples with questions of meaning, contingency, and history. Humanity's "enchantment" by "myth, philosophy or revelation," he observed, was displaced by the demands of democracy (freedom and equality) and the "overcoming of chance" (Grant 1969, 138). Any overarching—for Grant it is eternity, the topic of ch. 7 of this volume—meaning of our lives disappears in modernity's conflation of "freedom" with "will" (142). Emberley ([1994] 2005, lxxvii) employs "meditation" to describe Grant's *Lament for a Nation*; for me the term resonates with the doubleness of allegory (see Pinar 2012, 50), in that it moves us from the "familiar" and "near" to the "most enduring," inviting us to "reflect" on the "tension" between particularity and universality.

46.   See Grant (1965) 2005, 4. In a September 1940 letter to his mother—composed during an air raid in London—the young Grant wonders if "national existence" is "the best way of achieving happiness for Europe" (anticipating by three decades the formation of the European Union) and for Canada, if not part of the British Commonwealth (for which he argues remaining in a 1945 pamphlet; Davis and Emberley 2000b, 97) then "the U.S.A." (Christian 1996d, 64).

47.   It had been the fall of the Progressive Conservative government in 1963 and its replacement by the Liberal Party, and the new Prime Minister Lester Pearson's willingness to accept nuclear warheads and generally accommodate US interests, that provided the political provocation for George Grant's *Lament for a Nation*. It was the "shabby" treatment of PC leader Diefenbaker—of whom Grant was both praising and critical—by the "Canadian elite" that fuelled, Potter (2005, xvi) suggests, Grant's "seething, focused anger." See also Grant (1970) 2005, lxxi.

48.   Grant (1970) 2005, lxxii. "The universalization of technology," Angus (1987, 101) observed, "conceals the concrete and particular which it transforms." Among these is evidently philosophy itself: Heidegger, in 1964, announced the end of philosophy concordant with the triumph of technology, as Kittler notes (see 2013, 299).

49.   Doull 1983, 31.

50.   Sibley (2008, 152) sketches this scenario: "Left alone to face the unknowable will of God, the Puritans sought reassurance of divine favour in mastering nature and solving the practical problems of life.… The result was a restlessness to master the land for the sake of survival and to prove oneself worthy of God's favour. The problem, says Grant, was that this wilful restlessness eventually produced a society with little sense of inwardness or regard for reflection. With the waning of the Christian faith and its lingering moral restraints, what we have is a society of administrators, technicians, and consumers who try to satisfy themselves with ever more complex technological trinkets and a morality made up of banal slogans about values and process."

51.   Emberley (1994) 2005, lxxx.

52.   At first technology "shapes our ends," Cayley (1995, 12) summarizes, "and, finally becomes our end.… [I]n the pursuit of mastery, truth is destroyed." Why? O'Donovan (1984, 166) explains: "For these triumphs of mastery place us in a relation to human and non-human nature that conceals our own essence, that for which we are fitted." As Kittler (2013, 286) reminds: "As Nietzsche, Samuel Butler, and Alan Turing all prophesied, machines will one day assume dominion over the world."

53.   Sikka 1997, 260; she is discussing Heidegger. "Much" of Grant's oeuvre, Reimer (1990, 107) reminds, "clearly bears the imprint of Heidegger's ideas," adding that "[m]ore specifically, however, it is Heidegger's analysis of modern technology itself that shines through most clearly in Grant's writings" (108).

54.   Sikka 1997, 261.

55.   Emberley (1994) 2005, lxxx. "What I mean by technology," Grant told Cayley (1995, 133), "is the unity of art and science. Knowing has been put at the service of making," showing that it "has something to do with will and is a summons rather than a leading forth." As the exercise of will for its own sake, Grant continues, technology becomes nihilistic, a "self-propelling dynamo,"—"when you can do it, you should do it," is the "craziness" of the day (142–3).

56.   Grant (1965) 2005, 52. "With no common political intention beyond the lure of material benefit," Sibley (2008, 166) succinctly summarizes, "Canadians have given themselves over to the imperatives of technology. This ascription to the technological imperative has fated Canada to disappear."

57.   "At any stage of capitalism," Grant reminded, "the interests of all are contractually subordinated to the interests of some" (Davis and Roper 2009b, 288). Intellectually, he noted, "all questions are up for dispute except the proposition that the making of money is a good" (101).

58. Grant discerned, Sibley (2008, 152) suggests, "a deep connection between Protestantism and empirical science.... Protestantism led men away loving contemplation of the world and encouraged them to see the world as something to be mastered according to their will."

59. Grant (1965) 2005, 52n15. "In contrast with the moderns," Flinn (1990, 128) notes, "the ancients may be said to have had a *piety toward nature*, or, in the biblical case, a *reverence for nature.*" The "classical argument" is, Flinn continues, that humanity is "by nature ordered to the good" (129). Technology, Jersak (2012, 59) concludes, has "dimmed our ability to think the Good."

60. Grant (1965) 2005, 53. Nor time, as Angus (1987, 111–2) observes: "Scientific technology abstracts from the 'here and now'; it is precisely the lived dimension of this standardization and direction that is the *specific configuration* behind the contemporary universalization of technology."

61. Technologization and globalization have been intertwined from the outset, even before the Silk Road linked Europe to Asia through the Middle East. Al-i Ahmad's imagery links then and now (when China proposes a new Silk Road; see https://www.newyorker.com/magazine/2018/01/08/a-new-silk-road)—a virtual Silk Road recently denoted a "dark-Net marketplace...a bazaar of drugs and illegal services including, apparently, murder-for-hire...shut down by the FBI in 2013" (Halpern 2015, 55), rueing "an age when the machine not only is itself the greatest feudal lord, sitting on the throne of the Great Khan, but demands security, open doors, open borders, as well as naiveté (or rather credulity), obedience, trust in others, and confidence in the future" (Al-i Ahmad 1984, 68). Globalization, the age of progress, and uncritical acceptance of what technology brings, Al-i Ahmad reminds that these spell the fate of not only the West: "This in an age when the machine demands an end to all borders, an end to all gates, and the internalization of everything and everywhere" (74).

62. Umar 1992, 15.

63. Grant 1966, iv. In modernity, Grant noted, freedom means "the liberty to make happen what we want to happen" (Davis and Roper 2009b, 292; see also 950; 2005b, 230; Davis 2002b, 193). In modernity, Cayley (1995, 28) notes, "there are no longer any purposes outside freedom by which we could determine what freedom is for." The opportunity to "develop freely towards a higher and fuller destiny" (Davis and Emberley 2000b, 112) is a form of freedom Grant does endorse, at least in his *The Empire Yes or No?* (161).

64. Grant (1974) 1998, 2. And science seems a secularization of "Christian providentialism," as Cayley (1995, 10) explains, the conviction that God's will is evident in all occurrences, "summed up in the word progress: that human beings have a right and duty to alleviate evil and remake the world without limit." In contrast to the ancient sense of time as the moving image of eternity, he notes, "the Judeo-Christian view allowed for genuine novelty and progress. Truth had entered time and made of history the sphere in which good would finally overcome evil" (9). In late modernity, however: "Evil no longer means a disharmony of nature and reason, to be corrected so far as may be by the discipline of secular and sacred institutions," Doull (1983, 36) points out, "but is the accidental failure of technology and its agents."

65. Potter (2005, xxiv) points out that Grant's divination of technology as a universal homogenizing force is registered in the mainstream social sciences from the 1950s

to the 1970s. But this force was not contained there, as social science, Grant thought, radiated outward its technological force. The "new social sciences," Grant ([1965] 2005, 78) declared, dissolve "family, Catholicism, and classical education." The "worst abuses of the modern university," he tells Cayley (1996, 165), "have happened in the social sciences."

66.   Davis and Roper 2009b, 1053. Equality is now, Knopff (1992, 69) observes, "an entirely *willed*, rather than a *given*, end."

67.   "High technology," Grant knew, "enables more individuals to pursue their private interests" (Davis and Roper 2005b, 250). But then, he adds, "Most of us have no alternative but to find our freedom in private rather than in public life. This cannot be the era of the democratic citizen" (251).

68.   Grant 1969, 33.

69.   "Christianity in some sense brought individuality into the world," Grant suggests, "in a very strange way. Whether rightly or wrongly is very hard to say" (Davis and Roper 2009b, 766).

70.   Grant 1969, 33.

71.   To the extent such "reform" is associated with the No Child Left Behind (NCLB) Act, it ended in December 2015, as the US Senate approved a "sweeping revision of the contentious NCLB law, sending to President Obama's desk a proposal that ends an era of federal control in education policy after 14 years" (Huetteman 2015, A22). An examination of the first six months of the daily calendar of Trump's Secretary of Education Betsy DeVos discloses, Lipton (2017, A11) reports, that her primary priorities are "voucher programs" and "charter schools," adding that "[h]er calendar is sprinkled with meetings with religious leaders, leading national advocates of vouchers and charter schools, and players involved in challenging state laws that limit the distribution of government funds to support religious or alternative schools." Reforming schools in the United States has now given way to making money from them, that and religious proselytizing, perhaps intersecting enterprises.

72.   "The power of social technology," Knopff (1992, 71) points out, "depends on a behavioural view of life that threatens the dignity and integrity of intellectual life itself. In the end, social technology may confer power on intellectuals at the cost of undermining the very basis of intellectual life."

73.   Fierlbeck 2006, 56. Al-i Ahmad (1984, 31) notes that "the one who created the machine now cries out that it is stifling him."

74.   See Grant 1969, 34.

75.   If the public school as educational institution is dismantled in the United States, professional educators will no longer be required, as the curriculum would be moved online and assignments monitored by underpaid checkers. Such "school reform" is a subspecies of ongoing profit-driven corporate restructuring, downgrading professionals into interchangeable parts, easily replaced and paid accordingly. One hundred years ago the top executive of a business firm typically earned no more than twenty times the average wage of its workers. In recent years in the United States, that multiple has risen to 200, D. Cohen (2009, 30, 33, 34) reminds. The same greed drives the privatization of public schools in the United States today, as public funds are diverted from school children and their teachers into the pockets of profiteers (see S. Saul 2011), disguised as school choice. "I so dislike the exaltation of greed (in the name of liberty) which is so widespread in the English-speaking world that I

would be glad to vote for a non-capitalist party," Grant wrote within months of his death (Christian 1996d, 385).

76. Grant acknowledged that "there is such a thing as a problem to which there is a solution, but mysteries are things one lives in the presence of…. Darkness consists above all in cutting these mysterious out of our lives altogether. I have been trying, in talking about darkness, to hold the mysteries before people…. Darkness also hides problems, and it's very important to say what are real problems. But I think it is bad to look at the world as altogether problems" (Cayley 1995, 170–1). Athanasiadis (2001, 217) emphasizes: "Bringing to light the darkness as darkness was a central task for Grant."

77. Not only or even primarily scientific knowledge, it should go without saying, but also that associated with the humanities and the arts. But given that the former is "our dominant account of knowledge…at the heart and core of our education," Grant noted (Davis and Roper 2009b, 422), this point must be made, over and over again (for a recent rather American example, see Roth 2014). Grant worked within but went beyond academic knowledge, prompted by "great questions" that "research" cannot answer, among them "What is justice? How do we come to know what is truly beautiful? Were do we stand toward the divine? Are there things that can be done that should not be done?" (Davis and Roper 2009b, 422). He reminds that "for centuries" education was "about these questions," carried on by "sustained and disciplined conversation" (422). Consequently "we have to talk with the great minds of the past," (422) Grant admonished.

78. Speaking over the radio in 1954, Grant said: "Now I think that gives us the clue to what wisdom is. We call people wise if they know how to live—if they know what is important in living. And when we speak about living we mean something to do with the whole of the person—that which goes to the very roots of an individual's life" (Davis 2002b, 117). He adds that for those preoccupied with money—"and of course this kind of mood is present in all of us—there is little desire for wisdom, little desire to think what life is about" (117).

79. Continuing with the distinction between "information" and "knowledge," I am reminded of Grant's distinction between knowledge and opinion (like information, always changing): "Knowledge never changes—opinion always" (Davis and Roper 2009b, 938).

80. "When technologies assume dominance over science and aesthetics," Kittler (2013, 89) notes, "only information accounts." Grant thought the emphasis upon "information" would also intensify the tempo of homogenization, as, he noted, "abstracting facts so that the may be stored as 'information' is achieved by classification, and it is the very nature of any classifying to homogenize that may be heterogeneous" (Davis and Roper 2009b, 286). Certainly keywords structure the searches—online and within my notes stored on my computer and in the cloud—I undertake.

81. As Grant complained, "tucked away as part of one's own subjectivity" (Davis and Roper 2009b, 393).

82. "Originally an economic term expressing the relativity of supply and demand," Knopff (1992, 65) affirms, "'value' was transformed by Nietzsche and Weber into a term that now signifies a more general moral relativity." No absolute metaphysical value, but certainly a secular one, as Sibley (2008, 155) suggests: "To know the *use* of things is to know their *value*." Knopff (1992, 63) asserts that the "decay of rights into values in a symptom of the victory of technology over liberalism."

83.   Minogue (1990, 165) comments: "[G]oodness has, as it were, had the *telos* scooped out of it and can now only express preferences. At worse, 'goodness' is replaced by 'value.'"

84.   Cayley (1995, 121–2) asks Grant if "values are willed meanings," to which Grant replies "yes," adding: "You cannot look at human life without some idea of wiling and choosing and freedom; but in the ancient world these ideas of willing and choosing and freedom were seen in terms of the purposes that were given to man in the world. The central thing was to know those purposes and then one had freedom. Once you have gotten rid of the universe of meaning, then everything becomes our making, our willing, our choosing." Grant's critique of "values" had shifted over time. Early on he accepted such language (see Davis and Emberley 2000b, 161; Davis and Roper 2005b, 235), but by the time he is teaching Nietzsche at McMaster Grant tells students that "that the language of values is unequivocally an atheist language" (Davis and Roper 2009b, 966), a view apparently contrary to his spiritual teacher Simone Weil, who, Thibon ([1947] 2002, xxxv) suggests, regarded "values" as "intermediaries" between here and eternity.

85.   The private sphere of freedom is also where thought is relegated. In "capitalist democracy," Grant (1986, 10) notes, "differences" over "practice" matter; "theoretical differences" are best kept "private."

86.   Pérez-Gómez (2016, 4) reminds that the "public realm is inevitably the space where we appear for others as embodied consciousness, and...it is crucial to our self-understanding." Many (among them Jürgen Habermas) attribute a normative dimension to the public sphere as it housed the liberal idea of public discussion of different viewpoints. With Herf (1984, 24n17), "I am using the term in a strictly descriptive sense to refer to a forum in which politics is discussed without all points of view necessarily being represented." In a public sphere as market, politics becomes "retail" and public dialogue devolves into advertising (as McLuhan, in 1974, pointed out; see Cavell 2002, 186), often of the "false" kind. The point is private accumulation, not sacrifice for the common good, these last two concepts incomprehensible in the public sphere as market.

87.   Grant 1969, 26. "Pluralism" and "tolerance" for Grant are both "dogmas," Lampert (1978, 188) argues, "certainties that we uniformly and automatically assent to by our very way of being. Such absolutes constitute the public religion of our age even though they are infrequently recognized." Almost two decades later, also reflecting on Grant's analysis, Heyking and Cooper (2006, 178–9) write: "What remained of public life for the masses consisted of little more than sexually driven entertainment and political demagoguery, which was also served up as titillation and entertainment." They note that "Grant had in mind Kennedy and [P. E.] Trudeau" as emptying "public discourse of meaning," but of course I have Trump on my mind as the endgame, as even "pluralism" and "tolerance" are displaced by narcissism in public life as "reality TV."

88.   I am married to another man—Jeffrey D. Turner—and I am grateful for the legal protections and obligations its legalization affords. At the same time, a homosexual liaison connotes no insurrectionary potential, as it did during the days of "gay liberation," when sexual preference promised political protest; see, for instance, Marshall 1997. When returned from the social surface—politics, including identity politics—to subjectivity, perhaps another order of significance is revealed, perhaps even spiritual.

89.   "We purchase tolerance," Dart suggests, "at the price of relativizing all things" (Dart and Jersak 2011, 62).

90.   Not only gender becomes incorporated in the homogenous standardized state, culture does as well. This point Sibley (2008, 277) makes juxtaposing Grant with philosopher Charles Taylor: "Where Taylor sees multiculturalism as a means to help disparate groups find their identity within the whole, Grant sees multiculturalism as an expression of modernity's universalizing and homogenizing consequences. Multiculturalism is another means by which liberalism subsumes different cultures into the technological mixing bowl where once-authentic ways of life are reduced to cultural kitsch."

91.   "Everything must be said," Kittler (2013, 100) asserts, "because there is nothing to say."

92.   Kittler ascribes to a German company the creation of anti-encryption and decrypting machines (manufactured during the Second World War) and the invention of the first computer (although he acknowledges Alan Turing too; see Kittler 2013, 163, 186), adding: "Mass communication, in other words, was first admitted when it was a matter of consuming or hearing everything, and no longer listening in on anything" (158). Decades ago Grant was alert to the prospect of surveillance, noting that "[i]n Ontario there are cards on which local school authorities can assess children as to their intellectual 'skills' and 'behaviour.' This information is retained by computers" (Davis and Roper 2009b, 286). I appreciate too his quote marks: the jargon of "skills" remain omnipresent.

93.   Two threats to contemporary society—terrorists and child predators—have rendered retreat from the public sphere suspect.

94.   For Heidegger, Kleinberg (2005, 15) points out, *das Man* is an "essential structure" of *Dasein* because it is what accords *Dasein* its "values, norms, and practices." While the "basis for all shared practices," Kleinberg continues, "it is [also] the locus of conformity wherein the individual *Dasein* loses itself in the anonymity of shared practices" (16). The "rationality" and "universal principles" of the present age strengthen the "grip" of "das Man," Kleinberg explains, "obscuring" (16) the character, indeed the ontology, of *Dasein*. The materialization of that "rationality" is, in part, technology. Charles Larmore (2010, 142), in contrast, contests the idea that being authentic requires us to be "independent of what conventions and borrowed models have made of us." For him, authenticity turns on the self's relationship to itself (173).

95.   See Lasch 1984.

96.   Kleinberg 2005, 16.

97.   Including intervention in the 2016 US presidential election through the propagation of pseudo-news. Grant could have predicated this calamity, as he had become convinced, O'Donovan (1984, vii) notes, "that technological freedom will not admit of limitation, is inimical to restraint." At least by human beings, contrary to Andrew Feenberg (2010, 153), who affirms the autonomy of human engagement with machines (and computers specifically) when he writes: "Processes of interpretation are central there." Grant is not sure. "The truth is," Athanasiadis (2001, 201) observes, "that the ways computers are to be used are built into them."

98.   Reviewing the evidently escalating intensity of political exchange on the Internet, Manjoo (2015, B6) acknowledges that there is no culture of "nuance" or "complexity." He recalls the Internet's inception, when its "pioneers" promised that the

Web would expand "democratic discourse" (B6). In his 1996 "Declaration of the Independence of Cyberspace," addressed to the governments of the presumably disappearing "industrial world," John Perry Barlow, the Internet-freedom activist, wrote: "We will create a civilization of the Mind in Cyberspace" (quoted in Manjoo 2015, B6). Almost twenty years after Mr. Barlow's declaration, Manjoo notes, "it's obvious the effect that the Internet has had on the world's discourse has been more mixed" (B6).

99. Grant 1969, 26–7. The "political" character of modernity is itself obscured by modernity, Grant suggests, nowhere more evident than in the "inevitable relation between dynamic technology and imperialism" (72–3). In his *Lament for A Nation*, Grant ([1965] 2005, 9n1) defended his use of the phrase "American Empire" by noting "an empire does not have to wield direct political control over colonial countries." Indeed, decades before the "retreat of the state" argument (see, e.g., Strange 1996), Grant ([1965] 2005, 42) knew that the "capitalist system" renders "national boundaries...only matters of political formality." Is this prescience in part an acknowledgement of empire as a "non-place," as Hardt and Negri (2000, xiv) later suggest, as "characterized fundamentally by a lack of boundaries; Empire's rule has no limits." To guarantee "justice...for all peoples," Hardt and Negri continue, "the single power is given the necessary force to conduct, when necessary, 'just wars' at the borders against the barbarians and internally against the rebellious" (11). But all violence is not directed elsewhere, as "the totalizing social processes of Empire" (10) ensure that standardization—leaving no child behind—will be enforced at home. "One thing that is consistently forgotten among leftists of a certain class, the Anglophobe leftists," Grant wrote in a November 1942 journal entry, "is that English imperialism is not the only side to the life of England, and that English capitalists have performed almost as great an exploitation within their own country as without, that the average Englishman has had little benefit from empire other than fighting to maintain it" (Christian 1996d, 101). At home and abroad, then, Grant (1969, 73) discerned an "inevitable relation between dynamic technology and imperialism" accompanying "the practical tumult of the technological society" (Grant [1974] 1998, 88).

100. This is Grant's (1969, 28) phrase.

101. Grant 1969, 28.

102. Grant 1969, 2. "I am not such a believer in progress," Grant made plain, "and therefore do not assume that the thoughts of a generation ago are less valid than ours" (Davis 2002b, 206). As Benedetti (2005, 205) confirms, "modernity conceives of thought as a continual supersession of itself."

103. Grant 1969, 24. "Under the sway of modern epistemology," Sibley (2008, 149) summarizes, "even reason comes to be an instrument to satisfy subjective purposes." Is any activity exempt? Forty years ago Grant (1969, 24) named "art and sexuality," but I suspect he might today exclude these as well, given their commodification. Benedetti (2005, 115), for instance, references "modern artistic logic and its compulsion for the new," a compulsion that can encourage a very wide sort of sometimes dangerous sexual practices. "Repressive desublimation" (for a succinct summary see Savran 1998, 34–6) was a key concept in his time. Grant ([1969] 2001, 26) associated desublimation with the human will and the emancipation of passion; Marcuse had argued that desublimation could also be "repressive." But that politically reactionary risk is ignored by the confidence many express in electronic media, that an

"electronic enlightenment will overcome the old anal rationality of print and speech" (49). Grant may be referencing McLuhan here, who thought not only linear rationality but also nationalism itself had been a "product of print" (Cavell 2002, 186).

104. "To accept a void in ourselves," Weil ([1947] 2002, 11) said, "is supernatural."

105. And so, Grant knew, "the great question is one's egocentricity" (Davis and Roper 2009b, 127). Within modernity, Athanasiadis (2001, 81) suggests that "[f]reedom is crushed in the human spirit, not in terms of human dignity, humiliation or the capacity to transcend one's social assumptions, but rather in limitations to one's material and sexual appetites—in terms of a narcissistic injury, rather than in the affliction of the soul." What puzzled Grant, Sibley (2008, 153) suspects, "is how Calvinism's worldly asceticism, its attempt to manifest the kingdom of God in earthly good words, was reduced to secularized hedonism. How did the desire to obey God's will and self-disciplined practicality descend into individualistic narcissism? Or, to ask the question in another way, how were the principles of inward freedom and individuality that came to North America with the Puritans reduced to an egocentrism that regards freedom as merely the capacity to satisfy material desires? Grant finds the answer in Protestant theology's denigration of reason and the European contemplative tradition." As a young man, sexual adventure became for me a secular spiritual quest. For one brought up to care only about behaviour, changing behaviour became the route back to inwardness.

106. As Angus (1997, 59) observes, "A medium of communication is thus both a technology and a social relation," including an intrasubjective one, as Grant notes. Exhibiting a "public technicism and a private existentialism," Grant described the young of his era (Christian 1996d, 259). Technologism is not confined to North America of course; one hundred years ago it played a prominent role in the Weimar Republic and in its dissolution (see Peukert 1992, 241–2).

107. Nusselder's 2009, 23.

108. Grant (1969) 2001, 56. In modernity, O'Donovan (1984, 114) notes, willing "also pertains to the unique character of our action, directed to the continual creation of novelty." Baudelaire, Benedetti (2005, 105) reminds, discerned "a substantial affinity between the phenomenon of fashion and the logic of modernity." The "new" can amuse, titillate and mutilate. "Media enact a historical escalation of violence," Kittler (2013, 76) thought, "and they force those affected into total mobilization."

109. Grant (1965) 2005, 71. Much of Grant's thought during the second half of the 1960s was devoted, O'Donovan (1984, 89) notes, "to exploring the totalistic and nihilistic directions of the modern principle of freedom, which is, at one and the same time, the historicist and the technological universal…. From 1964 onward Grant examines two horns of the dilemma of autonomous freedom: on the one hand, existential despair [now rage—political, cultural, interpersonal], and on the other, immersion in the objectified world [non-online]."

110. Grant 1969, 76.

111. The Tyler rationale (Tyler 1949, 1)—with its four questions: (1) What educational purposes should the school seek to attain? (2) What educational experiences can be provided that are likely to attain the purposes? (3) How can these educational experiences be effectively organized? (4) How can we determine whether these purposes are being attached? —is yet another version of a decades-old procedure referenced earlier, for instance, in Hilda Taba's 1932 *The Dynamics of Education* (see 172, 246).

112. Callahan 1962.
113. Potter 2005, xliii. "Reason is just a little extra for calculation and for getting us comfortable and doing technology and things like that," Grant complained, adding that "modern science, which was an enormous rational activity, destroyed the idea of man as the rational animal, as the animal who is fundamentally called to a destiny which is more than instinct" (Cayley 1995, 114)."Our making," Grant reminds, "takes place within an ultimate givenness" (Davis 2002b, 60).
114. Grant (1974) 1998, 3.
115. Grant endorsed Heidegger's assertion that (in Grant's words) "capitalism and communism are just predicates of the subject technology" (Cayley 1995, 125). Coming from either communism or capitalism, colonization meant technologization, Al-i Ahmad (1984, 87) knew, approvingly quoting Charles Malik, the Lebanese philosopher and former president of the United Nations General Assembly: "Roads, dams, efficiency and the smile of rulers—that is all that matters; but spirit, freedom, joy, happiness, truth, man—that never enters the mind. A world of perfect technicians is the aim, not a world of human beings, let alone beings divine."
116. "Information" concerns "objects," Grant (1986, 24) points out, and belongs to those sciences that "summons subjects" as objects. In its very nature information is "homogenizing."
117. Potter 2005, xliii.
118. "We represent things to ourselves as potential resources," Grant appreciated (Davis and Roper 2009b, 1022).
119. Krauss 2007, 30.
120. (quoted in Potter 2005, xliii). "It has been made clear by both Grant and Heidegger," Nicholson (2006, 333) explains, "that technology is not the mere assembly of machines and devices that we make use of; beyond that, it is the form taken on by reality itself in the modern age, that reaches right into ourselves and so comes to constitute our way of thinking as well as acting." See too Angus 1997, 92; Planinc 1992, 40.
121. Silverman (2009, 107) recalls a 1945 Heidegger presentation ("What Are Poets For?") to a small group of listeners, in which he suggested that what "threatens" humanity "with death, and indeed with the death of his own nature, is the unconditional character of mere willing in the sense of purposeful self-assertion in everything." Such instrumental—technological—rationality has come to dominate thinking, now reduced to everyday calculation of self-interest, dignified in academic disciplines such as economics. Applied economics assumes, Coyle (2007, 124) asserts, "rational and self-interested behaviour by individuals."
122. Potter 2005, xlv.
123. *Webster's New Collegiate Dictionary*, 575.
124. Potter (2005, xlv) points out that Grant's analysis of technology as "universalizing" and "homogenizing," dissolving "all particularity," remains uppermost in today's anti-globalization activism, concerned that the "cultural uniformity that has swept through North America will soon extend to the rest of the planet." But like the Occupy movement all dissent within the technological statement is converted to assimilable form. "Dissent is built into the fabric of the modern system," Grant ([1965] 2005, 78) saw. "We bureaucratize it as much as everything else." That is to say, we incorporate dissent into existing structures, such as spectacle, as in the age of Trump.

125. In an August 1948 letter to his mother, Grant confesses that "the thought of the [academic] year ahead of pouring oneself out, I do not face with even any excitement. I guess it will come. But there is such an endless sense of what one could do, in the marvellous opportunity, if one only had more singleness of purpose and unity of character" (Christian 1996d, 150).

126. As Kroker (1984, 60) points out: "[B]ecause we live now, fully, within the designed environment of the technological sensorium…. We now take our 'environment' with us in the form of technical 'extensions" of the human body or senses. The techno-structure is both the lens through which we experience the world, and, in fact, the 'anxious object' with which human experience has become imperceptibly, almost subliminally, merged."

127. Grant was no fan of McLuhan's work, Davis and Roper (2005b, 752n2) tell us, explaining why Grant reference McLuhan infrequently. But references him he does (see, e.g., Davis and Roper 2009b, 491, 903; Christian and Grant 1998b, 99). There is one letter (dated April 19, 1978) to McLuhan (see Christian 1996d, 301), wherein he expresses his "admiration" for him. Davis and Roper (2005b, 752n2) tell us that Grant sometimes referred to followers as "McLuhanatics," a term evidently in circulation at the University of Toronto. In addition to Kroker's study, see Stamps 1995 for an extended analysis of McLuhan and Grant. See also Christian and Grant 1998a, 23.

128. Kroker 1984, 61. Kaethler (2009, 33) puts the point simply and forcefully: "We are technology; we think technology; we breathe technology; we worship technology."

129. As a structure-enabling subjective reconstruction, non-coincidence (see Pinar 2011, 158n13) is the space of freedom, wherein—I'm recalling Potter's phrasing quoted earlier in the main text—thought and action can occur. It is the space study can cultivate. Such freedom includes, as Grant rues, "the liberty to be indifferent to the good" (Davis 2002b, 60).

130. A point made by Pérez-Gómez (2016, 1), who argues (discussing architecture) "that environment *matters* in ways that perhaps we have not fully fathomed. It matters not only as a material ecology that must obviously be kept alive for the survival of our species, but also because it is nothing less than *a constituent part of our consciousness.*"

131. Also informed by Heidegger, Aoki's analysis of technology merits a separate section; suffice to say here that he concludes his essay by recounting a case in which life itself depends on technology. "Carol," Aoki ([1987] 2005, 157) informs us, "has been for 12 years a child of haemo-dialysis technology. She and her three siblings have been sustained by a dialysis machine at the University of Alberta Hospital…. She recently wrote of her experiences with technology: 'We acknowledge our indebtedness to technology; we refuse to be enslaved by technology.'" In another essay, Aoki ([1993] 2005, 292) reflects: "As I contemplate my relationship to technology, I affirm that it is both a blessing and a burden." Whatever his intentions, the terms "blessing" and "burden" convey Christian connotations, interesting in light of Grant's acknowledgement that technology, however it has undermined hierarchies and ended parochialism, cannot communicate spirituality (see Emberley [1994] 2005, lxxxi).

132. Emberley (1994) 2005, lxxxi.

133. It was McLuhan, Richard Cavell (2002, 170) points out, who "sought to convey the notion that the world around us, and the lived experience of it, had become

artifactual through the effects of media, such that nature could be said to have collapsed into culture." This seems to me more like an acknowledgement of pervasive narcissism than it does historical or empirical fact. With climate change, for instance, nature isn't collapsing into culture, but vice versa.

134. Grant (1965) 2005, 73.

135. Grant (1965) 2005, 71.

136. Grant (1965) 2005, 63. "Cultural/bio-conservatism," Bowers (1995, 165) taught, "involves a way of understanding time that is more attuned to the cycles of the different elements in the biome."

137. Emberley (1994) 2005, lxxxi. Or so it seems. "At the individual level," Sibley (2008, 117) summarizes, "the subordination of the private realm to the productive and administrative requirements of a technological order has meant that the formation of individual character, the attempt to manifest the good in one's daily life, is sacrificed to the imperatives of technological efficiency."

138. Christian (1996a, 177). I emphasize "relationship" as affirming non-coincidence with machines, washing machines being less threatening than computers and handheld devices, and certain medical products and procedures—while dangerous—potentially life-saving, as Grant noted: "When my children are sick, I want penicillin" (Davis and Roper 2009b, 1001). Grant imagined that the ancient political philosophers were more cautious about technology than we moderns have become, realizing, as they did, that among inventions "some led to good, some led to bad, and they had to be very cautiously controlled" (Cayley 1995, 78), adding that without certain inventions (like stoves, electricity) he and his wife and their six children would suffer, telling Cayley (1995, 79) "I don't want to...imply that we can all go back to a world that included slavery."

139. Christian 1996a, 177. In addition to the exhilaration associated with technology, there has been, Trilling (1972, 126) points out, also an "anxiety about the machine...commonplace in nineteenth-century moral and cultural thought." Of course the First World War and his father's injury made such anxiety personal for Grant.

140. "Men are going to do anything they can do," Grant feared, "and nothing that any of us can do will stop them" (Davis and Roper 2005b, 256).

141. Harvey (2010, 120) summarizes succinctly the sharply divided situation in which techno-capitalism leaves us: "On the negative side we have not only the periodic and often localized economics crises that have punctuated capitalism's evolution, including inter-capitalist and inter-imperialist world war, problems of environmental degradation, loss of biodiverse habits, spiralling poverty among burgeoning populations, neo-colonialism, serious crises in public health, alienations and social exclusions galore and the anxieties of insecurity, violence and unfulfilled desires. On the positive some of us live in a world where standards of material living and well-being have never been higher, where travel and communications have been revolutionized and physical (though not social) spatial barriers to human interactions have been much reduced, where medical and biomedical understandings offer for many a longer life, where huge, sprawling and in many respects spectacular cities have been built, where knowledge proliferates, hope springs eternal and everything seems possible (from self-cloning to space travel)." Grant's genius was to think both negative and positive sides together.

142. Willinsky 2006, 113.

143. Grant sees no promise in progressivism, as Sibley (2008, 149) summarizes: "Lacking any history prior to the age of progress, North America incarnates more than any other society the values and principles of progressivism, including a largely unquestioned subscription to mass production and its techniques, standardized consumption and education, and hedonistic entertainment." Certainly that is the underside of modernity which progressivism (in its various guises) critiques.

144. Two years later, it is not clear what "season" it is, as Egypt is once again engulfed in protests and Syria's civil war threatens not only to destroy that nation but destabilize its neighbours. The "Arab uprisings," Anne Barnard (2013, A10) reports, were "interconnected," as "movements inspire and instruct one another." If so, that suggests that the information technologies have played a role, although perhaps no uniform role with predictable outcomes. Activists, Barnard (2013, A10) continues, regard events as structured by both "domestic politics" and "foreign interests," not by a "uniform regional narrative," and thus not judgeable as a whole.

145. Davis and Roper 2009b, 295; see also 287.

146. Quoted in N. Cohen 2011, B3.

147. Quoted in N. Cohen 2011, B3. Rocha (2017, 13) points out that "when we are here [online], we are not elsewhere. Depending on where elsewhere might be, we can begin to see how—and perhaps why—this place is not a place at all: it is an anti-place, a site of virtual reality that exempts us from the real." Discussing the colonized, which is to say the technologized, Al-i Ahmad (1984, 92) decries the subjective consequences: "He is like a particle of dust suspended in the void, or a shaving floating on the water. He has severed his ties with the depths of society, culture, and tradition. He is no link between antiquity and modernity, nor even a dividing line between old and new. He is a thing with no ties to the past and no perception of the future." Seeking "ease," the technologized is "without belief or conviction, to such an extent that he not only believes in nothing, but also does not actively disbelieve in anything.... But everywhere is he is a spectator.... He never invests anything of himself" (94)—that last sentence the inverse condition of subjective presence.

148. Quoted in N. Cohen 2011, B3.

149. See, for instance, Watson 2007, 355, 406, 411. Writing about Innis in 1980 in the *Globe and Mail*, Grant acknowledged Innis as a "Canadian who was outstanding at what he did, by any standards anywhere in the world. He became a famous historian of the fur, fish and lumber trades early in his life. But he did not stick with his specialism. By the end of his life he was writing books which looked deeply at the question: what is a human being?" (Davis and Roper 2009b, 903).

150. Quoted in N. Cohen 2011, B3.

151. Streitfeld 2017, A1.

152. Streitfeld 2017, A1.

153. Quoted in Streitfeld 2017, A1.

154. Streitfeld 2017, A1.

155. Streitfeld 2017, A1.

156. Soon after white supremacists marched in Charlottesville, Virginia (murdering one counter-protestor), Sisario (2017, B5) reported that the music-streaming service Spotify deleted from its website several songs that it said incited hatred and violence. Such music (sometimes called hatecore), Sisario continued, had circulated for years, citing the 2012 assassination of six people at a Sikh temple in the United States by a

white supremacist who played guitar in hatecore bands. According to the Southern Poverty Law Center, fifty-four such bands sold their music on iTunes. While Apple has removed that music from its iTunes store, Spotify and Amazon are, according to the center, "slow to act." Sisario concludes: "Hatecore songs may make up a tiny fraction of the content available on YouTube, but the site has also been criticized as a gathering place for far-right agitators and an outlet for ISIS recruitment" (B5).

157.   "Call *presentism*," McDaniel (2016, 259) suggests, "the view that that presently existing entities are the only entities that there are." As such, it erases the sense of the present as wedged in between past and future, as having a multi-dimensional meaning, that it is a "situation" in any phenomenological sense (Pinar et al. 1995, 412).

158.   Grant (1965) 2005, 78. "Mathematizable research has been very deep in the social sciences," Grant reminded. "I mean, mathematizable research can tell you a lot about the planets…. But, in the social sciences, mathematizable research has been so pervasive that those people who haven't fallen into it have often fallen into some other kind of mumbo-jumbo. Now this is also true of the humanities, but there at least there is a given corpus" (Cayley 1995, 166–7).

159.   As the epicentre of modernity for the last one hundred years, the United States is the site of unlimited technological development. "In the U.S.," Doull (1983, 39) observers, "where it occurs in its purest and simplest form, it is commonly assumed that technology and a free naturalistic individuality can sustain each other." As educational research and school reform in the United States testify, that assumption is false.

160.   See, for instance, S. Saul 2011 and Spring 2012. Betsy DeVos, the US secretary of education, P. Cohen (2017, A1) reports, has been "an ardent campaigner for privately run schools and has investments in for-profit educational ventures."

161.   Grant complained about the influence of business from the onset of his career: "But we live under the continual tyranny of the rich—the oh so ignorant rich" (Christian 1996d, 172). But, he had written earlier, "No wonder the businessmen walk over teachers. Most of them are such ninnies" (Christian 1996d, 154).

162.   "It is hard indeed," Grant (1966, vi) observes in another context, "to overstate the importance of faith in progress through technology to those brought up in the main stream of North American life. It is the very ground of their being. The loss of this faith for a North American is equivalent to the loss of himself and the knowledge of how to live."

163.   Grant 1986, 15. For Grant, Sibley (2008, 151) states: "Technology is not simply oriented to freeing humans from nature, an expression of will and hubristic dominance; it is also an expression of charity."

164.   Grant 1986, 16. "Indeed," Flinn (1990, 123) comments, "it might be said that North Americans think about technology technologically."

165.   Jünger (quoted in Kaes, Jay, and Dimendberg 1995, 371). (We shall meet Jünger again in ch. 3.) "The danger of technology," Angus (1997, 93) appreciates, "is that it conceals its own essence—the world revealing itself as resource." For Reimer (1990, 115), "the danger inherent in technology" includes its effect on the body—the "sensory is de-essentialised"—and its idolatry, e.g., its adoration of "the will to power." It also, Reimer suggests (referencing a posthumously published interview with Heidegger), "uproots us from earth and leaves us with purely technical relationships…. Technology leaves us homeless" (119). How? Grant understood, R. Peters

(2006, 249) notes, that "technology as ontology produced a way of thinking that sought only man's comfort through control." Absolute control it sometimes seems.

166. Grant 1986, 16.

167. Ling (2008, 3) argues that "mobile communication...supports better contact within the personal sphere, sometimes at the expense of interaction with those who are co-present," but in doing so supports "social cohesion" (5). Ling's study is of cellphone use; Keller (2012, A19) reports that online sites—Facebook in particular—leave many "lonely, and narcissistic and actually ill."

168. "[A] suppression of the here and now," Angus (1987, 112) observes, a substitution of temporally empty space for historical place and time in my terms.

169. In France, a new law went into effect on January 1, 2017, that discourages employers from contacting employees during evenings at home, vacations, or Sundays. "Employers are more and more connected during hours outside of the office," Myriam El Khomri, the minister of labour, said last year, justifying the need for the law. "The boundary between professional and personal life has become tenuous," and cases of burnout are becoming more prevalent, she said (Rubin 2017, A6).

170. Grant 1986, 16.

171. Another instance of Grant's prescience is evident in a December 1941 letter to his mother, in which—I am writing this at the onset of the second month of the Trump presidency in the United States and the month the United Kingdom invoked article 50 of the Treaty of the European Union, toward Brexit—Grant appreciates, "although we have created a great industrialized world, it hasn't become positive for many" (Christian 1996d, 94). That resentment is painfully present today.

172. Grant 1986, 17.

173. For Lipari (2014, 186) *"bearing witness"* means to not "turn away from suffering but to look at it unflinchingly, lost neither in its ubiquity nor in its singularity. It is a kind of looking and listening without objectification or appropriation, but with a kind of awareness that makes space for the unthinkable, the unimaginable, the other."

174. Paras 2006, 85.

175. Thanks to Alan Turing, Kittler (2013, 178) suggests, "knowledge disappeared from human heads and moved into the small machines that (as technicians put it neatly) 'implement' it." Kittler adds: "Yet even though literature about computers grows daily—in professional journals, social critiques, software advertising, and popular writings—silence prevails about their military history" (180). In sync with that history, computers, Grant suggested, "can only be used in homogenizing ways" (Davis and Roper 2009b, 286).

176. Bowers (2000, 22) worries that "computers lead us to substitute decontextualized ways of thinking about the world for the sensory encounters with the natural world that intertwine our lives." Such dissociation occurs not only vis-à-vis the natural world, but within culture as well. "[T]he the electronic 'community,'" he argues, "is populated by individuals who are free both of the moral constraints and the wisdom contained in the intergenerational narratives of the cultural group" (46). Grant (1986, 26) notes that "computers...exclude certain forms of community and permit others." Such intergenerational isolation spells narcissism, implied in Bowers (2000, 47) observation that "[j]ust as data should be viewed as a degraded from of knowledge, computer-mediated communication should be viewed as a degraded form of symbolic interaction—one that reinforces the rootless individual who is comfortable

with the expressions of self-creation that the computer industry finds profitable to encourage." Concerning education specifically, Bowers cites evidence from the mid-1990s questioning the positive correlation between technology and learning (111). More recent reports—see, e.g., Ripley (2016, A3)—repeat those Bowers cites. Despite the evidence, that faith remains unbroken and aggressively promoted, as in the United States, where curriculum is developed by corporate employees—not academicians—and moved online (Spring 2012).

177. Grant 1986, 19. For Kittler, Gumbrecht (2013, 318) reminds, any idea of an "interface" between humanity and computers is "dangerous," a point Grant also emphasized, noting that the "simple characterization of the computer as a neutral instrument makes it sound as if instruments are now what instruments have always been and so hides from us what it is completely novel about modern instrumentality" (Davis and Roper 2009b, 285); namely, that we are becoming the devices we thought we were "using."

178. Greene (1973, 6) emphasized—almost as the aim of education—"the possibility of arousing individuals to wide-awakeness, to 'thinking' in Arendt's sense about their own commitments and action wherever they work and make their lives."

179. Davis and Roper 2009b, 284.

180. Studying Grant, it can seem that transcendence is foreclosed by technology—clearly, it often is—but Christian (1990, 193–4) reminds us "that Grant spoke merely of the improbability, not the impossibility of living the transcendence of justice in the modern world."

181. Davis and Roper 2009b, 284.

182. Emberley 1990, xvi. Kaethler (2009, 41) emphasizes, that "spiritual needs cannot be met by technology."

183. Kaethler 2009, 38.

184. As we will see in the next chapter. Why write about the Weimar Republic in a book about George Grant? "The very intricacy and variety of Weimar culture," Detlev J. K. Peukert (1992, 164) explains, "and the tensions it contained, have made it the archetypal emblem of what we understand by modernity."

185. Davis and Roper 2009b, 284.

186. Davis and Roper 2009b, 284–5.

187. Ronell 2003, 97. Discussing the work of Paul de Man, Ronell suggests that "technology's essence is disclosed in its moments of breakdown...the fact that 'l'effet machinal' is responsible for effects of meaning generated by sheer contingency, elements of uncontrol and improvisation" (98). Such disruption—the "technicity of a power failure" (97)—denotes, one might say, "the experience of permanent parabasis" (99). "Can this be an experience of ecstatic self-departure...a desubjectivizing rupture [producing] a medused effect, terrorizing and petrifying the other[?]," Ronell asks (193). Can it, she continues, underwrite "the radical vulnerability of the psychologically uninsured[?]" (209). Probably such "rupture" underwrites nothing but rupture.

188. Grant 1969, 142.

189. After achieving access to her childhood experience through painting, Alice Miller abandoned any concept of pedagogy, asserting that all pedagogies serve the needs of adults, not of children; she substitutes the concept "support" (Capps 1995, 8). Interesting in light of Grant's later critique of abortion, Miller is critical of opponents of abortion, who, she points out, substitute abstract conceptions of life for "lived life,"

thereby distracting our attention away from the need to work toward the protection of the right of already-born children to a life without parental violence. Miller points out as well that those who oppose abortion are often supporters of "traditional" childrearing practices (what she terms "poisonous pedagogies"), characterized by abusive ideas such as "spoil the rod and spare the child." These people exhibit no commitment to protect the children they insist be born from parental, social, and economic violence. They say they "love" the unborn child, but to claim to "love" without at the same time condemning traditional childrearing practices discloses the same confusion of love and cruelty that these "old-fashioned" childrearing practices themselves reproduce (see Capps 1995, 19).

190. Grant 1969, 78. "If there are genuinely courageous ways to face a reality in which the old forms of courage have to give way," Jonathan Lear (2006, 88) appreciates, "this must involve a process in which psychological structure is altered." In my terms, becoming historical—attuned to the moment in which one is enmeshed—requires subjective reconstruction, not to opportunistically take advantage but to attune oneself to what is ethically appropriate to do.

191. In contrast to Freud, for instance, who, Elsaesser (2009, 93) reminds us, was a "notorious technophobe, who, according to his son, hated both the radio and the telephone…. Freud's obdurate refusal to have anything to do with cinema…is well documented." While "refusal" is not an option for many of us, the great man's contempt for technology was no eccentricity.

192. As Emberley ([1994] 2005, lxxxi–xxxiii) points out. "Technology has undermined the independence of the indispensable prerequisites for political life," Angus (1997, 77) emphasizes. How? "Through the bringing of private life into the productive and administrative exigencies of technological society," he explains, "the formation of individual character has been entirely ceded to the imperatives of the technological conquest of nature."

193. In its "profound past form," Grant (1986, 24) reminds, "heterogeneity" conveyed "autochthony." From "autos" (self) and "chthon" (earth), we have now become machinic, everywhere the same: as O'Donovan (1984, 138) notes, "the computer *can only be used* in homogenizing ways."

194. Even as sympathetic a student of Grant as Cayley (1995, 44) judged Grant "too "starkly black and white," that "whatever the destination of technological society turns out to be, so far, it is not well described as the universal and homogenous state. The postmodern condition has turned out to be stranger, more various, and more 'historical,' in terms of the persistence of religion, war, and class conflict, than Grant foresaw." Such is the case twenty years on—I am writing during spring 2017—but to be fair to Grant he never announced a timeline for this "universal" state to become installed, nor did he exclude the possibility, indeed the inevitability, of violent resistance to it. On the other hand, in that interview with Cayley (1995, 107) Grant did suggest that "in Central Ontario particularly, we live in an advanced, industrial-technological society as much as Chicago or Buffalo do." From 1972 to 1985 I lived in Rochester, New York; for the last several years there I enjoyed a *pied–à–terre* in Toronto. Perhaps "much as" is accurate, but at that time I focused on the differences, and those were there.

195. Grant 1969, 34.

196. Grant 1969, 27.

197. Emberley (1994) 2005, lxxxiv.
198. Emberley (1994) 2005, lxxxiv.
199. Emberley (1994) 2005, lxxxiv.
200. Grant (1965) 2005, 41.
201. Christian 1996a, 358. Early on—this in a letter to his mother in April 1952—Grant though a prudential use of technology might be possible: "After the extremely hard year and Sheila with three children we thought a car would free us. Yet, we both feel guilty" (Christian 1996d, 172). That "guilt" presaged his later thought, focused in the following on the computer. "In short," Grant appreciated, "computers do not present us with neutral means for building any kind of society. All their alternative ways lead us towards the universal and homogeneous state" (Davis and Roper 2009b, 290).
202. "The question of technology," Angus (1997, 92) notes, "is often posed as: How can we bring technology under control? However, 'bringing under control' is an attitude inherent in technology…. Similarly, if we say 'technology must serve human purposes,' we fail to see the 'serving human purposes' is characteristic of technology."
203. Contemplating computer technology twenty-five years ago, Ted Aoki ([1987] 2005, 153) sounds a little like George Grant: "How, then, is this essence [of computer technology] revealed? It is revealed as an enframing, the ordering of both man and nature that aims at mastery. This enframing reduces man and beings to a sort of 'standing reserve,' a stockpile of resources to be at hand and on call for utilitarian ends…. But by so becoming, man tends to be forgetful of his own essence, no longer able to encounter himself authentically. Hence, what endangers man where revealing as ordering holds sway is his inability to present other possibilities of revealing. In this, it is not computer technology that is dangerous; it is the essence of computer technology that is dangerous." Aoki's distinction reminds us that it is the way of being technology invites that threatens revelation and that it is our responsibility to decline or least try to renegotiate the terms of the invitation. Still, the threat becomes "revealed" through the machine, and our "inability to present other possibilities of revealing" becomes installed (like a virus). That means that, as Grant—and later C. A. Bowers (1995, 12; 2000, 8)—knew, computer technology is indeed "dangerous."
204. Christian 1996a, 358. Athanasiadis (2001, 122) emphasizes that "choosing technology also meant being shaped and driven by it and toward it in all aspects of existence, from one's thoughts to one's activities, from the private to the public realms, out of one's fears and toward one's hopes."
205. Christian 1996a, 358.
206. Grant 1986, 3. "[T]echnique," Grant emphasized, can no longer be thought as an "external plaything which man can use as he wants, but as occurrence totally related to the way moderns have thought about what is and what ought to be" (Davis and Roper 2009b, 136). A "society given over to continual technical development," Grant continued, "cannot be one in which human excellence will be realized" (137). Human excellence requires subjective and social reconstruction toward moral improvement in the ethical care of self and others, actualizations of attunement to the transcendent.
207. To that concept I turn in ch. 5. Like Grant, Rigelhof (2001, 134–5) associates technology with will, specifically that secularization and materialization of will we worship now: "Technology emerged from a way of looking a life that elevates will power over every other consideration. Technology not only gives us what we want when

we want it, but it teaches us to want only what it's best at giving us…. In teaching this, technology changes the meaning of what it is to be human."

208. Quoted in Christian 1996a, 358.

209. Grant (1974) 1998, 84. O'Donovan (1984, 50) associates this concept with Leo Strauss's affirmation of "a classical Greek understanding of the unchanging and eternal 'whole' to which all men everywhere are open." It is "the whole"—contemplation of which affords humanity its only opportunity for self-understanding and transcendence—that has been progressive obscured in the history of the West (161).

210. Grant's condemnation of abortion and euthanasia derive from his moral concern for the weak (see Bradshaw 1996, 221; Ajzenstat 1992, 95n30). He tells Cayley (1995, 158) "everybody on earth should have moral concern as much as they can. One has moral concern for those one teaches, but one doesn't teach the people for whom we ought to have the greatest moral concern: the weak of society. This is why I have feelings about the mentally retarded, and people like that, as well as about the foetus. There's a way in which our society cares about the weak but there's a way in which technological society very much does not care about the weak." Reimer (1978, 51) emphasizes that in opposing abortion Grant is arguing against "the modern liberal criteria used to justify abortion," among them "convenience." "In doing so," Reimer continues, "Grant draws on other aspects of the liberal tradition—the political freedom of all Canadians, 'the sanctity of the individual,' the inalienable God-given rights of every human being to life, including the unborn child…. What he rejects is not every aspect of liberalism, but its dominant assumption; namely, that man is free to shape his life and the world the way he desires" (51).

211. Grant approved of birth control, and he supported abortion when the mother's life was threatened (Cayley 1995, 156; Davis and Roper 2009b, 493, 496; Ajzenstat 1992, 83) and in cases of rape (Cayley 1995, 154). "[W]hat I am fundamentally against," he made clear, "is abortion as convenience, abortion resulting from easy calculation" (Cayley 1996, 156). Mass infanticide resulted, he thought, from the "the disappearance of the idea of soul" (Cayley 1995, 157). Near the end of his life he wrote that for him "abortion quite transcends any issue but nuclear disarmament" (Christian 1996d, 378). He credits his wife, Sheila, for enabling him to see that the "abortion issue was very fundamental" (Cayley 1995, 145).

212. Christian 1996d, 345.

213. "Only twice in my life," Grant reports, "have I been so ravished with love for the works of an artist that the very substance of my soul seemed to be within these works. The first time was when I really listened to the music of Mozart in my twenties; the second when I read Céline's trilogy in my sixties…. I speak here of that sudden ravishment which changes consciousness, no more profoundly than the long sustenance of Bach or Shakespeare, but which happens so suddenly, and therefore surprisingly, that it can be compared to love at first sight. It is the unexpected, which means that one will never again as one was." In a January 1981 letter to William Christian (1996d, 313), Grant admits that "Céline is a mystery, just to me in the same way that Heidegger is a mystery. Both so great & yet both tied to the criminality of National Socialism…. But nevertheless they both see so much." In a 1983 letter to Dennis Lee, Grant wrote that "one of the reasons I do so love Céline is that I so identify with the wild old man and feel myself now one" (Christian 1996d, 335). Sheila Grant reports that she and her husband spent "innumerable hours discussing

both Céline and the wider questions raised by Céline's work…. [and] the enigma of Céline's racism" (Davis and Roper 2009b, 427; see also 922; Athanasiadis 2001, 196).

214. Davis and Roper 2009b, 451.

215. "Of course," Grant reminded, "finally a country and its traditions are not ends in themselves. They are only means of partaking in the eternal. But nevertheless we come upon that eternal justice through the mediation of particular traditions and the particular traditions of Canada in their wide diversity are worth loving and working for on the northern half of this contractual continent" (Davis and Roper 2009b, 419). Particularity is prized for its mediation of universality—a moment in time becomes precious as it radiates, e.g., a moving image of eternity.

216. Cayley (1995, ix–x) quotes the journalist Charles Taylor's description of Grant as "a burly man of impressive corporation," adding that "his trademark, as nearly every-one who sat with him has noted, was the cascade of cigarette ash that would tumble down his broad front as he became engrossed in conversation. I found him a touching, unguarded companion, whose intelligence seemed deeply rooted in his heart." In that last sentence we read a reassertion of Grant's integration of "precision" and "soul," as well as his hospitality, inviting others into his "home," his subjective dwelling.

217. Quoted in Christian 1996a, 354. Love is "one of those words," Trilling (1972, 120) muses, "which are best not talked about if they are to retain any force of meaning." Perhaps, but Grant tried: in 1966 he wrote "To love is to pay attention to other people and this means to communicate with them" (Davis and Roper 2005b, 419). Justice is ethics enacted, including in communication, teaching for instance.

218. "For what is peculiar to love," Marion (2012, 47) writes, "consists in the fact that it gives itself." It becomes a state of mind, even a *mode d'être*?

219. "Justice as liberty, equality, and the inalienable rights of the individual," Athanasiadis (2001, 209) summarizes, "could not be sustained by a contractual liberalism in the face of the technological will to power in the modern era. Grant saw this happening in a number of ways. He saw it in education and politics. He also saw it in the new possibilities opened up with medical technologies—abortion and euthanasia." For another insightful commentary on Grant's critique of contractualism, see Ajzenstat 1992, 87; see also Meynell 2011, 18.

220. Quoted in Christian 1996a, 358.

221. Quoted in Christian 1996a, 359. Kittler (2013, 249) asked: "My question is, how did it come that people in Europe do not know love, but rather love knowledge?" For Grant, to know love requires knowledge. "Love," Rigelhof (2001, 131) concludes, "was at the centre of George Grant's experience."

222. Marion 2001, 156.

223. Angus 1997, 232–3.

224. Flinn (1990, 139) invokes similar images: "[W]e have become not only the masters of technology but also its most willing servants."

225. Davis 2002b, 214.

226. That erasure is the human, as Kittler asserts. "A crucial implication of the ontological character of technology," Robertson (2006, 148) explains, "is that it cannot be itself mastered or taken in hand or subordinated to higher human ends." Andrew Feenberg (2013, 13) disagrees, insisting that the "technical system…is not rigidly constraining but on the contrary can adapt to a variety of social demands."

227. Kittler 2013, 298.

228. Davis and Roper 2009b, 134–5.
229. Weil (1947) 2002, 153.
230. I am anticipating here the Holocaust; in ch. 3 we revisit the period just before—the Weimar Republic—a time that for Grant anticipates the homogenous world order he dreads. But the term—"genocide"—also recalls the cultural genocide of Indigenous peoples and the spiritual genocide technology commits. As noted, Grant will reactivate the past—ancient Athens and Jerusalem—to extricate himself from this nightmare, but Minogue (1990, 170) is no fan of that move, pointing that "ancient wars were often genocidal." Omnipresence does not absolve one from decrying the phenomenon; Minogue would no doubt concur.

CHAPTER 3

Time

The fact that events happen does not imply they are good.[1]

George Grant

It is as if the love of justice atrophied during modernity, replaced by the pursuit of power, with its unimaginable twentieth-century effects, among them two world wars and the Holocaust. Studying that "modernity"—the time of his life—was George Grant's "life work," Andrew Potter concludes.[2] While the concept[3] can become complex, for Grant it could be summarized as the historical tendency toward the homogenization of human life,[4] "our rushing restless life,"[5] lived most intensely in North America, especially in the United States. It had been achieved through the substitution of technological progress for moral striving.[6] What constitutes the North American dream, Grant observed, is progress[7] through technological innovation.[8]

While that North American faith may not be as "religiously defined"[9] as the demand for economic justice had been for many Marxists, Grant wrote (at the end of the 1960s, when the Marxist dream was still alive) that our faith in technological advance requires that "freedom"[10] and "flexibility"[11] remove any "theoretical" reservation concerning its realization.[12] Decades before the disappearance of the Soviet Union and subsequent proclamations of the "end of ideology," George Grant chided the "clever" who proclaimed the "end of ideology."[13] As did our predecessors—in this chapter I focus upon the Weimar Republic as an allegory of the present[14]—we live within the ideology of technology, a pseudo-promised land where distraction[15] deters an intellectual life now devoted to control, an ideology that substitutes for moral striving momentary virtual satiation.[16]

Such secular salvation perforates the steady stream of searching, our constant craving refocused first from God to the public sphere, now to the screens in front of us, screens that stare back at faces transfixed as if by the presence of God.[17] Nothing—everything—has changed, as our new subject positions, subjects of the screen, subject us to the never-ending search for something we will never find there. We do not notice, however, as we have become "technique," Grant knew.[18] It is not we who search, as the phrase implies at least one degree of distance. Rather, we have become fused, as if we were prosthetic extensions of the screen. Searching is our sacrament, testimony to the truth that awaits, not necessarily in heaven but surely in the sequence of sites Google or Bing brings.[19]

Communion occurs no longer by consuming symbols of divinity or through acts of social solidarity.[20] Even in the presence of others we experience fusion[21] through devices that make us mobile while holding us steady, close in hand. In our screened workstations we live in "monistic vulgarity,"[22] a phrase Grant uses to emphasize the demeaned humanity homogeneity incurs. What have we become, Grant wonders. What were we already? While the vulgar and the sacred have always split the human condition, Grant is registering modernity's loss of at least the pretense that being alive has a moral purpose, however modestly and variously that purpose might be defined.[23] Whether focused on a personal god or an impersonal regime of self-divestiture seeking enlightenment or social justice, this sense of life having a meaning, a point, that life matters in and beyond itself—this sense of immanence or transcendence vanishes in the temporally empty "now"[24] that is staring at screens.[25]

Instrumental rationality is substituted for contemplation. Calculation replaces supplication. "The present darkness is a real darkness," Grant affirmed.[26] Not spiritual discovery or social understanding, but capital accumulation through technological advancement becomes the salvation to which one kneels, perhaps not in prayer. Pleading in the present becomes the disciplined demand for new product development and dissemination, with wealth—not absolution—as the fantasy of the future. In his genealogy of the present, the Weimar critic Siegfried Kracauer testified to "the *emptying out* of people's spiritual/intellectual space," and such "transformations of the self…are [also] transformations of the outside object-world, of reality, which is gradually robbed of its substance and compressed to a point where its structure depends on the self."[27] Long before Christopher Lasch,[28] Kracauer knew modernity meant cultures of narcissism and presentism.[29]

The "modern project," Grant lamented, has led us "away from excellence."[30] Kracauer sensed the same: "Value is not produced for the sake of value."[31] Seeking moral excellence—always aligning ourselves to the Good—requires acknowledgement of the Other.[32] "When life becomes dominated by self-serving," Grant reminded, "the reality of otherness, in its own being, almost disappears for us."[33] And "when otherness has become completely absent for us," Grant added, "we are hardly human beings at all."[34] The cultivation of our humanity occurs within the reality of our inhumanity[35] Grant knew, rendering the ancient aspiration for the ethical—summarized in Grant's question "what is worth doing with our freedom?"[36]—also political, as his citation of Plato makes clear. As the most "self-serving," the "tyrant" is for Plato "the worst human being" because he is the most "self-serving," Grant writes, and so "otherness has ceased to exist for him."[37] Are narcissism, presentism, and tyranny reciprocally related?

The disappearance of the Other—the "experience of time as presence, time as immersion,"[38] historical time[39]—is the chief sign of narcissism, that inability to escape one's own projections. Is narcissism the chief cultural consequence of modernity, modernity as our subsumption in the "technological sensorium"?[40] It has been the eradication of difference, through genocide, through the Holocaust specifically, that marks modernity as mired in its salvational undertow. For Grant, it is the denial of alterity—including the presence of God, the quintessential conception of Otherness—that severs subjectivity from its embeddedness in the world, from acknowledgment of the world as simultaneously inseparable from and ultimately opaque to us, irreducible to its use-value.[41] Now, attuning ourselves to what Grant termed "the Good," to right conduct in the world, sounds quaint. Now, Grant points out, "Good is what is present in the fulfillment of our given purposes."[42] It is that conflation of calculation with consequences that creates the vicious volatility of human action in modernity, as apparently intrinsic tendencies toward violence now become rationalized as collateral damage in accomplishing the objective of the day. While it has damned millions, it is the salvational potential of technology—its promise of progress, its subsumption of moral purpose within product development and profiteering—that calls us to worship today.[43]

Modernity is no despotic scheme imposed upon us against our will; modernity is the materialization of that will. Not always conscious, as the term "will" connotes in the vernacular, for Grant it has converted to a compulsion to materialize whatever is possible.[44] Indeed, the "possible" is preferred over "what is," Grant concluded.[45] What is—contingency—dissolves into fantasy in an era of virtual reality. "As a negation of impossibility," Doane observes, "contingency is a witness against technology as inexorability, a witness that it could have been otherwise."[46] Historical inexorability is not only a Marxist fantasy, it is the movement of modernity. Recall that Grant emphasized that within modernity a "universal" and "egalitarian" society represents the teleology of "historical striving."[47] Such a society—"a very tough, tight, twilight society"[48]—will be actualized, Grant explains, via "modern science," itself enabling the "conquest of nature," including human nature.[49] Where is the epicentre of this ongoing possibly history-ending event?[50] "Particularly" in the United States, Grant argued, "scientists concern themselves with the control of heredity, the human mind, and society."[51]

The totalizing scale of modernity's teleology—the "planetary" future is technological and that is "inevitable"[52]—and the location of its epicentre in the United States simultaneously abstracts and concretizes the catastrophe to come.

We live, Grant appreciated, when our only options seem to be either "planetary destruction" or "planetary tyranny."[53] The catastrophe to come—climate change, nuclear accident or terrorist attack, overpopulation, antibiotic-resistant disease—will come as yet *another* catastrophe. The catastrophe, and the tyranny that ensured it, has already occurred. Grant remembers: In his introduction to the 1970 Carleton Library edition of *Lament for a Nation*, he references the decade before the Holocaust begins. Reflecting on the United States (and the political protests there over the Vietnam War), Grant thinks of the "political polarization" during the Weimar Republic.[54] While that polarization was specific to German political culture and to that post–First World War historical moment, it also conveyed the violent multiplicity[55] of modernity.[56] While history may not repeat itself, remembrance enables reconstruction of the present, dislodging us from identification with it.[57] "What history can bring to moral and political life," Collingwood knew, "is a trained eye for the situation in which one has to act."[58] Grant worried that our very capacity to remember becomes dissolved in the imagistic "intensity" of our time; without "re-collection" there can be no "wisdom."[59] While the remembrance of Weimar cannot provide wisdom, perhaps it can provoke a reactivation[60] of a past that, while in very different imagistic forms, seems eerily similar.[61]

Lament for a Nation

> "The most absolute naiveté about time is
> to take the past as in no sense present."[62]
> George Grant

The tendency toward totalization that technology tempts is not democratic in character. In the service of capitalism—"society" has become a "machine for greed,"[63] Grant knew—technology enables totalitarianism.[64] When technological innovation substitutes for moral striving corruption can be the consequence, at least some ninety years ago, and not only in America but in Germany, where, Peukert explains,

> Part and parcel of the new [totalitarian] mood was an abandonment of the ideal
> of progress through technology that had originated with the Enlightenment
> but had become perverted into a merely materialistic utilitarian ideology in
> the course of the economic expansion of the nineteenth century.[65]

As moral aspiration morphed into technological advancement for the sake of profit maximization, the question of ethics became quaint.[66] The politics of resentment followed as Germans—outraged, humiliated, and suffering financial stress due to the military loss in the First World War, diplomatically aggravated at Versailles—experimented with a parliamentary politics unprecedented in their history.

Despite the political polarization and economic destabilization, the "Roaring Twenties" were celebrated by many as the "culmination" of modernization, and not only in technology and the economy but in social and psychic life as well, where, Peukert notes, "a substitute religion of social and technological utilitarianism and a euphoric faith in progress inspired a cult of 'Americanism.'"[67] Such optimism was erased first by the great inflation of the 1920s, followed five years later by the Great Depression, but even during the days of optimism, this "dream of modernity" was also a nightmare, shattered by deafening demands to return to traditional German values and assumptions, demands not only from the past but from the future, from "prefigurations of a critique of modernity we can now call post-modern."[68] These regularly violent repudiations of the present fused into a "conservative revolution"[69] that featured what Jeffrey Herf characterized as an "irrationalist embrace" of technology.[70] Over the decade this "reactionary modernism"[71] was formulated by a series of influential intellectuals, among them Hans Freyer, Ernst Jünger, Carl Schmitt, Werner Sombart, and Oswald Spengler. Martin Heidegger[72] formulated a more ambivalent analysis, one that would very much influence George Grant.[73] Eric Weitz reminds:

> The notion that right-wing politics generally and Nazism in particular were the work only of material-minded, self-interested elites coupled with a collection of thugs and brutes is one of the major misinterpretations that has managed to prevail over the decades. In fact, German conservative revolutionaries were, in many cases, serious thinkers and writers, who also happened to be profoundly antidemocratic and, in many but not all instances, anti-Semitic as well.[74]

Grant viewed "Nazism as a perverted eruption of the instinctual which had been repressed in technological society."[75]

For many Germans, such anti-modernism[76] was inseparable from anti-republicanism,[77] as the Weimar Republic was associated with the lost war, the Versailles Treaty, economic crises, cosmopolitan mass culture (itself associated with Jews), and political liberalism.[78] These affronts—symptomatic, conservatives insisted, of German political and cultural degradation—demanded cultural renewal through an energizing "barbarism."[79] For "reactionary modernists,"[80] Herf underscores, technology could come to provide the primary prospect of such renewal, provided it could be freed from the commercial (recoded as Jewish) interests the Weimar Republic served.[81]

There were several influential formulations of this fantasy that would, in decades to come, subsume national within technological progress. In this earlier still bifurcated version, the future didn't seem so bright, as the promise of technology had been usurped by those seized by the avarice of free-market capitalism. Oswald Spengler's "brooding pessimism," most famously articulated in his *The Decline of the West*, obscured (Herf points out) his embrace of technology, which he associated with the "creative, productive domination over nature" in contrast to the "alien world of parasitic, unproductive, cosmopolitan finance."[82] Despite this adversary, triumph was possible, Spengler asserted, depicting (in Herf's words) technological advancement as a "heroic ascent, a creative emancipation of the species from its natural limits."[83] That prosthetic potential of the body was also imagined by Ernst Jünger, whose writings of the 1920s, Herf summarizes, juxtaposed the "lifeless" and "mechanized" biological body with the "animated…instrument" of the "human will" that is technology; whatever "cultural renewal" to which Germans aspire could come only through technological advance."[84] About this time Freud was suggesting that the obsession with technological innovation was a sublimation of sexual energy, arguing it was "the diversion of primary destructiveness from the ego to the external world [that] feeds technological progress."[85]

It was during the Weimar Republic, then, that technological advance came to mean cultural renewal, and cultural renewal spelled self-regeneration.[86] Drawing on the *Fronterlebnis* (front experience) of the First World War to reconcile political reaction with modernity and modern technology,[87] Jünger affirmed the "man-machine symbiosis" as the dynamic fusion of human will and technology.[88] For Jünger, technology contributed not only to self-renewal, it revolutionized the body as well, as the machine does nothing less than biologize utopia with its promise of flawless functioning.[89] For Jünger, technology, sacrifice, and destiny were dynamically interwoven.[90] For us, sacrifice is not so alluring, and we prefer not to think about destiny (as the oceans rise, storms intensify, and technological warfare becomes ever more insidious). For us, the ruling triumvirate is technology, pleasure, and profit. In each series technology incorporates eschatology, materializing the future and its fantasies of an afterlife into a timeless perfectibility now.[91] Subjectivity dissolves into an updated behaviourism (performativity)— "modern life: a life that has more to *do* than ever, but less and less to *be*,"[92] Rocha reminds—alternating sequences of searching online and numbed satiation. Enter the era of the posthuman.[93]

For Jünger, whose life spanned the twentieth century, technology had eclipsed individuality.[94] In fusion with machines—"voluntary uniformity" in Jünger's phrase[95]—one is freed from self-limitation and external constraint, able to attain whatever the will wants. Like the conformity consumer capitalism compels, technology converts atomized individuals into instruments—"mass ornaments" in Kracauer's famous phrase[96]—of national will. While concern over "dehumanization" was "common coin" in Weimar Germany, Herf reports, Jünger[97] warmly welcomed the instrumentality of human life that technology promised.[98] Becoming flawless—in our time the cyborg or the "fyborg" ("any bodily enhancement/transformation through any temporary technological intrusion into the body"[99])—incurs an intoxicating tension[100] that promised to materialize transcendence through the rejuvenation of the *Volk*.

For Hans Freyer, the problem facing the people was the incorporation of technological advancement without destroying Germany's distinctive *Kultur*. For Freyer, only the political Right could foster the fusion of technology and soul.[101] For Freyer, what was necessary was the formulation of a "philosophy of technology" that reconciled *Kultur* and *Bildung* with *Technik* and *Zivilisation* by acknowledging the unrecognized contribution of the latter to the former.[102] In the political program of the Left, ending the economy's domination of society required a proletarian revolution.[103] On the Far Right, as formulated by Freyer, ending the economy's degradation of culture demanded the establishment of an authoritarian state. A revolution of the *Volk* against dehumanizing industrial society required the "unification" of the *Volk* and the state.[104] On both the Left and Right, the individual would disappear into the collectivity, into the workers or the *Volk*.

Millions of individuals did disappear. In *The Jews and Economic Life* (1911) and in *German Socialism* (1934), Werner Sombart converted questions of capitalism, technology, and cultural renaissance to questions of race.[105] Like Spengler and Jünger, Sombart associated technology with an active, Nietzschean will to power and, Herf points out, wrote more about "technology *and* culture rather than technology *or* culture."[106] It was soulless finance that had constrained culture *and* technology. What calamitous fate had befallen Germany, Sombart decried, that the will to power that creates technology had instead recast individuals as numerals, only objects of business transactions.[107] For Sombart, Herf explains, if "capitalism stood for the primacy of commerce over technology, then anticapitalism simply meant the reversal of this relationship by making technology predominant over commerce."[108] What was politically urgent, Sombart insisted, was the rescue of this finest form of the German will—technology—from its subservience to finance capitalism. "A 'technopolitics' must replace laissez-faire"[109] and before the decade was out, technology had come to signify national service, not private profit.[110] It also became associated with "fantasy and [the] imagination rather than [with] abstraction,"[111] the former animations of the German soul destined to prevail over the latter, the dry calculations of a predatory finance capitalism.

How, in one decade, could technology be detached from its association with death and destruction in the First World War and as an instrument of parasitic finance capital that had destroyed (in the 1923 hyperinflation) Germany's wealth, be recast as creative patriotic labour in the service of rejuvenating German culture and thus the German nation?[112] Herf summarizes: First, technology was reconceived as fundamentally aesthetic, not dehumanizing, in fact capable of "comprising new, stable forms that constituted beautiful alternatives to a flabby and chaotic bourgeois order."[113] Those "stable forms" would have their political correlates condensed into state authoritarianism. Second, technology was no mechanistic abstraction severed from our inner lives. Indeed, technology externalized that inner life, materializing the will to power. "This Nietzschean motif," Herf notes, "celebrated the domination of nature with Social Darwinist overtones and excoriated antitechnological romanticism as effeminate and escapist."[114] To unleash this cultural potential of technology required releasing it from finance capitalism and from the Jews who presumably controlled capitalism.[115] So freed, technology would produce politics—institutionalized in the German state—and not the economy as the dominant force in society. Fourth, technology was dissociated from the destruction and defeat of the First World War by realigning it (and this was the specific "accomplishment" of Jünger) with the masculine camaraderie of the *Fronterlebnis*. Fifth, technological development became a "uniquely German project," to be protected from "the financial swindles of the Jews."[116] As the key country located *between* East and West, Germany was destined to exceptionality. It alone could combine technology *and* soul. Whereas the Americans and the Soviets were both mired in materialism, Germany would become again a close(d) community, a society defined by its political coherence, its cultural purity and vitality materialized in its technological innovation. Technology would define the new German national identity.

Nationalism and reactionary modernism remain interrelated, Herf cautions, and the dangers they pose do not decrease "by an illiberal alliance between Western intellectuals who have lost faith in the Enlightenment, and those of the developing nations who mistakenly equate modernity with technology alone."[117] George Grant drew a distinction between nationalism and nationhood, implied in his definition of "national articulation" as a "process through which human beings form and re-form themselves into a society to act historically,"[118] as Doane remarks, "history as the mark of what could have been otherwise."[119] And what can be otherwise; in my terms, "becoming historical"[120] invites subjective and social reconstruction, ongoing enactments of remembrance and agency attuned to the Good, "justice"[121] in Grant's term. Justice, Grant pointed out,[122] cannot be derived from calculations of self-interest.[123]

Nor, Grant would add, can justice coincide with "the people" or the "state," however administered its legal codifications are by the latter, however contained in the social imaginaries of the former. "For justice," Grant suggested, "is the inward harmony which makes a self truly a self—or in more accurate language which today sounds archaic: Justice in its inward appearance is the harmony which makes a soul truly a soul."[124] Justice, Grant concluded, is not only a social concern: it is as well an "individual" condition classically called "virtue."[125] In my terms, reparation—making things right with others and within oneself, an enactment of virtue—requires remembrance and reconstruction, simultaneously subjective and social.[126]

Grant's Lament

> Life as little brother often leads to politi-
> cal naiveté and even self-righteousness.[127]
> George Grant

"There is no such thing as modernity in general," Herf concludes from his study of the Weimar Republic: "There are only national societies, each of which becomes modern in its own fashion."[128] Canada inherited two versions of modernity, one French and one English, the former, Grant thought, less inclined to emphasize the exercise of freedom over the cultivation of virtue, in part due to the character of Quebec Catholicism.[129] For Catholics, Grant suggested, "virtue must be prior to freedom."[130] In the secularization of Protestant Christianity[131] that had evolved into modernity, eschatology had morphed into absolute confidence in progress,[132] at times (as in Weimar Germany) tempting a fanatical fleeing from the present by embracing maniacal fantasies of the future.[133] Specificity—contingency—dissolves into virtual reality, as the anxiety of time shreds any stability, social or subjective. How did that happen? Doane provides a succinct summary:

> The reconceptualization of time as a source of anxiety is accompanied by the rationalization, standardization, and tight regularization of temporality effected by industrialization and the forces of modernity. Rationalization transforms time into a form of constant pressure and constraint. The lure of contingency in such a context lies precisely in its resistance to systematicity, in its promise of unpredictability and idiosyncrasy. This lure and promise have been, precisely, *historical*.[134]

To inhabit the present as temporal requires recollection of the past, in this chapter the moment before democracy dissolves and alterity annihilated.

Grant provides a succinct summary as well. North America, Grant reminded, had been imprinted by Protestantism, and for him the persisting puzzle was why "Protestantism, centered as it was on a great affirmation of freedom and the infinite, has been the dominant force in shaping a society which is now so little free and so little aware of the infinite."[135] To solve this puzzle Grant knew he had to work back from the present, that convergence of secularization, science, and technology known as modernity.[136] "A bloodless, sterilized world of secularism, possessive individualism, and nation-states, born from the liberal womb of modernity," Rocha rues, "is a toxic, disenchanting ideology that hides its absent core: nihilism."[137] Such modernity, as Herf reminds, took different forms according to the nation, its cultures, and the historical moment.[138]

The influence of location was central to Grant's analysis of Canada's modernity. In the United States, individualism, capitalism, and technology had fused with the nation's faith in its divinely inspired exceptionality, producing a volatile, at times explosive, mix of economics, politics, and culture. Canada had been destined to be different from the United States, Grant believed. Canada had intended to be a society, more "ordered" and "caring," decidedly "less violent."[139] Technology has its own intentionality, one that incorporates the manifest destinies of nations and their inhabitants through its totalizing—in Grant's terms its "universalizing" and "homogenizing"—tendencies. Contained within these deceptively simple terms, Emberley points out, are the progressive dreams and apocalyptic nightmares of modernity: universal liberation requiring universal tyranny, equality as the enforcement of "sameness."[140] For Grant, Emberley summarizes, technology compels a wrenching shift in the "human spirit."[141]

Efficiency, technology's "driving principle," Emberley concludes, suppresses "local differences, particular loyalties, and credible resistances."[142] Whether nations or cultures or classes within nations or across borders personify differences, "difference" is what disappears in modernity.[143]

Recall that for Grant technology includes not only gadgets but also modes of being, including structures of social organization and patterns of individual thinking. He attributed the death of democracy,[144] as had Harold Innis before him,[145] to the technology of information exchange, in particular to propaganda presented as news.[146] Now "power is legitimized by conscious and unconscious processes."[147] Grant could not have been surprised by the Murdoch mess—the phone hacking at News Corp., the corruption of the London police and apparently of British politicians[148]—but he would still have been dismayed by the public's willingness to allow the man to own *any* newspaper or media outlet.[149] The tendency toward hierarchies, even authoritarianism—must we invoke the historically specific term "fascism"[150] here?—in the very organizational structure of the contemporary corporation is clear enough in Rupert Murdoch's case, but "organization men"[151] have often risked political conformity when succumbing to the never-ending demand to maximize profits.[152]

"Populist democracy," Grant judged, prematurely,[153] is a "dying force" in the United States, but surely he was right to add that it is not exactly supported at "Simpson's-Sears or General Motors."[154] Not only do corporations—Grant characterized them as "private governments"[155]—destroy democracy, his examples underscore where. "A branch-plant satellite," Grant pointed out, that makes no "difficulties in foreign or defense policy, is a pleasant arrangement for one's northern frontier."[156] Here Grant is not naming a department store or a kind of car but Canada itself.

As it was the case in Weimar Germany, "nationalism" can be furthered by "technological advance," but, Grant noted, "technological advance entails the disappearance of those indigenous differences that give substance to nationalism."[157] Not only corrosively, from within, does technology destroy difference. It seduces with the promise of progress.[158] Canada's "independence," Christian suggests, had been "eroded" less by the "actions" of Americans that it had been "by the increasing acceptance of the attractiveness of the American vision of modernity."[159] Technology corrodes culture because it dissolves it, bleaching it of its multivariate dynamic distinctiveness—often contained in traces of the past—that is sacrificed for "modernization."[160] In modernization the very concept of "citizen" disappears, replaced by the "consumer." In consumer capitalism, Grant knew, we become "defined" by our "capacity to consume. All other differences between them, like political traditions, begin to appear unreal and unprogressive. As consumption becomes primary, the border appears an anachronism, and a frustrating one at that."[161] In the inexorable drive toward economic integration, Grant argued, Canadians will stop seeing "what all the fuss is about…. [After all] the purpose of life is consumption, and therefore the border is an anachronism."[162] Modernity means the universal corporate state.

What *is* the fuss all about? Or, as some might ask, what fuss? Has not modernity meant reduction in disease, overwork, hunger, poverty? That Grant acknowledged, but, he added, "as soon as that it is said, facts about our age must also be remembered: the increasing outbreaks of impersonal ferocity, the banality of existence in technological societies, the pursuit of expansion as an end in itself."[163] Modernity means demands for endless economic expansion, corporatization that enforces cultural homogeneity, the "fate," Grant warns, of "any particularity" in this technological era.[164] Indigenous cultures, singular individuals, distinctive nationalities—all face this same fate as does Canada. "Canada," Grant pronounced, "has ceased to be a nation."[165]

The nation and the memory of its peoples disappear, but the state—in service to the economy—remains. Affluence, we are persuaded, depends upon ongoing technological advancement, and that advancement "develops within a state capitalist framework."[166] Manufacturing profit through technological development, corporations control the state, evidently even in Canada too. "Decisive," Christian suggests, was that "large corporations…knew nothing of loyalty, only interest. That directed them south."[167] Grant knew that the "wealthy" would abandon their "nationalism" should it conflict with their "economic interests."[168] The wealthy are not the only guilty ones, as Grant allowed that "many" North Americans do not know "any ideology" but "affluence."[169] The ideology of affluence reproduces itself not only through the promise of profit and pleasure but also through its corollaries: pain and deprivation. It is, Grant advised, "only" by attuning ourselves to "deprival" that we can "live critically" in the "dynamo."[170] That "dynamo" is not only the constant cultural dissolution—so-called creative destruction—technology stimulates, but also its concomitants, among them the manufactured fear reactionary US politicians[171] propagate, and that quiet desperation Henry David Thoreau acknowledged before heading for Walden Pond.[172]

Siegfried Kracauer, Thomas Levin explains, linked the "intimations of deprival"—feeling uprooted, isolated, emotionally vulnerable—of the 1920s German white-collar class to the "new social obsessions," among them "consumption" and that "compensatory leisure" associated with Berlin's cafés and cabarets.[173] Kracauer focused on this historic redirection of human attention along lines, Levin notes, later taken up in Walter Benjamin's essay "The Work of Art in the Age of Its Technological Reproducibility."[174] Recall that Benjamin had been preoccupied with the perception that technology possessed, in György Lukács's phrase, "a phantom objectivity."[175] Haunted by devices, relations among those surviving in technological corporate states become task-specific and even numbered, measured not in meaning but in quantified outcomes.[176] Subjectivity and sociality become technologically contracted. Can they be reconstructed? To that question I return in the epilogue.

For cultures that had attributed social cohesiveness to God, the triumph of modernity was at once horrifying and liberating.[177] The Weimar Republic was not only democracy under siege, it was also culture in crisis. For Germany's right-wing intellectuals, the "liberation" of technology from the Weimar Republic's social and political regulation became synonymous with the recovery of the German soul. Reducing government regulation might free corporations to pursue profit even more aggressively, but that was, during the 1920s, incidental to Germany's right-wing intellectuals. The "profit" the right wing sought in liberating technology from government regulation was cultural and political. Their confidence that "economic"—and specifically technological—"advance could overcome a cultural crisis"[178] represented a novel idea for Germans, Herf points out. No longer "novel," this idea—that technological advance can overcome cultural, economic, educational crises—has faded into the background. It is our assumption. That faith prompts the purchase of new technology and assures us we can cure climate change. In its status as salvational, technology, George Grant understood, becomes "pervasive."[179]

Conclusion

> Who is to recount how and when and where private anguish and public catastrophe may lead men to renew their vision of excellence?[180]
>
> George Grant

"People have sometimes taken national socialism in Germany as an aberration," Grant told Cayley,[181] "and it certainly was in detail, but as a way of thought it was also something more universal."[182] When ideology—it was for Grant nothing less than a "surrogate" religion[183]—triumphs, idols (the state, race, the multitude, the nation) replace icons. Public figures can exploit the ideological force of the spectacle, infantilizing adults who then pretend to know.[184]

Idols destroy "common sense and moderation," Grant knew, "the two great protectors of the health of the public realm."[185] Grant cautioned: "English-speaking people are well advised to remember the German experience. The Germans were the first to build universities in which 'objective' science and scholarship was exalted above all questions of the good."[186] Instead of the eternal, we are left with "only the moving image, and our experience as listeners and as readers, and indeed as living human beings," and that "is grounded in temporal sequence."[187] Even the sense of temporal sequence, history as everyday memory, fades in our submersion in the screen. "What gets repressed is not the lost object," Benedetti suggests, "but the fact that it constitutes a loss."[188] Can reactivation of the past—not only lost good but nightmares under threat of being forgotten—encourage non-coincidence with what is, that double consciousness[189] that enables lived experience of the present as well as intimations of that to which one might become attuned, to the Good?[190]

Despite the political crisis[191] of our time, Grant's caution goes unheeded. STEM, not history, dominates the school curriculum of our era.[192] "The fact [is] that our ruling classes have become technicized," Grant lamented, "and our universities have largely excluded from the curriculum the serious study of the most important questions."[193] Excluded from the curriculum—from the life of academic study—can mean excluded from daily life. Grant worried that "the reading of the morning newspaper has taken the place of the morning prayer,"[194] rituals replaced today by staring at social media. Grant's point remains: "At the beginning of the day when we need to pay attention to what is necessary to our good we turn that attention to reading about public events, not to the eternal."[195] As I suggest in chapters 6 and 7, public (and private) events can provide portals to more eternal topics. When the curriculum is organized (in part) as allegories of the present or, more broadly, as iconographic (a topic of ch. 5), one's "morning prayer" becomes simultaneously a matter of worldliness and transcendence. Grant's teaching was, I suggest, just so doubly directed, as we will see in the next chapter.

Absent memory[196] and attunement to the Good, people become "extremely restless and willing to do anything," Grant worried.[197] "That the English, the Germans, and the French walked into the First World War is almost unbelievable," he mused, reflecting on a century that had been "a catastrophic era of the West," one that leaves us looking "for external enemies: it is always easier than facing the catastrophe within oneself."[198] From within subjectivity—"every moment of our living"—Grant suggests that we have moved "into the high noon of modernity."[199] For us now, high noon seems passed; late (or post)modernity is our present moment, our entrapment in a timeless present. "In reality there is no irreversible fate that weighs on late-modernity," Benedetti suggests, "so as to lock it into this dead end. If it is trapped, it is only because it itself has barred every possible exist."[200] She adds: "What brings on paralysis is precisely admitting the impossibility of the new."[201] Because we are materialists, attuned only to machine, we are mired here, now, neither concept intelligible while submerged in the screen.

Resetting the clock isn't possible, but re-experiencing—through reactivation of—time past is.[202] Such recollection, Grant seems to suggest, involves waiting. He reminded students that they ought not judge Nietzsche "too quickly" but instead "wait upon him and see what he is saying first."[203] That advice follows acknowl-edgement of "my purpose in teaching Nietzsche," which is "to understand moder-nity," and "in Nietzsche modernity is laid before us consummately."[204] Decrying Christians' "willingness to get into bed with modernity"—many had imagined that "they were going to impregnate modernity with the truth of the Gospels, when in fact what was going to happen was that they were going to be impreg-nated by modernity"—Grant tells students that his "chief purpose in teaching has been to expand what modernity is,"[205] to reconstruct it in my terms. But that cannot occur solely or even primarily through the engineer's science; it requires spiritual attunement. "That is why I wanted you to wait upon Nietzsche," Grant explained.[206] Let us wait upon George Grant; in his subjective presence we may find our way through the labyrinth that is the present.

Notes

1. Grant (1965) 2005, 37.
2. Potter 2005, xxxix. "Modernity is too enormous a human experience," Grant empha-sized, "which has brought into the light certain human potentialities which were hidden. It is too enormous to respond to it either in any easy acceptance or rejection but above all in understanding" (Davis and Roper 2005b, 678).
3. As there was no one Enlightenment, there was—is—no monolithic modernity, as it exhibits national and temporal differences. Referencing Leo Strauss, Grant suggests that since Nietzsche we've been living in a "third wave of modernity" (Davis and Roper 2009b, 1076). Just as waves crash on the same beach at somewhat different times, modernity came later to Germany than to England and other countries. "It was precisely because the process of modernization had been so blatant and rapid since the end of the nineteenth century," Peukert (1992, 187) explains, "and because even the last trappings of Wilhelmine tradition were then jettisoned after 1918, that opposition to modernization in Germany was so radical and so self-tormenting." Could something similar be said about the 2016 US presidential campaign—and the Trump presidency? Certainly these are "radical" and "self-tormenting" events. And, as during the Weimar Republic, vulnerable minorities are targeted (Jews then, Muslims, illegal immigrants, African-Americans now) as Trump and his supporters, like their Weimar right-wing predecessors, decry modernization (now automation, globalization, and the loss of working-class jobs).
4. "The fear that "modernity," Umar (1992, 4) appreciates, "culminates" in "universal-ity" and "homogeneity" constitutes the "connecting thread of all of Grant's work."
5. Grant, in Davis 2002b, 121.
6. "The dogma of progress is dangerous," Grant wrote, "as it eventually kills the criti-cal faculty. It prevents the mind from seeing things as they are. About universities it is particularly misleading, for it encourages that depressing industrial metaphor—that all expansion is good" (Davis 2002b, 22). Not only capitalism Grant rejects, but after 1960 history itself, as O'Donovan (1984, 58) reminds: "Grant's rejection of 'his-tory' is first and foremost his abandoning of hope in the attainment by the modern public of a new level of morality and piety on the basis of technological liberation."

7.   "What turned Grant from his initial acceptance of Hegel's notion of historical development," Sibley (2006, 97) acknowledges, "was his recognition that it carried too much of the positivist idea of progress as the ultimate aim of man and, worse, made even evil a purposive good. Such a claim ignores the idea of man's existence having a given highest purpose or good that transcends time or history."

8.   Grant 1969, 30. That "innovation" is often—catastrophically—military, as Grant knew. Kittler documents that "the United States, the new world power, took over—and in seamless fashion, at that—the military technology of the National Socialist state" (Gumbrecht 2013, 314). Kittler holds the United States "entirely responsible" for the replacement of soldiers with "self-guided machine-systems" (Gumbrecht 2013, 318).

9.   Grant 1969, 25.

10. "In every field," Benedetti (2005, 181) observes, "modernity has always moved to the cry of 'Long live freedom!'"

11. The curriculum of the future, B. Williamson (2013, 23) suggests, will be "negotiable and flexible," entirely "concerned with students' future employment and it adopts the flexible correspondence model that flexible learning = flexible labour" (49). In other words, flexibility is the capacity to do whatever is required.

12. Grant 1969, 25. Inner freedom involves obedience through attunement to the eternal, as we will explore in ch. 6 and 7. In contemporary North America, "freedom" converts to conformity, Grant asserted, living in an "ant-hill" that provides "security in the world—where they do not need to think or to be uncertain, and where they live with the certainty of authority" (Davis and Roper 2009b, 948).

13. Grant 1969, 25; see also Davis and Roper 2009b, 288. "Ideology is a particular characteristic of the modern world," Grant suggested, "and it is likely that our future will be characterized by outbreaks of it" (Davis and Roper 2009b, 184).

14. Not for the first time; see Pinar 2012, 69–101. Allegory occupies the space in between contingency and abstraction, an intermediary exercise, not unlike the index as Doane (2002, 219) describes it: "Yet the index also harbours within itself a temporal tension. On the one hand, the indexical trace—the footprint, the fossil, the photograph—carries a historicity, makes the past present. At the other extreme, the deictic index—the signifiers 'here,' 'now,' 'this,' 'that'—are inextricable from the idea of presence." Like the future, the present can be found in the past.

15. Within the operation of capital," D. Smith (2014, 51) explains, "cultivating distraction is foundational to all marketing psychology, and the maintenance of distraction is an absolute requirement for product innovation and production." For Dewey ([1934] 1962, 51), too, distraction was trouble: "In a distracted age, the need for such an idea"—for Dewey "a clear and intense conception of a union of ideal ends with actual conditions capable of arousing steady emotion"—"is urgent. It can unify interests and energies now dispersed." In our time, "interests" and "energies" are sucked into screens.

16. "[I]n our time-is-money world of 'sound-bite democracy,' political discussion has all but ceased to exist," Lipari (2014, 152) observes. In contrast to Lipari's affirmation of listening, Kittler (2013, 295) complains that since the radio "we Europeans have lived, 'more or less compelled,' with a technical medium that defines us solely as listeners." That passive conception is also in contrast to Lipari's, but it supports her observation concerning "political discussion," namely that in the United States there is often no dialogical encounter but rhetorical warfare.

17. "Madness," Kittler (2013, 66) asserts, "is technological, and God…is a deity of information channels such as Marconi and Siemens built…. What runs down the wire is the Real of the current century: electrical data flow."

18. Grant 1969, 137.

19. "For there is no truth which it concerns us to know," Grant complained, "there is only the truth with which we are concerned to do things" (Davis 2002b, 162). The "things" we "do" seem confined to eyes and fingers and the devices they (be)hold.

20. Referencing Arendt's analysis of totalitarianism, Bradshaw (1996, 231) points out that "what is destroyed in totalitarian regimes is the public space—the civic space in which people are visible to one another, are compelled to confront one another. The mere fact of visibility leads to empathy among human beings. This is why the secrecy of the concentration camps and the hiddenness of medical experimentation in Nazi Germany led to such horrific consequences. For the state to operate according to the triumph of the will, people have to be pushed back into an isolated and completely privatized existence." Isn't that what the information technologies do?

21. "The digital screen," Pérez-Gómez (2016, 101) notes, "easily furthers the delusion that the represented space in the optical image is homologous with the spatiotemporal reality appearing before us in our lives." (See also Kittler 2013, 81–2). "There is no space between the use of a technical artifact and the image of Being projected in the epoch of technology," Angus (1987, 101) appreciates. Can the concept of culture—as in "our lives"—survive the digital age? The concept of "digital culture," Pérez-Gómez (2016, 201) adds later, is a "lamentable contradiction in terms."

22. Grant 1969, 24.

23. "This technological paradigm of knowledge," Knopff (1992, 59) notes, "means that we not only make the world to suit our purposes, but also make up those purposes. There can be no 'given' purposes because the assumption of an uncaring and improvident world means that there is nothing or nobody to 'give' them. If the world is raw material for human mastery, then the purposes served by that mastery are also man-made. This is why Grant sees a gulf between technology and justice. Justice properly speaking (or at least speaking pre-technologically) is an expression of human purpose."

24. For Benedetti (2005, 207), "the historical process has gotten jammed," adding that history itself has become like "an immense, overstuffed library, to which nothing can now be added."

25. "Mass culture," Doane (2002, 162) suggests, "seeks to annihilate the possibility of boredom, of dead time, of a monochrome, unpunctuated time. Modernity, in contrast, becomes the persistent production of events."

26. Grant (1969) 2001, 68. In a 1950 letter, Grant invokes such imagery, writing to his mother: "Theology must be a study where one is surrounded by the dark" (Christian 1996d, 161). Writing decades later about Jewish theology, Fishbane (2008, ix) shares the imagery, writing that his book is an "attempt to 'do' theology in a dark and disorienting time—a time sunk in the mire of modernity." That "doing" I reconstruct from Grant as "attunement," a term in Fishbane's title. See ch. 6.

27. Kracauer 1995, 129, 130.

28. "The intense subjectivity of modern work, exemplified even more clearly in the office than in the factory," Lasch (1978, 102) observed, "causes men and women to doubt the reality of the external world and to imprison themselves…in a shell of

protective irony." Exhausted by psychological intensity and an acute, often physical, sense of threat, many retreat from a public sphere that no longer seems safe, let alone supportive or worthy of their engagement. In the apparent safety of private life, however, few find solace. "On the contrary," Lasch notes, "private life takes on the very qualities of the anarchic social order from which it is supposed to provide a refuge" (27).

29.   In late modernity, time disappears in fusion with the screen. In his era, Grant argued that time had been reduced to history—that absent eternity there is *only* history—a development he attributed, Sibley (2008, 142) suggests, to "Judaism's incorporation into early Christianity." Sibley explains: "The Incarnation made historical events absolutely important, lending weight to the sense that history can be the arena for man's redemption and salvation. However, to think this is to believe that time is not 'the moving image of eternity,' but rather the realm in which good overcomes evil" (142–3). The spiritual assurance that events are expressions of divine will slides, in secularity, into confidence in human will, redirecting humanity's attention away from eternity to history, and specifically the future. In late modernity (e.g., postmodernity), even the future fades as satiation in the present is all that matters. Given this scenario—not only has eternity evaporated but time (even as history, now only a narrative) too—recollection (in Grant's term) or reactivation ("becoming historical" in Toews's) becomes, in my judgement, politically progressive.

30.   Grant (1969) 2001, 65. For Grant, National Socialism was the "greatest modernity" (Davis and Roper 2009b, 327).

31.   Kracauer 1995, 78.

32.   Like Angus (1997, 242n81), "I use the convention of capitalizing the 'Other' when it refers not to the 'other' as constituted within one's perceptual-intellectual horizon but as opening to an Other beyond the domination of the self." Perhaps beyond materiality itself, as Grant might suggest.

33.   Grant 1986, 38.

34.   Grant 1986, 73.

35.   In postmodernity, the ancient war—good versus evil—intensifies, if Epstein (2010, 6) is right: "Digitization will amplify our better nature but also its diabolic opposite."

36.   Grant 1969, 138. Freedom affected "my own position as a teacher," Grant knew, crystallized in the question: "Is there any proposition which should not be questioned in the classroom?" While the answer must be affirmative, he adds a second question: "Hasn't every obscurantist used the affirmative answer to this question as the way he prevented the search for and spread for truth?" (Davis and Roper 2009b, 98). This is also the question the president of Bard College in the United States—Leon Botstein (2017, A25)—raised after the inauguration of Donald J. Trump as US president: "How is the university to function when a president's administration blurs the distinction between fact and fiction by asserting the existence of 'alternative facts'"?

37.   Grant 1986, 39.

38.   Doane 2002, 222.

39.   As O'Donovan (1984, 5) explains, for Grant history was "the central theoretical and practical idea of our age," structuring humanity's sense of itself as "unique," as dated, e.g., belonging to a specific unrepeatable era. The past becomes a foreign country, almost an absolute alterity. In postmodernity, I am suggesting, especially three decades after Grant's death, time itself—either as history or as a moving image

of eternity (those two are not mutually exclusive in my view)—disappears. Kearney (2005b, 145) even wonders "how can time be said to *be* since the future is always *not yet*, the past is always *no longer*, and the present is always not always?"

40. "[M]odernity is coeval with…the designed environment of the technological sensorium," Arthur Kroker (1984, 60) explains: "We now take our 'environment' with us in the form of technical 'extensions" of the human body or senses. The technostructure is both the lens through which we experience the world, and, in fact, the 'anxious object' with which human experience has become imperceptibly, almost subliminally, merged." It is this last point that points to the pervasiveness of narcissism in advanced technological societies. It is the impossible project of extrication from the "technological sensorium" that both Grant and, evidently, Marshall McLuhan endorsed. "No less critical than Grant of the human fate in technological society," Kroker tells us, "McLuhan's imagination seeks a way out of our present predicament by recovering a highly ambivalent attitude towards the objects of technostructure" (58). In Richard Cavell's (2002, 190) characterization ambivalence is nowhere in evidence: "Yet McLuhan does not posit a way outside his environment except through technology itself." It's not obvious to me how, if technology is the environment, it can provide passage "outside." Only nature—however socially constructed that term is (see, e.g., Wapner 2010, 6), but hardly "artifactual," as McLuhan argued (see Cavell 2002, 170)—can be "outside" technology.

41. An early and secular sense of Grant's appreciation for "difference" is evident in a December 1941 letter written to his mother where he expresses his admiration for the "tenacious courage" of the Russians in fighting the Germans. He continues: "What we all forgot about Russia…is…that the standards of our civilization just don't apply to theirs, that our ideas of the world moving forward in the liberal way just don't mean very much to them. They have their own that are as valid for them as ours are for us" (Christian 1996d, 93).

42. Grant 1986, 42.

43. "Technological civilization is not simply external to us," Athanasiadis (2001, 171) observes, "but molds us in all that we are, from our practical activities to our thoughts, dreams, and imaginings. The pursuit of technology has become the dominant purpose of our existence; it is our religion." It is idolatry, I argue, that informs Grant's critique, as technology substitutes for temporality, rationality, ethics, and education.

44. Athanasiadis (2001, 183) notes: "This sense of history also gave rise to the focus on doing…. The very concept of history was future-oriented and directed toward very concrete purposes."

45. Grant 1986, 34. Speaking to teachers in 1955, Grant observed that such "worldly materialism…exalts the salesman and the engineer above the teacher and the minister" (Davis 2002b, 183), both of whom he envisioned as nourishing the soul. When humanity becomes "so intoxicated by the achievement of finite ends that the idea of any spiritually infinite end is fast disappearing. And, of course, with the disappearance of the idea of spirit, of the idea of the infinite from consciousness, men fast become apes" (183).

46. Doane 2002, 232.

47. Grant (1965) 2005, 52.

48. Davis and Roper 2005b, 597.

49.   Grant (1965) 2005, 52. "We see," Grant lamented, "that freedom has only brought us enslavement by science. And enslavement by scientists is surely even more dangerous than enslavement by prelates" (Davis 2002b, 31). Why might he say that? Science led to "modern medicine," Grant noted, but it also threatens "modern nuclear war" (Davis and Roper 2009b, 539).

50.   "Grant begins to see human history," Athanasiadis (2001, 19) reminds, "not as a progression toward heaven, but a descent into hell."

51.   Grant ([1965] 2005, 52). Many concur with Grant, including Sibley (2006, 99), who positions the United States as "the center of the modern project."

52.   Grant 1969, 139.

53.   Grant (1970) 2005, lxxv.

54.   Grant (1970) 2005, lxxiii. In 1945 Grant knew that the "rise of fascism and organized barbarism in the 1930s should never be forgotten" (Davis and Emberley 2000b, 104). After the 2010 mid-term elections in the United States, I remembered the Weimar Republic (Pinar 2012, 62ff.). Americans needed no Hindenberg to surrender the reins of power; in the 2016 presidential election they demolished their democracy democratically. No surprise to Rocha (who ruefully predicted the event in 2011; see Rocha 2017, 23–5), nor to Grant, as Dart (Dart and Jersak 2011, 4) implies: "Grant thought that the USA (rhetoric aside about liberty and democracy) was a nation built on Power and Will."

55.   "Dynamism" was the term US progressives like Hilda Taba (1932, 38) embraced: "Meanings are dynamic, in the sense that they are a result of an active, shifting relationship within the experiential situation. They are produced and remodified in every act of experience. On the other hand, they enter as active participants in determining the processes of experience." For Taba and her progressive colleagues, such dynamism portended social progress, despite writing at a time when the future was foreclosed by political instability and economic collapse. Such was the power of progressives' faith in education, that secular version of Protestant Christianity (see Tröhler 2011) that promised social and economic salvation.

56.   "The greatest thinkers of that [modern] era have been Germans," Grant told Cayley (1995, 111), "and I would say the two supreme thinkers have been Nietzsche, about a hundred years ago, and in our time present time, Heidegger, Nietzsche's great epigone." Cayley remembers that when he interviewed Grant—in his home—Grant had a small photograph of Heidegger on the mantelpiece, "and I noticed one morning that it was facing the wall rather than the room, as it had been the previous day. When I asked him about this, he said that he changed the orientation depending on how he was disposed to 'the old bastard' that day" (25–6).

57.   That recollection and reconstruction can be correlative seems implied in Doane's (2002, 221) insight: "It is not only the past which seems 'lost' and in dire need of reconstitution, but the present as well, a present that is the victim of rationalization and estrangement."

58.   Collingwood 2002, 100.

59.   Grant (1970) 2005, lxix. "The past is the very character of time itself—to pass away," Grant writes (Davis and Roper 2009b, 1005). To pass away, even to be forgotten, but present as echoes perhaps, as the subsequent section on the Weimar Republic illustrates, time represents the movement from here to eternity.

60.   "Hermeneutic dialogue with our past brings our presuppositions to light," D. Roberts (1995, 175) notes, "thereby making self-criticism possible." True enough, but such self-criticism is not necessarily subjective, e.g., changing how we are, as Grant's sense of recollection suggests. "Grant tells us to make the deposit of history our own," Meynell (2011, 119) explains, "that we might see our own culture in contrast to that of our past and, through reason, discern the elements of the past are worth retrieving and which can be left behind. Studying history teaches us the proper form of philosophy, the importance of natural law, and the distinctive nature of our contemporary conception of time." That is quite an agenda, and O'Donovan (1984, 166) suggests that "the greatest paradox of Grant's writings" is "that he exhorts us to a task that he has rendered impossible, the task of thinking our fate in relation to what is remembered."

61.   Given the "dynamism" of technological present, Grant—also thinking of the Weimar Republic (and Montreal in the 1940s)—thought that "the great experiences of particular times and places soon [become] inadequate as the archetypal interpreters" (Davis and Roper 2009b, 916). Inadequate, I agree, but indispensable nonetheless.

62.   Davis and Roper 2005b, 623. "Historical thinking," Hutt (2013, 68) writes, "makes possible the actual rethinking of past thoughts." Such trans-temporal action does not strip historical persons or events of their specificity, as Hutt emphasizes: "[T]he so-called timeless message of such images [he is citing the crucifixion] is activated and makes sense only in specific presents" (77). When I first wrote this chapter, Weimar was apt; Trump had not yet been elected. "Only the past," Weil ([1947] 2002, 175) wrote, "when we do not remanufacture it, is pure reality."

63.   Grant 1969, 64.

64.   Grant was not alone. "According to Hannah Arendt," Planinc (1992, 25n19) reminds, "all ideologies have three totalitarian elements: a claim to total explanation, independence from all common sense experience, and a claim to perfect consistency…. Issuism is a totalitarian ideology of a new type. It is the ideology best suited to technological society, the society that deduces everything from technology."

65.   Peukert 1992, 241–2. For Grant, O'Donovan (1984, 167) notes, "each historical totality is an image of eternity, even if an inverted image."

66.   Why? Because, Grant asserts, "ethics depend on metaphysics." I'm not so sure, but even the secular can share Lipari's (2014, 179) suggestion that "an affirmation of the other's alterity—the otherness of others—is central to ethics." In the political polarization that followed the First World War, however, the demonization—not the affirmation—of alterity structured public life, and not only in Germany but the in the United States as well.

67.   Peukert 1992, 277. After the hyperinflation of 1923 had been stabilized, a "stabilization phase" (lasting until the Great Depression) began, inaugurating, Herf (1984, 19) explains, a "period of expanded investment and rationalization in industry. It was during this period of relative prosperity and political stability that Americanization, Fordism, and class harmony based on corporatist arrangements fostering expanded productivity reached their zenith." While "modern consumption was one sign of the golden years of the Weimar Republic," Weitz (2007, 149) points out, "'rationalization' was the other. The term meant, most basically, the application of scientific methods to production in order to expand output, with less labour. Technological and managerial improvements were all the rage. Businesses combined, mechanized

many processes, and shed workers." Isn't this what the insistence on technology in schools is partly about: increasing productivity, reducing costs (at least personnel costs), while rhetorically inflating the importance of teachers to rationalize the scapegoating and dismantling of the profession?

68.   Peukert 1992, 277–8.

69.   Peukert 1992, 278. The Austrian poet Hugo von Hofmannsthal, Herf (1984, 32n6) points out, was the first to use the term "conservative revolution," and in 1927, referencing the many Germans who sought "not freedom but communal bonds." Fifty years later, in the United States, those "communal bonds" would take not only the form of national culture—Ronald Reagan's uncritical embrace of patriotism was unrelenting—but of subcultural—some would say subaltern—forms as well. "[T]he conservative revolution of the Reagan years provoked the return of the repressed," Cusset (2008, 131) suggests, "the notorious *referent*, evacuated by these formalistic versions of French theory, made a sudden comeback under the name of *identity politics*." In Canada, the name of identity politics is of course Indigenous, in the United States, black. "[N]ot religion but revolution," Weil ([1947] 2002, 181) declared, is the "opium" of the people.

70.   Herf 1984, 3.

71.   Herf's phrase; see 1984, 1–2.

72.   Kittler (2013, 246) emphasizes Heidegger's military background, his deployment in summer 1918 in the "field of operation of the 1ˢᵗ Army on the Western Front," an imprinting experience Kittler implies: "Later, in summer 1923, Heidegger—leading 'a shock troop of sixteen men' against philosophical opponents—answered the call to the University of Marburg. Finally, in spring 1927, the first half of *Being and Time* was published." Kittler even traces the concept of *Dasein* to Heidegger's 1918 deployment: "In its torn state of having to be a thrown project, Heidegger's *Dasein* executes the competition between tactics and technology, 'in-each-case-mineness' and the work of the general staff shock troops, and the Supreme Army Command" (248). This is not the whole story, however; Sikka (1997, 265) demonstrates that, "in certain respects, Heidegger is himself a mystical theologian and metaphysician."

73.   Sikka (1997, 265) shows that "Heidegger's thought is original precisely in being an authentic retrieval of the past, a repetition of the possibilities handed down by the tradition," possibilities (as Weimar makes clear) horrific as well as inviting. As noted earlier, "authentic retrieval"—recollection is Grant's preferred term—is for me simultaneously subjective, spiritual, and scholarly. "Authentic retrieval," Sikka continues, "is transformative and critical, however, and, in looking at medieval thought through Heidegger's own confrontational appropriation of it, I hope that what has come to light is not merely the remains of what was once thought but also some directions for how these past thoughts may be translated into the future" (265). While her impressive and persuasive project—juxtaposing medieval thought with Heidegger's twentieth-century thought—is quite different from mine, her sense of what "retrieval" (or reactivation) promises seems similar.

74.   Weitz 2007, 334.

75.   Davis and Roper 2005b, 719. There are occasions when Grant makes remarks about "Jews" that seem questionable, as when he writes of "the mystery of the Jews," to which there is "no solution; one simply lives in their presence with reverence and good judgment" (Davis and Roper 2009b, 483). Juxtaposed with the virulent

anti-Semitism of his era, Grant's comment seems mild but questionable, especially in light of his admiration for Céline. Explaining the rise of that early twentieth-century anti-Semitism, Grant wrote: "To many European intellectuals, the Jews appeared to want the benefits of the homogenized society while maintaining as final their loyalty to their particularist community" (Davis and Roper 2009b, 484). With his affirmation of loving "one's own," did not Grant want the same?

76. For a definition that limits the concept to the last one hundred years, see Peukert (1992, 81–2). Grant's ([1965] 2005, 52n15) temporal scale is much broader: "I use 'modern' to describe the civilization of the age of progress. This civilization arose in Western Europe and is now conquering the whole globe and perhaps other parts of the universe. 'Modern' is applied to political philosophy to distinguish the thought of Western Europe from that of the antique world of Greece."

77. See Peukert 1992, 188.

78. Other important Weimar figures saw synergy where others experienced only irreparable conflict. Herf (1984, 40) points out that "Walter Gropius, the leading spirit of the Bauhaus, saw no conflict between cosmopolitanism, social democratic values, and reason, on the one hand, and beauty on the other. Given a sufficient measure of reason and passion, Gropius saw no reason why technology should post a threat to mankind. The Bauhaus embraced technology as part of modernity in a broader sense."

79. Herf 1984, 21.

80. Herf 1984, 32.

81. In Herf's (1984, 1–2) terms, Weimar's "reactionary modernists combined political reaction with technological advance." Rejecting the German Right's "backward-looking pastoralism," reactionary modernists pointed instead to "a beautiful new order replacing the formless chaos due to capitalism in a united, technologically advanced nation" (2). They did not succeed immediately, as "considerable antagonism to technology persisted in the Weimar Right" (38). Reactionary modernism was not limited to Germany; Herf cites Henry Ford as "American reactionary modernist" (219).

82. Herf 1984, 55.

83. Herf 1984, 65.

84. Herf 1984, 72. "Facing obscure orders and invisible foes," Kittler (2013, 87) writes, "literature became a matter of *Combat as Inner Experience* [*Der Kampf als inneres Erlebnis*, 1926], as Ernst Jünger aptly put it." Jünger was not the first: Trilling (1972, 128–9) points out that the "central doctrine of the Futurist Manifesto, which Marinetti wrote and published in 1908…is the beauty and vitality of the machine." For Marinetti, Trilling adds, "the mechanical is to be the authenticating principle of modern life" (129).

85. Quoted in Herf 1984, 72. In *The Mechanical Bride*, Cavell (see 2002, 44) points out, aggression is depicted as self-directed, as, McLuhan asserted, "the subject has become displaced in an 'annihilation of the human ego' that has taken place through the identification of humans with their machines." This is no self-enclosed affair however, as for McLuhan the unconscious itself—dramatically depicted as "the ever-mounting slag-heap of rejected awareness" is, in Cavell's words, "extruded into the technological environment." *That* too could help explain the narcissistic hold technology has over humanity, could it not?

86.   Angus (1987, 82) asks: "If the self is altered by technology, how can technology be measured? How can technology be evaluated if there is no standpoint outside technology which can establish the ethical value of the self?" As events after Weimar affirm, the answer to both is negative. One hundred years after, it is clear that technology replaces culture as it eradicates the self.

87.   Herf 1984, 70. For Grant, O'Donovan (1984, 49) writes, it was a different war—the US invasion of Vietnam—that bound "technological freedom to imperialism: that of an ever-expanding conquest of human and non-human nature in the service of freedom as the overcoming of chance." For Jünger, of course, this conquest was a great (specifically German) accomplishment; for Grant it constituted a catastrophe.

88.   Herf 1984, 79. In our time it is the fusion of man and drugs, in the case of Lance Armstrong, as well as with hardware, prostheses for US soldiers returning from Iraq and Afghanistan, that enables exceeding the limits of the biological body.

89.   Herf 1984, 79.

90.   Herf 1984, 84. Time disappears when, as Kittler (2013, 55) suggests, "machines themselves *are* the mind." Promoted to major in the Second World War, Jünger—"both an operations officer in, and the poet of, the Wehrmacht," as Kittler (2013, 135) casts him—lived in occupied Paris at the Hotel Raphael, from whose rooftop terrace Jünger would ascend to "enjoy the "great beauty" and "demonic power" of the multimedia "show" provided by the Royal Air Force bombing (136). "At such times," Kittler continues, Jünger would hold a glass of burgundy with strawberries swimming in it in his hand," a glass decades later French critics would raise to condemn "the drinker's nihilism and aestheticism" (136). Kittler reminds that in 1915 Proust joined a young French officer on leave from the trenches to "enjoy the play of light between attacking German zeppelins and French defensive installations" (136). The officer—Robert, Marquis de Saint-Loup—confessed to his companion his marvelling at "the beauty of moments when the zeppelins "form constellations"—and even more so when they crash and "form an apocalypse" (136–7). Kittler connects Wagner, opera, and film, and their acoustic special effects, with military savagery, conjoined in a wineglass. In contrast to natural beauty—which, like Weil, Grant associates with eternity—technological beauty is a pleasing poison that kills.

91.   In the late- or postmodern moment what for Grant was distinguishable—Jerusalem (with God's intervention in, indeed structuring of, history) and Athens (with time as a moving image of eternity—fuse in our idolatry of the device. Discussing Innis, Stamps (1995, 48) acknowledges "the modern denial of time—the key problem of the West." Revelation and eternity disappear; only the screen remains, flickering in front of us.

92.   Rocha 2017, 13.

93.   "[W]e have already become posthuman," Foster (2005, 5) announces, a state that "emerges when technology does in fact 'become me,' not by being incorporated into my organic unity and integrity, but instead by interrupting that unity and opening the boundary between self and world" (10). "Opening the boundary between self and world" invites fusion, indeed, narcissism, and the disappearance of the public, including civic, sphere. This calamity is then restated as a technical, even cultural, advance.

94.   "The so-called late Enlightenment…in Austria and in Germany," Kittler (2013, 146) chronicles, "simply exchanged modes of memory and installed a system that could not just store information, but erase it as well. The eraser swept over the individual."

Without memory, focused on affluence and pleasure, the self atrophies in symbiosis with the sensory, in our time with the virtual, and the character required for "moral intransigence and political activism"—namely "renunciation and sublimation"—dissolves, these among the "adverse political implications of reduced individuality" (Trilling 1972, 165–6). Trilling is discussing here the work of one refugee from Weimar's collapse, Herbert Marcuse, for whom the "adverse political implications of reduced individuality" (165) are among the most chilling.

95. Quoted in Herf 1984, 100.

96. The mass ornament, Kracauer argued, represents, in Thomas Levin's (1995, 18) words, a "new" form of collective organization, one not based in "community" but in functionality and instrumentality. In Kracauer's (1995, 83) terms: "The human figure enlisted in the mass ornament has begun the *exodus* from lush organic splendour and the constitution of individuality toward the realm of anonymity to which it relinquishes itself when it stands in truth and when the knowledge radiating from the basis of man dissolves the contours of visible natural form." Working from within is required to discern traces of humanity remaining within the anonymity of the contemporary living "ornament."

97. Heidegger was "personally close" to Jünger, Herf (1984, 108) points out, although characterizing Heidegger as a "reactionary modernist" would stretch the concept. "But," Herf adds, "it would be fair to say that his Nazi sympathies in the 1930s had a great deal to do with his views on technology, some of which bore striking resemblance to [Jünger's]" (108). Recent publication of Heidegger's philosophical diaries make clear that anti-Semitism was also in play: https://www.theguardian.com/books/2014/mar/13/martin-heidegger-black-notebooks-reveal-nazi-ideology-antisemitism.

98. Herf 1984, 103.

99. Weaver 2010, 193.

100. Humanity dwells within the "tension of time," Kaethler (2009, 29) suggests, in part because our "fundamental characteristic is possibility." The tension of time may be "fundamental," but recasting it in terms of the *Volk* and as intoxicating, as Jünger did, renders tension temporally empty.

101. Herf 1984, 125.

102. Herf 1984, 126.

103. Today only the prospect of planetary collapse due to environmental degradation provides any fantasy of revolution, and that fantasy is technological. Porter (2017, B1) reports that researchers from the physical and social sciences gathered during March 2017 in Washington, DC, to discuss the possibilities of "cooling the planet by shooting aerosols into the stratosphere or whitening clouds to reflect sunlight back into space, which may prove indispensable to prevent the disastrous consequences of warming."

104. Herf 1984, 128.

105. Herf 1984, 130. Grant made a somewhat similar set of associations, except to cultural degradation: "The contractualized life of the public world has an increasingly dog-eat-dog quality. This is particularly so as the industrial machine has required continual new waves of immigrants to do the dirty work of that expanding society. The society therefore has the quality of increasing racial disparity" (Davis and Roper 2009b, 491). What Grant termed "that hideous movement, German anti-Semitism" (992), becomes another allegory of the present.

106. Herf 1984, 134.

107. No longer persons, students are recast as scores on standardized tests; see Taubman 2009. This atrocity is conducted energetically, with moral righteousness, for the sake of the American nation, in the name of school reform, but its racial subtext is unmistakable, as it is the racialized underclasses in America that are said to be failed by so-called underperforming schools. It is the racialized underclasses who must be integrated in the economy. Teaching to standardized tests renders irrelevant functionally futile knowledge like that of lynching (see Pinar 2001, 1117).

108. Herf 1984, 143

109. Herf 1984, 150.

110. Herf 1984, 171.

111. Herf 1984, 175.

112. See Herf 1984, 224.

113. Herf 1984, 224–5.

114. Herf 1984, 224–5.

115. As noted, on occasion Grant made comments that sound, to my ears, a little too close to Weimar-era fantasies of pervasive Jewish influence. For example, on one occasion Grant asked: "Can we say that Jews are outsiders in the world when they exert such power over the politics and culture of the world's most powerful empire?" (Davis and Roper 2009b, 917) In an April 1952 letter to his mother, however, Grant clearly associates "plutocracy" with anti-Semitism (Christian 1996d, 172).

116. Herf 1984, 225. Many of these theorists of technology—"reactionary modernists"— were not biological racists like the Nazis, Herf (1984, 226) points out, "but by the time those who cared realized that differences existed, it was too late." Moreover, not only rightists were persuaded by the promise of technology. The trade unions and Social Democrats had also endorsed technological progress, Peukert (1992, 112) points out, judging it a "vehicle for the achievement of social reform. Increased productivity would, presumably, lead to higher wages and shorter working hours and would make for easier and safer working practices." As is the case today, there was then a political consensus on the centrality of technology in fantasies of the future. What is clear to us, living in the future (of the past), is that technology has, in many instances, decreased working wages as it has decreased the total number of jobs, as increasing productivity requires fewer workers, especially those without technical training. "Global economic forces have pummelled blue-collar workers more relentlessly than almost any other segment of society," Sullivan (2015, 36) reports: "No wonder suicide and mortality rates among the white working poor are spiking dramatically."

117. Herf 1984, x.

118. Grant (1965) 2005, 13n3. Grant associated nationhood with love of one's own, love anterior to love of others, no expression of ideology but a profound concern over Canada's vulnerability to the United States, that evident when Cayley (1995, 104) asks him: "But you're saying that your concerns are related more to national survival than to some a priori ideological position you were taking?" Grant replies: "Of course." On that point the Nazis said the same—National Socialism was in the service of national survival—but it was nationalism fuelled by demonization of others. Pacifism not militarism inspired Grant's sense of patriotism, an inclusive sense that in the 1960s welcomed even Americans. Grant tells Cayley: "I admired greatly from

a distance the fact that large numbers of young Americans wouldn't go along with the Vietnam War—and I saw a lot of these people coming and going in Canada, and I just liked them" (105).

119. Doane 2003, 88.

120. See Toews 2004; Pinar 2011, 126–40. Becoming historical emphasizes subjectivity and social agency, in contrast to "historicism," for Grant "the teaching that all thought is determined by belonging to a concrete dynamic context" (Davis and Roper 2009b, 342). Muggeridge (1978, 43) notes that "Grant shuns both historicism and determinism." And Arapura (1983, 60) suggests that "the transcendent is the only defence against the tyrannies of history and against history itself, which is probably the greatest of all tyrannies because it is the most transcendental form that immanentist reason arrogates to itself." After studying Grant, history can seem as if it is a moving image of eternity, not an idol unto itself.

121. "Justice had always had a central place in Grant's thinking," Cayley (1995, 31) reminds. Justice appears first, Grant suggests, in the love of one's own, of one's own body, of one's own children (see 102–3). As love enables attunement to the transcendent, one's love expands to include others.

122. Grant (1974) 1998, 43.

123. Calculating such "interest" is complicated by the fact, as Simone Weil ([1947] 2002, 9) noted, that one is "other" than what one imagines oneself to be.

124. Grant (1974) 1998, 45. "Justice is connected to the soul," Kaethler (2009, 45) emphasizes, "because it is part of our being. The only reparation is to pay what is due."

125. Grant 1986, 54.

126. Pinar 2012, 207–38.

127. Grant (1970) 2005, lxxi.

128. Herf 1984, 1. One technological-historical through line of America's modernity is Germany. "Already at the end of August 1944," Kittler (2013, 205) reports, "it was known in the Reich Central Security Office—from 'reliable' reports provided by agents abroad—that plans existed, 'in the event of a German collapse,' 'to transfer at least 20,000 German engineers to the United States.' This and nothing else, then, had prompted Major General Kammler to order his rocket technicians to the deepest south, that is, into American territory."

129. Quebec, Christian (1996a, 248) tells us, Grant "knew and loved." He had "experienced" French Catholicism during his youth, Christian continues; later he came to regard it as a "sustaining bulwark against the inroads of the universal and homogenous state" (248–9). Quebec enabled Canada to resist assimilation into the United States; without it, he told a CBC interviewer, Canadian nationalism could not be thought.

130. Grant (1965) 2005, 74. For a view of Catholicism in line with Grant's, see Kane 1990.

131. Confidence in our technological future derives from Christian eschatology, Grant understood, itself a "prophetic view of temporal events" in which, as O'Donovan (1984, 36) explains, "God acts directly and personally, giving to every fine occurrence uniqueness and irreversibility…. Thus, time is finite and oriented to the future, and human action is ultimately significant, being directed to an absolute fulfillment."

132. Dewey (1922, 176) questioned commonplace conceptions of progress too: "There is something pitifully juvenile in the idea that 'evolution,' progress, means a definite sum of accomplishment which will forever stay done, and by which an exact amount

lessens the amount still to be done, disposing once and for all of the many perplexities and advancing us on our roads to a final stable and unperplexed goal."

133. That modernity was secularized Christianity did not, for Grant, absolve the church from complicity with it, writing, in April 1952, that "Protestantism will kneel to the rich and the technicians and the military as much as anybody" (Christian 1996d, 173)

134. Doane 2002, 225.

135. Quoted in Christian 1996a, 173; see Davis 2002b, 163.

136. "In an argument that is again very close to Grant's," Sibley (2008, 198) writes, "[philosopher Charles] Taylor claims that this has in fact taken place because modern instrumental science denies its own spiritual sources and its original moral purposes." More than Grant, Taylor emphasizes the "positive aspects of modernity" (198).

137. Rocha 2017, 38. Of these concepts, a comment concerning "possessive individualism" is in order, given its conflation with individualism or individuality. In contrast to individuality, the concept of possessive individualism—associated with C. B. Macpherson—emphasizes freedom from constraint, converted by capitalism into the right to exploit labour and land for maximum profit; see Harvey 2010, 175; Meynell 2011, 61; see also Angus 2013, 42, 46; Martin and Barresi 2006, 180. As Huebner (1999, 76) explains, "the possessive individual denies the other's freedom and his own, for he is not open to the other but is walled off by his own self." While hardly interested in any "undoing of the distinction between the inner life of the subject and the external social and physical worlds" (Foster 2005, 176)—after all, social media threatens that (Foster suggests otherwise; see 229–30)—I emphasize that individuality is socially constituted, embedded, and embodied, in contrast to economistically inflected conceptions of "possessive individualism."

138. These concepts intertwine too, as Stamps (1995, 62) notes: "Cultures are necessarily historical things. Moreover, unlike the dichotomous space-time world described by Hobbes, they are interactively spatial and temporal, as Innis showed so well. Similarly, in contrast to the scientific view that separates objective from subjective processes, they are at once objective, by virtue of their materiality, and subjective, by virtue of the unique forms of consciousness that they produce. Hence, like language, cultures are innately decentered." This last point seems forgotten in the contemporary centredness—essentialism, strategic, and otherwise—of identity politics.

139. Emberley (1994) 2005, lxxx.

140. Emberley (1994) 2005, lxxxi. Planinc (1992, 20) suggests that the "universal and homogenous state has no specific political form."

141. Emberley (1994) 2005, lxxxi.

142. Emberley (1994) 2005, lxxxii.

143. In this revelation, Grant was not alone. Pasolini believed that consumer capitalism meant "cultural genocide" (Mariniello 1994, 115, 125). "Doctrine has eliminated idols but not idolaters," Mondzain (2005, 190) observes, "under pain of eliminating humanity in its entirety." Mondzain continues: "But have we forgotten that it is in the mercantile belly of collective narcissism that the sordid beast has always laid its first eggs?" (220).

144. Sometimes Grant seemed to think the claims of democracy were overstated. In a 1950 letter to his mother, Grant complains about post-war shortages in the United Kingdom—he is again at Oxford completing his DPhil—being attributed to labour

while ignoring "the fact that the old ruling class led them through two wars.... So many of them talk as if the Labour Party had introduced class struggle into England, when my God the middle class has waged it for years," inserting, almost parenthetically, "as you know I don't believe in democracy and think there have to be rulers, however controlled by elections" (Christian 1996d, 161). Four years later—yes, another letter to his mother—Grant notes his "dislike of the growing social democracy with its trust in psychiatrists and scientists to solve anything" (183). Twenty years later, in a letter to Dennis Lee, he writes of "the horror of modernity" (275)... reminding Lee, "I am not a democrat" (276). Well, yes and no, as Grant recognized the hierarchy of talents but not its capacity to exploit others. His affirmation of others as souls equal in the sight of God was enacted in his pedagogy of testimony, witness, and ethical concern for others. "And when I speak of loyalty of that democracy," Grant affirmed, "I do not mean to its political forms, but to its social forms as well. For instance, the idea of social equality, which is so much a product of the North American as against the English tradition, is something to which I give wholehearted allegiance" (Davis 2002b, 167).

145. Innis's first communications essay per se, "The Newspaper in Economic Development," had appeared in the *Journal of Economic History*, in 1942 (see Watson 2007, 249). For Innis, Watson explains, "newspaper technology was like an addictive drug that accelerated this destructive process while at the same time obliterating those long-term critical faculties that could identify the basis of the problem" (383), namely the loss of capacity to concentrate, to analyze, to think critically. Instead, a "new" form of "ecstasy"—titillation, expectation, appetite for constant change, as in ever-changing fashion—was introduced by contemporary communications technologies, in Innis's time most prominently the newspaper, now devoted, in Watson's words, to "fuelling the most banal forms of consumerism rather than towards the conservation of a cultural heritage" (384). Because the newspaper appropriated the vernacular, it was, in Innis's assessment, all the more predatory. Through the "mechanization, amplification, and transmission of the vernacular," communications technologies like the newspaper "increase social hysteria, irrationalism, and the appeal to force at the expense of rational, contemplative rule based on the an appreciation of the strengths and limitations of the social heritage of the West" (385). McLuhan argued—Cavell (2002, 35) explains, quoting McLuhan—"that it is the formal or structural implications of the newspaper that are significant, not its content, in the same way that modern art 'lack[s]...a message,' and that this form inevitably points towards unity." While I am not persuaded by this argument—that content does not matter, only its "structural implications"—McLuhan's conclusion (regarding "unity") seems similar to Innis's and Grant's. In an era of "fake news" (see Irwin 2017; J. Peters 2016), however, reputable newspapers—I rely on the *New York Times* (although the Toronto *Globe and Mail* must be included in any North American list of reputable sources of news and analysis)—become, if not truth-telling, at least truth-seeking institutions to be protected.

146. "Under the influence of Heidegger and Ellul," Gillespie (1990, 129) concludes, "Grant comes to overestimate vastly the power of a technologically-guided social science employing propaganda, polling, and so on, to subvert and subordinate all contemporary politics." Gillespie might revise this judgment today. While "spin" has often seemed omnipresent in US elections, outright lying and fake news characterized

the 2016 US presidential campaign of Donald J. Trump. "Over the years," admitted John Ziegler, a conservative radio host in the United States, "we've effectively brainwashed the core of our audience to distrust anything that they disagree with. And now it's gone too far" (quoted in Herrman 2016, B1). As Innis and Grant anticipated, now "every story, and source, is at risk of being discredited, not by argument but by sheer force" (B1).

147. Grant (1965) 2005, 41.

148. See https://www.bloomberg.com/news/articles/2014-06-24/phone-hacking-scandal-that-rocked-news-corp-timeline.

149. The chief executive officer of News Corporation, which owns the *Wall Street Journal*, Rupert Murdoch, Banchero and Simon (2011, C2) report, has been an "advocate" of "digital education." In 2010 News Corp. bought a 90 per cent state in Wireless Generation, an education-technology company that sells handheld computers to teachers to monitor student performance. From wiretapping to "monitoring" student performance seems a seamless move. After all, Grant pointed out, "How then do we know what purposes we should use computers for and what not?" (Davis and Roper 2009b, 119)

150. "One basic problem of Western civilization," Al-i Ahmad (1984, 122) observes, "is the constant need for vigilance against the seeds of fascism."

151. In his *Verbi-Voco-Visual Explorations* (1967), McLuhan comments that organization men "would be ashamed to be caught reading during business hours. Any activity so private, silent and meditative is disloyal to the ways of organization" (quoted in Cavell 2002, 109).

152. Teamwork and collaboration are among the keywords of organization "men," and questions of leadership—insofar as these imply ethical judgment—devolve into matters of management. "If economics and technology are taken to be the great inevitable forces of our day," John Ralston Saul (2005, 12) points out, "management is more like a support system that makes the other two seem inevitable. The abrupt rise to hyper-respectability of managerial schools and their matching with large corporations led by technocrats has had the astonishing effect of confusing management with leadership. And if leadership is reduced to management, well then, problems are not to be solved. They are to be managed. In fact, they are no longer problems."

153. "A new strain of populism is metastasizing before our eyes," Mark Lilla (2010, 53) suggested, a "politics of the libertarian mob." Galvanized by the 2008 financial collapse and the election of the nation's first African-American president, Lilla suggests this has been fifty years in coming, but Grant ([1974] 1998, 56) references Paine in his more nuanced view that the egalitarianism of US populism has "always" been "subsidiary." Demonization, not egalitarianism, characterizes the Trump election of November 2016, as reactionary populism triumphed.

154. Grant (1965) 2005, 14.

155. Grant (1965) 2005, 9.

156. Grant (1965) 2005, 85.

157. Grant (1965) 2005, 75. Whereas the Nazis emphasized racial purity, Grant affirmed diversity, telling Cayley (1995, 107) that he thinks "it's great that there's new nationalism in Canada; I think it's great that there has been new nationalism of an authentic kind in Quebec." In light of the residential-school scandals, I suspect he would

have also strongly endorsed Indigenous nationalism, including claims for cultural preservation and reparation (as noted in the introduction).

158. As Dewey and, no doubt, Grant would acknowledge, progress is possible, but the assumption that progress is inevitable and/or can always engineered is a "doctrine" of which Grant was critical as early as his DPhil thesis (see Davis and Emberley 2000b, 373). In late modernity, Benedetti (2005, 208) suggests, "having taken away the idea of progress, history becomes simultaneous, it curves around the subject, it turns it into a labyrinth." There is nowhere to go, a suffocating enclosure of our own making: technology, weaponized even more after Weimar. "[W]hatever we do," Benedetti continues, "we remain prisoners to the already-written or the already-thought" (208), emphasizing that point when she writes, "History, no longer progressive, piles up around one in an unwieldy heap: and the writer, not longer author, is asked to assume the role of an ironic (or melancholic) librarian of that immense accumulation" (200). As this book testifies—in our time of teacher as entrepreneur—teacher as ironic or melancholic librarian seems preferable.

159. Christian 1996a, 250. Grant, Christian reminds, did not "condemn" those who could not resist the "beguiling allure of modernity" (250), including America's version. "Those who criticize our age," Grant suggested, "must at the same time contemplate pain, infant mortality, crop failures in isolated areas, and the sixteen-hour day. But on the other side, other facts must be remembered: the increasing outbreaks of impersonal ferocity, genocide, the banality of existence in our concrete prisons, the pursuit of expansion as an end in itself. The powers of manipulation (not least man's ability to make man) may portend the most complete tyranny the world has ever known. When we contemplate these facts, we may wonder whether the age of progress has not been a tragic aberration in the history of the species" (Davis and Roper 2005b, 260).

160. School reformers in the United States frighten parents and policymakers by conjuring up the concept of the global workplace, intensely competitive, ever changing, increasingly technological, and for which—of course—schools fail to prepare our children. This secular salvational sermon (prepare for the next life or be damned!) is as old as its Christian substrate. In 1927, Kracauer (1995, 78) complained: "A system oblivious to differences in form leads on its own to the blurring of national characteristics and to the production of worker masses that can be employed equally well at any point of the globe. Like the mass ornament, the capitalist production process is an end in itself. The commodities that it spews forth are not actually produced to be possessed; rather, they are made for the sake of profit that knows no limit."

161. Grant (1965) 2005, 88.

162. Grant (1965) 2005, 87.

163. Grant (1965) 2005, 92.

164. Grant (1970) 2005, lxxii. A "love of particularity" is among the attributes of Céline's art that Grant admired, "in part the particularity of the nation against the universalizing and homogenizing power of the cosmopolis" (Davis and Roper 2009b, 483).

165. Grant (1965) 2005, 85.

166. Grant 1969, 74.

167. Christian 1996a, 248.

168. Grant (1965) 2005, 14.

169. Grant 1969, 74.

170. Grant 1969, 141.

171. I am thinking of the administrations of George W. Bush and Donald J. Trump, but the phenomenon is long-standing—see Hofstadter ([1965] 1996). With the selection of Betsy DeVos as US secretary of education, the "manufactured [school] crisis" (Berliner and Biddle 1995) is "solved" by consumer choice, as she endorses public funding of private schools (Green 2017, A16), a sector in which she and her family have significant investments (P. Cohen 2017, A1). David E. Kirkland, an education professor at New York University who has studied Ms. DeVos's impact in Michigan, suggested she could "badly hurt public education" by removing resources out of schools in need of federal funding. "Her extensive conflicts of interest and record of diverting money away from vulnerable students and into the pockets of the rich make DeVos completely unfit for the position she was just confirmed to," Kirkland observed (quoted passages in Huetteman and Alcindor 2017, A20).

172. See Kimmel 1996, 44.

173. T. Levin 1995, 25–6.

174. T. Levin 1995, 26.

175. Quoted in Herf (1984, 31). Stamps (1995, 49) credits Harold Innis with characterizing "objectivity" as "the philosophical version of imperial self-certainty."

176. "Without a standard of judgment," Fishbane (2008, 9) notes, "we cannot evaluate our actions in terms of what would constitute a just or human way of existing on earth; and in the process, measurement serves the most narrow or self-serving ends."

177. For Grant the triumph of modernity was the triumph of the will, a concept, Bradshaw (1996, 225) points out, meant "something quite specific to Grant: it is the assertion of the will of the individual over all else, including the sacred and the state. In our stage of modernity, the divine ground of meaning, and the political community of meaning have collapsed like a house of cards, and all that is left is the individual with his or her desire for mastery. This is fascism." Grant, Bradshaw reminds, drew "parallels between the propaganda campaign in Nazi Germany to turn Jews into nonpersons, and the propaganda in North America to prepare the general public for the acceptability of abortion" (229), parallels Bradshaw judges to be overdrawn.

178. Herf 1984, 32.

179. Grant 1986, 17.

180. Grant 1969, 132.

181. Cayley 1995, 149–50.

182. That "something," Grant suggested, was a "lower form of society even than contractarian capitalism" (Cayley 1995, 150), a somewhat eccentric explanation (in that it overlooks anti-Semitism, the Great Depression, the Versailles Treaty, and the miscalculations of Hindenberg and his Weimar Republic colleagues). I should have thought that in Grant's analysis it would have served as an exemplary instance of the tyranny of a homogenous society.

183. Davis and Roper 2009b, 185.

184. Doane (2002, 170) knows: "Spectacle functions to localize desire, fantasy, and longing in a timeless time, outside contingency. In this respect, spectacle, in contrast to the event, is epistemologically reactionary." Like its politics, one might add.

185. Doane 2002, 170.

186. Doane 2002, 170.

187. Davis and Roper 2009b, 464.

188. Benedetti 2005, 202.

189. The term is most often associated with W. E. B. Du Bois (see ch. 6, n183) but Aoki ([1979] 2005, 347) also reflected on especially the affirmative potential of what he termed "double vision," writing: "Instead of the power of monovision, the power of double vision may be what I should see.... Such an approach may reveal more fully within my lived human condition self-imposed or socially-imposed distortions that call for action—action that in the very acting will empower me to become a maker of my own history, a historical being engaged in his own personal and human becoming."

190. Such reactivation may prove to be not only a pedagogical possibility but also a spiritual necessity. "When revelation becomes foundation," O'Donovan (1984, 169) writes, "the truth is no longer present as present, but only present as past, as memory." Somehow the past becomes sacred, even (or it especially?) when it was horrific.

191. Crisis seems constant, indicative perhaps, of what Rotstein (1983, 126) terms "the hidden relation of the apocalyptic tradition to human consciousness."

192. As previously noted, science, technology, engineering, mathematics. Our era has been a long time coming and it is not confined to the West; in mid-twentieth-century Iran, for instance, Al-i Ahmad (1984, 81) complained: "In our schools we have for years been tiring our children's minds with the formulae and equations of physics, chemistry, and mathematics while all but eliminating literature from the curricula of our high schools and colleges."

193. Davis and Roper 2009b, 185–6.

194. Davis and Roper 2009b, 181.

195. Davis and Roper 2009b, 181.

196. In this instance, memory that "modern left-wing democracy, socialism, egalitarianism, liberalism is really a form of secularized Christianity" (Davis and Roper 2009b, 976). That is to say, that ethics—personal and social—remains imperative, even if without the doctrinal superstructure that commands it. Reimer (1990, 109) reminds that "there continues to be a strong residue of his [Grant's] early liberalism in his later thought."

197. Davis and Roper 2009b, 741. "Contemplation was once likened to virtue," Kaethler (2009, 50) observes, "and now 'willing' has replaced this."

198. Davis and Roper 2009b, 741. "Near the end of our five hours [of conversation]," Taylor ([1982] 2006, 132) reports, "Grant says suddenly: 'Do you know, the whole Occidental experience may be a failure? Has it never struck you?'... It's so bizarre, this momentous statement just dropping on us, almost as an afterthought, yet carrying the entire weight of our afternoon. Implicit in everything we have been discussing, yet none of us explicitly aware of it. Grant is still wrestling with the idea. 'Don't you see, the Western world might *well* be a failure now....'" As Weimar testifies, we live within that failure, if resolved to right it.

199. Davis and Roper 2009b, 971.

200. Benedetti 2005, 210.

201. Benedetti 2005, 210. Contradicting the reality, says Doane (2002, 218), is "the dream of modernity, to embrace the possibility of the emergence of the truly new." Instead, in the homogenous universal state we witness the recurrence of the old, in this chapter, Weimar.

202. "[T]ime must in part escape any definitive account," Bennington (2005, 59) concludes, a consideration to be explored in ch. 7.

203. Davis and Roper 2009b, 997.
204. Davis and Roper 2009b, 997.
205. Davis and Roper 2009b, 997.
206. Davis and Roper 2009b, 997. It was not only modernity that Nietzsche laid out before us, Grant thought, but also the ancient Greeks sense of tragedy, as in Athanasiadis's (2001, 186) words, "beings in a noble encounter with the chaos of existence, with resolute courage even in the face of profound suffering. For human beings such as these, suffering produced greater strength of character and resolve." Moreover, Athanasiadis adds, "Grant sympathizes with Nietzsche's hope for the emergence of those who will overcome the spirit of hatred or revenge in their existing. Nietzsche speaks of himself as a convalescent, letting go of the spirit of revenge and growing toward a positive love of the earth. Such love Nietzsche calls *amor fati* [love of fate], a term borrowed from the Stoics" (187). It is a concept Grant will borrow from Nietzsche.

CHAPTER 4

Teaching

[T]he [contemporary] purpose of education is to gain knowledge which issues in
the mastery of human and non-human
nature.[1]

George Grant

Like his colleague Harold Innis,[2] George Grant invoked a mythological image[3]—
that of the owl of Minerva taking flight at twilight[4]—to denote historical movement.[5] Citing Hegel, Grant acknowledged that this fading of the light invites
reflection on day's end and the night now underway, a moment for philosophy.
By philosophy Grant meant the "rigorous" and "consistent" effort to "think"
the "meaning of existence."[6] "[H]uman beings only pursue philosophy," Grant
writes, "when an old system of meaning is coming to the end of its day."[7] What
he means by "old system of meaning" turns out to be ancient indeed.

What were the markers of "twilight" in his day? One was the 1957 Sputnik
satellite, inaugurating fifty years of "school reform" in the United States,[8] and
in Canada precipitating political events that for Grant would indicate the end
of national autonomy. After the initial hysteria over Sputnik, Americans became
"deeply depressed" by the Soviet's technological "success."[9] Grant kept his
attention on the American elites, who, he suspected, were relieved, now free to
focus on conquering outer space, free from any obligation to "think about what
will make life meaningful when practical problems are settled."[10] While practical problems are rarely finally settled, evidently questions of meaning can be
deferred indefinitely.

Sputnik became the precipitating event for a constitutionally questionable
and ongoing federal intervention in the education of the American public.[11] Grant

is focused on Canada; Sputnik provided the rationale for the United States to stipulate the status of its ally in this perilous phase of the Cold War. Canada remained the neighbour to the north, but in the national panic over Sputnik "neighbourliness" meant more proximity than congeniality. Grant minced no words, noting "how rocked" North America had been when the Soviets launched "that piece of metal up into the sky before we did," providing provocation for "business and military leaders" to demand "we must be tougher in our education so that we can produce together history-makers."[12] Responsibility for the fiasco— failure to be first in space—shifted swiftly from government, the space program, or the US military onto an institution ill-suited to produce a national mobilization.[13] By relocating responsibility for Sputnik from government to schools, officials sidestepped accountability and ensured that schools would not escape theirs.

Sputnik signalled that the postwar period in American public education had ended.[14] There would be a decade—the 1960s—when US progressivism remerged and even more radically so, intensified by, as it was intertwined with, the racial, gender, and anti–Vietnam War politics of the period. With Richard Nixon's election in 1968, night falls. The military competition characterizing the Cold War had accelerated the technologization of culture and of the economy, prompting politicians and the increasingly powerful defence industry[15] to pressure schools to produce more scientists and engineers.[16] By mid-century, bureaucratization— in the early twentieth century judged "progressive" as it promised equal and fair treatment of the masses—seemed only oppressive. Grant goes so far as to say: "Every instrument of mass culture is a pressure alienating the individual from himself as a free being."[17] While today this judgment seems too sweeping, it is not mistaken. Then schools could curb creativity as they institutionalized instrumentalism: with "reform" schools could produce scientists who could produce the technology that ensured military and economic—national—superiority.

Such a scheme restated an American confidence in engineering[18] at least a century old, a nationally and historically specific modernity summarized as "Americanism," at least in Germany during the 1920s.[19] It had been Germans— Adorno and Horkheimer—who had argued that modernity meant the instrumentalization of reason,[20] its debasement into calculation, manipulation, exploitation.[21] In education "reason" becomes reformulated as objectives[22] whose organization of "learning experiences" promises to produce outcomes[23] assessed by standardized examinations.[24] While Grant was charting the calamity befalling Canada, Jerome Bruner was assuring Americans that any child could be taught sophisticated science at any age.[25] It was more mathematicians, scientists, engineers, and technologists the "power elite"[26] wanted then, and wants still.[27] Within the curriculum, one subset of instrumental rationality was academic vocationalism[28]—training students to think as professional scientists or mathematicians or historians think—that remains today, evident in the revision of the teaching of history in Canada.[29] Too rarely is reason imagined as enabling us to travel to destinations unknown at the outset, as our conveyance through uncharted realms.

Dewey cautions against such intoxication, reminding us that "reason is not an antecedent force which serves as a panacea. It is a laborious achievement of habit needing to be continually worked over."[30] Once "worked over," however, and "worked with," reason can become, I will suggest in chapter 6, an indispensable if imperfect medium of attunement. Grant recollected reason's ancient offering: "The old idea that 'the truth shall make you free,' that is, the view of reason as the way in which we discover the meaning of our lives and make that meaning our own, has almost entirely disappeared."[31]

Its disappearance was for a moment remembered, in the midst of America battling in Vietnam, embattled at home, protested and ritualized by 1960s youth cultures. Or so Grant suspected, suggesting that some, "whether they know it or not, hold in their very being the remnants of that tradition, the knowledge of themselves in their freedom…as standing against the pressures of the society which bind them in an impersonal grip."[32] Those pressures were multiple—institutional, political, racial, gendered—but also generational.[33]

To loosen that "impersonal grip" requires study,[34] then as now not foremost on the minds of those driven to extricate themselves from such pressures through what Marcuse imagined as "repressive desublimation."[35] Declining to coincide with "Americanism" took many forms—I have argued that "school reform" in the United States represented in part a reverberating repudiation of the 1960s, an effort to "grip" youth again—many studied those disciplines that articulated the alienation non-coincidence created. Harnessed to the military-industrial complex, schools complied with the directives of the power elite, producing "part of that alienation," Grant suggested, that will drive some to "philosophy" and "theology "…[and indeed there is] evidence" that "profound philosophical thought is arising," promising the "dawn" of an age of reason in North America.[36] Grant was not alone[37] in allowing himself this hope, and its mutilation by four decades of right-wing reaction does not diminish my determination to think our way through the calamity that shows no sign of conclusion.

As the ongoing ethical engagement[38] with alterity, study remains out of sync with the instrumentalism of the present moment, and not only in the United States. "Dawn" is a distant memory, but what "reason"—as Grant implies—offers us now is remembrance, the instantiation of temporality, not functionality, as the structure of subjective and social life.[39] Associated with psychoanalysis—over which Grant was ambivalent, although preferring it to the behaviourism[40] then in vogue—informed reason deciphers the past in the present, not the plotting of the future, a fantasy filtered through instrumental reason. Grant knew that reason today was regarded as a "subjective tool," useful in increasing "production," guiding the "masses," and maintaining national "power."[41] What, I wonder, is "subjective" about production, indoctrination, or military power?[42] What Grant means here by "subjective" is "will"—for example, the will-to-power, the historical relocation of "will" from God to man, and, in modernity, associated with the right to materialize whatever is possible.[43] For me this is decidedly "desubjectivized" reason, but for Grant the term is obviously associated not only with whim or (subjective) bias but with human hubris, specifically the institutionalization of will in science and technology. Education now aims at "dominance" over nature and humanity, Grant regrets, and "scientific reason is what we mean by reason."[44] The study of humanity, he adds, deteriorates into "social science, particularly psychology in its practical sense."[45]

In contrast to this historically specific psychologistic obsession—the advent of a culture of narcissism[46] and its cult of calculation—subjective reconstruction represents a moral striving for subjective synthesis.[47] Such moral striving invites an allegorical restructuring of experience. By remembering that one's lived experience exhibits this mythological significance—that it is not exclusively its contingency and idiosyncrasy but also a timeless (e.g., ongoing, can we say eternal?) ethical issue—one declines to coincide with what is, sculpting a continuous creative tensionality that curbs collapse into the quotidian while deferring disappearance into abstraction (including calculation), into moralism (and specifically its static, often authoritarian, adherence to abstractions). Subjectivity strewn as decentred (but not compulsive) openness to reality is worldliness, not wilfulness.[48] One studies—not only sculpts—the future, by becoming historical: reactivating the past, declining to coincide with the present, enabling another future (than the one in front of us) to unfold. For me, these are the subjective movements of a cosmopolitan curriculum.[49]

The force of history determines us, as victims and beneficiaries and all points in between , as it now demands that we reconstruct what it has done to us (including by ourselves), immersed in modernity obsessed with our calculations of what we can yet do. "The idea that we make history and that this is what is important," Grant appreciates, "is so completely taken for granted that we hardly think of it, let alone question it."[50] It is, he thinks, reflected in the respect accorded "engineers" and "businessmen," to all those "who are really doing something, because they are changing the world;" it is also reflected in the absence of respect accorded "artists" and "lovers," to "thinkers," and, he adds, to "people of prayer," as their endeavours do not, presumably, "change the world."[51]

The demand for progress—quantified as profit—and the cultural homogeneity it requires translates into various agencies and institutes of intervention. Anticipating by thirty years the rhetoric of US President Bill Clinton's school reform—"America 2000"—as well as the anxious symbolic significance the turn of the century would hold for billions of people, Grant predicted that as we move "towards" the year 2000,

> we [will] need all the institutes of urban studies and of race relations, all the centers of economic development and psychological adjustment we can get…. Add to these the international problems of how underdeveloped countries can be brought to share in the new possibilities by accepting the conditions of modernization.[52]

Here Grant anticipates the economic emergence of "emerging markets" and increased intervention in local and national economies—and educational systems—by the International Monetary Fund and the World Bank.[53]

The freedom modernity promised dissolved in front of our eyes. Various efforts are ongoing to explain how it can be that calculation and instrumentality fail to produce the realities we have decreed. The disciplinary ascendancy of sociology and its tendencies toward determinism—"the modern tendency to locate evil in social systems rather than in persons"[54]—threatens to condense any conception of individual agency and expressivity. It is no accident, as Grant noticed, that "sociology is central to our North American way of living."[55] The passivity sociology installed was accomplished in part by its "spectator theory of knowledge"—society is somehow separate from us, observable and measurable—with its associated authoritarian assumption that it is legitimate to study social reality only scientifically.[56] Despite the sophisticated theorization of the "crisis of western sociology" by Alvin Gouldner and his epistemologically altering acknowledgement of sociologists' "domain assumptions,"[57] the hubris of modernity, of science specifically, continued to assert itself in the disciplinary ascendency of social science, especially sociology but also psychology, itself antagonistic to psychoanalysis and indeed increasingly physiological.[58]

Grant saw that modernity's demand for nomological knowledge was not confined to the social sciences, imperfect if increasingly aggressive copies of natural science as they were. Philosophy—specifically its Anglo-American versions in which logic not experience governed—as well as the humanities more generally, became dominated by modernity's demand for objectivity.[59] The concept of "research" increasingly replaced "scholarship," Grant noticed, with the latter's acknowledgement that the craft was not unrelated to the craftsman, that the scholar's undertaking was a calling,[60] not a contract job. In contrast to the researcher—with that concept's expectation of new discoveries and solutions to social problems—the scholar sought truth. Demands for methodological uniformity—limiting the search to what was observable and, often, measurable—undermined the aspiration. As the calling became quiet, the name remained, as if on a tombstone. The "more traditional" notion of scholarship, Grant observed, has been replaced by "research."[61] In research, there are objects to be investigated, outcomes to be reported. In the humanities, Grant pointed out, that "object" has become "the past."[62]

The reconstruction of the past may be the vocation of historians, Tony Judt reminds, but (as he also notes), it cannot finally be separated from the ethical demands of the present moment.[63] The point of a cosmopolitan curriculum is not to reduce the past to the polemics of the present.[64] For Grant, the danger seemed in the opposite direction: objectivity froze the fluidity of the past by conceiving it scientifically, as if someone here and now could, spectator-like, apprehend the dynamics of then and there. The distinctiveness of the past communicates its present significance. That significance could surface—be articulated—in the teaching of the past, especially to undergraduates, Grant thought, as they constituted a public. When the past became an object, however, its meaning for us became mute. Both the dead and the living become entombed in the present.

Instead of the past speaking to us in the present, research requires, Grant complained, that its protocols provide us with practical information, techniques equipping us to profit from what we learn. The continuing emphasis upon "knowledge utilization" commands students and faculty alike to accent the practical point of what we study. Questions of meaning and significance become secondary, sometimes even socially suspicious. "Practice" has long been the byword not only of curriculum studies but of teacher education as well.[65] During my professional life "practice" has always had a self-evident ring, even while serious theoreticians—Ted Aoki[66] in Canada, James B. Macdonald[67] and Dwayne Huebner[68] in the United States—were noticing that the concept compelled conformity, not professional integrity. For Grant, not just public schools (and the profession that prepared professionals to teach in them) had succumbed to modernity's demand for functionality, universities—now "corporations for organizing the technical society"[69]—had as well; no educating the public toward truth but, instead, "teaching young people techniques by which they can do things in the world."[70] Absent, he observes, is "concern in our educational system with seeing that our young people think deeply about the purposes for which these techniques should be used," a matter now delegated to psychiatry and the ministry.[71] Today cognitive science threatens to reduce education to neurology, and psychotherapy to pharmacology.[72] In the above-quoted passage Grant was acknowledging the psychiatric profession's increasing importance, a fact that at that time spawned an anti-psychiatry movement.[73] Then, at least, psychiatry conducted its calling through conversation, asking patients to reactivate repressed memories.

Now education and psychiatry—the ministry seems somehow exempt—are all about outcomes, perhaps pharmaceutically induced. Rationalizing immoral behaviour as an acceptable means to whatever ends "freedom" allows, Grant realized, meant "personal power combined with social engineering."[74] Constant craving in search of satiation, such "activism" casts its counter-disciplines—Grant lists daydreaming, sensuality, art, prayer, theoretical science, and philosophy—as "leisure," endeavours that do not "directly" produce measurable outcomes.[75] "Non-manipulative" and with "joy" and "adoration" as their "ends"—not "power" and "control"—these antiquated disciplines are now entirely optional.[76] "Our practicality has made us uninterested in systematic thought," Grant rued, a "common moral language is seldom systematized."[77] Certainly a common moral curriculum could not be systematized, despite periodic calls[78] for "character education," as teaching became increasingly instrumentalized, substituting employable outcomes for ethical convictions. "Pragmatism has had such a pervasive influence in our schools," Grant thought, "because it…

was implicit in our way of life."[79] Kinzel points that "Grant did not treat pragmatism as a philosophy in its own right but only with reference to a particular historical situation."[80]

While also Canadian—versions of US progressivism made their way north[81]—the referent for Grant's use of "our" seems the United States, as the "spirit" of democracy, pioneering, and science converged in the educational theory the Puritans[82] and later immigrants devised to produce what Grant termed "egalitarian technologism."[83] Determined to find freedom in the land they took from Indigenous peoples, settlers were willing to destroy not only what was here but also whatever that remained from Europe, indeed anything that "limited" a supposed "open society."[84] "In the field of education," Grant concluded, "the decisive victory of the technical over the older studies has allowed...success to consist of purely technical skills: engineering, commerce, etc."[85] Were he alive today, surely he would cite STEM.[86]

Grant blamed Dewey.[87] Attributing to the American philosopher responsibility for "that change in our education whereby the individual has more freedom to express his individuality," Grant criticized "Dewey's belief that the intellect is an instrument for living," as that has, he judged, "directly led to a lowering of intellectual rigour in our education."[88] This oversimplification Grant repeats— and contradicts[89]—elsewhere. Grant critiques the pragmatist conception of "freedom" as misconstruing the "relation between freedom and thought," between "freedom and spiritual law."[90] Commenting on this issue, Kinzel bifurcates the matter less sharply, suggesting that Grant's point is that in pragmatism's "philosophical anthropology [there is] a fuller account of freedom than of the law, i.e. the moral law."[91] Perhaps, but Dewey's attentiveness to consequences hardly ruled out moral matters, as Grant himself knew: "Dewey's philosophy must be taken seriously, not as a system, but as it expresses the desire of the prospering democratic society to free itself from the transcendent and ironic elements of its Protestant heritage, without losing the old ethical ardour."[92] Exactly—no one doubts Dewey's social ethics. And "prosper" means not only profit but to thrive, another verb that includes intellectual, spiritual, and moral as well as worldly flourishing.

Grant predicted that "research" in the humanities would lose "significance," especially for the "best" faculty and students.[93] Why? He blamed the disinclination to construe scholarship as "knowledge necessary to human existence," one calling of American pragmatism.[94] It is Grant's calling, clear enough in his critique of researchers' tendencies toward objectifying the past. Instead of addressing the present moment, the humanities have become, he complained, a "museum culture."[95] The point is well taken, but it is an unfortunate choice of adjectives, not only because many museums take their educational obligations seriously but because historiography—one of Grant's formative fields—requires the reconstruction of history as it was, not only as we might find it pertinent to our situation today.[96]

While the relationship between the "object" of scholarship and scholarship itself is elusive and subject to ongoing critique and controversy, Grant is clear that what he terms its "sacralization"—due to its "marriage with research"—is destructive.[97] "This stance of command necessary to research," he continues, "therefore kills the past as teacher."[98] To the extent the humanities incorporate the language and methods of the social sciences, the less social significance he feels sure they will have.[99] By imitating the sciences, Grant warns, the humanities can "abstract" their concreteness, appear to end their "ambiguities," and render human experience into a "quantifiable" object; in so doing they end their "openness to all that is."[100] Nowhere is that choice clearer in recent educational research in the United States, now mandated to be "mathematical."[101]

Purporting to discover "what works" in classrooms, such "research" contributes to the destruction of education, its end as a public trust, increasingly privatized as products sold by software companies.[102] What Grant knew fifty years ago was that the "quantification-oriented behavioural sciences are wonderfully appropriate for serving the tasks of control necessary to a technological society" and they have been "well adapted to serve…corporations."[103] To the extent they become servants of capital, social scientists lose the thread of their own disciplinary commitments as they concede the primacy of priorities to those set by funding agencies, themselves pressured by corporate capital to enlist scientists in their profiteering. Without an ongoing disciplinary conversation[104] and one's self-critical engagement within it, faculty cannot communicate with those in their midst, and teaching becomes the dissemination of information[105] sprinkled with tips to get ahead. Self-advancement and cynicism supplant professional ethics and disciplinary intellectual advancement.[106] Walter Rathenau's cynical remark seems even more timely today, and Grant quotes it: "There are no specialists, only vested interests."[107] Intellectual curiosity—"wonder" as Grant remarks—becomes "subsidiary" to "power."[108] He complains that universities within technological societies privilege "those sciences" which promise mastery of human and non-human nature.[109]

What "sciences" are these? Grant references the "privileged place" of "mathematics" in the contemporary curriculum.[110] Those fields without obvious technological utility—the arts and humanities—recede in curricular significance, yet another "price" now paid, Grant notes, "for our long tradition of taking the goods of practical confidence and competence as self-sufficiently the highest goods."[111] Like the "scavenging mongrel" during a "famine," Grant rues, one can claim "no merit" in "scenting food"; perhaps in another time, he wonders, it will be possible to search for something "deeper" that is "publicly" available now.[112]

Reactivating the Past in the Present

> If one denies the possibility of any return-
> ing to the past, and yet does not believe
> in the assumptions of the modern experi-
> ment, what then is the task of thought?
>
> George Grant[113]

The past is a foreign country.[114] Grant journeys to ancient Greece, asking us to join him, "to think with" Plato and Aristotle, to discern "their vision of human nature and destiny."[115] In so doing, he imagines that "we come to see our own."[116] In the eighteenth century, Grant reminds, it had been common to acknowledge the differences between the ancients and moderns, providing "a way of understanding these different assumptions."[117] With philosophy "dying out," as we face nothing "foreign," only the familiar—"our dead-level, conformist society."[118] Presentism and narcissism ensure encapsulation within what is. When one has not considered concepts "quite different from their own," Grant reminds, one tends to coincide with what is, "not even conscious that they are living within those limits."[119] Through remembrance we might peer through the "principles"[120] of the technological sensorium.

Can there be another life than this one, submerged in the screen, observing images and information rather than seeking knowledge and the wisdom it can confer? Can we find passages to life not structured by the corporate triumvirate (calculation–competition–compulsory collaboration[121]) not focused on others as means to our ends but as intrinsically important (sometimes intellectually intimate[122]) relationships that render the present meaningful? Rather than a conveyance to accumulation, can experience become educational? Can ethics replace politics as the animating force in public life?[123] From the "dawn" of the West through the nineteenth century Grant positioned "piety" as prerequisite to the "public good."[124] Piety is less a set of observable behaviours than it is a state of mind, in educational terms a devotion to ongoing study, humbling oneself before the mystery of the world, seeking understanding.[125]

Revelation represents the results of such research. Engagement, not instrumentality, characterizes its *mode d'être*. It is spiritual. In contrast to Grant I shed supernaturalism, less transcendent than immanent, immersed in the moment that is simultaneously eternal and contingent, following from what preceded it, pregnant with what is now to come. For Grant, "contemplation" occurs after, in the (divine) light of, "revelation" and it is structured by "charity," obediently "giving oneself away."[126] For Jean-Luc Marion, "the theological teacher is not justified unless he serves charity."[127]

Here charity is no voluntaristic act of generosity that leaves the structure of subjectivity untouched.[128] In my terms, when we reactivate the past we are tourists no longer, still lodged within the temporally empty present. Returning to the past we are "going native," not as escapism or exoticizing alterity but in order to dwell within the world as it is as if our lives depended upon it.[129] Such aspiration is not ornamental as it recasts one's character. Educationally, it testifies[130] to the subjective reconstruction sustained study encourages.

Such study implies attentiveness but not only the instrumental observation scientific experimentation ritualizes. We are not testing hypotheses to produce outcomes we can operationalize as much as we are attuning ourselves to what is at stake in the situation that structures us. We are not only trying to solve a problem as much as resolve what remains leftover so we all can move on. Attunement reveals resolution; calculation reproduces the problem if in different forms, perhaps as collateral damage or unintended effects, variables (not yet) controlled whose movements perhaps cannot be predicted. Productivity is no working-through of the injustice of the past that structures the present.

In societies before the age of progress, Grant remembers, there was "education wherein the truth of justice was made central."[131] The problem of the present is that calculation substitutes for judgment that is not only expertise but also wisdom informed by love.[132] Knowledge, Grant suggests, depends on it: "The close connection between Socrates and Christ lies in the fact that Socrates is the primal philosophic teacher of the dependence of what we know on what we love."[133] Love enables attunement to passages from the present, not escape routes but reconstructions—transfigurations—of what has been bequeathed us. "Paul's hymn to love," Grant reminds us, "uses the word *agape* which is best translated as charity; Plato's symposium is concerned with *eros* which is best translated as desire."[134] The reconstruction of private desire into public service is the calling of a cosmopolitan education.[135]

Charity condensed to kindness obscures its educational potential.[136] One learns from others as one engages with the situation intersubjective presence reveals and can articulate.[137] One learns also from oneself.[138] When subjectivity no longer contracts—made minimal in Lasch's[139] spatialized metaphor of our cynical and futile withdrawal from the public sphere—we enlarge our domain of experience as we decline to reduce human relationality to contractual obligations. Openness to what is—willingness to allow reality to speak through us, acting as its self-questioning mediation—becomes one prerequisite of knowledge. For Plato, Grant reiterates, "the opposite of knowledge is not ignorance, but madness, and the nearest he can come to an example of complete madness is the tyrant, because in that case otherness has disappeared."[140] It is the apprehension of alterity—its recognition as difference and sometimes as resonance—not its disappearance into narcissism that the adjudication of justice demands.

Such adjudication is institutional and social, but it is also subjective and cultural, each informed ethically: what does the present moment require? Alas, the educational line through this ever-shifting simultaneity of domain, scale, and time has become not reparation but the triumph of technology. How did "hope," Grant wonders, become reduced to "technological regulation" and "expansion."[141] His narrative of this degradation of charity into calculations of productivity focuses on the faculty of will. It is the elevation of will—achieved through its detachment from agape, from community, from the humility alterity insinuates—into the idolatry of technology, an institutionalization not of charity but conquest, that propels us into a present shorn of ethics and education.[142] How could this have occurred? As Grant acknowledges above, the history is too "complex" to know, but he isolates education as one narrative trail to follow.

Grant appreciates the democratization of knowledge that progressives embraced, their commitment to cut learning free from the confinement of elitism.[143] "Influenced" by Rousseau, Grant acknowledges that Dewey did desire to provide "educational content" to the lives of "equal citizens."[144] But education's "elitism" remained, if taking different forms, reformulated not as the preservation of privilege but the privileging of reason as an instrument of engineering, stipulating justice as equality. "Unlike Rousseau," Grant continues, the progressives succumbed to an "unlimited faith" that the "conquest of nature" provided the "means" to such "equality."[145] Science would save society. That "dream" of liberalism—"equality"—could become a nightmare of social conformity and the extinguishing of cultural difference; political manipulation, Grant knew, accomplishes the promotion of "mastery" from "means" to "ends."[146] Discovery becomes an unquestioned end in itself, requiring the scientific sacrifice of animals—including humanity—as the will is unleashed, authorized to do whatever it can imagine. Humanity becomes a means to unspecified ends, no longer "equality" but always punctuated by "productivity," proliferating profits and bankruptcies of virtue.

We cannot undo what has been done. We cannot return to the past nor recast its injustices through reparation. "Socrates' prayer for the unity of the inward and the outward was spoken in an antique world," Grant acknowledges, "the context of which it could not be our historical business to recreate."[147] In one sense we need not, as the past is not past; modernity's morphing of "human excellence" into "human will" fails.[148] Isolated, unrestrained, authorized by its institutionalization, the will—as the scientific method, as the capitalist compulsion for profit, education as social engineering[149]—mutilates as it manipulates what is. Only when it is embedded in the inheritance we inhabit but cannot control can "will" strive for human excellence, an aspiration undertaken by "those who have glimpsed that it is sustained by all that is."[150] This glimpse is located not in the view from "nowhere," not in the omniscience religion reserves for God, nor in the certainty of progress, historical inevitability guaranteed by the outcomes of scientific discovery with its spectator concept of knowledge.[151] Indeed, such a "glimpse" may not be only ocular but also auditory, discernment as well as determination: attunement. Perhaps such "sustainment cannot be adequately thought by us," Grant wonders, due to the "fragmentation" and "complexity" of humanity's "historical inheritance."[152] Haunted by what we cannot think through but are obligated to try, our "will" extends from head to heart, enfeebled there but befriending so that we might remain "open…to all those occasions in which the reality of that sustaining makes itself present to us."[153] That reality is simultaneously historical and timeless, and its revelation requires contemplation, self-critique, and social engagement.

Complicated Conversation

> There is no bluffing in teaching because when it is present it is exposed, more so than in one's writing.[154]
>
> George Grant

These modes of "being-in-the-world"—writing and teaching, each intertwined with the other—typified George Grant's life. After the trauma of the 1940s London bombings, Grant returned to Toronto to recover. His first foray into the world was working with the Canadian Association of Adult Education (CAAE; now defunct), a challenge he accepted in February 1943 at age twenty-four.[155] Grant had "no inkling," Christian tells us, "how much the next two years would affect his mature views of politics and education."[156] Indeed, his work with the CAAE seems to have encouraged his lifelong[157] reflection on what is at stake in the education of the public.[158] Speaking on the air to a broad public, such "public engagement," Davis concludes, imprinted Grant's writing, rendering it "vital" and "immediately accessible."[159] The work at the CAAE enabled Grant, Davis continues, to integrate "both the poetic and religious passion that had been such an important part of his earlier experience, and the practical orientation of the progressive public servant he was raised to be but never became."[160]

Working with Jean Hunter Morrison, a permanent CAAE employee, Grant undertook an educational experiment in public broadcasting: the *Citizens' Forum*. In my terms, this was curriculum development dedicated to the social and subjective reconstruction of the public. Before each program, listeners who had assembled across the country in church halls, friends' living rooms, or wherever a radio could be shared perused a study guide prepared each week by Morrison and Grant. After the broadcast, discussion ensued, prompted by questions in the guide. Afterward, each group's secretary submitted a report to the respective CAAE provincial secretary, who in turn sent a summary to Grant. He studied the national results and composed a report for subsequent broadcast.[161] Without employing this phrase, George Grant was undertaking a complicated conversation with Canadians about themselves that would continue until his death in 1988.

It was indeed conversation, and not only over the air as Grant managed to visit nine provinces. By the end of his first term as national secretary, some 1,215 groups had registered to participate. Most adult educators were on the political Left, worried that, unless the postwar period was informed by a vigorous and critical public, Canadians could be manipulated by propaganda presented as news.[162] Many intellectuals, educators, and political activists of the 1930s and 1940s—in the United States as well as in Canada—appreciated that education was central to citizenship; being critically informed was the prerequisite for citizens' civic engagement in a democratic society.[163] Like many progressive educators in the United States, many Canadians thought the appropriate way to educate the adult citizenry was through small groups. On this point Grant agreed. The *Citizens' Forum* was an exercise in small groups whose members engaged in study, deliberation, communication, taking action.[164]

The CAAE, then, was engaged in the education of the public for the sake of a more just social order. It organized a nationwide conference in Montreal for September 1943 to coordinate the efforts of various interested groups. When the Liberal government noticed, it tried to intervene: the parliamentary secretary to the prime minister (Brooke Claxton) tried to block the broadcasts at the CBC.[165] Although opposed to ideologues who would propagandize—personified in the United States by the legendary George Counts[166]—Grant "staunchly defended" the *Citizens' Forum*'s "right to free speech" despite "government pressure."[167] While he defended their right to free speech, finally Grant could not endorse his colleagues' faith in progressive education. While education for the sake of democracy was a compelling concept, Grant concluded it risked ruining education. Education mattered in its own right.[168] By early 1945 he had come to realize: "I had to spend my life thinking out what were the consequences of not thinking progressive liberalism."[169]

We can glimpse Grant's grappling with this issue in a talk to teachers he gave in 1952.[170] By then teaching philosophy at Dalhousie,[171] Grant was ready to confront the progressive faith he had encountered—had enacted—during his work at the CAAE. The pragmatists, he told the assembled teachers, thought knowledge was useless unless it could change the world. Progressives' commitment to education followed not from its capacity to provide truth, but for its potential in creating well-adjusted human beings.[172] That meant, in our time, that education was worthwhile only to the extent that it leads to "money, comfort, success, and power."[173] Even if referencing only businessmen, this pronouncement oversimplified.[174]

Indirectly testifying to his conversion,[175] Grant invoked the Christian conviction that a person is a "free, rational being whose destiny is to live in the light of God." For Grant, such "light" was not tantamount to doctrinal conformity but, referencing Plato, a matter of freeing humanity from "finite chains to the love of the infinite."[176] He did not claim to comprehend the relationship between freedom and transcendence—it would preoccupy him for the remainder of the decade[177]— but he felt sure it could not be grasped by those who had been "swept away" by "technique and self-expression, prosperity and power," the cult of "convenience" and "worldly success," not "knowledge." "Time was short," Grant felt, but perhaps the preservation of "ancient spiritual tradition" was still possible.[178]

In a series of articles written for *Food for Thought*, the journal of the CAAE, Grant pursued this possibility. In "Philosophy and Education,"[179] Christian reports, Grant defined education as "any means that brings the human spirit to self-consciousness," and he cited Socrates as a "saint in whom knowledge of his own mind led to the presence of absolute mind."[180] The distractions[181] of the present age would lead to cynicism and despair, he prophesized, and it was the calling of adult education to offer an alternative:

> When men encounter nothingness they are at last driven to seek reality. As in the pointless universe days are spent in the beauty parlors…or in the search to prolong a dying virility, in the days when there is always economic plenty and even cruelty has become tedious, then, will be the moment to speak of education, of the journey of their minds to liberation.[182]

Despair demands reflection, study, thinking: the very processes of education.[183] But the "liberation" he has in mind is not the secular assurance of social improvement through reconstruction, but attunement, transcendence, "absolute mind," or the Good. Grant's rejection of progressive education would seem to be complete.[184]

Curriculum and Teaching

> [I]f we are to live in the modern university as free men, we must make judgments about the essence of the university—its curriculum.[185]
>
> George Grant[186]

The curriculum is indeed the "essence" of the university, Grant appreciated,[187] the intellectual centrepiece of any educational institution. More than teaching methods, organizational structure or outcomes, it is the curriculum that "determines" the "character"[188] of the university, Grant knew, contradicting one hundred years of educational research in the United States, focused as it has been on instruction linked to learning and its assessment. For Grant, learning is "largely shaped by what is studied and why it is studied."[189] Here he inverts organizationalism—the faith that policy, procedures, and personnel produce educational excellence—by casting the curriculum as determinative. However appealing this claim might be for curriculum theorists, it overstates the case, as Grant himself seems to have suspected. On one occasion he deflates the power he has accorded it, insisting instead that curriculum is determined by class.[190] This is so-called reproduction theory (that popular 1970s curriculum theory that relegated the curriculum to the reproduction of the social-economic status quo), if *avant la lettre*. Grant resented the rich businessmen[191] who served on the governing boards of the universities he knew—he found them overbearing, always steering the institution toward vocationalism[192]—but accounts of his own teaching belie his assertion of the curriculum's total determination of educational experience.

A teacher's son, George Grant was devoted to teaching,[193] and not only due to filial fidelity. Grant considered teaching—not research and the specialization and objectification it encouraged—as the central mission of the university. Why was Grant such a remarkable teacher? Christian suggests Grant enjoyed a "natural theatrical flair,"[194] which he had cultivated during his student days at Upper Canada College and at Queen's University. And he worked at it, explaining to his mother:

> To give oneself in [lectures] means three things which take all one's energy. (1) Preparation is necessary & often about subjects I am not trained in & this means extensive reading & thinking. This first year I am not going to be able to do much work but just prepare & give my lectures. (2) Preparation of stories, examples; that, particularly in an elementary philosophy course of 125, is vital. (3) Great emotional concentration at each hour of lecturing.[195]

Note that study comes first, not the formulation of objectives or the composition of lesson plans. Professional ethics—above all knowledge of subject matter accented (in the quoted passage) by efforts to engage one's students through anecdote,[196] emotional intensity and subjective presence[197]—precede any specification of outcomes.[198] And note that the lecture[199]—now discredited or converted to entertainment by PowerPoint—can be a compelling educational experience.[200]

Teaching is erudite ethical engagement in the complicated conversation that is the curriculum. Unless one is subjectively engaged[201] with what and whom one is teaching, teaching can become technical and formulaic, today tending toward entertainment not education. Note that in Grant's sequence (in the passage quoted above) contextualization comes second: stories associate abstract ideas with everyday experience, situating them in a coherence that is narrative as well as disciplinary.[202] Grant could be mesmerizing—that was his "theatrical flair" enacted in the service of communication and understanding.[203] Third, self-mobilization is prerequisite to becoming subjectively present and intellectually engaged with others, capable of glimpsing the singularity of others, even when they are too numerous (as in a large class) to be apprehended individually.[204] Here subjective presence[205] focuses that theatrical disposition, scripting a dialogic encounter that was the subject of a "poor curriculum";[206] for example, one stripped of technological props so it could become compelling in its immediacy.[207]

Grant's students "were drawn" to him, Davis and Emberley tell us, a "teacher embarked on a quest for answers to questions[208] that mattered to them,"[209] questions that were not always subject-matter specific (if almost always subject-matter informed[210]) but also located in their lives as students—and teachers—were experiencing them then. More specifically, Davis explains, students found Grant appealing because he seemed to sense "their lingering attachment to religious belief and also their excitement about the modern world."[211] When Grant invited his students to examine what was happening to them, what they wanted for themselves and for others in the future, he was, Davis and Emberley conclude, affirming "their questioning minds and spirits,"[212] uncommon then, they note, and perhaps even more uncommon today. Not only individually urgent, such questions—about "morality, religion, politics, economics, all intertwined"[213]— also concerned the future of Canada, as Grant would later make explicit in his *Lament for a Nation* and *Technology and Empire.*

Grant's lectures were not, then, monologues, even when he alone was speaking.[214] Grant's speech became an event, a subjective engagement with ideas and those who had formulated them with his students in that place at that time.[215] Grant was fond of students from rural areas, as they, he thought, had not yet been spoiled by modernity's compulsion for progress.[216] He reached out, enacting physically and emotionally his intense intellectual engagement, moving around the classroom, interrupting himself to ask students what they thought. Students quickly appreciated that philosophy was not only lists of facts to be memorized but a complicated conversation that was still underway, in fact, in front of their eyes and inside their minds and, possibly, their hearts. Greenspan remembers:

> Grant was sometimes a riveting teacher but his ideas are to me so inextrica-
> bly bound with his person, if I might say, with his own performance, as to be
> inseparable from it. The eloquence with which his voice could evoke the pres-
> ence of those archaic meanings that he finds lacking in modern life gave his
> ideas an embodiment that will be impossible to replace.[217]

That has been my sense all along, that Grant's embodiment and personification of what he thought and felt and knew invited his students to be subjectively present too.[218]

Grant could startle students with his direct questions, Christian reports. In fact, his conduct could not be predicted, as when he bypassed the blackboard and scrawled the concept he was explaining on a winter-frosted window. Sometimes he used the tail of his fraying Oxford academic gown to wipe the blackboard clean. Students were, Christian tells us, "captivated" by the "formality of his style," juxtaposed as that was with the informality of his appearance.[219] As he spoke of truth and eternity he seemed unmindful of a hole in his shoe or his untucked shirttail, or of a necktie doubling as a belt. In its eccentricity, contingency can communicate a sense of subjective engagement with students, oblivious to, perhaps contemptuous of, classroom convention. "The key to his teaching," Davis suggests, "was his attention to his students, to what mattered to them; he had high hopes for the young people he taught; he believed it was important to know what they were going through in order to teach them."[220] In this description, Grant comes off as the ideal progressive educator, attentive to students[221] and to their existential concerns, committed to helping them understand what they face, individually and together, through the complicated conversation that is the curriculum.

On occasion the conversation became so complicated that Grant fell silent, having been asked a question he could not answer. Such questions preoccupied him, Christian reports, and Grant took "whatever time it took, sometimes days, to reading and thinking about the answer."[222] Research—reading can be research in the humanities—followed questions, questions that pointed in directions he and the students had not yet explored. The unknown invites awe and humility, but it also demands devotion: careful reading, constant thinking, imagined rejoinders, associated questions, and sometimes silence. Grant's conversation continued outside the campus classrooms, including at the tavern at Halifax's Lord Nelson Hotel. "With his students," Christian tells us, Grant was "never off duty as a teacher."[223] Relationships with students support as it embodies[224] intellectual labour: the awkwardness of intellectual difficulty, the excitement of intellectual adventure, the vivid sense that education is not something done to one, but something requiring individual agency; for example, one's willingness to engage ideas that before might have seemed opaque, uninviting, even unintelligible.

On occasion being Grant's student might have been an edgy experience, listening to and perhaps talking with a man so profoundly engaged in his work. Given his humility and his receptivity, perhaps not; Colville remembers that "he [Grant] listened, and presumably looked, in the way that a few good students do, in that open and vulnerable way."[225] Grant's teaching was, obviously, no isolated "ivory tower" exercise; it seemed in fact an ongoing struggle to find one's way with others in a world that was always but now quite specifically in crisis. "For most people still teach philosophy," Grant wrote in a letter, "as if there were still a civilization in North America, instead of teaching it as if the old traditions were completely finished and one had to build new ones."[226] The present moment was no empty space[227]—an "environment" as educational research so often designates it[228]—waiting to be filled with new ideas; it was a wasteland piled high with wreckage in the wake of science and technology.[229]

Despite the devastation[230] teach Grant did. Not to increase students' scores on standardized tests, Grant taught the knowledge he deemed of most worth.[231] The introductory course, Philosophy I, was before Christmas focused on Plato's *Republic*; after the holiday it settled on Kant's *Critique of Practical Reason*.[232] In addition to Philosophy I, Grant taught a wide range of courses during those early years at Dalhousie: Medieval Philosophy, Modern Philosophy Since Descartes, Philosophy of History, and Logic and the Scientific Method. After a few years he was able to offer senior classes on Kant's *Critique of Pure Reason*, ethics, and early Greek philosophy. He taught a graduate class on Augustine, and, from time to time, a course on morals and politics with a colleague in political science. Grant was adamant in protecting his professional prerogative to teach the courses he judged important, assigning the readings he judged as appropriate, attending carefully to students, always on guard against attempts of the businessmen[233] to meddle with the curriculum.[234] "I see no alternative," he wrote, to fight when one is pushed into being a slave because in my opinion it is wrong to let the rich get away with it. I am, as you know, a conservative in politics[235]—that is I think change is dangerous—but it is exactly that conservatism which makes me so mad at the way a lot of wealthy people think they can dominate in their spare time as subtle an institution as a university.[236]

Today we see that there are those among the wealthy who feel entitled to dominate whatever institution they please.[237]

What Knowledge is of Most Worth?

> Surely the basic problem of our society is the problem of individuals finding meaning to their existence.[238]
>
> George Grant

Business does not operate in isolation, of course, but through technology and the sciences that support it.[239] The crisis of modernity crystallized the crucial questions of the curriculum, questions that came to consume Grant, especially after leaving Dalhousie for McMaster University in 1961.[240] At McMaster[241] Grant settled into that university's new Department of Religion.[242] In a sermon to students delivered on October 6, 1961, Grant invoked the scene between Jesus and Pilate to dramatize the role of religious studies in a secular university. Grant asserted that McMaster's new department should imitate

> this conversation, this dialogue between the transcendent truth of the soul and the wisdom of the world [that] has gone on in western society from that day to this. It is the tension in their meeting which has more than anything else given western society its greatness and only insofar as western society keeps that tension has it anything valuable in it.[243]

To engage in this dialogue[244] meant confronting the secularization of the contemporary curriculum, and this, Grant knew, would be contentious, as "the curriculum as it is based in our modern secular universities is radically at odds with Christianity."[245]

Grant knew what was at stake. Given the pervasiveness of the "now-dominant faith of objectivity and progress," the department must proceed cautiously, avoiding the extreme of scientistic positivism on the one hand and of religious proselytizing on the other.[246] The curriculum, in Christian's words, "must" include religion "without forcing students to accept positions in which they did not genuinely believe."[247] The core of the departmental curriculum, Grant argued, should be a clear, *factual* knowledge of Christianity—that is a knowledge of Judaism and the New Testament. *Subsidiary* to this there must be some factual knowledge of the Mediterranean civilization and its traditions (other than the Semitic) which were brought under Christ by the Fathers. Obviously, also, in a later year when the student has some knowledge of Western religion, he must look at the other religions of the world.[248]

Because Buddhism was being popularized in North America at this time, Grant thought that tradition must be included.[249] Because it was not at this time compelling, Islam would not be.[250]

Even more contentious was Grant's insistence that new faculty live within the religious traditions they were being hired to teach.[251] What can appear to be doctrinal conformity derived, Christian[252] points out, from Anselm's celebrated formula: *Credo, ut intelligam*: understanding arises from belief. Prerequisite to understanding Christianity, Grant felt sure, was the Greek philosophical tradition. These convictions followed from Grant's ongoing engagement with the historical moment. Despite the power of the present, Grant knew that "at all times and in all places it always matters what we do."[253] Ethics, not only politics, structures the complicated conversation that is the curriculum.

As Grant knew, what knowledge is of most worth remains the key curricular question. Because this is an ethical question, it can keep us open—to the subject we study, to the students with whom we are working, to ourselves as we discover anew who we are and might become, to the academic knowledge we are labouring together and alone to understand and extend.[254] What knowledge is of most worth invites us to discern what is at stake in time and place. The canonical curriculum question invites, but not compels,[255] ongoing openness.[256] "This quality," Grant understood,

> is the exact opposite of control or mastery. Mastery tries to shape the objects and people around us into a form which suits us. Openness tries to know what things are in themselves, not to impose our categories upon them. Openness acts on the assumption that other things and people have their own goodness in themselves; control believes that the world is essentially neutral stuff which can only be made good by human effort.[257]

Especially in our time, openness demands exertion; it "requires daily the enormous discipline of dealing with our closed-ness, aggressions and neuroses, be they moral, intellectual or sexual. To be open in an age of tyrannical control will above all require courage."[258] That courage cannot be innocent, I would add, as tyranny requires that virtue be communicated with caution, especially in public. Especially within the solitude[259] of ongoing study, openness animates our efforts to understand.

Conclusion

> At best, one's teaching is largely one's
> instruction of oneself.[260]
>
> George Grant

On the thirteenth of November, 1983, George Grant turned sixty-five. He decided it would be his final year of teaching.[261] At McMaster, he had felt constant pressure to publish "to keep the bastards in charge off my back as they examined each person's curriculum vitae minutely to see if they were fulfilling their job as a production machine."[262] In retirement, Christian reports, Grant would write only what he deemed to be of the greatest importance.[263] Ascertaining what knowledge is of most worth at any given historical and biographical moment not only structures the educator's participation in the complicated conversation that is the curriculum, it functions as a rudder, guiding us to the project on which we must work next. In ancient conceptions of education, Grant had written years earlier, when one discerned the "ultimate purpose" of human life, one was deemed "wise." The point of education was "wisdom," the "condition" at which one reached "through reason."[264]

Teaching required generosity, charity in Christian terms, and Grant knew that "those who care about charity must care about communication, and to communicate requires systematic thought."[265] "As we have seen, such "systematic thought" required "steadfast attention to the whole."[266] Steadfast attention to the whole is what Grant communicated in class, whatever the number of students. Such communication required his subjective presence, expressed in shared language but spoken singularly, frankly, as if in private. That ongoing enactment of the immediacy and intimacy of the complicated conversation that is the curriculum rendered his published works ineligible for his teaching. For Grant, teaching meant exploring matters he had not yet defined in print. He told students:

> Let me say in parenthesis that what I am certain about I generally write down and do not repeat in this class. I do not repeat them [sic] in class because I think it impertinent to you to repeat what you can read of mine in print if you so desire. Professors who go on repeating their books in a class are a bore; people who need that should just read the books. It is one's new and therefore uncertain thoughts one should give in class.[267]

"Indwelling"[268] between the "curriculum-as-planned" and the "curriculum-as-lived," Grant communicated with those in his midst, encouraging them to sustain "steadfast attention to the whole." Such attention was simultaneously subjective and spiritual, intellectual and emotional. The academic labour of study and teaching is not only a matter of acquiring and conveying information, it is the ongoing professional obligation to think through what one learns, maintaining one's openness to the world. For such an undertaking, Grant counselled, one must study "the thought of great thinkers," thought which is "not matter for the chit-chat of television and cocktail parties; nor for providing jobs for academics in the culture industry. In it the fate of our whole living is expressed."[269] Through sustained study understanding can occur. On their reciprocal relation our fate in part depends.

Neither study nor understanding comes automatically, as the triumphant omnipresence of machines and their applications might imply.[270] Study is not a matter of manipulation or convenience: its conduct requires commitment, conviction, courage. While "thinking in any era requires courage to sustain it," Grant warned, courage can condense into "ambition," thereby corrupting the courage on which thinking depends.[271] Every graduate student or assistant professor who has been advised to "brand" himself, to settle on a "line" of research and "sell" it, appreciates how intellectual curiosity can become commoditized in the contemporary corporatized university.

What is the fate of education in such an era? "At the heart of modern liberal education," Grant knew, "lies the desire to homogenize the world."[272] Homogenization means the obliteration of difference, including the erasure of that alterity that is the past. In contrast, memory and remembrance mean making conscious "continually" those "distortions" embedded in "one's individual and social history."[273] Such working through what we have been bequeathed forces the forefronting of difference, the courageous cultivation of openness to what is not obvious, what could become intelligible in the future if we can reactivate the past. George Grant faced the fate of education in a technological era; he taught with courage and conviction to name what imprisons us in a false—idolatrous—present. In the September 20, 1980, issue of *Today* magazine, George Grant was acknowledged as one of the great teachers in Canada.[274] Surely he remains so today.

Notes

1. Grant 1969, 118. Summarizing Grant, Fierlbeck (2006, 57) explains: "We have gained mastery over the our physical world, he [Grant] concluded, but we have lost touch with the sublime, the transcendent, and the virtuous. We are lost on a web of directionless and bleak concrete freeways, but—well, we drive great cars."

2. Harold Innis was among the names—Charles Cochrane and Northrop Frye were others—Grant referenced in his 1951 report on philosophy in Canada for the Massey Commission into the state of arts and culture in Canada. Innis and the others were thinkers "who have shown themselves willing to go beyond scholarship to more general questions of human import" (quoted in Christian 1996a, 154). Grant judged Innis a scientist, not a philosopher: "He did not ask those questions which belong traditionally to philosophy.... To put it mildly, the eternal was not his dish" (quoted in Christian 1996a, 406n13). Like Grant, Innis had a "fundamentally conservative attitude towards modern democracy," evident in his critique of the United States (see Watson 2007, 383). "Innis's intensely critical attitude towards the Liberal Party,"

Watson suggests, "was also similar to the later position of Grant" (391). Grant taught at McMaster; Innis studied there as an undergraduate.

3.   "The myths are not then the truth about human life," Grant wrote, "they are the enchanting images by which most men are led to apprehend some purpose in their existence" (Davis and Roper 2005b, 230). Are "enchanting images" educational ones, at least potentially? It would seem so in this instance. The danger of being enchanted by an image—idolatry—we explore in the next chapter.

4.   Grant was hardly the first to cite Hegel's famous phrase. Innis had chosen the myth of Minerva's owl to sketch his communications theory in an address to the Royal Society of Canada (as the newly elected president). For Innis, Watson (2007, 308) explains, the owl represented those "living traditions" of the West that link us to the "oral tradition of the ancient Greeks." While the centre of Western civilization moves from one people and place to another—symbolized by the owl's flight—cultural continuity can occur "only through the person-to-person dialogue of living individuals" (308).

5.   Grant (1959) 1966, 5.

6.   Grant (1959) 1966, 5. These views Grant first articulated in his 1951 "Philosophy" essay for the Massey Commission (see Christian 1996a, 151–2; Bruno-Jofré and Cole 2014, 85; Richardson 2002, 51; Cavell 2002, 201). This essay—Forbes (2007, 37) judges it his "first significant publication—begins, Christian (1996a, 153) recounts, with Grant's key question: How had philosophers in Canada "lost sight of the eternal?" Grant's answers included Canadians' historic preoccupation with survival, allowing little time for "speculation…[as] sureness and confidence were necessary for survival" (153). More broadly, Grant located the primacy of the immediate in the "spiritual climate" in the West with its obsession with "knowledge for power" obscuring "those disciplines that once had been considered a potent influence in preventing us from becoming beasts" (153). Professors of philosophy—notably Fulton Anderson, head of philosophy at the University of Toronto—took sharp exception to Grant's critique of philosophy in Canada (see Christian 1996a, 154–5; Davis 2002a, xxiv; 2002b, 3). (In a letter to his mother afterward—1952—Grant wrote that "[t]he only thing to do is write good stuff, teach well and live as best one can" [quoted in Jersak 2012, 175]).

7.   Grant (1959) 1966, 5. "For Heidegger," Sikka (1997, 252) explains, "it is being itself, from whose self-withdrawing giving the epochs of history, each of which is a determinate truth of being, arise. This abyss, for Heidegger, is not God but that which lets God and gods be." As you will see in the next chapter, this "withdrawing" is also the space of icon, between here and eternity.

8.   The national curriculum reform that followed Sputnik—led by the newly elected John F. Kennedy in 1960—positioned Jerome Bruner as its primary architect. "It is highly probable that certain changes in our educational system will occur in the years ahead," Bruner ([1960] 1977, 75–6) predicted, "given the demands placed upon it by the community. The first is that there will be an increasing demand for the teaching of science, technology, and supporting subjects." Presumably jobs would be abundant in the newer technical industries. For the story of how America moved from Sputnik to STEM, see Pinar 2012, ch. 4.

9.   Grant 1966 (1959), 87.

10.   Grant 1966 (1959), 88. Grant speaks of "that wonderful platitude that the purpose of the school is to teach people to think," but which "breaks down as soon as one

asks the simple question—why is it good to think?" (Davis 2002b, 174). It is not, he answers, to "help one to get on in the world" but "because it will teach you what is real, it will give you the vision of God" (174).

11.   The US Supreme Court had intervened in its landmark 1954 desegregation ruling; Sputnik provided the provocation for more comprehensive congressional action that incorporated then superseded the 1954 ruling (see Pinar 2012, xvi).

12.   Grant (1959) 1966, 24–5.

13.   In the curriculum reform that followed, the Kennedy administration drew on arts and science faculty at Harvard University, demonstrating its confidence that academically rigorous research should be integral to national mobilization. The tale is much more twisted than that sentence communicates (as I explain in *What Is Curriculum Theory?*), but the Kennedy administration's respect for academic elites does contrast with the attitude of the then Canadian prime minister, Diefenbaker, as Grant ([1965] 2005, 24) points out.

14.   Since the war there had been building criticism of public schools as insufficiently focused on mathematics and science. Schools' post-war embrace of "life adjustment" (Pinar 2012, 184) seemed vague, even anti-intellectual to those arts and science faculty now frustrated with teaching high-school graduates without adequate academic preparation, students who had not planned to attend university, until the GI bill enabled them to do so. Before this criticism gained traction with the public, professional educators were clear about what they faced: "Wartime developments in technology are forcing revisions in the teaching of science and mathematics," US curriculum-development specialist Hilda Taba (1945, 80) appreciated. After Sputnik, public criticism became deafening: "The sources of current criticism are multiple.... Some, no doubt, represent a coalition of citizens opposed to school taxes, radicalism, and progressivism in education. A deepening concern over the expansion of Communism at home and abroad plays a role, as the instant reaction to the technical feat of Sputnik demonstrated," Taba (1962, 2) summarized. But, she added, "the strongest pressure for re-examination of the curriculum comes from the drastic changes in technology and culture, ranging from automation to atomic power, the voracious demands of the expanding industry on intelligent manpower" (3). In an opinion piece on mathematics teaching in the United States, science historian Christopher Phillips (2015, A35), writing in the *New York Times*, reminds that the post-Sputnik "new math" curriculum—at first a bipartisan enthusiasm—became anathema to political conservatives by the 1970s: "[B]ack to the basics" they then demanded. "As long as learning math counts as learning to think," Phillips suggests, "the fortunes of any math curriculum will almost certainly be closely tied to claims about what constitutes rigorous thought—and who gets to decide" (A35). Political polarization was well underway.

15.   Even President Dwight D. Eisenhower, a five-star general, warned: "In the councils of government, we must guard against the acquisition of unwarranted influence, whether sought or unsought, by the military-industrial complex. The potential for the disastrous rise of misplaced power exists and will persist." See http://coursesa. matrix.msu.edu/~hst306/documents/indust.html.

16.   Indeed, "education" itself, Grant appreciated, "began to be thought of as a species of social engineering" (Davis 2002b, 67). In a 1955 talk to teachers, Grant complained that at Dalhousie "we are just becoming a factory for technicians—engineers,

scientists, accountants, doctors, etc., and I don't think any of us can gather how almost completely the old free rational traditions of human dignity are disappearing among those technicians."

17.   Grant (1959) 1966, 7.

18.   Engineering here means remaking the world, including humanity, by design. "[W]hen the possibilities of technological tyranny had become obvious," Grant ([1974] 1998, 51) observed, "the most popular academic theorizing about politics went no farther than the decent prescription that we ought to pursue 'piecemeal social engineering' so as to 'minimize misery.'"

19.   See Pinar 2012, 163.

20.   "For the basic proposition of Dewey is still there," Grant complained, "namely that reason is only an instrument for manipulating the world" (Davis 2002b, 177). Dewey (1922, 145) was in fact critical of "persons of a more practical turn of mind [who] accept the world 'as it is,'" concocting "aims…that may be turned to their own private account. They employ intelligence in framing ends and selecting arranging means. But intelligence is confined to manipulation."

21.   "It is hardly necessary to mention," Grant appreciated, "what the end result of a manipulative view of freedom must be on personal relations. The substitution of manipulation for contemplation turns other people into objects instead of subjects like ourselves. The loss of adoration of the other must here be most seriously corrupting" (Davis 2002b, 200). It becomes a form of idolatry.

22.   So-called goals of action, Dewey (1922, 140) knew, "are ways of defining and deepening the meaning of activity. Having an end or aim is thus a characteristic of *present* activity." Presumably future-oriented, objectives restate assumptions embedded in the present.

23.   "We know without thinking," Dewey (1922, 141) appreciated, "that our 'ends' are perforce beginnings."

24.   In earlier Christian conceptions of education, Grant wrote, "what mattered was not concrete results but the movement of the soul" (Davis 2002b, 26). That educators cannot know let alone predict—the pedagogical point seems to me is to support, as best one can, such "movement." In secular terms, although the two are obviously interrelated, study supersedes learning, implied in Grant's remarks to students (in a course on Plato) that because the *Phaedo* is an "extremely complex and brilliant piece of writing…I do not expect for the examinations that all of you will deeply understand it" (Davis and Roper 2005b, 704; see also 709). As Grant noted on another occasion: "In the way our conventional system is set up, one has to make clear the distinction between knowing what is necessary for exams and what is necessary for the soul" (Davis and Roper 2009b, 932).

25.   Pinar 2012, 105, 108, 183, 215, 216.

26.   The phrase is C. W. Mills's, the title of his 1956 classic text; see Mills 2000.

27.   Pinar 2012, 19–20.

28.   "Clearly the education of scholars is one end in any university," Grant acknowledged, adding: "Society needs scholars as it needs carpenters, postmen, doctors, etc. But also clearly to meet the needs of young North Americans in their present dilemma, a department of religion must pass to that which quite transcends scholarship—namely thought" (Davis and Roper 2005b, 665). Here the great anti-progressive invokes one of the key (if problematic) concepts of progressivism—"needs"—and

seems to make knowledge subsidiary to "thought," a positioning (making knowledge subsidiary to anything) other anti-progressives questioned. As becomes clear, Grant's anti-progressivism is complicated by his internalization of it during his childhood and youth.

29. See, for instance, Seixas 2011, 141. Sixty years earlier, in his 1951 Massey essay, Grant lamented that "even the traditional humane subjects such as history, the classics, and European literature are in many cases being taught as techniques by which the student can hope to earn his living, not as useful introductions to the sweep of our spiritual tradition" (Davis 2002b, 5). Academic vocationalism—studying history as vocational training to work as historians might work—is not as vulgar and misleading as the vocationalism Grant is referencing here, but it does remain an instance of ends-means thinking, confident of the transfer of skills across settings, both questionable secularizations of salvational thinking from which educational theory and research have suffered.

30. Dewey 1922, 123.

31. Grant (1959) 1966, 9. Repudiating calculation as the supreme role of reason, Grant confronted the tension between reason and revelation, between philosophy and theology. Like Leo Strauss, Heaven (2006, 315) points out that Grant knew one must "*live* the conflict between philosophy and theology, reason and revelation." Rather than living this conflict within the mind (which Heaven suggests Strauss did), Grant lived this tension "*in his whole being*" (315). This capacity to live "simultaneously" within these two—reason and revelation—marks, Heaven suggests, "the nature of George Grant's genius" (317). In the next chapter I invoke the concept of irony to gesture toward Grant's living in and between reason and revelation; that second preposition points to Aoki's ([1986/1991] 2005, 161) affirmation of the "dwelling in the zone of the between."

32. Grant (1959) 1966, 12. Holding "in their very being" such "remnants" invites reactivation of those remnants, encouraging subjective and social reconstruction. These possibilities represent not educational engineering but the lure of the transcendent (in Huebner's phrase), as we see in the chapters that follow.

33. Grant located himself generationally, encouraging, I suspect, his students to reflect on their own: "What it comes down to is the different stage of life I am at, compared to most of you in the room. As I have said I used to teach as an older brother—now I teach as a great uncle. When one is young, philosophy appears to one in the wholeness of life—in the immediacy of life. When you have reached my age, philosophy itself becomes the immediate" (Davis and Roper 2009b, 996).

34. Study, it bears emphasizing, is not test preparation, but subjectively animated ethical engagement with alterity, enabled by academic knowledge; see Pinar 2006a, 114; 2012, 231; 2017b. Describing Grant "leaving the library with an armload of books piled literally to his nose, heading for home on the edge of the campus," Davis and Emberley (2000a, xv) suggest that the "same intensity that drove him to read so widely made classes with him come alive." Minogue (1990, 161) observes: "Because he [Grant] took them [Plato and the ancient Greeks] to have thought through the question of justice, he believed it is educational duty to make this philosophy come alive for his students."

35. Free love—"rigorous genitalization" in Savran's (1998, 34) amusing phrase—was expensive; the price was depoliticization due to the satiation of frustration. Like the

conception of dance as quintessentially African, free love turned out to be, Sekyi-Otu (1996, 95) argues, "the function of a repressive desublimation,…a testimony not to the creative freedom of a people but of the futility of their dreams of action."

36. Grant (1959) 1966, 13.

37. "[T]here were a lot of very fine young people around, and I saw a dawning," Grant tells Cayley (1995, 66–7). "Now, I've taught a lot of wonderful young people, and there have been great dawnings in North America at certain points. I think the whole protest against the Vietnam War was a great dawning…. I was astounded by the excellence of the Nova Scotians I was teaching, and the capacity for reason and thought in them filled me with hope." I felt it too for a time (Pinar 1974).

38. Magrini (2017, 5) notes that *we become other to ourselves only in the face of the other.*"

39. "For Grant," Meynell (2011, 123) emphasizes, "subjectivity must involve more than being aware of ourselves as capable of thinking and choosing; it must include thinking about our proper ends and being a project for ourselves."

40. Grant (1969, 131) descried the "behaviourist psychology" that "dominates" the university curriculum, "geared" as it is to produce those who will manage the masses. "Whatever its defects," Grant ([1974] 1998, 104n27) admitted later, "popular Freudianism is surely superior to the 'new brutalism' of behaviour modification carried out by behaviourist techniques." (See Christian 1996a, 216. For a history of psychoanalysis in education, see Taubman 2011.) Collingwood (2002, 95) minced no words, declaring that "psychology…is not a science. It is what 'phrenology' was in the early nineteenth century, and astrology and alchemy in the Middle Ages and the sixteenth century: the fashionable scientific fraud of the age." He asks if we might not understand "human affairs" more deeply by studying history (95).

41. Grant (1959) 1966, 9.

42. Of course each of these is "subjective" in often irrecoverably indirect ways.

43. In classroom conduct too, as, tongue-in-cheek, Burke and Segall (2017, 103) suggest: "In all, we encounter God as a multifaceted teacher who is at times absent, provides confusing instructions, and is short-tempered but is also reflective, open to suggestions, adjusts instruction in light of student responses, and wants to be respected—even loved—by his students, not unlike most 'regular,' contemporary teachers." Conceiving of "God" in human terms is, of course, a form of idolatry, a topic of the next chapter.

44. Grant (1959) 1966, 9.

45. Grant (1959) 1966, 9–10. One disciplinary site where this degradation was fought—is being fought—is the academic field of education. "It is significant that at Dalhousie" [where he returned in 1980], Davis and Roper (2009b, 775) suggest, Grant supervised "only one graduate student, James Calder, who was not enrolled in the classics, philosophy, or political science departments but in the department of education. Calder's approach to Weil reflects Grant's interests at the end of his career." Entitled "Labour and Thought in the Philosophy of Simon Weil: Preface to a Philosophy of Education," Calder's thesis, Davis and Roper continue, provides "plausibility to the view that Gant was, at the end of his life, relying more and more on Weil's analysis of modern science as the basis for his critique of the technological society" (776). With University of British Columbia Faculty of Education Professor Anne Phelan, I am working to show Grant's continuing significance to curriculum theory and teacher education, fields Phelan links in her 2015 book (and the inspiration of my collaboration with her).

46. See Lasch 1978, 1984.

47. Technology erodes subjective synthesis (see Pinar 2012, 225). Despite such dissipation, Grant remained subjectively present: "Please remember that I am a very definite person—and therefore may seem a dominating person—but it is important therefore that you do not let yourselves ever be talked down. And let me say that I never resent in a foolish way people being clear about my unclarities" (Davis and Roper 2009b, 834). Subjective synthesis—or coherence—enables reconstruction through dialogic encounter.

48. "Our world only changes," Lipari (2014, 188) writes, "when there is a kind of decentring involved, when we come to question, or leave behind, shedding like a snake's skin, our old views and certainties about our world." Even that old certainty?

49. "We cannot study Nietzsche as scholars, simply objectively," Grant told his students, "we study him to teach us where we are now and as all of us are now" (Davis and Roper 2009b, 986). Reimer (1990, 120) reminds that Grant disdained a "shallow deracinating cosmopolitan culture and yearned for the 'love of one's own,' including one's body, family, nation and tradition." From the particular to the universal was the direction of Grant's thought, but sometimes the journey was jagged, telling students in 1977: "I find my life altering between periods of great darkness and then some light and that the periods of darkness are bad when one is teaching. I am sure that is why Nietzsche gave up teaching very early" (Davis and Roper 2009b, 1060). He apologized for "being an unclear director of this class" (1060), an apt noun choice. As teacher, one directs—but does not necessarily control—the conversation that is the curriculum.

50. Grant (1959) 1966, 23–4.

51. Grant (1959) 1966, 23–4. "Prayer" and "studies" are both forms of "attention," Weil ([1947] 2002, 120) writes, asserting that "each school exercise should be a refraction of spiritual life." Mental "exercise" suffers a discredited status in progressive educational theory, but Weil's recasting of it as a refraction of spiritual life echoes in James B. Macdonald's (1995) characterization of curriculum theory as a prayerful act. Insofar as teaching might also be a refraction of spiritual life, Grant's teaching seems a most suitable instance of it.

52. Grant 1969, 29.

53. For a short summary of the World Bank's leadership in global school reform, see Pinar 2015d, 3–5.

54. Trilling 1972, 14.

55. Grant (1969) 2001, 33.

56. "The major source of power in this society," Knopff (1992, 66) notes, "is the technological paradigm of knowledge itself."

57. Gouldner 1970, 31–5.

58. Psychology, Grant (1969, 116) observed, is being reduced to "physiology." Grant's prescience is confirmed when Taubman (2009, 189) registers that "for both neuroscientists and cognitive scientists consciousness and subjectivity remain a puzzle…. What they cannot explain is why we are obsessed with existential questions when we do not need them; why, that is, there is subjectivity." Given their inability to articulate "the experience and testimony of the individual mind," as Robinson (2010, 22) phrases it, many flee to "generalization, solemn efforts to tell our species what we are and what we are not, that were early salients of modern thought." Sociology and anthropology, she adds, are two "examples" (22).

59. Grant tells Cayley (1995, 164) that even "studies of literature are more and more technological." On another occasion Grant names Northrop Frye as complicitous (see Davis and Roper 2009b, 987).

60. Discussing (and quoting) Heidegger, Sikka (1997, 203) explains that "[t]he call does not convey information: *it summons*. Thus, that to which the call calls this self is one's *own self.*' This call to the self cannot be formulated in words since 'conscience discourses solely and constantly in the mode of keeping silent.' The force of this silent speaking presses *Dasein* that is summoned into the hiddenness and seclusion, the science of its own self." Sikka (1997, 203–4) reminds (quoting Heidegger still), "that, in this summoning call, both caller and called remain indistinct.... 'The call comes *from* me and yet from *beyond* me.'"

61. Grant 1986, 37. This complaint becomes curricular, as we will see in ch. 5.

62. Grant 1986, 37.

63. Judt 2012.

64. In April 2016, Princeton University announced that it will keep US President Woodrow Wilson's name on its school of public and international affairs and a residential college despite calls to expunge his name from those institutions due his support of racial segregation (Anderson 2016). Absent abrasive reminders, will not the past be bleached from the present?

65. "Professional knowledge," Anne Phelan (2015, 142) notes, referencing teacher education, "is restricted to strategy." In contrast, she affirms a concept of "study" in teacher education represents "the temporary suspension of those forces—economic, social, cultural, religious, or political pervading institutions—that would influence, cajole, or direct students. This is not to say, however, that the spirit of study is denial or destruction of those influences; it is, however, about rupture, interruption, and disorientation of the familiar and taken-for-granted" (31).

66. See Pinar and Irwin 2005.

67. See Macdonald 1995.

68. See Huebner 1999.

69. Davis and Roper 2009b, 156.

70. Grant (1959) 1966, 38. Writing to his friend Derek Bedson in June 1960, Grant observes that it can be "hard for them [educated Christians] to recognize that universities can be sources of evil as well as good" (Christian 1996d, 204). This comes during what Christian calls "possibly the worst year of his [Grant's] life" (198), having joined then resigned from the philosophy department at the newly established York University, having learned the curriculum would be controlled by his adversary at the University of Toronto, Professor Fulton Anderson. However upsetting the year was, Grant learned from it, writing Bedson again that "I would not have missed the last months of my life for anything because they have made me pull myself together and realize how slopping and wishy washy I had become and above all how intellectually lazy and content with an idolatry of education" (206–7).

71. Grant (1959) 1966, 38.

72. The so-called learning sciences, Taubman (2009, 160) points out, have "provided the switch point or transfer points that allowed the discourses and practices associated with the business world to enter education." One example is the rapid rise in use of the medications for "learning" problems, a development that has prompted criticism that pharmaceutical firms, pursuing profits in an $11 billion international

market for ADHD drugs alone, are driving the global increase in diagnoses. In 2007, for instance, countries outside the United States accounted for only 17 per cent of the world use of Ritalin; by 2012, that number had grown to 34 per cent (Ellison 2015). The overreliance on drugs is also evident in psychotherapeutic practices. "Doctors have long known that journal articles exaggerate the benefits of antidepressant drugs," Carey (2016, A19) reported, citing a review of research in the journal *PLOS ONE*.

73. "The roots of anti-psychiatry lay within psychoanalysis," Zaretsky (2004, 327) explains. Anglo-American anti-psychiatry, exemplified by Ronald D. Laing, descended from British object-relations theory. Trained as a psychiatrist at the University of Glasgow, Laing joined the staff of the Tavistock Clinic in 1956, where he worked with D. W. Winnicott, Melanie Klein, and Susan Isaacs; he underwent analysis with Charles Rycroft. For Laing, psychoanalysis was "the first lifting of the veil—the first detachment from the objects of consciousness to look at consciousness itself." In the early sixties, as did Thomas Szasz and others, Laing began to depict schizophrenia as a category imposed on the individual by the psychiatrist, not as an intrapsychic condition. Michel Foucault was another advocate of anti-psychiatry (see Zaretsky 2004, 327). It was Laing and David Cooper who informed my first scholarship on socialization in the school (Pinar [1975] 2000).

74. Grant (1959) 1966, 87.

75. Grant (1959) 1966, 87.

76. US politicians—especially those affiliated with the Republican Party—have expressed such sentiments. In January 2016, for instance, Kentucky Governor Matt Bevin asserted that students majoring in French literature should not receive state funding for their college education. Florida Governor Rick Scott criticized anthropologists, and North Carolina Governor Patrick McCrory belittled gender studies (P. Cohen 2016). On November 10, 2015, US Republican presidential candidate Marco Rubio asserted that "philosophy majors would be better off going into welding" (quoted in Rappeport 2015, A25). "Welders make more money than philosophers," Rubio said. "We need more welders and less philosophers" (A25). Perhaps we need more English teachers, too?

77. Grant (1959) 1966, 88.

78. In Baton Rouge, Louisiana, where I lived for twenty years, these sometimes took the form of public signs—billboards—demanding that children memorize the Ten Commandments, as if moral lapses occurred because people were uninformed or had simply forgotten.

79. Grant (1959) 1966, 89. It appears that here (again) Grant mistakes "practicality" for the distinctively American philosophical tradition known as "pragmatism." Kinzel (2009, 17) appreciates that "George Grant's philosophical position shares the democratic outlook with the pragmatists; however, he points to what he regards as the metaphysically inevitable ground of philosophy in God's love of being." That pragmatists did not tend to share, with William James (as Kinzel also appreciates) and, as Victor Kestenbaum suggests, even with Dewey, the primary philosopher of pragmatism. While pragmatism did emphasize the consequences of thought and action, Dewey's version eschewed a vulgar utilitarianism (see, e.g., Dewey 1922, 118). By Dewey's death in 1952 pragmatism as an educational philosophy and movement had almost disappeared (see Cremin 1961), replaced by a naked utilitarianism,

first in the service of American militarism (after Sputnik), then economism (during Ronald Reagan's presidency). In his analysis of pragmatism, Kestenbaum (2002, 1) reduces the distance between Grant and Dewey, if inadvertently, emphasizing the spiritual elements of especially the early work Dewey undertook: "The central aim of this work is to propose that at least one version of pragmatism, John Dewey's, has an important place for the ideal, intangible, and transcendent."

80.   Kinzel 2009, 11. That historical situation was also personal, reflected in his intellectual life history. At first, Kinzel reminds, Grant had endorsed Dewey and James, even claiming they were his "favourite philosophers" (10). At that time of his life, Grant latter suggested, he had been an "ambitious little pragmatist" and that his "whole mental being [had been] caught up in that [North American] tradition." That changed after his conversion one is tempted to say, but Grant's work at the CAAE was adamantly progressive in character. So sometime after the Second World War—perhaps while studying Oman—Grant became critical of the cultural consequences of pragmatism. As Kinzel notes, he developed a "distinctively 'Grantian' form of philosophy under the by no means congruent influences of Hegel, Simone Weil, Leo Strauss, Nietzsche and Heidegger, as far as the moderns were concerned, and especially Plato on the side of the ancients" (10–11).

81.   See Tomkins 1986, 106; Christou 2012.

82.   See McKnight 2002.

83.   Grant (1959) 1966, 84. Such "egalitarian technologism"—eradicating difference for the sake of equality, accomplished through technologizing society—was at odds with the spiritual purpose of education. "Grant admits," Athanasiadis (2001, 109) appreciates, "that it is difficult to reconcile the contradiction between loyalty to democracy and the recognition of its destructive tendency on education. But this is no excuse for seeking to escape this tension by pretending it does not exist. Rather, one is called to live within it." Aoki's ([1995] 2005, 310) "generative space of difference" hovers here.

84.   Grant (1959) 1966, 85.

85.   Grant (1959) 1966, 85. "Technological society requires an enormous number of highly specialized people," Grant tells Cayley (1995, 163), "and the multiversity is to a very great extent a product of that, is it not? It produces all kinds of specialists to serve the technological society." In effect extending Grant's prescient analysis, LaCapra (2004, 203–4) points out that "a more or less relativized market model is active not only in the conception of a university itself as a corporation but in its status as the complement of private-sector business enterprises, a conception in which the university is based on knowledge as information, and information technology is dominant, from the primacy of the 'hard' sciences to the restructuring and 'digitalization' of the library, even to the point of continual technical 'upgrades' of systems that far exceed (or even counter) the needs of those who use libraries most, the humanists." Once the core disciplines of the university, the humanities are now, and not only in budgetary terms, almost ornamental.

86.   Science, technology, engineering, mathematics. Or, as Weil ([947] 2002, 152) put the matter: "Money, mechanization, algebra. The three monsters of contemporary civilization. Complete analogy." There are those who, while sympathetic to Grant, take issue with his critique of technology. Andrew and Planinc (1990, 181) write that "Grant was wrong to think that pursuing the Platonic trinity of truth, goodness, and

beauty is difficult in a technological society. Truth is a matter of attitude, a willing-ness to know the truth however uncomfortable it may be.... The pursuit of truth is not implicated in, but rather is stimulated by, technological development." One can only hope, I suppose. At this point in technology's development—military threats to the species' survival as well as climate change and the spiritual genocide technology threatens—I confess to have no hope, only resolve.

87. Christian (1996a, 194) tells us Grant found the "pedagogical writings of Dewey... useful precisely because they were shallow," making it "easy to see aspects of the modern." If citation of specific textual passages is any indication, Grant read very little of Dewey.

88. Grant (1959) 1966, 94.

89. In mid-1941—after the London raids had subsided and before his breakdown, conversion, and return to Canada, Grant wrote his mother that in a bookshop he had noticed John Dewey's *Pedagogic Creed* (orig. 1897), which he considered "the complete justification, written well, of father's life.... In philosophy my favourite philosophers are William James and John Dewey" (quoted in Christian 1996a, 83). They did not remain his "favourites" for long, as after his conversion to Christianity ("likely on 11 or 12 December" 1941; see Christian 1996a, 85)—Grant blamed Dewey and James for promulgating the erroneous view that "traditional education was somehow cut off from life" (104).

90. Grant (1959) 1966, 96. Despite secularization, teachers—in the United States cer-tainly—are cast as "saviours," accountable for children's success to an extent even parents are exempt. "Our current ways of thinking in education," Burke and Segall (2017, 52) conclude, "could be traced to a foundational text such as the Bible by rousing its sediments in contemporary educational thought." Just as Judaism and Christianity are for Grant the antecedents of science and secularization (and remain embedded in each), they are also present in secular education.

91. Kinzel 2009, 12.

92. Davis 2002b, 199.

93. Grant 1986, 97.

94. Dewey ([1934] 1962, 26) appreciated that "understanding and knowledge also enter into a perspective that is religious in quality. Faith in the continued disclosing of truth through directed cooperative human endeavour is more religious in quality than is any faith in a completed revelation."

95. Grant 1986, 98.

96. For an intellectual history of historiography emphasizing issues of historical recon-struction, narrativization, deconstruction, see D. Roberts 1995. "In shorthand terms," Roberts writes, in terms that Grant would not, I think, find entirely mistaken, "the element of infinity operates within finitude and results in finitude. There is no limit to the ways we, looking into the past, may sort things out, dividing and combining and relating, but not everything has happened, and thus even the totality is a par-ticular. Still, the thickness of the particularity means that it is not to be confined to a single dominant strand—the dominant strand of the moment—but is always more even that the totality of our ways of understanding it" (296).

97. Grant 1986, 98.

98. Grant 1986, 99. Allegory enables the past to be at once unique and mythological, thus edifying; e.g., enabling educational experience. For an initial theoretical exposition

of this idea, see Pinar 2012, 49–55; for an illustration—the Weimar Republic—see 69–101.

99. See Grant 1986, 99.

100. Grant 1969, 45. For Walter Benjamin, Doane (2002, 130) reminds, "statistics have a levelling effect. Through translation into an abstract numerical system in which all phenomena becomes comparable and hence 'equal' to some degree, uniqueness and individuality are lost."

101. See, for instance, Sztajn et al. (2012). While not yet mathematicized, this acronym-riddled graphed exposition maps a micromanaging of teaching and learning that ensures that neither could occur "openly" in Grant's sense.

102. Facebook is a recent entry to the education market (as it is misconceived), focusing on "traditional student-teacher relationships" (Singer and Isaac 2016, B5). On Aug. 9, Facebook and Summit Public Schools, a non-profit charter-school network with headquarters in Silicon Valley, announced that nearly 120 schools would introduce a "free student-directed learning system," one that "puts students in charge of selecting their projects and setting their pace" (B5). Well, sort of. Singer and Isaac report that the "software gives students a full view of their academic responsibilities for the year in each class and breaks them down into customizable lesson modules they can tackle at their own pace" (B5). Note that that knowledge is of most worth doesn't enter the picture. For overviews, see Pinar 2013; Spring 2012.

103. Grant 1969, 119. "To the extent that chance consists in unpredictability," Knopff (1992, 71) knows, "modern technological reason has emphasized the possibility of prediction. A theory is adequate only if it can accurately predict, and if it can predict, it can, of course, control. Indeed, the ability to control is a good test of the predictive accuracy of one's theory. In the social realm, one might think that chance is impossible to conquer because of the unpredictability of the actions of others. But this is true only if people truly act. If they do not act, but merely behave predictably in response to environmental stimuli, then social engineering becomes a practical possibility. The behavioural view is the natural concomitant of the attempt to overcome chance in the social realm." Overcoming chance in the classroom ensures learning as it enacts totalitarianism.

104. As Thibon ([1947] 2002, x) wrote of Weil one is tempted to suggest of Grant, that her "extraordinary learning" was "so deeply assimilated" that it constituted an "expression" of her "inner life." Likewise, Grant's erudition became the medium of his self-expressivity, his capacity to communicate across difference.

105. It bears repeating, as Grant (1986, 24) himself appreciated, that "the word 'information' is itself perfectly attuned to the account of knowledge which is homogenizing in its very nature." Knowledge is a different matter, one requiring erudition, a subjective threading of information and experience that enables judgment, on occasion insight, possibly even wisdom. Despite being an uncritical "critic" of public schools in the United States, even the *New York Times* columnist David Brooks on one occasion endorsed schools for wisdom (see Brooks 2015)

106. These are intertwined in the complicated conversation that is the curriculum. As this student—the writer Matt Cohen—from the 1960s remembers, living, teaching, and philosophy were "the same thing" to Grant: "As with many other students who met him at the time, I was very impressed by his willingness or even eagerness to take what I said seriously. Because this, as I say, was his method of teaching: to

make people take what they thought seriously, and therefore possibly think different things and examine the conclusions…because he believed that was right and wrong was within people, within every person. Because that was his view of what people were. To him, the business of living and the business of philosophy were the same thing. And I think that that was one of the things that made him so attractive to students, because they felt that in a sense he was saying to them that the most important thing you've got is your life and how you live it" (quoted in Davis 2002a, xx).

107. Grant 1969, 81.
108. Grant 1969, 116.
109. Grant 1969, 115.
110. Grant 1969, 116.
111. Grant (1974) 1998, 89.
112. Grant 1969, 36.
113. Grant (1969) 2001, 65.
114. The nineteenth-century German architect Karl Friedrich Schinkel, Toews (2004, 175) reminds, was among those who imagined the "past as a foreign country," and one "that could function as a model and norm for the present. But for Schinkel the past lived in the present through all of the historical forms in which its principles had been transfigured and passed on through time. To think historically was not to make an imaginative leap into a past world, but to view oneself within the flow of time in which historical forms were in a constant process of making and remaking." For Schinkel those forms were architectural; they can also be curricular, evident in this present effort to reconstruct the present through "reactivating" the thought of George Grant.
115. Grant (1959) 1966, 26.
116. Grant (1959) 1966, 26.
117. Grant (1959) 1966, 26.
118. Grant (1959) 1966, 26. Thanks to the Bill and Melinda Gates Foundation, US public schools are now enlisted in the cause of "dead-level" conformity. Long committed to "reforming" public education in the United States, the foundation granted $900,000 to develop eighty videos, five to fifteen minutes in length, featuring "high-performing" teachers in the Washington, DC, district as they teach decimal numbers and the Marshall Plan. Rich (2012) reports that the videos function as a complement to Washington's teacher-evaluation scheme, known as Impact, in which teachers are judged on student test scores and classroom observations. (Versions of these are used across the United States.) Because observers assign numerical ratings, many teachers complained that they required demonstrations of "excellent" teaching. "Teachers were saying to us, 'Just be very clear about what good teaching looks like,'" said Kaya Henderson, Washington's school chancellor (quoted in Rich 2012, A14). If we can turn teachers into robots, perhaps students will follow? Of course teachers will fail—if they remain human—and school reformers will point out, indignantly, their imperfection, rationalizing the use of actual robots, boosting profits of those companies that manufacture them and cutting the costs of public education by eliminating health insurance (repair insurance instead) and pensions.
119. Grant (1959) 1966, 26.

120. Within technology, "principles"—once associated with ethics—imply "procedures," a degradation evident in the history of curriculum theory. For a discussion of the "principles" of curriculum development, see Pinar 2015a, 99.

121. Collaboration with colleagues, Collingwood (2002, 54–5) reports, "very soon taught me what it was important for me to learn: that I must do my own work by myself, and not expect my colleagues in the philosophical profession to give me any help." While Grant could not quite say the same—his Dalhousie colleague James Doull was invaluable—he could come close, especially after the dispute at McMaster, an event discussed at the outset of ch. 5.

122. Thibon ([1947] 2002, xxxi) acknowledges the "reserve" that accompanies "intimacy."

123. That would mean, for one thing, that honest or authentic dialogue—instead of sophistic assaults—would characterize public discourse, including among political candidates. Referencing the seminal work of Buber and Levinas, Lipari (2014, 188–9) cites the "co-constitutive relationship between ethics and dialogue."

124. Grant 1969, 50.

125. As Grant came to rely on Simone Weil, Barry Cooper (1978, 28) notes, he came to consider the "true purpose of education to be the cultivation of a capacity for attention…—which is to say the capacity to do right." As I too suggest in ch. 6, such attention—or attunement—enables ethics.

126. Grant 1969, 35; see also Davis and Roper 2009b, 943. "The supreme figure of the Western world other than Christ," Grant wrote, "is Saint Francis. He asserts the supremacy of charity" (Davis and Roper 2009b, 579–80). In his interview with Cayley (1995, 174), Grant worries the word has become convoluted: "*Charity* has become such a lousy word, I just like to use *love*." Heaven (2006, 312) would seem to agree, writing that "though revelation must be thought, the charity or love at its heart cannot be grasped by thought."

127. Marion 2012, 154.

128. For Marion (2001, 249) "charity" is "iconic…turned back, in a filial manner to Him whom it loves and from who it receives the very chance to love Him—the Father." Even in secular terms, this sense of charity as multidirectional and as exceeding itself associates it with iconography.

129. Perhaps this is a "third space," but it requires a "double consciousness," e.g., non-coincidence with the situation at hand. "[I]t is necessary on the one hand to avoid a scholarship that by its immersion in the past castrates our thinking about what it is to exist now," Grant ([1969] 2001, 32) understood, "and on the other to avoid an immediacy that trivializes by persuading us that we are understanding the modern when in fact we are being carried along by the waves of its dynamism."

130. Showing how Judaism and Christianity inform schooling still, Burke and Segall (2017, 58) assert that…teaching is still very much…a form of testament," adding that the "curriculum [remains] based on testament" (59). What Burke and Segall suggest is threefold: "The first approach is simple: engaging, as we do here and elsewhere in a frank, ongoing conversation that seeks to address the myriad ways in which history, culture, and discourse remain informed by religion and just what that might mean for the formation of schooling, of teachers, and of students. A second strand, we propose, might need to take seriously the ways in which love, as a concept—both in broad terms, as well as in how it underlies the very concepts of teacher as martyr and teacher as saviour—is leveraged and indeed compelled in schools" (95). And

third, "propose…a-religious teaching that will, somewhat oxymoronically, require attention to the religion that underlies schooling and its history but that also then moves away from notions of martyrs and saviours preaching at the podium or pulpit of the classroom" (96).

131. Grant 1986, 57.

132. "The unifying nature of love," Sikka (1997, 226) explains, "not only flows out and draws in; it also binds and holds together. It embraces in unity. With respect to creatures, this embrace is not an equalization of all but a holding together of what is ordered and distinct."

133. Grant (1986, 72). For Magrini (2017, 4), the "Socratic project of *care for the soul* is an *interpretative* project, focused on the normative issue of understanding and enacting the ethical life."

134. Grant 1986, 73. Desire demands satiation. Love invites devotion. "[E]ros is aspiration toward something beyond itself to something eternal, unchanging, perfect, and final," Grant wrote (Davis and Roper 2009b, 1008). In modernity *eros* becomes means to another secular ends: mastery, wealth, power. In the ancient world, Grant (1969, 99) suggests, we moderns would be considered fools, as "universal human satisfaction" was considered in principle impossible due to "human dependence" and "weakness."

135. "Properly understood," Lindenman (2017, xiii) suggests, "education is the 'craft of desire,' or an ordering of the soul that inculcates it with a reciprocal longing for God and holiness. The person who devotes herself to this ordering, the teacher, answers a calling no less noble than a priest's." Rocha (2017, 71) knows: "This is the vocational question: the question of what and who I am called to *be*."

136. This is a very different sense of potential that Tyson Lewis (2013) decries, i.e., monetizing talent. Grant historicizes this development within "English-speaking modernity," with its "exaltation of motion over rest, of potentiality over actuality, of interest as detached from virtue" (Davis and Roper 2009b, 84). Given these circumstances, Grant reaffirms the integrity of study when he asserts: "Learning—[one] must do it at one's own pace, must do it one's own way. I can point out places [he mentions Ellul] to learn, which may be helpful, [or] may not…. The great thing about learning is to keep one's proper independence and yet not stop listening to the other—sometime[s] [a] waste, sometime[s] not" (Davis and Roper 2005b, 677).

137. What Grant wrote about a superb storyteller seems pertinent here: "He or she must be there as an individual, and yet open to otherness" (Davis and Roper 2009b, 436). Perhaps the importance of presence derives from Christian culture as it summarized by Grant (referencing Strauss): in Islam and Judaism, "revelation comes in the form of law…while in Christianity it comes in the form of a being" (Davis and Roper 2009b, 829). Law becomes personified and enacted intersubjectively, a whiff of eternity within time.

138. See Davis and Roper 2009b, 775. The subjective site of educational experience renders it singular, not standardized, reconstructed not only received. Thibon ([1947] 2002, x) tells us Weil's "genius" was that her teaching was alive, an "original creation." Rocha (2017, 78) reminds: "As an art, teaching is so ancient as to be pre-institutional."

139. Lasch 1984.

140. Grant 1986, 73.

141. Grant 1969, 130.

142. See Moghtader 2015.
143. Meynell (2011, 158) suggests that "Christian teaching presents a conception of the individual that is distinct from that offered by classical philosophy. Freedom, reason, and fulfillment are available to us all equally, and are not exclusive to an elite of superior souls." In his 1970 lectures on Heidegger and Ellul, e.g., Grant reassured students what they were studying was "a general subject around which to see where we are—but don't be disturbed; learn at your own pace" (Davis and Roper 2005b, 676). This sounds close to classic child-centred progressivism; see Tomkins 1986, 65.
144. Grant 1969, 130.
145. Grant 1969, 130.
146. Grant 1969, 130.
147. Grant 1969, 133. "Socrates," Magrini (2017, 17) suggests, "is ultimately concerned with the individual," adding that he is "not a teacher but, rather, a *co-participant* in the process of questioning and learning" (83); such a "life-project" is to "examine" and "seek together" the "elusive philosophical understanding of the virtues" (21).
148. Grant 1969, 133.
149. The conversion of ethical aspiration into social engineering is evident in the career of the progressive curriculum theorist Harold Rugg. "Certainly if any single career symbolizes the constantly changing image of progressive education during the decades after World War I," Cremin (1961, 181) tells us, "it was Harold Rugg's. A New Englander originally trained at Dartmouth in civil engineering, Rugg had gone on to graduate study in psychology, sociology, and education at the University of Illinois, taking the Ph.D. in 1915. The shift from engineering to education was a painless one, he once noted, since both fields in that era were consumed with a passion for precise measurement." In the *Twenty-Sixth Yearbook of the National Society for the Study of Education*, at least, Rugg's passion was the reconstruction of the curriculum (Rugg 1926, 3) so that it might anticipate "social needs" (4), affirming, he argued, the public schools' "prophetic function" (4). Unable to save society, schools—in the United States at least—seem now unable to save themselves, capitulating to capitalism's latest lure, technology.
150. Grant 1969, 133.
151. Pinar 2012, 235.
152. Grant 1969, 33.
153. Grant 1969, 33. Grant would have agreed with Rocha (2017, 79) when he writes: "Many teachers, both those who quit the profession as conscientious objectors and those who hang on doggedly, know the voice that calls them to teach comes from a deeper and more intimate place than the school bell. The law of the teacher is the same law to which Martin Luther King Jr. appealed when he gave his national lesson in Washington, D.C. This is the law written on the heart of the person, the inviolable law that so many schools and nations fear and seek to control."
154. Christian 1996d, 347. This Grant wrote in a February 1985 letter to Joan O'Donovan, where, after praising her book (O'Donovan 1984), he expressed pleasure at learning that she was teaching, adding (just before the sentence I've used as an epigraph): "Teaching is not only good because of what is taught, but it is so good for the teacher because when he or she gets to his feet he finds out how clear or unclear he may be on the matter at hand, because he hears what he is saying in relation to the taught people" (Christian 1996d, 347).

155. Christian 1996a, 94. In Grant's collected letters, Christian (1996d, 97) uses the sub-heading "Adult Educator 1942-5," implying that the role extended beyond employment dates, as I am arguing here. Athanasiadis (2001, 20) reminds that through his "regular column on public education for the Canadian Association for Adult Education…he sought to foster people's involvement and participation in building up the nation at the grass-roots level." Education for civic engagement—indeed nation-building—was a primary motive for many progressive educators. For instance, the great progressive experiment in the 1930s United States—the Eight-Year Study—was committed to the realization of "our national democratic commitments" (Kridel and Bullough 2007, 2).

156. Christian 1996a, 96.

157. Almost literally, as there is in the collected works a review, written when Grant was nineteen and studying at Queens University, of University of Chicago President Robert Maynard Hutchins's *The Higher Learning* (1936). Hutchins criticized overspecialization and vocationalism in higher education, as well as non-academic pursuits such as sports. Grant deems Hutchins an "educational revolutionist" who decried the deterioration of higher education in America that had followed, the undergraduate Grant wrote, "the American worship of money and business has led to the position where nearly every student wants to train himself to become a large money-maker (which is unfortunately not uniformly possible) rather than to train himself to live 'the good life'" (Davis and Emberley 2000b, 6).

158. And like the progressive educators he criticized, Grant was quite responsive to the public, surveying forum participants to learn what topics seemed most important (see Davis and Emberley 2000b, 52), attentive to "purpose" and "growth," and even fiddling with format (54; see also 69, where Grant notes a "need in improvement in our techniques"), all in the service of "democratic living" (55), almost a moniker for progressive education. At this time, 1944, Grant seemed willing to take into account that "most" Canadians are "practical" and want knowledge to be "useful" (57). A year later, he decries "mass education" as a "myth" (64), while—paradoxically it would seem—"noting the wide potentialities for discussion in the schools through the use of *Citizens' Forum*" (67).

159. Davis 2000, xxvi.

160. Davis 2000, xxix. As noted in the introduction and elsewhere, I think Grant remained a progressive public servant—in my terms an educator of the public, a passionate life in public service—but time and place encouraged him to embrace a conservatism with strong socialist and nationalist elements. One of Grant's Dalhousie students shared this sense of Grant: "What struck me about his mind then, as today, was how modern he is…. Here was a man who was totally modern and totally traditional" (quoted in Davis 2000, xxx–xxxi). Grant's expansive interiority could accommodate contradictory elements, synthesizing them in his subjective presence.

161. Christian 1996a, 96.

162. This was Harold Innis's fear. "One of Innis's most bitter memories of the First World War period," Watson (2007, 235) explains, "was the propaganda that had sent idealistic Christian youngsters into the horror of trench warfare. While this had largely been a wartime phenomenon, he now confronted a situation where US propaganda was to be cranked up and continued as a permanent feature of peace under the banner of the Cold War." Now it is rationalized by the "war on terror."

163. In the United States today, businesses brazenly endorse education as job preparation. There is no mention of citizenship in the full-page advertisement in the *New York Times* signed by Alcoa, Bayer, Boeing, BP, Dollar General, Dow Chemical, Dupont, Eli Lilly, Exxon Mobil, General Electric, General Mills, Harley-Davidson, Intel, Manpower Group, McGraw-Hill, Microsoft, National Defense Industrial Association, Northrop Grumman, Raytheon, Rockwell, State Farm Insurance, Taco Bell, Texas Instruments, Time Warner, US Chamber of Commerce, Xerox, and others: "As business leaders, we believe ALL American children have a right to an education that prepares them to be successful in a competitive global economy. We also understand that in order to compete in a knowledge-based, global economy, we must improve the academic performance of our students" (Signatories 2013, A7).

164. See Christian 1996a, 100. One issue that the CAAE pursued with the Civil Liberties Association of Toronto was the campaign to restore the property and civil rights of Japanese Canadians. Grant himself became involved in a movement for public housing in Toronto (see Christian 1996a, 101).

165. For Grant, Umar (1992, 14) notes, the CBC was "one of the central national institutions," a countervailing influence to continental integration.

166. On February 18, 1932, George Counts, a sociologist at the Teachers College, Columbia University, challenged the annual meeting of the Progressive Education Association to articulate a critique of the social order so that their students could confront the misery and injustice of Depression-era America. In small groups, those present considered Counts's question—"Dare Progressive Education Be Progressive?"—as other conference presentations were cancelled. Later published as an article and expanded into a pamphlet, Counts's speech sparked an ongoing debate regarding the relationship between school and society. Schools inevitably indoctrinate, Counts insisted, and it was essential for educators to counter anti-democratic propaganda (see Perlstein 2000, 51, 55). Tomkins (1986, 191) tells us that "very few Canadian school reformers" advocated Counts's views.

167. Christian 1996a, 97.

168. Christian 1996a, 10.

169. Quoted in Christian 1996a, 104.

170. Grant's writing during the mid-fifties, Davis (2002a, xxi) notes, as well as his many talks to professional groups, were "linked closely with his experience of teaching."

171. During his first appointment at Dalhousie, Davis (2002a, xvii) tells us, Grant constructed a curriculum that included courses on ethics, Plato, St. Augustine, and Kant, asking still the ethical, religious, and political questions he had faced at Oxford. "With these as the medium," (Davis 2002a, xvii) explains, "he challenged his students to test their mid-twentieth-century Nova Scotian and North American ways of thinking against the intuitions of the older Greek and Christian traditions." (Characterizing the curriculum as a "medium" is central to progressive education.) Dalhousie seemed a perfect fit for Grant; President A. E. Kerr had hired him, Davis notes, "with the understanding that he was expected in part to teach a philosophy informed by religious and moral concerns" (xvii). But the perfect fit was maybe too tight, as in a 1948 letter to his mother, Grant complains that "[m]y department has 310 students with me the only full time teacher & they call that philosophy" (Christian 1996d, 154). The proposal of a graduate school at Dalhousie provoked Grant to write to Kerr complaining about the differential funding of the sciences and

the humanities (156; see also 169). Had Grant seen his 100th birthday, he would have noticed that such funding inequities have only multiplied.

172. "[W]hen you think the purpose of education is adjustment to this world as Dewey does," Grant observed, "then the emphasis of your curriculum will be entirely different and what students think important to study will be entirely different" (Davis 2002b, 173). Dewey (1920, 51) thought the point of education to be reconstruction not adjustment, positioning "the individual not as an exaggeratedly self-sufficient Ego which by some magic creates the world, but as the agent who is responsible through initiative, inventiveness and intellectually directed labour for re-creating the world, transforming it into an instrument and possession of intelligence."

173. Christian 1996a, 164.

174. Grant's caricature of progressive education seems shared by his biographer, who at one point decries "the progressive educational ideas of theorists like John Dewey in preaching the debased view that the aim of education was to adjust people to their society" (Christian 1996a, 176; see also 216). Davis (2002b, 104) gets it wrong as well: "This view of education as adjustment kills not only all real art, even worse it kills our relation to God, by making the idea of God a servant of our security and comfort." Evidently, Davis and Christian do not know Dewey's work. "Instead of accommodating ourselves to conditions," Dewey ([1934] 1962, 16) wrote, "we modify conditions so that they will be accommodated to our wants and purposes." In the next sentence Dewey uses the term "adjustment," but in this context the term conveys agency, not passivity. No doubt Grant would critique Dewey's emphasis on "our wants and purposes," but for Dewey these were not defined only in secular terms, as Kestenbaum (2002) documents.

175. In December 1941—see Christian 1996a, 85; Christian and Grant 1998a, 4.

176. Quoted passages in Christian 1996a, 164.

177. See Christian 1996a, 177.

178. This is Christian's summary of Grant's thinking at this time (both passages are in 1996a, 164).

179. Published in 1953 in *Food for Thought*: see Christian 1996a, 164.

180. Christian 1996a, 164. While a very different figure in a very different era, Sikka's (1997, 209) summary of Heidegger's thinking is evocative in this content too: "Existence, transcendence, means: understanding being, being understanding. That *Dasein* exists means that it understands possibilities of being and, in this understanding, transcends to being."

181. "Those exiled from the world of universals," Al-i Ahmad (1984, 118) predicted, "will clutch at minutiae."

182. Quoted in Christian 1996a, 165. O'Donovan (1984, 23) points out that Grant saw the situation educators faced as one requiring the "rescuing" of "modern minds for true thought from their captivity to the myths and 'illusions' of science. This is why adult education must be committed to the teaching of philosophy. Grant summarizes the purpose of education in words borrowed from Weil: to cultivate 'the faculty of attention, so that ultimately attention can be paid to the infinite'" (23).

183. While Grant emphasized "content" he was hardly inattentive to the forms subject matter took, e.g., these very processes of education the progressives emphasized. The teachings of the church, Ouspensky (1982, 29) notes, are transmitted not only by the content but its "mode of expression," the progressives' point precisely.

184. Christian 1996a, 176. Grant's intellectual rejection of progressivism did not purge it from his psyche, where it would continue to inform his life.

185. Grant 1969, 127.

186. Grant 1969, 127.

187. Grant 1969, 113.

188. Grant 1969, 113.

189. Grant 1969, 113. For Socrates, Magrini (2017, 12) points out, the process of learning was a "continual and ever-renewed process, or *way-of-life*, of examining the virtues." When not the main text of Grant's teaching, study of the virtues as a way of life was the subtext. In a Socratic education, Magrini adds, "the pursuit of the virtues is an extremely personal undertaking" (12), curriculum decoded as *currere*.

190. Grant 1969, 113.

191. Colonel Laurie chaired the Dalhousie University board, Christian (1996a, 136) tells us, for Grant yet another businessmen whose "benign…intensions…caressed and bullied, to transform the university into an appropriate instrument to serve…the progressive capitalist societies of North America." Earlier he decried "the tyranny of the rich men who control us, and let them turn our universities into instruments for their cheap version of the expanding economy" (Davis 2002b, 69). Professors are no longer persons "of thought" but "simple employees" (197). Under my photo on my University of British Columbia ID card I am listed as employee no. 1667203.

192. "I do not mean," Grant wrote, "that technical education is not important—of course it is important to teach people how to earn their living. But earning one's living is only a means so that one can live in the world and move one's mind to fuller and richer life" (Davis 2002b, 432–3).

193. Christian 1996a, 134.

194. Christian 1996a, 134. Rigelhof (2001, 88) concurs: "There's something theatrical in his dishevelment, something that goes beyond the shabbiness of a busy parent and underpaid professor who has neither the time nor money to dress well. In the eyes of some students, George is making a vivid visual attack on the superficiality and conformity of so much of life in the 1950s."

195. Quoted in Christian 1996a, 134; see also 147. Spring term 1949 started, he wrote to his mother, with a "class of 210" (Christian 1996d, 158). Grant was working with the tradition of rhetoric, at least insofar as (Mondzain 2005, 12) describes: "Rhetoric is the use of persuasive speech, the driving force of which is not cynicism or doubt as to the existence of truth, but the taking into account of the listeners and of the very possibility of communication on the moving ground of everyday reality." Sounds slightly "progressive" to me.

196. "Walter Benjamin," Trilling (1972, 84) reminds, "speaks of the impulse to impart instruction as a defining characteristic of story-telling and a condition of its vitality."

197. "It is all very well to talk of giving yourself away," Grant reminded, "but you must first have a person to give away" (Davis and Roper 2009b, 781). Subjective presence, in person, occurs in specific places (not so easily on screens, except, perhaps by great film actors and actresses).Subjective presence can seem magical (and not necessarily always admirable), even compensating, on occasion, for age, a point brought to mind by Grant's summer 1943 letter to his mother in which he describes seeing Henri Bourassa (1868–1952, founder of the Montreal newspaper *Le Devoir*, a federal Member of Parliament, and "one of the main early influences on French-Canadian

nationalism" [Christian 1996d, 112n5]). While physically infirm (Grant describes him being helped out of his car by a young man), he was nonetheless subjectively present, and "with an idea…not merely a man whose end was office…live, real, vital" (111).

198. Davis and Emberley (2000a, xv) tell us that Dalhousie students "sensed a fire within him. He obviously did not treat the academic life as detached from the concerns and suffering of everyday existence." Rigelhof (2001, 79) summarizes: "Preparation is one side of it. Performance is the other. George understands that a teacher giving a lecture has to be as emotionally concentrated as a dramatic actor. It isn't a question of entertaining students. It's a question of getting students to grasp that serious questions ought to be taken seriously as a search for wisdom. A search for wisdom is as great an adventure as any quest any actor might embark upon in any play. George creates this sense of adventure, this climate of risk in the classroom, by drawing students into his own enthusiasms and leading them to think about themselves in new ways…. [H]e blurs the borders between his own life and his teaching." Certainly Rigelhof is right to note the blurred boundaries between Grant's teaching and Grant's life, and there is too a reiteration of the Davis and Emberley observation in the concepts of "adventure" and "risk." That Grant's teaching led students to rethink themselves seems maybe the highest praise of all.

199. Grant, Rigelhof (2001, 133) suggests, "taught best when he could teach intimately. He was better in small classes than large, seminar rooms rather than lecture halls." His lectures were memorable but it is plausible that smaller groups enabled his subjective presence to fill the room.

200. Cayley (1995, 52–3) asks about Austin Farrer, one of Grant's teachers at Oxford; Grant replies: "Yes…I went to hear Farrer lecture on Descartes and fell in love. I knew this is why I had come to Oxford. I suddenly heard a great philosopher like Descartes being wonderfully articulated and so I always went to his lectures. This was what had been so deeply absent in North America: somebody who really had given his mind to the study of philosophers of the past and who could really expound them. You know how hard it is to read people like Descartes directly, you just don't know where you are. Farrer taught me how to read; I hardly ever spoke to him, I just heard him lecture. Later on he lectured on Aristotle, and it was just wonderful for me because it gave me an entrance into how to do it. This was a highly articulate, well-educated Englishman, who was also a priest of the Anglican Church. But you know it was just wonderful for me to hear something done as well as that." George Grant has provided something of the same opportunity to me that Farrer had provided Grant: giving my mind to the study of a philosopher of the past, and one, I must say, who does not seem to me at all "past."

201. Sounding once again like a progressive educator, Grant raises the question of curricular sequence, inviting students to participate in his decision: "But there remains the question of whether we should read *Beyond Good and Evil* or the *Genealogy* first, but since I am hesitating and I want to put the arguments on both sides for proceeding either way, and then you might then express your preference" (Davis and Roper 2009b, 964). Perhaps this a one-time-only event, but one suspects that Grant's subjective engagement with his subjects (e.g., his students) and his subject matter become interwoven one with the other.

202. Pertinent here is Annovi's (2017, 9) quotation of Pasolini: "[I]t is always necessary to talk and act in concrete terms." She comments: "The author is fully aware that the

recipient—as he stated in the context of another interview—has a relevant weight in a work of art. Similarly, in his essays, Pasolini feels the need to address the reader, not merely to provide information" (9). Grant addressed his readers and his students, providing more than information (as important as that is).

203. Grant's speech—in person and in his books—was often poetic prose, in which "the materiality of sound and construction demands notice. Instead of being a transparent medium aimed at its referents, poetic language," Benedetti (2005, 14) suggests, "attracts attention to itself, becoming a physical object," adding (referencing the literary text) "in short, everything is pertinent, 'everything signifies,' from the level of its sounds to that of its meanings" (149).

204. Like many educational institutions across North America, in 1947 Dalhousie was overcrowded due to returning Second World War veterans. As a result, Grant gave his lectures to the students enrolled in Philosophy I in Coburgh United Church Hall (Christian 1996a, 134). Thirteen years later, at McMaster University, conditions had not improved: in his first year he taught over 1,800 students (332). Despite his capacity to convert a lecture hall into something of a parlor for complicated conversation, Grant was clear that class size must be kept minimal so as to enable "contemplation" (144). The key culprit was not class size, however, but the "scientific world of the West," which formed Canada's "spiritual climate"; it was preoccupied with "knowledge for power," an imperative that displaced "those disciplines that once had been considered a potent influence in preventing us from becoming beasts." Even his grandfather's own institution, Queen's University, had severed its ties with the Presbyterian Church, which had founded the school in 1841; consequently "the content of the teaching in the Faculty of Arts at that university is found to be almost entirely secular" (Grant, quoted in Christian 1996a, 153).

205. Rocha's recounting of the presence of Maya Angelou makes my point. Expecting to be "underwhelmed"—he had "a thick layer of cynicism where celebrity artists and intellectuals were concerned"—he was instead astounded by "Maya Angelou's presence" [that] alone captured my attention and respect." She was, Rocha concludes, "a beautiful witness to me of something all too rare these days: a teacher" (quoted passages in Rocha 2017, 120).

206. Pinar and Grumet (1976) 2015.

207. "[J]ust like poetry," Annovi (2017, 87) writes, "film must express—at every level—the author's absolute individuality." I am suggesting the same of Grant's teaching.

208. Rigelhof (2001, 132) quotes Grant's McMaster colleague Eugene Combs: "Above all, his propensity to ask questions to answer a question, a condition he was born with, makes him the teacher he is. George's questions become part of your thinking. They tend to direct you, what to read and which other teachers you listen or talk to. His questions focus your attention where you've not quite focused before. Grant's questions change you." See http://samizdatpress.typepad.com/spring_summer_2013_hamilt/george-grant-js-porter-in-conversation-with-eugene-combs-1.html.

209. Davis and Emberley 2000a, xv. According to Matt Cohen, Cayley (1995, 42) reports, Grant's method of teaching was (in Cohen's phrasing) "to make people take what they thought seriously," a method, Cayley adds, Grant used in his "writing—to try to reveal the generative thoughts that people were half-consciously thinking as they went about their everyday affairs."

210. In vol. 4 of the collected works there is extensive documentation of Grant's teaching, especially during his McMaster years. As at Dalhousie, Grant devoted hours to preparation. For his 1975–76 seminar on Weil, Grant composed 140 pages of notes "to help him," Davis and Roper (2009b, 814) report, "direct the class discussion. These notes are at times fragmentary, elliptical, and on occasion unintelligible, but the excerpts presented here provide a sense of his teaching style and his immense appreciation" for Weil. For his 1977–78 seminar, Davis and Roper report that Grant's colleague Professor Ian Weeks worked with Grant: "Professor Weeks recalls that he and Grant responded to papers presented by students (from both political science and religious studies)" (1044). Davis and Roper provide three pages of Grant's commentary on students' papers (1054; for other instances of Grant's engagement with student writing, see 929, 977, 983, 985, 989, 1002, 1003, 1015, 1029; for instances of Grant's engagement with students in class, see 996, 998). Also included in vol. 4 of the collected works are lectures and other excerpts—including a list of thirty-six notebooks and a list of courses taught—that provide glimpses into Grant's teaching during his second decade at McMaster. Roper notes that these provide "access to that intimate engagement with students that such a vital part of Grant's life work" (Davis and Roper 2009b, 930). Grant's openness to students is also evident in the following: "Let me also say—break in at any time with questions. If I do not stop just force me to stop—and if there is anything you want to ask me, my office is 114, University Hall. I love to discuss these matters" (932). Clearly, Grant's curriculum included direct and ongoing engagement with individual students over what they wrote as well as what they said, both in the public space of the classroom or in the private space of his office.

211. Davis 2002a, xix.

212. Davis and Emberley 2000a, xv. Even as an undergraduate, Grant admired students who studied not only for vocational but for more fundamental reasons. As he puts it in a 1938 letter to his mother, "I have found many, many new and awfully nice friends who can be clever and intellectual and amusing and who are *students*. They came to the university to *find out*, not only through the classroom, but every way" (Christian 1996d, 32).

213. Davis and Emberley 2000a, xv.

214. The autobiographical accounts affirm that when Grant spoke students listened. Weeks (1990, 84n2) remembers the "first time I heard Grant speak in a relatively public setting, at a welcome to new graduate students at McMaster University in the very early 1970s. After a long statement about the going down of the West he was asked what could be said to people. At first he said this was very difficult, and then he brightened and replied, 'You would have to say the *Te Deum.*'"

215. Collingwood (2002, 73) affirmed that "my job, after all, was not with my colleagues but with my pupils. According to one very ancient Oxford tradition—a tradition far older than Oxford itself—philosophy is taught by reading, expounding, and commenting on philosophical texts." That would seem to be the tradition from which Grant worked, if in quite different circumstances. In a 1951 letter to his mother Grant laments that "in the fight [over salaries at Dalhousie] education is forgotten by both camps. I am going to reserve my energies for the students.... The strange thing about teaching is one never knows if one is accomplishing anything and whether one does is wasted effort or not. Anyway, lovely, lovely students" (quoted in Jersak 2012,

151–2). That is the timeless truth of assessment—authentic assessment that is, not test scores—is that one rarely has any sense of what students do with what one has given them. That is the nature of the gift that is teaching.

216. See Christian 1996a, 134.

217. Greenspan 1990, 5.

218. Students remembered Grant's generosity. On a 1983 visit to the home of his uncle George—"a huge presence in my childhood"—and aunt Sheila, Michael Ignatieff (2010, 25) (then a young academic attending Learned Societies' meetings in Halifax) reports: "Every few minutes as I sat with them, another student from the past would knock on the door and be admitted to sit with him. Some of them were very young, and some were very distinguished, but they all sat in reverent awe as he held forth, this great shambling patriarch with a straggly beard and a huge laugh that revealed a frightful set of crooked and stained teeth. His visitors came to be in his presence, and he was gracious and regal with all" (150–1).

219. Christian 1996a, 134.

220. Davis 2002a, xix.

221. "[G]rant developed a remarkable empathy for young people," Rigelhof (2001, 19) reports, adding: "It was a most charming part of the complex personality that made him an extraordinary teacher in his own classrooms at Dalhousie and McMaster universities, on lecture platforms, in newspapers and books, and on CBC radio."

222. Christian 1996a, 135.

223. Christian 1996a, 135.

224. "As with Levinas," Lipari (2014, 191) reminds, "Buber's face evokes an ethical response," not necessarily seen on Skype, I add, but "face as the sign of the other that transcends social categories of identity, a well as the idea that ethics derives from the recognition of this face in all its otherness. Levinas's interest begins with the transcendence of being through ethics, through the responsibility for the other." Of course being physically present does not guarantee ethically engaged teaching, but it encourages it. Online learning is perhaps preferable to no learning at all, but it cannot offer what embodied—subjective, intellectual—presence invites.

225. Colville 1990, 8.

226. Quoted in Christian 1996a, 143.

227. For the great Canadian political economist Harold Innis, Ian Angus (1997, 63) points out, "the emphasis on space is…characteristic of industrialization, mechanization, and modernity—connecting it to the colonial influence—in contrast to the localizing orientation of oral tradition." In that tradition there is place not space.

228. Grumet (1978, 278) criticized the language of "learning environments," a concept that "obliterate[s] all that is personal in favour of what is general. The outside is favoured over the inside in curriculum work in the United States."

229. Grant saw the catastrophe coming: in a 1948 letter to his mother he complains that, at Dalhousie, "science and applied science will be built up at the expense of education" (Christian 1996d, 152). Now moving online and taught primarily for the sake of profit, even science will become a shadow of its historical intellectually adventurous self, as the acronym STEM implies.

230. While depicting an extreme instance of the devastation Grant discerned, Jonathan Lear's (2006) study of the Crow people specifies what is at stake in living through "cultural catastrophe" (8). "We do not grasp the devastation that the Crow endured,"

Lear argues, "so long as we think that the issue is who gets to tell the story. For the problem goes deeper than competing narratives. The issue is that the Crow have lost the concepts with which they would construct a narrative. This is a *real loss*, not just one that is described from a certain point of view. *It is the real loss of a point of view*" (32). How can one locate oneself in a world in which "one"—the person, a human creature with a soul—has disappeared? "It is as though," Lear appreciates, "there is no longer an I there" (3). Grant—a subjectively present "I"—was committed to address the devastation he saw everywhere around him.

231. For a list of Grant's undergraduate and graduate courses, 1970–1980, see Davis and Roper 2009b, 1082.

232. In the 1950s a Platonist teaching Plato was "rather unusual," Davis (2002b, 445) suggests. In the 1960s, at McMaster, Grant continued to teach Plato "as he had done at Dalhousie," Davis and Roper (2005b, 669) explain, "adding now a more thorough exploration of myth and the Greek religion. He welcomed what he saw as the freedom to teach as a Platonist and to teach Christianity as a believer. As he put it, he was able to teach 'from inside' these traditions, in contrast to the scholarly or 'objective' examination of religious phenomena from 'outside.' He explained, of course, to his students that he respected their right to their own beliefs, and he encouraged them to think for themselves. He did not expect them to conform to his view in order to obtain good grades."

233. At one early point (1948), Grant imagined that obtaining a doctor of philosophy degree would save him from being "utterly at the beck and call of the businessmen" (Christian 1996d, 152). While he was never at their "beck and call," Grant did at McMaster succumb to the academic refraction of corporate capitalism—assessing faculty members not by their teaching but by their productivity (numbers of articles published, and the prestige of their publishers; conference and invited presentations, signalling celebrity). Always on the go, ambitious faculty had less time for students, something Grant noted in a 1972 letter to his close friend Derek Bedson: "I am asked to go away and speak so much that I have made a rule for myself not to be away from this university except rarely, and I have accepted too much for this year already. The rebelling students had one good part of their case, that too many professors spend their lives in airports and I am determined not to become one of them" (Christian 1996d, 265). For a contemporary reaction against the frequently frenetic pace of contemporary professorial life, see Berg and Seeber 2016.

234. Christian 1996a, 171. In a letter to his mother written soon after arriving at Dalhousie, Grant wrote that he has been "getting some stuff back from my first year students and it really is so full of vigour and energy when they drop the artificial form that makes them believe that academic subjects are cut off from the life they lead," an observation Jane Addams or John Dewey or any of the other great American pragmatists might have made and with the same satisfaction. Adding attentiveness to time and place to sensitivity to his students, Grant worries that becoming "committed to philosophy, which won't feed them," will fail to prepare students for the "growing technocrat civilization…now that it has come to the Maritimes" (quoted passages in Christian 1996d, 148). Like several of the US pragmatists—William Heard Kilpatrick for one—he sounds willing to sacrifice subject matter for the sake of his students' well-being. In 1977, in a course on Aristotle,

Grant admits: "I wanted to find out what you know" (Davis and Roper 2009b, 1060); knowing students' prior knowledge is canonical pedagogical practice, from Dewey to Piaget and beyond (see Trueit 2012 for William Doll's working through the two).

235. After the publication of *Lament for a Nation*, recall that Grant was sometimes termed a "Red Tory" (Forbes 2007, 10, 59), an appellation he disliked as he thought it vulgarized his political thought—see Christian 1996a, 266—but one that acknowledged that conservative tradition in Canada that, as Potter (2005, xxxi) puts it, endorsed economic intervention by the state and opposed "economic continentalism."

236. Quoted in Christian (1996a, 171).

237. US President Donald Trump's secretary of education, Betsy DeVos, is one conspicuous example. A beneficiary of the Amway fortune, DeVos worked as a lobbyist on behalf of for-profit education ventures but has no professional experience in education (Zernike 2016, A12). She does have experience in making a struggling public-school system self-destruct: as one of the architects of the Detroit, Michigan, charter-school system, Harris (2016, A21) reports, DeVos is "responsible for what even charter advocates acknowledge is the biggest school reform disaster in the country." The reciprocal relationship between for-profit and education and personal financial gain—a conflict of interest signalling corruption on a scale Grant seems to have been spared—is indicated in Patricia Cohen's (2017, A1; italics added) conjunction: DeVos, she notes, is an "ardent campaigner for privately run schools *and* has investments in for-profit educational ventures."

238. Grant 1969, 58.

239. This sequence is contested by some, as Ridley (2015, C1) summarizes: "Most technological breakthroughs come from technologists tinkering, not from researchers chasing hypotheses. Heretical as it may sound, 'basic science' isn't nearly as productive of new inventions as we tend to think." The Stanford University economist W. Brian Arthur, Ridley reports, is convinced that "technology is self-organizing and can, in effect, reproduce and adapt to its environment" (C1). I suspect Grant would not be surprised by such suggestions.

240. Grant went to McMaster specifically because he was "immensely impressed" by Paul Clifford's "understanding of the problems of the modern secular university." The founder of McMaster's Department of Religion, Clifford was determined that "the great questions we call religious, should be continued to be asked in the new university" (quoted passage in Davis and Roper 2005b, 663).

241. Rigelhof (2001, 9–10) provides a peek: "At McMaster, his [Grant's] office is located in University Hall, one of the original buildings of an old Baptist college that had been built to look as if it had always been there. University Hall is a stone building in the Gothic style. Vines grow on its walls and creep across the leaded glass panes of its windows. McMaster is undergoing a building boom, but Professor Grant's office looks away from it and on to the older part of the campus—trees, lawns, and other stone buildings in the Gothic style. He sits in a large, overstuffed chair."

242. Founded in 1959, the department was positioned between the divinity school on one side and the philosophy, history, and social-science departments on the other, Davis and Roper (2005b, 633) note; Grant was hired to attract students from each of these. That he did, as enrolment figures for his course entitled Philosophy and Religion document (633).

243. Quoted in Christian (1996a, 221). As Rigelhof (2001, 126) notes, Grant was "convinced that this department ought to be a place where students and faculty can think about the great religious questions we face in our time."

244. "The word 'dialogue' has been spoilt these days by over-use," Grant admitted, "but it is still the best word for the crucial activity of a department of religion." Dialogue was a way of "opening oneself to the reverences of other[s]" (quoted passages in Davis and Roper 2005b, 655), adding: "It need hardly be said that dialogue such as this is not cheaply achieved" (656). "To conclude," Grant wrote, "openness is both the purpose for which the study of religion exists and the quality which should be incarnated in its practice" (656).

245. Quoted in Christian (1996a, 221).

246. Christian 1996a, 221. Arapura (1983, 51) notes: "The most dominant trend in all modern thought, namely positivism, involves a radical turning away from the Eternal and the transcendent." So does proselytizing, I would add.

247. Christian 1996a, 221.

248. Quoted in Christian 1996a, 221.

249. Judaism figures prominently as well of course. Surprising was the absence of curricular emphasis upon Hinduism, given that, according to Christian and Grant (1998a, 30), Grant considered Platonic thought "closest to the Vedanta, the ancient Indian scriptures."

250. The cultural significance of Islam to North America—to Canada in particular—is obviously much increased since Grant's death, and not only due to increased immigration and violence throughout much of the Middle East, including, most recently, the civil wars in Syria and Yemen. Born out in the years since Grant's death is Benhabib's (2006, 171) concern that the "increasingly hostile security environment" and the "reality" of "fundamentalist Islamic terrorism" in Europe would mean that "pan-Europeanism may not result in heightened cosmopolitan consciousness but in a new form of chauvinism, heavily interlaced with racist attitudes toward the Muslim world." John Ralston Saul (2005, 279) suggested that "Islam, the religion that most concerns the West these days, is fundamentally open and has a more flexible history than Christianity." That history, however, is obscured by present perceptions, Butler and Spivak (2007, 99–100) note, that "Islam...is contaminated by reactive gender politics and 'terror.'" The former impacts not only women, Ruthven (2009, 54) points out, but also contributes to practices not exactly forefronted in social histories of Islam: boy concubinage and pedophilia. Although *liwat* or *lavat* (sodomy) is condemned in the Qur'an, Ruthven continues, "homosexual relationships between older men and boys were tolerated, not least because they posed a lesser threat to the patriarchal order than unregulated heterosexual interactions" (54). Would that fact recommend Islam to contemporary religious—or queer—studies? Or, as in France, especially after the January 2015 terrorist attack at the satirical magazine *Charlie Hebdo*, would secularism—*laïcité* in France—be affirmed? (See Lilla 2015, 14). For Grant, probably not.

251. This must have been a turbulent time, and not only due to tensions over Grant's theory of teaching. By 1970, Davis and Roper (2009b, 929) report, the Department of Religion at McMaster had "grown rapidly," and many faculty were teaching graduate courses and supervising MA and PhD theses (thirty-six of them in 1971), precipitating concern among the faculty that there was insufficient time to attend to the

undergraduate program. Grant taught graduate seminars and supervised "many theses," Davis and Roper note, "but still managed, along with teaching his section on Christianity for the department's introduction, 'World Religions,' to offer two new undergraduate courses" (929). In 1973 he taught The Meeting of Christianity and Philosophy, in Grant's words a "course [that] will concentrate on how the receivers of Christianity took Plato's writings as the means to understanding their religion. It will concentrate on this process as found in the writings of Augustine. The study will be of the writings of Plato and Augustine." In 1978 he began to teach The Question of Good in the Technological Age, an "exploration," Grant wrote, "of the private and public questions concerning right action in modern Canadian society. What light do religion and philosophy throw on these questions?" (929).

252. Christian 1996a, 222.

253. Quoted passage in Christian 1996a, 265.

254. The subsidiary relation of pedagogy to curriculum is indicated in Angus's (2006, 347) suggestion regarding justice and its enactment: "It seems rather that 'what is the due of humans' refers primarily to the *what* itself and secondarily, as a consequence of the specific nature of this *what*, to the account of *how* to fulfill it." Surely *what* knowledge is of most worth is the question that implies answers, at least in part, to the question of how.

255. If openness is compelled, e.g., rendered compulsory, it is no longer openness but another form of closure, one leaving the one always open vulnerable to assault. To be open or not, and to what extent, positions ethics as central.

256. "Freedom for Grant," Meynell (2011, 123) writes, "entails the ability to reflect on what we should want and not just the ability to get what we want." Sounds like an ethical translation of the curriculum question, does it not?

257. Quoted in Christian 1996a, 265.

258. Quoted in Christian 1996a, 265.

259. It is not only the acknowledgement of being "behind enemy lines" that requires caution and solitariness, it is study itself. After a period of public engagement, Grant himself realized that social withdrawal was indicated (see Christian 1996d, 267). We will return to this issue—quietude—in ch. 6.

260. Davis and Roper 2009b, 819.

261. "I'm at the point where I want to retire," Grant told Cayley (1995, 106), "I don't want to teach at the moment. I want to write and think and read things that I've never read, and at sixty-seven I have a right to do that." Later, in a 1985 letter, Grant reports that "[i]t is an immense joy to be retired, because it allows me to follow my own reading pattern [study] & not think of students" (Christian 1996d, 354), a sentiment he reiterates in another letter (Christian 1996d, 346). Commending his friend Dennis Lee for deciding to leave teaching, Grant said about his own impending retirement simply "thank god thank god" (Christian 1996d, 335).

262. Quoted in Christian 1996a, 348.

263. Christian 1996a, 348.

264. Grant (1959) 1966, 32. Reached through reason perhaps, but not isolated there, at least for Dewey ([1934] 1962, 48): "Aims, ideals, do not exist simply in 'mind'; they exist in character, in personality and action." There is, then, a "synthesis" (Pinar and Grumet [1976] 2015, 78).

265. Grant (1959) 1966, 102.

266. "Must communication with secularization mean the acceptance of modernity?" Grant worried (Davis and Roper 2005b, 420).
267. Quoted in Christian ([1995] 2001, xx).
268. Aoki (1986/1991) 2005, 159–62.
269. Grant (1969) 2001, 58.
270. "For those of us confronted with the application of computer technology in curricular situations as the task at hand," Aoki ([1987] 2005, 156), explains, "understanding of application as a technical reproduction problem shows itself as instrumentally reductive, and inadequate. Understanding of application as a hermeneutic problem seems to overcome the shortcomings of the technical by vivifying the relationship between computer technology and the pedagogical situation." Such a "vivifying" relationship recounts the ancient controversy between idols and icons, as we see in the next chapter.
271. Grant 1969, 44.
272. Grant (1965) 2005, 78.
273. Grant 1969, 45.
274. Christian 1996a, 331.

CHAPTER 5

Idolatry

[W]e have made of economic prosperity
and worldly success such idols that we
have forgotten the true end for which
education exists.[1]

George Grant

The dispute at McMaster University was institutional, focused on the changing
nature of the university's religion department and of the university itself.[2] It was
also an intellectual dispute, one with E. P. Sanders specifically. A Methodist minister who had studied at Union Theological Seminary, in New York, Sanders would
become one of the most respected New Testament scholars in the world, later
holding chairs at Oxford and Duke Universities. Sanders saw Christianity as an
"outgrowth" of Judaism, Christian explains, while Grant sought a bridge—"good
and necessity as both infinitely separated and at the same time related"[3]—between
the Gospels and Plato, between Athens (Greek philosophy) and Jerusalem (biblical revelation).[4] As a Christian Platonist, Grant taught from within[5] his faith[6]
while committed to communicating with those who did not share it.[7] It was to
this profoundly "engaged"[8] educator students were drawn.[9] By contrast, Grant
saw Sanders's approach as an expression of "museum culture"[10]—the past[11] was
presented as a "collection of objects,"[12] what can also be recoded as idols.[13]

"Something tremendously important is lost in the process of objectification," Anne Phelan appreciates, "and it relates to the kind of person that is
produced."[14] That person is the double subject of research: the person researched
and the researcher herself. Grant was focused on the former: stripped of the spirit
that animates them, creatures become cadavers to dissect, research[15] on which we
can project promise for the future, a future free from disease: biological, social,

psychological.[16] For those of us embedded in cultures of objects—"material possession may become a ghastly idolatry,"[17] Grant knew—the past itself can become another series of cadavers, images on screens sealed off from the temporal present.[18] Submerged in screens, many are unable to "find in it [the past] truths that might help them to think and live in the present."[19] These issues seem interrelated: (1) objectification[20] fragments life into atomized collectables, a series of self-identical items we can "worship" like relics from a "foreign country" one cannot comprehend; (2) when mastery and ownership dominate, humanity is prevented "from knowing that they are essentially owned by something beyond them";[21] and (3) objectification installs presentism, in our era existence without time, rendering the past (and thus the present) incomprehensible to us.[22] Time is—we are—no longer present.

It was E. P. Sanders not George Grant who was in sync with McMaster's administration.[23] Admitting defeat, Grant resolved to leave, returning—not without controversy[24]—to Dalhousie.[25] There was controversy too in Ontario, where his resignation from McMaster[26] had been reported in the press. First in the *Dundas Star Journal*, then in the *Hamilton Spectator* and the *Globe and Mail*, Grant was reported to be leaving because McMaster had become populated by Americans.[27] That was true, but it was also the cover story.[28] Grant's point was that in becoming more American, Canadian university faculty were losing interest in the enduring questions of human life, focused as they were on solving practical problems, on research not scholarship, not teaching.[29] This reversal of institutional priorities modelled universities after businesses[30]—emphasizing productivity[31] and consumption,[32] not teaching[33]—quickly became not only an institutional but also a public concern.[34] The truth is that George Grant had been concerned over the deterioration of academic learning since at least 1943, when (working for the CAAE) he wrote: "Universities have served to produce techniques and technicians rather than sane ideas and thinking citizens."[35] The association of these trends with America was accurate; it was also strategic.[36]

In an account of the McMaster dispute he wrote for the *Globe and Mail*, titled "The Battle Between Teaching and Research," Grant summarized succinctly his lifelong engagement with education, which William Christian dates as starting in 1938 as expressed in the *Queen's Journal*, when Grant asserted that Robert Maynard Hutchins's *The Higher Learning in America* (1936) posed "a challenge to the people of North America."[37] North Americans, Grant had written, aspire to build "a noble technological society of highly skilled specialists who are at the same time people of vision."[38] The institutionalization of this aspiration followed Sputnik,[39] an event provoking Ontario governments to expand education, including higher education, in the province. While there were many benefits, Grant acknowledged, this expansion had also emphasized what amounted to a "new paradigm of knowledge, research."[40] In the 1960s and the early 1970s a significant number of American scholars[41] had accepted positions in Canadian universities, bringing with them their American emphasis upon "research."

While "research"—specifically scientific research—brought many benefits, much had also been lost in the scientific era, including sustained scholarly attention to enduring (eternal) questions of justice, ethics, and religion.[42] Such questions invited not only activism but also quietude—solitary, social, and spiritual attunement to what and where these questions point.[43] They cannot be answered "objectively"[44] as research requires; the "answers should arise out of a sustained conversation between teacher and students."[45] Grant reminds us that "[s]cholarship is a means to thought, not a substitute for it."[46]

While that sentence sounds slightly utilitarian, I suspect Grant intends it spiritually—after the Eastern Christian tradition[47]—casting the subjects of scholarship as iconographic[48] and their study as sacred.[49] An echo of the iconoclastic crisis[50] resounds in Grant's critique of Western Christianity.[51] "Western Christianity," Grant complained, "became exclusivist and imperialist, arrogant and dynamic by the loss of this...truth that the orders of good and necessity are different."[52] It had, as Sibley summarizes, "sought to overcome the paradox of God's immanence-transcendence by blurring the distinction between God's essence and being, and it did this by identifying God with being itself," adding that "God, in short, was rationalized as little more, made more subject to man's subjective purposes."[53] Free from "subjective purposes" and from "being itself," the concept of "God" dissolves, leaving us, presumably, with a sense of the reality of what is beyond empirical reality.[54]

In modernity we focus on empirical reality, thanks. In an essay on Dostoevsky, Grant noted that Dostoevsky had "turned back to assert Eastern Christianity—what is known as orthodoxy" in part to protest against "Russia being Westernized."[55] Westernization—Western Christianity specifically—meant technologization, Grant knew.[56] From Eastern Christianity Grant learned, Angus, Dart, and Peters suggest, "how Christian Platonists understood knowing as loving rather than as power."[57] For Grant, they continue, "Eastern Orthodoxy represented a theological tradition that had been nourished outside the West and therefore was devoid of modernity's most devastating effects."[58]

In Eastern Christianity,[59] icons[60] can—presumably—provide[61] passage to the spirit or the Good they represent.[62] Unlike idols that substitute[63] for something else (in the Bible[64] for God[65]) icons in the Eastern Christian tradition remind the faithful of what lies beyond the visible.[66] As Grant's "saint," Simone Weil, put the matter: "The essence of created things is to be intermediaries."[67] This notion of "intermediary"[68] seems to me implied in the concept of "particularizing holy"[69] found in Grant's DPhil thesis:

> The particularizing holy is misused when the concentration on one object remains fixed simply on that object and does not pass over into an ethical judgment. The feeling fails to be related both to the undifferentiated holy and to our general moral duties. Thus the particularizing holy is the source of idolatry, whether that idolatry be the central factor or a more peripheral part in advanced religions.[70]

Here Grant is cautioning against positioning creation—including the curriculum[71]—as conceivably[72] an idol, affirming it as an icon, an intermediary[73] between heaven and earth.[74] The latter seems expressed in his commitment to hire faculty who dwell within the religious traditions they have been called to teach. Does that recast faculty as embodied intermediaries? Grant's motive seems more epistemological—for example, that belief precedes understanding.[75]

Being taught by believers did not mean being proselytized. Grant wanted the McMaster Department of Religion to communicate both belief and understanding, avoiding objectivism at one extreme, religious dogmatism at the other. The department would concern itself with the study of what humanity "at all times and places" has "reverenced."[76] The "central question of any real department of religion" becomes, Grant insisted, "What is worthy of reverence?" In modernity, he knew, technology[77] results in "the destruction of reverence."[78]

While not pressing students to share the teacher's specific faith, the curriculum must not, Grant thought, be "about" religion, objectifying it as a relic in the museum, another topic of scientific inquiry.[79] Like an icon, the curriculum can also convey religion on its own terms.[80] For Christianity that meant, Grant knew, starting with "clear *factual* knowledge"[81] of Judaism and of the New Testament, contextualizing that knowledge with study of the Mediterranean civilizations surrounding these. After studying Western religions, students would study religions worldwide.[82] Grant emphasized: "religion is not a subject that you are outside of."[83]

I consider myself "outside" at least organized or institutionalized religion, but I appreciate Grant's pedagogical point. Certainly I appreciate his insistence on studying factual knowledge, not only as an end in itself but also because it can provide passage to understandings to which it might not be intended to point. Weil's assertion that the things of this world can be "intermediaries," located between the "soul and God,"[84]—between self[85] and what one studies, I'd add— implies that the curriculum can also be cast as a moving image of eternity, as iconographic.[86] While created "in the divine image," Athanasiadis writes,

> humanity is now fallen and, therefore, need education to restore them toward his image again. This is a lifelong journey. Grant's model for education is Plato's allegory of the cave…. Rather than adjusting ourselves to society as it is, we must resist its allure and find our fulfillment in divine wisdom and charity. This also requires divine grace and illumination.[87]

The preposition "toward" implies that while the gap between here and eternity cannot be bridged—for Marion the "ontological difference can never become an object for representation"[88]—one can become attuned "toward" the Good in the image[89] in which we exist. That last line underscores the Christian conviction that education is not itself the exit from the cave, that (in secular terms) luck and insight are needed too.

"There must be somewhere out of here" sang Jimi Hendrix.[90] Finding the way—each of us, I suspect, has a way only we can discern[91]—requires study as prayer, attentive to the abrasive[92] specificities of "the cave" while attuned to what lies beyond. That cave includes us, of course. Self-study is surely as central to Grant's conception of education as is academic study: in the humanities the two can be irreducibly intertwined. What we experience when we study, what we are able to think and imagine through what we learn, illumines images on the wall, forms material and immaterial, intermediaries between where we are and what waits for us outside. In ways peculiar to our time and place, peculiar to each one of us as individuals, these images or forms,[93] Fishbane suggests, "come to us and are expressed through us; and insofar as we live with awareness of our participation in the reception and transformation of all these images, one may strive toward their enhancement and integration into larger wholes."[94] For Grant, that "larger whole" was the Good.[95] For Lints, "the image finds its flourishing in its relationship to the original."[96] If "the original" remains absent or is shrouded[97]— for Grant it is a "perfection beyond"[98] the image—then "finding its flourishing" (Lints's phrase) requires striving toward "enhancement" and "integration" (see Fishbane above), what we can also understand as modes of attunement (on which I focus in the next chapter).

Characterizing curriculum and teaching as "moving images of eternity" positions subjects (both school and human) as "intermediaries."[99] Each—the human subject, the school subject—is reciprocally related to the other.[100] "Not only does the rightness and degree of truth mediated to the understanding by image and mode depend upon the rightness of the one who understands," Sikka explains, "but also the appropriateness of the images and modes themselves depends upon the appropriateness of the person who produces them, upon the enlightenment of the reason which invents the image."[101] In more Platonic language, Athanasiadis writes: "Creatures were linked to the divine source of their creation through their intelligible nature, which participated in transcendent ideas."[102] The relative reciprocity of this relationship is embedded in Thibon's caution that because materiality is mixed one must undergone a subjective "stripping," lest one convert an icon into an idol."[103] Idols or icons, that is the question.

Idolatry

> What people revere, they resemble, either
> for ruin or restoration.
>
> G. K. Beale[104]

While that either/or seems too sharp a distinction—and the matter of resemblance no simple or self-evident matter[105]—the point remains: we are, Grant knew, "ultimately defined by the object of our desire."[106] Idolatry is not only a biblical concept, it can be psychological, intellectual, curricular. Grant's critique of the technical or vocational curriculum as potentially idolatrous—at one point he rues "the god of technology"[107]—would seem to stem from the term's biblical history.[108] The temptation to mistake the image for the original is, it seems, easy, given that in several ancient traditions, Beale explains, it was believed that "an idol or image contained a god's presence, though that presence was not limited to the image."[109] That an image[110] could contain a spiritual presence or, in simple secular terms, points beyond itself, is expressed more in Eastern than Western Christianity, a point not lost on Grant. But stripped of its spiritual presence, the image[111] becomes encased in its materiality, and the "semblance of something" else becomes mere mirage, a self-enclosed item[112]—an idol[113]—on which are projected powers residing elsewhere, including within the human subject.

That spiritual potential resides within the human subject is implied in the biblical conception[114] of humanity[115] as made in the image of God.[116] "Human identity is rooted in what it reflects," Lints asserts, although I wonder if "refracts" might be a more precise verb choice.[117] Perhaps the visual[118] verb is complicated when Lints suggests that because "an image is contingent upon the object [it reflects] for its identity, so the *imago Dei* is contingent upon God for its identity."[119] "Contingent" upon is not equivalent to being identical to or being the mirror[120] image of, although it does suggest dependence. If God is tantamount to absolute alterity, "attunement" seems to me a more promising choice of terms to denote the refracted connectedness that *imago Dei* implies.[121]

For Hans-Georg Gadamer, Jay reminds, "Key hermeneutic concepts like *Bildung* (self-cultivation)...derive in part from the ancient, mystical tradition of the imitation of God's image. *Bild*, he [Gadamer] notes, means both *Nachbild* or copy and *Vorbild* or model."[122] Academic study, then, can become a form of attunement, a "bridge" between here and eternity. However conceptions shift in time, something—a "soul"—remains, Lints suggests, that "has persisted across the ages and across our differences."[123] In that soul is somehow embedded a relationship to something else: God, the Good, the Whole.

Relationship seems central. Within an anthropomorphic concept of God, Halbertal and Margalit explain, idolatry becomes a sin of "relationship...such as betrayal and disloyalty," specifically adultery.[124] Biblical depictions of God's relationship to human beings incorporate images of human relationships, Halbertal and Margalit remind.[125] God is declared king, father, bridegroom, husband, woman in labour, and judge, all implying "flawed human relationships."[126] Of these, "marital relations" are, Halbertal and Margalit continue, the "root metaphor" in understanding idolatry, suggesting that this "central theological principle of the Bible—the rejection of idolatry—is actually based on an accepted moral intuition in human relationships."[127] There is a gendered, even sexual[128] element here, as within this metaphor, they suggest, the sin of idolatry is "whoredom," as Israel offers herself to "whoever pays her the highest fee."[129] No male prostitute mind you, Israel is woman, transgender,[130] even "children."[131] Halbertal and Margalit emphasize that the Israelites' "obligation" to God is "personal;"[132] it has a history that started with the exodus from Egypt. Implied in biblical denunciations of idolatry, then, is the impersonality of worshipping other gods, thereby betraying their—ancient Israelis'—"knowledge" or *"yedi'ah,"* Halbertal and Margalit explain, a term denoting a "personal and intimate relationship."[133] Explicit here is that the divine becomes manifest in personal terms.

Such betrayal of what the ancient Israelites knew, Halbertal and Margalit continue, was a form of "forgetfulness."[134] Their "obligation" of "remembrance" represents a "personal loyalty," an obligation sealed by an oath or "covenant."[135] These anthropomorphic metaphors themselves risk idolatry, not unlike material representations such as idols.[136] What rescues metaphors or material from idolatry—what implies their iconicity—is their capacity to bridge the gap.[137]

The Gap

> Concerning God, let us admit clearly that we can think him only under the figure of the unthinkable.[138]
>
> Jean-Luc Marion

For Grant bridging the gap seemed possible sometimes.[139] Not, however, on the day he said this to David Cayley: "I think that the idea that Providence is scrutable is a terrible idea. It's a blasphemy. It's a cause of unbelief."[140] And in a 1975 letter to Simone Pétrement—who wrote on Gnosticism and on Weil—Grant expressed his sense of the gap as unbridgeable, there aligning himself with Martin Luther (if in a "Platonic sense"), quoting him: "He is not worthy to be called a theologian who sees the invisible things of God as understood through the things that are made."[141] Yet there is the Christian faith in incarnation, and maybe that is in play when Grant tells students that "most of us can have a mediated vision of the divine" as least as it "mediated to us through human love, thought and science, beautiful things, just actions," and for Christians, "mediated to us through Christ."[142] Only the "very few" are "called to know God" in an unmediated way—"immediately" as Grant phrases it—and in doing so they "set aside all visions."[143] Visions here may be products of the imagination—against which Weil inveighed—and these are to be "set aside" when "personalities have been broken,"[144] a subjective shattering of the human prism so that then, presumably, attunement to the transcendent becomes unmediated.

In a 1978 letter to Derek Bedson, Grant again reserves direct experience of the divine for a very few but, in that letter, that has less to do with being called by God than with the confinement of institutional life. Here using (as he does in his DPhil thesis) the term "supernatural" for the "divine," Grant writes that "except for the saints who may reach the supernatural directly, most people have to glimpse the supernatural through the natural," adding that the "natural"—by which he means what is "our educational, economic, political and scientific systems"—ensures that the "supernatural" is severed from those trapped inside them.[145] Absent in that list is the church. And despite working in universities almost his entire life, the supernatural was not exactly excluded from Grant's life.

Grant may be ambivalent about the prospects for bridging the gap between the natural and the supernatural but not so Richard Lints, who asserts with almost complete confidence: "When God creates, he creates contexts reflective of his character. The analogies of his character are naturally found in the created order."[146] Lints regards these analogies as the "divinely appointed means of understanding him."[147] Fishbane prefers the metaphor of correlation to analogy: "Divine truth and human truth are correlated."[148] For me, both "correlation" and "analogy" over specify any relationship between the everyday and what is beyond the senses. What we can know (however tentatively) is the sphere of the subjective; it is there one might become attuned to the transcendent.[149] Perhaps "decreation"[150] (or self-shattering[151]) is a prerequisite, perhaps an effect, as implied in Alford's suggestion that "[f]or Levinas, infinity is the opposite of 'there is.' Infinity breaks me open in my own bag of skin."[152] After such self-shattering through self-synthesis[153] can one sew oneself together again, a living quilt of trauma, testimony, and teaching. There is nothing necessarily linear or chronological in subjective struggle within the "gap," also a space of study, struggle sanctified by (re)search. Grant reminds:

> That is why the hard grind of study should never be taken simply as if it were a tough means to be got over as soon as possible. It is valuable in itself, [and also] a means to something beyond itself. It is something necessary to becoming a human being in the fullest and richest sense of that world—a religious human being. In this fact there can be achieved a kind of union between the wisdom of the world and the ultimate truth of the soul. The attention gained in the first leads us to the second.[154]

For Alan A. Block study "acralizes the mundane."[155] Should it not point beyond itself, Grant cautioned: "Scholarship can be as much an idolatry as money…. If scholarship is limiting, it is such an idolatry."[156] Despite its worldly rewards, scholarship can also serve, Grant is implying, as an icon.

Recall Grant's characterization of the few who experience the divine as having set aside any "vision" of the supernatural. In that discussion we were focused on the subjective conditions necessary for setting aside "visions." Recall that in Deuteronomy the revelation at Sinai is depicted as "hearing the voice of God without seeing any shape."[157] In fact, sight[158] seems the sense central to idolatry, the error of "making an image of something that has no image."[159] Are the images on the ceiling of the Sistine Chapel idolatrous?

What can be the difference between painting God and writing about God? One view is that language—especially figurative[160]—has no concrete object that can then serve as God's substitute; as an idol, for example.[161] The distinction between language and its referent is mediated by the "idea," which, Halbertal and Margalit point out, is an "internal image," one that renders description in language "less intimate and more distanced from direct contact of the senses."[162] It seems to me that the contrary could be the case as well, as language's lack of material specificity, its figurative quality, could encourage the supplicant to imagine an intimate and unique relationship to God, a relationship (as Halbertal and Margalit point out) God demanded of the ancient Israelites. There is also the view that God forbids both material and linguistic representations.[163] By implication Grant and Weil would seem to share this view, as they sometimes stress the "absolute otherness"[164] of God and the "essential categorical difference" between God and all representations.[165] But both also affirm intermediaries that purportedly link this world to the other.

After the Enlightenment, idolatry loses its sacred sense, devolving into one more of the "great illusions."[166] From anthropomorphism to projection, religion is demoted from truth to obstacle to truth, one that blocks scientific progress as it preserves human subjection.[167] After the Enlightenment, Halbertal and Margalit suggest, the concept of scientific truth is the same for everyone who can comprehend it, but within religion "wisdom"[168]—acquired through revelation[169]—is distributed unequally. Within religion the past is where revelation[170] occurred; within secular society it is the future that beckons, expressing and creating a "vision of progress toward the recognition of the truth."[171] In such an era, idolatry becomes, Halbertal and Margalit explain, "the manipulation of the imagination for controlling the masses by means of an image of the world built upon meaningless promises and threats."[172] Among these, one supposes, are promises of wealth and well-being as well as the threats of war and terror.

Idolatry, then, is the elevation of worldly concerns to absolute significance, redirecting human attention from ethics and charity to success, prosperity, and power. For Halbertal and Margalit, "any nonabsolute value that is made absolute and demands to be the center of dedicated life is idolatry."[173] Even more strongly stated, no human value should be promoted as absolute,[174] a commandment (if made absolutely) that seems to me to risk contradicting itself. But Halbertal and Margalit state the matter so that it becomes sensible even to the secular: making something absolute—conferring upon it "ultimate value"[175]—is not necessarily metaphysical; what it implies is dedicating one's life to something or someone. "The falseness of idolatry," they continue,

> is that the object of this devotion is not worthy of it. Idolatry in this extension means leading a false life, a life dedicated to an unworthy cause. The opposition between idolatry and proper worship is not between the false and true god but between the unworthy and worthy god.[176]

What knowledge is of most worth?[177] The curricular question is both a personal and public question, thereby a metaphysical one, a matter of revelation and attunement as well as of reasoned deliberation.[178] So conceived, curriculum can be converted from idol to icon.

Iconography

> [T]he doctrine of the incarnation and the icon are one and the same.[179]
>
> Marie José Mondzain

In his infamous 1951[180] essay on the state of philosophy in English-speaking Canadian universities for the Massey Commission,[181] Grant's answer to the canonical curriculum question was unequivocal. There, Athanasiadis reminds, Grant associated the purpose of philosophy with the purpose of education: "to achieve a high degree of self-consciousness in reason, will, and imagination, and to seek out freedom and wisdom in the light of God, is the purpose of education."[182] Philosophy is no "technical subject," Grant asserted, but contemplation[183] of the Good[184]—an unceasing "judgment" of society's "traditions"—an "activity necessary for all sorts and conditions of men—politicians and saints, artists and businessmen, scientists and farmers."[185] In Grant's—classical—sense, the point of public education is, in Dart's definition, "to open the mind and imagination to the overtures of the divine."[186] Education of the public becomes a sacred calling[187] as well as a public trust, one betrayed by substituting idols (vocationalism for instance, including the academic kind) for icons, for example; academic knowledge as intermediary to the Good. Grant complained that "[e]ven the traditional humane subjects such as history, the classics, and European literature are in many cases being taught as techniques by which the student can hope to earn his living, not as useful introductions to the sweep of our spiritual tradition."[188] Grant blamed this state of affairs on the "short" history of Canada, consumed by "practical business," devoting itself to "material ends," positioning the "active" rather than "contemplative life" the "ideal."[189]

In this 1951 statement, Grant was asking philosophy departments to focus not only on teaching the past but also taking up the "prophetic aim of showing what those ideas mean in our actual present existence."[190] Becoming historical means recognizing that our existence is today technological, a fact Grant associates with the "dimming" of "hopes,"[191] hopes erased for Grant during the Second World War. To articulate this juxtaposition of intellectual histories and present circumstances, Grant called for an indigenous philosophy in Canada, a project not without precedent.[192] In this "rediscovery" of the "wisdom" of the past, today's "tragic split" between "action" and "contemplation" can be "overcome."[193] In this calling one discerns an iconographic potential for the curriculum.

In the present era,[194] the term "icon" may suggest to readers a small image on a computer screen that represents a machine program or function. The term is also used to refer to any widely known symbol,[195] but for the spiritually minded the term has been closely associated with idolatry. For some, icons become, as Halbertal and Margalit describe, "mere signs...serving only as reminders and transparent representations of the gods."[196] Accordingly, icons become "didactic artifacts" whose primary function is to "inspire" and "teach."[197] Others insist that icons are not "mere transparent signs" but convey "independent power," capable of healing and even performing "miracles."[198] Such spiritual power derives from the "special relationship" between the icon and what it represents.[199] That relationship is one of distance and withdrawal, it would seem, as made in the image of God the icon is not to "be expressive, signifying, or referential...not be inscribed within the space of a gap, but will rather incarnate withdrawal itself."[200] For Marion, "Only distance, in maintaining a distinct separation of terms (persons), renders communion possible, and immediately mediates the relation."[201] For Ware, the "icon bears witness to the nearness yet otherness of the Eternal. It introduces us to a world of mystery, yet at the same time we discover that this mystery is not far away, but is hidden within each one of us, closer to us than our own heart."[202] The icon is also construed as a "place of residence (like the soul in the body)" and on others as a material "concentration" of God's powers.[203] In this view, the icon becomes a "holy object," Nes notes, the "form being merely a receptacle for the content."[204] The "law of the icon," Mondzain suggests, is "its topical singularity, its phenomenological specificity."[205] Steimatsky specifies its phenomenology:

> The rhetoric of the icon—which, like the relic, claims to provide visual, material evidence for the incarnation of the sacred in the world—asserts Christianity's redemptive vision of God's materialization in Jesus. The iconic image is not simply "symbolic" or "allegorical" in relation to its divine referent, as it would be in a Protestant system that severs the manifest and the hidden, the flesh and the spirit. Rather, it is grasped as participating in what it represents: it is an index of Christ's humanity; in partaking of his body it incarnates God.[206]

Not "simply" symbolic or allegorical but both and more, as it beckons those in its presence to proceed beyond it.

This phenomenology of iconography seems embedded in Nes's elaboration of the icon, which, for him, is certainly more than object:[207] it exhibits subjective qualities, including agency: "The icon enfolds us; contemplation becomes participation,"[208] Ware writes. In so doing the icon "teaches" those in its presence biblical and church history, thereby not only "mediating knowledge about belief" but also stimulating "feelings that lead to an inner arousal of belief."[209] In secular terms, one might say "that book spoke to me." But the icon is "always more" than ideas and images on an educational mission: due to its subject matter the icon becomes itself "holy."[210] This no mere thematic association made by a believer but, presumably, an actual interpenetration of the spiritual and material realms authorized by the appearance of Christ. "The icon has, by implication, the properties of what it represents," Steimatsky explains, "hence it is expected to heal and to perform miracles, it participates in processions, it is venerated like a holy personage."[211]

Maybe no holy personage, Grant's subjective presence is nonetheless encoded in his texts. "The greatness of 'great' books," Rocha suggests, "is to be found beyond their pages. They must refer to an incarnational reality; in order to be great, the world must become flesh."[212] Nes asserts: "As a result of the Incarnation, matter has become able to carry the divine within itself."[213] Accordingly, Nes continues, an icon not only portrays the surface of its subject but also attempts to convey "inner, spiritual qualities which radiate from the whole person, especially the face."[214] What radiates from inside the icon positions the viewer in a suspended space in front, as Steimatsky suggests:

> The ceremonial frontality of the icon, which it shares with ancient portraiture, offers itself to the devout's bowing and prostration. It does not draw the viewer into its space but is directed forward: depth is conceived not as behind but in front of the icon, in the space of the devout.[215]

Because the space "actualizes the spiritual reality towards which the faithful turn," Nes suggests, the icon is to be "honoured."[216]

Conclusion

> I don't believe that technology is to be worshipped in place of God.[217]
>
> George Grant

Grant associated irony with living "within a double vision," Schmidt suggests during their interview, juxtaposing "eternal justice and those caricatures of justice which parade before us in the conventional world of our approbation."[218] Grant asks: "How can one live as a Christian in a modern university without irony? Yet is one just to give up these institutions? There I don't think irony is dishonest or wrong at such points."[219] Not only "nothing wrong" but maybe something obligatory: by naming himself a Platonist, Umar asserts, Grant affirms the "importance of irony and double vision. Things are as they appear on the surface, but that surface appearance bids us look further."[220] Further yes, but living within "the tension between nature and the ultimate good"[221] amounts to

> a requirement for human self-understanding and can only be maintained when the transcendence is set alongside the natural and the political to form the duality in which we must live without an unequivocal assurance that it is the working out of a higher good than we are able to understand.[222]

This represents, Aoki reminds, dwelling within the "both this and that and more"[223] rather than the "either/or," the space of generative tension[224] between what is and what might be.

This matter of double vision[225] comes into focus when Grant reminds Cayley that Weil[226] was a "perfectly practical person; she had run unions, she had worked as a schoolteacher, she had fought in Spain, and all this had to be thought in relation to this immense experience. She found that what is given in Plato allowed her to think the two together."[227] Does the juxtaposition—requiring a space in between, of non-coincidence—provides portals to transcendence? Does this inscrutable tension between the Good and Necessity inhere within the space—the frontality—of the icon? Does this position the scholar as supplicant?[228]

With this question we return to the dispute at McMaster.[229] Supplication would seem to be the supplement of scholarship that threads the tension between the Good and Necessity. Within that tension one waits for revelation through reason, an attunement to the Good in the midst of Necessity. The revelation reason can communicate follows from that attunement the position of supplication implies: that the intelligence is enlightened by love.[230] By "love," Grant emphasized, he meant no association with "sentimentality—but the recognition that others are, in the fullness of what they are."[231]

Such recognition can occur not only in public but also in private, wherein intimacy might support inhabiting the gap between this world and the transcendent.[232] Or so Grant seems to suggest in a strange (strange in the sense he suddenly sounds like Pasolini) passage about sexuality. After noting that sex can provide not only "gratification" but also "ecstasy"—"With my body I thee worship"—he cautions that when such "worship" is "limited to the immanent," it may be "justly characterized as idolatry."[233] But through this "very worshipping" it becomes possible, he offers, to discover something of the sacred in nature, what has been lost by those held by the philosophy of human power and self-confidence. The rediscovery of that sacredness may be a condition for the rediscovery of a worship that is more than natural. For all its dangers, idolatry may also open the way back to worship.[234] In the recognition of alterity love allows, in the fusion sexual passion enacts, the self-as-idol dissolves, and the pleasure of the body perforates the veil of the transcendent.[235]

What's love got to do with it? Without it sexual objectification, not spiritual union, follows. Within modernity, moreover, love gets in the way of the will. "If you take so much of the modern way of looking at things," Grant tells Cayley, "one says that one knows things by holding them apart from oneself as objects, that love really darkens the intellect."[236] While acknowledging "some truth in this in the law,"[237] science[238] (however frayed[239]) stumbles toward the transcendent, first by its internalization (as secularization) of Christianity's mission of salvation, and by its reasoned attentiveness to the unknown. "To put the matter crudely," Grant tells us, if I had authority over university curricula, I would eliminate all courses on the philosophy of science taught by people who were not primarily engaged in a particular science, and I would exclude from such courses all students who were not giving a large part of their lives to the practice of some science. Still greater foolishness is to write as if one wished to reform or even replace such science. General discussions about the sciences can only be usefully carried on by those who have given long years to the serious and successful pursuit of some modern science.[240]

This view aligns with his assertion that only someone inside religion should teach religion—the core of the curricular controversy at McMaster—but it ignores the idea of science in the public interest, which might not only be taught by scientists teaching from within their scientific disciplines.

Grant judged his efforts at McMaster—"to build a department of religion in which the people where inside the great religions of the world expounded the truth of these religions"—an "utter failure."[241] That failure he attributed to "mistakes I made,"[242] surely an overly harsh judgment given the power of the McMaster administration melding with the gravity-like force of technology. "Gradually," he continued, the department was "taken over" by those "who just did research about the great religions. You know, you can write endless books about the Bible without caring an iota whether what you've written has anything to do with the truth that is given in the Bible."[243] Such research, he lamented, is now the "very core of the university."[244] Grant acknowledged: "Research can be useful, but because it so dominates the university, it takes over those things that need to be known but which cannot be known by research."[245] To what cannot be known by "such research" we turn next.

Notes

1.   Davis 2002b, 184. There are many false gods, of course, surrogates slipped in, sometimes ideologically, as Grant knew: "Ideologies make public the modern denial that reverence is the matrix of human nobility; but as surrogate religions they slip reverence in. It is, however, reverence for something not truly worthy of reverence, such as the state, the race, the multitude, the nation. Those of us who are Jews or Christians would say they are idolatrous in the worst sense of the word. On the other hand, they claim to be rational, scientific, and philosophic, and therefore to be giving knowledge of what is happening, when in fact they do not. In this sense they are destructive of common sense and moderation—the two great protectors of the health of the public realm" (Davis and Roper 2009b, 185). And not only there, if Weil ([1947] 2002, 153) is right; in modernity, she declares, "immoderation invades everything: actions and thought, public and private life."

2.   "One of the nice things about being at Dalhousie in '47," Grant tells Cayley (1995, 164) "was that that transformation hadn't yet happened. Transformations that are necessary to the technological apparatus sometimes happen more slowly in Nova Scotia. Watching what happened to places like the University of British Columbia

and then to the State University of New York when I moved to McMaster impressed me very much." Grant remembers a different time, telling Cayley that "at a place like Oxford, there was more real education than in the mass multiversities" (106), the latter now as "soulless" as they are "technological" (22). Despite that, Grant had high hopes when he moved to McMaster; in a 1961 letter to Derek Bedson, Grant wrote: "What I will be doing is to teach Christian doctrine to non-divinity undergraduates. This dept. of religion is really introducing the faculty of theology back into the university in a big way in a Canadian university—the very thing that has always been my dream" (Christian 1996d, 207). In another 1961 letter: "We have fallen on good times. McMaster has been awfully good and it will be interesting to see what comes of a department of religion" (208).

3.   Ward 1990, 104. "How this could be so," Ward adds, "is one of those profoundly difficult questions so abundantly present in Grant's religious thought" (104). Perhaps Grant's conversion experience provides a clue. "Instead of the effort to bridge the enormous gap between here and there, between God and my sinful self," Rowan Williams (2012, 24) writes, "we have a movement—direct intimate, overwhelming, even embarrassing—from God to us." Working from this experience, Dart (Dart and Jersak 2011, 4) suggests, "Grant sought to understand the meaning of the Good and make sense of such a reality in the public square."

4.   Christian 1996a, 302. Grant drew a contrast between Judaism and Platonism: "For whatever else Hebraic faith may be, it is a worldly faith—a belief that God the creator acts in history and that history is a series of meaningful events in which human beings are called to realize righteousness in the world. In contrast to the Greek exaltation of reason as a contemplative act, of history as an image of nature and of God as uninterested in the particularity of the world, the Hebrews saw God as the molder of history and existence as a call to decision" (Davis 2002b, 242). Grant reminded students that "St. Augustine said that Plato knew the whole of Christian truth except that the Word (*logos*) had become flesh" (Davis and Roper 2009b, 935). During the iconoclastic crisis of the eighth century, Mondzain (2005, 79) reminds, "recourse to Plato is both tempting and embarrassing where Christian thought is concerned... [because] Plato was able to serve both iconoclast and iconophiles causes."

5.   Grant speaks of "lecturing about something from within" (Davis and Roper 2009b, 935). In an August 1950 letter to the president of Dalhousie University, who had asked him to look for a philosophy colleague while in Britain, Grant said he preferred someone from "within" Canada: "You mentioned before I went to 'the old country' that I might look around for somebody (preferably Scottish) to help teach philosophy. I came across nobody who seemed suitable.... Science is so objective and certain that the background of the teacher is not of its essence. Philosophy, because it deals with such personal mysteries, does depend on the teacher understanding and sympathizing with the background of his pupils. So many of the young English and Scottish teachers I met were able, but I doubted their ability to transfer that ability to a Canadian setting. This is not to say that I do not believe that Canadians have endless things to learn from the great tradition of European life and thought—but it does seem to me that somebody who was a Canadian and yet knew Europe would be better in the university teaching philosophy than somebody from the U.K." (Christian 1996d, 166–7). Fifteen years later, in a 1965 letter to Leo Strauss, Grant (now at McMaster) expressed a shift in preference: "[W]e would like somebody in

the department who lives *within* Judaism" (Christian 1996d, 226; emphasis added). Apparently Grant's concern over Americans teaching in Canada was overridden by his commitment to teaching from within one's faith.

6.   "I see faith as the union of love and knowledge," Grant explained (Davis and Roper 2009b, 577). "In Grant's view," Davis and Roper (2009a, xxii) report, "each religion should be taught by believing individuals, not for devotional reasons, but because religions such as Hinduism, Christianity, and Judaism could be more fully understood from within." Working from within does not imply the willing of belief or the suspension of critical thought, as faith, Grant affirmed, is a matter for "contemplation" (Davis and Roper 2009b, 389).

7.   "[W]e had to make clear," Grant wrote, "that any student who came into any classroom was not in any sense forced to any opinion which he had not reached on his own steam" (Davis and Roper 2005b, 664). That was the case the decade before: Dalhousie students remembered—Davis (2002b, 445) reports—that "it was possible to talk to Grant about religious doubts.... Grant became a mentor for many because he was willing to give time and attention to their questions. Combining Socratic questioning with an understanding of commitment and responsibility, he helped them examine their assumptions and face the life choices they had to make."

8.   Davis and Emberley 2000b, 163. That had been true at Dalhousie too; introducing a section on Grant's lecture notes, Davis (2002b, 443) reminds that they "do not always convey the excitement of the exchange between teacher and students that students of those years experienced." Grant's pedagogical engagement was, I suspect, iconographic; that is, yes about him, the students, and the subject matter, but also to what each—alone, together—testified. "Both in icons and in the lives of saints," Ouspensky (1982, 37) explains, "the first thing that emerges is not the individuality but its subordination to that of which it is the bearer."

9.   And not only students from the Department of Religion but from other departments and even visitors outside the university. Grant's McMaster seminars enrolled typically fifteen to twenty students, Davis and Roper (2009b, 961) explain, "mostly from religious studies and other departments like political science and philosophy," but "there were also occasional and regular visitors who sometimes annoyed registered students by drawing Grant into what seemed to be time-wasting debates. Participants recall that Grant lectured, commented on class presentations, and recommended secondary works to supplement the primary texts and themes of the course. The notebooks show that detailed responses to student papers were very important for Grant." Given the historic divide between curriculum and pedagogy, I want to emphasize that Grant's appeal was expressed through, not apart from nor ornamental extra to, the subject matter. That Grant was not submerged in subject matter—that he kept an educational perspective focused on what academic study offered students and society beyond itself—is clear in his question: "To what functions in life are we training those who are honouring in religion? Some indeed will just be taking the honours courses in general education. This, however, is not a sufficient answer in our highly technical society. Of course, the answer to this...point is closely related to what content we want in the curriculum" (Davis and Roper 2005b, 636). "Functions in life," allow me to point out, is a typically "progressive" concern, one Dewey very much shared. Referencing "our technical society" documents that Grant had become "historical," mindful of the moment, and linking these two

(technical society and the historical moment) to "content" shows that "content," not "style" or "teaching," is paramount, however fused the three were in Grant's own teaching.

10.   Christian 1996a, 304. Non-Western cultures were also objectified as relics, as Al-i Ahmad (1984, 34) rues, writing of mid-twentieth-century Iranians: "We are all equally acceptable to Westerners, the makers of our machines, as contented museum pieces."

11.   "For us moderns," O'Donovan (1984, 112) appreciates, "study of the past is a vehicle of *our specific accomplishment as moderns*, that is, the bringing about of novel events." LaCapra (2009, 24) cautions that "an extreme contextualizing, objectifying history serves a carceral and exoricistic function by eliminating a threatening 'other' from our society and confining it to the past." Such as fascism, as I suggested in ch. 3.

12.   Christian 1996a, 305. In such a "culture," Grant rued, the "religions become like flies caught in amber, worthy objects for libraries and museums, but not living realities in a living culture" (Davis and Roper 2009b, 395; see also 424). Not only religions but thinkers too, as Grant cautions while teaching a 1978–79 graduate course called Heidegger and Technology. "What I fear in much North American education," he told students, "is the tendency to put even the very great into neat pigeon holes [classification] and therefore safely put away. This is part of technological training. The thinker in question is placed at our disposal like standing reserve is made accessible to us" (Davis and Roper 2009b, 1029). For Grant even the self–self relationship can become objectified: "For as soon as I try to know myself, I turn myself into an object, and my subjectivity which tries to know escapes my knowing" (Davis 2002b, 286).

13.   This association of modernity with objectification is a long-standing one. For Georg Simmel (1858–1914), Levine (2007, 28) notes, "modernity was marked by the accelerated production of 'objective culture': all those created forms of symbolic work such as science, art, music, philosophy, and the like. This enormous output has taken place at the expense of subjective culture, that is, of the capacity of human subjects to engage and digest those objective forms for the sake of their personal growth." Growth—subjective and social, personal and public—was an enduring preoccupation of John Dewey and the progressives.

14.   Phelan 2015, 14. Reimer (1990, 120) reminds that Grant (and Heidegger, Reimer notes) rejected "the modern obsession with the objectification of everything, from the assault upon human and non-human nature from the reduction of the essence of human life to purely technical relations and instrumental reason."

15.   Grant had quite specific complaints about research, among them that it replaced teaching as the primary obligation of the university. Initially a late nineteenth-century German conception—"under historical conditions that reduced language and spirit to epiphenomena of a neuroelectrical data flow," as Kittler (2013, 61) provocatively puts it, Germany's universities had adapted, attaching "laboratories" to "lecture and seminar rooms"—the research-intensive university was transplanted to the United States, specifically at the University of Chicago, where, Levine (2007, 40) notes, "founder William Rainey Harper became the first American university president to make research the primary concern of an academic institution."

16.   In this, faith in the future science and its offspring technology plays the pivotal roles; Grant condemned the "current worship of science" (Davis 2002b, 31), asking in 1955: "what is there about the human race that makes it worthwhile that it

should survive? I can imagine a prosperous society, without war, of healthy animals adjusted to worshipping their machines which could be so disgusting that one could will that it should be destroyed" (157).

17. From Grant's DPhil thesis; see Davis and Emberley 2000b, 380. Later, Grant would expand contemporary forms of idolatry to include the "expanding economy" of the post-war period, pointing out that it is "no longer a means to us—a means for the liberation of the spirit—it has become an end in itself and as such is enslaving us" (Davis 2002b, 159). "Therefore," Grant continued, "the price we have paid for the expanding economy is that by making it God men turn away from their proper purpose in this life. There is nothing wrong with automobiles and washing machines, but they must be known as simply means—means of richness of life for individuals and society" (159). Dewey is deemed the demigod of such idolatry: "And the good side of Dewey is just like the good side of the expanding economy—that it is important that men should be encouraged to achieve finite ends, the bad side of course is also the same—these finite ends are turned into objects of idolatry in Dewey so that man's spiritual destiny is quite forgotten. This is why Dewey is such an important writer on education, because he expresses so forcibly the revolt of the expanding capitalist economy against the old Christian tradition of the west. That is why he has had such influence in the United States, a society where the new patterns of the secular post-Christian world are arising" (185). Here Grant's expansiveness becomes overstatement, making Dewey a strawman.

18. Idolatry, Weil ([1947] 2002, 60) concedes, is a "vital necessity" in the "cave." "We have minds to see," Fishbane (2008, 2) reminds, "but our minds are filled with idols. The result is a living death. Almost unknowingly we become caretakers of our moribund sensibilities. Only through self-examination may one hope to begin anew." For Fishbane, theology provides the portal to life itself; for Grant education can as well. What Grant faced at McMaster, Marion (2012, 153) might suggest, is that "the status of science makes of theology a the*ology*."

19. Christian 1996a, 306.

20. Minogue (1990, 165) finds the idea that the world as object is then "summoned" and "forced to justify itself by answering our questions" to be a "curiously melodramatic view of the relation between the knower and the known."

21. Cayley 1995, 82. "I don't mean as slaves," Grant adds, "here all language fails—but that there is something beyond the passing that we do not measure and define, but by which we are measured and defined" (82).

22. So Grant affirmed the significance of the past, including in his thinking about the religion curriculum at McMaster: "theology both ancient and modern should be in the curriculum, because it is a particularly important aspect of Western religion" (Davis and Roper 2005b, 651). Students must also study "some other great tradition which answers some of the religious questions in at least a superficially different way" (651). For Grant that was either Hinduism or Buddhism—also venerated by Weil (see Thibon [1947] 2002, xi)—as Islam was too close to Judaism and Christianity to be a "valuable means of comparison" (Roper 2005b, 651; see also Davis and Roper 2009b, 829). "It's very strange that Islam and Judaism should be politically at war now," he told Cayley (1995, 131), "because I find in both of them the same thing, something I am frightened of, the overwhelming power of this very bare monotheism."

23. One gains a glimpse of Grant's situation in a June 1979 letter to Dennis Duffy (principal of Innis College of the University of Toronto) and his wife expressing his thanks for the honorary doctorate the university had awarded him: "I am very grateful because it came at a time when I am rather under attack by the administration at McMaster. The words you introduced me with at the convocation were very well composed and much too generous, but I was grateful for them" (Christian 1996d, 305).

24. It was not Grant himself who was cause of the controversy but the means by which his appointment had been secured; see Christian 1996a, 325.

25. On his last visit to the Grant home in Ontario, journalist Charles Taylor ([1982] 2006, 128) "found the Grants in the midst of a strategic retreat. Grant had accepted a teaching post at Dalhousie and had prepared the move with an article in the *Globe and Mail*, assailing the way in which universities such as McMaster had become gigantic knowledge factories emphasizing research over teaching, technical excellence over the dialectical pursuit of truth."

26. In his letter of resignation—dated March 14, 1980, and addressed to the dean of the Faculty of Social Science, R. C. McIvor—Grant explained that he was leaving due to the "dominance" of "research," an "appropriate principle for those parts of the university concerned with the progressive sciences," but one that "cannot produce an account of knowledge adequate to an Arts Faculty" (Christian 1996d, 309). To Taylor ([1982] 2006, 129) he wrote: "I am hoping in Nova Scotia to get away from the silly involvement in McMaster which has stood in the way of thinking."

27. O'Donovan (1984, 134) summarizes: "The direction of past decisions has been, in Grant's judgment, unequivocally towards the 'Americanization' of McMaster. That is, these decisions have all conspired to the entrenchment within the university of 'technique' (to use Heidegger's term)—that ethos and paradigm of knowledge which has gained control of American education and scholarship. The issue of hiring policy is cardinal, as Grant attributes the Americanization of his university most directly to the influx of U.S. professors into its teaching ranks."

28. The "back pages" might have revealed the catastrophe Grant was contesting, namely (in Dart's [2006, 12] succinct summary): "[T]he empirical, scholastic, rationalist, scientific, mastering way had come to dominate the world of thought and university life to such an extent that the contemplative, meditative, receptive, listening, romantic, and attentive way of knowing had been exiled or reduced to the private and subjective."

29. For Grant, research implied the erasure of the eternal questions in its objectification of what it studied, substituting a crass materialism for spirituality. In a letter to the *Globe and Mail*, McMaster President A. N. Bourns and M. W. Kristofferson, president of the McMaster Faculty Association, pointed out that Grant's own superb work had been the product of countless hours of research (Christian 1996a, 328). Scholarship—study attentive to "the Good" and often aligned with teaching and associated with the humanities—contrasts with research as Grant defined it.

30. "Canadian universities are run by businessmen," Grant had complained in 1948, among whom, he continued, "the ethic of material success is overwhelmingly predominant" (Davis and Emberley 2000b, 152).

31. After Strauss, Grant (1969, 98) insists that philosophy serves the perfecting of the soul, a conception resting on faith in "an eternal and unchangeable order." When

time is history and contingency is chance to be controlled, productivity becomes a form of idolatry.

32.   Quantified in citation counts, conceptualized as impacts.

33.   I am thinking of teaching here as a form of charity in Christian terms, public service in secular. Cayley (1995, 24) comments that Grant blamed professors for using research as "an excuse for avoiding the ardours of teaching," including, I should think, those that accompany dialogical encounter and ethical engagement with students, requiring the teacher's subjective presence. Writing his friend Peter Self (from Oxford days) the year before he died, Grant described another friend's (Ian Weeks) experience teaching in Melbourne, enjoying there a very different experience than had Grant, e.g., the university as "research factory which plagued so much of my life. He really had a sense of the university as a place where the young were led out of the cave" (Christian 1996d, 365). Grant here seems more the Platonist pedagogue than the Christian committed to charity or the public servant engaged in complicated conversation with citizens, but—spanning his lifetime—the three seem held in generative tension, and, sometimes, they fuse.

34.   Christian 1996a, 326–8. "In his discussion of mechanical reproduction's destruction of the aura," Doane (2002, 129) reminds, "Walter Benjamin aligns the social bases of such decay with the growing importance of statistics." Quoting Benjamin, Doane defines the aura as "'the unique phenomenon of a distance, however close it may be.' Benjamin also allies the concept of aura with the notions of 'presence,' 'unique existence,' 'authenticity,' and the 'authority of the object'" (129–30). Destroying the aura—the iconoclastic crisis echoes here—the "masses are endowed with a form of agency," Doane explains, derived from "their desire to bring things closer and their 'bent toward overcoming the uniqueness of every reality by accepting its reproduction,'" here again quoting Benjamin, knowing that "mechanical reproduction robs the object of its uniqueness and permanence" (130). The subjective presence of the teacher is replaced by interactive curriculum online.

35.   Davis and Emberley 2000b, 92. Later, Grant complained: "The secular universities of Canada are more and more places where our clever young people are indoctrinated with an opposition religion to Christianity—secularized humanism. And this is becoming gradually the case in our schools" (Davis and Roper 2005b, 225). I dispute that "secularized humanism" is a religion; it is an agnosticism, I am emphasizing in this book, within which attunement to the transcendent remains an option. Within secularity, truth is not a command but a commencement, an undertaking of deciphering the meaning of any situation in which one is embedded. While not dogmatically anti-dogmatic I nonetheless prefer my spirituality without an institution or a saviour, although I remain open to revelation. With the eclipse of humanism—presumably we are now "posthuman"—and the reactionary rise of an intense parochialism (in his embrace of loving one's own Grant never advised demonizing others), secular humanism might be a "tradition" a progressive can endorse, depending on time, place, and circumstance, of course.

36.   Grant would not be alone—see Cormier 2004.

37.   Quoted in Christian 1996a, 328.

38.   Quoted in Christian 1996a, 328.

39.   See ch. 4. See Tomkins (1986, 290) for K–12 effects in Canada. Sputnik was also a pivotal event in the educational history of the United States. For details, see Spring

2006, 95; Zimmerman 2002, 155; Pinar 2012, 104; Harootunian 2002, 156; Clifford and Guthrie 1988, 8; Astiz, Wiseman, and Baker 2002, 77.

40. Christian 1996a, 329. Grant was quite aware, Christian (1996a, 329) notes, that his Grandfather Grant had been a key figure in this shift from a British tradition of education to that of Germany and the United States.

41. Not only Americans, but, as Grant complained in a 1979 letter, "most of them products of the Ivy League" (Christian 1996d, 308).

42. "The world of religion," Grant wrote, "constitutes a realm where the subject is confronted with something over which he can obtain no hold at all." Moreover, "religion," Grant wrote in his DPhil thesis, "should not be regarded as creed nor morality simply as conduct" (Davis and Emberley 2000b, 374), a view from which he departs in the 1970s when he fastens onto abortion and euthanasia as absolute issues.

43. In his introduction to *Time as History* (in the collected works), Roper writes that when time is conflated with history, when "horizon" becomes "simply a human creation, it is "no longer possible to live within it," as "will" becomes the centre of human life; as an "alternative," Grant pointed to the "possibility of an openness to what the ancients called a 'passion,' or in modern language, 'receptivity,' an intimation that activity is not simply a creation, but an intimation of something beyond human making" (Davis and Roper 2009b, 7). That "intimation" I recast as attunement, and among its prerequisites could be quietude, terms discussed in the next chapter.

44. Referencing Heidegger, Grant tells Cayley (1995, 126) that what is required of us now is "passing outside the position where everything is an object and our relation to it is to summon it before us to give us it reasons...[and instead] waiting upon what is…. The poets are those who listen to what is."

45. Christian 1996a, 329.

46. Quoted in Christian 1996a, 329. Referencing Owen Barfield, Pérez-Gómez (2016, 202) warns of the "grave dangers of identifying models with reality, a veritable idolatry that has dire consequences for scientific practices." Fishbane (2008, 155) would seem to state the status of scholarship in the other direction (as it were), affirming: "Such care for God, through the forms and images of the world, and most especially in their human manifestations, is the sacred labor of redemption." That sense of reality as (immanently) sacred is one Pasolini shared (Annovi 2017, 62).

47. "The Western church fundamentally chose Aristotle; the Eastern church fundamentally chose Plato," Grant tells Cayley (1995, 77), adding: "As far as my own thought goes, I have fundamentally chosen Plato." In July 1988—two months before his death and in conversation with William Christian—Grant reaffirms his allegiance: "I'm on the Eastern Church's side, because it's essentially Platonic against the Aristotelian" (Davis and Roper 2009b, 743). Philip Sherrard's *The Greek East and the Latin West* helped Grant to "clarify his misgivings about Western Christianity," Christian and Grant (1998a, 6) acknowledge. The "essence of what Grant took from Sherrard," Sibley (2008, 146) suggests, is that "the Eastern church remained closer to the Gospels, or biblical theology, and Platonic contemplative philosophy by claiming that both the Son and the Holy Spirit proceed from the Father alone. For the Eastern church, the Christian revelation demonstrated that the essence of God was ultimately unknowable in that it transcended all human knowledge and experience." Athanasiadis (2001, 137) summarizes—the "influence of Sherrard's ideas on Grant's thought are only too obvious."

48.   Ouspensky (1982, 27) writes regarding the icon: "The image is reduced to a minimum of detail and a maximum of expressiveness." Scholarship may include much more than a minimum of detail, but the montage details create can be expressive, in this book's case, of Grant's subjective presence as an educator.

49.   A view Alan A. Block (2017) has formulated.

50.   "The iconoclastic crisis in Byzantium," Mondzain (2005, 1) explains, "was essentially a Constantinopolitan political crisis, which is to say, a crisis over the symbolic foundation of authority," but it revolves too around "the fundamental interdependence that ties the fate of the artificial image, or icon, to the transfigured flesh of the natural, invisible image and to our living, corporeal reality as desiring, political, and mortal beings" (xiii). The iconoclasts, she adds, "were trying to separate spiritual power from temporal power" (5).

51.   As he often does, Athanasiadis (2001, 135) provides a succinct summary: "But with the advent of Constantine and the crowning of Christianity as the official religion of the empire, there was pressure to exteriorize the faith. Suddenly, the church was obligated to pronounce itself on all issues related to society and to shape society in a Christian way. This went hand in hand with the expansion of the empire, requiring greater order over a growing territory. The Platonic form of Christianity was not well suited to such 'secular' responsibilities. The focus now had to shift toward the shaping of history and society, and in biblical terms it meant the more eternal, concrete conception of the Mosaic law rather than the more internal, metaphysical interpretation of this law in Christ. Matter separated from its divine origin was now seen as evil and, thus, to be subjugated. Moreover, the human mind was now the ground of transcendence and, therefore, responsible for subjugating nature and shaping society to the order of its own reasoning." Behind modernity's objectification of everything (toward the end of control) was, Grant believed, Western Christianity. It would be in Eastern Christianity, Peters (2006, 238) notes, that Grant would find "theological concepts that had not fallen prey to the 'onto-theology' of the West." See also Angus, Dart, and Peters 2006, 224 .

52.   Davis and Roper 2009b, 397. That idea of "infinite distance" between "necessity" (or "gravity" in Weil) comes from Plato, Grant explains to Cayley (1995, 175). Heaven and Heaven (1978, 71) associate necessity with "chance," reminding us that for Grant "the attempt to overcome chance as the central aspiration of modern science and this aspiration is identical to the overcoming of necessity as Simone Weil understands it." Necessity and good can be related, they add, "only in such a way as to maintain the infinite distance between them of which Plato spoke" (71). Does the concept of iconography imply "such a way"?

53.   Sibley 2008, 146. Sibley suggests: "Grant's insistence on the distance between necessity and goodness is both a repudiation of Hegel and a moral judgment regarding the modern project" (114).

54.   Derrida remembers: "From my childhood home, this could be named God without any possibility of knowing what it is, or possibility of determining any content to his name—I won't say 'concept' but 'name' of God. It is the question of the addressee, that is, the other. The addressee—precisely because of the structure of the trace, when a trace is addressed and left without any firm and assured destination— [is indeterminate]; we don't know whom we are addressing" (quoted in Kearney 2005a, 35).

55. Davis and Roper 2009b, 948. It is obviously a very different matter for Dostoevsky to oppose Westernization and for Grant to oppose technologization, differences of time, place, and person. Cautioning students against making of Nietzsche an "externalized study," Grant advised them to study "through what he is talking about and see it—not only about a world outside oneself but as a world in which one is included" (Davis and Roper 2009b, 966). It is because he was such a historically situated teacher—one engaged in educating the public in particular places at particular times—that I admire Grant so. If I had been a nineteenth-century Russian, however, I can't imagine opposing Westernization. Embedded in the West, in late modernity structured technologically, the conception of icon in the Russian church has its appeal, however, as the following sections suggest.

56. "The triumphalist theology that developed in Roman Christianity," Cayley (1995, 38) explains, "was also connected, in Grant's view, to the fateful emphasis on the will which expressed itself in the restless technological dynamism of Western civilization…. This strenuous, expansive conception of divinity led to an account of religion as the exercise of will, rather than as the pursuit of knowledge."

57. Angus, Dart, and Peters 2006, 224. Knowing as loving has it subjective consequences, as Rowan Williams (2012, 46) suggests: "[A]s Eastern theology has consistently said, the 'divine humanity' of Christ, human nature restored and transfigured by the presence of divine 'energy' saturating yet not destroying it."

58. Angus, Dart, and Peters 2006, 224. For Eastern theologians, Randy Peg Peters (2006, 242) suggests, God "was beyond knowing and beyond Being," beyond humanity's capacity to understand. Caputo (2005, 106) confirms: "The name of God, which is the 'theological' name par excellence, at least the 'rationalist' pronouncement of it, is taken to be something that must be effaced in the name of God's utter transcendence of every name or concept," adding that the "name of God should be a self-effacing trace, like a comet that burns itself out and disappears as it streaks across the sky of language."

59. Grant's references to "the Eastern Church," Christian (1996a, 235) suggests, were not necessarily to the Orthodox Churches of Greece or Russia; the phrase was for him a "symbol" invoking a Christianity "more attuned" than Western Christianity to "Platonism" and the "ultimate mystery of God." Perhaps not precisely or specifically or only, but surely any reference to the "Eastern Church" includes the Orthodox Churches of Greece and Russia. "It can be said that if Byzantium was preeminent in giving the world theology expressed in words," Ouspensky (1982, 45) suggests, "theology expressed in the image was given preeminently by Russia."

60. In Western Christianity, as Marion (2001, 87n9) implies, quoting Colossians 1:15 where Paul defines Christ as "icon of the invisible God."

61. That verb might not be active enough for Weil ([1947] 2002, 90), who writes that "God" moves within the "thickness" of the "world" to become discernible. For me, attunement is prerequisite, adding to any agency of "God" that of humanity. Of course our agency may follow God's stimulation of it in us, requiring us to recast agency as obedience, as I suggest in ch. 6.

62. "The mystery of the Incarnation is itself," Nes (2004, 15) asserts, "the crowning argument for the icon." Sibley (2008, 146) summarizes: "God was both immanent (the Trinity) and transcendent (the unknowable essence)." Discussing the icon, Mondzain (2005, 24) writes: "Yet the mystery of divinity must remain whole, and it is worth repeating that it is impious to scrutinize it and to ask too many questions." Lossky (1982, 14)

writes that "icons, just as well as the Scriptures, are expressions of the inexpressible." In Mondzain's (2005, 85) phrasing, the "historical Christ is the existential manifestation of God in a synthetic unity that mysteriously links the two natures, human and divine, to each other without mixing them together or altering them." Ouspensky (1982, 25) traces the first icons back to the lifetime of Jesus and the period immediately after him.

63.   Understanding idolatry as "substitution" was, Halbertal and Margalit (1992, 42) note, "central" to Maimonides's thinking. Their view is that the basis of the prohibition against idolatry is the inappropriateness of representation, not that it threatens to substitute the representation for what it represents, namely God (48).

64.   It bears reminding that while Grant sometimes praised fundamentalists (in part because they opposed modernity and, specifically, abortion) he was not one himself, at least not when he wrote: "First, we can no longer believe that the Book is a sufficient and final authority. Secondly, the old Biblicism has gradually degenerated into a set of rules—don't drink, don't steal, etc. and when something has become a set of ethical rules it has lost its true power. It cannot endure because it has become sterile and rigidly legalistic" (Davis 2002b, 217). On the subjects of abortion and euthanasia Grant can sound "rigidly legalistic."

65.   Referencing "[t]he distance of God," Marion (2001, 76) emphasizes that "no idol can announce the death or life of God, because 'he dwells in an inaccessible light' (I Timothy 1:6) attained by no light, no access, no dwelling. But the distance preserves as well the most inescapable proximity to what we can no longer idolize." Marion continues that "[o]nly the infinite separation of distance ensures one of subsisting within the infinite proximity of God" (78).

66.   Ouspensky (1982, 34) underscores that the "very fact of the existence of the icon is based on the Divine Incarnation." The icon remains within this world even as it invites us to contemplate another; it can be not only a sacred object but any object or reality at all, even a nation, as Weil ([1947] 2002, 147) implies when admonishes us to make one's own country no idol, but instead a "stepping-stone towards God."

67.   Weil (1947) 2002, 145. Within Judaism, the *sefirot* are "aspects of the Godhead that are themselves beyond space and time, though manifested through both" (Mayse 2016, 232). For Weil, it is the gift of divine grace (see Weil [1947] 2002, 32–3; Davis and Roper 2009b, 773, 829; Athanasiadis 2001, 94; Thibon [1947] 2002, xxiv).

68.   "What it will be for the gods to make their appearance," Grant told William Christian, "I have no idea. You have to believe in the appearances; you have to say the epiphanies have occurred.... But where the epiphanies of the new gods will come, I don't know? And what their relation is to the other gods. I think there is something very dangerous in the monotheisms, the pure monotheisms, that have cut down all the intermediate forms" (Davis and Roper 2009b, 759–60).

69.   Doull (1983, 46) attributed "the subjective, individualistic revolt in which we still live—the modern sophistry it might be called—is not against the tradition as such, of which it has no grasp, but rather against particular historical forms...a purgation from such absolute particularities."

70.   Grant 1950, 61. Grant, Umar (1992, 9) notes, acknowledges that "no particular can be a full incarnation of the good."

71.   "The heart of any university or department is its curriculum," Grant knew (Davis and Roper 2005b, 651). From a 1966 letter Grant wrote to Anglican Archbishop H. H. Clark, the curriculum is also central to Sunday school (see Christian 1996d, 242).

72. In the quoted passage "ethical judgment" is required to avoid idolatry, but isn't such judgment embedded in those educational aspirations about which Grant complains as progressive: "[D]emocratic citizenship, economic prosperity, or sexual normality have been exalted into idols because they were not thought in proper subordination to what was more important than they" (Davis 2002b, 66–7)?

73. As the Torah can be for Jews, "nothing less," Mayse (2016, 233) explains, "than divine eternity manifest within words and letters. Novel understandings of Scripture emerge in every generation because the infinite Torah is always taking on new forms that are appropriate for each time and place." Becoming historical becomes iconographic. If study is a secular form of prayer, as Block (2001) argues, "through prayer one may glimpse the realm of God's eternity, and the worshiper becomes a bridge spanning divine infinity and human temporality," as Mayse (2016, 234) suggests. This is an awfully expansive suggestion, I should think, and surely intertwined with what is being studied (Mayse is focused on the Torah), where, and who is studying (and, perhaps, with whom). Burke and Segall (2017, 11) point out that Torah "stems from the same root as 'moreh,' the Hebrew word for teacher." They add that "the words 'teach,' 'teacher,' or 'teaching' appear 261 times in the Bible. Words such as 'learn' and 'learning' appear 244 times."

74. "[T]he world as an icon to God," Marion (2001, 178) writes, requires us "to relate the world back to him."

75. Christian 1996a, 222; Davis and Emberley 2000b, 163. It is a view Grant had expressed decades earlier, in a journal entry dated November 5, 1942 (see Christian 1996d, 104). "But at the same time," Davis and Emberley (2000b, 163) note, "he always tried to communicate to his students and readers in terms they could understand, faith or no faith."

76. Davis and Roper 2005b, 679.

77. "We have in effect," James B. Macdonald ([1975] 1995, 74) knew, "created our first man-made gods in material form." While never explicitly espousing a religious faith, the great US curriculum theorist here appreciates technology as idolatry. Perhaps not the "first" form, but certainly novel and perhaps unprecedented in its powers of corruption.

78. Davis and Roper 2005b, 680. "Reverence," Grant suggested, "may lead to contemplation" (740).

79. Athanasiadis (2001, 217) summarizes succinctly Grant's critique: "The scholarship that should have served as a means to thought had become the end in itself in terms of research. Even the study of the past, which had become especially important in the humanities, had become objectified. The past was no longer studied as a means to knowing ourselves in our present but, rather, as a relic which had been surpassed."

80. Aoki ([1979] 2005, 333) cautioned about objectifying what we study: "So much of what we see and read about ethnicity are object studies about ethnic people, and by being factual, they tend to conceal the experiences of life-as-lived earthly. Hence, my interest here is to disclose even to some extent that which we tend to conceal, by attempting to bring into fuller view reflection upon what, for me, experiencing ethnicity has been like. I regard experiencing ethnicity as experiencing subjectively one's lived situation from one's own ethnic perspective. From my personal standpoint, and this is the only standpoint I experientially know, experiencing ethnicity has been and is experiencing being a Japanese Canadian in the time-space coordinates of my

own historical situation in which I was born, and within which I have lived and am now living." The great Canadian curriculum theorist appreciates—as did Grant at almost the same time, although there is no evidence that they knew of each other—that concepts can become idols or icons, functioning as intermediaries or ends in themselves. Importantly, Aoki appreciates, as Grant does, although rarely explicitly, how "time-space" too is an "intermediary," in Grant's phrase (after Plato) a moving image of eternity.

81.   Davis and Roper 2005b, 625.

82.   Grant endorsed Buddhism and Hinduism (in his DPhil thesis even criticizing John Oman for failing to discuss "Indian religion"; see Davis and Emberley 2000b, 387). Grant found resonance with Hinduism (Cayley 1995, 175; Schmidt 1978a, 102), explaining that Hinduism is emphasized in the McMaster religion curriculum because it provides contrast. Like the US progressives he decries, Grant allows (worldly) educational considerations to inform his answer to the curriculum question: what knowledge is of most worth?

83.   Davis and Roper 2005b, 644. As the "religion" of our time, technology was also a subject Grant thought one could not be outside of.

84.   Thibon [1947] 2002, xxxv.

85.   In modernity, Grant knew, "we talk of people as 'selves' rather than 'souls,' but in that secularization "we have changed how we consider ourselves" (Davis and Roper 2005b, 234). He quotes Leo Strauss: "The self is obviously a descendant of the soul; it is not the soul. The soul may be responsible for its being good or bad but it is not responsible for its being a soul; of the self on the other hand it is not certain whether it is not a self by virtue of its own effort." Severed from its grounding in the Good, the self risks becoming an idol, worshipped (as it were)—e.g., narcissism and exhibitionism. "In a word," Mondzain (2005, 190) writes, "the idol resembles us." For Marion (2012, 113), "[s]elf-idolatry seemed to be the rule of the idolatrous gaze." For Elshtain (2005, 253), "Evil is the turning of a limited creature from God to himself, and hence to an absolutizing of his own flawed will."

86.   At one point Thibon ([1947] 2002, xxxiii) criticizes Weil for overemphasizing the "irreducible nature" of "supernatural reality," so that she sometimes overlooks, he thinks, those places where, by the grace of God, the supernatural and the natural meet.

87.   Athanasiadis 2001, 86.

88.   Marion 2001, 203. "How does one yet pass from one to the other," Marion (citing Colossians 1:15) asks, "if not in the person of Christ 'icon of the invisible Father'" (176)? Nineteenth-century African-American feminist Anna J. Cooper ([1892] 1998, 189) was skeptical: "The finite mind of man cannot conceive the Infinite and Eternal. And if such a being exists, he cannot be concerned about the miserable wretches of earth. Searching after him is vain. Man has simply projected his own personality into space and worshipped it as a God—a person—himself."

89.   "Such is the image," Mondzain (2005, 191) muses, "deceitful and truthful at the same time."

90.   The song, "All Along the Watchtower," is Bob Dylan's, however; see http://www.covermesongs.com/2014/03/the-story-behind-jimi-hendrixs-all-along-the-watchtower.html.

91.   Recounting his critique of Marx, Athanasiadis (2001, 83) points out that for Grant, "True freedom is not only transcending everything in the world that oppresses us,

but everything within us that prevents us from transcending ourselves and recognizing our true purpose."

92. "In a world of simulation," Mondzain (2005, 223) asks, "what does our flesh become? What can we resemble?"

93. Referencing Tillich, Huebner (1999, 413) cautions against "form," as it "loses its vocation, becomes idolatrous, and no longer points to the transcendent. Continual protest against form is necessary for reformation and renewal of vocation," specifically (but not only), for Huebner, teaching. Huebner might have altered—contained—his critique of form (idolatry) had his faith been Eastern rather than Western Christian, wherein consanguinity between form and faith seemed emphasized. "Through the Divine service and through the icon," Ouspensky (1982, 30) suggests, "revelation becomes for believers their property and precept for life. For this reason Church art acquires from the very beginning a form in keeping with what it expresses." See Shaw (1980) for a pedagogical elaboration.

94. Fishbane 2008, 155.

95. Grant reminded readers that "being open to the whole is being open to the evil...the whole is not [only] good" (Davis and Roper 2005b, 660).

96. Lints 2015, 39. "To be 'the image of' is to be in a living relation," Mondzain (2005, 78) explains, a "relation [that] is symmetrical, reciprocal, and simultaneous," adding: "This relation, however, does not refer to the essence of the terms, but only to the means by which they are related to each other." Ware (2012, x) also emphasizes relationship, depicted in the icon "through the gestures of the hands and the orientation of the eyes each icon brings before us not isolated figures but persons in relationship." Elshtain (2005, 249) concludes: "Created in image of God, human relationality defines us."

97. For a discussion of the Shroud of Turin—in terms of iconicity and idolatry—see Mondzain 2005, 192–208,

98. Davis and Roper 2005b, 705. Grant's distinction between the two may be driven, in part, by his study of Augustine, who, along with Plato, Grant thought "dominated" Western philosophy and theology; see Davis 2000, xxix; Davis and Emberley 2000b, 159. "If time is an image of eternity," Dinshaw (2012, 13) notes, "there is resemblance between the two but also difference, distance, and it is difference that is felt most keenly in the *Confessions*."

99. "Weil speaks of *metaxu*—the Greek word for 'intermediaries'"—Athanasiadis (2001, 92) points out, noting that "[t]hese include family, art, culture, tradition, and country. The love of such *metaxu* can lead the soul to the love of the ultimate good, so long as they are not idolized as absolute themselves." Discussing the medieval mystic John of Ruusbroec, Sikka (1997, 236) writes: "A person who is right to God, in the sense of only meaning God, sees the spiritual significance of the names which both utter and conceal God, for that persons sees God spiritually in and through all the names."

100. "This genuine turn to the afflicted neighbour," Athanasiadis (2001, 92) notes, "Weil calls 'attention.'" Such receptivity—even reverence—invokes the space of the icon, its "frontality" in Steimatsky's (2003, 255) terms.

101. Sikka 1997, 237. For Grant, Christian (1992, 56) suggests, "It is only through love and not by means of reason alone that human beings can experience existence as good and beautiful in its essence." Are not the two intertwined?

102. Athanasiadis 2001, 134. "Plato's thought was dualistic," Athanasiadis explains, "but not absolutely so. Form and matter were opposites, yet both had their origin in a

supreme reality. Moreover, Plato's 'ideas' or forms were not simply transcendent and ideal in relation to the multiplicity of sensible objects which they determined, but also immanent or present within them" (134).

103. Thibon (1947) 2002, xxxv. That "total stripping" is for Weil "decreation," a mystical version of the regressive phase of the method of *currere*, self-shattering for the sake of synthesis. We "participate" in the world when we decreate ourselves, Weil ([1947] 2002, 33) suggests, emphasizing that only when we become "nothing" can we discern the "right place" for us in the "whole" (36). Perhaps such "stripping" is a spiritual version of "self-shattering," what I conclude is the reparation racism requires (Pinar 2006b, 181), implying too the inevitable if indirect relation between subjective and social reconstruction.

104. Beale 2008, 16.

105. See Mondzain 2005, 3, 29, 66, 69–70, 72, 177, 221.

106. Umar 1992, 5.

107. Davis 2002b, 29. "The scientists," he continues, "never lack one central unified principle around which to organize education. A scientific world picture soon convinces men that only science is valuable" (29). The worship of science as humanity's salvation is a form of idolatry, as Grant appreciates, but it seems to me that very coding of social media disposes its platforms to be idolatrous, as its coding encloses experience and image within its own self-sealed simulated universe. Sikka (1997, 263) suggests otherwise: "Since enframing is still an essential destiny, a destined way of coming to presence and so a mode of the truth of being, a light from the flash of being still comes to presence within it." That light is what goes out, it seems to me, idolatrously replaced by the light of the screen. If Sikka is right (and if I understand her), then technology could become iconographic, a portal to what lies beyond it.

108. For Grant, Athanasiadis (2001, 229) writes, it had been the "particularistic, historical focus of Western Christianity [that had] encouraged an idolatrous understanding of divine providence in the world." In contrast, Athanasiadis points out, "The Greeks were more concerned about the temptation to treat history and the particular as absolute and final (idolatry), as opposed to perceiving in them a means through which one could access a deeper universal truth" (250).

109. Beale 2008, 17.

110. Idolatry seems often ocularcentric; that term is often associated with modernity; see Thomas Levin 1995; Jay 1988, 1993. "Any visibility can become an idol," Mondzain (2005, 189) notes, but not visibility itself. Only when it draws attention to itself—instantiates itself as the only sensory medium of apprehension, and its endpoint—does it becomes ocularcentrism, e.g., idolatry.

111. The legacy of the ancient Greeks seems imprinted in both Western and Eastern Christianity (especially given the blurred boundaries between idols and icons that Mondzain chronicles). Jay (1993, 32–3) summarizes: "In short, the faith in the nobility of sight bequeathed to Western culture by the Greeks had many, often contrary implications. It could mean the spectatorial distancing of subject and object or the self-reflective mirroring of the same in a higher unity without material remainder.... It could mean the absolute purity of geometric and linear form apparent to the eye of the mind or it could mean the uncertain play of shadow and color evident to the actual senses. It could mean the search for divine illumination or the Promethean wresting of fire from the gods for human usage. And it could mean the contest

for power between the Medusan gaze and its apotropaic antidote (a contrast with gender implications occluded until recent feminist critiques made them explicit)." Invoking Jünger's (see ch. 3) fusion of man and machine, can we not re-gender the screen at we stare as a male Medusa?

112. Anything could become an idol, including democracy. While an ambivalent democrat, Grant was loyal given "alternative systems," but that "allegiance must be limited, of course, for it is idolatry to give more than limited allegiance to anything as relative as the ordering of society" (Davis 2002b, 167).

113. Among the "casualties" of idolatry, Thibon ([1947] 2002, xxx) suggests, is "mysticism."

114. Genesis 1:26–7.

115. And not only humanity, at least for Fishbane (2008, 155), who asserts: "[T]he human is an image of God. Many and mysterious are the forms of this image (human and non-human), and so diverse are they in their realizations and kinds of fulfillment."

116. The visual element of "reflect" becomes auditory when Lints (2015, 32) characterizes Creation as "invested with the 'echo' of God's glory," the last term invoking Athanasiadis's (2001, 4) analysis of Grant's "theology of the cross," the "center of Grant's thought." Davis and Emberley (2000b, 164) explain: "The theology of the cross meant to Luther—and Grant—something broader than a reference to the crucifixion, or a doctrine of atonement. It meant that one could know the love and forgiveness of the gracious God only through 'faith,' that is, through receptive trust and openness to Christ's Passion as revelation of that love." The conjunctive relationship between Christianity and Platonism that Grant affirms seems challenged in his DPhil thesis when, writing about Oman's conception of "intuition," Grant registers "how much the Cross makes necessary a criticism of Platonism—its tendency towards an intellectualist ethics, its inability to find joy in God's world, its incipient dualism" (Davis and Emberley 2000b, 367).

117. Lints 2015, 30. Even "refract" doesn't seem complicated enough a word to register that oxymoronic "fact," but I'll stay with it for lack of a better one. ("Imprint" seems eligible, as it retains a visual meaning while losing the mirror image idea. Thibon ([1947] 2002, xxi) writes that because humanity has "*issued*" from divinity it means that it bear its "imprint.") In Hasidic Judaism "refract" would seem exactly appropriate, as Mayse (2016, 236) explains: "God's energy *must* be refracted through time and space, for otherwise it would overwhelm the cosmos and cause everything to sink back into the unlimited Divine." The classic Bible version is 1 Corinthians 13:12: "God—the Good—is everywhere but escapes our understanding; we cannot see it except through a glass darkly."

118. Halbertal and Margalit (1992, 239) point out that idolatry not only prohibits the worshiping of other gods but also the representing of God in pictures and images. Given that God has no image, the Deity cannot be represented imagistically, only linguistically. Perhaps, as Lints (2015, 60) emphasizes, being in the *imago Dei* is the "most" important fact of human existence, that image cannot be visual. The Christian acceptance of Jesus as the Incarnation of God would seem to contradict this tradition, despite Lints's (2015, 61) attempt to wiggle out of it: "Humankind is not fashioned after a pre-existing image of God, since God has no image. Rather humankind is created as the image or reflection of God himself."

119. Lints 2015, 30. Because one can substitute something for God as the basis of one's identity, Lints points out: "Identity and idolatry are intertwined" (30). Mistaking the

idol (e.g., identity) for what it invokes, "otherness is seen as something to be shaped according to one's own image of the good, which is, finally, idolatry and insensitivity" (Athanasiadis 2001, 176).

120.   "Whatever else the *imago Dei* might mean," Lints (2015, 32) concludes, "there can be little doubt that it stands as paradigmatic of all creation in its calling to reflect or mirror God." Naming the errors that follow from conceiving God as "first cause," Randy Peg Peters (2006, 241) cites two, the first replacing transcendence with immanence (rendering God knowable through reason), and the second, humanity seeing itself in the image of God as "co-creators or masters of their own wills." Ouspensky (1982, 34) quotes Genesis 1.27—"And God made man, according to the image of God he made him"—emphasizing that "nothing is said about likeness. It is given to man as a task, to be fulfilled by the action of the grace of the Holy Spirit, with the free participation of man himself." That free participation I discuss in the next chapter.

121.   Not only refracted but intermittent, it seems. "In Christianity there is always not only the presence of God," Grant tells Cayley (1995, 128), "but also the absence of God." That idea Grant expressed decades earlier, while recovering from his experience during the London Blitz. In a November 1942 journal entry we read: "God sees the truth but waits," adding "what a phrase that is. The whole tragic futile benighted sublime ridiculous grandeur of our lives is there…. Personally, it is a great emotional discovery—the discovery of God—the first glimpse of that reality—not amateurish or kind—not sentimental or moral, but so beyond our comprehension that the mere glimpse is more than we can bear. God, not as the optimist—nor as the non-mover, but God, *who sees the truth but waits*…. Of course, the approach to God is, I know not how. For me it must always be *Credo ut intelligam* the opposite of that is incomprehensible" (Christian 1996d, 104–5). Here he affirms the gap between this world and the transcendent, its inscrutability, except perhaps through "belief," not mindless mimesis but, I suggest, an ever-shifting attunement to what exceeds the "grandeur" Grant so poignantly complicates above.

122.   Jay 1993, 110. Jay points out that the "tradition of hermeneutics, which gained a new life in the early nineteenth century with Friedrich Schleiermacher, was also resolutely tied to aural experience. As one of its leading twentieth-century practitioners, Hans-Georg Gadamer has acknowledged that 'the primacy of hearing is the basis of the hermeneutical phenomenon'" (106).

123.   Lints 2015, 19.

124.   Halbertal and Margalit 1992, 1. They also acknowledge that the biblical metaphor of the marital relationship represents only one aspect of idolatry, specifically, the "worship of other gods." Idolatry also prohibits certain representations of God, specifically in images and paintings, while allowing others (1).

125.   Halbertal and Margalit 1992, 9.

126.   Halbertal and Margalit 1992, 9.

127.   Halbertal and Margalit 1992, 10. Lints (2015, 26) also affirms that "marital themes of fidelity and infidelity are played out across most parts of the canon because of the conviction that marriage was an institutional reflection of the relationship between God and his people."

128.   That the sin of idolatry is sexual, Halbertal and Margalit (1992, 23; see also 209) report, is indicated in a "number of places in the Talmud." Later the idol is characterized as a "fetish" (39).

129.   Halbertal and Margalit 1992, 13.

130. And not only Israel was transgender. Rabbi Mark Sameth (2016, A17) asserts that "[c]ounter to everything we grew up believing, the God of Israel—the God of the three monotheistic, Abrahamic religions to which fully half of the people on the planet today belong—was understood by its earliest worshipers to be a dual-gendered deity."

131. Halbertal and Margalit 1992, 20.

132. Ibid.

133. Ibid.

134. Ibid.

135. Ibid. For me, "covenant"—racialization, I argued (Pinar 2006b), is its curse—translates into resolve (Pinar 2015a, 180), a subjective synthesis structured by remembrance. Recall Grant's emphasis upon recollection: O'Donovan (1984, 103) underscores that "historical recollection is for Grant a way to knowledge of the eternal and unchanging good." For Badertscher (1978, 87), Grant affirms—against the lure of technological "freedom"—the "power of recollection or participation in a living tradition, desiring or love, and thinking. Taken together, these powers ground the possibility of reverence." And recall that for Grant, "reverence is the matrix of human nobility" (Davis and Roper 2005b, 647).

136. See Halbertal and Margalit 1992, 35. "In turn," Lints (2015, 96) laments, "they [ancient Israelites] made idols and became like their idols, without life."

137. While "bridge" implies passage, it is nothing material, as Aoki makes plain when he writes: "I understand conversation as a bridging of two worlds by a bridge, which is not a bridge" (Aoki [1981] 2005, 228). On another occasion, discussing a bridge in a Japanese garden, the concept of icon seems somewhere close when he writes: "But on this bridge, we are in no hurry to cross over; in fact, such bridges lure us to linger. This, in my view, is a Heideggerean bridge, a site or clearing in which earth, sky, morals, and divine, in their belonging together, belong together" (Aoki [1996] 2005, 316). Within the Christian condition, lingering becomes adoration, marvelling at "God's unknowability" (Marion 2012, 231).

138. Marion 2012, 46. "[T]he unthinkable can be aimed at as such only in remaining unthinkable," he (2001, 141) continues. "Between God and man," Marion (2001, 198) adds, "incommensurability alone makes intimacy possible."

139. "For Grant," O'Donovan (1984, 37), "the Incarnation unconditionally establishes history as the realm in which good is overcoming evil." In the final decade of his career, Athanasiadis (2001, 181) suggests that "Grant makes some bold attempts at expressing how the good/God can be manifested and experienced positively (as presence as well as absence)." Marion (2001, 89) seems to combine the two, asserting "withdrawal as the most radical mode of presence for God."

140. Cayley 1995, 83. Athanasiadis (2001, 49) also emphasizes the point: "The reality of the world is one of evil, suffering, misery, and affliction.… Thus, in order to maintain an honesty about reality, it is also necessary to maintain a certain agnosticism or mystery about God's presence and working in the world." Discussing Freud, Trilling (1972, 157) reminds that "[h]is imagination of the human condition preserves something—much—of the stratum of hardness that runs through the Jewish and Christian traditions as they respond to the hardness of human destiny. Like the Book of Job it propounds and accepts the mystery and the naturalness—the natural mystery, the mysterious naturalness—of suffering."

141. Christian 1996d, 283. Obviously there is no unanimity among Christians on this point. Thibon ([1947] 2002, xxxiii), for instance, criticizes Weil's "absolute division" between this world and the supernatural one, worrying that humanity might then lose our sense of the presence of "Providence" in history.

142. Davis and Roper 2009b, 926. As we see in next chapter, Grant reserved a special status for the beautiful. "Because we are situated in a world where we cannot contemplate this Good directly and without distraction," Grant wrote, "it is necessary for us to approach it through its presence in the world as the Beautiful" (Christian and Grant 1998a, 28). But beauty is not the mediation of the Good, as the quoted Grant sentence (in the main text to which this is an endnote), as Kaethler (2009, 92) notes: "[L]ove is a mediator of God's own goodness, bridging the gap of human misery and divine perfection."

143. Davis and Roper 2009b, 926.

144. Davis and Roper 2009b, 926.

145. Christian 1996d, 300–1. In the West, each of these systems may now have become subsumed in the economic, ground zero of objectification through quantification. Grant knows: "We have exalted the economic motive (call it if you will greed) to the highest place it has ever had in human history" (Davis 2002b, 205).

146. Lints 2015, 21.

147. Lints 2015, 21; see also 38, 41, 50, 52, 54, 57.

148. Fishbane 2008, 40.

149. My sense of sensing the Good through attunement is surely weak, but then it seems not altogether different from what O'Donovan (1984, 177) presents as a Christian view of these matters, criticizing Weil "because she does not conceive the relation between the divine work of creation and redemption in a sufficiently positive manner.... Against Weil's mystical and Gnostic theology, we would call for a Christian understanding of nature and freedom that preserves the theological tension between creation, redemption, and eschatological perfection. Such an understanding would provide a compelling criticism of the ideal of technological freedom, while at the same time offering positive guidance for our action in the present." My sense shares the critique of "technological freedom," but is minus the concepts of "creation, redemption, and eschatological perfection."

150. The term is Weil's (see, e.g., Weil [1947] 2002, 32, 33; Thibon [1947] 2002, xxiv), whose importance, Grant once suggested, is "her attempt to express the truth of Christianity outside the philosophy of will" (Davis and Roper 2009b, 833). He continues: "Yet for Simone Weil autonomy is just that which stands in the way of knowing we are the image of God. This takes us, it seems to me, to the heart of S.W. and decreation. To be created is to think one is autonomous, creation is autonomy. Decreation is our end and it is overcoming our createdness—our creating. Autonomy is the evil which separates God from God" (833; see also 773, 829, 842, 843.) (Perhaps I'm quibbling here, but mystical experience—maybe not always but sometimes I should think, and to some extent—requires at least assent, an expression of "autonomy.") In Athanasiadis's (2001, 94) terms, "decreation is the form that divine redemption must take in a world of sin," requiring "our free consent to be nothing as that which we are in reality. It is our acceptance that we are not the center and ought not to be." Through such subjective reconstruction, "one is purified from one's illusions and idols and brought to the foot of the cross" (95). "This means," Athanasiadis

concludes, "that our suffering of the weight of our sin will not destroy us, but purify us" (95).

151. Central to anti-racist education, I have argued, is self-shattering (2006b, 180). Thibon ([1947] 2002, xxix) suggests that among idols those constructed by the "collective" can be the most "powerful" and "dangerous." Among such idols is racialism, in the present era converted to identity politics.

152. Alford 2002, 68.

153. That fourth phase in the method of *currere*, a moment of subjective coherence achieved through analysis (itself meditative, attuned), what Grant might have termed more modestly as mediation: "And this bitter contrast [between the good and necessity, e.g., the gap] is in my opinion something which thought cannot escape. It is a contradiction which we attempt to reconcile, for as is clear, I hope, thought is always mediation; that is, it is the instrument of reconciliation" (Davis 2002b, 488–9). Subjective synthesis is surely also a (however momentary, open to revision) reconciliation with one's past.

154. Davis and Roper 2005b, 138.

155. Block 2004, 2–3.

156. Davis and Roper 2005b, 137

157. Halbertal and Margalit 1992, 38.

158. The association of ocularcentrism and racialization has a pre-modern genesis, perhaps (Pinar 2006b, 6–7). Is racism, then, a sin of idolatry, substituting skin colour (or whatever whites "see") for spirit?

159. Halbertal and Margalit 1992, 45. While forbidding "similarity-based representations" of God, Halbertal and Margalit (1992, 48) report, the Bible allows "metonymic representations," such as the cherubim. They cite this fact—that metonymic representations of God are allowed in the Bible—in support of their argument that it is inappropriateness, not substitution, that is the sin of idolatry (Halbertal and Margalit 1992, 48).

160. See Halbertal and Margalit 1992, 56.

161. Devices may be another matter. The "tendency of digital technologies," Pérez-Gómez (2016, 211) appreciates, "is reductive and substitutive."

162. Halbertal and Margalit 1992, 53. Jay (1993, 33) notes that the ancient "Greek privileging of vision meant more than relegating the other senses to subordinate positions; it could also lead to the denigration of language."

163. Halbertal and Margalit 1992, 54.

164. And not only God, the world is "other," as O'Donovan (1984, 90) explains: "At the same time, man as 'subject' encounters only and everywhere otherness—as recalcitrance, as external necessity to be overcome through manipulation and control. Modern man no longer participates in the meaning of otherness, of the world, by suffering it; rather, he bestows meaning on a meaningless otherness by subjecting it to the determination of his will. Technique is just that determination of the other as object by the human subject." Technique becomes an idol.

165. Halbertal and Margalit 1992, 59.

166. Halbertal and Margalit 1992, 115.

167. Theorists as different as Marx and Wittgenstein invoked idolatry, the former in connection to capitalism and the alienation it produced, the latter in reference to philosophy, as its function is to destroy idols of the mind (Halbertal and Margalit 1992,

243–4). Lints (2015, 133) terms these—including Hegel, Feuerbach, Nietzsche, Freud (see 134)—as the "secular prophets" who turned idolatry "on its head," insisting that "religious belief of every kind was intrinsically idolatrous."

168.   Halbertal and Margalit 1992, 120.

169.   "One of the wisest things Strauss ever said," Grant told Larry Schmidt (1978a, 64) "was that in Judaism and Islam revelation is received as law, while in Christianity it is received as the being—Jesus Christ. This difference above all affects the relation between philosophy and revelation in those religions."

170.   Not only in the past, and for Grant's teacher Simone Weil not only within Judaism and Christianity. "According to Weil," Athanasiadis (2001, 88) reports, "divine revelation was not limited to the sacred texts and traditions of Christianity, but was equally present in Hinduism, in the ancient mystery religions crushed by Rome, and in certain Gnostic traditions condemned by the church. At the same time, Weil rejected portions of the Bible, particularly the Old Testament, which seemed to emphasize the exclusiveness, conquest, and interventionism of God in history, as well as the scrutability of divine providence to the human mind."

171.   Athanasiadis 2001, 88. Like Grant, Weil ([1947] 2002, 162) decried the "lie" of "progress." For Grant, Athanasiadis (2001, 158) suggests, our confidence in progress positions as close "necessity" and "the good," rationalizing even "the loss of Canadian sovereignty, sacrificed to the larger progress of history toward universal freedom and equality. For Grant, this is blasphemy and idolatry." But does not condemning "progress" risk simply reversing its valence, thereby preserving its allure?

172.   Halbertal and Margalit 1992, 127.

173.   Halbertal and Margalit 1992, 246.

174.   Halbertal and Margalit 1992, 246. Ajzenstat (1992, 95n30) points out that Grant names "few such absolutes," but one of them the "judicial condemnation of the innocent," complicated by his "unhesitating acceptance of abortion when the mother's life is threatened." So Grant's "absolute" may be less a non-negotiable belief than, in Ajzenstat's term, a "counterweight" against the press of circumstances.

175.   Halbertal and Margalit 1992, 245.

176.   Halbertal and Margalit 1992, 245–6.

177.   The canonical curriculum question is posed always from within specific situations—historical, political, spiritual, subjective—and its answers start with what is known, a point with which Grant grapples: "If, as is obvious, the university decides its curriculum on some principle more than scholarship, what is it that it considers are really worth a man or woman knowing? And let me make the obvious explicit—if something is considered worth knowing what is known is not an open question in the university. It is not an open question I hope in the classrooms of this university that the peace of Westphalia was signed in 1648. Can then the principles on which it is decided that something is worth study be open questions?" (Davis and Roper 2009b, 104) Does not limiting the curriculum to facts risk rendering facts idols not icons?

178.   "The office of deliberation is not to supply an inducement to act by figuring out where the most advantage is to be procured," Dewey (1922, 124) explains. "It is to resolve entanglements in existing activity, restore continuity, recover harmony, utilize loose impulse and redirect habit" (124).

179.   Mondzain 2005, 15. Mondzain is here posing the equivalence as a question structuring her study.

180. Perhaps not coincidently, it was 1951, Davis (2000, xxxi) suggests, when Grant discovered Weil, reviewing her *Waiting on God* for the CBC, "beginning a lifelong encounter which was to influence his thought decisively."

181. Officially the Royal Commission on National Development in the Arts, Letters and Sciences (see Davis 2002b, 3).

182. Athanasiadis 2001, 86. For Fishbane (2008, 35) this aspiration is restricted to "theology...whose principal task is to guide human thought and sensibility toward God." For Grant, however, it is education that bears the burden of "cultivating this spiritual attunement" (37).

183. For Rowan Williams (2012, 4), "the icon...[is] an invitation to a continuing action of contemplating."

184. In iconographic terms, the "sensitive contemplation of a glittering absence, made by the hand of man" (Mondzain 2005, 90).

185. Davis 2002b 4.

186. Dart 2006, 12. For Mondzain (2005, 91), "the contemplative gaze produces the truth of the icon, the truth as an existential relation."

187. The concept is spiritual of course, and teaching is not the only profession with its sacred subtext. While the call comes from the world, that world is also inside us, as Sikka (1997, 202) makes clear in her association of Heidegger with the medieval German mystic Johannes Tauler: "Like Tauler's notion of call, then, this voice [of conscience, in Heidegger] provides an 'interior' and thus individual attestation of a higher possibility for the self, and in recalling it to this possibility, it calls the self back in from its everyday lostness and falling, its average absorption in the world. Furthermore, while the actual performance of the call does not, for either Tauler or Heidegger, lie within the self's own power of choice, the failure to hear the call does, at some level, involve a decision for which the self is responsible." Ethical engagement with one's self is a prerequisite to profession, a term also defined as taking the vows of a religious community.

188. Davis 2002b, 5.

189. Davis and Emberley 2000b, 380. On occasion Grant seemed to focus blame solely on his colleagues, telling Taylor ([1982] 2006, 134): "I'm contemptuous of modern academia," he told me. "All those pompous charlatans...most write very poorly."

190. Davis 2002b, 12. These two emphases have also been my own, expressed as studying "intellectual histories" and "present circumstances" (see Pinar 2010, 2011a, 2011b, 2013, 2014a, 2014b, 2015b).

191. Davis 2002b, 12. "Hope can be a false idol," Lipari (2014, 222) reminds.

192. Grant references the work of C. N. Cochrane, Northrop Frye, and Harold Innis (see Davis 2002b, 13). Given differences among the first English-speaking settlers—the English, the Irish, the Scots—it became obvious that reason alone could provide the only non-violent means to solve problems of irreconcilable difference. Leslie Armour and Elizabeth Trott (1981, 4) suggest that this earliest accommodation of difference among English-speaking Canadians led to a "concern with public education which the need for public reasoning was bound to feed." While not unique to Canada, that educational concern (the cultivation of not only academically specific but also public reasoning) coupled with the federal system of government designed in part to protect regional interests led to systems of thought with "distinctive national characteristics" (14). Armour and Trott add that given the great diversity of early Canada—a

diversity only multiplied many times since the early colonial period—there developed a sense that "society must be held together by aims of great generality and of fundamental importance" (21). It is these scales of aims, they suggest, that held Canadians together, scales sharply imprinted in the thought of George Grant.

193.   Davis 2002b, 14–5. In education, this is the long-standing tension between "theory" and "practice" (Pinar and Grumet [1981] 1988).

194.   In its spiritual sense the icon is ancient, at least to contemporary sensibilities, legitimated, Tradigo (2006, 6) reminds, in the year 843, with the Triumph of Orthodoxy, a struggle against, he explains, "the early heresies that...rejected any representation of his [Christ's] image." He continues: "[W]hat people worship in the icon are not the wood and colors, but what it represents as it travels a path from the visible to the invisible, the material to the spiritual" (6).

195.   For instance, Walsh, Mehsud, and Khan (2016, A10; emphasis added) reference the "Taliban attempt on the life of the schoolgirl activist Malala Yousafzai in 2012, [thereby] transforming her into a global *icon* of course and energizing other educational campaigners in Pakistan."

196.   Halbertal and Margalit 1992, 39.

197.   Halbertal and Margalit 1992, 39–40.

198.   Halbertal and Margalit 1992, 40.

199.   Halbertal and Margalit 1992, 40. Mondzain (2005, 95) is adamant that an icon "never *represents*" but reiterates" the "incarnation and resurrection." The agency implied in that conception is repeated in Mondzain's suggestion that the icon "institutes a gaze" (70) that can transfix those in its presence. "As a child," Ryan-Scheutz (2007, 135) reports, Pier Paolo Pasolini "loved to look at icons of the Virgin, observing them with such fervour and emotion that he was sometimes convinced that they smiled or moved. This affection for the Holy Mother influenced Pasolini in deep and lasting ways—from his own identification with the son who revolutionized and suffered, to his adoration of Susanna Pasolini, and the innumerable references to the mother-son bond found throughout his works." Such references are rendered iconographic in his 1964 *Il Vangelo secondo Matteo*, wherein, Steimatsky (2003, 256) notes, "Pasolini's pervasive frontal mode may be traced back to the Byzantine icon." I focused on that film as an evocative instance of reactivation (Pinar 2017c).

200.   Mondzain 2005, 81. She adds: "Christ is not in the icon; the icon is toward Christ, who never stops withdrawing" (88).

201.   Marion 2012, 169. Jay (1993, 31) reminds: "The Latin *speculatio*—along with *contemplatio*, the translation of *theoria*—contained within it the same root as speculum and specular, which designate mirroring. Rather than implying the distance between subject and object, the specular tradition tended to collapse them."

202.   Ware 2012, x.

203.   Halbertal and Margalit 1992, 40. In the Kabbalah, Halbertal and Margalit explain, the forms of divine revelation are termed "*sefirot*" (95), as noted above.

204.   Nes 2004, 12. Rowan Williams (2012, xiv) writes: "What we call holy in the world—a person, a place, a set of words or pictures—is so because it is a transitional place, a borderland, where the completely foreign is brought together with the familiar. Here is somewhere that looks as if it belongs within the world we are at home in, but in fact it leads directly into strangeness." Ouspensky (1982, 38) emphasizes that "holiness has no external characteristics."

205. Mondzain 2005, 96.

206. Steimatsky 2008, 138–9.

207. Or "image," as the term "icon" is derived from the Greek *eikon*; it is, for Tradigo (2006, 6), "a sign of the presence of God."

208. Ware 2012, xi.

209. Nes 2004, 14. "The church fathers," Mondzain (2005, 57) reports, "believed that truth only obtained its authority by means of its emotional power, its direct access to the heart. The speaker must touch his listeners in order to convince them and change their attitudes. Intelligence is not enough—it can even corrupt by the perverse manipulations of its arguments. Pathways must therefore be found that lead the intelligence directly to the enthusiastic passion for the truth." Recall Grant's affirmation of emotional intensity in planning for his teaching, discussed in the previous chapter.

210. Nes 2004, 14.

211. Steimatsky 2008, 140–1.

212. Rocha 2017, 93.

213. Nes 2004, 16. And not only in Christ, it would seem. In his eulogy for Jelte Kuipers (see Christian and Grant 1998a, 29), Grant seems to locate the beautiful and the good in a former student, and in a young man, as ancient Greeks often suggested sculpturally, and as Grant himself mentions in reference to Venus: "[T]he human body divinized" (Davis and Roper 2005b, 685).

214. Nes 2004, 20. The capacity to hold "inwardness and outwardness together" is one reason Grant admired Céline's art (Davis and Roper 2009b, 478).

215. Steimatsky 2003, 255. Pasolini was parsimonious: "Sacrality: frontality"(quoted in Steimatsky 2008, 143). Without using the term "frontality," Rowan Williams (2012, xv) nonetheless sets the stage: "There is the reality of the icon, which is a picture of some bit of this world, so depicted and so constructed as to open the world to the 'energy' of God at work in what is being shown. And, most importantly, there is the person who stands on the frontier between promise and fulfillment, between earth and heaven, between the two Testaments: Mary…how she stands for the making strange of what is familiar and the homeliness of what is strange."

216. Nes 2004, 23.

217. Davis and Roper 2009b, 537.

218. Schmidt 1978a, 19. Grant finds the "secular democrat difficult to understand" (Davis 2002b, 168), holding two (for Grant) opposing ideas: equality and secularism. "If, as they do, one holds that man's destiny is only in this world, how is it possible to believe in equality? In a worldly sense, men are so obviously unequal" (168). He adds: "It has, however, been the genius of Christianity, at its richest, to hold together in tension both sides of the truth at this point. It has remained clear that men are not equal in talents and yet has insisted on the more mysterious truth that all persons being called by God to salvation are equal before His majesty" (168).

219. Schmidt 1978a, 19. Double vision contracts into single vision on occasion, as in his defence of fundamentalism in the United States (see Davis and Roper 2009b, 574). In my view, he's just wrong about fundamentalism; it is a literalism and, as such, an idolatry, mistaking the Word—the semantic icon—for the spirit infusing it.

220. Umar 1992, 2–3. Internally too, as Grant acknowledges in a 1982 letter to William Christian: "[I]t depressed me that my ability to maintain outward calm is not

equalled by one's inward state" (Christian 1996d, 322), a divided self he acknowledges to another correspondent (as we see in 322n225).

221. Ajzenstat 1992, 96.

222. Ajzenstat 1992, 96–7.

223. Aoki (1993) 2005, 295.

224. Aoki (1996) 2005, 318.

225. Double vision becomes "divided state" in a letter Grant sent Peter Self in 1987: "I go on in my usual divided state," Grant wrote, affirming that "Christianity is 'theoretically' best expressed for myself" in "a kind of gnostic Platonic way, but in my life I remain a very sensual bourgeois. I have had to give up some of the pleasures because of heath and I regret every [forgone] drink of wine and every cigarette. Having it both ways was a great mark of my mother's failing; so perhaps I just took it in my youth" (Christian 1996d, 365). Writing Joan O'Donovan five years earlier, Grant wrote, characteristically humbly, "To be personal, I am a lazy, lecherous, self-centered person who knows hardly anything about giving oneself away. It would presumptuous of me to write of matters of which I know only indirectly…. Therefore, I write about those intermediate questions" (324). One is reminded of the space of those "intermediaries" Weil affirmed, the space of the iconographic.

226. In Cayley's (1995, 39) view, Weil "furthered both Grant's thinking and his work in building the Department of Religion at McMaster University between 1961 and 1980, by demonstrating an approach to Christianity that was intellectually honest, non-dogmatic, and open to other ways of understanding the divine. She believed that the same truth that was manifest in Christianity had been manifest in all the ancient civilizations."

227. Cayley 1995, 180.

228. "Language only ever speaks following the difference," Marion (2001, 204) explains, adding: "Here again, language does not express distance, since it expresses itself in distance, just as it receives itself from distance" (205).

229. O'Donovan (1984, 133–4) summarizes: "His resignation is provoked by a protracted and bitter battle waged with his colleagues and the university administration over fundamental policy issues affecting the fabric of university life. These issues concern the aspiration and orientation of his own department—the department of religion—and of the larger university, as reflected in decisions about curriculum content, procedures and criteria of evaluation, academic priorities, and staffing."

230. Referencing Plato, Christian (1992, 56) reminds that the "ultimate nature of existence is not susceptible to reasoned proof," that "the most" science can provide are "reasonable" accounts according to "available evidence," adding that "reason" is "limited" to that which resides within our experience. "Because the Good is beyond being," he continues, "it is apprehensible only through faith" (56). Comprehension (or reasoned revelation) sometimes follows, sometimes precedes, and can accompany apprehension. "To be a Platonist and Christian," Umar (1992, 3) summarizes, "is to believe in the necessity of reason and revelation."

231. Davis and Roper 2009b, 415. "For Grant," Randy Peg Peters (2006, 246–7) explains, "it is only when the Good is understood as 'beyond' and uniting both Being and reason that love rather than science or an ethically neutral openness to Being can be understood as the height of humanity. If Plato argues, as Grant suggests, that the Good is 'beyond Being' and that which one seeks through love, then to seek the

Good by objective reasoning would be to miss it. For Grant, the Good is not subject to human reason, instead we are subject to its rule." We turn to the matter of obedience to what attunement reveals in ch. 6.

232. Referencing Hölderlin, Marion (2001, 80) acknowledges the "unthinkable paradox the intimacy of man with the divine grows with the gap that distinguishes them, far from diminishing it." Rocha (2017, 54) suggests that "[w]e can locate God within the intimacy of love as an iconic gift."

233. Davis and Roper 2005b, 177.

234. Davis and Roper 2005b, 177.

235. Fishbane (2008, 155) affirms "the living divine image that appears to each person through the other." Sexual exploration can be a form of study and experiment, then, not only self-referential satiation, a point Athanasiadis (2001, 110) seems to overlook after he rightly laments the positing of "prosperity and success, which lead to leisure, have become the goal of education rather than the means to opportunities for deeper education. But," he adds, "leisure without any greater purpose can only bring meaningless or perverted forms of pleasure-seeking." I share his sense of the first risk—meaninglessness—but dispute the second: "pleasure-seeking" can provide "deeper education" by providing self-knowledge and knowledge of others.

236. Cayley 1995, 178–9.

237. Cayley 1995, 179.

238. Grant admires Socrates' turning away from science, preferring instead "human beings," he tells (Cayley 1995, 76).

239. Tips of the iceberg include that "sting operation by the environmental group Greenpeace" that found that "some researchers who dispute mainstream scientific conclusions on climate change are willing to conceal the sources of payment for their research, even if the money is purported to come from overseas corporations producing oil, gas and coal" (Schwartz 2015, A26). There is the 2015 report of the Reproducibility Project that "found that fewer than 40 studies in a sample of 100 psychology papers in leading journals held up when retested by an independent team" (Carey 2016, A3). There is the "blurring the line between researchers and lobbyists" in so-called think tanks (Lipton, Confessore, and Williams 2016, A1).

240. Davis and Roper 2009b, 270.

241. Cayley 1995, 165.

242. Cayley 1995, 165.

243. Cayley 1995, 165.

244. Cayley 1995, 166.

245. Cayley 1995, 166.

CHAPTER 6

Attunement

What is it exactly which lies beyond thinking?[1]

George Grant

"Technology," Grant knew, was "the one activity outside thought. Thought is permissible about politics, sexuality, art, God etc. but not about unlimited technological advance."[2] In this chapter I chronicle—and extend—Grant's effort to attune himself and us to what lies beyond "technology," to that which transcends material existence. "The spiritual realm," Weil writes, is "precisely the realm where we can obtain nothing by our own efforts, where we must wait for everything to come to us from outside."[3]

Attunement tries to traverse the gap between our world and what is outside it, from particularity to universality.[4] "Particularity need no longer be defined as against universality," Angus observes, "but as the *very condition* for whatever universality the human being may be able to apprehend."[5] For Grant, Rigelhof reminds, "the first thing to do is to allow ourselves to be 'nudged, claimed, inflamed by the good' by being 'open' to the real stuff of everyday living."[6] Stressing its "uniqueness," Dewey affirms that "[i]n quality, the good is never twice alike. It never copies itself. It is new every morning, fresh every evening. It is unique in its every presentation."[7] Attunement is the bridge—that is, not that which traverses the abstract and the concrete, the bridge that, in Aoki's famous phrase, is not a bridge.[8] It is not another tool in modernity's toolbox, as it not to be used instrumentally, even if one can make efforts, however clumsy, to attune. Like revelation, attunement cannot be possessed or summoned; one decentres and waits, open—listening—to what lies beyond.[9] Not predicated upon privilege—"it is easier for a camel to go through the eye of a needle than for someone

261

who is rich to enter the kingdom of God" (Matthew 19:24)—even the desperate attune themselves to realities beyond those they suffer, a point to which not only biblical verses testify.

Desperation takes many forms, of course, as does enduring it, imagining life beyond the degradation of the present. Discussing Dostoevsky[10]—before Simone Weil and Leo Strauss only Henry James had influenced him as much[11]—Grant suggested that "what he means by freedom or *svoboda* is best transited as openness to eternity,"[12] what on other occasions Grant appreciates as attunement.[13] "It is to me clear that human beings are open to the whole, and [to] the question of what constitutes the good life, which it seems to me is an unavoidable question for each of us."[14] Grant continued: "It becomes clear that there is some connection between what knowledge we can have of the whole and what is the good life for us."[15] That "connection," I suggest, can be construed as attunement. Modifying "connection" with "some" implies the luminous link to what lies beyond everyday life. In this experience of apprehension through a glass darkly,[16] freedom is enlisted in becoming open to that beyond.[17] "Freedom, as being one's own," Grant notes, "here meets the vision that one is not one's own."[18]

Not one's own—whose am I replaces who am I?—freedom is finding out not only what one wants (and why) but what the moment, the situation, requires.[19] Emberley is confident that "at the experiential level, we are always capable of the meditative enactment of those spiritual experiences given to us as human beings."[20] Grant not so much, as for him such sensitivity to the situation is insufficient. As Athanasiadis appreciates:

> There is no transcendent standard of judgment and justice the free obedience to which leads to ultimate fulfillment. The question is, can such free inner obedience to the good be consistent with the free changing of the world, involving as it does the use of manipulation and force on the human and natural environment?[21]

Not every situation is one of force and manipulation of course. Indeed, to be educational the situation should be free of the latter. Grant exhibited force in his teaching—the force of erudition threaded through his subjective presence while attuned to the eternal[22]—but it was not in the service of manipulation.[23]

Sensitivity to the situation while attuned to the Good does not necessarily result in moral relativism, only in behavioural variability.[24] One's wants and wishes may not coincide with what one intuits one must do. Propriety, profit, and pleasure—for instance—may fade as revelation relegates these from idols to be worshipped to possible (even unintended) consequences of action originating and directed elsewhere.[25] But can knowing what to do be that straightforward: attunement followed by obedience?[26] "[E]thics arises," Grant notes, "at the point where one is a person without an alternative."[27] Does it not also arise when one faces alternatives? Without alternatives knowing how to proceed would become self-evident. The complexity of ethics[28]—"right conduct"[29]—resides in not only summoning the courage[30] to proceed when there are no alternatives; it resides also in determining where to go when several paths—with uncertain destinations—present themselves.

When rational deliberation by itself seems insufficient, attunement may provide a nudge to move this way or that. "All deliberation," Dewey decrees, "is a search for a *way* to act, not for a final terminus. Its office is to facilitate stimulation."[31] For Grant, revelation constitutes "stimulation," and the "office" of deliberation is to disclose it in decodable terms. In this sequence, rational deliberation follows attunement[32] to the Good—the role of reason[33] can be the comprehension[34] of what is apprehended[35]—and it through this attunement one is situated ethically. "To recognize the link that attaches every man to the Good," O'Donovan explains, "is to incur the obligation of treating each human being as something 'sacred,' worthy of love."[36]

And worthy of justice,[37] O'Donovan might have added, as love is expressed according to person, place, and circumstance. Obeying what is indicated through attunement threads the need through these domains and modalities of being-in-the-world. In a poem Grant wonders: "The question then / is what is taken out of the word good / when you use it without the presence of obedience."[38] Aoki seems in sync with Grant even though he is not Christian and is speaking about educational leadership: "A leader must be a true follower—in leading, he must follow. But follow what? If he is a good leader, he must lead by following that which is true to that which is good in the situation within which he dwells."[39] Freedom becomes not license but recognizing—then acting in congruence with—one's duty, animated by attunement to the "that which is good," as Aoki phrases it.

The forms freedom takes, it seems, follow from the revelation attunement affords. In his introduction to his interview with Grant, Cayley summarizes that "our freedom consists only in our capacity to accept or refuse a timeless order which we did not make, which we cannot fully comprehend, and for which we cannot finally be responsible."[40] When freedom becomes an end itself—"systemic" and "pervasive" in O'Donovan's phrasing—it becomes "idolatrous," thereby a "challenge to Christian belief and action in the present."[41] Action, then, becomes obedience—freely chosen—to revelation.[42] Athanasiadis reviews this point:

> Along with consent and obedience, Grant stresses the importance of attentiveness. In particular, he also uses the word 'consent' to give spiritual content to a more immediate attentiveness towards otherness through which love receives the deepest kind of knowledge of the other.[43]

One consents to obey what attentiveness reveals.[44] "Obedience always means in part transcendence," Grant asserted.[45] "In this account of things," Cayley explains, "obedience is higher than freedom."[46] I would say that in this account of things, obedience constitutes an enactment of freedom.[47]

"Obedience" is another one of those words of eras gone by, a word that rankles still, often relegated to unreasonable demands by authorities uniformed and not.[48] Such obedience is political or perhaps familial but not necessarily spiritual. We moderns wouldn't know. Modernity's emphasis upon "autonomy" and "freedom," Grant knew, had erased ancient traditions of "virtue as obedience to a divine order."[49] Obedience to what attunement affords—"virtue"[50] is Grant's term—offers opportunities (yes, through autonomy,[51] exercising freedom) for self-legislation,[52] even self-reconstruction.[53] No self-evident matter—I will emphasize its elusiveness in mood and thought[54]—such attunement is surely central to spiritual life.

David Cayley associates attunement and obedience not in a sequence but in a hierarchy: "[O]bedience, or attunement in this account of things, is higher than freedom."[55] Such attunement constitutes an enactment of freedom—I can stay with their association as sequential—as one chooses[56] to obey "not my will but thine,"[57] reflecting, for Fishbane, "the double-faced nature of attunement: it involves both perception and performance."[58] These two seem implied in Lipari's suggestion that "ethics arises from listening rather than speaking.... It is an entering into, an attending, an obedience."[59] To what, an intuition, an idea, a mood, an inner voice? Inadvertently invoking "the gap" between the contingent and the eternal, as well as Jean-Luc Marion's insistence on divine presence as withdrawal, Mondzain—referencing the icon—reminds that "[t]he distance is rather inside the icon itself, and it allows us to hear the echo of a voice within it...it is the voice that provides that linkage."[60] To what or whose voice is one listening, and under which conditions—within the "acoustics of the soul"[61]—does it become audible and identifiable? What (revealed) knowledge is of most worth?[62]

These questions dare not disappear into any self-satisfied assurance that one has become "tuned in" to the "truth."[63] A subliminal skepticism seems to me another form of devotion.[64] Uncertainty keeps one in the current, but not coinciding with it.[65] Through attunement to "eternity"[66] one can recalibrate oneself within the world, lived experience experienced as an ongoing revelation,[67] informed by the omnipresence of alterity, for Grant, the Good or God.[68] Attunement is not tuning out the world—although retreat[69] and quietude[70] could be required on occasion—but attunement to the Good within as well as beyond this world.[71] For to know, as Grant appreciated, that the "purpose of life is transcendent...[but] this is no reason for a false and empty denial of this world. We are saved in the world—not out of it."[72]

Dewey too affirmed the omnipresence of the good: "The powers that generate and support the good as experienced and as ideal, work *within* as well as without."[73] Early on Grant emphasized that "what we are as we are is always subjectivity and to find that subjectivity we must be continually transcending ourselves."[74] For Dewey, as for the pragmatists, the proof is in the pudding; transcendence[75] implies consequences, a "learning that takes us back not into an isolated self but out into the open-air of objects and social ties, terminating in an increment of present significance."[76] From the ideal to the real and back again, a sense of dialectics and of the whole Dewey may have derived (as Grant did during the 1950s) from his study of Hegel.[77] And on at least one occasion Dewey does invoke the phrase "the whole," a concept dear to Grant.

> Infinite relationships of man with his fellows and with nature already exist. The ideal means...a sense of these encompassing continuities with their infinite reach. This meaning even now attaches to present activities because they are set in a whole to which they belong and which belongs to them. Even in the midst of conflict, struggle and defeat, a consciousness is possible of the enduring and comprehending whole.[78]

To a man almost crushed[79] by conflict—the Blitz—Dewey's assertion of conviction, openness, and belonging could only be confirming.

Referencing Aristophanes's account of Socrates in *Clouds*, Grant confers upon the soul the capacity of openness "to the whole and therefore more like the whole than anything else,"[80] implying an almost gnostic faith that God dwells within.[81] The "locus of human participation in the good," Planinc points out, "is the soul. A human being is thus torn between necessity and goodness."[82] How to dwell in between, to linger—as Aoki invites us—on the bridge? "The task," Emberley suggests, "is to think together the law of love and the rule of law without being drawn into either rigid doctrinairism on the one hand, or the charm of ineffability or transcendent mystery on the other."[83] Recall Weil's dictum: "Faith is the experience that intelligence is enlightened by love."[84] In Grant's terms: "Therefore the whole is interpreted in terms of the highest we know in it. Nature is interpreted in terms of the soul, as the virtues—justice, moderation, courage, and wisdom—are seen as natural."[85] Perhaps Dewey's sense of "nature" and Grant's are necessarily dissident.[86]

Besides the emphasis upon qualities and conduct over consequences, another difference between Grant and Dewey would seem to be that for Grant attunement emphasizes attentiveness[87] to what is not necessarily visible, or imaginable, or even thinkable. Yes, Dewey emphasizes ideals[88] but these are always associated with activity.[89] Like Dewey—and Edward Said[90] a generation later—Grant worried that a self-enclosed "intellectual integrity" could "easily lead to narrowness of vision."[91] Focused only on "accuracy and competence in our own subject," he continued, we lose the questions "which lie beyond our subject and to which we...should be open."[92] In such self-enclosed study, Grant cautioned, "we will be good scholars; but poor human beings."[93] For Grant, attunement to the transcendent animates authentic academic study.[94]

In a sermon delivered at the McMaster Divinity School in October 1961, Grant acknowledged that a "dialogue between the transcendent truth of the soul and the wisdom of the world" is an ancient one in the West, but now has become a "tension," and one that "anybody who wants to experience the full force of a university education must experience."[95] Grant suggested that "we should be making ourselves competent to understand the wisdom of the world—with all the disciplined study that that requires; we should at the same time be opening for ourselves those ultimate questions of the meaning of human existence which I have called the transcendent truth of the soul."[96] He admitted that achieving "both requires great discipline."[97]

For Fishbane (as for Grant) such doubled "forms of attention" are "cultivated by sacred study, both alone and in partnership," thereby preparing students to "engage in the world, through the reflective consideration of textual scenarios and topics; and they cultivate both an inner and an outer discourse, through the ways one speaks about things to oneself and with another person."[98] For Weil "attention" is a form of "humility."[99] Grant reminds that "those of us who are called to be students are called to hard work, to paying attention and to the virtues of moderation and courage required for that attention."[100] Are these virtues gifts or also autonomous acts of subjective reconstruction?

Whether gifts or goals, attunement to the Good does not come easily. It can occur through dialogue within oneself and among others, in the presence of texts—again, understood broadly to include experience[101]—that do not break the circuit (as it were) but direct it beyond.[102] Such attunement—for Weil attention, "full attention," affirms "truth, beauty and goodness."[103] And "teaching," she adds, "should have no aim but to prepare, by training the attention, for the possibility of such an act."[104] Recall that the concept of teaching I am invoking here incorporates content, teacher, and student subjectively present in complicated conversation.

Texts, then, can also become conveyances of transcendence. If icons are material objects, crafted in time and place, why can't historical time—advantaged maybe by being immaterial, as a moving image of eternity—also serve as a moving site of transcendence? Grant juxtaposes Heidegger's historicism (e.g., the certainty that humanity achieves authentic freedom only when we recognize we are thrown into a particular historical existence) with Plato's certainty that thinking, including philosophy, depends upon its capacity to "rise above the particularities of any historical context...to transcend the historical."[105] Why can't Heidegger's claim not contradict but confirm Plato's? How can one discern time as a moving image of eternity unless one has become attuned to infinite transcendence as well as—perhaps *through*—historical contingency?[106] Without such contingency there is free-floating abstraction.[107] Without transcendence there can be shifts in narrative—progress through class struggle rather than free markets—but no outside to, non-coincidence[108] with, history. "Grant contrasts historicist consciousness with ancient consciousness," Sibley reminds, "the former regards the world as an unending flow of unique and irreversible events that have to be dominated and controlled through creative will. The latter," Sibley continues, "considers time as the moving image of eternity and in which daily events of life hold meaning insofar they lead us toward eternity."[109] Especially now—with the disappearance of historical time into fusion with the time-empty *now* of the device screen—affirming the space in between represents, I should think, a "progressive" move. After all, becoming historical means becoming historical about being historical.[110]

The blurred boundary between material and virtual reality parallels that between pornography and sexual love.[111] While becoming sexually stimulated can of course accompany the former, it remains within fantasy and often with oneself, even when enacted with partners. While there is nothing necessarily wrong with that, my point is this: it is when attention shifts from the screen to specific—acknowledged—others that non-coincidence can occur, even while absorbed in—perhaps through—sensation. Grant tells us:

> Love is only love insofar as it has passed through the flesh by means of actions, movements, attitudes which correspond to it. If this has not happened, it is not love, but a phantasy of the imagination by which we coddle ourselves. As far as love is concerned, and particularly love of justice, "matter is our infallible judge."[112]

The quoted phrase in the above passage is Simone Weil's. Grant thinks of Weil; I am reminded of Pasolini, for whom sexual encounter could become a consecration.[113]

For Grant attunement—again Cayley understands—follows the exercise of "our capacity to accept or refuse a timeless order which we did not make, which we cannot fully comprehend, and for which we cannot finally be responsible."[114] For me, that decision "to accept or refuse" is not one made in an instant and for evermore, nor once made can it be enacted fully. It is an ongoing decision, requiring (for me at least) constant contemplation[115] of what might be beyond empirical (observable, audible) experience, what might be, even in some incomprehensible indirect way, influencing it. While one cannot be responsible for what lies "beyond time and space," ethically one can act *as if*[116] one were (at least partly) responsible for what happens here, as implied, it seems to me, in Grant's supposed "synthesis" of Athens and Jerusalem.[117] Non-coincidence with what is—living within the gap[118]—installs subjective freedom, implying that there is always, or almost always, a move to make, even if only inwardly. Whether that makes us responsible for what happens is an even more complicated story, as ethicists testify.[119]

Responsibility[120] for what happens starts inside us. After attunement—in religious traditions through prayer, worship, study—obedience occurs inwardly, however also focused outwardly. While not only sensory, attunement occurs through the body. Lipari reminds us that the word "listen" has been traced to the Sanskrit *srosati*—translated as "hears, obeys"—and that "obey" follows from the Latin *obedire*: to "give ear, literally 'listen to,' from *ob* 'to' + *audire* 'listen, hear.'"[121] Etymologically, then, "listening" emphasizes "attention and giving to others, while 'hearing' comes from a root that emphasizes perception and receiving from others."[122] Both can become forms of attunement, which, like listening, is "multimodal."[123] Like Dewey's ideals, attunement invites action.

"As an enactment of ethics," Lipari tells us, "listening, like quickening, brings a recognition of an unknown other to whom we are bound and about whom we feel care and concern."[124] "Obligation"—and "obedience"—are terms decidedly out of fashion in an era of idolatry, one of self-worship in which ethical questions have been replaced by one: what's in it for me? Obligation is an acknowledgement of duty; like obedience it is an exercise of subjective agency[125] to follow what we know needs to be done, what we are instructed to do, however open to reconsideration—even skepticism—such instruction is.[126]

Surely we are skeptical when we hear someone claim they are instructed by God to act, especially if that act is one of aggression or violence. Grant is hardly endorsing such scary self-absolution, such complete confidence that the Good could cause one to act so counter to the teachings of the wisdom traditions worldwide.[127] On the other hand, I cannot completely share Ian Angus's characterization of "obedience" as a "closing of the openness of thought."[128] In certain circumstances certainly it could be, but not necessarily.[129] That Angus seems to acknowledge when he suggests "that Grant desired—perhaps believed—that obedience could itself be an opening, even though he could not think so."[130] "Obedience may be the product of thought," Grant wrote, "but it is in that the enemy of thought."[131] The enemy of self-enclosed thought, perhaps, but must it be the enemy of insight inspired by revelation? If obedience occurs through attunement, after revelation (however modest, momentary,[132] and open to reconsideration), then "openness"—including to obligation even when we do not fully understand[133]—seems one prerequisite. Through such attunement one pauses to reconsider—to question, to study—what is being revealed, how one might act in accord with it.[134] Obedience is no simplistic submissive or even self-evident act but one more adequately appreciated as an elusive form of educational experience.

Learning from experience requires engaged embodied experience, I suggest[135]—"engagement as the body's attunement"[136] in Nagatomo's phrase—and ongoing (academic, when possible) study of it, threaded through self-reflection.[137] Educational experience can also involve quietude, sometimes physical, sometimes psychological (of course these can be reciprocally related), to a place[138] where and when contemplation[139] can take place, including analysis that can on occasion encourage subjective reconstruction.[140] Grant required it from time to time, as he recorded in a 1967 letter to Nita and John Graham.[141]

> [T]here was some deep need in me to be far away within myself and, therefore, an impossibility to speak about the most important matters. I know that a certain period of my life has come to an end and that I must reform myself to move on, but in doing that I have to retreat away from conversing with people, even those who are most meaningful and most interesting to me. I am sure that such periods must occur in different ways for you both. If you were aware of this retreat in me I hope you will excuse it. For me superficiality is always easier than intimacy.[142]

As is so often the case in Grant's letters, there is here a sense of revelation, not only to his readers but also to himself, insight he undergoes as he composes.[143] Note the reliance of inner movement upon inner reform: "I must reform myself to move on," he writes.

Perhaps Grant's sense of inner—subjective—necessity[144] had been building slowly, and perhaps it had been postponed given the pull of family and professional obligations. In either case it seems to have become compelling by July 1967. In a sense this seems a letter to himself as much as it is to the Grahams (and now also to us), confiding that within withdrawal—inner quiet—attunement can occur.[145] Grant reflects on the time of his life now ending, and he wonders what might come next. It is no passive matter; he mentions he must "reform" himself so that he can be in accord with what is required of him. He acknowledges that this process of attunement, obedience, and subjective reconstruction may be shared by others, including by the Grahams, if in different ways at different times. Attunement occurs in the midst of living, even on occasion interrupting it.

Within that an inner space[146] of felt freedom wherein attunement becomes possible, there can be—there was for Grant—an experience of "eternity" that, as Cayley explained, "reminded people of something lost, but at the same time gave them hope—both in his person and in his writings—that it might be recovered."[147] Cayley recounts Grant's conversion experience, his sudden sense that outside human experience, beyond time-space, there is order. That sense of an outside— he named it God—left him certain he was not his own, that we are not our own,[148] that we belong to that spiritual order to which we can become attuned. Within that ongoing attunement, requiring ongoing adjustment of apprehension,[149] one becomes recast, recalibrated, reconstructed. This is where the wisdom traditions— spirituality, "religion" in its various cultural and institutional forms[150]—meet everyday life within modernity, including those forms of reasoning and deliberation known as philosophical—specifically Deweyan—pragmatism.[151] Writing his friend Derek Bedson in 1962, Grant the Christian Platonist seems to accede if not to pragmatism, at least to the need for flexibility: "Clarity and absoluteness at the level of doctrine needs to be mixed with moderation and relativeness at the level of the day-to-day."[152] Within the gap between "absoluteness" and "relativeness" one is steadied[153] by attunement to the Good.[154]

In a sense, one can think of theology as a form of attunement. Grant distinguishes between two traditions in Christian theology, one "positive," the other, Grant tells Cayley, "negative": the former "moves to God through the world, and the negative tradition moves to God by negating the world."[155] Grant continues: "The negative tradition is in its essence Platonism, and the positive tradition is in its essence Aristotelianism and certainly Simone Weil is on the side of the negative tradition."[156] Despite drawing a sharp distinction between the two in this passage, on occasion Grant suggests there can be a link, however enigmatic and elusive, what might be recoded as irony. Ward wonders whether Grant's "thinking that is so close to immediate experience might not always enjoy the detachment required for irony, but it does possess an urgency that speaks to a wide range of readers within and outside the university."[157] In the West, is "duality the very being of meaning"?[158]

It is through studying Grant I have become open to this idea that beyond time and space, as we apprehend these in everyday life,[159] there could be order, but I do not know that beyond as "God," at least as depicted in the Bible.[160] Dewey's concept of "ideals"[161] has seemed to me an adequate affirmation of what lies beyond the observable. For Grant however, the concept of "ideals" seems secular, epiphenomenal, inspirational perhaps but incapable of defining and guiding humanity. Dewey would, I think, share Grant's concern over the bleaching of "ideals"—for Grant, the Good, including public good—in contemporary "empirical" social science.[162] By insisting that their research be value-free, Grant allowed, social scientists may have thought that they were clearing away ideology, religious beliefs, and metaphysical superstitions, and thereby affirming their intellectual independence, but, Grant continues,

> what in fact they have been doing is clearing out of the universities any coherent discussion of the political good, and so eliminating small barriers which stood in the way of the general public identification of that good with the totally technicized and administrative society.[163]

In such a society, intellectual independence becomes the first casualty, as one finds oneself embedded in an administrative apparatus and technological labyrinth which leaves little liberty.[164] Any sense of "public good"—of "ideals"—fades, as one becomes attuned to the next move to make, not to what is revealed through embodied experience.

In such circumstances, how can one understand attunement to the Good? The crux of the matter, as it seems to me now, resides in the relation between apprehension and comprehension, a matter addressed by much greater minds than mine but about which I venture a simple statement. Apprehension may provide passage to comprehension, however swiftly comprehension can become a tower of Babel. Attunement to what seems beyond time and space may not reveal in any empirical sense "order" and it may not, again in an empirical sense, be timeless ("eternity"[165]) but acting *as if* [166] it were so provides an "outside" to the confinement of the everyday. Such an outside—for Grant "the Good" or "God," for Dewey "ideals"—is a subjective necessity if one is not to coincide with what is, crushing one's capacity for what Dewey termed "growth," what Grant termed "transcendence."[167]

That constructed non-coincidence with the world we know provides opportunities to learn from it, to learn from experience; from educational experience, for example. That includes the cognitive concerns for calculation that characterize instrumental rationality, but also for the extra-cognitive, what filters through our minds and bodies and originates—or so it seems—outside us, and not just with other people and human events generally, but to what we cannot see or name, the presence of something outside our comprehension of it.[168] Outside and also inside, however inscrutable revelation or manifestation can be to those of us skeptical of the empirical truthfulness of the holy books, and even to those who are not. As noted but bears repeating, Grant often insisted on an almost absolute gap[169] between the eternal and the everyday.[170]

So, while staying alert to everyday events but apprehending "as if" there were an outside to empirical reality, one can become, in Fishbane's language, "a creature attuned to the unfathomable, and the capacity or willingness to stand in the silence of God's mystery."[171] Grant quotes Psalm 46:10—"Be still and know that I am God"—lamenting that "[w]e live in a world dominated by words and pictures, the media dominate our lives. We live in a world in which there is little silence."[172] For Grant, that attunement achieves sensibility as a form of "piety," what he termed "reverence," itself seemingly a subset of "justice," the very "matrix of all morality," given that one can "only act well" when one's actions are "attuned to the very nature of things."[173] This faith in the "nature of things" Grant associates with Socrates, for whom, he suggests, the gods were "personifications" of that eternal order.[174] Suddenly the gap seems not so "absolute" but maybe bridgeable, if in Aoki's sense.[175] The bridge provides passage from one reality to another; it is a metaphor for attunement.[176]

For those of us enmeshed in modernity, reality is material and historical but, for Grant, decidedly not only. While these moving images—time, materiality—can be idolatrous they can also remind us of the transcendent.[177] That seems so when Grant reminds professionals that they bear a "great responsibility" in a "situation" such as ours, namely "modern technological society."[178] In such a situation, Grant continues, the professions can become "creative intermediate institutions,"[179] in this quoted passage between the state and the individual person, but specifying the bridgeable, explicitly ethical, relation between acting in historical time and attuning oneself to "the nature of things."[180] Piety is primary, as one can never become completely confident one is attuned, however tentatively, reverently, one proceeds. It is as if there were two antennae attached, one for this earthly plane and the other for what lies beyond it. Such "double consciousness" is a familiar if usually secular[181] characterization of human apprehension,[182] specifically racial awareness in the well-known theory of W. E. B. Du Bois.[183] Rather than a consequence of racism, today one might embrace the capacity to see the natural as also supernatural. Such an embrace occurs in private, in quietude, in the company of others.

Quietude

> Society is the cave. The way out is solitude.[184]
> Simone Weil

That space in between—three decades ago heralded as a third space[185]—enables one to become attuned to the endless ways the nature of things is particularized. "Moral life is bound up with concrete determinations and the ongoing explication of norms and ideals," Fishbane notes, adding that "our moral lives must be more precise if we are ever to live with the implication of our terms."[186] Such precision of attunement—the comprehension of apprehension requires knowledge[187] and reason[188]—realigns subjectivity[189] not only with the eternal but also with the historical, including the political, the gendered, the racialized, world.

"Revelation as precept or command," Heaven explains, "requires obedient love as a response."[190] But "changing the world," Athanasiadis points out, "can become self-centered and destructive."[191] This risk becomes, he continues, "all too evident in an era when change has become idolized as an end in itself beyond the recognition of otherness as sacred."[192] Intervening in the social "for the sake of convenience or comfort"[193] is self-referential, not socially focused. "If meaning and purpose are to be perceived," Athanasiadis suggests,

> a transformation is required in the human soul, a transformation activated and directed by the good/God. Such a transformation can open the soul to experience the good/God in the world (faith), think according to the good/God in relation to the world (love), and act in obedience to and love of the good/God in the world (justice).[194]

While formulaic, this sequence—faith, love, justice—embeds quietude within activism[195] in a time when, as Benedetti observes, "action" (like "scandal") sometimes seems "impossible."[196]

The influence of the ancient Greeks may (once again) be in play here. If politics is the public space of debate where the means and ends of society are debated, one must, in Sibley's summary, "remain rooted in a private realm that satisfies their requirement for the necessities of life, including the psychological necessity of love and intimacy."[197] The private is not only a refuelling station for the public, it is where ethical engagement begins. Sibley—whom I am following here—invokes Plato in suggesting that the Good is refracted (however elusively) through daily life. Sibley writes:

> Grant makes this point when he says that only in loving our own—our families and friends, our neighbourhoods, cities, and countries—is it possible to experience that which is beyond calculable reason and will-to-power, and gain some insight into what it means to "not be one's own." In the knowledge of such experience, we are vouchsafed a glimpse beyond the cave…. In other words, only through the everyday realities and particularities of the material world is knowledge of a transcendent good possible.[198]

Being grounded in the private sphere—wherein one becomes attuned to the transcendent—enables citizen to engage others in the common or public realm. "For

Grant," Sibley states, "statecraft requires soulcraft."[199] Not wrong but perhaps too pithy, this statement is also incomplete.

For as politically engaged as Grant could be, "politics," he confessed, "are not an ultimate issue to me."[200] That adjective implies Grant's recognition that for some politics had become idolatrous, writing: "Indeed in their allegiance to the great ideologies—communism, English-speaking liberalism, national socialism—men have seemed to commit themselves to the belief that salvation is attained in the political."[201] Reimer reminds that Grant turns away from "the modern preoccupation with radical political doing and human construction to thought and contemplation of that which is granted to human beings to think."[202] Near the end of his life, writing Gaston Laurion (who had translated *Lament for a Nation* into French), Grant affirmed: "[W]e must put little trust in politics, except that in the case of Quebec there is hope of non-assimilation."[203] In a 1967 letter, Grant described *Lament* as no "practical political book, but to point to what always lies beyond and is more important than the political, the eternal order."[204] Writing Derek Bedson in 1962, Grant confided that he had been asked to stand for election, with the NDP, but he declined, as "my job is to be a theologian."[205] Recall that Grant is a theologian who juxtaposed Jesus and Socrates, neither of whom adored politics. Penelhum reminds that Jesus "refused to allow anyone to interpret his mission as one involving political action, the ultimate refusal of which is the famous Render unto Caesar the things that are Caesar's and unto God the things that are God's."[206] Regarding Grant's other icon, Magrini writes that "Socrates eschews practical involvement in politics," reasoning that a person committed to justice must lead a private, not a public, life, adding that Socrates practiced political engagement unconventionally.[207]

Attuned to the Good, political conduct is not necessarily self-consistent or even expressed in forms ordinarily associated with the political. The English critic Walter Pater is often associated, Heather Love notes, with a politically discredited aestheticism that elevated beauty above justice.[208] "Beauty is the cause of love,"[209] Grant asserted; beauty and justice could be reciprocally related.[210] Weil would have agreed, asserting that in "beauty" one can experience the "presence of God."[211] Christian explains:

> In order to be aware of this beauty, we have to hold in abeyance the forces of modern rationalism which issue forth in technology. Should we manage to do so, we might be able to gain an insight into the transcendent world by a means other than faith. We might be able to achieve a poetic insight into the nature of transcendence. Grant was later to offer Mozart as the most perfect example of his phenomenon.[212]

Christian emphasizes that for Grant art has a "mystical quality which lifts us out of the morass of historicism and positivism,"[213] something study can do as well. Both, however, can convey truth, a capacity obvious in the icon but absent today, as Grant complained to Cayley: "[A]rt has more and more become entertainment."[214]

For Christian, Grant's awareness that art can betray truth represents an anomaly, but if we acknowledge the historicism (like the progressivism) Grant could never entirely shed, the anomaly dissolves.[215]

In such an era—well underway in the second half of the nineteenth century, when Pater wrote and taught—seeking beauty was a spiritual undertaking, as, in Weil's words, "all art of the highest order is religious in essence."[216] In such an era, it can also be decoded as a political one. Pater's presumed lack of political commitment was, Love suggests, "a politics of refusal to the experience of social exclusion."[217] She explains:

> The key practices of such a politics—secrecy, ascesis, the vaporization of the self, and temporal delay—depart significantly from the modernist protocols of political intervention. Nonetheless, I argue that we should understand his backwardness as an alternative form of politics—one that is consonant with the experience of marginalized subjects.[218]

While few could characterize Grant in such terms—he seems not so secretive or self-disciplined (in any strictly ascetic sense), although he did affirm "temporal delay" (through "recollection") and self "vaporization"[219] (through "decreation"[220])—he did find himself marginalized, first by professional philosophers after his 1951 Massey Commission essay, then, two decades later, by the McMaster colleagues[221] who demanded that religion be regarded not as a way of life but as another topic of research.[222]

However unwelcome—and often dangerous—suffering social exclusion is, if it is not crushing it can engender double consciousness. For some that would be the consolation prize, but double consciousness does allow one to keep one's eyes on the prize: the contemplation of beauty and the presence it can convey.[223] The quietude that accompanies such contemplation—keenly conscious of injustice[224] while attuned to what we are fitted for—can constitute a subjective act of political intransigence, as Du Bois's analysis implies and Fanon's makes explicit.[225] Pater's rebellion is, shall we say, more gay (Love calls it queer), as he sees it as (in Love's terms) "sedate, retiring, shy," (in Pater's) "the revolutionism of one who has slept a hundred years."[226] Love explains:

> Pater's turn toward the past aims to transform the present and the future; he explored such moments in an effort to ignite a cultural revolution in the present. He drew on the past in part to break with it; his thoroughgoing critique of religious, moral and social tradition is legible as modernist.[227]

Grant's modernism—his progressivism—is in the service of anti-modernism, a reactivation of the pre-modern: Socrates and Jesus.[228]

For Pater, Love argues, quietude also implied a refusal to play politics by modernity's terms of *intervention*. There is a gendered dimension to interventionism—the machismo of it[229]—but perhaps Pater, like Grant and Dewey, is concerned about consequences. Even "to engage actively in trying to bring about the best," Reimer writes (referencing Grant), "would simply harden the directions in which society is already going."[230] For Grant, Reimer continues, the "impossibility of politics and radical activity for social change leaves...philosophy, art, and imagination [as] the only true enemies of modern tyranny."[231] The three stand apart from those eddies of so-called creative destruction demanded by contemporary investors. Art had become, Grant thought, a "kind of religion in our time, because it appears as a means of transcending society at a time when other means of such transcendence are no longer available."[232] Other efforts at transcendence—Grant invokes meditation, contemplation, and recollection[233]—can also be protests[234] against the violence of intervention[235] characteristic of modernity, even if they do not necessarily resolve the ethical tensions encountered there.

That painful point became evident to Grant in the thought of John Oman (the subject of Grant's DPhil thesis research), conflicted as it was between "quietism" (which would have produced pacifism in 1914) and the "liberalism" (implying complicity with, even participation in, the Great War) that triumphed.[236] Grant's use of the term "quietism," Davis and Emberley explain, does not point to a "passive or apolitical withdrawal from the world, but rather a detachment from the purposes of the state when they were in conflict with Christian principles."[237] At one point Grant thanks God "for our activist tradition"—contrasting the West with "quietist societies"—but he adds that activism has become "an excuse for idolatry."[238] For particular people at certain moments in specific places, attunement to the eternal may mean quietude.[239]

So might physical and emotional exhaustion. Writing at the end of spring term 1952, Grant admitted to his mother: "I live only for one event, the end of lectures, when I don't have to get up and open my mouth and when people aren't pulling at one for decisions a thousand times a day," adding that "[i]t has been a wonderfully rewarding year, however, as last year I hated teaching and this year I loved it again and learnt a lot myself—particularly the infinite resources of Plato's thought."[240] Enlivened (and exhausted) by teaching, Grant knew that study required solitude, writing his mother in August 1948 that "tomorrow we go to the country for two weeks. Its greatest joy is getting enough seclusion to write, as already the students are coming back and one can't get that environment of concentration which one must selfishly push for."[241] Solitary study, Alan A. Block reminds, can become sacred.[242]

Quietude can encourage contemplation, perhaps prayerfully undertaken, but it—and the attunement that it supports—cannot compel coherence. Within Christianity, Grant observed, and from its "beginning," "there has been a consistent tension between pacifism and the just war theory."[243] For Grant, the cross[244] represents a "very powerful argument for pacifism," acknowledging that

> my life has always been caught between these two in a way that I have never been able to work out. It is just a tension, as you would say, between these two. I was twenty-one when the last world war broke out. Both my wife and I were pacifists. For a while after the war I thought I had been entirely wrong. But I am not sure.[245]

"The order of things is riven in two," Cayley notes.[246] One point of quietude is social withdrawal for the sake of subjective reconstruction, registering in—maybe working through—mind and mood the tension between what this world demands and what might be beyond invites, then mobilizing that synthesis (should things congeal) for social reconstruction. All my terms, but they anticipate Reimer's claim that "Grant's conclusion is a hopeful one: that nature itself will revolt, that the noble, the great, and the good will ultimately triumph."[247] Surely this is over-statement, but I concede that it does not seem "triumph" will be brought about by political activity as it is perceived and practiced in modernity.

While Pater's and Grant's politics, place, and time were quite different, there seems, at least in these quoted passages by Heather Love and by Arthur Davis and Peter Emberley, a certain similarity: when faced by an intractable cal-culus of events one may decline to be coopted. And in so doing one registers disagreement while declining the terms of defeat. In that subjective space of quietude, attention to and detachment from modernity's enactment of the politi-cal invites non-coincidence with the historical moment, a double consciousness within which attunement to what is outside it could occur.[248] For both Pater and Grant art—for Grant specifically its beauty[249]—testified to the world that exists outside time, while manifesting materially in this one.[250] "In what sense is beauty sacred?"[251] Mondzain asks? She replies:

> In effect, if the icon is a memorial to the incarnation, that is, to God's assump-tion of human misery, his splendour can only be spiritual, whereas in the case of the ornamentation of objects and liturgical places, beauty is not only the motif of decoration itself, it also becomes an anagogical factor in the contem-plation of divine splendour.[252]

Mondzain concludes: "In this sense, the beauty of the décor has a protreptic and pedagogical intention."[253]

That juxtaposition of two worlds Grant might have also experienced during the Blitz, a trauma imprinting not only his critique of technology. That experience might have left, in Eric Santner's terms, an inner "archive," ever-present in the man as "mood," in which remain "traces" of trauma, an "opening or attunement to 'otherness' below the level of intentional states and propositional attitudes."[254] Santner references Heidegger's discussion of mood or *Stimmung*, its meaning for a human being to be "in" or "open to" the world.[255] "For Heidegger," Santner emphasizes, "mood registers our sense of 'always already' finding ourselves stuck in a specific historical constellation, which means first and foremost being stuck with, being riveted to, ourselves."[256] Such "riveting" can become embodied, as when Andrew Feenberg suggests that

> Marcuse's "erotic" resembles Heidegger's concepts of "attunement" or "state-of-mind." These concepts refer to the fact that sensory experience is always colored by a general quality of perception such as fear or anxiety, joy or hope. These questions reveal the worlds in its various aspects and are not merely subjective.[257]

"Merely" might bifurcate what are inevitably intertwined. Did Grant's trauma in East London—and his father's in the First World War—leave him lamenting what was lost?

Kaja Silverman draws a distinction between "mood," "internal to the psyche," and *Stimmung*, a "relationship" between the psyche and something outside: "[T]he affective attunement of the former to the latter."[258] Through such attunement, Silverman continues, we are linked to "other creatures and things, thereby actualizing their redemptive potential."[259] For Fishbane, "the living divine image...appears to each person through the other."[260] Pérez-Gómez sees *Stimmung*—"tone" or "mood"[261]—as pertinent to "realizing architecture's contemporary potential for attunement."[262] Architecturally, *Stimmung* is associated with "ambiance" and "atmosphere."[263] While abstractions—Pérez-Gómez emphasizes that "atmospheres are spatial phenomena, but always intertwined with temporality; they are never 'outside time'"—atmospheres are also concrete, focusing attention on "locality" and "physical presence."[264] For Grant, such "abstractions" and "atmospheres" point to both "locality" and universality, "physical presence" but also spiritual, inside and outside time.

Perhaps—despite differences in its secular and spiritual senses—*Stimmung* can be an iconographic conception, enabling attunement to the transcendent? Frederick William seemed to think so, as Pérez-Gómez (not only a theorist but also a historian of architecture) might appreciate. Toews tells us that Frederick William chose for the architectural representation of the "present moment" (the 1840s) in the "sacred history" of the "relationship" between the divinity and humanity "a late-antique, early Christian basilica in the form he imagined as authentic to the era of the first Christian emperor, Constantine, and that conformed to his idea of the original apostolic church."[265] William was sure, Toews continues, that the early Christian basilica was the "authentic spatial form for the apostolic church," as it reminded those who saw it that "transcendent paternal authority was the dominant factor in producing a redeemed, ethical community out of the ethnic substance of the *Volk*."[266] That "ethical" and "spiritual" community came from the "spontaneous religious energies"[267] the church encouraged, a church unified by the transformed subjectivities of its members rather than uniformity of doctrine or external organization. It was this inner transformation, the identification of the individual with the revealed truth through submission to the will of the heavenly father, that provided the transfiguring power that turned ethnic Germans into ethical Germans.[268]

Is that not the task of curriculum conceived as iconographic, including—post-identity politics—the conversion of the ethnic into the ethical? More precisely, does not, as Grant affirmed, love of one's own provide passage to love of others? "Even if the ordered, intersubjective cosmos is gone," Pérez-Gómez reminds, "metaphoricity is at work everywhere in human experience, as is the central metaphor: *the inner is the outer.*"[269] Perhaps not fused as he implies, but in relationship, each providing passage not only to the other but also to what lies beyond. Is the icon one answer to Grant's question: "[H]ow is good to be brought down into our existences, insofar as these existences attempt to be more than private?"[270] Does not the structurally same relationship—in the gap, the space in front of the icon into which we are invited—structure mood and mind?

In 1952 Grant characterized "reason"[271] as enabling humanity to conceive of "the Good," itself a Platonic conception that for Grant becomes embedded in "the Christian belief of the image of God in all men."[272] In his review of a book by Bertrand Russell, Grant emphasized the consequence of denying reason's role[273] in attuning us to the Good; rendering reason technical rather than attuning represents "the denial of the only possible theoretical grounds for democracy,"[274] namely that each of us is created in God's image. In this conception reason's role—like that of mood—lies in its alignment with the order to which it can become attuned.[275]

Educators can be committed to the cultivation of reason, if after progressivism conceived as "intelligence."[276] Not a quantified "quotient" but "passionate," as Dewey acknowledges, merged with "emotion," and "inherently involved in action."[277] While "action" for Dewey was worldly, for me it can include attunement to what in a behavioural sense could be called "action," including inner action; for instance, Pater's quietude.[278] What animates "action" can be injustice in the world or personal obligation, but in either category it can take the form of obedience to what is revealed through attunement to the Good. In secular terms such action expresses the "synthesis" subjective reconstruction through attunement enables. Such synthesis is embodied thought and emotion merged and enacted, for educators, as devoted—attuned—participation in the complicated conversation that is the curriculum. At one point Dewey invokes the concept of "devotion," something, he suggests, that can be "so intense as to be religious."[279] At one point Weil suggests that we "substitute *devotion* for *obedience.*"[280]

For one student of Dewey—Victor Kestenbaum—attunement represents a form of "vigilance," attentive to "difference, otherness, and plurality," so that we may "do justice to the phenomenon."[281] Such "justice," Kestenbaum continues, enables us to recognize "possible or essential otherness."[282] Such attunement occurs within subjectivity—within that structural non-coincidence between me, myself, and I—as Kestenbaum appreciates: "Without this split between me and myself—the dialogue of myself with myself—I would never experience the tension or insufficiency which leads me to new possibilities of meaning, to 'values yet unknown,' to vigilance."[283] "Resolve" requires "vigilance," a capacity for conviction that accrues through study,[284] self-reflection,[285] passion expressed as public service, a form of "synthesis," however momentary and situational its expression is. It is "vigilance," Kestenbaum suggests, that "keeps watch over the mind, reminds us what to keep in mind."[286] Grant keeps in mind that "the end of life is [not] thinking...[it is] doing what is good."[287] Figuring out (or waiting[288] for the revelation of) what "doing good" is can take thinking, as well as its momentary cessation.

Writing in 1945, Grant thought that "freedom" and "international security" demanded "eternal vigilance."[289] So might be "internal" or subjective security. Such "vigilant attentiveness"[290] can be enabled by candour, that "truth-telling" known as *parrhesia*, without which, Nancy Luxon points out, "ethical self-governance" cannot occur.[291] Truth-telling is no exercise of unrestrained speech,[292] as attunement requires "coherent subjects" capable of forming relationships characterized by "constraint,"[293] resisting, Luxon notes, that objectification of the individual[294] into a "body of knowledge," so common in identity politics when race or gender or class (only) predominates. For Luxon, *parrhesia* constitutes a "set of practices" encouraging "individuals to become grounded and to thoroughly inhabit themselves."[295]

Psychoanalytically—at least for Winnicott, Alford suggests—"attunement" originates in "symbiosis, a mutual attunement between mother and child,"[296] an insight that seems in sync with object-relations theory.[297] "Winnicott was preoccupied with gaps and spaces," Alford explains, those "gaps and spaces in the experience of the self that arise from a lack of attunement with mother and others."[298] However non-coincidence—and attunement—begins, it can enable as well as disable the formation of human relationship, including, perhaps pre-eminently, with oneself. Without that inner space in which one can reflect, learn, and choose, no "knowledge"—including of another person—seems possible. That complexity of subjective formation and human relationality acknowledged, "Winnicott is talking about attunement," Alford emphasizes, "the sense one has of being in emotional contact with a separate human being. It is through attunement that one is able to recognize another's moods and feelings and response appropriately, which does not mean identically."[299] Moods, Pérez-Gómez reminds, are not exclusively "subjective but, rather, are primary in perceptual experience, intertwined with *place*, setting the tone for cognition, action, and thought."[300]

In the "language of human relatedness," Alford suggests that "play" is "the paradigm of attunement," something altogether absent, he thinks, in Levinas.[301] "Or if there is," Alford adds, "it is the attunement of the hostage, infinitely sensitive to the other, but always in the spirit of perfect service."[302] In Lipari's "ethics of attunement," public service seems paramount, as it emphasizes "interconnection and generosity, impermanence and humility, iteration and patience, and invention and courage."[303] Mood and mind, subjective and social, worldly and otherworldly; attunement is multimodal but merged. Referencing Weil, Grant affirms that the "mistake is personal, truth is universal."[304] Is the former a matter of misreading the "signal"?

Listening

> [T]here are important aspects of human existence that are, simply, ineffable.[305]
>
> Lisbeth Lipari

Like the more expansive concept of attunement, listening too is multimodal, as one listens not only to "words," Lipari reminds, "but also to the music of the voice" while observing "the posture and gesture of the body with my eyes, the vibrational rhythm of others' pulsations, movements, and intonations in my body."[306] After asserting that "appreciation for the fundamental role of music as a carrier of intellectual and emotional knowledge"[307] underlies European spiritual history,[308] Pérez-Gómez invokes Aristotle's sense of "friendship as a musical performance emerging from the tuning of two souls."[309] Attunement aligns us with each other even while accenting the alterity to which each of us can be attentive.

In a sense one listens while reading—in Grant one can sense his subjective presence (what Planinc terms his "*daimon*"[310]) in his writing—but maybe only those who were in his physical presence can be confident they heard his teaching. Grant "heard" his listeners, as the conversational structure of his prose testifies that he was simultaneously student and teacher, supplicant and prophet. Listening, Lipari emphasizes, is "inseparable" from speaking, and vice versa: "[T]o cleave them apart would be like touching without being touched in kind."[311] Sound, touch, sight— the sensory becomes a space of the iconographic.

Listening, Lipari suggests, can constitute "a kind of dwelling place from where we offer our hospitality to others and the world."[312] Such hospitality requires subjective reconstruction, and listening can be the catalyst: "By interrupting our habitual conceptual systems, listening being [*Homo audiens*] enables us to step outside of the quotidian order of things, of knowledge, conviction, and fundamentalism of all kinds. In this way, listening being involves a dangerous encounter with alterity, outside of understanding, beyond temporality."[313] We have slipped, it seems, back into the gap, or is it the space in front of the icon, as opening one's ear to the embodied other means openness to the immaterial and disembodied, what Lipari describes as "a space of being in which we may hear things not otherwise audible: the absent, the broken, and the radically strange."[314] Rather than what is summoned, she is speaking of what might be retrieved, even reactivated.

"Communication," Lipari concludes, "is not merely an instrument for accomplishing goals, it is the way we do human being."[315] Is attunement not only our way of being-in-the-world but also beyond it? The iconographic potential of language is implied in Lipari's discussion of the work within dialogue, not an "object" but rather, she asserts, "an energy, a living vital force, élan vital."[316] As such, she continues, "communicative acts are always already vibrating with traces or echoes of the resonance of other relations,"[317] including temporal ones: "[T]he dialogicality of communication means that our words with others stretch far into the past and in the future, and into worlds both familiar and strange."[318] In reactivation of the past—"a momentary obedience to the past"[319] Grant might put it—we resurrect what lies buried alive in the present, potentially freeing us to live more abundantly[320] in a present more fully multi-modally if elusively "now."[321] An ethics of attunement is simultaneously subjective and social, past and future stretched across, focused on, enacted in, being present.

Like the moods with which they are often enmeshed, thoughts too pass through us, subjectivity as a prism[322] for those frequencies being broadcast within and beyond what we see in front of us. Referencing James Carey, Lipari registers that "even the 'innermost' thoughts in our head are permeated with words from 'outside,' and these 'exterior' voices echo and resonate in our most 'interior' thoughts."[323] Indeed, even the revelation of our most "innermost" thoughts can occur through language that originates from "outside," Lipari continues, "forever obscuring the boundaries between inside and out."[324] Listening is where thought comes to "completion," Lipari suggests, "giving," in effect, "birth to thought."[325] Private thought expressed becomes public property, not only socially (and legally, where copyright laws are respected) but temporally, as the complicated conversation in which we are engaged as students and teachers is not only with those who have authored what we studied but those with whom we have studied, now internalized, a cacophony rendering attunement not only multimodal but polyphonic.

"But just as past, present, and future voices blend and interact to make us who we are," Lipari appreciates, "so do the inner and outer conversational selves and other selves that we inhabit and which inhabit us."[326] With boundaries blurred (between inner and outer speech, between inner self and others), and like others before her,[327] Lipari emphasizes the significance of "the *between*" in "creating a new, generative, and shared collaborative process in which self and other are less differentiated."[328] In an era of narcissism—aggravated by social media—any further erosion of differentiation would be concerning, as distinctions between fake and real news, for instance, fades. Within a culture of simulation reality is virtual, unreal.

There is, Lipari acknowledges, "a politics to listening,"[329] a fact emphasizing ethics cannot obscure. While listening may well constitute, in Lipari's phrasing, an "ethics of attunement,"[330] it provides the information we can then analyze, drawing upon knowledge and discernment to make judgments, including political ones. The "providential economy," Mondzain emphasizes, "does not blindly put back in our hands some incomprehensible power that will only demand from us blind passivity or renunciation; rather, it leads us to administer and manage for ourselves, to the best of our ability, what it is given to us to endure in the full exercise of our judgement."[331] She adds that the motion of revelation occurs in its "incessant coming and going between the visible and the hidden, enigma and mystery."[332] Attunement reveals but cannot resolve "enigma and mystery," but it might enable the "coming and going."

The *Oxford English Dictionary*, Lipari notes, defines "attunement" as a "bringing into harmony," linking the concept etymologically to the noun "attune" (tuneful accord or harmony[333]) as well as with archaic usages ("atone," as in "agreement," "reconciliation," from "at one").[334] Contemporary usage, she continues, includes broadcasting (as in "stay tuned"), mental attention ("don't tune me out"), social control ("he calls the tune"), and repair (as in "give the car a tune-up").[335] The juxtaposition of these meanings—the conventional ones next to the spiritual, the contemporary with the archaic, and the political with the mechanical—underscore that attunement does not shed its critical cognitive elements. Whether attuned to the transcendent or the tawdry, critical questioning structures the deciphering of what is revealed. Yes, attunement communicates "interconnectedness, congruence, and attention,"[336] but these do not come unsullied. Attunement may transcend thought and mood but it is hardly free of them.

Lipari recalls two concepts from the ancient Greek that, to my mind, illustrate the interplay between the worldliness and otherworldliness of attunement: "[K]airos, most superficially understood as 'right timing' or the 'opportune moment,' and *akroasis*, translated as listening and invoking the idea of secret, esoteric teachings."[337] To Lipari, these concepts inform a sense of "attunement as the relation between resonance and temporality,"[338] terms that traverse this world and transcend it. The former is evident when Lipari notes that "calling *kairos* an 'opportune moment' seems at first glance to cultivate an ethos of opportunism that certainly runs counter to an ethics of attunement."[339] The latter is hinted when she points out that *kairos* came to mean "propriety,"[340] a concept that can connote conformity, but human decency too. Inflated, the term can imply "situational ethics," Lipari observes, itself vulnerable to "opportunism" and "instrumentalism."[341] But propriety also can invoke the ethical obligation to assess the context in which we are embedded, a term that then testifies to teaching.[342]

That context is multidimensional is made manifest within attunement. When conceived only materially, or, as Pérez-Gómez points out, "environments valorized in terms of the economic payoff their novel monuments may yield, tend to conceal autochthonous values, natural beauty, and biological purpose."[343] Attunement to these can be amplified, he suggests, by the arts, including architecture, whose "fundamental task" is "nothing less than a possible unveiling of truths."[344] Among those truths, he continues, is "a disclosure of human purpose in the face of mortality, through specific contexts and actions," revelation that occurs when one is at home, multidimensional as that concept can be, for Pérez-Gómez "a place of fruition and completeness analogous to erotic experience, a place for dwelling and not merely a shelter for our physical bodies."[345] Like Grant, Pérez-Gómez focuses on beauty, suggesting that it attunes us to our surrounds and in so doing provides a "gift of meaning" that is "life-affirming," concluding that "[o]ffering such attunement through the human actions to which it *gives place* is perhaps architecture's most durable contribution to humanity through the ages."[346] It is through the specificity of place one transcends its parochialism.

Transcendence

> Why does Grant so often call "transcendence" a dangerous word?[347]
> William Christian and Sheila Grant

William Christian and Sheila Grant answer that by telling us Grant felt the term had become conflated with immanence.[348] In the past I have tried to keep the terms separate, perhaps simplistically so, reserving transcendence for the otherworldly, a move Grant makes too, if affirmatively. It was because transcendence no longer pointed to an eternal unchanging order that Grant worried it no longer provided a measure of humanity but rather, in modernity, signalled our freedom, our capacity to exceed what is.[349] That conception of transcendence as "freedom" through "autonomy," Christian and Grant continue, "is itself just part of the loss."[350] To "think the loss a loss," they conclude, requires "purging" the " language" of such convoluted terms.[351] Enclosed in "acts of self-transcendence," Grant warned, one becomes "less and less able to rely on any objective authority at all—be it eternal values, political creeds, or the dogmas of science given by psychics or psychology."[352] Without such "authority," one finds "freedom," Grant suggests (freedom from, not to, as his ambivalent embrace of "obedience" implies), found in alienation from the world and themselves, what Sartre termed "nothingness."[353] In such a time, perhaps what is required is, in Fishbane's phrase, the "transcendence of transcendence,"[354] in Grant's terms, attunement to the Good.[355]

Could such transcendence start by reactivating the past to reconstruct the present? Grant's referencing of Plato implies no disinclination to confront his historical moment, Christian and Grant emphasize, noting that Grant insisted that we must meet technology directly, know it for what it is.[356] For Grant, transcendence requires recollecting, a form of non-coincidence with what is. Such juxtaposition of past and present might enable one to feel what is lost in fusion with the device, namely "now," not only sensory but also temporal, pulled, as Heather Love has noted, between the past and the future. It might also traverse time as one attunes oneself to what was and can no longer be. So it seems to me that immanence and transcendence may not conflict but enable each other.

Losing time is also a political and ethical loss, the two for Grant interrelated. For me, the primacy of politics in the present era renders ethics[357] mute, replaying politics as reality TV. Despite this civilizational calamity, Grant demands we remember not only what is lost but also what can be gained.[358] For Aoki, what could be gained is life itself, but that "good" signals the "significance of that which is beyond the technological in the technological."[359] This is no reframing of technology as iconographic, as "beyond" makes explicit that the good is non-coincident with (in the Aoki instance) the dialysis machine, spatially and temporally, as "beyond" also suggests a "later time," the time detached from the machine.

Such a separation from the technological—inhabiting that gap, attuned to the transcendent—does not necessarily imply agreement that, in Lear's language, "there is a transcendent source of goodness," in part because (as Grant and Weil admit) "the goodness of the world transcends our finite powers to grasp it."[360] Transcendence enables acknowledging this incapacity to think "the whole" that follows from acknowledging the "limited nature of our finite conceptual resources."[361] Like mood, mind becomes one (albeit extremely important) medium of attunement, itself multimodal as Lipani would remind us. Recollecting the past, reconstructing the present: these are affirmations—enactments—of temporal transcendence but they are not necessarily stairways to heaven.[362]

In our time the danger is that recollecting or reactivating—even attunement itself—becomes reduced to strategies of social engineering, not subjective reconstruction.[363] No transcendence, thanks, just do it. In Grant's terms, we moderns "make the future by mastery, and the closing down of all thinking which transcends calculation," as technological advance becomes the "sole context within which all that is other to it must attempt to be present."[364] The attempt to dominate necessity, Grant notes, directs attention toward the immediate, ignoring an "eternal" and "unchangeable order," an order that "transcends history and in which history takes its place."[365] Because the prospect of human excellence depends upon attunement to eternity, fixated on mastery humanity cannot transcend itself. "Negation" can become a substitute stairway to heaven, Grant implies, as through a "continual negation of the self" can a "continual self-transcendence" occur, including a "negation of what is most dear to one's own society."[366] In my terms, transcendence is what subjective and social reconstruction through the reactivation of the past can precipitate.

"We are always a project to ourselves," Grant acknowledged, noting that we can, on occasion, choose to "negate what we are in the name of what we ought to be."[367] His point here seems to be that self-understanding cannot occur objectively, in part (I would add) because it is temporal and situational and ongoing. Grant is emphasizing humanity's capacity to "transcend any worldly situation," a capacity for non-coincidence, in his phrase "freedom of the spirit."[368]

Moreover, he reminds that one cannot experience "completeness" through "any finite object of desire,"[369] a reiteration of the injunction against idolatry. Yet the ascetic avoidance of such desire and its "objects" can leave us moderns feeling incomplete and even more needy: even a slight asceticism became possible for me only after a lifetime of satiation. To put the matter another way, everyday life—in its voluptuousness,[370] not its suppression—provides passage to transcendence, a sequencing with which, Christian and Grant assert, Grant agreed: "Grant makes it clear that the most important knowledge is given us in the ordinary occurrences of daily life, and through the concrete more readily than through philosophical abstractions."[371] For me, the abstract and the concrete are not only epistemologically and temporally related, they are situationally so.[372]

While I am drawn to the idea that justice is what human beings are fitted for—an idea, Christian and Grant remind that both Grant and Plato accepted[373]—I cannot comprehend why the idea implies that justice is "an unchanging good," unless it is precisely the infinity of forms justice takes that is the "unchanging good." But if justice implies a universal standard of behavioural conduct—as Grant's opposition to abortion and euthanasia implies—it seems we have smuggled back in long-standing ecclesiastical efforts at establishing its own universal and homogenous state. While the contrary, anything goes, cannot constitute justice either, what human beings are fitted for—"the always immediate demands of charity"[374] in Grant's phrasing—obviously shifts according to time, place, and circumstance.[375] If the secular conception of the "individual" bears the trace of the spiritual concept of "soul," can that creature's efforts to transcend the technological be decreed by abstraction? For me one's spiritual journey, while it can be shared, is individuated[376] as it becomes revealed through everyday life, through attunement to the transcendent while immersed in the moment, life reconstructed through ongoing study of it, what can become educational experience.

That seems to have been the case for Grant while at Oxford, surrounded by students for whom, "if not yet for George, adjusting oneself to the transcendent was vastly more important than being well adjusted socially."[377] In Grant's life, at least during that time at Oxford, these were coextensive. Often, as you recall from earlier chapters, associated disparagingly with Dewey, adjustment, at least during Grant's first time at Oxford, seems to have supported his attunement to the transcendent. Recall that for Dewey "adjustment"—on one occasion he likens it to harmony[378]—includes modifying conditions according to our "wants" and "purposes,"[379] enactments of the "will" (which worried Grant so). But for Dewey "adjustment" also "pertain[s] to our being in its entirely," a "change *of* will conceived as the organic plenitude of our being, rather than any special change *in* will"[380] traceable not to "*a* religion" but "from whatever cause and by whatever means, there is a religious outlook and function."[381] Grant himself was not always pleased with the church or the university: faith and education[382] for him did not necessarily coincide with either institution. Still, he worked within and through both.

Everyday experience is not often voluptuous. It can be painful (Weil and Grant underscore this fact[383]) but it can also be redemptive.[384] But must suffering[385]—affliction for Weil—become the substructure of everyday experience, as Christian and Grant imply when they reify the good—"this hard standard"—as demanding we "pay its price in the ordinary occurrences of space and time?"[386] Sometimes being fitted is pleasurable, and becoming "tailor-made" can be joyous as well as irksome, even sometimes painful. Whatever one's experience—and the adjustments one can make in it—it seems for Grant attunement to the transcendent focuses that suffering or joy, making it a matter not only of irritation or pleasure but contemplative attentiveness, too. Referencing Heidegger, Grant depicts such attentiveness, such attunement, as taking "something to heart," meaning "that one is not detached from it as one is detached from an object which stands over against one. To take something to heart is just the opposite of thinking about something as if it were an object, concern about which we could choose or not choose."[387] No sterilized receptivity to a signal, attunement is embodied: it opens one's head and heart, perhaps one's soul, mindful of mood. As Grant acknowledges, "our dilemma always is to combine that right combination of openness and commitment that our lives require."[388] Cultivating that "combination" is the very "purpose of education," Grant teaches us.[389]

Conclusion

> To say the Good is beyond being, which I think is essential, is a fantastic transcendence.[390]
>
> George Grant

Attunement can occur when one enters the space of an icon, for Grant listening to Mozart, for me in the absent presence of one George Grant. While subjectively decentred[391]—decreation seems extreme, but something like self-shattering[392] might sometimes be required—one works from within, attentive to the inner source (mood, mind) as well as to the natural world in its endless (if threatened) particularity. It does not end there, as whatever we experience can remind us of what is beyond: in the past, in the future, but also "beyond" any term we can postulate. "In knowing necessity as necessity," Grant asks, "does not our intelligence transcend necessity?"[393] Being in the world, then, requires double consciousness. The present can be an allegory of the past, and in the gap between the two can be an opening to what is outside history, if not outside time itself. O'Donovan summarizes:

> Grant's writings, therefore, imply an understanding of revelation as foundation, as the truth of our beginnings which is recollected…. For us moderns, who belong to the tradition of technological freedom, the foundations are present only in the solitary act of recollection, which must be solitary because

what is recollected lies outside the public realm. It lies outside the realm of public speech, lacking a coherent language of communication in the present.[394]

Quietude, then, not only reflects Grant's aging and his disquiet over politics (perhaps sensing its impossibility in late modernity or postmodernity), but also his sense that Christianity is as much about personal as it is about social salvation, although they may well be interrelated. "Keep your solitude," Weil recommended.[395]

Self-critical and interpretive receptivity to what experience reveals is a form of listening: it is as if we are straining to hear what we're being told. Structured by certain receptivity, relationship—with others (including the dead and not yet born), with ourselves, with the biosphere in which we are embedded, and with what is beyond—may be functional, maybe even foreordained. It might be moral. "Human life is in essence the moral life," Grant knew, adding that "human beings are such that they are good and bad, can become better or worse. But it is a fact that they cannot become better by trying to be less imperfect. They can only become better by paying attention to and desiring perfection."[396] Such perfection is sometimes beautiful in ways others apprehend but more often, it seems to me, "perfection" is a private aspiration, fine-tuning the instrument one is, worked out in idiosyncratic terms perhaps heard only by oneself—"one man's making may be another man's unmaking,"[397] Grant himself once acknowledged—and affirmed, *amor fati* (love of fate).[398] Such affirmation occurs within and beyond time and space.

Time and space—these are, Ian Angus suggests, the coordinates of Grant's thought. They could also be the coordinates of attunement, as the inner perfection of which Grant speaks is not only revealed but reconstructed from the remains of the day, lived experience that is simultaneously temporal and spatial. One of the key metaphors for curriculum is "journey," and it is one Grant invokes on occasion, as when he writes that the "journey to liberation is an infinite journey in which there is no stopping place and where no formulations are adequate."[399] Death may be its destination but death too seems shrouded in mystery; it is as utterly incomprehensible as it is utterly inevitable. Grant counselled acceptance, noting that "the religious spirit of acceptance has always had within it the element of mystery," adding that "to assert transcendence was to assert mystery."[400]

In time and place the pilgrim plots his unpredictable course, attuned to what surrounds, obeying (or not) what is revealed, engaging (or not) with what and who appears. It is a pilgrimage that demands fealty in finding one's way along a trail that sometimes fades away. "Therefore," Grant knew, "we must discipline ourselves so that we all have a constant life of controlled study from which our public life flows."[401] In this "constancy" resides the "discipline," perhaps through habit or ritual, by which one structures one's day, structure in service to study. One registers one's experience, perhaps through note-taking, life-writing, a daily journal, an ongoing dialogical encounter with that experience, including with the past and those absent others within us, and those we did not know except through reading what they wrote. Not always affliction, my life—even before age set in—is an ongoing effort, in part because, as Grant knew: "To achieve this is hard because the modern world presses men into the life of manipulation and organization and considers contemplation a waste of time."[402] Profit and pleasure—the idols of our time—impose disciplines and distractions of their own, but as Grant appreciates: "Freedom and subjectivity mean the same thing, the ability to transcend ourselves."[403]

For Nietzsche, Grant taught, freedom and subjectivity meant the same thing, but in modernity the good was not beyond both. What is good is what is good for me: "[O]ne's project is to realize one's individuality in the face of chaos," as Grant phrased it, and it must be undertaken "at high noon—that is, in love of the earth and the body—and the assumption that there is no transcendent good."[404] Why must what is good for me and what is Good be mutually exclusive? Of course the transcendent Good to which sometimes I feel attuned is no personal "confederate," as Grant once snarled at those who position God thusly,[405] but something—eternity—beyond what I can think or imagine. Of course there is considerable "noise" in my signal (however inadequate that image is) in deciphering it. Mind not to mention mood—translated into academic knowledge, especially in the humanities and arts—are indispensable.

The curriculum invokes all these, but also what is beyond them. *Currere*—the lived experience of curriculum—can become iconographic in its invocation of both the here and now and what is beyond. The role of reason[406] in *currere* is at first meditative then analytic, in the service of regression (the past), progression (the future), analysis, and synthesis, reconstructing one's character, now structured by conviction and resolve. For Grant, Athanasiadis suggests, "the world as ruled by necessity and chance is not the highest truth. In the end, Grant is a 'rationalist.' He believes that there is an order of the good/God that provides a *telos* for human life and the world."[407] While I am agnostic on this last point, I do share the first two: that what we see is not necessarily what we get, and reason plays a pivotal role in rendering intelligible what we can apprehend through attunement to the Good.

Important in themselves, then, facts and concepts function as receptacles of, as well as portals to, experience no longer immediately available to us, palimpsests of the past that can pull us from disappearing into the temporally vacant present. In a technological era, "the intimate and the ultimate are being eclipsed by the immediate."[408] The facticity of the material world can testify to what transcends it: "All our worldly experiences," Fishbane appreciates, can become "prismatic revelations" of a "deeper elementariness."[409] Everyday experience can become educational, as one's worldliness[410] wields its way beyond itself. For Fishbane it is the task of theology—for Grant also the task of teaching—"to attune the self to the unfolding occurrence of things in all their particularities and conjunctions," attunement itself requiring that "one remain steadfast at each new crossing point where raw elementariness...becomes human experience."[411] Human experience can become educational—indeed iconographic—if we are attuned to what it teaches us.

Attunement is listening, feeling, thinking, sometimes separate sometimes fused attentiveness to what is revealed to—and what is withheld from—us. Through the prism of the personal we try to decipher the meaning of the moment, its materiality, temporality, calling us to coincide with neither. Distracted by devices, we lose ourselves in obsession, for many emotions obscured by the affliction of hard labor, the piercing pain of hunger and illness, humanity struggling to survive. "Modern life," Grant tells Cayley, is "hard," and leaves "most people" unable to engage in

> sustained thought.... When a society is in as great an intellectual chaos as the Western world is, where nobody knows what anything is about anymore, then I think that his mass public confusion is terribly hard for people. With most people, their main life is not to think, and therefore they can be easily driven here and there.[412]

Such manipulative circumstances require inner withdrawal, quietude not as civic ineptitude but as political activism through academic study and inner reform.

The spiritual not the political is the paramount consideration, a social as well as subjective necessity. That positions each of us in the gap. "We are not so situated," Grant mused, that the "death of the spirit" is something we can ignore, adding that we are obligated to "deal with that ambiguity from day to day" by "attempting to incarnate meaning in those very structures which we know inhibit or even negate its very possibility."[413] Incarnation is precisely that mediation between the empirical world and its transcendent ground, that space in front of the icon. "Mediation constitutes the sole given that merits immediacy," Marion muses, "because it produces that immediacy," adding: "Only mediation produces immediacy; abolished, it would give way to barbarism."[414] Attunement to the Good keeps us minding the gap.[415]

Distracted by devices, we are now attuned to virtual—not historical or transcendent—reality.[416] No longer supplicants on a spiritual mission too many have become, in Grant's terms, "clever ape[s]" fastened on finding "comfort and security through techniques."[417] For Grant our "destiny" is to find ourselves "in the infinite."[418] Attunement to the eternal can yield guidance in the present. Those who attain "perfect obedience," Weil writes, become a "unique, irreplaceable form of the presence, knowledge and operation of God in the world."[419] The presence of the infinite—of the eternal—manifests subjectively, within subjective presence. While perhaps not perfectly obedient—he suspected only the saints could be—Grant personified such subjective presence, attesting to what that, as icon, communicated. Toward the infinite, the eternal, we turn in chapter 7.

Notes

1. Davis and Roper 2009b, 129.
2. Davis and Roper 2009b, 134. Unlimited because, as Robertson (2006, 148) notes: "All such efforts to get control of technology are themselves technological." Athanasiadis (2001, 116) asks if "there is any limit to human freedom in manipulating and controlling the world," asserting (with Grant) that the "idea of limit is the idea of God." Surely the idea of limit is not equivalent to "God," and deciding when, where, how to proceed or not, to what extent—within technology, with other persons and creatures, in relation to the planet—remains the ethical dilemma.
3. Weil (1947) 2002, 127. Weil, Kaethler (2009, 75) notes, emphasizes "receptivity rather than initiative."
4. For Grant, O'Donovan (1984, 103) reminds, "love of the particular good is, then, ordered to love of the universal good. There is an ascent of love from particular goods to the universal good." An interesting instance of this "ascent" occurs in Jeffrey Stewart's biography of Alain Locke, Howard University philosophy professor and the intellectual architect of the Harlem Renaissance. Along with Montgomery Gregory, Stewart (2018, 306; italics added) tells us, "Locke had started the *Stylus*, a literary magazine at Howard, to publish the writings of students and encourage them to *explore race aesthetically as a doorway to a unique universalism in modern spiritual life*." In that passage there is Weil's door ([1947] 2002, 145; discussed again in the next chapter), emphasizing both that it blocks and allows passage. Does current-day identity politics risk idolatry?
5. Angus 1997, 159.
6. Rigelhof 2001, 121.
7. Dewey 1922, 131.
8. Aoki (1981) 2005, 228. It is a space in between, an empty space of juxtaposition, at the least non-coincidence with that is. One risk is hubris, self-assurance that one is attuned. A second is denial of what one cannot see or measure. "To imagine that they [the gods] have a particular destiny in mind for humans and that they intervene in human affairs," Angus (2006, 359) reminds, "is to imagine the beyond as simultaneously present."
9. Referencing Heidegger, Sikka (1997, 247) explains: "Being is realized as the center only when *Dasein* stands within its truth as center, only when the subject is de-centered. The decentering of the subject is at the same time the realization of *Dasein*, and that means also the realization of being, not as perfect presence, but as a lighting which conceals and shelters truth within itself, a lighting that grants truth to *Dasein*, but 'in modes,' one might say—according to the historical finitude proper to *Dasein*." Grant would contest any acceptance of "historical finitude," but Sikka's depiction of the decentred subject inhering within truth seems in sync with his sense of attunement to eternity.
10. Dostoevsky, Randy Peg Peters (2006, 239) explains, "allowed Grant to work out his final position on how it live his faith in the midst of the Western dynamo. Dostoevsky's notion that faith was not about controlling people but about freeing people to love justice buttressed Grant's deep sense of the equality of all people." In her commentary on Peters's essay, O'Donovan (1984, 26) concludes that through his study of Dostoevsky Grant was reminded that "while freedom is man's individuality and his dignity, it is not man's salvation."

11. In a spring 1946 letter to his friend Alice Boissonneau, Grant wrote: "Two or three weeks ago I wrote you a letter after my first wave of Henry James.... Nothing that I have read in my life has influenced me more than James and only Dostoevsky has influenced me equally" (Christian 1996d, 128). James's "style," Grant continued, "is the full revelation of beauty" (129).

12. Davis and Roper 2009b, 950. (Grant's commentary on Dostoevsky, broadcast on the CBC, was composed also by Sheila Grant—see Davis 2002a, xviii—but this quoted passage comes from one of Grant's five lectures on Christianity.) So freedom has to do with time, or being beyond time, as in "eternity," the topic of the next and final chapter. As we saw in ch. 3, in modernity time is (nothing but) history, but Grant wants to reaffirm (by reactivating Plato) time as non-coincident with history, and eternity beyond both. He makes a sharp distinction during the interview with Cayley (1995, 89): "[H]istoricism is the exact opposite of Platonism.... Platonism is the belief that thought can transcend its context."

13. "Freedom is to be directed by one's own inner light," Grant affirmed, "not by things external" (Davis 2002b, 215). Attunement allows revelation to be apprehended (as reason allows apprehension to be comprehended); as such it enables one's spiritual quest. Almost needless to say, attunement is no technique one refines to gain competitive advantage.

14. Davis and Roper 2009b, 962. Athanasiadis (2006, 264) notes its double-sidedness for Grant: "Openness is directed toward otherness in the world, but it is also inspired by a larger openness to the transcendent Other, the sacred, the Good that is God."

15. Davis and Roper 2009b, 962. "While the ancients held a concept of the good which defined what everything in creation was fitted for," Athanasiadis (2001, 200) points out, "modern science does not understand nature in these teleological terms. It replaces the concept of 'good' with that of 'value'—the evaluation of things according to human standards." Recall Grant's critique of the concept of "value" in ch. 2. Today there is constant talk of "value added," as if none is intrinsic to human activity.

16. See 1 Corinthians 13:12. "We live in darkness about important matters, about what nature is, what a person is," Grant told Taylor ([1982] 2006, 80). "Bringing to light the darkness as darkness was a central task for Grant," Athanasiadis (2001, 217) observes. Weil ([1947] 2002, 51) seemed pessimistic about the prospect of that: "We only possess shadowy imitations of good," she felt sure.

17. "Perfected freedom," O'Donovan (1984, 180) explains (referencing Grant's invocation of Augustine), "is freedom not to be able to sin, the freedom of perfect obedience. And perfect obedience is freedom from bondage in all its aspects, including bondage to tradition." Kaethler (2009, 74) too suggests that "[i]ndividual freedom is at its height when we are obedient to God. Belief in God is a matter of knowing rather than choosing." The freedom to attune oneself to the Good is the freedom lost in modernity, Randy Peg Peters (2006, 251) points out, "an ethical freedom that was rooted in notions of justice and responsibility to the 'other.'"

18. "Davis 2002b, 264; see also Davis and Roper 2005b, 231. "Western ethics," Grant complains, "has substituted freedom for virtue as its central concept" (Davis and Roper 2009b, 811); it is no longer attuned to the transcendent.

19. This idea seems implied in Thibon's ([1947] 2002, xxxiv) suggestion that there are many paths to "heaven." In secular terms, Collingwood (2002, 103) knows that

"[t]here must, therefore, be a kind of action which is not determined according to rule, and where the process is directly from knowledge of the situation to an action appropriate to that situation, without passing through the stage of formulating a rule appropriate to the situation." He adds: "Rules of conduct kept action at a low potential, because they involved a certain blindness to the realities of the situation" (2002, 106). Finding out whose am I enables answering who am I, self-knowledge in the service of "decreation" so that "the realities of the situation" are not silenced by inner noise or outer distraction.

20.   Emberley 1990, xx.

21.   Athanasiadis 2001, 117. For Weil ([1947] 2002, 49) obedience is the "only pure motive," the one non-instrumental motive, provided, she cautions, that one obeys "necessity" not "force." Obedience is a "very central idea for Weil," Athanasiadis (2001, 99) notes, requiring "complete consent to God's will which is love, even through affliction." Grant may have also derived his sense of obedience from Hegel, or so Sibley (2008, 25) suggests, quoting Hegel: "In duty the individual acquires his substantive freedom."

22.   'Supposing, indeed, presence as the privileged temporalization of Being," Marion (2001, 203) writes, "it falls to beings to concentrate that presence in themselves, without Being ever being able 'to be' in accordance with that presence." Subjective presence, Marion's words remind, is not narcissistic but decentred, attuned to—but not "in accordance with"—the eternal, as it is refracted through subjectivity which cannot coincide with either. "Man does not hold under the wind," Marion (2012, 126) makes clear, "man does not hold the spirit; his presence floats, in suspension, in the flux that comes to him from elsewhere."

23.   "The difference between theology and economy," Mondzain (2005, 24) explains, "is the difference between believing without seeing and believing while seeing," adding that the "economy thus determines a field proper to speech and to showing. This field does not put an end to the mystery of what determines it; it gives word and visibility access to it" (25). Substitute "teaching" for "economy" Grant's iconographic calling becomes visible.

24.   Mondzain (2005, 20) observes: "Making justice reign amidst humanity cannot be achieved by the pure and simple application of a transcendent law. An adaptive concept is needed," adding that "speech, remedy, guile, condescension, punishment, or lie...all the means of the economy are good when one uses them with economy, that is to say, while remaining loyal to the spirit of the divine, providential economy" (21). In his critique of "application," Aoki ([1987] 2005, 155) writes: "Mindfulness of the situation allows the person in the situation to recognize that application is a hermeneutic act, remembering that being in the situation is a human being in his becoming. This mindfulness allows the listening to what it is that a situation is asking."

25.   "For the truth to be 'made' as an event," Derrida (2005, 23) suggests, "then the truth must fall on me—not be produced by me, but fall on me, or visit me."

26.   Not so fast, Athanasiadis (2006, 264) would caution: "Waiting, then, involves the loving hesitation of restraint in order to become 'open' to otherness." Once clarification occurs, then action might be swift and straightforward. Regarding restraint, see also Athanasiadis 2001, 148.

27.   Davis 2002b, 448. "In light of God's self-revelation in the person of Jesus," Scanlon (2005, 163) notes, "personhood for Christians becomes discipleship."

28. Angus (1997, 98) identifies "a fundamental issue concerning the interrelationship of technology and ethics: any ethics that begins from a distinction between a means and an end-in-itself will be inadequate to judge technology because technology itself is developed from precisely this distinction."

29. Referencing Grant's reflection on Plato, O'Donovan (1984, 21) summarizes, "man's final end is union with the transcendent Good, and his most urgent questions in this life concern the nature and grounds of right conduct."

30. "Courage is a high virtue for Grant," Taylor ([1982] 2006, 155) notes, "along with hope and love."

31. Dewey 1922, 120.

32. The sequence could be reversed too; for Magrini (2017, 108), "Attunement occurs in moments of understanding or enlightenment."

33. "For Plato," Sibley (2008, 192) suggests, "rational contemplation is an attempt to attune human consciousness to the proper order of the cosmos and, in this attunement, to perceive the ethical truth intrinsic to that order. The best function of a man is to use his reason to attune himself to the external order of the cosmos."

34. "Standing within such readiness," Sikka (1997, 247) writes, "is a thinking that grasps inwardly."

35. Whillier (1990b, 77) notes that the "biblical tradition also holds that thought is fundamentally transformed by revelation. Revelation has priority over thought, at least for the prophets. And surely the Bible holds that there is an intimate relationship between thought, revelation and action." Does attunement enable revelation? O'Donovan (1984, 84) implies as much when she writes: "True knowing is loving contemplation, is adoration of the Good in what is illumined by it." Weil ([1947] 2002, 128) goes further, writing that through "our intelligence" we know that what we cannot know through intelligence is "more real than what it does comprehend." Marion (2012, 45) seems to share this sense: "God, if he must be thought, can meet no theoretical space to his measure, because his measure exerts itself in our eyes as an excessiveness. Ontological difference itself, and hence also Being, become too limited."

36. O'Donovan 1984, 85.

37. "Justice," O'Donovan (1984, 59) reminds, "is man's highest good, Grant holds; justice is what man as man is fitted for."

38. Davis and Roper 2009b, 304. "What is the Christian life," Grant asked, "without a doctrine of obedience?" (Davis and Roper 2005b, 423). Grant suggests that the "unique revelation" to which the Bible testifies "concerns what is most important for man to know: the purpose in obedience to which he can alone fully realize himself" (647). Obedience, then, can be a spiritual (not necessarily biblical or doctrinal) idea; e.g., following what is revealed through attunement.

39. Aoki (1987) 2005, 351.

40. Cayley 1995, 8.

41. O'Donovan 1990, 147. Athanasiadis (2001, 149) expands the point: "Idolizing freedom, history, or progress, and identifying these with the working of divine providence, is…a deification of human activity and thought" (see also 133).

42. "Once the will becomes severed from obedience to God," Athanasiadis (2001, 172) cautions, "it becomes the servant of the human passions." If incarnation is a central fact of Christian faith, why can't the passions—I'm thinking of sexual desire

specifically—be in fact a gift from "God"? Yes, sexual desire can be a curse too, but in old age it now seems to me that sexuality is another site of spirituality, as well as intense unforgettable pleasure. And are these two inevitably contraries? The father of six children, could George Grant disagree?

43.   Athanasiadis 2006, 266. "In contrast to Athens and its progeny—the West—Grant looked," Randy Peg Peters (2006, 252) writes, "to the kenotic, self-emptying love that he believed characterized Jerusalem and the East."

44.   "Attention is bound up with desire," Weil ([1947] 2002, 118) writes, "or more exactly, consent."

45.   Davis and Roper 2009b, 307. Referencing his *Time as History*, O'Donovan (1984, 106–7) points out that "Grant is still obedient to the Socratic challenge to 'Know thyself!' As a decade before, he remains dedicated to the task of bringing his age to self-awareness as the appropriate (and appropriating) response to the novelty of our situation."

46.   Cayley 1995, 8.

47.   "But through freedom is the possibility of transcending any contingent situation," Grant acknowledged, "it is a transcendence which is always afflicted by the very contingency it transcends" (Davis 2002b, 287). Obedience in the service to transcendence might be embedded in notions of "bound writing," at least as Benedetti (2005, 162) explains the practice: "What characterizes bound writing is therefore not simply the reliance on chance but the assumption of a constraint, whatever kind of constraint it may be, as long as it succeeds in withdrawing a good portion of the task of thinking up or composing the text from the author's discretion."

48.   For Grant the concept may have gained spiritual salience at his conversion experience, during which he learned he was not his own (see Davis 2000, xxii), an idea Davis associates with John Calvin and the biblical personage Paul (1 Corinthians 6:19) (xxiii). That experience, Davis continues, "revealed to him the existence of an order beyond the world of space and time, an order which would endure no matter what happens here" (xxiii).

49.   Davis and Emberley 2000b, 160. "Whereas the Greeks regarded their deeds, and that determination necessary to them," O'Donovan (1984, 114) emphasizes, "as *obedient* to 'the very structure of what is,' we regard our doing and our willing as *creative*, as originating structure." Davis and Emberley locate Grant's insight in his 1970s study of Kant, pointing out that while Kant argued we human beings are finite, incapable of knowing nature as it is in itself (even scientific categories are ours; we project them onto nature) or knowing God through reason, Kant did insist, Davis and Emberley suggest, that we nonetheless know what moral conduct is, know that we are subject to duty, that what we are to do is inscribed in the conscience of all human beings. While the first two points seem obvious, the third not so much, as "conscience" (if imprinted at all) can so easily fade in a culture of calculation, competition, and greed.

50.   Virtue requires understanding and affirms charity, Grant thought, admitting to Charles Taylor ([1982] 2006, 132) that "[i]t has taken all my energy just to understand what virtue might be, the nature of a virtuous life." Cayley (1995, 18) tells us that "Strauss, in Grant's view, tended to identify virtue too exclusively with understanding, and not enough with charity." If knowledge is enabled by love, surely the two are entwined. For Athanasiadis (2001, 128), "Virtue emerges through education, which is the formation of character through habituation."

51. Grant was ambivalent about autonomy, recoiling from its adoration in modernity as idolatrous interference in necessity (technology). Acknowledging that such interference is sometimes "good," and while the autonomy behind it (like everything else) must have been created by God, Grant concludes that the "fulfillment of life is consent, which is the denial of autonomy" (Davis and Roper 2009b, 834). Does not the former rely upon the latter?

52. Self-legislation, Grant worried, "facilitated that readiness for constant change while maintaining the discipline of the will" (Davis and Roper 2009b, 121). For those attuned only or even primarily to "getting ahead," such caution is advice well taken; for those attuned to the Good, subjective reconstruction is not for the sake of success but for making those inner adjustments required by obedience to revelation.

53. In the subjective reconstruction attunement invites, the central status of the will is itself challenged, as Grant notes: "The self-overcoming is not only the self-overcoming of the lower by the higher will, but of the will as such. It must be in some sense redemption from the will" (Davis and Roper 2009b, 1003). Redemption but not relinquishing it altogether, as will enables the subjective reconstruction attunement invites. That fact is implied in Athanasiadis's (2001, 169) suggestion: "We need, rather, to admit change within ourselves in order to see otherness and all that is as good."

54. For Plato and Socrates, Grant suggested, "thought was a divine activity—the pursuit of truth was the center of existence" (Davis and Roper 2005b, 686). Obviously it is not only that, but I accept it can be.

55. Cayley 1995, 8. Grant thought true freedom, as Davis (2002a, xxi) points out, could be found "through truth experienced in faith." That experience may well be private, shared but in quietude, a form of monasticism. At a conference in Grant's honour, Kane (1990, 153) reminded his listeners: "Yet the authentic heart of the Catholic tradition in the U.S., the conscious assertion of the priority of virtue over freedom, will be kept alive, if at all, in forms and places roughly analogous to the monasticism of an earlier barbarian age. For then, too, authentic faith lived side by side with Christian barbarism."

56. Athanasiadis (2006, 265) explains: "Grant uses the words consent and obedience, then, in order to help express the active side of openness in the spirit of waiting."

57. Not only in Judaism but also at "the very height of Christianity," Grant notes, "is the statement 'not my will but thine,' but Western Christianity has still been very concentrated on the will" (Cayley 1995, 140), one's own that is. Not only Jerusalem but Athens was also a source for Grant's thinking, and, as Athanasiadis (2001, 113) points out, the "ancients believed the human will would find fulfillment in obedience to reason, and freedom in obedience to the good."

58. Fishbane 2008, xii. This "double-faced" structure recalls Grant's appreciation of irony (as noted in ch. 5's conclusion) and Du Bois's "double consciousness," referenced in the introduction and to be invoked again later in this chapter.

59. Lipari 2014, 188. Not blind obedience of course, or so it would seem when Grant affirms that the "new ethics" will arise through "thought," "insight," and "understanding" (Davis 2002b, 217). The resounding question—"how should I live?"—is, for Grant, "an ethical question" (428).

60. Mondzain 2005, 107.

61. The phrase is Novalis's (see Pérez-Gómez 2016, 90). Because "obedience" is freely chosen, an exercise in autonomy as well as an opportunity afforded by attunement,

it recalls acts of reactivation and reconstruction, precisely because "our emotional, prereflective life imposes its feelings on us, like musical modulations inspired by a condition of being that escapes external determinism and conformity" (90).

62. Heaven and Heaven (1978, 69) remind that "the highest knowledge is open only to those who love the good; or, only insofar as the soul loves it is qualified to know and understand." Still, some sense of utility—however folded into ethics, even metaphysics—remains, as Davis (2002b, 444–5) suggests that "[t]he question Grant wanted students to ask was, Which of the philosophic traditions offer the best guidance concerning how we should live our lives as thoughtful more individuals, as citizens, and as participants in the expanding economy and mass society of North America?"

63. Reason can adjudicate what can seem the demands of revelation. Kirby and Greenspan (1990, 155) point out that "whereas the natural law tradition emphasized a political rule based on reason, rule by revelation could mean an authoritarian rule by the few who had received the divine word." Revelation reasoned summarizes too simply the sequence, but reason remains the (rarely self-evident) means of comprehending revelation.

64. Muggeridge (1978, 47) implies that Grant's skepticism made him a contrarian, writing "he is perfectly willing to swim against the tide in obscurity." It was "yearning for a homeland" that led to "his Loyalism" (47). In the end "not a nationalist," Muggeridge reminds us that Grant was brought up a progressive, a formation he contradicts in adulthood with conservatism (47). This situated—some would say dialectical—sense of thought is in play in my suggestion that the form progressivism might take in our era is a version of Grant's conservatism.

65. Craiutu (2017, 190) recalls Leszek Kolakowski's admonition "to combine the faith of the priest, who perpetuates the absolute and is vigilant to keep the reverence for it in society, with the sceptical philosophy of the jester who systematically questions the accepted truths," adding: "We always thirst for the absolute, Kolakowski wrote, and we can never turn our ears deaf to its calls and signs" (191).

66. In this next chapter I'll attend to this term. For now let's say simply what is beyond time as we know it.

67. Athanasiadis (2006, 259) asserts that Grant's "focus on the cross" enables him "to speak about the primacy of experience for knowing and doing, as well as the critical content of such experience." Such emphasis upon experience—minus the cross—Grant shares with Dewey, Jane Addams, and the progressives. There is another utterly secular view of the matter: "[S]omething to write is always there," Kittler (2013, 54) says, "simply because there is something that never stops transmitting."

68. Such a decentring supports subjectivity's expansiveness (which I associate with cosmopolitanism; see Pinar 2009), in contrast to the contraction or minimalization of the self (see Lasch 1984) to which psychological survivalism attests. While civic and interpersonal engagement may become unpleasant, the single-minded attempt to protect oneself through psychic withdrawal may undermine the self as social strife might not, e.g., by encouraging the onset of that self-enclosure we call narcissism (Lasch 1978). Citing Buber and Levinas, Lipari (2014, 190) affirms that the "subject of the self is not a self-same subject, but is a relational intersubjective subject." Subjectivity requires engagement with the other—including the spiritual other attunement allows—but separation too, even quietude, as I discuss later in this chapter.

69. Interesting, in regard to this concept, that organizers Denise Taliaferro Baszile and Thomas Poetter choose "retreat" to designate their *Currere* Exchange Conferences. See https://www.currereexchange.weebly.com.

70. Quietude recalls the pacifism of Grant's youth. Quietude is not necessarily physical withdrawal from the public sphere, although for Grant it did at one point. Quietude can mean being an activist in the public domain—as Grant so often was—not as a polemicist or social engineer but as a servant of the truth. Both pacifism and quietude represents forms of non-violence. Weil ([1947] 2002, 85) admonished us to "substitute...non-violence for violence," as has Hongyu Wang (2014).

71. For Athanasiadis 2001, 179, "it is in listening and waiting (openness) rather than through active doing that we come to know, experience, and grow in the good/ God."

72. Davis and Roper 2005b, 17. McCarroll (2006, 272) puts the matter this way: "Grant, following Weil, affirms the experience of reality in the realm of necessity, within the larger unknowable connectedness of the Whole."

73. Dewey (1934) 1962, 54. While both subjective and social, Dewey's emphasis was this world, in sync with Welchman (2016, 186) when he writes: "Transcendental conditions are conditions of experience, that is, of the way things must appear to us in order to be experienced as any kind of objects." Grant's emphasis is elsewhere: ideals are "imperfectly embodied in the natural," as they "are of the supernatural" (Davis and Emberley 2000b, 381). We are back to the gap (recalling ch. 5), with Dewey (and Welchman) leaning one way and Grant the other, but everyone minding the gap.

74. Davis 2002b, 427.

75. Referencing idealist philosophers, among them Plato and Aristotle, Dewey (1922, 179) complains that "they set up a transcendental meaning and reason, remote from present experience and opposed to it; or they insist upon a special form of meaning and consciousness to be attained by peculiar modes of knowledge inaccessible to the common man, involving not continuous reconstruction of ordinary experience, but its wholesale reversal. They have treated regeneration, change of heart, as wholesale and self-enclosed, not as continuous." Does Dewey think his own sophisticated thinking is available to the "common man"? As this chapter suggests, "transcendental meaning" is not necessarily "remote" from "present experience." Through attunement such meaning informs present experience.

76. Dewey 1922, 179. "Our moral measure for estimating any existing arrangement or any proposed reform," Dewey emphasized, "is its effect upon impulse and habits. Does it liberate or suppress, ossify or render flexible, divide or unify interest?" (181). If, as Athanasiadis (2001, 127) phrases it, classical thinkers imagined "the goal of human and social life was not freedom but virtue," then emphasizing consequences is not exactly new to the pragmatists.

77. See, e.g., Westbrook 1991, 20.

78. Dewey 1922, 203.

79. "Nothing is worse than extreme affliction which destroys the 'I' from the outside," Weil ([1947] 2002, 26) writes, "because after that we can no longer destroy it ourselves."

80. Davis and Roper 2009b, 1074.

81. Planinc (1992, 43) suggests that "Grant also accepted Weil's contemplative gnosticism as a technique of ecstasy—that is, a technique through which one may

escape the activistic gnosticism of technological society, understood as necessity, and become aware of the transcendent realm it denies—but he refused to accept Weil's own activism." Contrary to Planinc's conclusion that Grant could not then be conscripted by the Left, he did participate in the NDP's founding, although he abandoned the party soon enough. "Grant understood," Planinc continues, "that if Heidegger's account of technology is true, Weil's attempt to escape modernity through contemplative gnosis was the only possible alternative" (44).

82.   Planinc 1992, 36.

83.   Emberley 1990, xxi.

84.   Weil (1947) 2002, 128. Jersak (2012, 65) explains: "The faculty of the soul designated for illumination and designed to perceive the Good in Plato is the *nous*—commonly translated 'intelligence,'" adding that "[n]ous is not to be confused with 'reason.' We might better translate it 'heart' or even 'spirit'" (67). As if anticipating a concept of attunement, Jersak writes: "[T]he meditative thinking of the *thanc* or *nous* is a steadfast, intimate concentration on things that speak to us, thought-encounters with things that cannot be apprehended by logic" (68).

85.   Davis and Roper 2009b, 1074. In Minogue's (1990, 167) summary: "The Greeks construed nature as a kind of living whole animated by a principle of reason which allowed Man (as represented by those few possessing real rational capacity) to align [attune] himself with the principles of the universe. Such alignment was the key to harmony, both inner and external, and it required understanding of the ideal world and some knowledge of the place of the disorderly passions." More confident of Nature's divinity it would seem—and, if so, undermining her assertion regarding the unbridgeable gap between here and eternity I quoted in ch. 5—nineteenth-century African-American feminist Anna Julia Cooper ([1892] 1998, 135) wrote: "Nature's language is not writ in cipher. Her notes are always simple and sensuous, and the very meanest recesses and commonest byways are fairly deafening with her sermons and songs. It is only when we ourselves are out of tune through our pretentiousness and self-sufficiency, or are blinded and rendered insensate by reason of our foreign and unnatural 'cultivation' that we miss her meanings and inadequately construe her multiform lessons." One is reminded of Weil's suggestion that attunement requires self-stripping or "decreation."

86.   "Now faith notoriously has degrees," Penelhum (1983, 93) reminds, "and insofar as it is weak it is primarily because the person who has it is nevertheless also partly secularized." Secularism too "has degrees" (92).

87.   Grant's words for Weil's conception of "attention" were "admire or wonder," but "concentrated on nothing in particular; attention is finally attention to the void." Grant adds: "It is waiting for something to appear" (Davis and Roper 2009b, 828).

88.   "Morals is connected with actualities of existence," Dewey (1922, 202–3) emphasizes, "not with ideals, ends and obligations independent of concrete actualities." The Greeks, Grant reminds, "had no word for the ideal" (Davis and Roper 2009b, 1056).

89.   Even "non-acting acting"—for Grant the "heart" of what Weil means by "attention" (Davis and Roper 2009b, 827)—seems like a form of activity to me.

90.   Said (1996, 82–3, 11) invoked the concept of "amateur" to indicate that the intellectual is obligated to raise "moral issues" even within "technical and professional activity" and on the basis of "universal principles."

91. Davis and Roper 2005b, 137.

92. Davis and Roper 2005b, 137.

93. Davis and Roper 2005b, 137.

94. "We know that intellect is superior to good sense," Whillier (1990b, 79) reminds, "but does not the example of Socrates' fate teach us the necessity of both?" For Magrini (2017, 96): "Transcendence is an event of learning and a moment and mode of disclosure where the *intimation of truth* manifests...an educative event highlighted by a form of attunement."

95. Davis and Roper 2005b, 135. I am reminded of Aoki's ([1995] 2005, 310) affirmation of such juxtapositions of difference as "generative."

96. Davis and Roper 2005b, 136. "This is the peculiarity of modern man," O'Donovan (1984, 114–5) notes, "the degree to which his relationship to himself and his world is one of making." Note that "making" shows up in that Grant passage I quoted in the main text, but implicitly supportive of my point that the will is hardly to be discarded because it has become overly elevated. In its proper place (one that moves according to time and circumstance), "making" too can be put to good use.

97. Davis and Roper 2005b, 136. "Truth is sought not because it is truth," Weil ([1947] 2002, 118) suggests, "but because it is good.

98. Fishbane 2008, xiii. There is a danger in studying with others, as Harold Innis appreciated. Recall that for Innis "talk" could destroy the possibility of intellectual contemplation; in fact, Watson (2007, 182) points out, "Innis ironically associated the silence of reading, writing, and thought, far more than the sound of public debates and pronouncements, with the oral tradition." Angus (1997, 64) suggests that "two major aspects of orality are relevant to its contemporary critical function: the role of memory and the central importance of the concrete situation in the here and now."

99. Weil (1947) 2002, 128. Weil regarded attention, Thibon ([1947] 2002, xxv) pointed out, as more important than will. Jersak (2012, 19) suggests that "Weil's 'attention' unfolds in five stages: (i) ascent, (ii) arrest, (iii) attention, (iv) awakening, and (v) activation," adding that activation means returning to the cave (36). "In other words, *only by returning to the cave do we fully escape the cave*" (37). Through the particular one can attune to the universal.

100. Davis and Roper 2009b, 832. Such sustained attention suspends one's personal purposes, encouraging a transparency that opens one to alterity. "In turning us out from ourselves towards the exterior," Grant told those in attendance during his 1975–76 graduate seminar, "it empties our spirit of the purposes of the self.... Attention empties us of these purposes and therefore leads us to decreation" (829; see also 823).

101. But maybe not every text, as at one point Grant makes clear that it is "impossible to reach any conception of transcendence through scientific activity, because by definition science deals with what is immanent" (Davis 2002b, 26).

102. Marion (2012, 163) writes: "The Eucharist requires of whoever approaches it a radical conceptual self-critique and charges him with renewing his norms of thought. We will attempt to show this with regard to one precise and fundamental case: the application of the Eucharist of the concept of 'presence.'" Marion's association of presence with ritual (for Christians a sacred rite) reminds that study encourages "self-critique" as it invites one to renew or reform one's "norms of thought." Allowing Grant to become present to you through studying his texts—and through my citations of those texts here—transports him from a time gone by to now.

103. Weil (1947) 2002, 120. Reminiscent of the icon, Weil writes that the past when present in its "purity," is "time colored with eternity…. There we have beauty" (175). Rocha (2017, 110) reports: "Beauty saved me and showed me, again, the invisible face of God." Invoking the title of his book, Rocha admonishes us: "Instead of speaking the truth, pure and simple, speak beautifully. Beyond sterile data and information, offer the truth that can only be known through love and loving" (8).

104. Weil (1947) 2002, 120.

105. Davis and Roper 2009b, 557. "Particulars," Grant said, "are beings which partake of universals" (Davis and Roper 2005b, 689). Referencing Heidegger in her study of Grant, O'Donovan (1984, 109–10) writes: "The *particularity* of Being's self-revelation in language is what determines human existence as radically finite, temporal, historical. The finality of the trans-subjective mediation of language is at the core of Heidegger's understanding of history as 'fate.' It is language that gives the thought of individuals their destinies; words are 'fateful' above all else." As iconographic, can language not only represent house arrest but also point to parole?

106. Eternity is implied in Grant's sure sense of historical contingency, embedded in the ethical question: "How will it be best to live in a society on the further side of industrial growth? Those of us who have been conscious of living in North America have known what it is to live within industrial growth…. The situation in which we find ourselves seems obvious: we are faced with calamities concerning population, resources, and pollution if we pursue those polices (here designated as industrial growth) which have increasingly dominated societies over the last centuries" (Davis and Roper 2009b, 281). Here Grant demonstrates he has his feet firmly planted on earth but knows it, as one eye is focused on infinity.

107. Within a modernity structured by a "technologically mediated rationalization," Doane (2003, 85) appreciates, "the lure of contingency is that it seems to offer a way out, an anchoring point for the condensation of utopian desires. It proffers itself as a way out of systematicity—both that of a tightly regulated classical system and that of its vaguely oppressive abstract analysis." She names statistics as "one form, in modernity, of the project of making the contingent legible" (87), but statistics seems to me an abstract erasure of specificity.

108. "For Augustine," Capelle (2005, 120) explains, "this non-coincidence [of the mind with itself] makes possible two dispositions of the spirit *curare* (*Bekümmerstsein*): man can choose between two directions: he can turn away from good; or he can actively listen to that which inhabits him, exceeds him, and constitutes his memory."

109. Sibley 2006, 97.

110. Throughout I have noticed that Grant's affirmations of an idea or activity originate in a specific situation and a particular time, a structure of double consciousness that depends upon attentiveness outside what confronts him at the moment. An instance of this double consciousness surfaces in his praise of his colleague James Doull, who, Grant tells us, "never reduced his study of the past to antiquarianism. Although a remarkable and careful student of the past, he has always known that philosophy is an activity practiced now, and that its end is far higher than that of scholarship" (Davis and Roper 2009b, 550). Like Grant, Doull was attuned to the transcendent because he was historically attentive.

111. While "[p]atristic teaching puts us perpetually on guard against any confusion of the incarnation with the materiality of the visible," Mondzain (2005, 175) notes. She

also writes: "The corporeal reality of the sacred is corporeal reality in that it is sacred, in that it is the object of a scopic exchange where the body only allows itself to be seen gloriously and miraculously" (177). Referencing the iconoclastic controversy, Mondzain concludes: "Considering that the Byzantine debate was centered on the incarnation, it must be acknowledged that for both camps, the icon was situated on the side of the body" (178). If modernity is an age of idolatry, can the body become iconographic?

112.   Davis and Roper 2009b, 387. Matter may be our guide—Dewey could concur—but perhaps as the icon references both itself and what it cannot in material form represent but merely gesture toward, a matter of, as Angus (2006, 348) poetically puts it, "[i]ntellect reaching towards flesh, flesh opening toward intellect; one teaching philosophical, the other religion."

113.   For Grant, too, I suspect, as implied in his 1978 observation that the "interdependence of love and knowledge is most clearly manifest when we try to understand what it is to love—(and it must be remembered that the love of justice is what all human beings are primarily called to)" (Davis and Roper 2009b, 387). Recognizing what one is fitted for occurs within sexual encounter too.

114.   Cayley 1995, 8.

115.   After the ancient Greeks, O'Donovan (1984, 100) points out, Grant conceived of "contemplation [as] a way of surrender to natural necessity; it finds meaning in the constraints of what is given." As the sentence in the main text implies, I am more aligned with psychoanalysis, wherein such contemplation and meaning found are in the service of unknotting the past and allow the contorted present to dissolve into a freer future. In the disappearance of contemplation Grant discerned—as O'Donovan puts the matter—"the loss of all human pursuits that transcend the technological" (91). On that point our view of contemplation coincides.

116.   Conducting oneself "as if" is hardly the only sleight-of-hand one commits, as behaving as if one will live through the day is a baseline assumption of many who do not suffer terminal illnesses, starvation, military or terrorist threat. In thinking about Nietzsche and historicism, Grant concludes that the latter communicates that "[t]here is no thought that man can ever possess, which will not prove to be in need of radical revision.... We cannot love on the basis of the purely personal and relative character of our principles" (Davis and Roper 2009b, 974–5). Of course we can, and we do. It is indeed the "personal" and "relative character of our principles" that implies alterity, yes even alterity, and makes our attunement to it so crucial.

117.   "Western civilization has two sources," Grant tells Cayley (1995, 141), "one saying the highest human act is contemplation, the other saying the highest human act is charity." The idea that these two conjoin in a synthesis is explored in several secondary sources; it is the title of Kaethler's (2009) study. "Mediation, according to Weil," Kaethler notes, "is central to the synthesis between Athens and Jerusalem" (92). Juxtaposition might be a more apt term than synthesis, as mediation—the space of the icon—occludes neither here nor eternity but invites one to enter. And elsewhere during the Cayley interview the two concepts remain two: "Revelation doesn't teach you many things," Grant tells Cayley (1995, 62), "but it teaches you the end for men.... Yes, and it also puts something higher than philosophy: it puts charity higher than contemplation. I think there's no getting away from this, that Christianity is in some sense a break with Plato." Strauss too saw no synthesis, for

him between philosophy (Athens) and faith (Jerusalem); see Havers 2006, 124. Recall Angus's (2006, 343) argument that Grant's attempt at synthesis fails.

118. "Now what the believer in transcendence would say," Grant explained, "is that this unity which we seek we can neither know in principle nor in detail. To put it in theological terms, God's essence is unknowable.... This is the idea that the One or the Good or God is beyond knowledge" (Davis and Roper 2009b, 953). On other occasions Grant insisted that we can—must—know, e.g., his condemnation of abortion and euthanasia.

119. Discussing the widely held view in the United States that corporate leaders have not only the business savvy but also the "moral status" to successfully solve "public school problems," Shipps (2000, 97–8) reviewed three theories that, "according to business ethicists, characterize the ethical aspirations and behaviour of corporate leaders": (1) the relatively unusual belief that "corporations have an ethical duty to ameliorate social problems"; (2) the so-called stakeholder view that businesses have an ethical responsibility to their customers, employees, suppliers, and, occasionally, to society at large (e.g., avoiding environmental degradation)"; and, after Milton Friedman, (3) the "Friedmanite" non-ethics, wherein business is held to have no ethical responsibility of any kind. In the United States, teachers have been made responsible for student learning, a scale of "accountability" spared parents and, for that matter, priests (for the souls of their parishioners).

120. Smith (1983, 83) suggests: "Irresponsibility is hopelessly bad; but responsibility is, at best, inadequately good."

121. Lipari 2014, 50.

122. Lipari 2014, 50.

123. Or "polymodal," as Lipari (2014, 51) prefers. Emphasizing listening, Lipari affirms "harmonic attunement" (182) and "the sounds of alterity" (183). "The answer to the call of conscience is not a speaking," she concludes, "but a listening. It is, moreover, a *listening otherwise* that suspends the willfulness of self- and foreknowledge in order to receive the singularities of the alterity of the other" (185).

124. Lipari 2014, 176.

125. Penelhum (1983, 97) accents the Christian's "autonomy of moral decision," stressing that not only does Jesus teach "that one has to use one's own powers of moral discernment to decide what God commands for us and what he does not," but "for our conduct to be accepted in God's sight it is not even necessary that we should think of our actions in the context of God's command at all." Penelhum adds: "With these inner springs toward an insistence on moral autonomy, Christianity contains within it a major thrust toward the secularization of its moral teachings" (97). Maybe modernity emerges from Jerusalem *and* Athens? There seems a "synthesis" on this point, namely the situated character of ethical action. Magrini (2017, 182) argues "there are no absolute or objective ethical principles that can be gleaned from or established through Socratic questioning. There can't be 'universalizable' ethical norms (agent-neutral prescriptive norms) because these norms are always dependent on agent-relative conditions, situations, and consensus."

126. Penelhum (1983, 95) scoffs at the idea that "Christian morality is a morality of simple obedience to divine commands," adding that the "authority of any allegedly divine command comes from the moral correctness of what is commanded, instead of the correctness of the command being guaranteed by the statement that it comes from the

gods" (96). This teaching is associated with Jesus who, Penelhum suggests, insisted that "moral action is not a mode of self-protection, but an open-ended risk; and one of its risks is that you cannot read off detailed answers to your individual moral dilemmas from previously existing commandments" (96). Penelhum concludes: "For Christianity teaches the need for every man to use his own moral judgement even in the application of rules that are thought to have a religious source" (97).

127. For a summary, see Smith 2014 and Wang 2014. "Perhaps not surprisingly," Lipari (2014, 99) reminds, "spiritual traditions and practices are some of the last places that cultivate and preserve...some form of meditative or contemplative practice for sustaining the kind of silence required for deep listening to the ineffable and the incomprehensible. Similarly, many world religions, from Vedic to Baha'i, find in listening a means of spiritual development." Listening is here a metaphor as well as means of attunement, Aoki's bridge (that is not a bridge) to the transcendent.

128. Angus 2013, 63.

129. Dewey ([1934] 1962, 9) was alert to the dangers that dogmatism—including religious dogmatism—pose to (not only secular) open-mindedness, alleging that "religions now prevent, because of their weight of historic encumbrances, the religious quality of experience from coming to consciousness and finding the expression that is appropriate to present conditions, intellectual and moral." Obedience, like faith, can enable understanding. Or it can foreclose it, if attunement is skewed. While not necessarily thinking spiritually, Lipari (2014, 8) suggests "misunderstanding is not only an inescapable aspect of communication, it is, moreover, both valuable and indispensable." She explains that "misunderstanding opens the doorway to the ethical relation by inspiring (or frustrating) us to listen more closely to others, to inquire more deeply into their differences, and to question our own already well-formed understandings of the world." I am suggesting that remembering misunderstanding as an ever-present possibility can keep a critical questioning in one's efforts to comprehend revelation through attunement. Obedience requires keeping an open and critical mind.

130. Angus 2013, 63.

131. Davis and Roper 2009b, 305.

132. Revelation is for me incremental, clues noticed here and there, punctuating the steady stream of experience, but "revelation" can, as Trilling (1972, 90) notes, take "place suddenly, in a flash."

133. "[W]hile many of us think we must understand in order to feel compassion," Lipari (2014, 182) points out, "the engagement with alterity instructs that I may not, in fact, be able to understand. Events and experience may be unimaginable to me, beyond my comprehension."

134. "Negative theology," Sibley (2008, 128) summarizes, "while acknowledging biblical theology, focuses on the limitations of temporal existence in an effort to dissociate those limitations from men's claims to possess knowledge of the eternal and from their use of that knowledge to satisfy their selfish desires. In this way, negative theology seeks to place limits on man's doing and making by pointing out that the tension between the temporal and the transcendent and thereby offering the possibility of the experience of the divine."

135. Pinar 2015c. "Visceral interiority itself," Mondzain (2005, 43) asserts, "prepares the way for the enigma of the inscription of the uncircumscribable."

136. Nagatomo 1992, 190. Mondzain (2005, 48) suggests: "Let us call existential wisdom every act of interpretation and adaptation to circumstances that chooses never to separate thought from life, or the concept from the flesh that makes it manifest. It is always exemplary in method, but never in the content of what it does or decides in each circumstance."

137. "But texts do not teach on their own; neither does life. There is no mere matter of fact," Fishbane (2008, 83) reminds.

138. That safe—subjective, physical—place we can call home, a "fundamental existential condition" Pérez-Gómez (2016, 6) terms it, "even when [we are] separated by global technological civilization from an innate sense of place," a "pressing" and "profound" point made graphic and tragic by images of refugees fleeing Syria and Afghanistan and elsewhere, refugees whose homes have become uninhabitable, even destroyed.

139. Contemplation involves detachment in the service of understanding, for Grant, in the service of solidarity with the suffering of others (see Athanasiadis 2001, 149).

140. Referencing both Pasolini and Roland Barthes, Annovi (2017, 125) enables one to understand how subjective reconstruction can constitute political intransigence within late modernity: "For Barthes, there is no way for the author to resist and survive power other than to constantly shift ground, just as for Pasolini the author's performance must be a 'continuous struggle' through 'permanent invention' and, consequently, constant self-reinvention." In this sense, subjective reconstruction can be not only moral improvement but function as political intransigence as well, allowing one to cast Grant—like Pasolini—as a "living protest" (11).

141. John Graham (1924–1990) was a professor of economics at Dalhousie. His wife, Nita Graham (1933–), was a former student of Grant's. Christian (1996d, 247n1) describes them as "very close friends."

142. Christian 1996d, 246.

143. Fishbane (2008, 113) acknowledges "the need to attune oneself to the specifics of the moment."

144. I am reminded of Jane Addams's sense of the subjective necessity of social settlements, as well as their "objective value" (Pinar 2009, 67).

145. "The withdrawal does not distress as much as ignorance of it threatens," Marion (2001, 128) cautions, adding: "For man then forgets what remains most proper to him, in withdrawal, namely, 'poetically to dwell' in it." Grant's poetic indwelling might have been inspired by ancient spiritual exercises. Referencing Pierre Hadot, Vries (2005, 76–7) notes "the tradition of spiritual exercises expresses the need for the self to turn away from everydayness." Kaethler (2009, 41) comments: "Plato, according to Grant, contends that the best politician is the person who contemplates the Good." Immersion in immediacy punctuated by withdrawal toward eternity: lingering in between could be the poetic indwelling Marion mentions.

146. It is a space often described as meditative. In contrast to calculation, "meditative thinking," Lipari (2014, 86) suggests, "is a pondering and a questioning that is not attached to a particular perspective." Barry Cooper (1990, 103) characterizes Grant's thinking as meditative, as acknowledging that "the purpose of thought was to open the eyes of the mind" or, in Christian terms, "to prepare the soul for intuitions of the perfection of God." For a study of such space as curriculum inquiry, see Kumar 2013.

147. Cayley 1995, 6.

148. It bears emphasizing that this is a spiritual not a sexual idea, as abused children—and not only girls (Gartner 1999)—often report that through abuse they learned their bodies were not their own.

149. "[I]f our ears were ten times more sensitive," Kittler (2013, 170) notes, "we would hear matter roar—and presumably nothing else." Surely reality is, in part, dependent upon our capacities for apprehension.

150. Dewey ([1934] 1962, 9) drew a distinction between "religion" and "religious," writing that "a religion...always signifies a special body of beliefs and practices having some kind of institutional organization. In contrast, the adjective 'religious' denotes nothing in the way of a specifiable entity, either institutional or as a system of belief." While "spiritual" shorn of its institutional and historical forms and traditions has been criticized—Wexler (2013, 15) dismisses it a form of "consumerism"—it has also been endorsed; see Huebner (1999, 342, 344).

151. "[W]hatever introduces genuine perspective is religious," Dewey ([1934] 1962, 24) wrote, "not that religion is something that introduces it. There can be no doubt...of our dependence upon forces beyond our control." We are obligated, he continued, "to insist upon the capacity of mankind to strive to direct natural and social forces to humane ends. But unqualified absolutistic statements about the omnipotence of such endeavours reflect egoism rather than intelligent courage" (24–5).

152. Christian 1996d, 210–11.

153. Perhaps. But perhaps the ride is rocky and one must toss aside what one doesn't need: decreation. "The ab-solute dissolves the tie that ties it to our thought," Marion (2001, 141) suggests, "it undoes itself, whence our undoing, which, rigorously, is attuned to the ab-solute as such and, in its undoing, honours the ab-solute."

154. While his terminology differs, Dewey (1922, 190) would seem to concur with Grant, writing: "Invariant virtue appears to be as mechanical as uninterrupted vice, for true excellence changes with conditions. Unless character rises to overcome some new difficulty or conquer some temptation from an unexpected quarter we suspect its grain is only a veneer."

155. Cayley 1995, 177. For Sibley (2008, 131), "Grant's negative theology, his rejection of a theology of glory, both contains and embodies his metaphysical alternative, as well as his epistemological and pedagogical challenges to modernity. Grant seeks to bring his readers to a remembrance of those animating experiences of eternity by which men once defined their purposes and meanings." Among those "animating experiences of eternity" might have been attunement, with its acknowledgement of the absolute but maybe bridgeable gap between humanity and divinity. Caputo (2005, 105) comments: "If the God of negative theology is called unknown, this is meant as a compliment, as praise, and it is to be taken strictly in the sense of the cloud of unknowing and the learned ignorance." Learned ignorance remains learned does it not? And to discern a "cloud of unknowing" demands apprehension, even incipient comprehension.

156. Cayley 1995, 177. "[D]espite his view that Christianity and Platonic philosophy are finally at one in their account of the Good," Angus (2006, 361) explains, "there is a *tension* between what is given in these sources.... Thus, it would seem that George Grant had an independent commitment to philosophy in order to diagnose this tension." That tension would seem to ease when philosophy becomes subservient to revelation, as Athanasiadis (2006, 259) implies: "Philosophy or thought, then, is second-order reflection on a more first-order experience of the Good."

157. Ward 1990, 94.

158. Mondzain 2005, 159.

159. "Our lives are thus grounded in worldly phenomena," Fishbane (2008, 14) acknowledges, "but there is conceivably something more that we may hope to intuit and bring to thoughtfulness." That something "more" is the "spiritual," at least as Huebner (1999, 344) suggests: "This going beyond, this 'moreness' of life, this transcendent dimension is the usual meaning of 'spirit' and 'spiritual.'"

160. "Simone Weil is certainly gnostic," Grant writes Joan O'Donovan in 1985, "but she is also agnostic; all her writing is also about the absence of God" (Christian 1996d, 351). Is this an instance of double consciousness? Of proceeding as if? Or is God's absence an expression of divine presence? For Jean-Luc Marion, that last question is to be answered affirmatively, but for me it remains entirely speculative.

161. For Dewey ([1934] 1962, 27) "Any activity pursued in behalf of an ideal end against obstacles and in spite of threats of personal loss because of conviction of its general and enduring value is religious in quality."

162. Recall Grant's objection at McMaster to research as the summoning of objects for scrutiny, e.g., classification, quantification. "[T]he right principles I must seek to know," Grant emphasized, "cannot be derived from the world as object, but only from the world as subject" (Davis 2002b, 429).

163. Davis and Roper 2009b, 184.

164. In "its alteration of the temporal, perceptual and social constitution of the practical world," Angus (1987, 110) points out, technology "also affects the ethical subject.... It is not that technology requires us to choose this over that value, rather, it cuts the ground out from under the subject presupposed by humanist ethics."

165. A term, as I learned preparing for the next chapter, with several meanings and a long history.

166. In his essay review of Kwame Anthony Appiah's As If: Idealization and Ideals, Thomas Nagel points (2018, 35) out that the book's title and theme references Hans Vaihinger (1852–1933), whose The Philosophy of "As If" (1911) suggested that, in Nagel's summary, generative thinking often depends on "idealizations" or what Viahinger termed "fictions," an instance of which is Adam Smith's proposal that human beings are motivated mostly by self-interest. While Vaihinger appreciates the utility of idealization, Nagel continues, he was also aware of its risks, reminding readers that fidelity to a concept of truth remains necessary. Nagel acknowledges "that our best understanding may come from theories or models that are not strictly true, and some of which may contradict each other," a fact one should not allow to "undermine our belief in the existence of the truth" (38). My point is that thinking and acting "as if" allows us to understand (however partially, momentarily) what otherwise we might not, a view echoing Grant's invocation of Credo ut intelligam.

167. On occasion Grant termed transcendence "a dangerous word," Christian and Grant (1998a, 26) report, explaining that "Grant makes it clear that the most important knowledge is given us in the ordinary occurrences of daily life, and through the concrete more readily than through philosophical abstractions."

168. Like Grant, Fishbane (2008, 12) wonders: "But is there more?" Like Grant, Fishbane appreciates that any affirmative answer must acknowledge "what we know and experience as moderns, or relegate this to some separate cognitive sphere" (13). And like Grant, Fishbane proceeds by "paying close attention to the concrete realities of

our lives, as we experience them on earth; and by rethinking how we constitutes our daily existence through thought or action and how we fill in or explain unsettling events that occur all around" (13).

169. Grant spoke of the "absolute distance between the necessary and the good" (Davis 2002b, 486). "Grant's thinking always turned to the mystery at the heart of things," Dart (2006, 24) observes, "the God of Love whom we could sense but never fully know."

170. Not only between the eternal and the everyday, but within the everyday too, as Fishbane (2008, 173) acknowledges: "Things come and go with no apparent sense, and the true interconnections between things elude and mock our vain pretensions at wisdom." Rocha (2017, 193) writes: "The finite cannot grasp the infinite."

171. Fishbane 2008, 145. "Our aversion to silence," Lipari (2014, 2) suggests, "masks our failure to listen in the same way it disables our ability to listen." And for her, "listening" is "both an ethical relation and a way of being in the world" (3).

172. Davis and Roper 2009b, 948. "What might have driven Grant into solitude," Greenspan (1990, 5) suggests, "is the speed with which philosophy becomes kitsch. He lived to see his ideas, the critique of technology, become fashionable." As Lee (1983, 6) quips: "[Y]et it is better to speak in silence than squeak in the gab of the age." Still, Grant did speak, perhaps inspired by his faith, as Weeks (1990, 83) suggests: "[G]rant did not ultimately disagree with some form of Christian proclamation and that he agreed that such practice was central to Christianity even when he was in his most gnostic times."

173. Davis and Roper 2005b, 741. Unconnected to the Good, attuned only to appetite, morality becomes, Grant knew, "just a matter of opinion or subjective. You have your values, I have mine" (Davis and Roper 2009b, 1056).

174. Davis and Roper 2005b, 741.

175. See Aoki (1981) 2005, 228.

176. Lints (2015, 38) insists that "the chasm between Creator and creature is not so great that God cannot bridge it." While we cannot bridge the chasm from our end, might we attune ourselves to it?

177. Referencing Heidegger's historicizing of humanity, Grant complains (it seems) that if one is "a totally historical being...[then one must] act resolutely in the face of the knowledge of his own finiteness in a particular historical situation" (Davis and Roper 2009b, 1021). That sounds right to me, as such knowledge depends upon attunement to extra-historical reality. Moreover, the sentence seems to describe Grant's life exactly.

178. Davis and Roper 2009b, 543.

179. Davis and Roper 2009b, 543. Exactly, as creativity is called for when occupying the gap, the space of non-coincidence between what is and what is not. On another occasion, however, Grant disdains creativity as an absolute right (but not as an option within obedience): "I have never felt that repugnance so greatly as in thinking about Nietzsche this year. Nothing could be more repugnant than the doctrine of human beings as creative—indeed of philosophy itself as creative" (1010).

180. Almost invoking the concept of idolatry, Dewey ([1934] 1962, 54) cautions: "A humanistic religion, if it excludes our relation to nature, is pale and thin, as it is presumptuous, when it takes humanity as an object of worship."

181. Radhakrishnan (2008, 67), for instance, speaks of a "double consciousness that transforms the givenness of history into a project of agential intervention." That

description might fit Alain Locke during the late 1930s; Stewart (2018, 769) summarizes: "Locke decided to believe in a positive double consciousness—that he could will himself to be both queer and race conscious in America, and succeed." O'Donovan (1990, 139) provides a spiritual version: "Thus, there is expressed in the biblical vision of creation a double teleology: a double directedness of every creature to God as its transcendent end, and to the perfection of its form as its immanent."

182. "Consciousness is 'always-already' differentiated," Caputo (1987, 130) emphasizes, adding: "Difference is not the external, the accidental, but a kind of a priori which inhabits things from the start."

183. Bergner (1999, 221) points out that while Du Bois's term became "standard shorthand to describe African-American subjectivity, the condition of double consciousness remains relatively undertheorized." Hazel Carby (1998, 37) reminds that the concept, as expressed in the first chapter of *The Souls of Black Folk*, is a "product of a world," in that it has allowed the black man no (quoting Du Bois) "true self-consciousness but only lets him see himself through the revelation of the other world" ([1903] 1969, 45). Carby (1998, 37) argues for a revision of the concept to acknowledge that "gender is an ever-present, though unacknowledged, factor in this theory," that racial self-consciousness is also "a gendered self-consciousness." The primacy of gender is also evident in (white) feminist theory too. Oliver (2004, 36), for instance, reminds that "notions of debilitating alienation and double consciousness, and resistance to them, may be inflected by gender." Inflected indeed, and also blurred with other "objects" of consciousness, the multiplicity, even contradictoriness, of which can carry challenges. Reflecting on Du Bois, Posnock (1998, 156) concludes: "Even for a man who prized 'double consciousness,' the pressure of multiple allegiances— to Negro Americans, to America, to anti-imperialism, to patriotism, to equal rights, to nationalism, to Pan-Africanism—proved almost overwhelming."

184. Weil (1947) 2002, 165. Probably neither Weil nor Grant would appreciate my association here with Barthes who, Shatz (2018, 12) reports, "harboured a profound bias against the spoken word," quoting Barthes's definition of fascism as "any regime that not only prevents one from speaking but above all obliges one to speak" (12).

185. For its expression in curriculum studies, see Wang 2004.

186. Fishbane 2008, 83.

187. While knowledge—obtained and reconstructed through study and the educational experience it can afford—is indispensable to understanding, it is insufficient in itself, as Grant himself makes plain when complaining about "intellectual Protestants," who, he alleges, "so worshipped 'education' as almost to believe that knowledge by itself could provide men with salvation" (Davis 2002b, 30). Not salvation, but understanding (including of what is at stake in such concepts) can be pursued via education. Grant seems to agree, at least in 1953 when worrying that American Protestantism risks "rely[ing] on faith and forget[ting] the duty to understand" (49).

188. Articulation and explication accompany attunement—certainly biblically as the word of God—but also among the pre-Socratics, to whom Lipari (2014, 68) traces the word *logos*, referencing not only Heraclitus but also Epicharmus, whom she quotes: "[T]he *logos* guides men and keeps them always on the straight and narrow. A man has reasoning, but there is also a divine *logos*. Human reasoning is born from the divine *logos*." For Grant, too, reasoning can seem sacred, if it is enlightened by love and faith. Christian (1992, 56), however, seems to bifurcate the two: "Reason,

powerful though it is, is limited to that which lies within the realm of Being. Because the Good is beyond being, it is apprehensible only through faith."

189. "In our modern 'subjectivity,'" Grant complains, "we are all entitled to see anything the way we want to see it" (Davis and Roper 2009b, 453–4). In the contrasting "classical" view, Grant points out, "freedom" meant "the ability to live by practical principles and not simply to be at the disposal of varying passions" (Davis 2002b, 277). Our capacity for cognition, for Grant, is "not simply an instrument which helps us to get what we want," but affords us "with the idea of a highest good and makes us desire that good wherein not only this or that desire will be satisfied but in which that very unity which is ourselves will find its completeness. Freedom is, therefore, the gift of truth" (277)

190. Heaven 2006, 304.

191. Athanasiadis 2001, 232.

192. Athanasiadis 2001, 232.

193. Athanasiadis 2001, 232.

194. Athanasiadis 2001, 218.

195. With the simulation (e.g., destruction) of politics as "reality TV" in late modernity, activism risks amounting to little more than a subspecies of innovation, the mechanical reproduction of the "new." Benedetti (2005, 209) understands the command of innovation as a double bind: "It is useless to continue the series of innovations now that the 'law' of innovation is already familiar, now that it is known that sooner or later we will all be surpassed and kicked out in our turn…. If you innovate, you will soon be made part of the future norm, but if you don't innovate, you are already part of the norm of the past. In short, every possible route seems to be blocked off in this jam." She concludes: "Late-modernity is littered with double binds of this kind" (209). While activism is obligatory, it seems useless, except as expression of inner conviction, unconcerned with effects. One acts because to do so is right not because it is effective.

196. Benedetti 2005, 209. Not for all of course: Horowitz (1990, 77 reminds: "In my review of *Lament* ("Tories, Socialists and the Demise of Canada," *Canadian Dimension*, May-June 1965) I strongly criticized Grant precisely for his failure to call for action." While then sixties activism was underway, not a decade later the space contracted, as Atwood ([1972] 2012, 278) appreciated: "A successful revolution in the present is not imaginable."

197. Sibley 2008, 116.

198. Sibley 2008, 116.

199. Sibley 2008, 115. Religion, Fierlbeck (2006, 92) observes, has played an important role in the history of Canada's political culture, once explicitly but now indirectly. While "the Church in contemporary Canada plays little direct role in influencing the current direction of policy-making," Fierlbeck explains, "its historical legacy in Canadian political thought is considerable. The first reason underlying the import of religion in Canadian politics is precisely that the political elites and the traditional social establishment in Canada were irretrievably connected with the Anglican church (also known as the Church of England)" (93). Recall that Grant was no stranger to that church: Christian (1996s, 180) reports that "[o]n 31 March 1956 George was confirmed a member of the [Anglican] church and Sheila was also admitted…. It was not until the abortion question came to the fore in the 1970s that George again began to question his denominational affiliation."

200. Davis and Roper 2009b, 569. "For classical thinkers," Athanasiadis (2001, 129) reminds, "the highest virtue was the life of contemplation rather than action."

201. Davis and Roper 2009b, 180. Even within the Second World War Grant worried that "politics" was finally a form of willfulness, asserting power to install one's preferences for another's. Admitting to his mother in early 1942 that he had been "for three days...on the point of suicide," Grant wondered if the triumph of the Allies would enable humanity to become "much nearer to God than the other alternatives?... We have just presumed that our standards fit others, that ours are best, that other people can find their God through our way of life. *We have created God in the image of our own wills*" (Christian 1996d, 95; emphasis added).

202. Reimer 1990, 120. "Where Greek thought emphasized contemplative reason," Sibley (2008, 153) summarizes, "biblical thought focused on acting in the world, reworking it in conformity with what was assumed to be God's will."

203. Christian 1996d, 371–2. Angus (1997, 85) points out that "Grant's choice [of lament over activism], which retains a respect for politics, nevertheless becomes increasingly divorced from action, and for this very reason it is the most significant course of philosophical questioning that we possess."

204. Christian 1996d, 243.

205. Christian 1996d, 210. While affirming overall Grant's theology, Athanasiadis (2001, 248; see also 52) is critical of his references to contemporary Protestant theologians, to neo-orthodox theologians in particular; he suggests his comments "reveal a significant lack of understanding.... In speaking about Christian hope, they did not see it as a human possibility or an inevitable outcome of history, nor did they subscribe to the progressive doctrine of providence.... They, too, came to experience salvation as rooted in the cross." In Grant, O'Donovan (1984, 161) perceives "a three-way tension: between the Bible, liberal historicism, and classical natural law."

206. Penelhum 1983, 101.

207. Magrini 2017, 127.

208. And beauty, Love (2007, 8) implies, may be found in the past. The "future" for which Pater yearns, she suggests, "will be the result of reanimating the dead" (8). Mondzain (2005, 59) suggests: "Beauty, like the lie, has the advantage of seduction and emotional arousal, and such weapons must only be used by the hand and mouth inspired by the grace of the Holy Spirit."

209. Davis and Roper 2009b, 392. "The fulfillment of love," O'Donovan (1984, 127) suggests, "is assimilation to the Good, to God, through adoring contemplation."

210. In iconographic terms, Ouspensky (1982, 35) writes, "beauty is holiness, and its radiance the participation of the creature in Divine Beauty." Athanasiadis (2001, 90) puts it this way: "Beauty is a divine snare for this drawing out of self."

211. Weil (1947) 2002, 150. Bradshaw (1996, 225) underscores that "[t]ruth, beauty, and goodness—the three things that Grant cites as objects of veneration which ought to guide considerations of justice—have been eclipsed by the will to power."

212. Christian 1990, 194.

213. Christian 1990, 197.

214. Cayley 1995, 185. Benedetti (2005, 42) confirms as she expands Grant's critique: "[M]ost modern works have abandoned this ideal of beauty. The ugly, the discordant, the slipshod, the casual can just as well aspire to being valorized artistically as long as there is a poetics capable of giving them an artistic meaning, as, for example, a

certain idea of realism, or of expressionism, or of alienation, or of experimentation."

215. See Christian 1990, 198.

216. Christian 1990, 198. In the second and third decades of the twentieth century in the United States, Alain Locke, as Stewart (2018, 334) reminds, "sought to encourage Howard's students to break with the society that lived only in the material present, and instead live boldly for their spiritual selves by cultivating a self, borrowing from the self-indulgence of Walter Pater, that viewed Beauty, Justice, and Truth as its highest personal goals." That judgment of Pater—and, implicitly, of Locke and Grant, insofar as each beauty, justice, and truth as aspirational and reciprocally related— seems overstated.

217. Love 2007, 58.

218. Love 2007, 58.

219. "Throughout his writing," Love (2007, 59) points out, "Pater evinces a fascination with the disappearing subject."

220. Recall that for Weil, Thibon ([1947] 2002, xxiii) notes, decreation is enacted "from within by love." For her, Thibon emphasizes, decreation was the "work" of "grace," not of one's "will" (xxiv). Maybe so, but surely being open to the "work of grace" requires willful attention or attunement.

221. "I spend a lot of my life in meetings with colleagues," Grant averred, "and to put it mildly, my intellect is not lit up by love" (Davis and Roper 2009b, 388).

222. Angus (1997, 230) notes that "time after time Grant met the challenge of speaking to the central political currents that have formed the country. For this he was marginalized by the intellectual establishment in Canada." Love (2007, 62) suggests that Pater's "experience of displacement leads him not only to a politics of camouflage and disappearance but also to a politics of deferral." Love quotes Pater: "Those who prosecute revolution have to violate again and again the instinct of reverence. That is inevitable, since after all progress is a kind of violence" (63). Grant could only concur.

223. Indeed, in an article, "The Drama of Negro Life," that appeared in the October 1926 issue of *Theatre Arts Monthly*, Alain Locke—Stewart (2018, 531) points out—"was resurrecting Du Bois's earlier, more complicated notion of Negro identity, 'double consciousness,' as potentially a positive, not a debilitating divided self, but a dialogic American. The Negro drama was become a means of revelation and reconciliation of the two sides of Negro/American identity."

224. "For Socrates," Angus (2006, 360) points out, "ignorance masquerading as knowledge is precisely what allows humans to turn away from the good. Ignorance, not of details but of that which is due to humans, cannot be forgiven. Or, more precisely, acceptance of ignorance, abandonment of the search for knowledge, is culpability itself." Ignorance of what is due ensures injustice; accepting such ignorance as knowledge could be construed as idolatry.

225. See Fanon 1967; Pinar 2011, 38–48. Referencing the preference of Hannah Arendt and Mary McCarthy for "solitude over solidarity," Phelan notes (2015, 147) that the "aloneness that Arendt and McCarthy cultivated entailed resensitizing" (148).

226. Love 2007, 25. "Pater's shy refusals," she adds, "give way to the antimodernism and the explicit homophobia and misogyny of Willa Cather" (25).

227. Love 2007, 57.

228. Like Christianity's adoration of Jesus, Love (2007, 57) suggests that "Pater's writings [are] dedicated to the figure of the victim: in this sense, he cultivates a modernist

aesthetic based not on violent transgression but rather on refusal and passivity." Redemption through affliction, one might remind, involves a profound refusal to accept the world as it is.

229. "Pater's withdrawal," Love (2007, 60) notes, can be decoded as a "renunciation of dominance. In Pater's case, such a willed act of self-overcoming can often have the air of a forced march." She adds: "In this sense, we may understand Pater's moment of ascesis not only as a withdrawal of the subject from the world but also a withdrawal of the world from the subject" (61).

230. Reimer 1978, 56; see also Cayley 1995, 24. "Contemplation, or understanding," Heaven (2006, 303) suggests, "is more fundamental than action. In fact, action is strictly secondary in the sense that intellectual virtue takes precedence over moral virtue." Whatever the sequence surely they are intertwined.

231. Reimer 1978, 55.

232. Davis and Roper 2009b, 907.

233. See Reimer 1978, 55. "The agentless action that Pater describes ('the moment of delicious recoil from the flood of water in summer heat') recalls," Love (2007, 58–9) suggests, "the dynamic that Eve Kosofsky Sedgwick identifies in her work on Henry James as 'queer performativity.' For Sedgwick, this term describes a combination of reticence and virtuosic stylistic performance; she traces this dynamic to the experience of queer childhood, with its combination of alienation, extreme self-consciousness, and lots of time for reading." Except for the period of his recuperation from the London bombings, Grant's life—including his childhood—seemed filled; somehow he made time to read.

234. For Grant, Rigelhof (2001, 115) reminds, protest was to be conducted with dignity.

235. "Even dissent is built into the system," Athanasiadis (2001, 162) observes.

236. Davis and Emberley 2000b, 166.

237. Davis and Emberley 2000b, 166. "There is a certain side of myself which can be seen as fighting that surrender," Grant suggested to his students, "or retreating before the surrender" (Davis and Roper 2009b, 986). He was here discussing the collapse of British and Catholic traditions of university education in Canada, but the political point—intransigence through withdrawal—remains.

238. Davis and Roper 2005b, 167. Given the historical moment, I am suggesting, quietism becomes a form of activism (and vice versa): like Pasolini, sheer survival—an echo of Atwood here—becomes a "living protest" (Annovi 2017, 11; see also 150).

239. "This is surely one of the complexities of life," Grant tells Schmidt (1978a, 17), "that those who are taken up with doing necessary and practical things just don't have the time to think through the central issues of their society." Or of their lives, he might have added.

240. Christian 1996d, 173.

241. Christian 1996d, 150.

242. "It seemed disingenuous for a figure as public as George Grant," Greenspan (1990, 1) reports, "to emphasize the solitude of the philosopher." Aside from the exhaustion that follows being in public, there is the interplay between private and public, as the one enables the other.

243. Davis and Roper 2009b, 566.

244. "First," Athanasiadis (2001, 40) explains, "the cross is the clearest revelation of God's distance from and judgment on the sin and evil in us and the world. This is reflected in the suffering, agony, and death of Jesus." He continues: "This leads to the second

component of the redemptive revelation of the cross: our inner preparation to receive it" (41). For Weil, you recall, that involved "decreation," akin to "self-shattering" and, more generally, "subjective reconstruction."

245. Davis and Roper 2009b, 566.

246. Cayley 1995, 12.

247. Reimer 1978, 56.

248. "If the historian acts on historical relativism," Grant knew, "he cannot be a historian. Why? The historical relativist, the man who sees the changes of values and principles as a panorama, stands absolutely outside of the historical process and violates it" (Davis and Roper 2009b, 975). While I can't share Grant's insistence that historicity requires an "absolute" transcendence, non-coincidence with history is clearly an epistemological prerequisite for writing history, and for becoming historical.

249. "By the beautiful," Grant explained to students, "I mean the image of the Good in the world" (Davis and Roper 2009b, 939). Sounding slightly like a spiritual version of Susan Sontag in *Against Interpretation*, Grant complains to Cayley (1995, 164) that the "great industries in the analysis of literature and the history of literature...seem to me to take one quite far, often, from the beauty of literature."

250. "We must not say the purpose of a beautiful work of art...lies outside itself," Grant appreciated, "Yet at the same time we must also say, always with the greatest hesitation and bewilderment, that it points beyond itself" (Davis and Roper 2009b, 436). In doing so, he suggested, "great art...show[s] the truth about reality" (452; see also 461). It becomes, in a certain sense, "iconic."

251. Mondzain 2005, 147.

252. Mondzain 2005, 142.

253. Mondzain 2005, 144.

254. Santner 2006, 45. Kittler (2013, 303) appreciates that "the essence of the human being involves, before all knowledge, moods."

255. Santner 2006, 45. "Originally," Pérez-Gómez (2016, 34) tells us, "*Stimmung* suggested a stable 'tunedness' of the mind, *the attunement of embodied consciousness*." During the Romantic period, he notes, "*Stimmung* became an explicit program for the arts, a means for humanity to seek new forms of attunement" (87), as curriculum—whose central subjects should include the arts—could become today.

256. Santner 2006, 45–6.

257. Feenberg 2010, 210.

258. Silverman 2009, 203. For Pérez-Gómez (2016, 144), "enactive understanding and embodied perception are crucial to our grasp of *Stimmung*."

259. Silverman 2009, 203.

260. Fishbane 2008, 155. And in ourselves: "[W]e know ourselves *through* the other, in embodied communication," Pérez-Gómez (2016, 228) points out, "and for which Skype on the computer screen is always a poor substitute."

261. Pérez-Gómez 2016, 15.

262. Pérez-Gómez 2016, 11.

263. Pérez-Gómez 2016, 16.

264. Pérez-Gómez 2016, 18.

265. Toews 2004, 56.

266. Toews 2004, 56. Interesting, in light of Grant's critique of immanentism (during his time with Hegel), William was also committed, Toews tells us, to "cleansing

university theological faculties of rationalists, liberals and pantheists—that is, of all proponents of 'immanent' interpretations of the sacred. In the 1830s he became especially interested in the struggle against Hegelian influence, which in his view combined the errors of both rationalism and pantheism" (59).

267. Toews 2004, 59. 2008

268. Toews 2004, 63. 2008

269. Pérez-Gómez 2016, 24.

270. Davis and Roper 2009b, 82–3.

271. In natural-law theory, Athanasiadis (2001, 114) notes, "reason, which is the means of deriving natural law, can lead us to know what is right." In "natural law as rational necessity, as specifiable good," O'Donovan (1984, 160) explains, one can know "that for which something is fitted." In my terms, reason renders intelligible what revelation reveals through attunement to the Good. Reason can convert apprehension to comprehension, thereby providing leadership or guidance. "True freedom is obedience of the reason and will to the good or God," Athanasiadis (2001, 87) clarifies. Elevating reason above translation—and the comprehension that it can provide— risks, I should think, idolatry, mistaking the world (and oneself) as self-enclosed.

272. Davis 2002b, 43. It is a view he repeats: "[R]eason, practical and theoretical, is the faculty by which man apprehends ultimate reality and that therefore that reality is supersensible" (177). In a conversation two months before his death, Grant told William Christian that "reason at its best is a kind of illumination" (Davis and Roper 2009b, 739). He was not only affirming reason, however, but cautioning us about it, too: "Reason in the deepest modern account of it teaches us to be atheists. Therefore, if for whatever causes we reject that, we must seek another account of reason than the modern" (Davis and Roper 2005b, 675).

273. At one point Grant speaks of the "divinity of reason" (Davis 2002b, 30). Discussing differences between Plato and Aristotle in 1953, Grant notes for each, humanity finds in reason that which is most akin to God. In this language, the word "freedom" means the "individual's acceptance, conscious and intelligent, of what he most truly is" (52).

274. Davis 2002b, 43.

275. "The encounter with the gods, the beyond-human forces of creation and destruction," Angus (2006, 359) notes, "throws the philosopher back to human experience and thought as the only available resource to determine right action." For Dewey (1922, 201) the very concept of "Right is only an abstract name for the multitude of concrete demands in action which others impress upon us, and of which we are obliged, if we would live to take some account." Taking account is one role of reason I should think. Nicholson (2006, 325) suggests that reason can become "a source of moral directives—indeed, as the illumination of existence. It is not merely our desires and inclinations that are fit to guide us, but above all our rational insight into what is right and good."

276. A subset of which is so-called critical thinking, assessed, remarkably, by standardized tests. In the United States, university freshmen and seniors at approximately 200 institutions take the College Learning Assessment Plus each year. The test, presumably, measures "how much better they get at learning to think" (Belkin 2017, A1). At more than fifty percent of institutions, at least a third of seniors failed to make a cohesive argument or assess the quality of evidence in a document or interpret data

in a table. The reporter notes that critics of the exam have observed that disentangling cause and effect is complicated, and "students don't always try their hardest when they take the exam, since there is little at stake for them" (A10). Never mind the political scapegoating of educational institutions evident in the article's title—"Many Colleges Fail in Teaching How to Think"—this reductionistic conception of intelligence, and its reduction further by standardized assessment, mirrors modernity mutilation of reason.

277. Dewey (1934) 1962, 79. Dewey's definition differs from Grant's decrying of the progressive "intellect" as reduced to "a tool which can help one to do certain things in the world more efficiently" (Davis 2002b, 162). Grant accuses Dewey of theorizing education as an "adjustment to the lowest common denominator of desire" (169), but in the one Dewey book Grant cites, Dewey is clearly critical of such utilitarianism (see Dewey 1922, 118).

278. Grant knew that "at its heart, knowing (which is the essence of education) is not a political act" (Davis and Roper 2005b, 605).

279. Davis and Roper 2005b, 605.

280. Weil (1947) 2002, 157.

281. Kestenbaum 2002, 95.

282. Kestenbaum 2002, 95.

283. Kestenbaum 2002, 95.

284. Study, Lewis (2013, 17) suggests, can attune "us to the *significance of a loss of significance* in our technological age. For Lewis, such a loss—for Grant a sense of "deprival—can trigger concern for "im-potentiality," the Agambenian term he defines as "an active capability for not doing or not-being." (7) That seems to me to only invert the current compulsion to act—of which Grant was constantly critical—rather than transcend it.

285. "[R]eflection circles around non-coincidence and," Wiskus (2013, 5) observes, "thanks to the temporal dislocation, projects backward into perception what it had already formulated." In that sense, she continues, self-reflection can be characterized as "dynamic process of thought, attuned to non-coincidence" (5).

286. Kestenbaum 2002, 99.

287. Cayley 1995, 58. In his 1975–76 graduate seminar, Grant told students that Heidegger's "thinking without willing" resonates with Weil's conception, implying that it resonates with his own as well (Davis and Roper 2009b, 828).

288. "Waiting is no passive inactivity," Athanasiadis (2006, 267) suggests, "but active charity wedded to contemplation and contemplation shaped by the transforming experience of sacred charity." Rowan Williams (2012, xvii) writes: "We, watching and waiting for Christ to come more fully to birth in us, are waiting for our lives to become 'iconic,' to show in their colour and line and movement how God acts, Christlike, in us."

289. Davis and Emberley 2000b, 61. Even the nation was not sacrosanct—that would be committing idolatry—but, he suggested, a "means of partaking in the eternal. But nevertheless we come upon that eternal justice through the mediation of particular traditions and the particular traditions of Canada in their wide diversity are worth loving and working for on the northern half of this contractual continent" (Davis and Roper 2009b, 419).

290. Fishbane 2008, xiii.

291.   Luxon 2013, 177. For Grant, Athanasiadis (2006, 262) suggests, the "purpose of speaking the truth, however, is not simply to expose the darkness for what it is, rather, exposing the darkness for what it is, Grant believes, is essential for cultivating the kind of ground out of which the experience of God can be authentic and true rather than false and idolatrous."

292.   Grant endorsed "moderation...tact in speech—saying certain things carefully and leaving other things unsaid" (Davis and Roper 2009b, 418). In the social sphere, tact and truth-telling are not mutually exclusive of course. In the private—especially within the self–self relation—"unrestrained speech" may, however, be a prerequisite to truth-telling and to the possibility of the subjective coherence Luxon mentions. In his first journal entry—October 21, 1942—Grant starts by explaining: "I decided to keep a journal, partly for the sake of recording events, but mostly for the practice in permanence it would give me, the discipline. So here it is; I don't know what caused the mood last night, but it was as if suddenly the sickness that had enveloped me since 1940 was over" (Christian 1996d, 99). The "sickness"—its trace, lifelong lament—starts with the Blitz. In mourning this trauma he links "discipline" with "permanence," reminiscent of Dewey's (1922, 16) reminder that "habits...constitute the self," not as "repetition" so much as "special sensitiveness or accessibility to certain classes of stimuli" (26)—and that having finally reached an emotional clearing could Grant record with candour his condition.

293.   Luxon 2013, 177. But not only, Craiutu (2017, 63) points out that "there can be no objective, eternally valid definition of constraint and liberty, since general rules, too, may sometimes be oppressive."

294.   So obviously tempting, since, as Knopff (1992, 63) observes, "the individual is constituted *qua* individual most obviously by his body."

295.   Luxon 2013, 196.

296.   Alford 2002, 44.

297.   For me the canonical summary remains Chodorow 1978.

298.   Alford 2002, 45.

299.   Alford 2002, 45.

300.   Pérez-Gómez 2016, 27.

301.   Alford 2002, 46.

302.   Alford 2002, 46.

303.   Lipari 2014, 6.

304.   Davis and Roper 2009b, 1080.

305.   Lipari 2014, 8.

306.   Lipari 2014, 9. The root of *Stimmung* in German (*Stimme*), Pérez-Gómez (2016, 90) points out, means "voice," the "atmospheric" conveyance "that carries human language, song, and melody, our original expressive utterance, continuous to gesture. It implies the primacy of orality over writing."

307.   Pérez-Gómez 2016, 38. Mondzain (2005, 59–69) references music as having an "important role to play in the emotional economy." She suggests: "Emotion is the trick of God who forces a path to our soul through our body, who dispenses his grace within everything that carries the mark of life in order to lead us to the heart of institutional and salvational virility" (59).

308.   Not only European history, of course: consider the African-European hybrid musical genre of the spirituals. Speaking on December 20, 1940—during the bombing of

Britain that traumatized Grant—at the seventy-fifth anniversary celebration of the thirteenth amendment to the US constitution, held at the Library of Congress, Alain Locke told his listeners: "For the spirituals are, even when lively in rhythm and folkish in imagination, always religious in mood and conception...always the voice of a naïve, unshaken faith, for which the things of the spirit are as real as the things of the flesh. This naïve and spirit-saving acceptance of Christianity is the hall-mark of the true spiritual" (quoted in Stewart 2018, 804).

309. Pérez-Gómez 2016, 45.

310. Planinc 1992, 28.

311. Lipari 2014, 9. Lipari crafts a concept of "interlistening" to show that "listening is itself a form of speaking that resonates with echoes of everything we have ever heard, thought, seen, touched, said, and read throughout our lives" (9).

312. Lipari 2014, 102. See also Ruitenberg 2015.

313. Lipari 2014, 103.

314. Lipari 2014, 103.

315. Lipari 2014, 113.

316. Lipari 2014, 117.

317. Lipari 2014, 117.

318. Lipari 2014, 119.

319. Davis and Roper 2009b, 309.

320. See Jardine, Clifford, and Friesen 2006; Salvio 2007.

321. "In fact," Dinshaw (2012, 2) points out, "the *now* is never purely there at all: it is a transition, always divided between no longer and not yet: each present *now* is stretched out and spanned by a past *now* and a future *now*." Like Aoki's bridge that is not a bridge, "now is ever now" (3).

322. "Truth is not personal," Kaethler (2009, 11) asserts, "and therefore philosophy should not be the expression of particular personalities." Truth may well be impersonal, but as the metaphor of prism implies, it is mediated through the person. Even so, it hardly becomes a subset of personality, but, rather, restructures personality.

323. Lipari 2014, 121.

324. Lipari 2014, 121.

325. Lipari 2014, 123.

326. Lipari 2014, 129.

327. In education, see Wang 2004 (as cited above) and also Taubman 1990.

328. Lipari 2014, 131.

329. Lipari 2014, 198.

330. Lipari 2014, 206.

331. Mondzain 2005, 38.

332. Mondzain 2005, 38.

333. "There is a natural harmony between the human mind and everything," Grant suspected, "that is, between the human mind and the whole." Within the "whole" one's "place" becomes revealed (Davis and Roper 2009b, 953).

334. Lipari 2014, 206.

335. Lipari 2014, 206.

336. Lipari 2014, 207.

337. Lipari 2014, 207.

338. Lipari 2014, 207.

339.   Lipari 2014, 209.

340.   Lipari 2014, 212.

341.   Lipari 2014, 212.

342.   Lipari 2014, 212.

343.   Pérez-Gómez 2016, 7.

344.   Pérez-Gómez 2016, 6–7.

345.   Pérez-Gómez 2016, 7.

346.   Pérez-Gómez 2016, 9.

347.   Christian and Grant 1998a, 26.

348.   Christian and Grant 1998b, 440. For Arapura (1983, 61), "There are three forms of temporal immanentism: past (history), present (social reality), and future (technology). Those who are consumed by any of these are usually hostile to the Eternal, while those who are consumed by the Eternal are always benevolently disposed to these three realms," adding that "total concentration on the immanent makes the immanent monstrous and diabolical. It generates the tyranny of immediacy, which is impatience with the need to be patient, with delay of fulfilment, in fact frustration of transcendence itself. Do not call it freedom" (61)

349.   In Lacanian psychoanalysis, James Penney (2014, 193–4) summarizes, "desire, on the level of what he calls its real, immanently lifts the subject out of the constraints of life; separates this subject from the chronological and teleological historicity of human time." For Lacan, Penney continues, desire installs immanence "by affirming a sort of background or underground non-temporality—eternity, in other words" (194). Eternity is within, then, including within immanence.

350.   Christian and Grant 1998b, 440.

351.   Christian and Grant 1998b, 440. Loss may be an "eternal" human experience. Heather Love (2007, 5) posits as "a central myth of queer existence...the paralyzing effects of loss," referencing Lot's looking back at—against God's command—the "lost world" of Sodom and Gomorrah. In so doing, "she becomes a monument to destruction, an emblem of eternal regret" (5). Does "recollecting" (Grant's term) or "reactivating" (my term) the past contain a similar danger? In an earlier analysis, it was the danger of "looking" (Pinar 2006b, 65) and patriarchal possession (82) in antiquity that captured my attention. Love's (2007, 5) study is intriguingly entitled *Feeling Backward* and "is populated by iconic figures that turn backward." While not in her book, Grant—and those of us looking at him—becomes such an "iconic" figure, and in the sense I suggest in ch. 5.

352.   Davis 2002b, 129.

353.   Davis 2002b, 129.

354.   Fishbane 2008, xi.

355.   "Liberation by the transcendent is not an end in itself," Athanasiadis (2001, 250) cautions, "nor is it an escape from the world."

356.   Christian and Grant 1998a, 27.

357.   There is, for Lipari (2014, 6), "an ethics of attunement: interconnection and generosity, impermanence and humility, iteration and patience, and invention and courage." I endorse such an ethics with the proviso that in certain circumstances what is revealed indicates an ethics of self-withdrawal, stinginess, permanence, aggression, silence and impatience, doing nothing while enveloped in fear.

358.   See Christian and Grant 1998a, 27. Even the concept of civilization—of course contentious and for good reason—becomes a casualty. For one curricular consequence, see

https://public-history-weekly.degruyter.com/5-2017-41/culture-civilization-and-historical-consciousness/.

359. Aoki (1987) 2005, 158.

360. Lear 2006, 121.

361. Lear 2006, 121–2. On occasion Grant seems to think one can if not think at least apprehend "the whole," as when referencing Mozart's experience of composition as working in "wholes," as he tells Cayley (1995, 59): "As Plato said, the idea of the good is just the idea of final purpose. The whole is opened to one when one asks the question of final purpose." Even one's own "final purpose" may not become clear except at death—if then—but to imagine one can discern or attune oneself to the (metaphysical) "final purpose" contradicts the idea of the inscrutability of God.

362. And not only because, as Grant (1986, 34) complains, the "possible is exalted above what is."

363. Engineering is design in the service of functionality, hardly always irrelevant in self-reflection, but a different emphasis from self-knowing through dialogical encounter—including dialogue with oneself—expanding inner space to emphasize alterity through attunement to the transcendent.

364. Grant 1969, 40.

365. Grant 1969, 98. While emphasizing here the otherworldly emplacement of history, Grant would, I suspect, appreciate that transcendence occurs in place (as, for instance, his conversion did at a gate in natural surrounds). Not necessarily metaphysical, Pérez-Gómez (2016, 10) acknowledges "the ontological primacy of place and its connections to language." In its modernistic degradation, place becomes, he laments, a site of "transit and never lingering" (15), that last word recalling Aoki's invitation.

366. Grant (1959) 1966, 15. "Negation," Marion (2001, 147) asserts, "if it remains categorical, remains idolatrous," adding that "[n]egation and affirmation bear upon the same attributes, only envisaged from two points of view" (148).

367. Grant (1959) 1966, 70.

368. Grant (1959) 1966, 70.

369. Grant (1959) 1966, 70.

370. A strange term, I suppose, but one that supports reparation, I suggest, through a reconstruction of white racist subjectivity (Pinar 2006b, 182).

371. Christian and Grant 1998a, 26.

372. Pinar 1994, 101. "Philosophy must arise in the most immediate and concrete experience of our lives," Grant tells Schmidt (1978a, 67), "both public and private."

373. Christian and Grant 1998a, 47.

374. Davis and Roper 2009b, 131. "The pressing question for Grant," O'Donovan (1984, 101) asserts, "is whether Christianity can offer an account of charity that is an antidote to technological striving." That phrasing implies Grant's progressive positioning, casting "charity" not only as important in itself but also as a means to an ends.

375. Ethics is implied in attunement, as Athanasiadis (2001, 45) seems to suggest: "Finally, if faith is 'passive' receptivity of divine love and active obedience to that love, then faith is also active love in relation to the neighbour." The forms that "active love" take are surely situation specific.

376. "Every act, every deed," Dewey (1922, 149) knew, "is individual."

377. Christian 1996a, 62. Perhaps so, but one of his closest friends Peter Self—whom he met at Oxford in 1939 and who shared Grant's pacifism (Christian 1996c, x)—expressed sharp disagreement with Grant's thought at a conference a year after Grant's death. Likening Grant to Isaiah Berlin's "hedgehog" (who knows one big thing rather than many little ones), he "questioned whether Grant knew what the big thing was anyway" (Andrew and Planinc 1990, 180). Self also contested Grant's critique of technology as structuring truth and society; how he reconciled that with sharing "Grant's concern about the unlimited exploitation of nature for the sake of human comfort" (181) is unclear.

378. See Dewey (1934) 1962, 14.

379. Dewey (1934) 1962, 16.

380. Dewey (1934) 1962, 17.

381. Dewey (1934) 1962, 17.

382. For Grant the two intermingled of course, including in the church's educational efforts. "If the Christian church surrenders at the level of curriculum," Grant wrote his friend Rhoda Palfrey Hall and her husband, Douglas Hall, in 1961, "it will be a sad day for generations of students" (Christian 1996d, 200).

383. "Suffering," Grant once said, "is the very heart of human life, and animal life." For him it had a recuperative—if not redemptive—potential, as "self-emptying" (Davis and Roper 2009b, 940). That said, he added: "Happiness is what we are fitted for" (941).

384. A certain abrasiveness (associated with embodied not virtual) experience is, I suggest, a precondition for experience itself (Pinar 2015c). "In a future where...we remain mostly fixed to computer terminals, live isolated lives protected from disruptive desires while exchanging memories of previous lives with others to pass the time in a pleasurable daze," Pérez-Gómez (2016, 7) cautions, "we would effectively exist out of human time and place."

385. Perhaps, as Magrini (2017, 125) explains: "To be attuned, here, indicates that when exposed to the *pathos* of the dialectic—*pathein*, 'to suffer'—we undergo an *educative* transformation to our Being through the 'clarification' (*katharsis*) of our understanding of the virtues, and thus we see, interpret, understand, and discourse in new and different ways as we are simultaneously opened up and *released over* to new possibilities as we learn." Suffering may be inevitable, but must it be a prerequisite for learning? I say learning can also be pleasurable, indeed, follow from pleasure. Grant was hardly opposed to pleasure.

386. Christian and Grant 1998a, 47.

387. Davis and Roper 2005b, 625.

388. Davis 2002b, 451. Nicholson (2006, 334) suggests that "[l]etting-be is, perhaps, what fulfills the very idea of freedom, in opposition to the project of control. This is the crucial possibility of a freedom that is self-limiting."

389. Davis 2002b, 107. Here Grant is referencing Weil.

390. Davis and Roper 2009b, 758.

391. Athanasiadis (2006, 266) seems to suggest the same: "Given our human tendency to preoccupation and absorption with our own selves, we need to be broken out of ourselves." He adds: "Weil calls this process 'decreation.'"

392. For Grant, Cayley (1995, 35) explains, only the saints had become, "at the cost of everything, transparent to the truth." Such transparency ensured ethics. As Grant

put it: "The height of the Christian religion is certainly the lives of the saints and what is a saint? Somebody who gives themselves away. Charity—the divine charity, or love, what word do you wish—is giving oneself away" (Davis and Roper 2009b, 1061–2). No saint, Grant nonetheless gave himself away: to his students, his family, his nation.

393. Davis and Roper 2009b, 823. Heaven (2006, 304) explains: "Goodness, for Grant, is beyond being and therefore beyond necessity. Necessity cannot be understood; it can only point to the mystery beyond being."

394. O'Donovan 1984, 167–8. "The art of speaking, as will prove to be the case with painting," Mondzain (2005, 66) explains, "is in an immanent and existential relation with our incarnation."

395. Weil (1947) 2002, 67.

396. Davis and Roper 2009b, 812.

397. Davis and Roper 2009b, 277.

398. "I start from the assumption," Grant once said, "that the height for man is what in Latin is called *amor fati*.... *Amor fati* is for me that which forms together—philosophy and revelation" (Davis and Roper 2005b, 682).

399. Davis 2002b, 107.

400. Davis 2002b, 224.

401. Davis 2002b, 224.

402. Davis 2002b, 224.

403. Davis 2002b, 125.

404. Davis and Roper 2009b, 318.

405. Davis 2002b, 104.

406. Such an expanded sense of reason has its antecedents not only in psychoanalysis, but also in pragmatism and its antecedent (and apparently antagonistic) traditions, implied in Posnock's (1998, 308n6) observation that "Nietzsche, like James, urges that we learn to reason differently by attending to what lies 'beyond,' to the residues which escape reason's drive to categorize." Historical residues may be reactivated and ethically engaged, spiritual ones apprehended through attunement.

407. Anthanasiadis 2001, 200.

408. As Davis (2002a, xxxi) succinctly puts the matter. In the urgency of the immediate that technology installs, Grant feared that any sense of ethical limits to behaviour would also disappear.

409. Fishbane 2008, 34.

410. Grant could be worldly, noting on one occasion that "it has always been true that human beings have exploited other human beings for their own convenience. We have had slavery and murder and oppression since the world began. Children have long been starved and killed. The fetuses are generally killed quickly and with little pain" (Davis and Roper 2009b, 494).

411. Fishbane 2008, 34. Attunement to the Good can enable understanding; theology, Athanasiadis (2001, 49) explains, "proceeds from 'faith seeking understanding,'" the simplicity of these phrases belying the complexity of the undertaking. Theology, Athanasiadis cautions, is the "most difficult of studies because it deals with 'the ultimate,' and its truth can only be discovered through deep experience and rigorous thought"; moreover, it must be "rethought and relived in every generation of the church" (49). Particularly pertinent to the concept of icon, theology, Anthanasiadis,

continues, "comes to existence in the meeting between the infinite and the finite in a particular time and place" (49–50).

412.   Reimer 1995, 57.

413.   Davis and Roper 2005b, 237.

414.   Marion 2001, 170.

415.   "Participation therefore never jumps over distance in claiming to abolish it," Marion (2001, 156) counsels, "but traverses it as the sole field for union." Moreover, "it is participation itself that presupposes and reinforces transcendence. To participate in the unthinkable is to do so in order to know it, to acknowledge it as such—as unthinkable" (157).

416.   "Some people dream of the icon, of a redeemed body or a new ethics," Mondzain (2005, 174) quips, "whereas others get drunk on numerical virtualities."

417.   Davis 2002b, 426.

418.   Davis 2002b, 426.

419.   Weil (1947) 2002, 48.

CHAPTER 7

Eternity

Eternity is humanity's greatest need. I
mean eternity in truth, in moral decision,
and in beauty.[1]

George Grant

"Modernity seemed to be the autumn of eternity," Yitzhak Y. Melamed observes.[2]
The "modern era," George Grant suggested more specifically, "substituted orientation to the future for orientation to eternity."[3] The substitution may not be
so substantive, as neither is necessarily temporal; each involves an imaginative[4]
extrapolation from the present, itself containing (if in modernity obscured) traces
of each.[5] To learn from experience requires reactivating and reconstructing those
traces, bringing them to consciousness[6]—subjective reconstruction[7] through
study.[8] One's "greatness" resides in the effort to "recreate" one's life, Weil wrote,
to "recreate what is given to him."[9]

Such subjective reconstruction requires judgment as to what to study: how,
when, why, and with whom. Judgment requires agency, a certain "autonomy,"[10]
which, Grant writes, "is at the final point the principle of the unity of the self as an
infinitely continuing person."[11] From such subjective synthesis engagement with
the world can occur.[12] In the present historical moment, when the political predominates, progressives might restructure such engagement as fundamentally
ethical.[13]

Such an emphasis—and the contemplation, mindfulness, and sustained
study it implies—requires if not quietude at least on occasion retirement from
the vortex of daily life in the "dynamo." Having formally retired from Dalhousie
University, Grant writes Joan O'Donovan that "Nova Scotia is good for us
because we live so quietly and from day to day,"[14] an affirmation of a present

moment predicated upon the eternal: "[M]y thoughts turn away more & more from political philosophy [to] the attempt to participate intellectually in the mystery of Christianity," he tells her, having admitted that "Canadian politics & life seems to go on in its pedestrian way.... What a queer place North America is. I can understand no other society and am very fearful of the self-righteous capitalism here."[15] These specific judgments seem secondary to the detachment they imply: Grant demonstrates the consciousness contemplation encourages.

The second side of such consciousness is immersion in daily life, the activism of quietude—for example, ethical engagement with others. For Grant, questions of "ethics arise" from everyday life, in "moments of time."[16] His verb implies that transcendence of time and circumstance that can occur through attunement, indwelling[17] the gap between here and eternity.[18] "[W]e can only act well," Grant wrote, "in so far as our actions are attuned to the very nature of things and we are attuned to the very nature of things by paying reverence to the eternal principles of order in the world."[19] As we saw in chapter 6, such reverence implies obedience to what revelation reveals.[20] For the medieval mystic Johannes Tauler, Sikka explains:

> Free bondage to this eternal will is also…bondage to what is eternal in the self. Through this commitment to the perfection of itself, a perfection known in its particularity through the commanding voice of God in the innermost point of the spirit, the soul is said to exchange the unsteadiness of its temporal and changeable life for the stability and constancy of its eternal one.[21]

For me the temporal cannot be exchanged for the eternal, but it is "as if" the two can be juxtaposed.[22]

Grant contrasts such transcendence of the contingent[23] and the embrace of "eternal principles" with historical engagement, starting with recognition that one is embedded within a particular historical existence.[24] "Experience is no argument," Grant wrote, "yet I cannot help believing that I am not much different from others in finding in the everyday pattern of life the content of my freedom. To speak thus personally is only to raise the general question."[25] For Angus, "particularity is more than an example of universality; it refers to the fact that a temporally and spatially bound being is thrown into a situation that it does not create."[26] For me, the two poles—particularity and universality, but also historicity and eternity, constraint and freedom—are reciprocally related, and each is unimaginable without the other.[27] Just as for Grant "ethics arise" from the everyday, does not eternity occur to us within the experience[28] of contingency[29] and temporality?[30]

Grant grapples with this issue during the Cayley interview, saying that Christianity, either Eastern or Western, or Hinduism or Buddhism must "reject" the rationale—here he associates it with Marxism but it seems to me equally entrenched in capitalism—"that good ends can be achieved by bad means."[31]

Grant ties this instrumental rationality to the idea of "limits," that one knows there are "things that one can know would be wrong at all times and in all places."[32]

I wonder what would these be? Murder seems justified in self-defence and during war; stealing seems right to stop the starvation of one's children, and so forth.[33] For Grant the "idea of limit is the idea of God,"[34] but I thought "God"— "the Good"—was beyond ideation, certainly beyond one, albeit important, idea like "limit." Kaethler reminds that "for Grant there are intimations of the whole that can be understood if one is open to the Good," adding that "what may be understood or perceived from the whole is supra-historical truth: truth that exists outside of the individual and outside of time."[35] Is the concept of "limit" one such "intimation"? Or is it a conceptual idol? Is not any conception of God inevitably idolatrous as it projects human attributes on what is beyond humanity and attributes? Metaphorically, "God" could be imagined (momentarily, provisionally) as authority that is not tyrannical, obedience to which one chooses, that there are indeed few "things"—like homosexuality, from which Grant turned[36]—a singular soul must never do.[37]

I can appreciate Weil's assertion—for Grant "the great teaching concerning the eternal in this era"[38]—that the "only good" that is "not subject to change is that which is outside the world,"[39] but even for her the eternal *does* seem to intersect with time[40] when it becomes what is beautiful. Weil writes: "Among other unions of contraries found in beauty there is that of the instantaneous and the eternal."[41] Immediacy and infinity: between them—among the intermediaries—is the icon, the incarnation, lived experience as (un)endurable affliction *and* as consolation, even redemption, attuned to the eternal.[42] Steimatsky suggests that the icon reiterates the "incarnation," reminding humanity that the divinity became "form" and "flesh," emphasizing that the "icon, like the relic, is a memento left by Christ as a promise of the vision of God in eternity."[43] The icon, she continues, is "grasped as participating in what it presents."[44] The icon as intermediary, then, becomes a precious relic of the past.[45] No one should be deprived of one's "*metaxu*," Weil writes, including those "relative" and "mixed blessings" that can "warm" even "nourish" a "soul," without which a "*human life*" is "not possible."[46] One thinks of Grant's love of one's own, his reverence toward beauty, "the visibility of the invisible,"[47] as Mondzain depicts the icon. But the concept of *metaxu* exceeds the relic, as "stars" and "blossoming fruit-trees," instances of both "utter permanence" and "extreme fragility," Weil writes, emanate an "equal sense" of the eternal.[48] "Beauty captivates the soul," she suggests.[49] Grant asked: "Does the experience of the beautiful help to overcome our oblivion of eternity?"[50] For Weil, it seems that the "value" of "experience" is that it can reveal what things are "fitted for," the "eternal."[51]

From here to eternity is not only a movie title: the phrase conveys movements from the particularities of place[52] and experience[53] to their elusive associations with what is outside them, transcendent and eternal.[54] None of this is self-evident or obvious, at least not to the aged[55] Grant, as when he told a journalist that it was a "struggle...to relate the idea of eternal truth—the immutable nature of justice—to the constantly mutating world."[56] That term—"struggle"—suggests attunement to the transcendent may be meditative but momentary, however eternal its referent.[57] Often the culprit in Grant's thinking, the will has its proper place here, if in a spiritual sense; the "perfecting of the will" occurs privately, in secret, if surrounded by, if not structured by, "incidents" of "action" and "passion" that are often "public."[58] For the mystics Tauler and Meister Eckhart, Sikka suggests:

> the soul is itself both temporal and eternal. It is temporal through its involvement with creatures, an involvement in which it is situated, first and foremost, by the manifold acts of attention and intention on the part of the will. It is also, however, eternal in the freedom of its innermost ground, the dwelling place of the presence of God. Because it is capable of entering into this ground, it is capable of entering into eternity, into the moment in which past, present, and future are comprehended, and when it does so it sees what God sees and will what God wills.[59]

For Grant such a moment—"both temporal and eternal"—is possible for the saints but not so much for us mere mortals.[60] What I know is that the struggle for soul is solitary and subjective, sometimes shared and social, but—despite the dismissals of the concept of soul—"*something* must persist in order for change to be possible."[61] That something—call it soul or self or transcendental ego—enables one, through reactivation of the past, to attune to the eternal.

Reactivation

> How, then, is one to link Being and being, eternity and time?[62]
>
> Robert C. Sibley

The religious might reply through prayer or other forms of ritual. The secular might suggest that even these, words and ritual, belong to us—humanity, that is—however they point to what might be beyond. Dewey suggests as much when he asserts that "infinite relationships" within humanity and nature "already exist."[63] For him the concept of "ideal" conveys "a sense of these encompassing continuities with their infinite reach,"[64] that final term a spatial more than temporal one. Cannot the former be a portal to the latter? That "whole" would then seem to be simultaneously spatial and temporal, stretching from here (this place, this time) to eternity (other places, other times, timelessness itself).

Referencing R. G. Collingwood, Grant suggests that there are no "absolute presuppositions which divide men of different civilizations in a way which cannot be overcome," but adding that neither are there "universal men who can overcome any division."[65] Invoking the space of the icon, Grant adds: "I simply assert that it is good that faculty and students should be faced in the academic environment with what is, at the level of common sense at any rate, an unequivocal religious otherness."[66] "Without the recognition of otherness," Kaethler reminds, "Grant believes we will lose our humanness."[67] Our humanity, then, is predicated upon the academic acknowledgement, even nurture, of alterity.

Recall that at McMaster Grant required students to study more than one religion and each in its historical context. In terms of time and space, then, historical and "religious otherness" would seem to intersect as well as diverge. Hutt points out that "Collingwood never thought that knowledge of events in the past—which are genuinely unique and unrepeatable—could be attained through attending to laws formulated in the present," noting that Collingwood "emphasized the otherness and alien character of the 'spectacle' which is past."[68] Hutt also notes that Collingwood later "retreats on this last skeptical point and argues that through a special historical form of experience or mediation…we can rethink the thoughts of those who have come before us."[69] While Collingwood does allow that "historical knowledge is the re-enactment in the historian's mind of the thought whose history he is studying," he adds that such "re-enactment…is a re-enactment with a difference."[70] To the person in the past whose thoughts one is thinking—reactivating, rendering them present—"that thought was a present thought; to me, it is a past thought living in the present but (as I have elsewhere put it) encapsulated, not free."[71] Collingwood concludes: "[H]istorical knowledge is the re-enactment of a past thought encapsulated in a context of present thoughts which, by contradicting it, confining it to a plane different from theirs."[72] Collingwood may have here conceded too much, confining himself to the present (which empirically he must do[73] but which mystically he must not do and, psychoanalytically, is ill-advised to do). Collingwood does reintroduce an element of that last mode of "re-enactment" when he writes:

> If what the historians knows is past thoughts, and if he knows them by re-thinking them himself, it follows that the knowledge he achieves by historical inquiry is not knowledge of his situation as opposed to knowledge of himself, it is a knowledge of his situation which is at the same time knowledge of himself.[74]

That is a fundamental psychoanalytical—for Collingwood a historiographical—insight, namely that understanding the past includes the capacity to re-experience it. There would seem to be, then, some sort of acknowledgement of the reciprocity between subjectivity and objectivity, past and present.

Once Collingwood has registered such reciprocity, he can also acknowledge that "something" that notices both, that "something"—call it soul or self or transcendental ego—traverses the here and now to the there and then, moving from this immediate moment to the whole that we can also call eternity. We might call this capacity to traverse time and space attunement, and its educational utility the reactivation of the past. But (as usual) I get ahead of myself. Let us return to Collingwood, who, speaking of the historian, suddenly sounds almost Jungian:

> If he is able to understand, by rethinking them, the thoughts of a great many different kinds of people, it follows that he must be great many kinds of man. He must be, in fact, a microcosm of all the history he can know. Thus his own self-knowledge is at the same time his knowledge of the world of human affairs.[75]

I am referring of course to Jung's concept of collective unconscious.[76] For Collingwood, these are conscious thoughts, moving images of eternity, universal singulars Sartre might have said.[77]

Time

> There are in history no beginnings and no endings. History books begin and end, but the events they describe do not.[78]
> R. G. Collingwood

In modernity, Doane suggests, "time seems to change its contours, to become more insistently present as a problem, to be subject to acceleration and manipulation."[79] "Representational systems"—she names art and literature, but what system is exempt?—"address themselves to the ephemeral, the contingent, the moment," and "the credibility of any static universal or eternal is diminished."[80] Must it be? No universal is static, at least to the extent it becomes embodied in the moment, a live, not simulated, "now" that flows from the past toward a future that cannot be foreclosed. How to conduct ourselves in that iconographic space between singular and universal, between now and then, here and eternity? Doane reminds us that "the ancients believed in 'privileged' instants, characteristic and essential poses," emphasizing that "these were the embodiments or actualizations of a transcendental form, eternal and immobile."[81] The space of engineering—getting from here to there—was less important, as transitions took second place to "certain moments" that were deemed "as the actualization of an ideal or essential form."[82] History, then, was both time and timelessness. In Scanlon's terms: "History is the content of eternity, while eternity is the issue of history."[83] Like Augustine, Grant may have deemed "eternity as superior to time in that it is something that exists that was *not created*."[84] Spiritual reality is, in this sense, empirical.

Over the two and a half millennia[85] of Western philosophy, Melamed explains, a distinction[86] between two conceptions of eternity has been constant: "[E]ternity as *timeless* existence, as opposed to eternity as existence in *all times*."[87] While a definite distinction, these seem also interrelated, as "timelessness"[88] could be conveyed from a sense of continuity[89] threaded through "all times."[90] For Aristotle, Wilberding reports, "time and eternity both involve duration, [but] temporal duration differs from eternal duration insofar as what is in time is subject to change whereas the eternal remains always the same."[91] While mortal, each of us can change over time and through effort (ah, the will) but noticing that we have implies an unchanging position or presence informed by, but not identical to, memory.[92]

"Although eternal truth is not entirely present to the human spirit," Capelle acknowledges, "it is nevertheless not entirely absent from it," adding that "this is the reason why...'memory,' inasmuch as it represents the habitation of the Verb in the human spirit, can be understood, within Augustine's logic, as a notion of factical life."[93] That Augustinian logic Grant may have internalized, discernible in his being struck one day while shopping, by the store clerks' "dull jobs," by the almost endless display of consumer goods, the combination of which led him to ponder the "whole question of industrial society," leaving him puzzled by his "own place" in it, wondering "was there purpose and point."[94] It was at "that place and at that time" the "eternal question" was posed to him, a question asking if he could look at "all these faces" and still "believe...there was purpose."[95] Grant was—remained—clear he could find point and purpose for himself—the Sartrean solution in *Nausea*—but in this passage Grant is wondering about the rest of us, whether he can "objectively...assert what is real—whatever that reality may be."[96] Is that reality concealed within eternity? Can it be glimpsed in everyday reality?[97] Among consumer goods?

For those of us embedded within modernity, reality often ends at the everyday, even and except with science, which also starts with the everyday but then (apparently) sees to the ends of the universe, presumably rescuing "eternity" from its metaphysical muddle.[98] It turns out that time and duration may have "no place in the most fundamental ontology," or so recent developments in physics and philosophy suggest, Melamed reports.[99] For Grant "the Eternal and Becoming are exact opposites," warning that "to unite them is to destroy the eternal."[100] When eternity disappears, so does ethics, precipitating the current crisis that compelled Grant to question not only science but also modernity itself.[101] It is the ethical calamity[102] that has accompanied modernity that animated Grant to see "faces" of shop clerks as afflicted, moderns adrift in riptides of exchange where time means (only) money. To encounter the soul in another's—and in one's own—face, shining through skin and eyes, embodied[103] as a "person," is, for Dwayne Huebner, "the essence of life. In it life is revealed and lived."[104] In such an educational encounter, the "student is not viewed as an object, an *it*; but as a fellow human being, another subject, a *thou*, who is to be lived with in the fullness of the present moment or the eternal moment."[105]

The capacity for such an educational encounter requires at least a moment of extrication from exchange, a moment that can be extended by sustained study, a duration of openness that can restructure the self–self relation to support ethical engagement with others and attunement to the Good.[106] Extrication from the grip of exchange requires not the instrumental rationality that structures social engineering but the ethics arising from the everyday, animating subjective reconstruction. "Only through some set of particulars or other," Lampert suggests, "can one glimpse or embrace the good."[107] The task of education, Grant asserted, is the encouragement of "that receptivity to the infinite which will not allow them [people] to rest."[108]

If philosophy—for Grant the "crown"[109] of education—is cultivating the excellence of the soul, Grant concludes that philosophy so conceived cannot exist "unless there is an eternal and unchangeable order."[110] Grant goes on to point out that the domination of necessity—the clarion call of modernity—precludes any such belief, but my point is, I suppose, faintly Kantian: why not suppose such an order if it allows one to measure one's conduct outside the norms of modernity? If we're so sure what you see is what you get, then mired we must be in the muck we have made, in Grant's terms, "that history is consciously and voluntarily made by human beings."[111] There is, in David Roberts's phrase, nothing but history.[112] For Grant, O'Donovan emphasizes, history became "the central religious and moral idea of our age."[113] Contemporary North Americans, Christian notes, "simply take for granted that time is history and we live our lives beyond good and evil (that is, oblivious of eternity), unaware of the moral abyss into which we are falling."[114] Enclosed inside it, anything goes.[115]

Believing now that "excellence" is defined by making history, Grant continues, we who live now could not be more different than those who lived in ancient times.[116] For those living then, history had been a moving image of eternity.[117] Grant emphasizes again and again that the ancients "did not see themselves as making events but as living out divine established patterns."[118] As Cayley puts it: "In ancient and medieval thought, what was good was known by intuitions reaching outside time."[119] For "ancient civilizations," Forbes summarizes, "justice…was the living out in time of a transcendent eternal model."[120] He asks if those who lived thusly were "perhaps right to focus, not on humanity's future development, but on its present existence within an eternal order?"[121] How might we moderns know how to live ethically, having long shifted from "eternal being to eternal becoming"?[122]

While Grant does not invoke the word, attunement to the transcendent—entertaining (invoking that "as if") the eternal through the temporal—would seem to me to be one means.[123] Working historically, Grant put the matter this way: "In this ancient vision," one discerns "reality solely through repetition of and participation in a divine reality."[124] After Weil, meaning is made through self-immolation as, Grant suggests, one "ceases to be himself and imitates and repeats the eternal archetypal gestures of the divine, such as the creation of the world and the bringing forth of life."[125] The self becomes a staircase to heaven.[126] "Within the flickering inconsequential acts of separate selves," Dewey writes, dwells a sense of the whole which claims and dignifies them. In its presence we put off mortality and live in the universal. The life of the community in which we live and have our being is the fit symbol of this relationship. The acts in which we express our perception of the ties which bind us to others are its only rites and ceremonies.[127]

That "community" is for Grant not only contemporaneous but also ancient, not only here but also beyond time and space.

I accept Grant's characterization of time in antiquity not as being *made* but as being *lived through*—"time ran its course through an infinite series of cycles, no event is new or unique"[128]—but I do not see why the two modes of being must be mutually exclusive. Nor can I assume that any infinite series of cycles are copied, only. These cycles—birth and death[129]—are everywhere the same but they are also everywhere different, re-experienced in time, place, and circumstance. Birth and death are not universals only, they are also intensely personal: we are talking about my—your—birth, my—your—death here. While Grant emphasized that we belong to "particular traditions and communities," he also appreciated that, as Davis suggests, "within these, each of us, as individuals, must also do our own thinking, believing, and dying."[130] For me, that means that manifestations of "the Good" must mutate, not opportunistically nor at the expense of others, but the justice of "what we are fitted for" shifts in time even if the maxim does not.[131] The civilizational shift toward the temporal as historical Grant tends to associate with Judaism and Christianity's emphasis upon a God "who reveals his will through particular events,"[132] or in Combs's phrasing, "the biblical teaching about the historicity of the whole."[133] Still worldly, such "images" of eternity become "concrete expressions of the divine will."[134] But as divinity disappears, all that matters—all that there is—is history. Not the past[135]—"there is no sense of the past,"[136] Grant appreciates—but "the future" substitutes[137] for the transcendent as eternal, a world where "everything is new every moment."[138] In antiquity, "the urgent present of the eternal"[139] made moral what today might seem exclusively economic or political.

The Perpetuity of the Past

Temporality is so strong.[140]
George Grant

In modernity what Grant thinks is required of us is the recollection[141] of the "tension between what comes to us from Athens and what comes from Jerusalem," abstractions[142] that Grant embodies in the historical figures of Socrates and Jesus, noting that "these beings were both condemned by their cities and in those condemnations and consequent deaths we touch the 'beyond'—use if you will the difficult word 'eternal.'"[143] In these deaths does space become time, the transcendent intertwined with the eternal?[144] As iconographic figures of mediation,[145] each figure embodies both.[146] Is what is required of us a subjective decentring—even a self-shattering or, in Weil's term, "decreation"[147]—so that inner space and time might dissolve into attunement to the Good?[148] "In the inner life," Weil writes, "time takes the place of space."[149]

For Socrates, Maxine Greene suggests, the student was to "be brought, on his own initiative, to regard virtue."[150] Moreover, the student was "stimulated to take an active role in the search for his perfection; he had to be courageous enough to turn toward the Good."[151] Like a midwife, Socrates brought a person to term through "two modes of teaching—questioning and eliciting"—that followed from the educator's location in two worlds at once: "[O]ne part of him was caught in the flow of time and imperfection; the other belonged to eternity."[152] A Socratic education, Magrini suggests, is *care for the soul,*[153] the student as icon not idol.

"The reality of the 'idea' was invented by Socrates," Grant tells us, determined to "overcome tragedy and who therefore posited that the immediate world was just the moving image of a real eternity."[154] Grant acknowledges that there could be a tendency, should one view the world as a "mere image" of the eternal, "to devalue the world."[155] He asks: "How can one affirm the eternal order which is the principle of this world and then say this world is all corruption? This is one side of the tension."[156] The question reverberates—is the gap between the two traversable? Or is human life—however culturally variable, economically exploitative—dwelling in between, lacerated by necessity while attuned to the eternal? Both Weil answers, asserting at once that while the world is a "closed door" it is also "the way through."[157] Sibley puts the matter this way: "The ancients distinguished between eternity, the good, and necessity, the realm of becoming that remains separate even while participating in it."[158]

"Grant stands in the middle," Kaethler emphasizes, "embracing both Plato and Christianity, connecting *eros* and *agape*, desire and charity."[159] Grant describes the tension between Jerusalem and Athens, the latter associated with reason[160] and the former with revelation.[161] For Fishbane there is no tension: "[F]or those in the know, there was no gap between scripture and philosophy."[162] If the gap between revelation and philosophy can be traversed, I ask again: can there be a bridge[163] between time and eternity?[164] Humanity stands, Ouspensky suggests, "at the start of a pathway which is not concentrated on some point in depth, but which unfolds itself before him in all its immensity."[165] For Thibon, the imagery is more temporal than spatial, writing that while time contrasts with eternity, it is nonetheless an "opening" to eternity.[166] How to walk through?[167] Through death? If alive, can one traverse—inhabit—the threshold through attunement?

Can't say I have, but can attunement to the eternal remove one from its mirage, that endless if emptied "now" devices decree? Ah yes, the future is now we say, surrounded by things, including the Internet of things. Replacing the present as a moving image of eternity or a distinctive moment wedged between past and future is a present emptied of eternity *and* time—that is, presentism.[168] "The modern," Benedetti explains, "is an eternal present that keeps shifting with use; it is a kind of temporal deictic, like the adverb 'now,' to which it is etymologically related."[169] This "false eternity" follows from refusing to be bored, treating "time as something to be overcome," entertainment for sure but also amounting to an "attempt to opt out of the awful responsibilities by flying away from time… [that] leads us to a false eternity."[170] What Weil is teaching, Grant suggests,

> is that orientation to the future is the assertion of our autonomy, and we assert our autonomy so that we can expand our personality in the future…so that it becomes a false eternity. Eternity becomes an endless extension of the self. This is why decreation of the personality is necessary, because it is that which in its expansion into the future stands between us and our meeting with the true eternity…. But positively, she goes much further, because this negation of the false eternity—or pseudo eternity—is to open the way for the affirmation of the supernatural good.[171]

Mesmerized, the posthuman subject tends toward fusion with the virtual reality the device screens.[172] The "temporal simultaneity in the *now*"[173]—the past and future restructuring the "infinite impermanence of the present moment,"[174] "everyday life…punctuated by eternity,"[175] freezes, Medusa-like, in the alluring stare of the screen. Those of us who can focus on "neither" the "past" nor the "future," Weil warns, become "reduced" to "matter."[176]

Presentism might be pathological not only culturally but also psychologically. Judith Stamps references Joseph Gabel, who suspected that the schizophrenic was a "person psychically locked into an eternal present, a state with no apparent differentiable past and, hence, no hope for an alternative future."[177] In video games and hook-up apps there are "alternative" futures, but these seem not exactly eschatological, not that I share any sense of that kind, either. Putting down the device, altering the object of one's attunement, may be no simple move, as you are already (it seems) connected. What may be involved, as Grant's summary of Weil above implies, is decreation (or self-shattering) so that one re-experiences not the slick surface of simulation but the abrasiveness of actual lived experience. Teaching Weil, Grant reminds that for her "living time…is related to decreation."[178] Grant urged students to live "only in the present so that one is oriented to eternity."[179] The temporally structured present, that is.

In its obliteration of time and eternity, presentism amplifies the political, in part by its ocularcentrism. "Virtual reality seems particularly oriented towards the spectacle," Rocha writes, adding: "No wonder politics proliferate online."[180] Anti-politics one might add, as spectators can't be citizens: "Without a *polis*," Rocha notes, "there can be no politics."[181] Without a common faith one is left to watch, susceptible to the spectacle and its mesmerizing spell, the spell cast by the idol, substituting itself for what it pretends to represent. Rocha knows:

The sign of ideology is the spectacle. The sign of truth is the real. One is an idol, made and loved by a culture that, in its blindness, mistakes it for real, as some shiny new thing: an opportunity for making money, for feeling better about ourselves, for justifying our misery. The other is an icon, mysterious and fleeting, visible mainly to children—the ones who know better than to pretend to know what they do not, and cannot, know.[182]

Note it is not the innocence of children Rocha invokes but their instinct that ignorance of eternity is the natural state, pretension its cover-up. Stripped of such inner spectacles, one waits, in time, for what the icon invites.

Being-in-time—for Grant "time [is] enfolded in eternity"[183]—within humility, can encourage transcendence, compelling continuity, a spiritual sense of the constant in one's life.[184] In inner movements from particularity to universality,[185] from temporality to eternity, can come recognitions of a shared fate, of a shared problematic, of a moral obligation to act.[186] Such movements are evident at almost every twist and turn of Grant's life. Grant's turn from law to theology to philosophy, Davis and Emberley suggest, represented his effort to "make sense of his experiences during the Second World War."[187] Recall that his service in East London during the Blitz subjected him to suffering on a mass scale, suffering he internalized and which was redeemed by his conversion. But even revelation of such a specific sort requires reflection, rendering lived experience educational: Davis suggests that "Plato's philosophy helped Grant make sense of his philosophical and religious conversion."[188] Grant's faith[189] in "an eternal order grounded," Davis continues, "rather than contradicted, his progressive desire to seek economic and political justice."[190] From here to eternity a line was drawn.

A decade later Grant faced another spiritual challenge, as he contemplated the confusion he felt in the faces of his students at Dalhousie. "While lacking his experience of the Blitz," Davis and Emberley report, "many were confused or uprooted from their religious traditions, and thus needed a philosophy that would respond to their confusion as they were drawn into mass secular society."[191] Grant's sense of eternity seemed to originate in everyday life as much as it does in faith or abstract forms.[192] To reply to the present he returned to the past.[193]

What Grant offered, Forbes emphasizes, was an ancient conception of "virtue," one that precedes "freedom," virtue that emanates from an "eternal order" against which human action is to be judged.[194] I cannot share Grant's conviction that without such a conception humanity dissolves into greed and sectarianism. After all, these have been characterized as (what a century ago was termed) "the human condition," a condition that takes different forms in different periods, but which itself seems "eternal," at least in the lifetime of the human species. So any conception of "virtue" and "eternal order" cannot be "objective" but strictly spiritual; for example, an invitation to become attuned anew in each circumstance to the conduct that "virtue" summons, and reflect on the judgment it implies (and upon which it rests), and these cannot always be known in advance. So for me what Grant is terming "virtue" is less observable behaviour than "internal harmony," an inward attunement toward the good or the right, an invisible rudder (as it were) that could be re-experienced in each setting, at each moment. This "eternal" if always shifting sense of "virtue" informs "justice," or so Grant also seems to say, if as a warning: "As justice is conceived as the eternal convenience of contract, it obviously has less and less to do with the good ordering of the inward life."[195] Justice is finding what one—what each of us, what the situation— is "fitted for."[196]

Such attunement to the eternal disappears once humanity considers itself beyond good and evil.[197] Then, Grant notes, the "strong are moved to the violence of an undirected willing of novelty."[198] It was Nietzsche's formulation of eternal recurrence, he continues, wherein "nihilism becomes therapeutic," enabling one to "will novelty in joy."[199] In such acceptance of the past as never completely past, that there can be no future which has (in some sense) not already happened and "yet in which there is openness to the immediate future," Grant judged that "the conception of time as history reaches its height and yet is not hypostatized into a comforting horizon."[200] Eternal recurrence may be "in accordance with the deadly truths of evolution and historicism," Grant continued, but it does represent "an infinite affirmation of life with all its suffering and defects in a way that is not possible in the base interpretation of historicism."[201] Could this be, as Christian suggests, the "heart of the noble teaching," the divination that there is "nothing eternal except individuals in their individuality," affirming "life with all its sufferings," enabling one to experience "harmony and unity within the cycle of nature."[202] For this aged secular educator—remembering those students with whom and the ideas with which I have worked over a lifetime—can there be a teaching more noble? Yes, Grant answers, there can be.

Eternity in Time

> Time is an image of eternity, but it is also a substitute for eternity.[203]
>
> Simone Weil

Weil did not doubt the "dignity" and "necessity" of "temporal values," Thibon tells us, deeming them "intermediaries,"[204] moving images of eternity. "But," Thibon adds, for Weil these can only be apprehended as such when, "out of love for God,"[205] one strips oneself of identification—fusion—with what is. Such love, McCarroll suggests, "dwells in the in-between of relationships and verifies itself as the real, the essence of things. As a relational reality, love presupposes contradiction and distance but also relationality and otherness."[206] Fishbane might agree, if allowing that the self must first be devoted to the tasks of worldly facticity and their cultivation. Gradually, the rungs of awareness are ascended—an expansion of consciousness within the self and beyond, toward the great circumscribing vastness. It is at these peaks of sensibility that the self is a reborn creature of God, attuned to the silences of eternity and the infinite harmonic of freedom and necessity—at once so elusive and so impinging.[207]

From here to eternity: the everyday affords us not only idols but also icons, evident in what are and who[208] is lovely, not ornaments but instances of beauty[209] that can provide epiphanies.[210]

"My reaching for the eternal," Grant wrote, "is through the images of it which appear to me through justice and knowledge and beauty."[211] For Plato, Grant reminds, such images are "preparations."[212] Like Grant's DPhil thesis: Grant's analysis of John Oman, Davis and Emberley suggest, became the "point of departure of his thought."[213] It is important as well because, Davis and Emberley suggest, it reveals Grant's

> lasting position—an agnostic believer, a moral egalitarian, a pacifist, an ambivalent critic of liberal modernity, and a Christian Platonist who argued the case for forgiveness not from the safe haven of eternal certainty but inside the doubt and despair of the modern world.[214]

From this multivariate position, the moving images that comprise the world we inhabit become points of preparation and departure through revelation: one's attunement to the transcendent reveals rudders for right conduct.

Not only for me is the concept of the eternal empirically impossible. Instead eternity becomes an "as if"[215]—something speculated not something known—that can enable one to disengage from the hurly-burly, if not to find forgiveness, to at least forget about it for a while. "Don't sweat the small stuff" was a slogan circulating some time ago, but that advice I had always decoded from within the logic of calculation: it was advantageous to stay cool while in competition. From eternity the small stuff definitely does not matter. "No matter how transcendence is conceived," O'Donovan writes (quoting Grant), "it amounts to the same thing: the will to overcome 'time's thrall.'"[216] Neither does the large stuff, finally. What matters are those truths revealed through attunement from which one learns—educational experience—rendering all stuff moving images of something sacred, a structural relation between here and eternity that icons convey.[217]

During the 1960s, Christian notes, Grant came to see that this—the Platonic—idea of time as the moving image of eternity had definitely disappeared, replaced by the idea of history as the total reality within which events took place.[218] "Oblivious to eternity," Emberley appreciates, "we have replaced receptivity to the transcendent with…indefinite tasks of mastery—a nihilistic purposiveness without purpose."[219] Focused on mastery, not only eternity disappears. Also missing in our ahistorical pseudo-eternal "now" is, Christian suggests, Marx and Hegel's sense of teleology, that history had an end and a meaning that was intelligible within that directional dynamic.[220] After Nietzsche, Grant appreciated that events were, in Christian's terms, "merely episodic moments of pure becoming, and all meaning was subjective."[221] Goals were accomplished or not, but even living aimlessly was a matter of personal gratification, not spiritual satisfaction. Can't living be both?

To talk about time or history one cannot coincide with either, inhabiting that "in-between" or intermediary space of non-identification where one hovers, a space of subjective freedom wherein one might attune to the eternal.[222] In that quietude it is "as if" there is an eternity—a transcendence—that enables one to sense the omnipresence of time. Is this what Weil intends when she writes that the "limitless is the test of the one: time, of eternity: the possible, of necessity: variety, of the unvarying"?[223] Conversely, can there be any sense of eternity without time, any sense of continuity without constant change?

Something similar may have been in play when, in the heyday of cultural studies, there was a rush to the "margins," and not only as a site of political "marginalization" and vulnerability, but as an epistemologically safe space, not yet appropriated by the hegemonic forces that be.[224] A passage from Ted Aoki illustrates the point. Referencing post-colonial scholars Stuart Hall and Homi Bhabha, "both of whom speak from the liminal margins of Eurocentric modernity," Aoki suggested that "we need to question this very imaginary that construes the Pacific Community as diversity," sensing that the concept relocated cultures in a "universal time frame."[225] He acknowledged that such an abstraction constitutes an "outside"—a self-constructed universal—from which omniscience can be constructed, construed as consensus so as to disclaim one's self-positioning as central and controlling. Keeping eternity outside time—incapable of being occupied by anyone or thing—provides at least a metaphoric sun illuminating everywhere obscured by mountains or molehills nowhere. Its character is always outside because it is unknowable; its intermediaries—objects and events—refract what is constantly in motion. Are such intermediaries akin to "illusion" if such a "veil" is "necessary" to conceal any "infinite meaning"?[226]

That question recurs when, discussing Kant with students, Grant wonders "how can I myself who am the minutest speck in the totality of things...be at the same time the center of the universe, the maker of the world—a self-legislating member of a Kingdom of Ends"?[227] "How" I do not—perhaps cannot—know, but for Grant art too can sometimes serve as such a "speck," as an "intermediary" between now and then, here and there, finitude and infinitude.[228] Grant provides a negative instance, warning that if art becomes devalued—if it becomes only "an imaginative coating to existence rather than as the recognition and statement of reality, then necessarily it is a less fundamental activity than the science which then becomes the only gate to reality."[229]

Halbertal and Margalit depict "divine revelations" as having a "complex structure," one "represented by a symbol that stands in a causal relation to the divine that cannot be analyzed," in a phrase "the infinite."[230] For Grant, O'Donovan notes, "knowing…involves man's infinite desire for self-transcendence, and the end of knowledge, the highest human freedom, is man's contemplation of this infinity."[231] Is infinity the spatial correlate of eternity? So the "symbol" functions like Weil's "intermediary"? Lints put it this way:

> God has made us in his image and that imprint in some sense has persisted across the ages and across our differences. Cultural influences are important but an enduring human identity is not thereby dissolved under the conditions of modernity. Or so the biblical witness amply testifies.[232]

I cannot follow Lint into his doctrinal certitudes, but this idea that identity is an image—not visible to the eye, one assumes—remains with me. Spiritually understood, then, human beings are, like everything else, moving images of eternity: again, not observable copies but, as Lint's use of "imprint" implies, a being (that is more than itself: a "symbol"[233]) that refracts frequencies from elsewhere, for Lint, from the Christian God of the Bible.[234] For the curriculum, not only one's worldly identity but also academic knowledge itself seems somehow reflective of "larger"—not exclusively empirical—realities.

For Grant these are contingent and specifically political—"equality should be the central principle of society"[235]—but ultimately transcendent, having to do with "the transcendent truth of the soul."[236] For many, Grant realizes, these realities—questions of "my eternal destiny," of "truth," "beauty," "love," and "goodness"[237]—are now the province of ecclesiastical, not academic, institutions. Even those who concede that the curriculum is "concerned with the wisdom of the world"[238] relegate issues of eternity to the church. That "won't do," Grant retorts, as such "questions are real questions, they are intellectual questions, and above all they are questions for which education is required to give if a clear and cogent answer."[239] Actually, many answers, Grant concedes, characterizing the two—"wisdom of the world and the questions of eternity"—as matters of individual labor: "Each must work it out as best he or she can."[240] Does eternity here become "the name for the path, now not in addition to but instead of the goal?"[241]

For Weil, Grant tells us, modernity's preoccupation with the future represents the "assertion of our autonomy" for the sake of "expand[ing] our personality in the future."[242] Such a false eternity represents "an endless extension of the self," and thereby a "false" one, escape from which requires "decreation of the personality,"[243] so that one can become attuned to what lies beyond: not only beyond the screen but also beyond—if through—materiality itself.

Conclusion

> Although trust in the eternal was the
> essence of Grant's thought, there were
> many tactical twists and turns along the
> way.[244]
>
> William Christian

"In all the great traditions of the world," Grant wrote, "education...was...the journey of the mind beyond all myths out of the shadows and imaginings into the truth."[245] While Grant admits this classical system was "often abused...confused and it was limited to the few," but at its core (invoking a term Dewey too endorsed: "ideal") education was "the practice of that ideal that men did anything by which we can call human existence meaningful."[246] That term "anything" implies an agnosticism regarding content or means, a situated ethics of education, not "anything goes" but keeping open the canonical curriculum question: what knowledge is of most worth?

In our time, that question has been answered almost exclusively in economic terms,[247] so that, as Grant notes, this ancient idea of education as the ways humanity was "freed to come into the light of infinite truth has largely disappeared," replaced by an education for "economic success," emphasizing the production of the "technical expert."[248] Invoking Plato's allegory of the cave, Grant quips: "[W]here the end of the old education was to free men so that they were out of the cave; the purpose today is to equip them to be successes in the cave."[249] Given this historical actuality, what is an educator to do? Grant answered: "There is, of course, no easy answer to how we should face this tension between the wisdom of the world and the questions of eternity. Each must work it out as best he or she can."[250] Study can help, as Grant reminds:

> The proper use of our worldly studies can lead us beyond them to the realm of religion. This is because all study, if properly undertaken, has a sacred content. And this sacred content is that it teaches us attention. And how can we ever pay attention to deity if we have not first paid attention to the world.[251]

Such worldliness provides passage to what is beyond the tomb in which technology encases us. In my rereading of Grant it is "as if" the intensity of sustained self-critical attentiveness—attunement—starts and sustains the journey.[252] "Because we have to give our full attention to it," Grant writes, "if we are to understand, and in it we learn *that* attention which we can then use for fuller purposes."[253]

Such faith—that knowledge is inspired by love[254]—seems especially fragile when we face political and economic instability, especially destabilizing now when we know that time is running out to correct climate change. While attentive to the earth Grant might not have been thinking of that threat but another—the nuclear arsenal surrounding us still[255]—when he wrote that "misdirected efforts may lead [us] away from human excellence, they may even succeed in destroying all our species, but they can never succeed in the total perversion of nature," from which he concludes: "A fundamental optimism is possible because despite all that men do, what happens does not ultimately depend on our freedom."[256] Surely such faith follows—as it precedes—attunement to eternity.

Notes

1. Davis and Roper 2009b, 573.
2. Melamed 2016b, 6. Reflecting on Grant's reticence to speak about "the other side of necessity," Heaven and Heaven (1978, 73) note: "It is neither smart politics nor timely pedagogy to speak publicly of the eternal." Perhaps the two are intertwined for Grant, as it seems to me he was teaching even when engaged politically, or drawn into quietude. But then these "progressive" considerations may not have been in play at all, as Grant freely admitted: "I simply have not crossed to the supernatural side" (Davis and Roper 2009b, 841). One cannot speak of what one does not know.
3. Davis and Roper 2009b, 841. "Grant realized that these old words" [the good, the eternal]," Rigelhof (2001, 120) writes, had "been used up. Over the past four hundred years, they've been emptied of their original content." That insight seemed confirmed as I read through the Melamed collection on eternity. How is the term defined there? Offering a negative conception, McDaniel (2016, 245) defined eternity as what is "atemporal, that is, neither in time (and hence not in space-time) nor subject to temporal (or spatiotemporal) properties or relations." Egginton (2016, 282) offers: "Indeed, it may be that each [eternality and finitude] is only conceivable against the absent ground of the other." Like "liberty," then, eternity seems defined here as "negative" rather than "positive."
4. We tend to imagine the future, Weil ([1947] 2002, 175) worried, adding that "only the past"—when it is not a fantasy—is "pure reality." McDaniel (2016, 264) reports, according to C. D. Broad, "the present and the past are equally real while the future is unreal." Certainly it can't be predicted. Grant told Cayley (1995, 120) that "nobody who has their brains about them at all can predict the future in any detail—where it will come, or how it will take place."
5. Recall that Grant had studied (Davis 2000, xxix) and taught (Davis 2002a, xvii) Augustine, who, during his DPhil studies, had become, along with Plato, "central figures for him" (Davis and Emberley 2000b, 159). Augustine, Kearney (2005b, 145) reminds, conceived of the present as 'threefold.'... In other words, if we cannot consider the past and the present to exist as such, we must rethink them as temporal qualifications which can exist in the present. Past, present, and future must thus be reconsidered as qualities existing *within* the soul as implied by our experiencing of narrating the past and expecting the future." For Grant the past was not only a "temporal qualification" of the present, it could be recollected. I tend to see fantasies of the future as projections from the present. Not always, of course, but within self-study—the method of *currere*—it seems so.
6. "And finally," Planinc (1992, 37) points out, "is it possible to recognize the enduring presence of the transcendent in reality, and in the contemporary society whose

predominant faction represents modernity, without also hoping for the very thing the representatives of modernity claim to have achieved: the redemption of mankind in time." Reactivation and reconstruction promise no redemption; they are, alas, only moves to make, a thoroughly modern idea…maybe.

7. Weil ([1947] 2002, 124) would seem to oppose such an idea, advising against changing ourselves. I would note that subjective reconstruction is not so much changing what we are as reworking what it is others have made of us. While no analogue to Christian conversion, subjective reconstruction does acknowledge that revelation— through study and lived experience—alters how we are, what we think and do.

8. Study can be, as implied in that last endnote, an iconographic space of sustained encounter with alterity intellectually, emotionally, temporally, in the presence of others, within oneself, a certain secular form of liturgical service one might say. "By 'translating' the specificity of place and its spatial connotations into the narrative-temporal dimension of the liturgical order," Steimatsky (2008, 130) suggests (speaking of Pasolini), "a re-siting of the sacred becomes possible." The room that serves as your study might suffice, as might a shared space in a library or reading room, could serve as such a sacred site, as finally, you yourself can serve as such site. "The secondary, local site tied to accidents of place and history, even to regional folklore," Steimatsky continues, "can be consecrated and hence endowed with the sacred value of the original. The sacred is thus made available. The very tenet of Christian culture, the doctrine of the Incarnation, is informed by this paradigm: the historical and the eternal, mortal flesh and holy spirit are identified in the Christian sacraments under God's generous allowance of a sacred *praesentia* and bear upon the Christian understanding of time, of place, and of the image" (131). In study, the topic may be irreligious, but the dynamics of study—reactivation of the past, "re-siting" of the sacred, spurring subjective reconstruction—remain. .

9. Weil (1947) 2002, 178. This apparent affirmation of subjective reconstruction is contradicted elsewhere in her writing; see n7 above.

10. Grant thought that "equality should be the central principle of society since all persons, whatever their conditions, must freely choose to live by what is right or wrong. *This act of choosing is the ultimate human act and is open to all.* In this sense all persons are equal, and differences of talent are of petty significance…. Because of this fact, no human being should be treated simply as a means, like a tree or a car, but as an end. Our moral choices matter absolutely in the scheme of things. Any social order must then try to constitute itself within the recognition of this basic fact of moral personality which all equally possess" (Davis and Roper 2005b, 41; emphasis added). While Grant is emphasizing morality here, my point is that it revolves around autonomy, the capacity to act, attuned to the Good.

11. Davis and Roper 2009b, 842. Sikka (1997, 201) shows that for both Johannes Tauler and Heidegger "the human self is viewed as standing in an intrinsic relation to the infinite, which it itself is not, but towards which it exists as what it is. A central observation of both Tauler and Heidegger is that the self has a tendency to forget this relation, and to evade it, thereby evading the responsibility for self-perfection which the relation imposes upon it. There is, however, a phenomenon which calls the self to this relation; for Tauler, it is the call of God the Father, for Heidegger, the call of conscience." I am reminded of Grant's call for teaching from within one's faith, thereby honouring the inwardness on which attunement relies.

12. In the method of *currere*, synthesis is the final (if recurring) moment of autobiographical study of educational experience, not "infinite" in any empirical sense, but sometimes seemingly "without limits," sacred even when momentary, a formation of soul (or spiritual self) from which engagement with the world flows. Grant might have dismissed such thinking, at one point saying "I don't think personal life is very important at a certain level and I don't want to talk about my psyche" (Davis and Roper 2009b, 164). Unless one confronts one's psychic embeddedness in technology I can't imagine how one can begin to extricate oneself from it. For Grant God intervenes. I am open to that, but while waiting I want to work on the problem myself.

13. "If you look at the ancients," Grant reminded, "there is the clear subordination of politics to philosophy. One's participation in the eternal through philosophy determines one's political wisdom" (Davis and Roper 2009b, 991). The ethical consequences of modernity's eclipse of the eternal, Grant appreciates, is that "the Good has been emptied of content and collapsed into necessity" (McCarroll 2006, 274). Wisdom, political or otherwise, becomes inaudible.

14. Christian 1996d, 351.

15. Christian 1996d, 351. Christian (2006, 58) concludes that Grant had "loyalty" to no political party. That is not to say he was not political: Christian suggests Grant was politically "precocious" in that "he showed evidence of a social conscience at an early age" (41). Ethics is surely that site of mediation between the eternal and the everyday.

16. Davis 2002b, 446. I cannot but think of the fiction of Virginia Woolf. Dinshaw (2012, 64) thinks of Henry Wadsworth Longfellow, in whose *The Golden Legend* (1851) "eternity, the everyday, change, hope, intimacy are all present, as is an expanded sensory perspective on the mundane." The point seems the same; perhaps she is right: "[A] synchrony is in our bones, providing the ground for that constant sense that other times press upon merely sequential chronology" (59).

17. Aoki ([1986/1991] 2005, 159) describes the "pedagogic situation" as "living in tensionality—a tensionality that emerges, in part, from indwelling in a zone between two curriculum worlds: the worlds of curriculum-as-plan and curriculum-as-lived-experiences."

18. "At least in theology," Hall (1978, 123) asserts, "there can be no depth of thought about the 'things eternal' if there is no deep dis-ease with 'things temporal.'" For Grant (in 1953), "theology is that study which teaches us of the final purpose and unity of our existence" (Davis 2002b, 50). Not once and for all as, like education, "theology must be rethought and relived in every generation of the Church. It arises," Grant continues, "with the crisis of the meeting of the temporal and the eternal and springs from every such meeting" (51). Sibley (2008, 133) summarizes succinctly: "Theology, Grant argues, is born of the encounter between time and eternity. As such, theology is an attempt to work out in a particular time and place the truths of eternity."

19. Davis and Roper 2005b, 741–2. Grant's emphasis upon the eternal as distinct from the temporal may derive, in part, from his study of Augustine, at least as Dinshaw (2012, 12–3) describes his conception of time: "For Aristotle," she writes, "the universe itself was infinite; for Augustine, time is created and bounded by the infinite, the eternal, God Himself. For Augustine, time is a good, because created by God, but is also associated with life on earth, which is ultimately an exile from the timeless

divine realm, eternity." In the *Confessions*, she continues, Augustine directs the reader's attention "away from the everyday toward the eternal" (16).

20.   Memory is one mode of revelation of course. *"Remembering with reverence* is a special kind of thinking," Rigelhof (2001, 122) reminds. *"Remembering with reverence* seeks out the ways that people lived—not what they did or said as such but as the life that animated their actions and their words. Those of us who can reverentially remember can come to know something of what others knew and feel something of what they desired and be nudged by what they loved" (122–3).

21.   Sikka 1997, 195.

22.   Grant, Angus (1987, 93) understands, "points to a civilizational contradiction that underlies the contemporary situation—we are beyond metaphysics but can't do without it. Grant's philosophy illumines but does not remove the contradiction." Can we convert contradiction to juxtaposition, living within a "doubled consciousness"?

23.   Schelling—in Pérez-Gómez's (2016, 87) words—urged a "gnostic turn vis-à-vis the rational world of dominant culture and mechanical time and space. He thought it our prerogative to effect a distance from the times in which we live and contemplate within ourselves eternity in its immutable form, this being the only way to access our most precious certainties…. This intuition appears to us whenever we stop being an object for ourselves." That last thought recalls Grant's critique of research.

24.   See Davis and Roper 2009b, 557. The eclipse of "eternal principles" also occurs due to modernity's affirmation of life's purpose as "comfortable self-preservation" (which Grant attributes to Hobbes and Locke), a "lowering of the sights" that led to an eclipse of eternity (Cayley 1995, 74). While not doubting the overall narrative here, I do doubt that comfortable self-preservation and an ongoing affirmation of eternal principles (e.g., justice as finding what one is fitted for) must necessarily be mutually exclusive. As Grant tells Schmidt (1978a, 19): "[T]here are worse accounts of politics than comfortable self-preservation."

25.   Davis and Roper 2005b, 268. For a Christian, Sikka (1997, 194) writes, "to will redemption is to come into accord with the will of God, where that will is manifested in the call of God that comes both inwardly in the ground of the soul and outwardly in the events that befall a person. According to Tauler, coming into accord with God's will means coming into accord with what God destines in the moment of eternity." For Augustine, Kearney (2005b, 148) explains, "to engage with this divine language of interiority is to learn from the eternal Word and, heeding divine teaching, redirect our lives from the fallenness of non-being toward a new quest for reconciled being," adding that "it is, paradoxically, when we attend to the still and steadying character of the eternal Word that we fully realize just how distended and scattered our temporal lives are" (149). "[I]t is from our insights into the experience of time that our longing for eternity arises" (149).

26.   Angus 1997, 158.

27.   "Grant [too] combines the historical and the eternal," Kaethler (2009, 90) reminds.

28.   Weil ([1947] 2002, 121) writes that the "transcendent can be known only through contact since our faculties are unable to invent it."

29.   Referencing Nikephoros, Mondzain (2005, 123) suggests "we come close to believing that the sacred's point of departure is the profane itself, just as Christ's humanity remains the center of the incarnation." The icon is suggestive of the space wherein eternity and temporality intersect.

30.   In Hasidic Judaism, Mayse (2016, 238) reports, "there is an element of the Divine that remains elusively eternal, but it is precisely within the temporal that God and man truly enter into a relationship." So time itself can be iconographic, reminding us of timelessness? Charting time through space, Vettius Valens (c. 120–185 CE) found the study of astrology iconographic, finding "an approximation of eternity both in studying astrology and the doctrine itself," providing "a path for the soul to the immortal, divine, and eternal" (Greenbaum 2016, 63). Weil ([1947] 2002, 37) considered the concept of immortality "harmful," given that we are incapable of conceiving of the "soul as really incorporeal."

31.   Cayley 1995, 68.

32.   Cayley 1995, 68.

33.   "Situation ethics" depends on an "outside"—God or the Good—I realize, and complicating further knowing what to do is skepticism concerning any self-evident sense of obedience to the "outside." As it was for Grant, pacifism appeals to me, as does non-violence generally. One winces at Grant's prescience when he does name acts which seem almost always unjustifiable that have been conducted in democracy's name: "Now, in our era, torture has come back in a big way," Grant tells Cayley (1995, 70) and long before waterboarding, "and by people who believe in progressive ideas."

34.   Cayley (1995, 68).

35.   Kaethler 2009, 31.

36.   Recall that Grant asked himself if "my turning away from homosexuality made me see God?" (Davis and Roper 2009b, 316).

37.   "In this love," Sikka (1997, 195) explains, "the self's willing is a willingness, a preparedness to do and to be what it is called to do and to be. This is a readiness to undertake what it is called to do and to be." My point (again) is that these commands are personal not social or legal, a point Dewey (1922, 204) makes: "Religion as a sense of the whole is the most individualized of all things, the most spontaneous, indefinable and varied. For individuality signifies unique connections in the whole. Yet it has been perverted into something uniform and immutable. It has been formulated into fixed and defined beliefs expressed in required acts and ceremonies. Instead of marking the freedom and peace of the individual as a member of an infinite whole, it has been petrified into a slavery of thought and sentiment, an intolerant superiority on the part of the few and an intolerable burden on the part of the many."

38.   Schmidt 1978a, 66. That said, Grant did on occasion become frustrated by Weil's work, writing in a 1958 letter to Sheila Grant: "I really am going to give up trying to be a philosopher. *I just know nothing after reading Miss Weil…. I have been reading Miss Weil but she gets on my nerves and her absolutist mysticism is tiring*" (quoted in Jersak 2012, 154).

39.   Weil (1947) 2002, 108.

40.   For Weil ([1947] 2002, 82): "Time does us violence," adding that time "casts" a "veil" of "unreality" (52).

41.   Weil (1947) 2002, 148. Interesting, in light of Grant's affection for Mozart, is Frisch's (2016, 283) observation that music is often regarded as one of the "most temporal of the arts," as "musical notation" can be considered an effort to render time "visual" and "reproducible." It is, Frisch adds, "perhaps not surprising that creators of music have associated the two, since temporality extended can become eternity" (283). For

"many centuries," he concludes, "Western composers have been preoccupied with ideas of eternity—in the realms of the secular or sacred, the physical or metaphysical, or the natural or supernatural" (289). For Grant: "Mozart—at one moment— eternity" (Davis and Roper 2005b, 689).

42. "Yet from religion as it vanished," Trilling (1972, 157) reminds, "Freud was intent upon rescuing one element, the imperative actuality which religion attributed to life." Life's imperative quality suggests its immanence, as if we are commanded to endure what befalls us, to (modifying Grant's phrasing) "live through the awful responsibilities of time" (Davis and Roper 2009b, 679–80n69).

43. Steimatsky 2003, 254.

44. Steimatsky 2003, 255.

45. Recall the end of ch. 1 and the association of Grant's presence in his text as a "relic." Gillespie (1990, 129) points to the distinction between modern and ancient conceptions of the past: "Grant thus admires the way the ancients understood their mortality in terms of the eternity of nature or the gods, the manner in which they grasped their own past in terms of this eternity as a tradition rather than as history, and the notion of human excellence that was developed by Plato in his portrayal of Socrates. None of these aspects of antiquity, however, is especially political, although each finds its echo in Grant's religious stance and his defense of localism and parochialism."

46. Weil (1947) 2002, 147. Casting doubt on the concept of *metaxu*, Weil emphasizes that "God" and the "supernatural" are "hidden" and "formless," not only in the "universe" but within the "soul" as well, complaining that the church talks too much "holy things" (56). Grant focused specifically on Protestantism's role in what in his DPhil thesis he termed "particularizing holy" (see ch. 5 here), a role Sibley (2008, 140) suggests is evident in Martin Luther: "Luther posited an inner freedom that rejected the ostensibly oppressive mediations of Catholicism's finite images in defining the individual's relationship to God. But, according to Grant, in doing so Luther effectively undermined the moral and spiritual foundations of the medieval institutions that had traditional mediated time and eternity." Given his historical moment, Grant affirmed such mediation while, I suspect, accepting Weil's cautionary note quoted above.

47. Mondzain 2005, 90.

48. Weil (1947) 2002, 108.

49. Weil (1947) 2002, 148. Beauty renders the soul, Weil writes, "tense" and "silent," beyond affirmation or denial, adding that "faith" too is such an "adherence" (129).

50. Davis 1996, 14. This ancient truth—obscured by modernity's commodification of art—must have seemed embarrassingly out of fashion when Grant pronounced it, not that "fashion" mattered to Grant or to truth. But if Benedetti is right, beauty's transcendental character may once again becoming recognized. Benedetti (2005, 183) writes: "Of the three fundamental aesthetic concepts—beauty, the sublime, and grace—the last, understood by Schiller as immediacy constructed without effort, as a union of the voluntary and the involuntary, seemed to have completely disappeared from modern theories of art. In modern poetics one could resort to either beauty or the sublime, which oriented in various ways the opposition between avant-garde and tradition. In late-modernity, however, grace seems to have made a comeback, having been called on by many writers with the aim of realizing, as [Walter] Benjamin wrote in regard to [Robert] Walser, the perfect fusion of will-lessness and intention."

Might attunement be a version of such a "perfect fusion"? Regarding "the sublime" and "beauty," Trilling (1972, 95) reminds that Edmund Burke "explicitly connects the sublime with masculinity, with manly *ambition*.... Beauty, on the contrary, is to be associated with femininity. It seduces men to inglorious indolence and ignoble hedonism."

51.   Weil (1947) 2002, 56.

52.   In a CBC documentary, Charles Taylor ([1982] 2006, 80) reports, Grant referred to a particular place, a rocky cove in Nova Scotia where his ancestors had lived: "That's why I love this place. It gives me a sense of holiness, of eternity. It reminds me that our traditions, both Greek and Christian, saw the universe as essentially good. The old beliefs recognized limits to man's abilities. They gave us a picture of nature and of man as part of an order, and not a man-made order."

53.   Weil ([1947] 2002, 56) writes that which is "fitted for all things is eternal," comprising the very "value" of "experience." Finding what one is fitted for takes place through experience, it bears repeating, if attuned to the eternal.

54.   Or universal, as when Grant distinguishes between the two: "We speak of whatever is given in sensation, that is, through our senses, as particular. In opposition [really, it seems continuous] to this, a universal will be anything which may be shared by many particulars" (Davis and Roper 2005b, 687). Listening to Mozart Grant seems to glimpse eternity (689).

55.   "For most people the end of life is a time to turn away toward eternity," Grant muses, "to be peaceful and less busy.... I've lived a very practical and busy life. I'm glad to be free of that now" (Davis and Roper 2009b, 581).

56.   Interview with Judy Steed of the *Globe and Mail*, July 9, 1983; quoted in Davis and Roper 2009b, 497. "Eternal justice, or transcendence for that matter," Kaethler (2009, 22) summarizes, "rejects time and nature by seeking to find meaning outside of the temporal." It is as if through attunement, intimations of the eternal become audible.

57.   Athanasiadis (2001, 23) reminds that "Kant drove a clear wedge between the finite and the infinite. The finite mind is unable to reach the infinite. This, of course, was an attack on all form of natural theology which attempt to build bridges to the infinite through human rationality." As noted, on occasion Grant is confident such "bridges" can be built; on others not so much. And Aoki reminds such bridges are not in fact literal. Attunements seems the more suitable (if ultimately unsatisfactory) metaphor.

58.   Davis and Roper 2009b, 805. "As far as the Vedanta is concerned," Arapura (1983, 56) writes (recalling Grant's interest in Hinduism), "the metaphor of gnosis being its own activity is important also for negating the impression that the knowledge of the Eternal that man gains is the result of any activity on his part.... Gnosis is never produced; it is what is there, inseparable from the Eternal or Ultimately Real."

59.   Sikka 1997, 194.

60.   "Both temporal and historical," Vries (2005, 76) suggests, "the movement of faith—conversion, confession—'is' at the same time not of this world, eternal, the annulment of time and the transformation of its ordinary concept." In this "movement," then, attunement to eternal can occur?

61.   Welchman 2016, 185. Grant's teaching seems to me similar to Pasolini's public pedagogy through cinema, at least as Steimatsky (2008, 165) describes it: "Pasolini seeks to capture in the filmed surface, in the 'things of the world,' a glimpse of the iconic image of God: seen but not quite nameable, exceeding the particular and the

historical in its apotheosis in the landscape." For Grant that landscape was meta-phoric as well as literal, as it was for Pasolini.

62. Sibley 2008, 133.
63. Dewey 1922, 203. "[T]he name 'infinite' is a finite name," Caputo (2005, 107) points out, "the concept 'inconceivable' is conceivable, and the name 'ineffable' is very speakable."
64. Dewey 1922, 203.
65. Davis and Roper 2005b, 655.
66. Davis and Roper 2005b, 655.
67. Kaethler 2009, 85.
68. Hutt 2013, 67.
69. Hutt 2013, 67.
70. Collingwood 2002, 112.
71. Collingwood 2002, 113.
72. Collingwood 2002, 114.
73. "[O]nce we have been through the era of subjectivity, science, and technology," David Roberts (1995, 175) appreciates, "there can be no question of merely recon-necting with phronesis or any other aspect of the Greek past. What is possible, again, is a creative fusion of horizons, an encounter with the past that destabilizes our present and enhances our possibilities for the future." From this empirical reality, reactivation requires acting "as if."
74. Collingwood 2002, 114.
75. Collingwood 2002, 115.
76. "The collective unconscious is common to all," Jung (1965, 138) explains, "it is the foundation of what the ancients called the 'sympathy of all things.'" Explaining a contrast between Jung and Freud, Zaretsky (2004, 92–3) provides some context: "For Carl Jung in Zurich…the ego was nothing. He despised its petty hurts, its 'oversensi-tivity,' its prickliness, its obsession with its standing in the world, all traits for whose tolerance he eventually blamed the Jewish character of psychoanalysis. A man of aristocratic temperament, Jung believed that a valid life was one lived in the shad-owed valleys of what he came to call the collective unconscious, the great cosmic for-mations that harbour the archetypes—trans-historical structures such as the Great Mother, the Anima, and the Shadow. Viewing modernity through the prism of loss and decline, he sought to halt its impoverishment of meaning by restoring contract with the sacred. Accordingly, he aimed to assimilate psychoanalysis to myth and religion, although not to any organized religion of his time." The term has circulated widely in several scholarly (and non-scholarly literatures), for me most memorably in Fanon (1967, 187): "European civilization is characterized by the presence, at the heart of what Jung calls the collective unconscious, of an archetype: an expression of the bad instincts, of the darkness inherent in every ego, of the uncivilized savage, the Negro who slumbers in every white man....all the peoples he has known—whether the Pueblo Indians of Arizona or the negroes of Kenya in British East Africa—have had more or less traumatic contacts with the white man."
77. "For a man is never an individual," Sartre (1981, ix) asserted, "it would be more fitting to call him a universal singular. Summed up and for this reason universal-ized by his epoch, he in turn resumes it by reproducing himself in it as singular-ity." Here the "epoch" constitutes "the whole," but even such historicism implies

its transcendence, evident in Combs (1983b, 24) assertion that "[w]ithin this view of the historicity of creation as distinct from the eternality of nature there can be no teaching that is eternally true; there are only historical truths that come to be and pass away." That last assertion Combs makes as if it were "eternally true." And why cannot such "historical truths" be at the same time moving images of eternity?

78.   Collingwood 2002, 98. "In general terms," Collingwood explains, "the modern historian can study the Middle Ages, in the way in which he actually does study them, only because they are not dead. By that I mean not that their writings and so forth are still in existence as material objects, but that their ways of thinking are still in existence as ways in which people still think. The survival need not be continuous. Such things may have died and been raised from the dead, like the ancient languages of Mesopotamia and Egypt" (97).

79.   Doane 2002, 176.

80.   Doane 2002, 176.

81.   Doane 2002, 180.

82.   Doane 2002, 180.

83.   Scanlon 2005, 165.

84.   Kearney 2005b, 147.

85.   Wilberding (2016, 14) reminds that it is common now to use the word "eternity" to mean merely "a very long period of time."

86.   Melamed (2016b, 2) traces this distinction between eternity as "timelessness" and eternity as "everlastingness" to Plato, Aristotle, and Parmenides. Platonists, Wilberding (2016, 17) tells us, regarded Parmenides as a "major forerunner of the Platonic tradition." It was Parmenides who conceived of eternity as "timelessness" (18). Philosophy starts, Grant told his students, with Parmenides (Davis 2002b, 464).

87.   Melamed 2016b, 1.

88.   At one point Grant defines eternity as the "opposite" of time, "expressed vaguely as timelessness" (Davis and Roper 2009b, 934). Logically at least, but for me also interrelated, as in the phrase "time as the moving image of eternity."

89.   Continuity is "lacking," Grant notes, in a technological era (Davis and Roper 2009b, 490). On October 21, 1942—home in Toronto recovering—Grant started keeping a journal (see Christian 1996d, 99). Through registering the moving images of daily life one acknowledges that subjective continuity attunement to the eternal allows.

90.   "The word 'eternal' is here used in no transcendent sense," Grant comments in his review of Carl Jung (but applicable here). Within Jung's psychoanalysis, Grant decodes eternity as "re-activating the collective unconscious [so that] we cease to be simply individual human beings and partake of 'human being-ness' in general" (quoted passages in Davis and Roper 2005b, 186). Grant seems to overstate Jung's view here: the individual remains, if collectively informed. Subjective continuity, then, is simultaneously specific and universal, contingent and timeless.

91.   Wilberding 2016, 23. Discussing Strauss, Sibley (2008, 271–2) reminds that "history demonstrates that all human thought is concerned with much the same fundamental themes and problems, regardless of time and place."

92.   "Eternity is not just secularized out of existence," Welchman (2016, 180) suggests, "but becomes understood as an entailment of, and somehow imbricated in, the conditions of our practical existence." He associates that idea with Kant's idea that

"practical reason involves a kind of eternal, nontemporal action" (181). By being associated with practical action, eternity has become a "more important" even "urgent issue" (187), Welchman writes. "And more recently," McDaniel (2016, 249) reports, "some physicists and philosophers of physics have entertained the hypothesis that spatiotemporality is itself a derivative feature that emerges from a more fundamental nonspatiotemporal framework."

93. Capelle 2005, 123.

94. Davis 2002b, 446. "Grant is otherworldly," Kaethler (2009, 84) notes, "but his otherworldliness leads him back into 'worldliness.'" Colville (1990, 4) puts the matter this way: "Persons are living in history, in the specific here and now, while attempting to be congruent with some transcending essence beyond history."

95. Davis 2002b, 446.

96. Davis 2002b, 446.

97. When "freedom" becomes conflated with "progress," Grant warns, "when it loses all sense of the transcendent purpose of righteousness from which it sprang, will becomes a sheer urge to power and love of consumption" (Davis 2002b, 252). It is no accident he thinks about ethics in a commercial establishment.

98. For the past two centuries, Melamed (2016b, 12) acknowledges, metaphysical concepts such as eternity have been discredited as "backwardness (religious or otherwise) or a kind of eccentricity." Melamed regards eternity as a "fundamental notion of metaphysics" (13).

99. Melamed 2016b, 2.

100. Davis 2002b, 480. Perhaps Grant derived this view from his study of late Greek antiquity, when the "eternal" meant a mode of being that was "removed from time altogether" (Wilberding 2016, 14).

101. "The gist of Grant's refusal of the modern," Lampert (1978, 189) asserts, "is this: we are not fit for it. The truth of the modern world is untrue to man; that is to say, unnatural to human nature, for man *has* a timeless nature." Humanity is—or can be—ethical.

102. For Grant, modernity, in particular, "modern liberalism," McCarroll (2006, 273) notes, accompanied uncritically the "collapse of the concept of the eternal into the temporal order (the Good into necessity)," precipitating "injustice, moral blindness, and the seemingly relentless compulsion of the human will to change and master the world."

103. Recall that Grant too affirmed embodiment, in part—like Augustine, as Elshtain (2005, 246), notes—because the "body is epistemologically significant, a source of delight, of travail, of knowledge of good and evil. The body is the mode through which we connect to the work and through which the world discloses itself. Mind is embodied; body is thought." Elshtain adds: "We come to knowledge through our interaction with the world" (247).

104. Huebner 1999, 110.

105. Huebner 1999, 110.

106. At one point, O'Donovan (1984, 157) notes, "Grant suggests that the end of human knowledge, the highest human freedom, is to contemplate the infinity of our desire for self-transcendence."

107. Lampert 1978, 185. But "love of the good," Athanasiadis (2001, 127) counsels, "must transcend love of one's own.

108. Davis 2002b, 68. In this passage Grant is embracing engagement, specifically "political activities" that "may be" for many "the most educative moments of their existence in this world" (68). The point of such engagement is educational; even the "best form of government"—"democracy"—should be "education's servant" (68).
109. Davis 2002b, 68.
110. Grant 1969, 98. "Drawing on Mircea Eliade," Sibley (2008, 140) summarizes, "Grant describes how, in pre-modern consciousness, events in time have significance only insofar as man is a participant in an overarching and unchanging cosmos. Temporal events reflect the eternal order. Human meaning and purpose are not to be found in the making of history, but rather in the capacity of humans to comprehend and thereby participate in divinely given archetypal patterns.... And individuals are free to the degree that they are able to use their faculty of reason to comprehend and thereby participate in the order of the cosmos and the natural limits it imposes."
111. Grant (1959) 1966, 15.
112. Roberts 1995. That fact would seem to contradict itself, as O'Donovan (1984, 121) implies: "Historical sense, then, is sense of the 'finality of becoming' that undercuts all philosophical definition and generalization." Except, apparently, the "finality of becoming."
113. O'Donovan 1984, 155. I understand but I can't help but wonder why history cannot be associated—humbly, self-critically—with "eternity" as we apprehend it or imagine ourselves attuned to it. After all, ethics is enacted historically—in time, place, with others—and for Grant, O'Donovan (1984, 152) notes, ethical engagement with others both rests as it invites (she quotes Grant) "an inward openness to eternity."
114. Christian (1995) 2001, vii.
115. Freedom for its own sake, moral anarchy, indications of the decline of the West—it was from his study of Leo Strauss, O'Donovan (1984, 161) suggests, that Grant came to a "more pessimistic understanding" of the Western tradition as a "progressive obscuring of 'the whole,' of 'the eternal things,' in the light of which alone man truly understands himself." Absent the knowledge of what we are fitted for, anything goes.
116. Grant (1959) 1966, 15.
117. Time provides passage to eternity (Thibon [1947] 2002, xxix) reminds, as can the icon. "The image is eternal similitude," Mondzain (2005, 3) explains, "the icon is their *relation* and their *intimacy*. The image is eternal similitude, the icon is temporal resemblance. The economy was the theory of the transfiguration of history."
118. Grant (1959) 1966, 15. See Forbes 2007, 89.
119. Cayley 1995, 29–30.
120. Forbes 2007, 90. Justice, Weil ([1947] 2002, 139) wrote, resides where the "natural" and the "supernatural" intersect.
121. Forbes 2007, 113.
122. Grant attributed to Nietzsche understanding "the meaning of this shift from eternal being to eternal becoming was unveiled" (Cayley 1995, 30).
123. Attuned to the eternal by becoming historical, e.g., reactivating the past, a juxtaposition implied when Weil ([1947] 2002, 175) writes that "time as it flows wears down and destroys that which is temporal. Accordingly there is more of eternity in the past than the present."
124. Grant (1959) 1966, 19–20. See Forbes 2007, 90.

125. Grant (1959) 1966, 15.

126. More specifically, the self's shattering serves as passage, at least for Weil ([1947] 2002, 83): "Time's violence rends the soul: by the rent eternity enters."

127. Dewey 1922, 204.

128. Grant (1959) 1966, 23. Discussing psychoanalysis, Grant notes that for Jung humanization—and, presumably, healing—follow from reactivating "eternal archetypes" (Davis and Roper 2005b, 186). Grant seems sympathetic, decrying the technological world as "emptied inwardly," and "cut off…from the eternal archetypes…ever more prone to outward violence and inward meaninglessness" (187). Given Jung's intellectual dependence on (if reconstruction of) his work, why Freud gets positioned as an enemy of eternity is not obvious (see Davis and Roper 2009b, 839).

129. Birth is often regarded as a gift but for Weil ([1947] 2002, 85), "death" is the "most precious" gift given to us.

130. Davis 2006, 69.

131. Could this be what Weil ([1947] 2002, 56) means when she suggests that what is universal is "eternal," the very value of "experience?" Her invocation of the cross later in the passage affirms the redemptive character of such experience, e.g., as "affliction"; see Weil (1947) 2002, 19, 78, 81. While affirming a theology of the cross, Athanasiadis (2001, 49) emphasizes that Grant kept open the matter of its meaning for individuals: "The reality of the world is one of evil, suffering, misery, and affliction…. Thus, in order to maintain an honesty about reality, it is also necessary to maintain a certain agnosticism or mystery about God's presence and working in the world." In his DPhil thesis Grant wrote: "[T]he present writer must admit his own agnosticism as to how universalist and individualist 'oughts' may be reconciled" (Davis and Emberley 2000b, 350). My point exactly.

132. Grant (1959) 1966, 45. Not only intervention but also infusion, as Hasidic teachings position God as "beyond time and outside all human notions of temporality…not the ultimate being but…the totality of Being itself" (Mayse 2016, 231). Mayse continues: "God continuously infuses the cosmos with sacred vitality, without which the universe would instantaneously collapse. This sacred energy represents God's immutable and immanent presence in the physical world. The cosmos is a temporal embodiment of the infinite and eternal Divine, and it is constantly being revitalized with God's life-force" (232).

133. Combs 1983b, 25.

134. Grant (1959) 1966, 45. From the apprehension of revelation to its comprehension is not only elusive. Mondzain (2005, 23) suggests: "The discourse of divine substance, of its eternal, transcendent essence that surpasses all comprehension and escapes all visibility, can only be hostile to all possibilities of portrayal and even to each of the historic figures of the redemption." Referencing Augustine, Elshtain (2005, 248) emphasizes: "Full knowledge is not available to human knowers, no matter how brilliant and learned that knower. We are both limited and enabled by the conventions of language." The gap between revelation and reason remains.

135. "The past, Weil ([1947] 2002, 175) writes, is time "coloured" with "eternity."

136. "More than an erasure of the past," Maggi (2009, 336) writes, referencing Pasolini's *Salò*, "we should speak of a metamorphosis of the past. Human beings, *Salò* tells us, have metamorphosed into monsters of an eternal present. Their monstrosity lies in a denial of time; they have changed into beings who do not change."

137. Modernity becomes for Grant "the thrust toward a contentless future, with the consequent loss of eternity," Beiner (1996, 130n5) explains, the explication of which was Grant's "chief purpose in teaching."

138. Grant (1969) 2001, 74. If not "new," a device or a practice—or a person—is dismissed as "dated." Recalling that the "great criticism of Diefenbaker was always that he was 'out of date,'" Grant focuses on the phrase, pointing out that it follows from faith in technological progress, so that "anything that is technologically and administratively necessary is also good. This expresses that oblivion of eternity which now defines the West" (Davis and Roper 2009b, 406). If all materiality is a moving image of eternity, then so are youthfulness and novelty.

139. Davis 2002b, 159.

140. From a November 1985 letter to Joan O'Donovan; see Christian 1996d, 350.

141. O'Donovan (1984, 165) suggests that "the ground for recollection for Grant...is the self-revelation of Eternal Justice to the human soul, the illumination of the mind by divine grace, which has the appearance for us of chance." O'Donovan may be quite right that for Grant recollection occurs as a kind of visitation from the divine. For me psychoanalytic-like reactivation of the past is an ongoing act of will, open to revelation but not dependent upon it. Unless of course "revelation" becomes conflated with Totality, in which case the distinction—between being visited or acting in the service of—seems inconsequential.

142. For Zylstra (1978, 156), Grant is grappling with "two deities," one a God of "perfection," a deity who "bears a remarkable resemblance to the God of Greek philosophy. And there is also the God who wills, who creates, who commands. He accepts the God who *is* love while he hesitates before a God who *wills* love." For Kaethler (2009, 5), Athens and Jerusalem form an "interdependent relationship" in Grant's mind, allowing him to harmonize "interrelated concepts of love, grace and justice," constituting the very "crux" of Grant's thought, his "critique and defence against modernity and Heidegger." Reimer (1990, 120) writes: "For Grant, that which grants and is granted is permanent, immutable and eternal as envisioned most adequately within classical Platonism and Christian theism. For Grant the love of one's own particular is only a means to the experiencing of that which is universally and eternally good. Only such a supra-historical anchor can secure true justice for the weak and the strong alike and limit our arrogant human drive into a tyrannical future. The eternal is the standard by which the temporal scientific and political ideologies of histories can be measured and judged." The eternal may provide the standard by which ideologies can be judged, but "it" cannot insulate humanity from the ravages of our inhumanity.

143. Davis 2002b, 61.

144. It would appear so in architecture, it seems. "Another important aspect of architecture's gift of *place*," Pérez-Gómez (2016, 227) asserts, "is to reveal in itself *the true temporality* of this space of human experience, a constitutive dimension of what we may call our access to *spirituality*. This is the experience of a present moment that, while it can be conceptualized by science (and our clocks) as a quasi-nonexistent point between past and future, is experienced as thick and endowed with dimensions—in a sense, eternal."

145. Grant blames Protestantism (following ancient Judaism) for erasing what for the ancient Greeks and Christians had been essential to religion, namely, "mediation" (Heaven 2006, 305).

146. "Socrates as Eros mediates both ways between the temporal and the eternal," Heaven (2006, 307) writes, "allowing the temporal to be 'the moving image of the eternal.'" It is Christ of the Gospels and not the historical Jesus of which Grant writes, Heaven notes (310), adding that the "cross" serves as the "supreme image of the ways things are for humans, bound up a they are within the desire for good and simultaneously crushed by necessity" (311).

147. "Driving the work of Weil, Thibon ([1947] 2002, xx–xxi) suggests, is an "intense desire" for "inward purification," that stripping away of fusion with what is, enabling to experience an "absolute goodness." For the secular such "inward purification" might be prerequisite for attunement.

148. In Hasidic Judaism, Mayse (2016, 235) explains, only the "one who journeys into the innermost recesses of the mind can cleave to the eternal unity that undergirds the temporal cosmos," adding that "Hasidic teachings situate this contemplative process in sacred rituals like prayer, study, or the other commandments, but many sermons extend this paradigm to seemingly mundane actions performed with the correct mindfulness. This means that all human deeds are potential access points for attaining God's eternity." Teaching too, it bears repeating. For a secular (and unfortunately formulaic) outline of mindfulness in education, see Ergas 2017.

149. Weil (1947) 2002, 120.

150. Greene 1973, 72.

151. Greene 1973, 72.

152. Greene 1973, 72. "Socrates as Eros," Heaven (2006, 307) suggests, "mediates both ways between the temporal and the eternal, allowing the temporal to be 'the moving image of the eternal.'"

153. Magrini 2017, 114.

154. Grant (1969) 2001, 52. For Kittler (2013, 25), the "death of tragedy coincides with the birth of science."

155. Davis and Roper 2005b, 706.

156. Davis and Roper 2005b, 706.

157. Weil (1947) 2002, 145.

158. Sibley 2008, 127.

159. Kaethler 2009, 86.

160. Referencing Aristotle, Grant asserts that "central to the philosophy of education" is that "the final object of the cultivation of reason is that we may know what is ultimately real—that is, God" (Davis 2002b, 172). In modernity, as Nicholson (2006, 326) reminds: "Reason has, as it were, migrated away from nature and the eternal, to take up residence within the freedom of subjectivity itself." In late modernity reason seems to have been banished from subjectivity as well.

161. In his DPhil thesis, Grant pointed out (approvingly it appears) that "Oman would affirm that reason has an Idea of Spirit (so many different vocabularies might here be used) and with that Idea so much content as always to pass beyond the known or the possessed—very much in the way that scientific knowledge always points beyond itself" (Davis and Emberley 2000b, 357–8).

162. Fishbane 2008, 6.

163. The "temporal" is a "bridge," Weil ([1947] 2002, 147) writes.

164. Sikka (1997, 252) suggests: "What brings Heidegger into proximity with the strand of mystical thought to which Ruusbroec, among others, belongs is the notion of being

as an abyss that refuses and denies any final conceptualization or expression but which, at the same time, is the source of all the finite modes in which it reveals itself, a source that conceals and shelters the inexhaustible wealth of those modes within itself.... It means being 'attuned' to it in its self-manifestation." Bridging the "abyss" through attunement seems, in Sikka's study, simultaneously sacred and secular.

165. Ouspensky 1982, 41.

166. Thibon (1947) 2002, xxix.

167. Liturgical art generally, Ouspensky (1982, 36) suggests, constitutes "not only our offering to God, but also God's descent into our midst, one of the forms in which is accomplished the meeting of God with man, of grace with nature, eternity with time."

168. We are "attached" to the present, Weil ([1947] 2002, 175) observed. Grant knew that "living without future and without past" collapses any distinction between "beasts from the human animal" (Davis and Roper 2009b, 1014).

169. Benedetti 2005, 22. In late modernity, Benedetti suggests, "there is no longer anything that is truly created; every form is an imitation, a citation of someone else's work.... With that, art condemns itself to necrophilia. The medicine turns out to be a poison. Sure, it allows one to elude the modern artistic logic entered on the value of the new and to get around its paralysis, but only on condition that creation no longer exists" (190). This book would seem to be another instance of what Benedetti depicts.

170. Davis and Roper 2009b, 844.

171. Davis and Roper 2009b, 842.

172. As Mondzain (2005, 224) observes: "The era of simulacra has taken place of the era of the image, of icons, and the word, all of which were originally indistinguishable from each other." Technologization, Mondzain might be implying, is the material-ization of the spiritualization that once characterized the West.

173. Dinshaw 2012, 116.

174. Lipari 2014, 186.

175. Dinshaw 2012, 109. Huebner (1999, 104) speaks of "the fullness of the eternal pres-ent" being eclipsed by "the sterility of the known future," referencing educators' preoccupation with "purpose" or "goal."

176. Weil (1947) 2002, 82.

177. Stamps 1995, 7. Hope is no help either, associated as it so often is in modernity with scientific discovery and technological production. In this sense, as Athanasiadis (2001, 162) points out, "Hope in the future is the 'chief opiate' of the modern world because it teaches people to dream rather than come to terms with reality." Without hope I labour toward resolve (Pinar 2015a, 180): mindful of but not determined by outcomes. "In every situation," Athanasiadis (2001, 161) appreciates, "it matters ulti-mately what one does."

178. Davis and Roper 2009b, 843.

179. Davis and Roper 2009b, 842.

180. Rocha 2017, 13.

181. Rocha 2017, 203.

182. Rocha 2017, 12.

183. Quoted in O'Donovan 1984, 123.

184. Melamed (2016b, 1) defines eternity as a "unique" order of "*existence*" belonging to the "most real being or beings...not shaken by the common wear and tear of time."

For me, time cannot be apprehended unless there is also a sense of being outside time, a sense of being present through time, a sense technology obscures.

185. Like Innis, Angus (1997, 201) notes, Grant embraced "particularity," enabling attunement "from one's own body, through local oral traditions to Canada itself, and perhaps beyond." Angus continues: "Particularity is not a defined arena of social life, but a concept that pertains to the character of one's encounter with any given arena of that life as a legitimation of a less universal, but necessary and good, moment of belonging, or being-at-home. It is because it is not a defined sphere of social life that particularity must be actively embraced. We may say that particularity is a mode of concern in which the specificity of the initial encounter is deemed worthwhile precisely insofar as it is one's indispensable way towards the universal" (201–2).

186. As suggested at the end of the last note, this "mode of concern" denotes, in our era, a moral not political obligation. O'Donovan (1984, 67) registers Grant's rejection of "modern political philosophy, so he must perceive the universal of technological freedom as the 'false universal.'"

187. Davis and Emberley 2000b, 158.

188. Davis 2002a, xix. Grant tells Cayley (1995, 57): "What Plato enabled me to do was to see some unity between thinking about ordinary things and my belief in God."

189. "Faith," Athanasiadis (2001, 159) writes, is "not absolute certainty. It has glimpsed the truth of the eternal order of divine perfection, the good which is love and the hidden presence in all of reality. But it has glimpsed this love from afar, crucified on a cross."

190. Davis 2002a, xix–xx. Contra Davis, O'Donovan (1984, 166) concluded that Grant could not "think together 'history' and 'eternity.'" But ethics requires we must, does it not? The inconsistency is, I think, Grant's. On some occasions he connected the two (as in the abortion issue, for instance) and on others he insisted the gap was unbridgeable.

191. Davis and Emberley 2000b, 158.

192. Weil, Thibon ([1947] 2002, xxxiii) concludes, chronicles the "journey" of the "soul" seeking "God." In my secular educational terms, I seek to register—through reactivation and reconstruction—the lived experience of curriculum: *currere*.

193. "The most absolute naiveté about time," Davis and Roper (2005b, 623) assert, "is to take the past as in no sense present."

194. Forbes 2007, 67. "Freedom means for us," Grant noted, "external freedom," meaning that "when we want to do something, nothing stands in the way of us doing it" (Davis and Roper 2009b, 950). Rejecting the idolatry of freedom modernity installs does not dissolve it, as even obedience to what attunement reveals requires one to exercise one's freedom. Such double consciousness is implied in Davis's (1996, 146) observation that Grant "was driven by the conviction that neither historical freedom nor eternal good could be evaded or compromised."

195. Grant (1974) 1998, 84.

196. Grant knew that "we have lost our way in thinking what anything is fitted for" (Davis and Roper 2005b, 623). What is lost can be found, Grant also knew.

197. "In other words," Meynell (2011, 138) reasons, "without a notion of an authoritative God beyond rational comprehension, we mistake our own ideas for ultimate truth, and thus act according to our pure will, while claiming to do so in God's name."

While that error occurs commonly, positing an "authoritative God beyond rational comprehension" risks merely restating the problem of knowing what things are fitted for.

198. Grant (1969) 2001, 56. Weil ([1947] 2002, 130) concurs, pointing out that our obsession with the "new" distracts us from the "transcendent, undemonstrable meaning" of what is here already. While contemptuous of capitalism's compulsion to create "the new," I don't see why one must forego novelty altogether in the attempt to attune oneself to eternity. If time is a moving image of eternity, surely the image can take novel forms, provide unprecedented experiences, and even afford some progress— ending poverty and pollution, for instance—while still acknowledging, even reverently, the mysterious and cyclical if chance-driven character of human life.

199. Grant (1969) 2001, 56. Praising a student's essay in class one day, Grant pronounced the eternal recurrence "the most abysmal thought" (Davis and Roper 2009b, 1002). In another class he discusses eternal recurrence in "light of [a student's] essay" (1003), for the moment sounding like a student-centred progressive.

200. Grant (1969) 2001, 56. Athanasiadis (2001, 188) suggests that with his "eternal recurrence of the same…Nietzsche transferred the eternal completely into the realm of history and becoming." To be sure, comfort and security hardly automatically ensue—whether eternity infiltrates history or remains removed in some transcendent realm—but overcoming requires attunement to what exceeds the empirical.

201. Davis and Roper 2009b, 1013.

202. Christian (1995) 2001, xxxi. There is also the unity of "whole" of course. That scale of unity, McCarroll (2006, 273) observes, "is known primarily by its absence, which transcends this realm."

203. Weil (1947) 2002, 19.

204. Thibon (1947) 2002, xxxv.

205. Thibon (1947) 2002, xxxv.

206. McCarroll 2006, 272. "Bonds of affection," Elshtain (2005, 250) remarks, "tied human beings from the start."

207. Fishbane 2008, 129.

208. Referencing Weil, Heaven and Heaven (1978, 78) note that "beauty is manifested not only in nature but in certain rare human beings who are like 'shafts' or 'pinpoints' of light whose very being is a radiant manifestation of eternal truth."

209. "The beauty that is seen, known, and loved in the other," McCarroll (2006, 279) suggests, "is the very mirror of eternity experienced in the particularities of life." At one point Grant asks: "Does the experience of the beautiful help to overcome our oblivion of eternity?" (Davis and Roper 2009b, 430) Referencing the Gospels, Grant defines beauty as "the image of the Good in the world" (Davis and Roper 2009b, 939). Indeed, such "intimations" (of the eternal through beauty), Christian and Grant (1998a, 29) write, "are precious and should be treasured, because they may be the way that the good for human beings, unspeakable in public terms in the contemporary world, may yet appear to us in the darkness of our situation."

210. Discussing James Joyce's conception of the "epiphany" (literally a "showing forth"), Trilling (1972, 89) concludes that an "increasing concern with the actual, with the substance of life in all its ordinariness and lack of elevation, was not directed to practicality alone. It also made the ground of a new, or rediscovered, kind of spiritual experience. To emphasize the intractable material necessity of common life and

what this implies of life's wonderlessness is to make all the more wonderful such moments of transcendence as may now and then occur."

211. Davis and Roper 2005b, 693.

212. Davis and Roper 2005b, 693.

213. Davis and Emberley 2000b, 157. One enters a complicated conversation through sustained study, one that shifts in space and time as one is reconstructed by educational experience. Not only Oman and theology, but philosophy and "modern scholarship" more generally enabled Grant to attune himself to the eternal, through time, a point Schmidt (1978b, 131) makes: "It was his experience of a society where time had been reduced to history that provoked Grant to study—and affirm—Plato's conception of time as "the moving image of eternity."

214. Davis and Emberley 2000b, 157.

215. "I must posit something which is eternal and lovable," Grant tells us, "that it has never appeared to me directly" (Davis and Roper 2005b, 696). Acting "as if" there is "something eternal and lovable" is no matter of "must," but, instead, more like a thought experiment. "I say to make a novel education," Deborah Britzman (2006, ix) asserts, "we need to stay close to this affected improper study. Then, research itself can be conceptualized as a thought experiment, as a note of counter-discourse." I am reminded too of Montaigne; of him, Weintraub (1978, 186) reports: "His uncontrollable imagination, leading the logic of his argument astray, involved him in thought experiments taking him back to the inner experience with vastly expanded understanding." These lines suggest the role of reason in apprehending the eternal: postulating "as if" allows attunement to what thought by itself obscures.

216. O'Donovan 1984, 124.

217. Like the incarnation, an icon is "extra-temporal revelation manifested in a given concrete event," Ouspensky (1982, 38) suggests.

218. Christian (1995) 2001, xiv.

219. Emberley 1990b, xviii. "For Grant," Sibley (2008, 171) says, "Strauss' account shows that modernity has become nihilistic because of its disconnection from eternity."

220. Christian (1995) 2001, xiv. "For Hegel," Meynell (2011, 136) notes, the concept of "spiritual" is "infinite" but does not reference a "world beyond ours, physically separated from us either by space or death, but to this world. It is the realm or aspect of experience that connects us with our history and each other and it makes itself apparent in myriad ways, including acts of charity and self-sacrifice." For Marion (2012, 183), "[f]aith would be worth nothing without charity," suggesting that "faith must be absorbed in charity." I'm reminded of how theory becomes "absorbed" by practice in curriculum theory.

221. Christian (1995) 2001, xiv. The eternity Nietzsche offered, Grant complained, was one "of becoming and perishing" (Davis and Roper 2009b, 1005). "Willing the eternal return is the peak of the will," he noted (1006).

222. "Where the ancients believed that man achieved his greatest fulfilment through a reasoned comprehension of and obedience to the cosmic order," Sibley (2008, 142) notes, "moderns regard freedom as a reflection of their ability to impose their will on a word devoid of any intrinsic meaning or teleological purpose." Like Grant, I aspire to house both ancient and modern conceptions within the same subjectivity, an expansive and at least "double consciousness."

223. Weil (1947) 2002, 106.

224. That space could sometimes be gendered, as Izenberg (2000, 99) notes in his study of the works of Thomas Mann: "The older equation artist = marginal man = criminal has been amended to artist = marginal man = criminal = homosexual."

225. Aoki (1995) 2005, 307.

226. Davis 2002b, 224.

227. Davis 2002b, 496.

228. Especially liturgic art would appear to occupy this position between here and eternity. Such art is, Ouspensky (1982, 36) suggests, "not only our offering to God, but also God's descent into our midst, one of the forms in which is accomplished the meeting of God with man, of grace with nature, eternity with time."

229. Davis 2002b, 200.

230. Halbertal and Margalit 1992, 96.

231. O'Donovan 1984, 22.

232. Lints 2015, 19.

233. "A conception which begins by ignoring or denying the symbolic character of history," Schmidt (1978b, 136) concludes, "must end with the oblivion of eternity and the reduction of Being to the temporal."

234. Secularizing God by humanizing the concept, Dewey ([1934] 1962, 42) noted: "On the one score, the word [God] can mean only a particular Being. On the other score, it denotes the unity of all ideal ends arousing us to desire and actions." Yet, that word "unity" implies something beyond specific "ideal ends," a composite of ends perhaps but nonetheless something independent of them. Not the God Lints knows, but something transcendent all the same.

235. Davis and Roper 2005b, 41.

236. Davis and Roper 2005b, 136.

237. Davis and Roper 2005b, 136.

238. Davis and Roper 2005b, 136.

239. Davis and Roper 2005b, 136.

240. Davis and Roper 2005b, 137.

241. Norman 2016, 230.

242. Davis and Roper 2009b, 842.

243. Davis and Roper 2009b, 842.

244. Christian 2006, 42.

245. Davis 2002b, 102.

246. Davis 2002b, 102.

247. For an even more chilling instance than Ben Williamson 2013, see Caplan 2018, where the educational exploitation of children for economic ends becomes only and explicitly economic exploitation.

248. Davis 2002b, 184.

249. Davis 2002b, 184.

250. Davis and Roper 2005b, 137.

251. Davis and Roper 2005b, 137. "[I]t is easy to underestimate the extent to which Grant's thinking was rooted in the world," as Whillier (1990a, v) emphasizes.

252. My thanks to Professor Rong Tingwei for bringing to my attention Romans 12:2: "And do not be conformed to this world, but be transformed by the renewing of your mind, that you may prove what *is* that good and acceptable and perfect will of God."

253. Davis and Roper 2005b, 138.

254. For Grant, love or faith precedes understanding, but for Augustine, Scanlon (2005, 159) points out, the relationship was not only sequential; for Augustine, "faith not only precedes understanding but is its very condition."

255. "[T]he final hour," for Al-i Ahmad (1984, 139), is "when the machine demon (if we don't rein it in or put its spirit in the bottle) will set the hydrogen bomb at the end of the road for humanity."

256. Davis and Roper 2005b, 269.

Epilogue

<blockquote>
If we aren't constantly recreating ourselves in thought and in imagination, the
people we come near won't learn anything from us.[1]

George Grant
</blockquote>

George Grant, the journalist Charles Taylor reminds, was "the most public of
philosophers," teaching us to grapple with "the ultimate meaning of the whole
Western experience," a panoramic preoccupation that was "rooted in his particular situation as a Canadian living in the second half of the twentieth century," animated, Taylor adds, by "his need to communicate his perceptions and his fears."[2]
For Grant it was the world that was the site of education, but it was also the place
from which education led, as he made clear:

> The very word education comes from an allegory of that great thinker, Plato.
> He describes human beings as living chained in a dark cave and their lives as
> a struggle to free themselves from those chains, to struggle up the steep ascent
> to the mouth of the cave and out into the sunlight which is the radiance of
> God. That is where the word education comes from. *Educo*—to lead out. And
> it seems to me that all of us are doing with ourselves and with the youngsters
> we teach—leading ourselves out of the chains of ignorance into the freedom
> of knowledge. That is, obviously, what Jesus meant when he said, "The truth
> shall make you free."[3]

The "very purpose" of education is education.[4] So understood, the world becomes
an iconographic space encouraging attunement to what it is not available to the

senses. Yet we cannot call Grant only otherworldly: "You have to live in the world," Grant told Taylor. "I can't imagine not living in the world. Sheila and I have raised six children. I can't imagine not having a family. You learn so much."[5] The love of one's own, as Grant's teaching testifies, can be reciprocally related to the love of the Good.[6]

Like the progressives, then, Grant regarded lived experience—being subjectively present, ethically engaged with others in the world as it is and might become—as educational, at least potentially so. Unlike the progressives, Ajzenstat argues, Grant was convinced "justice" and "liberty" rest upon "an experience of love that limits our manipulative activism and for which progressivist liberalism consequently makes no public room."[7] Not explicitly, but progressivism does affirm, as Grant did, that just as it matters what we do it also matters what we know. These intertwining domains—knowledge, thought, and action—are reciprocally related; perhaps love, in Grant's sense, unnamed in progressivism, is what threads them together. Now, however, each—knowledge, thought, action— is increasingly confined by soft and hardware.[8] Attending to the three enables us to learn from experience, and (in Grant's word) "recreate" ourselves, reconstruct what we have been conditioned to be in light of what is revealed through attunement.

Subjective reconstruction is, then, spiritual as well as social and psychic, a reasoned participation, even intervention, into what has happened to us, into what is happening now. "Transcendent reason is how we discover the meaning of our lives and make that meaning our own," Sibley suggests, adding: "The world is not of human making or willing, but one in which we must harmoniously abide in order to know our proper ends."[9] For me the three—making, willing, abiding—are co-extensive, not simultaneous but a situated series. Not procedure but improvisation, as Grant acknowledges: "We make ourselves as we go along."[10] That line can seem too simple, "but on a deeper level," Athanasiadis suggests, Grant appreciates "that life is a continual process of 'remaking oneself,' and this is part of the 'wonderful mystery' of divine providence through which disappointments teach one what is worth trusting and what is vanity and pride."[11] That line may seem facile, too, as surely the "mystery" of human life is not only "wonderful," nor do "disappointments" always teach so straightforwardly, but— significantly—Athanasiadis emphasizes that subjective reconstruction is not only psychosocial but spiritual. And in a somewhat specific sense, as Grant qualifies: "What is the most important to be thought is the rethinking of what things are fitted for."[12] Rethinking what things are fitted for requires the invocation of icons not idols, neither (despite the origins and histories of these concepts[13]) necessarily, strictly speaking, religious.[14] Yet like religion, subjective reconstruction occurs through study, less a matter of engineering than transmutation, in Fishbane's terms a "gravitational settling of thought into behaviour; and concomitantly, it is the nexus where physicality becomes spirit, infusing the forms of worldliness with transcendent dimensions."[15]

Whether we can reconstruct our idolatrous relationship to technology could be the key question of the present historical moment, "this immoderate age"[16] Grant knew. As we saw in chapter 2, Grant himself was not optimistic. As Ian Angus appreciates: "Escaping the technological empire requires, in the first place, understanding how deeply we are each caught up in it."[17] Rigelhof reminds: "Technology has a way of extending its reach until it claims us entirely for itself."[18] It becomes a simulation of eternity. To extricate ourselves from this virtual eternity is surely a subjective and spiritual and intellectual[19] undertaking, not a technological one. Like Andrew Feenberg and other (guarded) optimists, the great American curriculum theorist James B. Macdonald also felt confident: "Humanity will eventually transcend technology by turning inward, the only viable alternative that allows a human being to continue to experience oneself in a world as a creative and vital element. Out of this will come the rediscovery of human potential."[20] Macdonald was writing when Grant was writing, the moment before the computer became personal, before the person disappeared into the screen, first our idol now our abode, consuming first our attention then our very subjective presence in the world.[21]

Like the owl of Minerva, subjective presence engages as it withdraws, creating a space in between, where passage away from the present becomes possible. Like Pasolini, I suggest, Grant "continues to project signals of his authorial presence even in the darkness he has created, as a firefly continues to emit intermittent light."[22] Illumined is not the object but its movement within the cave. In its occupation of and moving within space—being (t)here—subjective presence contradicts that dissociation submergence in the screen installs.[23] In contrast to the vacancy of the device, the person occupies space through withdrawal from it. That vacant look could be reoccupied by the radiance subjectivity can emanate.[24]

By invoking Grant's subjective presence[25]—no monolith[26]—imprinted variously within his texts, we can work to extricate ourselves from the machine, labouring to reposition ourselves in front of this embodied icon, wherein we can be transported from here to there, listening carefully to Grant as he teaches at a moment just before technology becomes totalizing, a moment when we could still see each other's eyes rather than the screens we hold in our hands but which hold us in theirs. By regressing from this virtual and temporally empty moment to that actual, still vibrantly historical present, it is "as if" we can reactivate that iconographic space of non-coincidence between us and the screen with which many are fused.

I make no promises; I have no (conceptual) products to sell. The terrible truth is that we cannot be sanguine about our situation, as Grant knew, insisting as he did on seeing the present darkness as real darkness. To live with hope is like living inside virtual space, wagering that with the next click things will turn out better. I have no hope. What I have is resolve. Because resolve is embodied and thereby temporalized, it provides firmer footing. There can be no disappointments with resolve, no wagers gone wrong, no sense of having bet on the wrong horse. Ethics, not economic gain or political power, structures one's resolve to remain in study.

Easy to say, hard to live, perhaps even harder to understand. After all, living in a tower of Babel, words easily mislead. Even when we can decode the print we read we can stop there, fixed on the words only, according them the status of idols. In our age everything is eligible for idolatry, including Grant and his teaching. To keep him an icon requires us to sense his subjective presence[27] embedded in that historical moment, animating the words we study now. Grant was alert to these complexities of communication, as O'Donovan reminds:

> Even our language, although it belongs to *"the* tradition," is not an avenue of recovery *in itself*. For its meaning has been so perverted that it is now "incomprehensible" in its denial of the truths that were once affirmed through it. Thus our emancipation must come from without.[28]

For Grant, that "without" was conveyed as "the Good" or "God,"[29] terms, Athanasiadis points out, "outside the modern."[30] We moderns can live "as if" we can be guided through attunement to what lies beyond language, but we cannot in any scientific sense "know" what Grant termed "the whole."[31]

When the gap between here and eternity is imagined as bridged—as when fundamentalists decide the Bible and other holy books represent dictation by the Deity—"the whole" becomes scriptural, reduced to discourse, including commandments and other—including the Leviticus—prohibitions. Eternity would seem outside time; God, as Jean-Luc Marion would have it, is "without Being." What we mortals can discern is what attunement reveals, constrained by our apparatus of apprehension, by our capacity to comprehend. As Dewey knew:

> Religion as a sense of the whole is the most individualized of all things, the most spontaneous, indefinable and varied. For individuality signifies unique connections in the whole. Yet it has been perverted into something uniform and immutable. It has been formulated into fixed and defined beliefs expressed in required acts and ceremonies. Instead of marking the freedom and peace of the individual as a member of an infinite whole, it has been petrified into a slavery of thought and sentiment, an intolerant superiority on the part of the few and an intolerable burden on the part of the many.[32]

Grant affirmed the gift of egalitarian—not possessive[33]—individualism Christianity conferred. Taking that back in the name of doctrinal truth seems a cruel—idolatrous—fate indeed.

While no fundamentalist (except on the issues of abortion and euthanasia), Grant was reluctant to abandon institutionalized Christianity. "Grant treated religion, and especially religious institutions and establishments," Christian points out, "as topics within the general subject of political philosophy. From this perspective, what counted with regard to religion was its civil implications."[34] Because Christianity emphasized the spiritual subtext of human existence, it provided inspiration for critiques of human action, including technological action.[35] Its church, however, had obviously failed to restrain unbounded human willing; by 1969, Christian points out, Grant had "abandoned all hope that institutionalized Christianity would provide the needed shackles."[36] Consequently, Christian concludes, Grant felt that Christianity could no longer be an "adequate public religion in a technological age," that as a "public alternative to technological modernity, Christianity was effectively finished."[37] Sans spiritual subtext, we are adrift in time: historicism.

Today time is a casualty of unbound human willing, concentrated in technological development and the endless distraction it installs. So we suffer timelessness of another type—that presentism that is submergence in the screen—that requires the recovery of time, and as a moving image of eternity. Becoming historical[38] through academic study we might make time again, no steady stream of progress but advancement in attunement to the Good. Reactivating[39] Grant's critique of technology, time, and teaching reminds us of what has happened, of what might happen.[40] O'Donovan summarizes: "The first phase is the infinite subjectivity of the Reformation religious consciousness. The second is the externality and determinism of technological conquest. The third is the future reconciliation of technological determinism and infinite subjectivity in a new age of contemplation."[41] That hope belonged to Grant during the 1950s, as later—by the 1970s, when Macdonald expressed faith that the transcendence of technology was possible—Grant had lost faith that any such sequence could occur.[42] Indeed: "To change everything," Rocha writes (almost fifty years on), "we must be willing to change nothing and simply recover what we have lost, holding tight to hope, that nostalgia for the future."[43] Roger Simon concurs, affirming that "the promise of remembrance...is always about the future."[44]

By the 1970s the future seemed foreclosed. Almost suddenly it seemed clear that (not only) North Americans' intensifying addiction to technological novelty *and* our determination to master nature human and non-human had fused. "For these triumphs of mastery," O'Donovan appreciates, "place us in a relation to human and non-human nature that conceals our own essence, that for which we are fitted."[45] Such justice seems especially elusive in our time; to the past we must flee to experience any sense of what justice might mean now.

How can one reactivate the past from within the present? Thinking—let alone living—outside the historicist[46] and liberal assumptions of "late modernity,"[47] as Grant knew and Athanasiadis acknowledges, is an "immense"[48] challenge. Risking reduction of the past to the terms of the present requires "partaking" (in Grant's gerund) of the past, so that it can become incorporated in one's fiber, as was Grant's own hybrid philosophy: progressive and Christian and Platonist. The phrase is not only a juxtaposition of discrete (and contradictory) conceptual elements; it denotes the temporal layering of belief, identity, and practice in Grant's life history, implied in Davis' summary statement:

> Grant understood the belief in progress because he himself was raised to be progressive. At the same time, however, his progressive stance had been weakened by the shattering experiences of the war. Grant believed the tragedies of the twentieth century demanded a more religious stance, one that should replace progress. He knew a return to the old religion was neither possible nor desirable. Rather, he hoped for reverence inside the modern world with a greater awareness of its limits and dangers.[49]

Reactivation of the past initiates a self-reflexive subjective reconstruction.[50] It is an intellectual, emotional, and spiritual undertaking.[51]

Of course the odds are against both reactivation and reconstruction. "How can any reverence be sustained," Athanasiadis rightly asks, "when the dominant religion is one of greater progress beyond what has been and is presently?"[52] Reverence, reactivation, and reconstruction are animated by experiencing the deprival—and authoritarian appeal—of the present. Grant asks:

> Why if, as I have affirmed, the central purpose of all education is to teach us about the good life—what is the good life for man and society—why should one turn back several thousand years—why not start in the here and now—is not this our first concern?[53]

Grant's answer, Athanasiadis reminds, is that "any knowledge of the good that is outside technological society must come by intimation of the deprival—that is, negatively."[54] The negation of the present through the reactivation of the past can occur in the quiet cacophony of one's study.

Grant had prepared himself for—engaged in—such study: history at Queens, law then theology at Oxford. "[O]ne of the most articulate and probing theologians Canada has produced,"[55] Grant lived his theology through teaching. That teaching featured three elements, Dart argues, and the three must be held together, in "tension."[56] The first is Grant's incorporation of what Dart terms the "Orthodox way," one emphasizing the "sheer mystery and unknowability of God"[57] that acknowledges that (sometimes) absolute gap between here and eternity.[58] Theologically, Dart adds, such a gap positions us in humility,[59] requiring from us a "greater openness to the divine love that can be received only as a mystery and gift."[60] The second element is (as we have seen) Grant's tendency to conflate God with the Good; the third (as Athanasiadis has emphasized) is Grant's theology of the cross.[61] That, Dart concludes, "led him straight into the mystery and redemptive nature of the cross and suffering."[62] In Grant's theology, Athanasiadis reminds, the ethical charge is not only to work to eliminate "suffering in the world, but of being opened to the good through it."[63]

For O'Donovan, Grant's oeuvre is also driven by tensions, these between "faith and reason, between revelation and philosophy, between 'Jerusalem and Athens.'"[64] His early thought was driven, she suggests, by efforts to bridge the gap between these pairs. In addition to the ancients, he admired (O'Donovan continues) "those modern minds who have attempted to hold faith and reason together, in varying degrees of synthesis," among them Kant and Hegel, Simone Weil, as well as Grant's teachers and colleagues: Austin Farrer, Charles Cochrane, and James Doull.[65] That last colleague (and teacher) affirms Grant's insight when he writes:

> But the overcoming of technological naturalism is not in that immediacy but in a concrete intellectuality, as in classical and Christian thought. To regain a knowledge of this thought—and better founded than the older knowledge of it—appears to be the principal intellectual work of the present time.[66]

Despite their disagreements over Hegel and the current state and future of Canada, the two Dalhousie professors seem to be on the same page here.[67] For me such "concrete intellectuality" includes immediacy *and* eternality, however "as if" the latter must be for the secular, self-conscious now of secularity's sacred subtext.[68]

Juxtaposition not synthesis might well have been the move to make concerning ancient Athens and Jerusalem. In his 1988 addendum to his early essay "Two Theological Languages," Havers notes that Grant "insists" that ancient Athens and Jerusalem can be "united."[69] Grant "assertion" of a synthesis between the two traditions leaves Grant's work "vulnerable,"[70] Havers judges. Angus suggests that Grant corrected the ancient Greek inattention to charity[71] by emphasizing the Christian insistence that justice is due to all, concluding that the "synthesis of these two elements can be called Christian Platonism."[72] But "Grant's attempted synthesis fails,"[73] Angus agrees, due to his privileging of Jerusalem over Athens, Christ over Socrates. Grant does accord a greater status to Christianity.[74]

It also seems that both religion and philosophy replaced history and law in Grant's life as part of his ongoing response to the historical moment in which he was struggling and from which he attempted to extricate himself through teaching the progressive potential of the past, a past wherein charity and reason might thee wed. To reiterate this point: Grant retained his upbringing as he embraced the second two bodies of knowledge, becoming a hybrid sometimes paradoxical—often original—thinker. Davis himself implies as much, when— after allowing that Grant lost confidence that modern society could any longer "accommodate the Good"—Davis writes that "in my view, a careful examination shows that Grant believed that modern society needed to change fundamentally for goodness to prevail."[75] That it can—indeed must—be changed for the sake of goodness is the progressive creed.[76] That was Grant's "calling," Lee concludes, "to dwell nobly in the muteness of mind which he had uncovered, while cleaving to older truths in memory and desire, and living the best practical life he could."[77]

The tensioned reciprocity of the reactivation of the past in service to the reconstruction of the present for the sake of a just future was lived through by one exemplary Canadian citizen: George Grant. This tensioned, indeed dynamic—if often ironic—state of being subjectively present characterizes the dramatic intellectual life of George Grant, an immersion in the present moment with an eye to eternity through the peephole that is the past. "One of the remarkable features of Grant's writing," Ward notes, "is the manner in which his attempt to understand the times in which we live leads him and his readers into the presence of the great religious questions rooted in our past."[78] Partaking of that presence requires reactivation—recollection for Grant, re-enactment for Collingwood—of that past. But, Ward points out,

> If our present situation is like being lost in the wilderness, the way out does not depend simply on bringing out again the ancient compasses. For Grant these compasses too have been put in question. If Christianity is indeed the antidote to the crisis of modernity, it is also in some way responsible for modernity, and is therefore itself part of the problem.[79]

However secular—adamantly atheistic—one is, working through the present moment requires unearthing, reactivating, the early Christianity—and Judaism—that remain its subtext.

Reactivation is not rectification. If modernity represents a mistake, as Grant once termed it, "recovery of the pre-secularized sources of our thought and practice"[80] will not, as Ward notes, fix it. Any acceptance of such a conclusion is "precluded" by Grant's conviction that the "modern secularization of Christianity was inevitable and justified,"[81] in part because as a theology of glory it had invited its secularization as the age of progress, thereby treating necessity as justified, a means to the ends (or in Grant's theological terms, evil as good). Secularization was inevitable and justified also due to the ancients' incapacity to address injustice. "The seeds of modern nihilism may, then, be discovered in the Christian past," Ward concludes, referencing Grant's suggested locations as the tenth century in the West, or earlier, "even the time of Augustine."[82] Grant's critique of the Western Christianity, Ward reminds, occurs within his "explicit acceptance of Christianity as true."[83] In Ward's wise explication of his historicity *and* eternality we can appreciate Grant's indwelling within the space of the icon, here but also elsewhere, attuned to eternity while immersed in the present moment.[84] That moment is modernity, now, we say "late" or "post." For Reimer:

> The entire corpus of George Grant's thought is essentially a musing, a meditation on what it means to partake of the assumptions, values and language of the modern era rather than those of the age of Athens and Jerusalem. As

Grant so frequently reminds his readers, however, his is no simple rejection of "modernity" in favour of "antiquity." The task of the philosopher is not to make such simple choices but rather to consider deeply the meaning of the whole. He recognizes the strengths of the Enlightenment tradition, the extent of our captivity to the assumptions of an all-pervasive scientific-technological culture, and our need to transcend those assumptions if we are to avoid disaster and find what "we are fitted for." It is precisely the complexity of Grant's perspective on modernity that precludes any easy caricature of his conservatism as a romantic or even as a reactionary lament for the lost world of the past.[85]

Recall that lament means mourning, expressing grief over the loss of someone or something; that is, the remembrance that something *is* lost. And remembrance—let alone reactivation, recollection, or re-enactment—is what is lost in modernity. In contrast to melancholy, mourning implies working through loss, a renewed conviction that through analysis synthesis is possible.[86]

For others any such synoptic sense of Grant's oeuvre—as Reimer expresses—is unjustified. Grant was not "systematic in his thinking," Dart asserts; instead he "points, probes, tosses out flares."[87] Gillespie agrees that "Grant is not a systematic thinker," sometimes "changing his mind on certain fundamental questions."[88] Planinc points out that "Grant often contradicted himself; his arguments were paradoxical.… The truth of Grant's words is not a function of language or argument, but rather of the spiritual polyphony expressed in them."[89] Grant himself once conceded: "Life is too hard to try to be consistent."[90] Neither systematic nor consistent: despite the range, contradictoriness, and lived complexity of that thought, Grant threaded it through his teaching, his provocative participation in that complicated conversation that is the curriculum, "attentive and alert to what might speak to us if we have contemplative and meditative ears to hear."[91] That is the teacher's professional challenge, the challenge of the ethically animated, politically engaged, historically situated educator attuned to the eternal not only through erudition.

It is a challenge Grant had to lose, as teachers everywhere must, the impossible profession that teaching is. Annovi reminds that "Pasolini presents himself as an author without authority. He glimpses a solution to his crisis of representation in the accumulation and superimposition of imperfect material—that is, in the idea of work as failure."[92] Robert Meynell notes that despite many disappointments, Grant "fought on in his writings to the bitter end, and for him the end was bitter indeed."[93] Like Pasolini, Grant's work may be judged a failure but even so—one could say precisely so—it remains a powerful testament to the concept of teacher. That concept includes subjective presence, his teaching embedded in his texts, like an icon providing a portal to the person and the worlds wherein he dwelled.[94] "There are many of us," Angus observes, "who will not forget George Grant."[95]

Politics

> [F]reedom in a purposeless world involves
> commitment to total politics.[96]
>
> George Grant

This almost oxymoronic phrase—progressive Christian Platonist—depicts not only the philosophical sources of Grant's teaching but also of his politics, two intertwined engagements.[97] For the political domain another apparently oxymoronic term is invoked: Grant the Red Tory. Canada may not have contributed many terms to political discourse, William Christian allows, but "Red Tory" is one of them.[98] As noted in chapter 1, the concept contains collectivism and conservatism in service to nationalism,[99] a "patriotic nationalism [that] looks backward, not forward," as Warren noted.[100] Grant was not sanguine.[101] Two months before his death he wrote:

> The sadness of English-speaking nationalism in Canada is that so much of it wants nationalism, but wants to be the same American capitalism, with a maple leaf flag put at the top. You rarely meet people who are outside the determining power of that American dream.[102]

Grant would not have been surprised, then, when the former premier of British Columbia, Christy Clark, pronounced: "Vancouver has a lot more in common with Seattle than we do with Calgary, Montreal, Toronto, anywhere else in our country. We should make the most of those cultural commonalities."[103] Technology, Grant might have pointed out, is no cultural commonality; it eviscerates culture, including regional and national culture.

For Grant, Christian emphasizes, "Canadian politics came down to one thing only—nationalism, and nationalism meant opposition to big business."[104] It was big business that was selling Canada to the United States, and it was big business that demoted human beings from the status of individual souls—of intrinsic worth—to exchangeable employees and compliant consumers, about whose lives there could be only instrumental interest. "Distaste" for "big business" and "fear" of its corrupting effects on social and political life were lifelong features of Grant's thought.[105] Grant lamented the passing of the Canada as it had been conceived as well as the Canada he had known and had imagined might be.[106] The conception of public life that he associated with his parents and his grandparents had dissolved before his very eyes, as capitalism—the institutionalization of greed and exploitation—replaced the civic square with the marketplace.

Recall that Grant's conservatism—outlined in chapter 1—was different from what passed for conservatism in America. Republicans—even those like Barry Goldwater, who seemed far to the Right in Grant's era—were, to Grant's mind, merely another species of liberals, substituting private gain for public trust. No conservatism, such revolutionary radicalism had nothing to do with the British tradition that had characterized Canada, a tradition Fierlbeck traces to the "arch-Tory Edmund Burke" and the settlement of the 1689 English Bill of Rights "as the set of principles on which conservatism was to be based," securing "to a certain extent the political space necessary for the stable (if unpredictable) social development of organic communities."[107] Given the sheer scale of the human population today, relatively few focus on "organic communities," but it is within this centuries-old tradition that one can characterize Grant as a Tory, "but," Christian adds, "only a nostalgic one. He did not intend it as a relevant contemporary political stance."[108] Not "relevant" to present politics, perhaps, but decidedly subjectively present.

The "Red" element—for Grant less Marxist (an ideology of the age of progress[109]) than Christian[110]—conveyed his concern for the human person, no authorization of that "possessive individualism" that sanctions exploitation of the public for the sake of private gain, but an insistence that the particular is primary, perhaps an anticipation of the philosopher Charles Taylor's affirmation of "recognition."[111] Democratization is not only a political concept, but a social and economic one as well. It is threatened by Canada's proximity to the United States. If skepticism toward capitalism was one element of Grant's politics, Christian suggests, his lifelong concern over Canada's absorption by its neighbour to the south was another.[112]

We can also glimpse Grant's concern for Canada in Robertson's discussion of differences between Doull and Grant over the state of the nation. Doull concurs with Grant's conclusion that the quiet revolutions in both French- and English-speaking Canada in the post–World War period "destroyed the older forms of Canadian self-definition,"[113] but, Robertson points out, Doull judged this to have been a "positive development,"[114] one not necessarily leading to Canada's absorption by the United States but, instead, providing an opportunity for "real self-definition and independence on the part of Canadians."[115] To achieve such "self-definition" and "independence," Doull continued, Canada could be no narrative of tradition trashed by technology, but, in dialectical fashion, one in which can emerge a "certain form of the unity of the two."[116]

Dialectics aside, Grant might have been persuaded such a "unity" could be achieved, provided it be threaded through "Canada's past," from which, he speculated, "we might be able to build a more ordered technological society, a society which isn't as demanding on the individual and in that sense, as de-rooted as the great American society."[117] That sense of "ordered" may be embedded in the organic communities the Tory sensibility affirmed, but for Grant it was also, primarily, located in an eternal order.

As William Christian reminds, for Grant the heavenly—not earthly—city is "primary," and "politics takes place within the context of eternity."[118] That view meant to Grant that pacifism was morally mandatory, that abortion was "evil."[119] Such translation of the "eternal" into the "temporal" seems too simple. Acceptance of the situated historical character of ethical action does not authorize moral anarchy. Institutionalized in law, traditions of authority regulate but cannot prevent violence that seems sometimes justified, as the case of the Second World War—so pivotal in Grant's self-formation—demonstrates.

"Grant's strongest political assertion," Davis suggests, "may have been his attack on the *allegiance* of North Americans to the purely historical technological-capitalist order."[120] Insofar as the technological-capitalist disorder installs presentism it is decidedly anti-historical, obliterating past and future in an endless temporally empty "now" through submergence in the screen. Resistance to such disorder requires meaning-making in time, however attuned to the eternal historical action can become. Presentism is a repression of time that reactivation of the past can puncture. How? Return to the emphasized "allegiance" in the quoted passage above, denoting as it does what might be altered. What might be altered is our relationship with what is. Grant taught *as if* everything could be changed, *as if* he knew time could be a portal to what exists beyond it. That imaginative act of agency, incorporated into pedagogical action and internalized intellectually and psychically, seems to me the only avenue out of late or postmodernity. "The essential requirement for change," Davis explains,

> is that we change our minds about what we are here for, what we are fitted
> for as human beings and therefore what our stance or comportment should be
> inside modern technology and the empire where we find ourselves. A change
> in the way we act towards each other and towards the earth would flow natu-
> rally from our changed allegiance.[121]

Such wagers—risks taken without certain knowledge of the outcome—require conversion, for Grant to Christianity, for me to continuing education, ongoing study of self and situation through academic knowledge, animated by the insight of teachers, in print and in person. Changing one's mind is no self-evident undertaking.

Living *as if* one is in the presence of icons not idols I learned from George Grant. As McCarroll points out, Grant teaches us to look "upward," which is to say "beyond the realities of necessity and the dynamics of force and gravity."[122] Those concepts—associated with Weil—bifurcate this world into two, the latter one (presumably) of grace. "Grace, not gravity, is the deepest truth," McCarroll continues, however "hidden beneath its opposite"[123] it is. "Evidence" for this truth, she adds, can be found in "beauty,"[124] a portal to the transcendent for Grant, as we saw in chapter 6.

There is as if there is something active in beauty, especially but not only natural beauty: the sight of something or someone catches your eye; the look of a person slows one's movement; the fragrance of a rose or lily requires a deeper inhalation; the sound of Mozart (for Grant, Bach or Beethoven for me) astonish and stir one. This certain "agency" of beauty recalls the action of the icon, before which one is called to worship, which engenders a sense of reverence and reflection. Of course the agency of objects is not limited to these instances: smart phones and automobiles and opioids also pull one in. But the distinction I'd make between rose bushes and smart phones, between icons and computers, is that the former category of objects acts as intermediaries, transporting one to a place—call it transcendent[125]—where one senses that maybe this human life does not coincide with itself, that there is something else that exists beyond the sensory even when it is those same very senses that suggest that.

Devices take you somewhere all right, but it's a horizontal not a vertical move, somewhere else on the knowable plane of existence. Without a vertical move to make, one stays stuck in the muck, however well informed or constantly connected one is, however high[126] one feels. The idolatry of the technological age, as Flinn notes (interpreting Grant), is a "new piety toward technique."[127] Piety is perhaps too elevated a term, as addiction denotes a sordid state of affairs.[128]

Can computers function as icons rather than idols? Can we recast our relationship to them?[129] What if we made our relationship to devices less personal (the impersonal often alienating computer) and, say, more formal, even diplomatic, acknowledging that devices are alien even adversarial powers to which one is representing and protecting one's homeland, one's self or soul. Ongoing negotiations are required to ensure the safety of the homeland; ongoing study of the relationship is required to understand the alterity the alien power is, including its subtle effects on subjectivity. If negotiations break down, breaking off diplomatic relations may be recommended: one might actually withdraw from the phone for a while. Obviously imperfect, this analogy will strike some as absurd: for Kittler we have no relationship as we are already extras; for Feenberg the power we confer upon devices is our own. Like psychological projection, the power we confer on others can come back to bite us. At the least we might say with Aoki: "As I contemplate my relationship to technology, I affirm that it is both a blessing and a burden."[130] Aoki was not concluding that the two somehow balanced each other, or cancelled each other out: surely the issue is situational, a matter of time and place, a burden from which must learn, a blessing from which we must demur.[131] Within subjectivity—the subject we are—there might still be some wiggle room. If that subjectivity is attuned to the eternal, Grant would add. As O'Donovan explains:

> Against the loveless totality of technological mastery, in which is united the absolute and purposeless freedom of men and the absolute and purposeless determinism of nature, Grant sets the totality available to men's admiring contemplation, which undergirds their manifold loves with an unconditional, constraining claim ("as beyond all bargains and conveniences"). Only in loving surrender to this totality can men find purposes for their technical calculations. Outside of this stance they cannot invent (in the archaic sense of "come upon"—from the Latin *invenire*) the common good, in the service of which along their inventions (in the modern sense of "fabrications") receive sufficient justification.[132]

First is the insight that mastery—first as prosthesis, now as artificial intelligence mastering life—is the inversion of that obedience to what apprehension of the Good reveals. Second is the same space the icon creates—in-between both what is and might be—that aligns us with the Good as it grounds us in the particular. Only within this space might the technological serve as servant, not master, of us all.

Freedom

> Freedom and subjectivity mean the same thing, the ability to transcend ourselves.[133]
> George Grant

"Absolute and purposeless freedom," O'Donovan described the human condition within modernity. As Davis reminds, when Grant deemed modernity a "mistake," he was referencing our embrace of "unlimited human freedom," a move away from "reverence (and obedience)."[134] Grant turns my modernity on its head. Maybe the most difficult matter for me is freedom. I came of age accepting it as a right; it rationalized many of the moves I made, even when the rationalization was "why not"? Freedom can be such a commanding ideal one might be tempted to flee it—Fromm's *Escape from Freedom* resonated at that time—and reading Fromm reaffirmed my fidelity to it. That reaffirmation required psychological labor, as the limits to my freedom were not only outside but also—maybe most of all—inside me. Surely that insight led me to study humanistic psychology—at that time (1960s) it also permeated the scholarly literature in US curriculum studies—and later, after graduation, teaching at the University of Rochester, it led me to study autobiography. It was during my undergraduate days at Ohio State that I became determined to be (in O'Donovan's words) a "sovereign self," the "source" of my "own order," succumbing to (her gerund, I'd say preoccupied with) the "arbitrariness" and "contingency" of "existence."[135] As Grant once was, I was under the sway of (the early) Sartre then. It sure *felt* like freedom.

From Grant's—and I suspect O'Donovan's—point of view, I had moved "outside of a common moral world," by which I think she means natural law (not, as I would have seen it, conformity to whatever is *au courant* in society): O'Donovan deems the common moral world accessible to those who "recognize and accept their dependence on certain non-objectifiable conditions."[136] Certainly narcissism starts when one accepts that what you see is what you get, that everyone is out for themselves, and so on. But becoming a subject meant something rather different for me: an often decentred but internally coherent subject obligated to acknowledge alterity in whatever form it presents itself, a capability dependent in part on sorting out the splinters of internalized others within. And now, having studied Grant (and the others who have known and studied him), I see that the subject also enacts freedom by attending to what attunement reveals, including in obedience to it.[137] What Lasch expressed in secular language O'Donovan restates in theological language: "Sovereignty, self-determination, as the element in which man moves, dissolves the meaning, the weightiness, the claim of all otherness."[138] Narcissism and its dissolution of ethics are among what freedom leaves in its wake.

Self-absorbed, the supposedly sovereign subject is less likely to notice that the "inner, spiritual dimensions" of freedom can be paved over by those "very technological necessities" designed to enhance our freedom and reduce physical "suffering."[139] Not only does technology tend to determine our course of action now, it can recast what we imagine as both "our course" and "our action," confining these to what software allows. Attunement to the external is excluded as we become preoccupied with pressing keys and following the cues web pages provide.[140] Any understanding of freedom as "obedience to the truth"—Athanasiadis associates this with ancient Greek philosophy but I associate it also with phenomenology and psychoanalysis—tends to disappear. Such a sense of freedom—acting to obey what is revealed[141] through attunement—rested on a faith that there is an order and structure to the universe, again for Grant theological not only astronomical. This was an order that could disclose a "common moral world"—that is "more hesitating about changing the world, fearful of the destructive potentialities of such change."[142]

That is not to say—I am still following Athanasiadis here—that such quietude[143] numbs one's social or political sensitivity. Athanasiadis knows that "prolonged relationships of inferiority and subordination can have devastating consequences on people's spirits,"[144] an understatement to be sure, but one that also acknowledges that even "privileged" people suffer psychological forms of "inferiority" and "subordination." As for Dewey, private and public freedom seemed reciprocally related, an insight Athanasiadis seems to share when he acknowledges the "larger purpose of bringing people toward greater inward freedom and self-realization. This would involve greater participation of people in the decisions, goals, and directions society will take."[145] Grant might find more hope in fidelity to "the Good" than in the outer freedom "democracy"[146] affords.

If democracy guarantees equality (with its ironies of standardization through quantification) and affirms freedom, perhaps it provides, along with opportunities, obligations, and not only to each other. "[W]hat makes us all equal," Davis suggests, "is that we are challenged to love what is good."[147] Freedom, Athanasiadis emphasizes, enables us to "know the truth"—see through propaganda and other misrepresentations of empirical reality—but freedom is no "political slogan," no license to impose mastery over nature human and nonhuman.[148] Freedom, he understands in Grantian terms, is the "quest for knowledge of reality, the whole of it."[149] Of course the preposition "of" does not imply being outside of it—an omniscient point of view Athanasiadis and Grant would reserve for God—but attuned to it from the specificity of one's singular location, a multidimensional (including) temporal conception of space and time.

The question of quietude resurfaces here. While political freedom supports the "quest" Athanasiadis affirms, it cannot substitute for it, as political protest—Athanasiadis is here referencing the 1960s anti–Vietnam War protests and Grant's participation in and reflection on them—itself occurs "within the grid of mastery and force."[150] Like Frantz Fanon, Grant appreciated—from his study of Weil and his knowledge (through his father) of the First World War and his experience of the Second—that the oppressed can become oppressors once the tables are turned. While later in life he muted the pacifism he had espoused as a young man, he kept true to his faith that, as Athanasiadis phrases it: "Restraint and order rooted in charity and openness, even toward one's enemies, was the only means of keeping oneself pure and unstained from the world."[151] This is no accession to fastidiousness or self-righteousness, but a profound appreciation that, as Grant put it, it always matters what you do, including to and with yourself.

Quietude can also take the form of (provisional) deference to the young (who can be quite convinced they can set things right) and to the old (who can be not so sure they can). Quietude appreciates that generational location can prompt preoccupations, alter apprehension, recast comprehension. After praising Hinduism[152] and its ordering of the lifespan, Grant suggests that "For most people the end of life is a time to turn away toward eternity, to be peaceful and less busy.... I've lived a very practical and busy life. I'm glad to be free of that now."[153] Perhaps one need not wait for age to set in before hearing such whisperings of wisdom? The answer to that question may revolve around one's capacity to convert lived experience into educational experience.

Teaching

> This is an extremely difficult era to live in because we are asked to know so much so [as] not to be entrapped in it.[154]
>
> George Grant

The difference Warren discerns between the younger and older Grant is a "change of mood."[155] The younger Grant—"an inspired schoolteacher and fighting patriot, progressively disengaging himself from illusions about the modern world"—becomes in time the scholar who wants "serenity without illusions."[156] Warren attributes the shift less to age than to a "deeper Christianity,"[157] a point I appreciate but do not share. Like an icon, Grant withdrew from direct engagement with the world to create a space of "adoring contemplation" (in O'Donovan's phrase), an attunement to the eternal that would encourage him as he undertook that final project his death would not allow.

Not that what he contemplated was adorable. Grant knew[158] that "the disappearance of the liberal university" would be an inevitable outcome of the "expanding economy," but what might not be obvious immediately, he added, is "what this disappearance means to the kind of world that is coming into existence."[159] That world would be most obvious in the United States, Grant suspected, as Canada's neighbour was the epicentre of modernity, e.g., technological capitalism. In the United States not only does economics replace education— STEM replace the liberal arts as central to the curriculum—there are even politicians who attack the liberal arts as subversive and irrelevant.[160]

This assault on liberal arts—criticized[161] by Grant as vestiges of what they have been and ought to be—might seem ideological but if so it is no coherent one: it can be more precisely characterized as reckless rhetoric in the service of a know-nothing populism.[162] For Grant, "the most important thing to notice about this new view of education, in whatever of the multiple modes it may appear, is that it always makes of education as a means, something to serve some other good which is the end."[163] Whether it is for "good citizenship, education for a proper sexual life (call it, if you will, mental health), education for economic prosperity, etc., etc., etc.," Grant felt sure that this prostitution of education in service for something other than itself was the reason "the education profession is looked upon with such contempt in Canada and why fewer and fewer young people are going into it."[164] While I share his critique of instrumentalism, I wonder if education as depicted in the allegory of the cave is not also a means to an end.

For me, any wiggle room inside the cave—inside the technological sensorium—is to be crafted and travelled by individual souls, students in study of subjects that in themselves can subject them to edifying encounters with alterity of various orders. Such encounters can occupy the same space icons are said to stipulate, one in which an intensified experience of the immediate stimulates (not simulates) a seemingly extra-sensory experience of the sublime, of the Good. Speaking about such spiritual studies Fishbane understands that:

> It is only when the textual content is humanly appropriated as a living truth of existence that our own life fills out its exegetical spaces, and its linguistic features infuse our consciousness with challenge and possibility. Then the scriptural text offers models of theological living, of life lived in the context of God, and we live a citation-centered existence.[165]

During this study of Grant I have lived a citation-centred existence. For the secular, this fact—that "neither originality nor repetition exist since every word is citation"[166]—means we inhabit "a tomb-world, where everything that happens has already happened, and where nothing can happen ever again."[167] Even eternal recurrence can be, as Deleuze knew, repetition with a difference.

Quantifying the ends of education—even in the humanities and the arts— shows that policymakers are positioned inside the technocratic "tomb-world" while pretending to be outside it. Grant appreciates this point—the arrogance on which technocratic teaching rests—noting on one occasion that the very question ethically engaged teachers might pose—"how can we help others to find meaning?…implies too great a certainty about our possession of it; it implies that we are in some absolute situation outside the very pressures that negate meaning for others."[168] This is the point I emphasize when I disagree with Grant's stance that specific laws or academic subjects ensure such meaning, a stance contradicted by his testimony to contingency, its variability, transmutability, illusoriness.

How did Grant help others find meaning? By communicating—in exemplary progressive fashion—in language he hoped his listeners could hear. "[W]e do not get to the heart of the Grant that Canadians knew," Davis points out, "if we concentrate only on his religious faith. He had a passion to communicate about what was going on in the world. He wrote also for non-religious people in the terms of their experience."[169] Grant knew that curriculum is no procedural strategy to operationalize objectives into outcomes; it is a complicated conversation from which the infinity of human experience becomes focused on the meaning of the moment. Grant associated such meaning-making with ethical conduct itself, that

> [t]he self-liberation of the human soul by the systematic examination of its own activities; and that all the programs of teaching business men to be good business men and farmers to be good farmers and parents to be good parents and all to be good citizens were just preliminaries to that end.[170]

Like icons, the occupations are not self-enclosed ends in themselves in competition with each other, but also preoccupations, efforts to apprehend the Good.

Such apprehension of revelation and our varied efforts at its comprehension implies the role of reason, as we have seen. "For me," Grant told Taylor, "thought is redemptive."[171] Surely we can be—often are—stumped by what we sense, by that to which we are attuned; maybe words fail us, our narratives remain fragmented, strewn about in bits and pieces, and yet we are obligated to proceed. Grant appreciated this basic ethical dilemma, one also specific to the present historical moment:

> To combine the life of thought and responsibility in the modern world is almost an impossibility. But it is obvious that thought without responsibility becomes attenuated, while responsibility without contemplation becomes vacuous and diffuse. The agony of combining the two is the good life.[172]

In that last line is an association of affliction and supplication. In secular and pedagogical terms, I am reminded of Aoki's affirmation of the creative character of tension[173] in the juxtaposition of non-coinciding elements, requiring us to linger in-between, an iconographic space between here and eternity.[174]

That can also be the in-between space study affords: learning new material (and relearning old), questioning certainties (including, on occasion, the questioning of questioning), realizing (and recoiling from) revelations to be obeyed or reconceived. While the space of study can be solitary—alone in one's study or among others at a public library—that space can also be shared. In diverse settings dialogical encounter—with oneself and with others (in one's head or in a classroom)—affords opportunities for encouraging contemplation and enacting responsibility. Teaching can become a form of study: in communication with others one enters an inner space perhaps not yet mapped, as Grant makes clear:

> Let me say in parenthesis, if you will allow me a personal remark about teaching because some of you are going to be teachers. Let me say this: try always as much as you can in teaching—to deal with something where your mind is just moving to. Don't repeat things which your mind has already gasped and put in perfect order. That is, always teach what is really grasping you because otherwise teaching becomes a routine in which one is killed or else one becomes a pompous propagandist. And that is true at any level of teaching from kindergarten to PhD.[175]

Teaching as a routine, teacher as robot—each testifies to the ascendency of technology in what was once professional life, a life structured by study, thought, and responsibility. I am reminded of Aoki's affirmation of improvisation[176] when reading Grant's phrase: "[W]here your mind is just moving to." Surely that is an implicit acknowledgement of attunement, of one's inner space as also potentially iconographic. That is, if one doesn't routinize, objectify, and otherwise idolize, freezing what is in fact a fluid ongoing revelation.

In the statement quoted above Grant the progressive has offered pragmatic advice. He did not often do so. Recall that his teaching was less a posing of "how" than of "why" and "what." *Why* was the question he posed of the historical moment, the question he saw imprinted on the faces of his Dalhousie undergraduates, in the actions of the anti-war protestors in Toronto, on the frozen faces of McMaster colleagues as they rendered research a matter for the morgue. *What* he answered by teaching the history of the West, philosophically decoding what each of those terms means, had once meant. *How* he answered through dialogical encounter with Hegel, Nietzsche, Heidegger, and others who provided him ways by which he could decode those terms, decipher what he saw around and within him and those he knew and loved. Like Fishbane, Grant knew that "[t]he teachings of scripture become known only through exegetical engagement with their concrete expressions—not through any abstract deliberation or reflection. This is an essential principle of hermeneutical theology."[177] Exegetical engagement could be said to be an essential principle of Grant's teaching, too.

How, what, and why invites a fourth question: who? *Who* was this man who became subjectively present through his questions, through his efforts to provide replies, in communication with others close and distant? Those internalized influences denied, others affirmed, combined as progressivism, Christianity, Platonism, configured his critique of teaching, time, and technology. "None of

Grant's various critiques can be understood on its own," Planinc appreciates, as "the significance of each ultimately depends upon the manner in which Grant made it his own and integrated it within his polyphonic account."[178] Not only the account was polyphonic, so too was the man who studied and taught amidst the ruins of modernity. That person, that spirit, that daemon—"in ancient Greek belief a divinity or supernatural being of a nature between gods and humans"[179]— Planinc points out,

> presented itself in each of his critiques; and his *daimon* kept each of the critiques in check, determining its extent and significance, and preventing it from developing independently as an abstract argument. Without hearing the voice of Grant's *daimon* in the voices of his polyphony, no particular critique can be understood properly.[180]

Daemon inspirits[181] one's subjective presence,[182] providing subjective coherence and continuity through shifting subject matter[183] Grant sought to understand and communicate to students, both those formally enrolled in the university and those (we can say) non-formal "students"; for example, his fellow residents and citizens of Canada. Grant taught them all.

The human subject and subject matter are intertwined, each extending the other. Pérez-Gómez could have also been referencing that reciprocity when he writes about architecture: "It accommodates and furthers the appropriate moods for focal actions (unfortunately not always appreciated in our era of distraction and electronic gadgets) that allow humans the possibility of *being present*."[184] One's scholarly specialization can become the conceptual architecture in which one dwells, the medium through which the specialist and the student can become present to themselves and to each another. "In the end," Rocha reminds, "the teacher is not there to facilitate learning, the teacher is there to be there."[185] Through subjective presence—the person not as idol but as icon—the teacher testifies to the revelation of the realities in which students and teachers are embedded and can transcend.

Grant's subjective presence—a portal from here to eternity—was not the point of his teaching. How he taught was exemplary but what he taught was at least as significant: the "how" and the "what" merge in the teachings of George Grant. His critique of teaching, time, and technology is, as Robertson notes, polyphonic. But it could also be characterized as spare, calling us not to quietism but to quietude, wherein idols can become icons. Within solitude one strips, laying oneself bare, a psychological asceticism (as Weil's concept of "decreation" implies). Grant could also be ascetic sometimes, evident in a 1948 letter he writes to his mother. Like his Christian Platonism, his asceticism was spiritual and worldly, in this instance a response to what he worried he and his family—that year his wife, Sheila, was pregnant with their first child—might have to endure:

> We already have enough possessions. Too many. I want to keep everything to a minimum as I really feel that, in our lifetime, we may be called to the utterest precarious existence in a depression or another war. That is my first feeling against buying or possessing furniture. I even dislike my own books.[186]

In the same letter he writes that "we are leading very full and happy lives."[187] The capaciousness of his personality is polyphonically present during his interviews with Charles Taylor and David Cayley.

Grant's teaching was a portal not only to his own very human being but also to humanity and to what might be beyond us, also evident in that same letter, wherein he acknowledges the assassination of Mahatma Gandhi. "Gandhi's death," he wrote, "sort of stopped one up short and made one realize how utterly meaningless is any accomplishment now but that of the depths, and that one sees no prospect of such accomplishment coming from oneself."[188] Note his worldliness, his attunement to humanity, to what can become incarnate in us: the "supremely great."[189] Even the great can become crushed—as the Gandhi assassination makes clear—and four decades later Grant felt he had been too, writing two months before his death that "I think I have broken or the world has broken me."[190] In that same 1988 letter, however, he closes by affirming that "[m]ost people have learnt to live happily in hard political eras and we do that here."[191]

Grant taught us that technology, time, and teaching are moving images of eternity. When they become idols, they short-circuit our transmissions from elsewhere. To restore revelation idols themselves must be crushed, converted to icons, provoking one's attention not only on but also beyond what is material. As iconographic, objects take their proper place in a life ordered from elsewhere. Ordered not according to someone else's scheme, but according to one's own signal, honed through one's attentiveness, attunement, to the Good. For Grant, Davis points out, the "human dispensation includes being and loving our own; we belong to particular traditions and communities and, even within these, each of us, as individuals, must also do our own thinking, believing, and dying."[192] From the universal to the particular, from the eternal to the contingent, it always matters what we do, including with ourselves.

Time

> Only fools predict the future, particularly as the complex technological civilization totters to its apogee.[193]
>
> George Grant

In modernity, you recall, time became conflated with history. And "history," Grant suspected, had become (as O'Donovan phrases it) "the central religious and moral idea of our age."[194] Not that it came out of nowhere, as O'Donovan reminds: Judaism and Christianity installed the certainty that God had intervened in history, that history was itself an instrument of God's revelation. These beliefs, O'Donovan's explains, "bind freedom inextricably both to the finite, contingent event, in its relative independence from the infinite, and to the impulse for reforming the actual."[195] In science, she adds, the actual is manipulated, justified in the name of humanity.[196] In this reading, science becomes a secularized version of the coming kingdom of God. Perhaps pushing back against this secularization of eschatology, Grant declared: "I'm not terribly interested in the future."[197]

The trouble with technology is that the future becomes represented by novelty, a new device or idea, not the ethically animated reconstruction of what has before been revealed. Even the present as a distinctive, meaningful, temporal moment disappears once we're inside the screen, a web of both external and internal necessity, in which thought and action, desire and thought, become fused, extinguishing that light shining, however faintly, on the wall of the cave we inhabit. "The impossibility of the new is both the loss to be worked out and the means to work it out," Benedetti suggests, "both the ailment to be cured and the medicine with which to cure it."[198] Thinking our deprival and recollecting the Good are one, Grant knew.

"To see our minds in the atomic age," Grant suggested, "it is particularly necessary to look at our schools, our universities, and our churches. For the schools, the universities, and the churches are the chief institutions which can lead men to freedom in the truth."[199] As his experience at McMaster taught him, there could be little hope there either, as these institutions promising to be iconographic portals to eternity had instead become idols, corporations committed to their own advancement in a society reduced to a marketplace of products and services. Grant knew that "technological society is against human excellence and, yet, where does that leave one?"[200] It left him in public protest—Grant wrote that line in a 1968 letter, at the height of anti–Vietnam War protests in Canada and the United States—and in quietude, as he positioned the particular within the panoramic, the juxtaposition of which ensured subjective coincidence with neither. Worship—for the secular, study—can provide a place to hover (in Musil's language[201]), to linger (in Aoki's[202]), to testify, witness, and contemplate. Could the school and university recover what for Ouspensky the church remains?

> The Church does not reject particularities connected with human nature or with time and place (for example, national, personal or other features), but sanctifies their content, filling it with new meaning. In their turn, these particularities do not interfere with the unity of the Church, but bring into it new forms of expression, peculiar to them.[203]

As Grant's critique implies, the school and the university could become—or at least accommodate—such sanctification and expression.

While Grant was intrigued by the Eastern Christian Church—it is that church of which Ouspensky writes—he remained a Protestant, finally an Anglican, one focused, after Luther and Weil, on affliction, a theology of the cross. Athanasiadis reminds us that Grant "found his way to its meaning through his studies of the Psalms, Paul, Augustine, and the German mystics, coupled with his inner struggle to find redemption in his life."[204] That theology, Athanasiadis continues, "was not only a way of thinking, but also a way of existing, and because such existing drove Luther out of the monastery into the wider world, it intensified both his thinking and existing."[205] Might one say the same of Grant, focused as he was on time as transcendent and as contingent, however elusive their link might be? Ethical engagement is informed by time as history, itself not self-enclosed or sequentially progressive, but always associated—humbly, self-critically, elusively—with "eternity," as we apprehend ourselves in attunement to it.

It is hard to write those words without sounding sure of myself, terms arranged as if in a formula. My empiricism enters even during my attempts to write of the non-empirical, ensuring that my attunement is not to the eternal but to promises for the future. Empiricism infects my prose, my thinking, my experience. Like Grant, like each of us, I am dated, a creature of my time and place. Each time and place affords access to the eternal, if differently, something shred into infinity by the individuality of the human species. Each of us within the cave, a different cave: we North Americans now inside a glittering distracting all-consuming one, the light on the wall no longer faint, even blinding. In this glaring darkness it still matters what we do, Grant's affirmation now a mantra for me, the progressive in him (and in me) refusing to accept subjectivity's erasure in our technological moment, even when that meant for him carrying on in withdrawal from the public sphere, cultivating the quietude he knew was the sacred space where time moved more slowly, where the image he was/we are might be detected in more detail. Heidegger he wanted to confront during the days before death confronted him.

George Grant bequeathed that progressive challenge—it always matters what you do—but in an ancient guise, as ethics not politics. Politics is no longer the main arena for subject formation, instead the site of subject manipulation, the search for truth sacrificed for power and the lies that can conjure it. In the dark we look for the light, attuning ourselves to what might be outside the cave that confines. That looking for the light is study: of the wall, of the world, of what might be beyond our capacity to comprehend. Study is what we owe ourselves, what we owe each other, what we owe God, whatever that last word— and its associated terms (the Good, the Whole, Eternity)—signifies. Study is what society owes itself: education not only for vocational training but also for the formation of the human subject. Grant knew that "society, as a natural entity, has its highest end the education of its members."[206] That "highest end" is surely spiritual knowledge, an embodied state of mind structured (perhaps) like that of the icon: subjective presence that is a portal to what is beyond it. The canonical curriculum question is also a spiritual question, the posing of which is—as James B. Macdonald knew—like a prayer. In keeping the curriculum question open one can attune oneself to where that "next step" is, why and when it is to be taken, where and possibly with whom.

Subjectivity is no longer a hall of mirrors the technological sensorium constructs then occupies and hollows out; it becomes the capacity for non-coincidence, contemplation in front of the icon that is the world. There one might obey what attunement reveals. Cautioned by self-questioning, humbled by the scale of what we study, subjectivity can become another moving image of eternity, traces of which are refracted through the details of daily life.[207] That attentiveness (as Weil would have it) becomes more a virtue one cultivates than a resource on which one draws to get a "leg up" in a race to nowhere. Western Christianity, Grant lamented, had blinked in that competition, and he looked East, first (and momentarily) to Catholicism, then to Eastern Christianity, wherein icons not idols still preserved, he imagined, mystical revelation. Perhaps Grant might have entertained (to invoke Aoki's move[208]) "both and," as one speaker (at a conferencing honouring Grant) suggested:

> Yet the authentic heart of the Catholic tradition in the United States, the conscious assertion of the priority of virtue over freedom, will be kept alive, if at all, in forms and places roughly analogous to the monasticism of an earlier barbarian age. For then, too, authentic faith lived side by side with Christian barbarism.[209]

Activism and quietude, the twin sometimes merged poles[210] of Grant's life, structure as they at once animate and sustain study: solitary, spiritual, in solidarity (even when in disagreement) with those in our midst, each working from within, together.[211]

There were a series of poles supporting the tent wherein Grant taught: Western and Eastern Christianity, time and eternity, technology and attunement, idol and icon. Grant's accomplishment was his incorporation of ancient and modern thought, his refusal to conform to what is. "For Pasolini," Annovi reminds, "the authorial figure, far from dying off, was an antagonist who would challenge all forms of conformism merely by existing."[212] Grant too was a living protest, personifying contraries as he reactivated the past in search of a future. The creative tension the juxtaposition of contraries can create was what Grant had admired in the fiction of Céline:

> I think it is the very mixture of cynicism and love in Céline that moves me most; because both those rather conflicting attributes are used by him to express the nearest he can get to the truth of what is. This is what distinguishes him from a nihilist or a liberal. Human beings are not often very good—we are selfish and devious and broken.[213]

Attuned to eternity, resolve enables immediate action in the midst of the darkness, yes the present technological darkness but also the human darkness: we are "selfish" and "broken," not only theologically but also obviously empirically. Despite circumstances—internal and external, as Grant knew "the thing is as it is"[214]—we can become devoted to justice, in search for what we are fitted for.[215]

Technology

> Technology is not something over against ontology; it is the ontology of the age.[216]
> George Grant

Grant was no Luddite, Davis reminds.[217] He knew that returning to pre-modernity—to an agrarian economy or one of hunting and gathering—was neither possible nor desirable. What *is* possible, in Davis' terms, is "changing our awareness of who we are and where we stand in relation to what is other than us—nature and other beings—inside the modern world where we are situated."[218] Subjective reconstruction is not subjective engineering; it is, rather, attunement to what we are fitted for. Again, for Grant, as O'Donovan reminds, recollecting the Good and thinking our deprival are co-extensive, reciprocal.[219] No formula, neither is easy and conjoining them even harder. To make the task manageable I want to render them together, yes, but sequential, a methodizing move that is no doubt modernistic but maybe with a different motive and result. The first problem I face in thinking my deprival is that it is not obvious, materially speaking. For as many as one-third of the Earth's humanity, that is not the case. No fan of discomfort I am grateful to have been, thus far, spared starvation, seeing my children unnourished, stuck simply struggling to survive. Appreciating being spared such suffering, how do I think my deprival? It is, following Davis' advice, to alter my awareness from the material to the spiritual. That third of humanity struggling to survive would be fed and housed if the two-thirds of us who are both could feel inside ourselves the unendurable pain of others suffering. While ancient, is such ethical numbness now an indication of the "profundity with which technological civilization enfolds us?"[220] Technology has seeped into us over the centuries, Grant reminds: "Coming to meet us out of the very substance of our past, that destiny has now become, not only our own, but that of the species as a whole."[221] The accretion of endless actions our ancestors undertook has become embedded in our very flesh, Grant seems to be suggesting, numbing us.

When our awareness changes, we are met by what one has not expected, so confident (and in denial) many of us have become that progress is inevitable. Our pores seep the stench of a past we can no longer conceal, however frenetically we make babies and new technologies as if to distract ourselves from the dreadful sense of ending we now know will come somewhat soon if we fail to correct the errors technology has committed in our name: rising sea levels, intensifying storms and temperature extremes, political and social instability (ancient dangers now intensified thousands-fold with nuclear weaponry and social media), economies predicated on productivity (will what is discarded fill the rising dying seas?), an economic scheme that has now structured all aspects of contemporary life.[222] These are, as Grant termed them, "obvious externals."[223] His examples were "that we can blow ourselves up or ameliorate diabetes or have widespread freedom from labor or watch our distant wars on television."[224] All these remain among those circumstances that constitute our "deprival," but they are not, Grant reminds, the main one, namely our utter inability to

> think of the whole, with what we think is good, with what we think good is, with how we conceive sanity and madness, beauty and ugliness. It is a destiny which enfolds us in our most immediate experiences: what we perceive when we encounter a bird or a tree, a child or a road. It equally enfolds us in less tangible apperceptions such as temporality.[225]

Witless and machine-like many of us have become, posted online as one idol among billions, exhibitionism numbing any sense of deprival we cannot quantify.

Condemnation of our present circumstances is the flip side of the same coin that is confidence in the future, that Manichean tendency to divide into twos from which coding has capitalized. "Of course," Grant knows,

> this is not to say that we can or should turn back from the technological society. What I am saying is that the great job in Canada now does not lie in further economic expansion and quantitative progress, but in trying to bring quality and beauty of existence into that technological world—to try and make it a place where richness of life may be discovered.[226]

Yes this is early Grant, the almost optimistic Grant, but like his progressivism this inner resolve does not desert him, as he was always enacting his obligations to family, friends, humanity. Like the progressive Platonist he was, the Christian he was, Grant never abandoned his duty to do the right thing, that which revelation required him to do. "Overcoming technology," as Angus knows, "implies an ontology of participation and an immanent concept of the sacred."[227] Substitute "transcendent" for "immanent," and Angus's insight conveys the iconographic character of Grant's critique of technology, time, and teaching, embodied in and enacted through his subjective presence.

Grant could not categorically reject technology, as it had, in Angus's terms, "brought forth essential new human possibilities."[228] Nor could Grant accept it, given (again Angus's language) "the threat it poses to justice as individuality and equality."[229] The threat doesn't end there, as technology encapsulates our very capacity to think. "Uncertainty about any form of knowledge but technologized science is our present destiny," Grant knew.[230] Threatened but unable to flee how are we to survive? Aoki would point to the danger of dualism, of either/or rather than both/and.[231] Aoki tells the story of Carol, who has been for a dozen years a "child of haemo-dialysis technology," writing to him recently that she feels she must "acknowledge" her "indebtedness to technology" but "refuse to be enslaved by technology."[232] That refusal is not behavioural but subjective and spiritual. Grant knew:

> The trouble about asking the question How does one live with technique? is that in asking that question one sees technique as something external to us— "means out there"—but that is just exactly how not to see it. That is exactly how to be so unaware of it that one is it.[233]

Not only hooked up to a machine through which one's blood moves and is purified, one is now also psychically fused with the screen, a symbiotic interconnectivity from which complete extrication seems impossible: we are now, Grant lamented, "it."

Perhaps a small space of non-coincidence remains, however confined we are within the worldwide Web, a virtual cave generating its own unnatural light. How? For Grant, Robertson reminds, any transcendence of technology requires either the recollection of a pre-modern ethos (remnants of which remain among the ruins[234]) or technology's intensification to the point of civilizational collapse due to its "own inner nihilism."[235] In either case, Robertson continues, technology allows "no mediation" between itself and a "humanly livable order,"[236] a point you recall Kittler makes too.[237] Robertson envisions both past and future converging upon the present as technology increasingly consumes itself, an iconoclastic "self-dissolution" that he imagines "will purge the Western tradition of all voluntarism and open us to participatory and receptive relation to the divine."[238] This is a horrifying fantasy—is it a secular version of the Christian concept of rapture?— of civilizational crucifixion followed by resurrection.

While one can rule out neither, for me no such eschatology seems inevitable, given that technology has become, as Grant knew, "an end in itself."[239] (In other words, we might suffer civilizational collapse but its renewal remains unimaginable.) Attention evaporates in the face of the idol rather than, in the presence of the icon, rerouted to what exists beyond it. "The very being of technology, of modernity, of a self-contained secularity," Robertson summarizes, "can be ontologically established only by a negating or occluding of the order of what is."[240] Technology short-circuits that capacity for attunement by absorbing all that is into its software designs, requiring us to update to stay in sync with them. Now the materialization of our "will" seems to be incorporating a mind of its own— artificial intelligence—that threatens to end any non-coincidence with it as we become obedient to the instructions the screen shows.

Now almost omnipresent, technology's coming omniscience could be a clue to its Christian and Judaic prehistory, specifically these religions' confidence in

God's will merging with ours (and vice versa). Angus suspects so, asking: "Is a concept of Christianity (or Judaism) entirely without will conceivable? And, if not, is not Christianity unredeemably implicated in technology?"[241] Grant could only concur, realizing, as he did, that science was indeed the secularization of Judaism and Christianity's conception of God as guiding humanity from the wilderness to the Promised Land. Athanasiadis recalls science's sacred calling:

> In the early stages, modern science was put in the service of charity through the struggle to overcome scarcity, disease, and overwork. Later, it also shaped the thought of Protestants by cutting them off from apprehending the world as anything beyond a field of objects.[242]

This sense of the nobility of science has not vanished entirely, but surely it suffers under the rule of technological rationality, under the economistic commands that even basic research should produce profitable outcomes.

After interviewing Grant, Taylor reported "feeling less terminally pessimistic,"[243] despite the possibility that Grant might prove prescient, that Canada—that every particularity[244]—will be absorbed in the global hegemony that is technology. Despite economic and cultural continentalism, Taylor felt that "significant numbers of Canadians were concerned to remain distinctly Canadian, and that Grant may have overemphasized the homogenizing power of liberal technology."[245] That hope would seem somewhat shared by Heyking and Cooper, who suggest that for Grant the "individual may be redeemed…but civilization… not."[246] For a man who affirmed that individuality was also "communal,"[247] I'm not so sure redemption is possible for one without the other.

Conclusion

> Life becomes mystery for me more and
> more—but a wonderful mystery.[248]
>
> George Grant

In an era dominated by the virtual not the actual, by "phantasmagoria," notions of "uniqueness" or "individuation" amount to mere "window dressing for mass-produced sameness."[249] When conformity becomes compulsory, opportunities for "meaningful individual expression" become fewer; communication can end.[250] Where there are no actual individuals, Stamps concludes, "there can be no genuinely expressed ideas, and where there are no such ideas, there can be no exchange of them."[251] A conception of reason as affording us the concept of the Good and directing our attention toward it[252] morphs in modernity into instrumental rationality: calculation, assessment, manipulation. The self as soul becomes sealed off from eternity, now defensive and self-enclosed, narcissistic. No longer a spiritual or philosophical question, what is the meaning of life becomes repurposed:

what's in it for me? Grant wonders "what then will provide that source of attention for the masses without which life will be a frittering away in listless and increasingly perverted pleasures?"[253] He knew the answer:

> It can only be provided by an enormous program of education at all levels in society. In the affluent mass world, education must then become the great affair of all societies and not only vocational education to make us prosperous—but education dealing with the meaning and purpose of life. Mass leisure without mass education can obviously only lead to disaster. Even mass leisure with flaccid education will lead to disaster.[254]

Grant saw it coming; we are almost there now. Children stare at screens, unending distraction, completing tasks online in a curriculum designed by software engineers, teachers relocated to the "gig economy" wherein they are hired as contract workers—no longer public but now decidedly domestic servants—checking to see if the kids have completed their "individualized" assignments for the day.[255]

Grant could only recoil in horror when children themselves become the latest opportunity for predators promising high-paying jobs plunder public budgets. Coding not decoding becomes the buzzword of the day.[256] Within these circumstances in the United States—the reduction of education to vocational training and the commercial exploitation of children—Grant's question concerning Canada resounds as the question facing humanity: "I mean the question of Canada is: Are we going to build an alternative kind of technological society to what they have in the United States?"[257] To answer such a question one must think one's deprival by becoming historical, reactivating the past, including within one's subjectivity.

Technology is the materialization of human will and imagination. For centuries a series of prostheses, technology now—through artificial intelligence—is achieving a will of its own. Havers reminds that "the Will creates rather than contemplates: it masters nature rather than accepts it."[258] Such hubris, Grant knew, represented a secularization of spiritual faith in God's intervention in history. In the loss of that faith, replaced now by faith in science and technology, one locates the genesis of modernity, itself a historicizing, materializing concept Grant wanted to escape.

But a man of modernity George Grant most emphatically was, a fact registered in his teaching: at once Christian and Platonist and progressive. Grant taught attuned to the eternal through the historical, focused on those immediate concerns of individual existential selves, students struggling within a technologizing society exploiting them and the Earth, itself now only a resource, students converted to human capital.[259] "The question for Grant," Davis appreciates,

> was whether and how freedom and reverence exist together in our human experience. Being free, we must acknowledge and revere what makes us free;

being reverent, we have the freedom of responsibility for judgments and interpretation in our situation.[260]

It always matters what you do, Grant repeated, in the immediate moment and
forever more.

George Grant inhabited an iconographic space between here and eternity,
no static space but one strewn with bombs, bodies, and breakdowns, one requiring perpetual repositioning through teaching and study: first history, then law,
theology, philosophy, politics. A sequence yes but also a whole, subjectively
present(ed) to students young and old, submerged in the present, haunted by the
past, pressured by the future. "In later life," Davis tells us,

> he was tired and sometimes embittered by what he saw as his failure at
> McMaster, as well as by his long struggle with the progressives. He then
> tended to move towards certainty of the anti-progressive positions and to fall
> silent about his social-democratic convictions. Yet it would be wrong to con-
> sider the later Grant to be the "mature" Grant, as if what went before had
> been transcended.... There is indeed wisdom in the later work that had not
> yet unfolded in the earlier. But the early work boldly asserts the need for social
> change and Grant's thought, as a whole, stands up when we retain and reiter-
> ate his earlier insight and rebellion, which then were deepened and balanced
> by the wisdom of age and experience.[261]

Social change in the service of salvation, secular or not, is the progressive's dream,
a dream that by Grant's time had morphed into a nightmare. Social change was
no longer the lever by which the world would be uplifted; it was now the uncontrollable, unpredictable collateral damage done the name of the idol of the age:
technology.

Inherited from his family, inhaled from his culture, and in England converted into an articulate faith, Grant made the progressive dream a reality not
through revolutionary but through spiritual action, teaching and studying as
a supplicant, ennobled by reverence and resolve. For those of us who have
come after him it is past time to acknowledge the sacred subtext of secularity. As Grant knew: "A lot of people in the modern world, fine people, whom
we might call 'liberal secularists,' still want a continuation of the morality that came essentially out of Christianity, without belief."[262] Not only out
of Christianity but out of every major religion; still, Grant's point stands. In
reclaiming the non-doctrinal but spiritual subtext of human life, one might
move through the muck we're in. Now that social amnesia has set in, it is time
to reactivate the pre-modern past and, specifically, its acknowledgement of our
dependency upon what is beyond our capacity to comprehend, upon what we
cannot observe and measure, that which is revealed, that to which one can still
become attuned.

For the strictly secular epistemology and ethics evaporate in an ether of the "beyond." For those whose secularity is fundamentalist, attunement is best left to one's devices. Even that great, hardly shallow secularist John Dewey was unwilling to relegate conduct to the software of connectivity, temporally and ethically eviscerated. "In morals," Dewey insisted, "the infinite and the imperative develop from the participle, present tense. Perfecting means perfecting, fulfillment, fulfilling, and the good is now or never."[263] Like Grant, Dewey was affirming that it always matters what we do. Unlike Grant, Dewey rarely restated a fundamentalism (except as anti-fundamentalism). Into fundamentalism Grant lapsed, contradicting his conversion, his refusal to rationalize necessity in the name of the Good, and (not that he noticed) Dewey's conception of growth. While it can, as conversion did for Grant, occur in an instant, growth takes a lifetime. While clearly dissonant in temperament and philosophy, the two men harmonize when they teach us to study not only what surrounds us (although surely that) but also what the present occludes.

To live the progressive dream today, this progressive is suggesting, might mean deemphasizing Dewey for the moment[264] and reconstructing oneself to become a singular, contemporary version of the conservative Grant personified, not the anti-abortionist advocate (one of those anti-progressive positions Davis mentions above), but the Canadian in tune with the past, with those in his midst, including the victims who haunt this colonized place, as well as with those who can come after us. For Grant such attunement to the whole is philosophical, literary, musical, but also subjective, social, and spiritual. For Dewey not so spiritual[265]: his sense of the "whole" seems more akin to Jung's collective unconscious, except that Dewey's is more social than psychic, more present than past:

> Within the flickering inconsequential acts of separate selves dwells a sense of the whole which claims and dignifies them. In its presence we put off mortality and live in the universal. The life of the community in which we live and have our being is the fit symbol of this relationship. The acts in which we express our perception of the ties which bind us to others are its only rites and ceremonies.[266]

Note that the whole becomes particularized through action in the world, not only individuated but communal, the atomistic and the collective united in one's participation in those rites—teaching and studying primary among them—that reflect the social bond and the organic community through which the Good is refracted.

After studying Grant a strictly social sense of the whole becomes insufficient. Grant affirms that the whole incorporates the social, but it also houses the historical. And it is in the past—for him ancient Athens and Jerusalem—we can attune ourselves to the Good. Despite the presence of pedagogues Grant admired—Jesus and Socrates pre-eminently but also Strauss and Weil and, if ambivalently and at times only negatively, Hegel, Heidegger, and Nietzsche—teaching the whole is practically an impossible undertaking, as Weil herself appreciates when she charges humanity to "rediscover" the "original pact" between the "spirit" and the "world" in which we are embedded, an undertaking beyond our capacity to accomplish but one which we are obligated to try. Likening our situation to Socrates learning to play the lyre as he awaited death, she concludes: "At any rate we shall have lived."[267] Likewise beyond our capacity to accomplish, we teachers might nonetheless insist that pedagogy not politics become the primary preoccupation of humanity: teaching and studying what matters, always asking that canonical curriculum question.

What matters—knowledge of most worth—is not necessarily one subject: philosophy or art or STEM. "We are on our own, up to a point," Davis appreciates, "and must look to our own lights to interpret and decide how to apply within our new situation what we inherit in our language and traditions."[268] Maybe not "apply"—our duty is not only to deduce but also to divine—but to attune ourselves to what needs to be done, in this place, in this moment. As Magrini advises:

> *Become open* to new possibilities of our Being with the understanding that the potential for *transcendence* is to be found within the "present," as *in-between what is, what has been* (past), and simultaneously that which *has not yet been fulfilled*. The authentic potential for learning lives in a mode of attunement, revealing to us that when pursuing a life of moral excellence we are confronting the most elusive and recalcitrant aspects of human existence, engaged in the struggle for knowledge of the "good" in the face of human *finitude*.[269]

Grant—and I—would add a second "face," that of infinitude.

Teaching moral excellence, for knowledge of the good in face of facticity, must seem so yesterday to those connected to what's happening on social media. Attuned to what has not yet been fulfilled is quite different from looking to get off while watching the screen, a decentring and attuning to what is invisible, presence that might reveal itself by being here now. While the words are ancient, the sense of the possible they support may not be. "All that is needed," Benedetti suggests,

> is a little fissure that grants us a viewpoint external to the universe in which we are locked. The new might be conceived in a manner unlike that of the differential logic of the modern. But to do so, we must come up with something that has not already been thought. We must reopen the realm of the possible locked up in the vision of history as labyrinth. We must free ourselves from the epochal misrepresentation that characterizes postmodern common sense. This is the gamble that we must now take. This is the challenge facing art and thought today.[270]

Can reactivating the past—specifically the critique of time, technology, and teaching George Grant composed[271]—create one of those fissures?

However sealed, surely such a fissure remains within us. Opening it might be like threading a needle only we can see.[272] Is the crux of the matter the relation of apprehension and comprehension—in Grant's terms, revelation and reason?[273] Attunement to what seems "beyond time and space" may not reveal "order" (natural law for the ancients) nor timelessness ("eternity") but acting as if there were an "outside" to the everyday. That subjective non-coincidence with the world we know enables us to learn from it, from our experience of it, lived experience we can reconstruct: educational experience. That expansive concept includes cognitive concerns for calculation that characterize instrumental rationality, but here, in the subjective presence of Grant,[274] I am focused on what filters through our minds and bodies that originates—or seems to—outside us, and not just in other people and human events, but invisibly, the presence within which we experience daily life.[275] Through subjective presence, conscious embodiment in the natural material world, we can live attuned to what we might not, perhaps cannot, comprehend, but which we suspect or through love (as Grant would have it) know— informs what has happened, what is happening, and what we might do about it.

How might we proceed "as if" this were the case? Grant's answer, you recall, begins with acknowledgement of the historical moment: "[W]e must," he urges, "recognize that we are at a bad time in human history,"[276] by which he means many things, among them that teaching has become reduced to vocational training. The sacred calling of teaching had been silenced by the clamour of the economy, entrepreneurs insisting that the innovation depends on education. If they do not become rich it is teachers' fault for failing to adequately train those who work for them. Grant asks:

> What then can we do about this? First and foremost we must do things with ourselves. We must have the courage to be. What do I mean by that? Men and women do not automatically become human. We have to make for ourselves the decision to be human unless we are to slip back into being clever (or less clever) apes. To affirm, that is, in every situation the values that we know to be true. And that affirmation may mean in a very real sense the taking up a cross. Well this is, I think, what teacher must do—they must have the courage to be teacher even when that does not seem important to the world.[277]

Note his acknowledgement that presence—being here—requires courage, the courage to become human, to listen to the calling of teaching despite present circumstances and the suffering present circumstances can enforce. Quietly and insistently we teach the truth through the subjects we are qualified and contracted to teach.

For Grant that subject was philosophy; at the time of the passage quoted above he was teaching at Dalhousie. The circumstances he references then were twofold and interrelated, one public one private. The first was "a society…dominated by the values of the expanding economy," wherein "practically nobody I meet would consider it important to be a teacher of philosophy."[278] When "tired or depressed," Grant confesses, he found himself "taking their view of the matter, really unconsciously believing that the teaching profession is a haven for those who are not tough enough to pursue power or make money."[279] In such private moments, he lacked "courage," allowing these circumstances—"this lie—creeping like a nasty cancer into my soul. Now I think it is the fight against that lie which I mean by the courage to be a teacher."[280] That "fight" was simultaneously subjective and spiritual, requiring inner strength and attunement to what the soul suggested.

What Grant's soul suggested was keeping in mind—like insulation, sealing off his soul from the lies seeping into him—a "proper philosophy of education," by which he means, first, the "holding in one's mind that the end of all life is the journey of the mind into God (that is, into realty) and, second, "the holding in one's mind the value of each step of that journey a means in that journey."[281] Notice the association of "God" with "reality," or what he also terms "the whole," within which is "the Good." Students remain students but they are also fellow pilgrims, if at very different moments of their journeys from their teachers and other students. Such a doubled conception—students and supplicants—can be iconographic, terms Grant does not invoke but which seem to me implied when he notes that "the very act of attention required by the youngster in that study [of Latin in his example] may be exactly the act which may make the difference for him between being a slovenly beast and a child of God."[282] For Grant, then, the teacher is iconographic: embedded in the historical moment, teaching a specific subject in a specific school in a specific classroom on a specific morning while at the same time testifying to eternity and universality.[283] "The first duty of the teacher these days," Grant knew, [is] "to hold constantly in his mind the purpose of what he is doing for children and the necessary means of doing it."[284] He concludes: "For great teaching only comes out of the riches of a spiritual life."[285] To that truth Grant's teaching testifies.

Notes

1. Davis 2002b, 108.
2. Taylor (1982) 2006, 133.
3. Davis 2002b, 431.
4. Athanasiadis 2001, 86. "[S]ocrates seeks after truth," Magrini (2017, 70) reminds, he "is not someone who possesses truth." Surely truth presents itself along the way, however it dissolves in light of new information and insight. But this teaching—that the point of education is education—is one that links not only Grant and Socrates but those two with Dewey, for whom the educational point of growth (intellectual, emotional, social) was more growth. While students of Grant may not associate such metaphors with Grant's conception of education, in Cayley's (1995, 23) account not

a dissimilar biologistic metaphor is invoked: "In fact, Grant insisted to the end of his career that what was wrong with universities was not the students but the lack of moral and intellectual nourishment in the curriculum."

5. Taylor (1982) 2006. 133.

6. As Angus (1997, 202) notes: "Particularity is embracing one's own as a first meeting with a belonging that extends indefinitely beyond towards universality." Referencing Grant's spiritual teacher, Weil, Rigelhof (2001, 135–6) writes: "Her key teaching is that 'Faith is the experience that the intelligence is enlightened by love.' What this means is that love is the one thing that always and everywhere can escape the power of technology. Love insists that there is more to life than what we want and obtain by the power of will. We cannot will love into being. Love is other than us and insists that there is something other than us."

7. Ajzenstat 1992, 83. Because justice is what we are fitted for, Kaethler (2009, 52) suggests that justice "may connect with our self-interests," adding that: "Justice is not about comfortable preservation but about being whole, about finding one's self." To be faithful to Grant, one must add that such "finding" what one is "fitted for" occurs within the experience of transcendence attunement invites.

8. For those, Grant felt sure, "trying to incarnate meaning into the structures of the automated age...above all [what] will be necessary [is]: a much higher degree of theoretical sophistication than has yet been generally vouchsafed in your profession. By theory I mean the attempt to have knowledge of the whole" (Davis and Roper 2005b, 242). To the extent the screen short-circuits attunement to the eternal it becomes an idol, not an icon. Grant has provided theoretical sophistication but I remain spellbound by the screen; only shutting it down, walking outside, engaging others can I restore any (indeed inchoate) sense of attunement to "the whole."

9. Sibley 2008, 154.

10. Grant (1969) 2001, 41.

11. Athanasiadis 2001, 103.

12. Davis and Roper 2005b, 626.

13. See, e.g., Mondzain 2005.

14. "Religion has lost itself in cults, dogmas and myths," Dewey (1922, 204) complained, "Consequently the office of religion as sense of community and one's place in it has been lost. In effect religion has been distorted into a possession—or burden—of a limited part of human nature, of a limited portion of humanity which finds no way to universalize religion except by imposing its own dogmas and ceremonies upon others; of a limited class within a partial group; priests, saints, a church." While Dewey overgeneralizes, certainly it is the case that for many "religion" risks becoming another idolatry of the age.

15. Fishbane (2008, 108) is discussing here the subjective reconstruction religion can animate.

16. Davis and Emberley 2000b, 152.

17. Angus 1997, 96.

18. Rigelhof 2001, 121.

19. "The relationship between the received text and life-situations," Fishbane (2008, 63) notes, "unfolds in the course of interpretation." Substitute "revelation" for "received text" and, of course, add the human subject capable of interpretation, and I concur that interpretation can be an act of reconstruction.

20.   Macdonald (1975) 1995, 75. Contemplating the screen as spiritual, Barry Cooper (1990, 116) asks: "What is the spirituality that is expressed in or through technology?"

21.   Friedman (2017, A23) suggests that recently (winter 2015, he says) "we realized that a critical mass of our lives and work…had moved to a realm *where we're all connected but no one's in charge*," adding that during the 2016 US presidential campaign "we fully grasped just how scary that can be—how easy it was for a presidential candidate to tweet out untruths and half-truths faster than anyone could correct them."

22.   Annovi 2017, 140.

23.   Inadvertently, Annovi (2017, 3) provides another depiction of Grant when she acknowledges "Pasolini's haunting power to interrogate the present," adding: "Like a specter, Pasolini seems to wander through the ruins of a present unrecognizable to him or to us."

24.   The emphasis in that sentence is decidedly on the conditional. As Doull (1983, 41) points out: "[M]odern subjectivity has not grounded itself and found its justification."

25.   Planinc (1992, 28) quotes Barry Cooper: "George Grant's work is accompanied by the voice of his personality. He appears in the world along with his work.… The *daimon*, the personal element in a man, is neither subjective nor recognized by the one who reveals it, and yet it is public and real without being objective." From this insight Planinc derives his sense that "Grant's *daimon* provides the poetic unity to his work," noting that its "philosophic unity" is undetermined.

26.   "In private," Rigelhof (2001, 110) confided, Grant was "much funnier than in public and more ruthless."

27.   While the two terms do not conflate, *sentiment of being* does specify an element of subjective presence I have always acknowledged but not in this text emphasized: its association with social and political life. Discussing Wordsworth and Rousseau, Trilling (1972, 92) calls attention to "the passionate emphasis each of them put upon the individual's experience of existence." Both Rousseau and Wordsworth called this the "sentiment of being," for both "an unassailable intuition" that, Trilling adds, also figured "in the mind of Walt Whitman, who said that it is the hardest basic fact and only entrance to all facts,'" a fact that entranced one to "social and political life—it is through our conscious certitude of our personal selfhood that we reach our knowledge of others" (92). The inner life is prerequisite to a public life lived justly.

28.   O'Donovan 1984, 129.

29.   In a March 1988 letter, Grant writes: "God appears to me more as absence than as presence. Of course, God is both" (Christian 1996d, 379).

30.   Athanasiadis 2001, 190.

31.   Discussing Strauss, Athanasiadis (2001, 126) notes that "knowledge of the whole includes knowledge of all reality—God, world, humanity. It is not a possession of such knowledge but a quest." Certainly the quest metaphor resonates, but the positing of such knowledge of the whole seems scientific or theological, adjectives for me with sometimes blurred boundaries, given the scale of their concerns and their once fused history.

32.   Dewey 1922, 204.

33.   The phrase is C. B. Macpherson's and emphasizes the atomism of an individual whose freedom represents freedom from dependency upon others; see, e.g., Angus 2013, 46.

34.   Christian 1992, 47. "Implications" implies a kind of consequentialism associated with pragmatism, does it not?

35. Christian 1992, 49.

36. Christian 1992, 50.

37. Christian 1992, 51.

38. As it did for Pasolini, becoming historical affirms, as Steimatsky (2008, 133) points out, "the persistence of archaic forms within the contemporary world.... He further suggests that this overlapping of historical moments is also a way for the present to experience, to *think*, history." To be historical—it is a "condition"—in a time of presentism bears "an ideological charge," as the concept of "archaic" did for Pasolini (133–4). Rather than position the "archaic against progress," Steimatsky explains, Pasolini "embraces it as a vital and even dialectical force, analogous to what he reads in Matthew's Gospel as Christ's challenge to *his* contemporary establishment" (134). For me, these conceptions point to the past as also a state of mind, a structure of subjectivity that keeps one foot in the past in anticipation of the future.

39. According the concept a poetic quality, Taylor's ([1982] 2006, 88) quotation of Al Purdy conveys the pedagogical point: "[T]he privilege of finding a small opening / in the past, shouting questions and hearing echoes / whispering in the tents of the living."

40. As Caputo (1987, 241) observes, "Looking backward is the best way to look ahead." Trouble is, "[w]e have become deaf and blind to the *message* which is sent across the epochs" (162).

41. O'Donovan 1984, 157. "In the best traditions of Western Europe," Athanasiadis (2001, 174) reminds, "contemplation was not discarded but made subservient to revelation and put into the service of charity." In the United States, as Posnock (1998, 136) points out, "W.E.B. Du Bois's discovery of contemplation reverberates beyond the realm of self-culture to become an urgent part of his project to democratize access to the aesthetic as cultural capital." Depending upon circumstances, contemplation becomes political as well as spiritual, Weil's "door" that functions both as a barrier and a passage, in this case to a "new age."

42. Knopff (1992, 66) summarizes succinctly: "To repeat, in our time, thought is not contemplative, but active and transformatory. To use a famous formulation, it seeks not to understand the world but to change it. In the technological age, in other words, the life of the mind is little more than will to power."

43. Rocha 2017, 94.

44. Simon 2005, 2.

45. O'Donovan 1984, 166. Recall that Grant's conversion included the insight that we are not our own. What we are fitted for, it would seem, is not necessarily what we imagine we are fitted for. The experience of love—of another, of the Good—discloses the double nature of being fitted: "Our ability to love other people does seem to be a gift," Davis (2006, 68) reminds, "not something that we can generate with our wills," adding: "Are we not 'our own' as well as 'not our own' in this most important of experiences?"

46. "Historical thinking," Athanasiadis (2001, 184) reminds, "means that all thought is subject to the limitations of the context and perspective of the thinker." In this sense reactivation becomes a secular form of transcendence.

47. Benedetti 2005, 17.

48. Athanasiadis 2001, 189. The challenge comes from within as well, in Grant's case from his childhood imprinting of progressivism, leaving traces, as Ajzenstat (1992,

80) detects, in the adult Grant, who retained, he writes, "a certain sympathy" for elements of liberalism.

49. Davis 2002a, xix.

50. As noted earlier, subjective reconstruction through academic study can occur through the method of *currere*: regressive, progressive, analytic, synthesis. The movement of that curriculum theory—working from within—is implied in Angus's summary of the thought of Innis and Grant. "In both thinkers," Angus (1997, 101) writes, "there is a characteristic turning away from the universal orientation of contemporary civilization—by defining it in terms that reveal its actually deficient universality—back towards the local and particular, which is the provenance of every movement outward to universality. It is a regressive form of thought towards what is prior in the logical [and lived] sense. It devolves inward rather than moving outward. It is in search of its own foundation rather than moving confidently towards explaining the world." Exactly.

51. And perhaps a sexual one as well: in 1981, while his wife is away, Grant writes William Christian that he misses her sexually, admitting that "I am still in my heart a modern in which physical love is at the core" (Christian 1996d, 320). While that seems a confession, it does not contradict his Christianity nor his Platonism, in which the body is the site of intersection as well as separation of the here and now and what is forever more.

52. Athanasiadis 2001, 190 .

53. Davis and Roper 2005b, 728.

54. Athanasiadis 2001, 174. In a December 1976 letter, Grant describes his essays as "negative...namely that they exist to clear away the junk of the modern era and to say how difficult it is to make positive affirmations" (Christian 1996d, 296). Christian (1992, 54) affirms this sequence when he writes: "But was there anything that could withstand the power of the dynamo? Grant thought there was, but he had to clear away the old idols with his destructive work before he could attend in a forthright way to the task of reconstruction." Atwood ([1972] 2012, 13) observed that "Canadians show a marked preference for the negative."

55. Dart 2006, 26.

56. Dart 2006, 25.

57. Dart 2006, 25.

58. Magrini (2017, 171) suggests that "the human condition [is] suspended, as it is, between, finitude and transcendence." While that space—that of the icon—can be experienced it seems not so often occupied by humanity. Idolatry is the (in)human condition.

59. Grant's humility I documented in ch. 1. Humility, Dewey (1922, 178–9) knew, "is not caddish self-depreciation. It is the sense of our slight inability even with our best intelligence and effort to command events; a sense of our dependence upon forces that go their way without our wish and plan. Its purpose is not relax effort but to make us prize every opportunity of present growth. In morals, the infinite and the imperative develop from the participle, present tense."

60. Dart 2006, 25. I suggest such openness can be construed as attunement. In obedience to what is revealed comes freedom, a concept that once connoted, Davis reminds, being "loved," e.g., "those individuals who were sheltered, protected, and thus given the leeway to live and carry out their responsibilities as loved members of the

tribe, in contrast to the unloved, unfree slaves taken in battle" (69). Open or attuned to the Good can feel like being loved.

61. Davis and Roper (2009b, 960n13) note: "Grant strongly opposed the conception of the resurrection as a heroic triumph over the crucifixion seen as a defeat." Like Fishbane (2008, 11) I wonder "whether theology is even possible in our time."

62. Dart 2006, 25. For Luther, Athanasiadis (2001, 40) explains, the "cross has as much to do with us as it has to do with God."

63. Athanasiadis 2001, 176. Does not being open to the good in suffering risk the rationalization of suffering?

64. O'Donovan 1984, 17. While conjunctive, these are not always for Grant equal relationships, as Davis (2006, 73) notes, referencing John Porter's *Spirit Book Word*: "Grant's most powerful insight is that what is given to us overwhelms what is made by us."

65. O'Donovan 1984, 17.

66. Doull 1983, 47.

67. For Horowitz (1990, 81): "The Americanization of Canada is 'fated,' 'inescapable,' and not at all bad. The only question now is: what can we…do now to protect the human spirit from materialism?"

68. I can imagine the idea of theology without God (see Kaethler 2009, 70), accepting Marion's (2012) insistence on God "without Being," e.g., the absoluteness of the gap between here and eternity (but allowing for the latter to "exist").

69. Havers 2006, 127.

70. Havers 2006, 133. Specifically, he adds, to any critique inspired by the work of Leo Strauss.

71. It was less inattention than assertion of the unequal presence of reason among peoples, Angus specifies. In Minogue's (1990, 172) view Grant "goes wrong" in reactivating the ancient Greeks in support of a search for morality today. He explains: "This is a mistake for both historical and philosophical reasons. The historical reason is that the Greeks had no particular view of the sanctity of life. They seem to have practiced infanticide without any scruple. The philosophical reason is that Greek humanism is in the highest degree qualitative. 'Man' is not a creature made by God in his image, but a rational part of nature graded in terms of participation in reason" (172). "The idea of attaching rights to human beings as such," Minogue concludes, "is not something that would have detained Plato for long. He was not, after all, an Anglican" (172).

72. Angus 2006, 343.

73. Angus 2006, 343.

74. There were moments, it seems, when Grant wasn't so sure. In a June 1979 letter to Mary Ann and Dennis Duffy (the dean of Innis College, University of Toronto, thanking him for his role in the awarding of an honorary doctorate) Grant admitted "how shallow and uncertain is my partaking in Christ" (Christian 1996d, 305). There is that verb—"partake"—again, suggesting a degree of intensity and immediacy that might have grown faint during not quite four decades since his conversion.

75. Davis 2006, 64.

76. "Grant did side with the modern idea of changing the world to make it a more just place for the many," Davis (2006, 68) writes, even affirming "the liberation of the instincts, for example, *up to a point*." Moderation was Grant's mantra.

77.   Lee 1990, 20. Colville (1990, 4) emphasizes Grant's ethics over his practicality, writing that "George embodied the idea of a man thinking about how one might be good in the present and actual world."

78.   Ward 1990, 95.

79.   Ward 1990, 98. "For Grant," Ward (1990, 99n15) emphasizes, "the modern situation cannot be known clearly unless the role of Christianity in bringing it about is recognized."

80.   Ward 1990, 99.

81.   Ward 1990, 99.

82.   Ward 1990, 101.

83.   Ward 1990, 101. For Whillier (1990b, 72) as well, "Grant's solution to the problem is unabashedly theological: God is the only final limit on human freedom as an end in itself; God alone is that which we cannot manipulate."

84.   I am reminded of the description of study sketched by late-nineteenth/early-twentieth-century African-American educator, activist, and intellectual Charles W. Chestnutt, as "working in the dark. I have to feel my way along.... I have become accustomed to the darkness," an affirmation of intellectual life, as Posnock (1998, 109) puts it, "subterranean, liminal, as if in the midst of his community he is adrift, present but not present." Activism and quietude, attuned to the eternal: like Chestnutt, Grant too found his way through the darkness of his time.

85.   Reimer 1990, 105–6.

86.   Sibley (2008, 279) is not so sure, pointing out that the word *lament* derives "from the Latin *lamentum*, referring to a condition of wailing or grieving. There is no suggestion in the word that something can be saved or revived."

87.   Dart 2006, 26.

88.   Gillespie 1990, 126. "His thinking," Gillespie continues, "is united not by a single principle or doctrine but by a particular way of life. He draws upon the thought of others but he does not synthetize it into a new whole" (126–7). That might be a fault were Grant a philosopher first of all. As I trust I have demonstrated, Grant was, first of all, an educator. His calling was to testify to what he had learned during study, addressing those teachings to those in his midst while attuned to the whole.

89.   Planinc 1992, 41. "Polyphony has a distinctive content and form," Planinc explains. "Its content is spiritual and meditative; its form is the orchestration of a plurality of voices that best expresses such content. Cadence is the experience of a particular meditation seeking the appropriate orchestration of voices to express itself" (27). Polyphony is also an important concept in Aoki's oeuvre; see Aoki (1993) 2005, 209.

90.   Davis and Roper 2009b, 412.

91.   Dart 2006, 26.

92.   Annovi 2017, 61.

93.   Meynell 2011, 211. Meynell argues that Grant's work typified a Christian idealism common in Canada before the 1920s (211). While there are elements of that tradition, especially in Grant's early work, Meynell's thesis risks overstatement concerning Grant's oeuvre overall.

94.   Annovi (2017, 7) points out that "Pasolini's emphasis on the author's presence is a rebuttal to the poststructuralist approach to authorship, particularly to the Barthesian death of the author." Grant's subjective presence as an educator

provides another rebuttal to poststructuralist pronouncements of the author's—the person's—passing.

95. Angus 1997, 233.

96. Davis 2002b, 292.

97. In both teaching and politics, Grant's subjective presence was paramount. I am reminded of a review of Robin Campillo's film *PBM (Beats Per Minute)*, in which it is said of one of the film's characters that "he lived in his politics in the first person" (quoted in Scott 2017, C5). So did Grant, and not only his politics but his teaching, too.

98. Christian 2006, 39.

99. As late as July 1988 his nationalism remained unbroken, decrying the copycats he saw selling off his homeland: "It is for this reason that I detest [NDP Leader Ed] Broadbent's supposed nationalist rhetoric. It is just the Democratic Party North. And [Conservative Leader] Mulroney is the Republican Party North" (Christian 1996d, 388).

100. Warren 1990, 67.

101. Even about the state, complaining to his sister in an April 1988 letter that "the growth of the state automatically means the growth of the bureaucracy" (Christian 1996d, 383), on this occasion no welcomed development despite decades-earlier comments on the necessity of civil servants.

102. Christian 1996d, 387–8. "The major source of power in this society," Knopff (1992, 66) knows, "is the technological paradigm of knowledge itself."

103. Wingfield 2016, 1A.

104. Christian 2006, 52.

105. Christian 2006, 42. While it no doubt derived from his observations—recall he decried the influence of the corporate class on universities—his biographer suggests "that he absorbed it from his father over the dinner table, since it was present even in his youthful comments" (42).

106. For Parel (1992, 145) lament is a "biblical, not philosophical, notion," and that invocation of the theological is "what is original and bold in Grant's analysis of Canadian nationalism." Barry Cooper (1992, 160) reminds that a lament is also a "musical form that upon occasion has been piped before a battle," a form Grant associated with "necessity," another name for "fate." Cooper characterizes Grant's 1965 book as a "meditative lament of ancestral memories, as an act of piety." In its theological and aesthetic senses, lament might be a characterization one might extend to Grant's teaching as a whole.

107. Fierlbeck 2006, 157.

108. Christian 2006, 57.

109. Grant tells Cayley (1995, 119): "I blame St. Augustine. I think it was Augustinian Christianity that shaped both Catholicism and later Protestantism and in turn led to this extreme secularized form of itself as progress. I have no doubt that Christianity is true, and therefore, I think it has to be reformulated."

110. While some degree of social and economic inequality may be inevitable, Christian (2006, 41) reminds that for Grant "extremes of wealth are unacceptable, as are extremes of power."

111. See, e.g., Fierlbeck 2006, 39, 136–8; Angus 1997, 155; Meynell 2011, 201.

112. Christian 2006, 50. In a 1988 letter to his sister Grant noted his "general anti-American tendency" (Christian 1996d, 383).

113. Robertson 2006, 140.

114. Robertson 2006, 140.

115. Robertson 2006, 140.

116. Robertson 2006, 141. In that unity, Robertson adds, is integrated "North American freedom" and the traditions of "Jerusalem and Athens" (142).

117. Davis and Roper 2005b, 441.

118. Christian 2006, 40. Perhaps one could say about Grant what Thibon ([1947] 2002, xvii) writes about Weil, e.g., that she could be as passionate about politics as she was about religion, if maintaining the same critical distance from government as she did from the church, aware, Thibon continues, that the "social field" can be made into an idol, in fact "evil."

119. Christian 2006, 41. I share neither Grant's pacifism nor his anti-abortion politics, although his critique of the latter has its point, e.g., the cult of convenience and, as Ajzenstat (1992, 75) notes, liberalism's failure to protect the weak from the powerful (a pre-modern failure as well I might add). Appealing is Ajzenstat suggestion that pregnancy represented for Grant "a call to both men and women to live within the demands of a good beyond themselves, which is a condition of human fulfilment" (79). From this perspective, Ajzenstat adds, "the prevalence of abortion and especially its legalization would be symptomatic of a general tendency to close our lives to what transcends our pre-formed plans" (79).

120. Davis 2006, 72.

121. Davis 2006, 72.

122. McCarroll 2006, 276.

123. McCarroll 2006, 276.

124. McCarroll 2006, 276.

125. "[W]ithout the transcendent," Arapura (1983, 60) asserts, "the immanent has no bite."

126. Drugs have been and can be used as passages to transcendent experience; see, e.g., Castaneda 1985.

127. Flinn 1990, 125. Perhaps "piety" is not strong enough: "worship" may be appropriate, although that term too implies a separate subject capable of worshipping. In the idolatry of technology there exist no other Gods. "Grant perceives," Kaethler (2009, 44) summarizes, "that technology is a paradigm that assumes that Good is not beyond Being; there is nothing beyond being."

128. Recall that Kittler asserts humanity has no longer a relationship with technology; the only relationship that obtains today is among devices in the cloud. No longer standing reserve, we are epiphenomenal, extras on a movie set where the director is absent, except as the unconscious. "[In] mass media," Kittler (2013, 126) asserts, "the Unconscious turns into the main event."

129. Even arch-critic of technology Al-i Ahmad (1984, 30) allows: "History has fated the world to fall prey to the machine. It is a question of how to encounter the machine and technology." I'd supplement "how" with "why;" the emphasis upon "encounter" I share. For Al-i Ahmad "encounter" seems close to subjection, which is ambitious but appealing. Invoking imagery I associate with idolatry, he writes: "The third road—from which there is no recourse—is to put this jinn back in the bottle. It is to get it under control, to break it into harness like a draft animal. The machine should naturally serve us as a trampoline, so that we may stand on it and jump the farther by its rebound. One must have the machine; one must build it. But one must not

remain in bondage to it; one must not fall into its snare. The machine is a means, not an end. The end is to abolish poverty and to put material and spiritual welfare within the reach of all" (9). That last aspiration seems iconographic in character.

130. Aoki (1993) 2005, 292.

131. This verb I invoke in both its contemporary meaning (to object due to one's scruples) and its archaic meaning (to linger).

132. O'Donovan 1990, 139.

133. Davis 2002b, 125.

134. Davis 2006, 68. That freedom has been exploited to wage war, so that for Grant, as for Pasolini, modernity "was itself tainted by Fascism and the war...its contents and uses bent and exploited...a ruin itself in need of neorealist reconstruction" (Steimatsky 2008, xxii). Maybe the two very different men might have even agreed on the "neorealist" qualification as Grant had his feet firmly planted on earth—conscious of inequality and human suffering—as he attuned himself to the eternal.

135. O'Donovan 1984, 89.

136. O'Donovan 1984, 89.

137. Recall that for Weil ([1947] 2002, 44): "Obedience is the supreme virtue."

138. O'Donovan 1984, 89.

139. Athanasiadis 2001, 84.

140. Christian (1992, 56–7) succinctly summarizes: "Technological rationalism rejects the existence of the good because it is incapable of comprehending it within its paradigm. It cannot accept the existence of authentic otherness because it can only account for that which it has itself created; and one thing that we surely cannot create is authentic otherness. However we encounter it, whether through sexual love or through a higher and more spiritual longing, we experience it as something ultimately beyond our capacity to manipulate or transform."

141. Was Grant's "most powerful insight...that what is given to us overwhelms what is made by us?" (see Davis 2006, 73). If we are attuned to it, one might add.

142. Athanasiadis 2001, 84.

143. One might think of such quietude as, after Posnock (1998, 293), "serenity without complacency," the intellectual figured as (here Posnock is quoting Pierre Bourdieu) a "paradoxical synthesis of the opposites of retreat and engagement" (305–6n23).

144. Athanasiadis 2001, 108.

145. Athanasiadis 2001, 108.

146. Grant emphasizes: "I am not speaking against the fine system of constitutional government and its liberties which is the political mark of the English-speaking peoples. And which is the best thing about us. All I am saying is that that constitutional system of government and its freedoms now operates within something greater than itself—state-corporation capitalism. Our lives and our freedoms are exercised within that system and that means that often within our technological society it seems as if there is nothing between them. So many of the intermediate institutions such as the family and the churches [and now the schools] have been destroyed" (Davis and Roper 2009b, 543).

147. Davis 2006, 67.

148. Athanasiadis 2001, 162.

149. Athanasiadis 2001, 162.

150. Athanasiadis 2001, 167.

151. Athanasiadis 2001, 167. I am reminded of the important work done on non-violence in curriculum studies; see, e.g., Wang 2014.

152. Angus (1997, 248) reports that "Grant said somewhere—I believe it was in his seminar on technology at McMaster University, which I attended in the winter term of 1973—that his conception of Anglicanism was that variant closest to Hinduism. This remark was made in the context of the commitment of Western Christianity to the centrality of will since Augustine. I do not know what it means." Does Arapura's (1983, 59) observation concerning the Vedanta—that in it "there is no such thing as a mere appearance without a transcendent substratum"—provide a clue? See also Wilfred Cantwell Smith (1983, 81), who suggests that "Hindus have not had a Day-of-Judgment concept, have not been eschatologically minded (nor even much, historically minded), and strictly speaking have had no concept to which our term 'moral responsibility' is exactly applicable," adding that "Hindus live responsible lives as surely as do any other people, in any but the most precise meaning of the term. What I have called their counterpart vision, dramatic and powerful, is their so-called '*law of karma.*' This has hardly been a doctrine, so much as a proposition—in that it has underlain and coloured all their doctrines, and most Buddhist ones too."

153. Davis and Roper 2009b, 581.

154. Christian 1996d, 380.

155. Warren 1990, 61.

156. Warren 1990, 61.

157. Warren 1990, 61.

158. What Elshtain (2005, 246) writes of Augustine I would write of Grant: "Augustine is an epistemological sceptic who believes, nonetheless, that we can come to know certain truths."

159. Davis 2002b, 162.

160. And Caplan attacks education itself as irrelevant, a waste of time and money.

161. As we saw in ch. 5, the liberal arts have too been studied scientifically (e.g., objectified) and taught as vocational subjects (students of historians taught to think like historians).

162. Certainly this contemporary reiteration of populism shares anti-immigrant sentiments with its predecessor (see https://www.smithsonianmag.com/history/immigrants-conspiracies-and-secret-society-launched-american-nativism-180961915/), but its economistic outlook—life is all about making money—seems perhaps more prominent now.

163. Davis 2002b, 104.

164. Davis 2002b, 104.

165. Fishbane 2008, 63.

166. Benedetti 2005, 211.

167. Benedetti 2005, 211.

168. Davis and Roper 2005b, 237. "[M]eaning," Minogue (1990, 173) comments, "unlike truth, is partly made and partly discovered. Further, it is never absent from a human life. Nothing is ever strictly meaningless. When Grant talks about meaning becoming obscure he is expressing dissatisfaction with the trivial and unstable meanings people actually entertain, and with this it is easy to sympathize. It is conceivable that some new, overpowering religion might sweep the world, as Christianity did before it, and install a new moral order in which due and proper limits to man's

technological possibility were imposed. Indeed, this is the only thing that would meet Grant's dissatisfaction with the modern world. But it is unlikely, because of the pluralism of modern societies and the end of the conception of the good life." This is, it seems to me, a secular and historicist view of the matter, omitting altogether the fact that subjectivity is the ongoing site of meaning making and discovery. Even within secular society or one enforcing a specific religion, one can make and discover meaning through subjective attunement to that which exceeds the empirical, the historical. That is one meaning of Grant's work, I suggest.

169. Davis 2000, xxxi.

170. Davis 2002b, 69.

171. Taylor (1982) 2006, 131.

172. Davis 2002b, 107.

173. "Miss O, our teacher," Aoki ([1986/1991] 2005, 163) writes, "knows that indwelling in the zone between curriculum-as-plan and curriculum-as-lived experience is not so much a matter of overcoming the tensionality but more a matter of dwelling aright within it." I take "aright" to mean acting obediently in attunement to what needs to be done, who needs to be addressed and how and regarding what, haunted by the curriculum question: what knowledge is of most worth?

174. Not necessarily a comfortable space of course, for student or teacher. Magrini (2017, 124) reminds us of Socrates' "acute 'pain' associated with his 'midwifery' when watching over the labour of his interlocutors' souls."

175. Davis and Roper 2009b, 968.

176. Aoki 2005 (1990), 367.

177. Fishbane 2008, 63.

178. Planinc 1992, 41. Planinc borrows the term "polyphonic" from Dennis Lee's depiction of "poetic cadence," a rhythmic element, I suggest, of Grant's subjective presence. In that sense, Planinc continues, "polyphony is also a unity. The meditating consciousness, the content of its meditation, and the single voice that emerge from the orchestration of many voices are all one" (27). Subjective presence one might say.

179. https://en.oxforddictionaries.com/definition/daemon.

180. Planinc 1992, 41–2. The movement of Grant's thought is not readily periodized, Planinc concludes, noting that "Grant developed a large repertoire of critiques during his life. Some are compatible with one another and some are not. The only feature they all have in common is the fact that they are critiques of modernity.... And the force of his character provided the polyphony with its unity" (27). That Grant had character fated him to oppose technologization, as one who is technologized, Al-i Ahmad (1984, 95) complains, "has no character. He is a thing without authenticity. His person, his home, and his words convey nothing in particular, and everything in general. It is not that he is cosmopolitan, that the world is his home. He is at home nowhere rather than everywhere." Nowhere is online.

181. Aoki ([1987] 2005, 359) called for an "inspirited curriculum."

182. "There is no unmediated self-identity which precludes the need to inform itself of its own doings," Caputo (1987, 135) reminds. "On the contrary," he continues, "the inner life of consciousness is a flux, constituted by the gaps and interstices of flowing time which needs constantly to be repaired by the work of synthesis" (135–6), that latter term suggesting that the coherence of subjective presence is compensatory, the consequence of subjective reconstruction.

183. "The totality of Pasolini's work should be understood as a macrostructure with Pasolini at its center," Annovi (2017, 7) notes, "which does not impose a 'Ptolemaic' authorial point of view but asks the audience to participate in the creation of the author's performance." Likewise, Grant radiates from within his texts, inviting us to participate in the text as we attune ourselves to what lies beyond it.

184. Pérez-Gómez 2016, 30. Do we escape into the screen in flight from our era? "We live in a time stunned by fate," Angus (1997, 5) appreciates.

185. Rocha 2017, 117.

186. Christian 1996d, 149.

187. Christian 1996d, 149. In fact, he adds "I have never felt so full of power and so integrated since I was born—but one is always chastened…[by] the supremely great and humble and self-discipline[d] and I haven't even started on the beginning of the road to any of these" (149–50). This juxtaposition of capaciousness (even voluptuousness: Pinar 2006b, 182) and asceticism in the presence of what lies beyond either restates his juxtaposition of progressivism, Platonism, and Christianity.

188. Christian 1996d, 150.

189. See n187 above.

190. Christian 1996d, 387. Writing his mother on Christmas Day 1941 Grant was intact but felt *like a piece of stick being carried by the strength of the current*" (quoted in Jersak 2012, 169).

191. Christian 1996d, 388.

192. Davis 2006, 69. Recall that Grant wrote his DPhil thesis on the Scottish theologian John Oman, whose "greatness," Grant felt sure, concerned his capacity to thread through the particularity of personality, place, and time what lay beyond these: "As a philosopher of religion that greatness appears in the way all problems are taken up into his own powerful individuality, and yet by his concentration on essentials that unique interpretation brings out the universality of the questions" (Davis and Emberley 2000b, 367).

193. Davis and Roper 2009b, 413.

194. O'Donovan 1984, 155.

195. O'Donovan 1984, 24.

196. O'Donovan 1984, 24.

197. Davis and Roper 2005b, 409.

198. Benedetti 2005, 211.

199. Davis 2002b, 161.

200. Christian 1996d, 247.

201. F. Peters 1978, 10.

202. Aoki (1996) 2005, 316.

203. Ouspensky 1982, 28.

204. Athanasiadis 2001, 33.

205. Athanasiadis 2001, 33.

206. Davis and Roper 2005b, 240.

207. Perhaps this realization Grant threaded through his study of Martin Luther. Athanasiadis (2001, 34) explains that "Luther believed knowledge about God to be intimately related to knowledge about ourselves in relation to God and in relation to the world…. Because we refuse to let God in our lives, we forge our own idea of God in our image and confuse God's will with our own." Here is a succinct statement of subjectivity as iconographic rather than idolatrous.

208. Aoki (1993) 2005, 295; Aoki (1996) 2005, 318.
209. Kane 1990, 153.
210. Discussing Grant and Harold Innis, Angus (1997, 103) concludes that "their position might be more completely characterized as involving a polarity between humanism and archaism."
211. "That is our solidarity with George Grant," Angus (1997, 233) points out, "our needing, remembering, and questioning the George Grant trail, leaving some markers as we go our own way."
212. Annovi 2017, 19.
213. Davis and Roper 2009b, 466.
214. Davis and Roper 2009b, 467
215. Ajzenstat (1992, 82) reminds finding what we are fitted for means rendering "what is due to them," adding that although Grant accepted that "justice was in our natures, he was far from thinking it was the only thing in our natures" (83).
216. Davis and Roper 2009b, 294.
217. Davis 2006, 73.
218. Davis 2006, 73. As the term implies, the supernatural can occur within the natural world, a point Trilling (1972, 90–1) makes in a different context (he is discussing the Wordsworthian epiphany) but relevant to Grant's sense of the relation between the two: "[S]pirit shows forth from Nature; the sudden revelation communicates to the poet a transcendent message which bears upon the comprehension of human existence or upon the direction his own life should take." Perhaps Grant felt that way about Terence Bay.
219. O'Donovan 1984, 129. In Angus's (1997, 96) terms: "Escaping the technological empire requires, in the first place, understanding how deeply we are each caught up in it."
220. These are Grant's words; see Davis and Roper 2009b, 294.
221. Davis and Roper 2009b, 294.
222. "Pasolini's last projections," Steimatsky (2008, xxxi–xxxii) reminds, "were of a vacuous Italy, homogenized by corporate mergers and consumer culture that subjugates bodies, identities, the nation as one, to the all-consuming morbid power of commodities and the media."
223. Davis and Roper 2009b, 294.
224. Davis and Roper 2009b, 294.
225. Davis and Roper 2009b, 294–5.
226. Davis 2002b, 163–4.
227. Angus 1997, 102.
228. Angus 1997, 95.
229. Angus 1997, 95.
230. Davis and Roper 2009b, 920.
231. "What is worrisome about this framework that valorizes the either/or binary," Aoki ([1993] 2003, 294) wrote, "is the way it seduces many of us into the language of either 'boosters of technology' or 'knockers of technology.' Trapped within the either/or realm, we can become either promoters or opposers of the value of technology."
232. Aoki (1987) 2005, 157.
233. Davis and Roper 2005b, 678.

234. See Robertson (2006, 148). Robertson associates this view with Grant's "conservatism." May I add that Pasolini shared this conviction that the past could be reactivated, if (in his case) through film.

235. See Robertson (2006, 148). For Robertson, Grant's consideration of civilizational collapse suggests his "extremism."

236. Robertson 2006, 148.

237. There remains for Kittler (2013, 301) an outside, not spiritual as in Grant's case but psychic: "As Lacan would have put it, the Real—because its body exceeds counting operations—persists as the Impossible, beyond all 'computability' (as one says in English)."

238. Robertson 2006, 148. That voluntarism—in Angus's term "will"—would seem to have been displaced from humanity to the machine, but Robertson is right to remember that the machine is the materialization of that voluntarism, that willfulness.

239. O'Donovan 1984, 59.

240. Robertson 2006, 147–8.

241. Angus 2006, 351.

242. Athanasiadis 2001, 173.

243. Taylor (1982) 2006, 150.

244. Parel (1992, 142) reminds us that while "the *modus vivendi* achieved by the English and the French was the keynote of the Canadian particularity, Grant also recognized the existence of other particularities within the Canadian particularity, namely the ethnic communities of Canada. These two were part of the Canadian historical experience; they too had to be loved. But there was to be a qualitative difference between the love for the English-Canadian and the French-Canadian particularities, on the one hand, and the ethnic particularities, on the other. It is for failing to grasp this distinction that Grant criticized Diefenbaker's 'One Canada' nationalism." I would reassert my claim that had he lived longer, Grant's sense of particularity would be extended further to affirm Indigenous peoples, especially as these preserved elements of pre-modern even anti-modernistic *modus vivendi*.

245. Parel 1992, 142.

246. Heyking and Cooper 2006, 172.

247. Davis and Roper 2009b, 416.

248. Christian 1996d, 183.

249. Stamps 1995, 31. Stamps is here discussing Adorno.

250. Stamps 1995, 31.

251. Stamps 1995, 31.

252. Athanasiadis 2001, 50.

253. Davis and Roper 2005b, 16–7.

254. Davis and Roper 2005b, 17.

255. Even in 2011, estimates ran from 200,000 (S. Saul 2011, A1) to 250,000 (Banchero and Simon 2011) of the number US children who were enrolled in full-time virtual schools, up 40 per cent since 2008. More than two million pupils took at least one class online, according to the International Association for K-12 Online Learning, a trade group. Banchero and Simon reported that while some US states and local districts operate their own online schools, many others hire for-profit corporations such as K12 Inc. of Herndon, Va., and Connections Academy in Baltimore, a subsidiary of the technology company Pearson PLC (C1). Collins (2017, A21) reports that the

family of US Secretary of Education DeVos holds investments in K12 Inc. The Walton Family Foundation, a strong supporter of school choice in the United States, funded a recent study which concluded that if the virtual charters were grouped together as a single school district, "It would be the ninth-largest in the country and among the worst performing" (quoted in Collins 2017, A21). These companies—not school-district selected professional directors of personnel—hire teachers, provide curriculum, and monitor student performance as they lobby to promote on-line education. No longer public services, these are now products sold to the public, substituting corporate profitability for professional commitment to the education of children.

256. In the United States, Kang (2017, B6) reports, tech companies, among them Amazon, Facebook, Google, Microsoft, and Salesforce, have "pledged a total of $300 million for computer science education, in partnership with the Trump administration meant to prepare students for careers in technology."

257. Davis and Roper 2005b, 446.

258. Havers 2006, 126. Ajzenstat (1992, 89) decodes Grant's account of modernity's demand for ever-increasing productivity, in the first instance, as "production for its own sake, unlimited production understood as the triumph of the will as creativity, centered finally on self-creation as the making of new human natures." In the second, modernity leads "not to intransigent self-assertion but to a dull, conformist mediocrity in which equality stifles individual freedom" (89).

259. For its most recent reiteration, see http://www.worldbank.org/en/news/speech/2014/11/04/human-capital-in-the-21st-century.

260. Davis 2006, 68.

261. Davis 2006, 76.

262. Cayley 1995, 147.

263. Dewey 1922, 178.

264. Of course Dewey's progressivism exceeds the moment in which he formulated it—a long moment occasioned by his long life and the confidence embedded in the larger progressive movement evident in his pragmatism—but now (what Grant insisted we acknowledge as a darkness) what remains of that century-old North American (or American) confidence is faith in technology, a faith that for a while Grant hoped to share: "We must have faith that the technological world can be shaped to richer ends than now seems likely. But the first thing necessary to that shaping is to see the transition we are in" (Davis 2002b, 214). Like Dewey, then, Grant discerned the singularity of the present historical moment, but managed not to become mired in it, as he also prophesized where that moment might go, yes that moment in which we find ourselves today, evident when he writes: "That is, we must recognize that we are at a bad time in human history. We must recognize that the very values that we as teachers affirm are largely defined by society as a whole" (Davis 2002b, 187).

265. Kestenbaum (2002) would disagree.

266. Dewey 1922, 204.

267. Weil (1947) 2002, 153.

268. Davis 2006, 65.

269. Magrini 2017, 179.

270. Benedetti 2005, 212.

271. As I did in ch. 1, I acknowledge that, especially in ch. 5–7, I have blurred the boundaries between Grant's critique and my thought. Like Marion (2001, 137) I must admit

that "my reading has perhaps seemed at times 'to force the text.' And the text has, to be sure, been forced, not as one violates, but as one forces a door." That judgment I hope the reader of this text shares.

272. "It is not that I have a long journey to undertake in order to get to God," Williams (2012, 35) writes, "but that I have a long journey to my own reality. It is my heart, the centre or source of my own being, that is furthest away from my surface mind and feelings, and pilgrimage is always a traveling to where I am."

273. Sibley (2008, 151) summarizes: "Grant sees the Western tradition rooted in two primals: reason and love, thought and charity, or, if you will, reason and revelation."

274. As if, of course, one imagines him present in his words. Many whom I have cited did meet Grant, Minogue (1990, 161) among them: "I met George Grant only once, in 1979, on what was, I think, his sixty-first birthday. It was with Bill Christian and Julie Beatty, who sat in the back of the car icing the cake. There was a seminar which made clear what a born teacher Grant was. At the end of it I think I said that he had turned Plato into an Anglican and he expressed surprise that I should find this an odd idea. Grant was a philosopher, and the way to keep a philosopher's ideas alive is by rethinking and testing them." Such is my aim here.

275. Kaethler (2009, 52) suggests that what Grant means by thinking "'openly about the nature of the whole' is that we must seek to understand the visible by contemplating the invisible." Here contemplation becomes attunement.

276. Davis 2002b, 187.

277. Davis 2002b, 187.

278. Davis 2002b, 187.

279. Davis 2002b, 187.

280. Davis 2002b, 187.

281. Davis 2002b, 187.

282. Davis 2002b, 188.

283. Discussing Joyce's epiphanies, Trilling (1972, 91) notes that they have their "locus and agency [in] some unlikely person...who, without intension, by something said or done, or not done, suddenly manifests the quality of his own particular being and thus implies the wonder of being in general." I am reminded of Grant's advice to teachers to allow oneself to follow not what one already grasps but what is grasping one, to allow oneself to be led from the particular to the universal, from the mundane to the wondrous.

284. Davis 2002b, 188.

285. Davis 2002b, 188.

References

Adams, Michael. 2009. *Fire & Ice: The United States, Canada and the Myth of Converging Values*. Toronto: Penguin Canada.

Ajzenstat, Samuel. 1992. "The Place of Abortion in George Grant's Thought." In Umar and Cooper, *George Grant and the Future of Canada*, 75–101.

Alford, C. Fred. 2002. *Levinas, the Frankfurt School, and Psychoanalysis*. Middletown, CT: Wesleyan University Press.

Al-i Ahmad, Jalal. 1984. *Occidentosis: A Plague From the West*. Translated by R. Campell. Annotations and introduction by Hamid Algar. Berkeley, CA: Mizan Press.

Anderson, Nick. 2016. "Princeton Keeps Wilson's Name on 2 Institutions." *Washington Post*, April 5, 2016, A5.

Andrew, Ed, and Zdravko Planinc. 1990. "Technology and Justice: A Round Table Discussion." In Emberley, *By Loving Our Own*, 175–87.

Angus, Ian. 1987. *George Grant's Platonic Rejoinder to Heidegger: Contemporary Political Philosophy and the Question of Technology*. Lewiston, NY: Edwin Mellen Press.

———. 1997. *A Border Within: National Identity, Cultural Plurality, and Wilderness*. Montreal: McGill-Queen's University Press.

———. 2006. "Socrates' Joke." In Angus, Dart, and Peters, *Athens and Jerusalem*, 341–68.

———. 2013. *The Undiscovered Country: Essays in Canadian Intellectual Culture*. Edmonton: Athabasca University Press.

Angus, Ian, Ron Dart, and Randy Peg Peters, ed. 2006. *Athens and Jerusalem: George Grant's Theology, Philosophy, and Politics*. Toronto: University of Toronto Press.

Annovi, Gian Mara. 2017. *Pier Paolo Pasolini: Performing Authorship*. New York: Columbia University Press.

Aoki, Ted T. (1979) 2005. "Reflections of a Japanese Canadian Teacher Experiencing Ethnicity." In Pinar and Irwin, *Curriculum in a New Key*, 333–8.

———. (1981) 2005. "Toward Understanding Curriculum." In Pinar and Irwin, *Curriculum in a New Key*, 219–28.

———. (1986/1991) 2005. "Teaching as Indwelling Between Two Curriculum Worlds." In Pinar and Irwin, *Curriculum in a New Key*, 159–65.

———. (1987) 2005a. "Toward Understanding Computer Application." In Pinar and Irwin, *Curriculum in a New Key*, 151–8.

———. (1987) 2005b. "Revisiting the Notions of Leadership and Identity." In Pinar and Irwin, *Curriculum in a New Key*, 349–55.

———. (1987) 2005c. "Inspiriting the Curriculum." In Pinar and Irwin, *Curriculum in a New Key*, 357–65.

———. (1990) 2005. "*Sonare* and *Videre*: A Story, Three Echoes and a Lingering Note." In Pinar and Irwin, *Curriculum in a New Key*, 367–76.

———. (1992) 2005. "Layered Voices of Teaching: The Uncannily Correct and the Elusively True." In Pinar and Irwin, *Curriculum in a New Key*, 187–97.

———. (1993) 2005a. "Legitimating Lived Curriculum." In Pinar and Irwin, *Curriculum in a New Key*, 199–215.

———. (1993) 2005b will amend textual reference. "Humiliating the Cartesian Ego." In Pinar and Irwin, *Curriculum in a New Key*, 291–301.

———. (1995) 2005. "In the Midst of Doubled Imaginaries: The Pacific Community as Diversity and as Difference." In Pinar and Irwin, *Curriculum in a New Key*, 303–19.

———. (1996) 2005. "Imaginaries of 'East and West': Slippery Curricular Signifiers in Education." In Pinar and Irwin, *Curriculum in a New Key*, 313–9.

Arapura, John G. 1983. "Modern Thought and the Transcendent: Some Observations Based on an Eastern View." In Combs, *Modernity and Responsibility*, 51–61.

Armour, Leslie, and Elizabeth Trott. 1981. *The Faces of Reason: An Essay on Philosophy and Culture in English Canada 1850-1950*. Waterloo, ON: Wilfred Laurier University Press.

Astiz, M. Fernanda, Alexander W. Wiseman, and David P. Baker. 2002. "Slouching towards Decentralization: Consequences of Globalization for Curricular Control in National Education Systems." *Comparative Education Review* 46, no. 1: 66–88.

Athanasiadis, Harris. 2001. *George Grant and the Theology of the Cross: The Christian Foundations of His Thought*. Toronto: University of Toronto Press.

———. 2006. "Waiting at the Foot of the Cross: The Spirituality of George Grant." In Angus, Dart, and Peters, *Athens and Jerusalem*, 256–69.

Atwood, Margaret. (1972) 2012. *Survival: A Thematic Guide to Canadian Literature*. Toronto: House of Anansi.

Austen, Ian. 2017. "Canadian City Remembers Great Explosion, 100 Years Later." *New York Times*, December 7, 2017, A6.

Autio, Tero. 2006. *Subjectivity, Schooling, Society: Between and Beyond German Didaktik and Anglo-American Curriculum Studies*. Mahwah, NJ: Lawrence Erlbaum.

Badertscher, John. 1978. "George P. Grant and Jacques Elul: On Freedom in Technological Society." In Schmidt, *George Grant in Process*, 79–89.

Banchero, Stephanie, and Stephanie Simon. 2011. "My Teacher is an App." *Wall Street Journal*, November 12–13, 2011, C1–C2.

Barnard, Anne. 2013. "As Arab Spring's Glow Fades and Turmoil Rises Unsettling Questions." *New York Times*, February 1, 2013, A10.

Bauman, Zygmunt. 1978. *Hermeneutics and Social Science*. New York: Columbia University Press.

Beale, G. K. 2008. *We Become What We Worship: A Biblical Theology of Idolatry*. Downers Grove, IL: InterVarsity Press.

Beiner, Ronald. 1996. "George Grant, Nietzsche, and the Problem of a Post-Christian Theism." In Davis, *George Grant and the Subversion of Modernity*, 109–38.

Belkin, Douglas. 2017. "Many Colleges Fail in Teaching How to Think." *Wall Street Journal*, June 6, 2017, A1, A10.

Benedetti, Carla. 2005. *The Empty Cage: Inquiry into the Mysterious Disappearance of the Author*. Translated by William J. Hartley. Ithaca: Cornell University Press.

Benhabib, Seyla. 2006. *Another Cosmopolitanism*. With commentaries by Jeremy Waldron, Bonnie Honig, and Will Kymlicka. Edited and introduced by Robert Post. Oxford: Oxford University Press.

Bennington, Geoffrey. 2005. "Time—for the Truth." In Caputo and Scanlon, *Augustine and Postmodernism*, 53–67.

Berg, Maggie, and Barbara K Seeber. 2016. *The Slow Professor: Challenging the Culture of Speed in the Academy*. Toronto: University of Toronto Press.

Bergner, Gwen. 1999. "Politics and Pathologies: On the Subject of Race in Psychoanalysis." In *Frantz Fanon: Critical Perspectives*, edited by Anthony C. Alessandrini, 219–34. London: Routledge.

Berliner, David C., and Bruce J. Biddle. 1995. *The Manufactured Crisis: Myths, Fraud,and the Attack on America's Public Schools*. Cambridge, MA: Perseus. [can you fix this spacing?]

Block, Alan A. 2001. "Ethics and Curriculum." *JCT* 17, no. 3: 23–38.

———. 2004. *Talmud, Curriculum, and the Practical*. New York: Peter Lang.

———. 2017. "Study as Sacred." In Ruitenberg, *Reconceptualizing Study in Educational Discourse and Practice*, 84–96.

Bobbitt, Franklin. 1918. *The Curriculum*. Boston: Houghton Mifflin.

Botstein, Leon. 2017. "American Universities Must Take a Stand." *New York Times*, February 8, 2017, A25.

Bowers, C. A. 1995. *Educating for an Ecologically Sustainable Culture*. Albany: State University of New York Press.

———. 2000. *Let Them Eat Data: How Computers Affect Education, Cultural Diversity and the Prospects of Ecological Sustainability*. Athens: University of Georgia Press.

Bradshaw, Leah. 1996. "Love and Will in the Miracle of Birth: An Arendtian Critique of George Grant on Abortion." In Davis, *George Grant and the Subversion of Modernity*, 220–39.

Britzman, Deborah P. 2006. *Novel Education: Psychoanalytic Studies of Learning and Not Learning*. New York: Peter Lang.

Brooks, David. 2015. "Schools for Wisdom." *New York Times*, October 16, 2015, A29.

Bruner, Jerome S. (1960) 1977. *The Process of Education*. Cambridge, MA: Harvard University Press.

Bruni, Frank. 2015. "Can We Interest You in Teaching?" *New York Times*, August 12, 2015, A17.

Bruno-Jofré, Rosa, and Josh Cole. 2014. "To Serve and Yet Be Free: Historical Configurations and the Insertions of Faculties of Education in Ontario." In *Teacher Education in a Transnational World*, edited by Rosa Bruno-Jofré and James Scott Johnson, 71–95. Toronto: University of Toronto Press.

Burke, Kevin J., and Avner Segall. 2017. *Christian Privilege in U.S. Education: Legacies and Current Issues.* New York: Routledge.

Butler, Judith, and Gayatri Chakravorty Spivak. 2007. *Who Sings the Nation-State?* London: Seagull.

Caldwell, Gary G. 2006. "Grant and Quebec." In Angus, Dart, and Peters, *Athens and Jerusalem*, 29–38.

Callahan, Raymond E. 1962. *Education and the Cult of Efficiency.* Chicago: University of Chicago Press.

Capelle, Philippe. 2005. "Heidegger. Reader of Augustine." In Caputo and Scanlon, *Augustine and Postmodernism*, 115–26.

Caplan, Bryan. 2018. *The Case Against Education: Why the Education System Is a Waste of Time and Money.* Princeton, NJ: Princeton University Press.

Caputo, John D. 1987. *Radical Hermeneutics: Repetition, Deconstruction and the Hermeneutic Project.* Bloomington, IN: Indiana University Press.

———. 2005. "Shedding Tears Beyond Being." In Caputo and Scanlon, *Augustine and Postmodernism*, 95–114.

Caputo, John D., and Michael J. Scanlon. 2005. *Augustine and Postmodernism: Confessions and Circumfession.* Bloomington: Indiana University Press

Capps, Donald. 1995. *The Child's Song: The Religious Abuse of Children.* Louisville, KY: Westminster John Knox Press.

Carby, Hazel V. 1998. *Race Men.* Cambridge, MA: Harvard University Press.

Carey, Benedict. 2016. "Report Questioning Psychology Studies is Criticized." *New York Times*, March 4, 2016, A3.

Carr, Nicholas. 2017. "How Smartphones Hijack Our Minds." *Wall Street Journal*, October 7–8, 2017, C1–C2.

Castaneda, Carlos. 1985. *The Teachings of Don Juan: A Yaqui Way of Knowledge.* New York: Washington Square Press.

Cavell, Richard. 2002. *McLuhan in Space: A Cultural Geography.* Toronto: University of Toronto Press.

Cayley, David. 1995. *George Grant In Conversation.* Toronto: House of Anansi Press Limited.

Chambers, Cynthia. 1999. "A Topography for Canadian Curriculum Theory." *Canadian Journal of Education* 24, no. 2: 137–50.

Chodorow, Nancy J. 1978. *The Reproduction of Mothering.* Berkeley: University of California Press.

Christian, William. 1978. "George Grant and the Terrifying Darkness." In Schmidt, *George Grant in Process*, 167–78.

———. 1990. "The Magic of Art." In Emberley, *By Loving Our Own*, 189–202.

———. 1992. "Religion, Faith, and Love." In Umar and Cooper, *George Grant and the Future of Canada*, 47–57.

———. 1995. Introduction to *Time as History*, by George Grant, vii–xli. Toronto: University of Toronto Press.

———. (1995) 2001. "Editor's Introduction: George Grant's Nietzsche." *Time as History*, by George Grant, vii–xli. Toronto: University of Toronto Press.

———. 1996a. *George Grant: A Biography.* Toronto: University of Toronto Press.

———. 1996b. "Selected Letters on Universities and Education by George Grant." In Davis, *George Grant and the Subversion of Modernity*, 304–27.delete: I can't seem to find your #5

———. 1996c. Introduction to *George Grant: Selected Letters*, edited by William Christian, vii–xiii. Toronto: University of Toronto Press.

———, ed. 1996d. *George Grant: Selected Letters*. Toronto: University of Toronto Press.

———. 2006. "Was George Grant a Red Tory?" In Angus, Dart, and Peters, *Athens and Jerusalem*, 39–61.

Christian, William, and Sheila Grant. 1998a. Introduction to *The George Grant Reader*, edited by William Christian and Sheila Grant, 3–32. Toronto: University of Toronto Press.

———, ed. 1998b. *The George Grant Reader*. Toronto: University of Toronto Press.

Christou, Theodore Michael. 2012. *Progressive Education: Revisioning and Reframing Ontario's Public Schools, 1919-1942*. Toronto: University of Toronto Press.

Clarke, Matthew, and Anne Phelan. 2017. *Teacher Education and the Political: The Power of Negative Thinking*. London: Routledge.

Clifford, Geraldine Joncich, and James W. Guthrie. 1988. *Ed School: A Brief for Professional Education*. Chicago: University of Chicago Press.

Cohen, Daniel. 2009. *Three Lectures on Post-Industrial society*. Translated by William McCuaig. Cambridge, MA: MIT Press.

Cohen, Noam. 2011. "In Unsettled Times, Media Can Be a Call to Action, or a Distraction." *New York Times*, August 29, 2011, B3.

Cohen, Patricia. 2016. "A Rising Call to Foster STEM Fields, and Decrease Liberal Arts Funding." *New York Times*, February 22, 2016, B1, B3.

———. 2017. "New Optimism in Education's Profit Industry." *New York Times*, February 21, 2017, A1, A18.

Collingwood, R. G. 2002. *An Autobiography*. Introduced by Stephen Toulmin. Oxford: Clarendon Press.

Collins, Gail. 2017. "Trump's War On Public Schools." *New York Times*, January 28, 2017, A21.

Colville, Alex. 1990. "A Tribute to Professor George P. Grant." In Emberley, *By Loving Our Own*, 3–10.

Combs, Eugene. 1983a. Preface to Combs, *Modernity and Responsibility*, vii–xiii.

———. 1983b. "Spinoza's Method of Biblical Interpretation and His Political Philosophy." In Combs, *Modernity and Responsibility*, 7–28.

Cooper, Afua. 2006. *The Hanging of Angélique: The Untold Story of Canadian Slavery and the Burning of Old Montréal*. Athens, GA: University of Georgia Press.

Cooper, Anna Julia. (1892) 1998. "A Voice from the South." In *The Voice of Anna Julia Cooper*, edited by Charles Lemert and Esme Bhan, 51–196. Lanham, MD: Rowan and Littlefield Publishers, Inc.

Cooper, Barry. 1978. "*A Imperio usque ad Imperium*: The Political Thought of George Grant." In Schmidt, *George Grant in Process*, 22–39.

———. 1990. "George Grant and the Revival of Political Philosophy." In Emberley, *By Loving Our Own*, 97–121.

———. 1992. "Did George Grant's Canada Ever Exist?" In Umar and Cooper, *George Grant and the Future of Canada*, 151–64.

Cormier, Jeffrey. 2004. *The Canadianization Movement: Emergence, Survival, and Success*. Toronto: University of Toronto Press.

Coyle, Diane. 2007. *The Soulful Science: What Economists Really Do and Why It Matters*. Princeton, NJ: Princeton University Press.

Craiutu, Aurelian. 2017. *Faces of Moderation: The Art of Balance in an Age of Extremes*. Philadelphia: University of Pennsylvania Press.

Cremin, Lawrence A. 1961. *The Transformation of the School: Progressivism in American Education, 1876-1957*. New York: Alfred A. Knopf.

Cusset, François. 2008. *French Theory: How Foucault, Derrida, Deleuze, & Co. Transformed the Intellectual Life of the United States*. Translated by Jeff Fort. Minneapolis: University of Minnesota Press.

Darnton, Robert. 2018. "The Greatest Show on Earth." *New York Review of Books*, June 28, 68, 69, 72.

Dart, Ron. 2006. "Stephen Leacock and George Grant: Tory Affinities." In Angus, Dart, and Peters, *Athens and Jerusalem*, 5–28.

Dart, Ronald S., and Brad Jersak. 2011. *George P. Grant. Canada's Lone Wolf*. Abbotsford, BC: Fresh Wind Press.

Davidson, R. C. 1992. "Military Integration and George Grant's *Lament for a Nation*." In Umar and Cooper, *George Grant and the Future of Canada*, 123–37.

Davis, Arthur, ed. 1996. "Justice and Freedom: George Grant's Encounter with Martin Heidegger." In *George Grant and the Subversion of Modernity: Art, Philosophy, Politics, Religion, and Education*, edited by Arthur Davis, 139–68. Toronto: University of Toronto Press.

———. 2000. Introduction to *Volume 1: 1933-1950* (xxi–xxxvii). Toronto: University of Toronto Press.

———, ed. 2002a. Introduction to the *Collected Works of George Grant, Volume 2: 1951-1959* (xvii–xxxvi). Toronto: University of Toronto Press.

———, ed. 2002b. *Collected Works of George Grant, Volume 2: 1951-1959*. Toronto: University of Toronto Press.

———. 2006. "Did George Grant Change His Politics?" In Angus, Dart, and Peters, *Athens and Jerusalem*, 62–79.

Davis, Arthur, and Peter C. Emberley. 2000a. Editorial introduction to the *Collected Works of George Grant*, xv–xix. Toronto: University of Toronto Press.

———, ed. 2000b. *Collected Works of George Grant, Volume 1: 1933-1950*. Toronto: University of Toronto Press.

Davis, Arthur, and Henry Roper. 2005a. Introduction to the *Collected Works of George Grant, Volume 3: 1960-1969* (xvii–xxv). Toronto: University of Toronto Press.

———. 2005b. *Collected Works of George Grant, Volume 3: 1960-1969*. Toronto: University of Toronto Press.

———. 2009a. Introduction to the *Collected Works of George Grant, Volume 4: 1970-1988*. Toronto: University of Toronto Press.

———. 2009b. *Collected Works of George Grant, Volume 4: 1970-1988*. Toronto: University of Toronto Press.

Derrida, Jacques. 2005. "Composing 'Circumfession.'" In Caputo and Scanlon, *Augustine and Postmodernism*, 19–27.

Dewey, John. 1897. "My Pedagogic Creed." *The School Journal* 54, no. 3: 77–80.

———. 1920. *Reconstruction in Philosophy*. New York: Henry Holt and Company.

———. 1922. *Human Nature and Conduct: An Introduction to Social Psychology*. New York: Henry Holt and Company.

———. (1934) 1962. *A Common Faith*. New Haven, CT: Yale University Press.

Dinshaw, Carolyn. 2012. *How Soon Is Now? Medieval Texts, Amateur Readers, and the Queerness of Time*. Durham, NC: Duke University Press.

Doane, Mary Ann. 2002. *The Emergence of Cinematic Time: Modernity, Contingency, The Archive*. Cambridge, MA: Harvard University Press.

———. 2003. "The Object of Theory." In *Rites of Realism: Essays on Corporeal Cinema*, edited by Ivone Margulies, 80–89. Durham, NC: Duke University Press.

Doll, William E., Jr. 1993. *A Post-Modern Perspective on Curriculum*. New York: Teachers College Press.

Doull, James. 1983. "Naturalistic Individualism: Quebec Independence and an Independent Canada." In Combs, *Modernity and Responsibility*, 29–50.

Du Bois, W. E. B. (1903) 1969. *The Souls of Black Folk*. New York: New American Library.

Duff, Alexander. 2006. "Response to the Strauss-Kojève Debate: Grant's Turn from Hegel to Christian Platonism." In Angus, Dart, and Peters, *Athens and Jerusalem*, 108–23.

Egginton, William. 2016. "Reflection: Borges on Eternity." In Melamed, *Eternity*, 277–82.

Ellison, Katherine. 2015. "A.D.H.D. Rises, but Support Lags." *New York Times*, November 10, 2015, D6.

Elsaesser, Thomas. 2009. "No end to *Nosferatu* (1922)." In *Weimar Cinema*, edited by Noah Isenberg, 79–94. New York: Columbia University Press.

Elshtain, Jean Bethke. 2005. "Why Augustine? Why Now?" In Caputo and Scanlon, *Augustine and Postmodernism*, 244–56.

Emberley, Peter C. 1990. Preface to *By Loving Our Own: George Grant and the Legacy of Lament for a Nation*, edited by Peter C. Emberly, xi–xxvi. Ottawa: Carleton University Press.

———. (1994) 2005. Foreword to the Carleton Library edition of *Lament for a Nation*, by George Grant, lxxviii–lxxxv. Montreal: McGill-Queen's University Press.

Epstein, Jason. 2010. "Publishing: The Revolutionary Future." *New York Review of Books*, March 11, 4, 6.

Ergas, Oren. 2017. *Reconstructing "Education" through Mindful Attention. Positioning the Mind at the Center of Curriculum and Pedagogy*. New York: Palgrave Macmillan.

Fanon, Frantz. 1967. *Black Skin, White Masks*. Translated by Charles Lam Markmann. New York: Grove Weidenfeld.

Feenberg, Andrew. 2010. *Between Reason and Experience. Essays in Technology and Modernity*. Foreword by Brian Wynne. Afterword by Michel Callon. Cambridge, MA: MIT Press.

Fierlbeck, Katherine. 2006. *Political Thought in Canada: An Intellectual History*. Peterborough, ON: Broadview Press.

Fishbane, Michael. 2008. *Sacred Attunement: A Jewish Theology*. Chicago: University of Chicago Press.

Flinn, Frank K. 1990. "Technology and the Masks of Prometheus: A Post-Grantian Meditation." In Whillier, *Two Theological Languages by George Grant and Other Essays in Honour of His Work*, 121–41.

Forbes, Hugh Donald. 2007. *George Grant: A Guide to his Thought*. Toronto: University of Toronto Press.

Foster, Thomas. 2005. *The Souls of Cyberfolk: Posthumanism as Vernacular Theory*. Minneapolis: University of Minnesota Press.

Freire, Paulo. 1970. *Pedagogy of the Oppressed*. Translated by Myra Bergman Ramos. Foreword by Richard Shaull. New York: Herder and Herder.

Friedman, Thomas L. 2017. "Online and Scared." *New York Times*, January 11, 2017, A23.

Frisch, Walter. 2016. "Reflection: Music and Eternity." In Melamed, *Eternity*, 283–89.

Garb, Jonathan. 2011. *Shamanic Trance and Modern Kabbalah*. Chicago: University of Chicago Press.

Garrison, Jim. 1997. *Dewey and Eros: Wisdom and Desire in the Art of Teaching*. New York: Teachers College of Press.

Gartner, Richard B. 1999. *Betrayed as Boys: Psychodynamic Treatment of Sexually Abused Men*. New York: Guilford.

Gillespie, Michael Allen. 1990. "George Grant and the Tradition of Political Philosophy." In Emberley, *By Loving Our Own*, 123–31.

Goldstein, Dana. 2017. "In High School, the Workplace Comes to Class." *New York Times*, August 11, 2017, A1, A14.

Gouldner, Alvin W. 1970. *The Coming Crisis of Western Sociology*. New York: Basic Books.

Grant, George. 1950. "The Concept of Nature and Supernature in the Theology of John Oman." PhD diss., Oxford University.

———. (1959) 1966. *Philosophy in the Mass Age*. Toronto: Copp Clark Publishing.

———. (1965) 2005. *Confessions and Circumfession*. Montreal: McGill-Queen's University Press.

———. 1966. Introduction to Grant, *Philosophy in the Mass Age*, iii–ix.

———. 1969. *Technology & Empire*. Toronto: Anansi.

———. (1969) 1995. *Time as History*. Edited and with an introduction by William Christian. Toronto: University of Toronto Press.

———. (1969) 2001. *Time as History*. Toronto: University of Toronto Press.

———. (1970) 2005. Introduction to the Carleton Library edition of *Lament for a Nation*, by George Grant, lxix–lxxvi. Montreal: McGill-Queen's University Press.

———. (1974) 1998. *English-Speaking Justice*. Toronto: Anansi.

———. 1986. *Technology and Justice*. Toronto: Anansi.

Grant, John N. 2002. *The Maroons in Nova Scotia*. Halifax: Formac Publishing Company Limited.

Green, Erica L. 2017. "Saying Money Isn't the Answer, DeVos Calls for More School Choice." *New York Times*, March 30, 2017, A16.

Greenbaum, Dorian Gieseler. 2016. "Eternity and Astrology in the Work of Vettius Valens." In Melamed, *Eternity*, 56–63.

Greene, Maxine. 1973. *Teacher as Stranger*. Belmont, CA: Wadsworth.

Greenspan, Louis. 1990. "George Grant Remembered." In Whillier, *Two Theological Languages by George Grant and Other Essays in Honour of His Work*, 1–5.

Grimmett, Peter P., and Mark Halvorson. 2010. "From Understanding Curriculum to Creating Curriculum: The Case for the Co-Evolution of Re-Conceptualized Design with Re-Conceptualized Curriculum." *Curriculum Inquiry* 40, no. 2: 241–62.

Grumet, Madeleine R. 1978. "Songs and Situations." In *Qualitative Evaluation*, edited by George Willis, 274–315, Berkeley, CA: McCutchan.

———. 1988. *Bitter Milk. Women and Teaching*. Amherst: University of Massachusetts Press.

Gumbrecht, Hans Ulrich. 2013. "Media History as the Event of Truth: On the Singularity of Fredrich A. Kittler's Works." In Kittler, *The Truth of the Technological World: Essays on the Genealogy of Presence*, 307–29.

Gutek, Gerald L. 2006. George S. "Counts and the Origins of Social Reconstructionism." In *Social Reconstruction: People, Politics, Perspectives*, edited by Karen L. Riley, 1–26. Greenwich, CT: Information Age Publishing.

Halbertal, Moshe, and Avishai Margalit. 1992. *Idolatry.* Translated by Naomi Goldblum Cambridge, MA: Harvard University Press.

Hall, Douglas John. 1978. "The Significance of Grant's Cultural Analysis for Christian Theology in North America." In Schmidt, *George Grant in Process,* 120–9.

Halpern, Sue. 2011. "Mind Control & the Internet," *New York Review of Books,* June 23, 33–5.

———. 2015. "In the Depths of the Net." *New York Review of Books,* October 8, 55–7.

Hardt, Michael, and Antonio Negri. 2000. *Empire.* Cambridge, MA: Harvard University Press.

Harootunian, H. D. 2002. "Postcoloniality's Unconscious/Area Studies' Desire." In Miyoshi and Harootunian, *Learning Places,* 150–74.

Harris, Douglas N. 2016. "The Wrong Way to Fix Schools." *New York Times,* November 28, 2016, A21.

Harvey, David. 2010. *The Enigma of Capital and the Crises of Capitalism.* New York: Oxford University Press.

Havers, Grant. 2006. "Leo Strauss's Influence on George Grant." In Angus, Dart, and Peters, *Athens and Jerusalem,* 124–35.

Heaven, Edwin B., and David R. Heaven. 1978. "Some Influences of Simone Weil on George Grant's Silence." In Schmidt, *George Grant in Process,* 68–78.

Heaven, Ted. 2006. "George Grant on Socrates and Christ." In Angus, Dart, and Peters, *Athens and Jerusalem,* 300–22.

Herf, Jeffrey. 1984. *Reactionary Modernism: Technology, Culture, and Politics in Weimar and the Third Reich.* Cambridge: Cambridge University Press.

Herrman, John. 2016. "The Trap of Exposing Fake News: Eroding Trust in Real Reporting." *New York Times,* November 19, 2016, B1–B2.

Heyking, John Von, and Barry Cooper. 2006. "'A Cow Is Just a Cow': George Grant and Eric Voegelin on the United States." In Angus, Dart, and Peters, *Athens and Jerusalem,* 166–89.

Hirsch, E. D., Jr. 1999. *The Schools We Need.* New York: Anchor Books.

Hofstadter, Richard. (1965) 1996. *The Paranoid Style in American Politics and Other Essays.* Cambridge, MA: Harvard University Press.

Horowitz, Jason. 2016. "Fake News Provokes Anxiety in Italy Ahead of Key Referendum." *New York Times,* December 3, 2016, A8.

Horowitz, Gad. 1990. "Commentary." In Emberley, *By Loving Our Own,* 75–82.

Huebner, Dwayne E. 1999. *The Lure of the Transcendent.* Mahwah, NJ: Lawrence Erlbaum.

Huetteman, Emmarie. 2015. "Education Law Changes Approved by the Senate." *New York Times,* December 10, 2015, A22.

Huetteman, Emmarie, and Yamiche Alcindor. 2017. "DeVos Confirmed for Education by Pence's Vote." *New York Times,* February 8, 2017, A1, A20.

Hurtig, Mel. 1990. "One Last Chance: The Legacy of *Lament for a Nation.*" In Emberley, *By Loving Our Own,* 43–58.

Hutt, Curtis. 2013. *John Dewey and the Ethics of Historical Belief. Religion and the Representation of the Past.* Albany: State University of New York Press.

Ignatieff, Michael. 2010. *True Patriot Love.* Toronto: Penguin.

Irwin, Neil. 2017, January 26. "Fake News? Welcome to 'False Remembering.'" *New York Times,* January 26, 2017, A3.

Izenberg, Gerald N. 2000. *Modernism and Masculinity: Mann, Wedekind, Kandinsky through World War I.* Chicago: University of Chicago Press.

Jardine, David, Patricia Clifford, and Sharon Friesen, ed. 2006. *Curriculum in Abundance*. Mahwah, NJ: Lawrence Erlbaum.

Jay, Martin. 1988. "Scopic Regimes of Modernity." In *Vision and Visuality*, edited by Hal Foster, 3–23. Seattle: Bay Press.

———. 1993. *Downcast Eyes: The Denigration of Vision in Twentieth-Century French Thought*. Berkeley: University of California Press.

———. 2005. *Songs of Experience: Modern American and European Variations on a Universal Theme*. Berkeley: University of California Press.

Jersak, Brad. 2012. *George P. Grant: Minerva's Snowy Owl: Essays in Political Theology*. Abbotsford, BC: Fresh Wind Press.

Judt, Tony. 2012. *Thinking the Twentieth Century*. New York: Penguin.

Jung, C. G. 1965. *Memories, Dreams, Reflections*. Translated by Aniela Jaffé. New York: Vintage.

Kaes, Anton, Martin Jay, and Edward Dimendberg, ed. 1995. *The Weimar Sourcebook*. Berkeley: University of California Press.

Kaethler, Andrew. 2009. *The Synthesis of Athens and Jerusalem. George Grant's Defense Against Modernity*. Saarbrücken, Germany: VDM Verlag Dr. Müller.

Kane, John F. 1990. "Lament and Hope: Thoughts on Roman Catholicism in the United States." In Whillier, *Two Theological Languages by George Grant and Other Essays in Honour of His Work*, 142–54.

Kang, Cecilia. 2017. "Tech Titans to Pour Money Into Push to Teach Coding." *New York Times*, September 27, 2017, B6.

Kearney, Richard. 2005a. "Confessions and 'Circumfession': A Routable Discussion with Jacques Derrida." In Caputo and Scanlon, *Augustine and Postmodernism*, 28–49.

———. 2005b. "Time, Evil, and Narrative." In Caputo and Scanlon, *Augustine and Postmodernism*, 144–58.

Keller, Bill. 2012. "Wising Up to Facebook." *New York Times*, June 11, 2012, A19.

Kestenbaum, Victor. 2002. *The Grace and Severity of the Ideal: John Dewey and Transcendence*. Chicago: University of Chicago Press.

Kimmel, Michael S. 1996. *Manhood in America: A Cultural History*. New York: Free Press

Kinzel, Till. 2009. "Metaphysics, Politics, and Philosophy: George Grant's Response to Pragmatism." *Cultura. International Journal of Philosophy of Culture and Axiology* 6, no. 1: 7–21.

Kirby, John, and Louis Greenspan. 1990. "Grant, Natural Law and Simone Weil." In Emberley, *By Loving Our Own*, 153–59.

Kittler, Friedrich A. 2013. *The Truth of the Technological World: Essays on the Genealogy of Presence*. With an afterword by Hans Ulrich Gumbrecht. Stanford, CA: Stanford University Press.

Kleinberg, Ethan. 2005. *Generation Existential: Heidegger's Philosophy in France, 1927-1961*. Ithaca, NY: Cornell University Press.

Knopff, Ranier. 1992. "Rights, Power-Knowledge, and Social Technology." In Umar and Cooper, *George Grant and the Future of Canada*, 59–73.

Kögler, Hans-Herbert. 1999. *The Power of Dialogue: Critical Hermeneutics after Gadamer and Foucault*. Cambridge, MA: MIT Press.

Koopman, Colin. 2009. *Pragmatism as Transition: Historicity and Hope in James, Dewey, and Rorty*. New York: Columbia University Press.

Kracauer, Siegfried. 1995. *The Mass Ornament: Weimar Essays*. Translated, edited, and with an introduction by Thomas Y. Levin. Cambridge, MA: Harvard University Press.

Krauss, Rosalind. 2007. "Who Comes after the Subject?" In *The Life & The Work: Art and Biography*, edited by Charles G. Salas, 28–33. Los Angeles, CA: Getty Publications.

Kridel, Craig, and Robert V. Bullough Jr. 2007. *Stories of the Eight-Year Study: Reexamining Secondary Education in America*. Foreword by John I. Goodlad. Albany: State University of New York Press.

Kroker, Arthur. 1984. *Technology and the Canadian Mind: Innis/McLuhan/Grant*. Montreal: New World Perspectives.

Kumar, Ashwani. 2013. *Curriculum as Meditative Inquiry*. New York: Palgrave Macmillan.

LaCapra, Dominick. 2004. *History in Transit: Experience, Identity, Critical Theory*. Ithaca, NY: Cornell University Press.

———. 2009. *History and Its Limits: Human, Animal, Violence*. Ithaca, NY: Cornell University Press.

Lampert, Laurence. 1978. "The Uses of Philosophy in George Grant." In Schmidt, *George Grant in Process*, 179–94.

Larmore, Charles. 2010. *The Practices of the Self*. Translated by Sharon Bowman. Chicago: University of Chicago Press.

Lasch, Christopher. 1978. *The Culture of Narcissism: American Life in an Age of Diminishing Expectations*. New York: Norton.

———. 1984. *The Minimal Self: Psychic Survival in Troubled Times*. New York: Norton.

Lathangue, Robin. 1998. "Introduction to George Grant." In Grant, *English-Speaking Justice*, vii–xxi.

Lear, Jonathan. 2006. *Radical Hope: Ethics in the Face of Cultural Devastation*. Cambridge, MA: Harvard University Press.

Lee, Dennis. 1983. "The Gods." In Combs, *Modernity and Responsibility*, 3–6.

———. 1990. "Grant's Impasse." In Emberley, *By Loving Our Own*, 11–39.

Levin, David Michael, ed. 1993. *Modernity and the Hegemony of Vision*. Berkeley: University of California Press.

Levin, Thomas Y. 1995. Introduction to *The Mass Ornament: Weimar Essays*, by Siegfried Kracauer, 1–30. Cambridge, MA: Harvard University Press.

Levine, Donald N. 2007. *Powers of the Mind: The Reinvention of Liberal Learning in America*. Chicago: University of Chicago Press.

Lewis, Tyson E. 2013. *On Study. Giorgio Agamben and Educational Potentiality*. New York: Routledge.

Lilla, Mark. 2010. "The Tea Party Jacobins." *New York Review of Books*, May 27, 53–6.

———. 2015. "France on Fire." *The New York Review of Books*, March 5, 14, 16.

Lindenman, Max. 2017. Foreword to *Tell them Something Beautiful*, by Samuel D. Rocha, xi–xvii. Eugene, OR: Cascade Books.

Ling, Rich. 2008. *New Tech, New Ties: How Mobile Communication is Reshaping Social Cohesion*. Cambridge, MA: MIT Press.

Lints, Richard. 2015. *Identity and Idolatry*. Downers Grove, IL: InterVarsity Press.

Lipari, Lisbeth. 2014. *Listening, Thinking, Being: Towards an Ethics of Attunement*. University Park, PA: The Pennsylvania State University Press.

Lipset, Seymour Martin. 1990. *Continental Divide: The Values and Institutions of the United States and Canada*. New York: Routledge.

Lipton, Eric. 2017. "DeVos's Schedule Shows an Emphasis on Vouchers and Alternative Schools." *New York Times*, October 28, 2017, A11.

Lipton, Eric, Nicholas Confessore, and Brooke Williams. 2016. "Top Scholars or Lobbyists? Often It's Both." *New York Times*, August 9, 2016, A1, A12.

Lohr, Steve. 2017. "A.I. Today May Underwhelm, but Before Long It May Overtake Expectations." *New York Times*, December 1, 2017, B3.

Lossky, Vladimir. 1982. "Tradition and Traditions." In *The Meaning of Icons* (rev. ed.), by Leonid Ouspensky and Vladimir Lossky, 11–22. Crestwood, NY: St. Vladimir's Seminary Press.

Love, Heather. 2007. *Feeling Backward: Loss and the Politics of Queer History*. Cambridge, MA: Harvard University Press.

Løvlie, Lars. 2003. "The Promise of *Bildung*." In *Educating Humanity: Bildung in Postmodernity*, edited by Lars Løvlie, Klaus Peter Mortensen, and Sven Erik Nordenbo, 151–70. Oxford: Blackwell.

Luxon, Nancy. 2013. *Crisis of Authority. Politics, Trust, and Truth-Telling in Freud and Foucault*. Cambridge: Cambridge University Press.

Macdonald, James B. 1995. *Theory as a Prayerful Act*. New York: Peter Lang.

———. (1975) 1995. "The Quality of Everyday Life in Schools." In Macdonald, *Theory as a Prayerful Act*, 111–26.

Maggi, Armando. 2009. *The Resurrection of the Body: Pier Paolo Pasolini from Saint Paul to Sade*. Chicago: University of Chicago Press.

Magrini, James M. 2017. *Reconceptualizing Plato's Socrates at the Limit of Education: A Socratic Curriculum Grounded in Finite Human Transcendence*. New York: Routledge.

Manjoo, Farhad. 2015. "The Internet is Breaking the Outrage Meter." *New York Times*, December 10, 2015, B1, B6.

Mariniello, Silvestra. 1994. "Toward a Materialist Linguistics: Pasolini's Theory of Language." In *Pier Paolo Pasolini: Contemporary Perspectives*, edited by Patrick Rumble and Bart Testa, 106–26. Toronto: University of Toronto Press.

Marion, Jean-Luc. 2001. *The Idol and Distance*. Translated and with an introduction by Thomas A. Carlson. New York: Fordham University Press.

———. 2012. *God Without Being*. 2nd ed. Translated by Thomas A. Carlson, with a foreword by David Tracy, and a new preface by Jean-Luc Marion. Chicago: University of Chicago Press.

Marshall, Bill. 1997. *Guy Hocquenghem: Beyond Gay Identity*. Durham, NC: Duke University Press.

Martin, Raymond, and John Barresi. 2006. *The Rise and Fall of Soul and Self: An Intellectual History of Personal Identity*. New York: Columbia University Press.

Mayse, Ariel Evan. 2016. "Reflection: Eternity in Hasidism: Time and Presence." In Melamed *Eternity*, 231–38.

McCarroll, Pam. 2006. "The Whole as Love." In Angus, Dart, and Peters, *Athens and Jerusalem*, 270–85.

McDaniel, Kris. 2016. "Eternity in Twentieth-Century Analytic Philosophy." In Melamed, *Eternity*, 245–76.

McKnight, Douglas. 2002. *Schooling, the Puritan Imperative, and the Molding of the American National Identity*. Mahwah, NJ: Lawrence Erlbaum.

Melamed, Yitzhak Y. 2016a. *Eternity: A History*. Oxford: Oxford University Press.

———. 2016b. Introduction to Melamed, *Eternity*, 1–13.

Meynell, Robert. 2011. *Canadian Idealism and the Philosophy of Freedom: C.B. Macpherson, George Grant, and Charles Taylor*. Montreal: McGill-Queen's University Press.

Mills, C. W. 2000. *The Power Elite*. 2nd ed. New York: Oxford University Press.

Minogue, Kenneth. 1990. "Grant's Technology and Justice: Between Philosophy and Prophecy." In Emberley, *By Loving Our Own*, 161–74.

Moghtader, Bruce. 2015. *Foucault and Educational Ethics*. New York: Palgrave Macmillan.

Mondzain, Marie-José. 2005. *Image, Icon, Economy: The Byzantine Origins of the Contemporary Imaginary*. Translated by Rico Franses. Originally published in 1996 by Éditions du Seuil. Stanford, CA: Stanford University Press.

Muggeridge, John. 1978. "George Grant's Anguished Conservatism." In Schmidt, *George Grant in Process*, 40–8.

Musil, Robert. 1990. *Precision and Soul: Essays and Addresses*. Edited and translated by Burton Pike and David S. Luft. Chicago: University of Chicago Press.

Nagatomo, Shigenori. 1992. *Attunement Through the Body*. Albany: State University of New York.

Nagel, Thomas. 2018. "As If!" *New York Review of Books*, April 8, 36–8.

Neatby, Hilda. 1953. *So Little For The Mind*. Toronto: Clarke, Irwin & Company Limited.

Nes, Solrunn. 2004. *The Mystical Language of Icons*. Grand Rapids, MI: William B. Eerdmans Publishing Company.

Nicholson, Graeme. 2006. "Freedom and the Good." In Angus, Dart, and Peters, *Athens and Jerusalem*, 323–40.

Norman, Judith. 2016. "Reflection: Eternity in Early German Romanticism." In Melamed, *Eternity*, 226–30.

Nusselder, André. 2009. *Interface Fantasy: A Lacanian Cyborg Ontology*. Cambridge, MA: MIT Press.

O'Donovan, Joan E. 1984. *George Grant and the Twilight of Justice*. Toronto: University of Toronto Press.

———. 1990. "Law, Love and the Common Good." In Emberley, *By Loving Our Own*, 135–51.

Oliver, Kelly. 2004. *The Colonization of Psychic Space: A Psychoanalytic Social Theory of Oppression*. Minneapolis: University of Minnesota Press.

Ong, Walter J. 1971. *Rhetoric, Romance, and Technology*. Ithaca, NY: Cornell University Press.

Ouspensky, Leonid. 1982. "The Meaning and Language of Icons." In *The Meaning of Icons* (rev. ed.), by Leonid Ouspensky and Vladimir Lossky, 25–49. Crestwood, NY: St. Vladimir's Seminary Press.

Pagels, Elaine. 1989. *Adam, Eve, and the Serpent*. New York: Vintage.

Paras, Eric. 2006. *Foucault 2.0: Beyond Power and Knowledge*. New York: Other Press.

Parel, A. J. 1992. "Multiculturalism and Nationhood." In Umar and Cooper, *George Grant and the Future of Canada*, 139–50.

Penelhum, Terence. 1983. "Faith, Reason, and Secularity." In Combs, *Modernity and Responsibility*, 85–105.

Penney, James. 2014. *After Queer Theory. The Limits of Sexual Politics*. London: Pluto Press.

Pérez-Gómez, Alberto. 2016. *Attunement: Architectural Meaning after the Crisis of Modern Science*. Cambridge, MA: MIT Press.

Perlstein, Daniel. 2000. "'There is no escape … from the ogre of indoctrination': George Counts and the Civic Dilemmas of Democratic Educators." In *Reconstructing the*

Common Good in Education: Coping with Intractable Dilemmas, edited by Larry Cuban and Dorothy Shipps, 51–67. Stanford, CA: Stanford University Press

Peters, Frederick G. 1978. *Robert Musil: Master of the Hovering Life.* New York: Columbia University Press.

Peters, Jeremy W. 2016. "Wielding Claims of 'Fake News,' Conservatives Take Aim at Mainstream Media." *New York Times*, December 26, 2016, A11.

Peters, Randy Peg. 2006. "Three Wise Men from the East: Eastern Orthodox Influences on George Grant." In Angus, Dart, and Peters, *Athens and Jerusalem*, 238–55.

Petitfils, Brad. 2015. *Parallels and Responses to Curricular Innovation: The Possibilities of Posthumanistic Education.* New York: Routledge.

Peukert, Detlev J. K. 1992. *The Weimar Republic: The Crisis of Classical Modernity.* Translated by Richard Deveson. New York: Hill and Wang.

Phelan, Anne. 2015. *Curriculum Theorizing and Teacher Education: Complicating Conjunctions.* New York: Routledge.

Phillips, Christopher J. 2015. "The Politics of Math Education." *New York Times*, December 3, 2015, A35.

Pinar, William F. 1972. "Working from Within." *Educational Leadership* 29, no. 4: 329–31. Reprinted in Pinar, *Autobiography, Politics, and Sexuality*, 7–11.

———ed., 1974. *Heightened Consciousness, Cultural Revolution and Curriculum Theory.* Berkeley, CA: McCutchan.

———. (1975) 2000. "Sanity, Madness and the School." In *Curriculum Theorizing: The Reconceptualization* (359–83), edited by William F. Pinar. Troy, NY: Educator's International Press. Originally published in *Curriculum Theorizing: The Reconceptualists*, by William F. Pinar, 359–83. Berkeley, CA: McCutchan.

———. 1988. "Time, Place and Voice: Curriculum Theory and the Historical Moment." In *Contemporary Curriculum Discourses*, edited by William F. Pinar, 264–78. Scottsdale, AZ: Gorsuch Scarisbrick.

———. 1994. *Autobiography, Politics, and Sexuality: Essays in Curriculum Theory 1972-1992.* New York: Peter Lang.

———. 2001. *The Gender of Racial Politics and Violence in America : Lynching, Prison Rape, and the Crisis of Masculinity.* New York: Peter Lang.

———. 2004. *What Is Curriculum Theory?* Mahwah, NJ: Lawrence Erlbaum.

———. 2006a. *The Synoptic Text Today and Other Essays. Curriculum Development after the Reconceptualization.* New York: Peter Lang.

———. 2006b. *Race, Religion, and a Curriculum of Reparation.* New York: Palgrave.

———. 2009. *The Worldliness of a Cosmopolitan Education: Passionate Lives in Public Service.* New York: Routledge.

———, ed. 2010a. *Curriculum Studies in South Africa: Intellectual Histories, Present Circumstances.* New York: Palgrave Macmillan.

———. 2010b. "The Eight-Year Study." *Curriculum Inquiry* 40, no. 2: 295–316.

———. 2011. *The Character of Curriculum Studies: Bildung, Currere, and the Recurring Question of the Subject.* New York: Palgrave Macmillan.

———, ed. 2011a. *Curriculum Studies in Brazil: Intellectual Histories, Present Circumstances.* New York: Palgrave Macmillan.

———, ed. 2011b. *Curriculum Studies in Mexico: Intellectual Histories, Present Circumstances.* New York: Palgrave Macmillan. Spacing please

———. 2011c. "Nationalism, Anti-Americanism, Canadian Identity." In *Curriculum in Today's World: Configuring Knowledge, Identities, Work and Politics*, edited by Lyn Yates and Madeleine Grumet, 31–43. London: Routledge.

———. 2012. *What Is Curriculum Theory?* 2nd ed. New York: Routledge.

———. 2013. *Curriculum Studies in the United States. Intellectual Histories, Present Circumstances*. New York: Palgrave Macmillan.

———, ed. 2014a. *Curriculum Studies in China: Intellectual Histories, Present Circumstances*. New York: Palgrave Macmillan.

———, ed. 2014b. *International Handbook of Curriculum Research*. 2nd ed. New York: Routledge.

———. 2015a. *Educational Experience as Lived: Knowledge, History, Alterity*. New York: Routledge.

———, ed. 2015b. *Curriculum Studies in India: Intellectual Histories, Present Circumstances*. New York: Palgrave Macmillan.

———. 2015c. "Without Experience Is Teacher Development Possible?" In Hua and Pinar, *Autobiography and Teacher Development in China*, 179–92.

———. 2015d. Introduction to Zhang and Pinar, *Autobiography and Teacher Development in China*, 1–47.

———. 2017a. "Rethinking Authority in Educational Leadership." In *Bridging Educational Leadership, Curriculum Theory and Didaktik*, edited by Michael Uljens and Rose Ylimaki, 395–408. Gewerbestrasse, Switzerland: Spring International Publishing AG.

———. 2017b. "Study: Concerning Relationship in Educational Experience." In Ruitenberg, *Reconceptualizing Study in Educational Discourse and Practice*, 97–109.

———. 2017c. "'The Scandalous Revolutionary Force of the Past': On Pasolini's *The Gospel According to Saint Matthew*." In *Catholic Education in the Wake of Vatican II*, edited by Rosa Bruno-Jofré and Jon Igelmo Zaldivar, 301–17. Toronto: University of Toronto Press.

Pinar, William F., and Madeleine R. Grumet. (1976) 2015. *Toward a Poor Curriculum*. 3rd ed. Kingston, NY: Educator's International Press.

———. (1981) 1988. "Socratic *Caesura* and the Theory-Practice Relationship." In *Contemporary Curriculum Discourses*, edited by William F. Pinar, 92–100. Scottsdale, AZ: Gorsuch Scarisbrick. First published in *Rethinking Curriculum Studies*, edited by M. Lawn and L. Barton, 20–42. London: Croom Helm, 1981.

Pinar, William F., and Rita L. Irwin, ed. 2005. *Curriculum in a New Key: The Collected Works of Ted T. Aoki*. Mahwah, NJ: Lawrence Erlbaum

Pinar, William F., William M. Reynolds, Patrick Slattery, and Peter M. Taubman. 1995. *Understanding Curriculum: An Introduction to Historical and Contemporary Curriculum Discourses*. New York: Peter Lang.

Pinker, Steven. 2010. "Mind Over Mass Media." *New York Times*, June 11, 2010, A27.

Planinc, Zdravko. 1992. "Paradox and Polyphony in Grant's Critique of Modernity." In Umar and Cooper, *George Grant and the Future of Canada*, 17–45.

Posnock, Ross. 1998. *Color & Culture: Black Writers and the Making of the Modern Intellectual*. Cambridge, MA: Harvard University Press.

Popkewitz, Thomas S. 2008. *Cosmopolitanism and the Age of School Reform: Science, Education, and Making Society by Making the Child*. New York: Routledge.

Porter, Eduardo. 2017. "Planet-Cooling Technology May Be Earth's Only Hope." *New York Times*, April 5, 2017, B1, B4.

Potter, Andrew. 2005. Introduction to Grant, *Lament for a Nation, 40th anniversary Edition*, ix–lxviii.

Power, Joseph F. 1978. "Grant's Critique of Values Language." In Schmidt, *George Grant in Process*, 90–98.

Radhakrishnan, R. 2008. *History, the Human, and the World Between*. Durham, NC: Duke University Press.

Rappeport, Alan. 2015. "Philosophers Say View of their Skills is Dated." *New York Times*, November 12, 2015, A25.

Ravitch, Diane. 2000. *Left Back: A Century of Battles over School Reform*. New York: Simon and Schuster.

Reed, Arden. 2017. *Slow Art: The Experience of Looking, Sacred Images to James Turrell*. Berkeley: University of California Press.

Reich, Charles A. 1970. *The Greening of America*. New York: Random House.

Reimer, A. James. 1978. "George Grant: Liberal, Socialist, or Conservative?" In Schmidt, *George Grant in Process*, 49–57.

———. 1990. "Do George Grant and Martin Heidegger Share a Common Conservatism?" In Whillier, *Two Theological Languages by George Grant and Other Essays in Honour of His Work*, 105–20.

Rich, Motoko. 2012. "Show and Tell for Teachers, Inspired by Reality TV." *New York Times*, August 16, 2012, A14.

Richardson, George H. 2002. *The Death of the Good Canadian: Teachers, National Identities, and the Social Studies Curriculum*. New York: Peter Lang.

Ridley, Matt. 2015. "The Myth of Basic Science." *Wall Street Journal*, October 24–25, 2015, C1–2.

Rigelhof, T. F. 2001. *George Grant: Redefining Canada*. Montreal: XYZ Publishing.

Ripley, Amada. 2016. "What the U.S. Can Learn From Other Nations' Schools." *New York Times*, December 8, 2016, A3.

Roberts, David D. 1995. *Nothing but History: Reconstruction and Extremity after Metaphysics*. Berkeley and Los Angeles: University of California Press.

Robertson, Neil. 2006. "Freedom and Tradition: George Grant, James Doull, and the Character of Modernity." In Angus, Dart, and Peters, *Athens and Jerusalem*, 136–65.

Robinson, Marilynne. 2010. *Absence of Mind: The Dispelling of Inwardness from the Modern Myth of the Self*. New Haven, CT: Yale University Press.

Rocha, Samuel D. 2017. *Tell them Something Beautiful: Essays and Ephemera*. Eugene, OR: Cascade Books.

Rohdie, Sam. 1995. *The Passion of Pier Paolo Pasolini*. Bloomington: Indiana University Press.

Ronell, Avital. 2003. *Stupidity*. Urbana and Chicago: University of Illinois Press.

Rorty, Richard. 1982. *Consequences of Pragmatism: Essays, 1972-1980*. Minneapolis: University of Minnesota Press.

Roth, Michael S. 2014. *Beyond the University. Why Liberal Education Matters*. New Haven, CT: Yale University Press.

Rotstein, Abraham. 1983. "The World Upside Down." In Combs, *Modernity and Responsibility*, 106–32.

Roy, Christian. 2006. "Echoes of George Grant in 'Late Boomer' Critiques of Post-Quiet Revolution Quebec." In Angus, Dart, and Peters, *Athens and Jerusalem*, 190–219.

Rubin, Alissa J. 2017. "'Right to Disconnect' From Work Email and Other Laws Go Into Effect in France." *New York Times*, January 3, 2017, A6.

Rugg, Harold. 1926. "The School Curriculum and the Drama of American Life." In *The Twenty-Sixth Yearbook of the National Society for the Study of Education. The Foundations and Technique of Curriculum-Construction.* Part I, "Curriculum-Making: Past and Present," edited by Guy Montrose Whipple, 3–16. Bloomington, IL: Public School Publishing Company.

Ruitenberg, Claudia W. 2015. *Unlocking the World. Education in an Ethic of Hospitality.* Boulder, CO: Paradigm Publishers.

———, ed. 2017. *Reconceptualizing Study in Educational Discourse and Practice.* New York: Routledge.

Rumble, Patrick. 1994. "Stylistic Contamination in the 'Trilogia della Vita': The case of 'Il fiore delle mille e una notte.'" In *Pier Paolo Pasolini: Contemporary Perspectives,* edited by Patrick Rumble and Bart Testa, 210–31. Toronto: University of Toronto Press.

Ruthven, Malise. 2009. "Divided Iran on the Eve." *New York Review of Books,* July 2, 53–6.

Ryan-Scheutz, Colleen. 2007. *Sex, the Self, and the Sacred: Women in the Cinema of Pier Paolo Pasolini.* Toronto: University of Toronto Press.

Said, Edward W. 1996. *Representations of the Intellectual: The 1993 Reith Lectures.* New York: Vintage.

———. 2004. *Humanism and Democratic Criticism.* New York: Palgrave Macmillan.

Salvio, Paula M. 2007. *Anne Sexton: Teacher of Weird Abundance.* Albany: State University of New York Press.

———. 2017. *The Story-Takers: Public Pedagogy, Transitional Justice, and Italy's Non-Violent Protest against the Mafia.* Toronto: University of Toronto Press.

Sameth, Mark. 2016. "Is God Transgender?" *New York Times,* August 13, 2016, A17.

Santner, Eric L. 2006. *On Creaturely Life: Rilke, Benjamin, Sebald.* Chicago: University of Chicago Press.

Sartre, Jean-Paul. 1964. *Nausea.* New York: New Directions.

———. 1981. *The Family Idiot: Gustave Flaubert 1821-1857.* Translated by Carol Cosman. Chicago: University of Chicago Press.

Saul, John Ralston. 2005. *The Collapse of Globalism: And the Reinvention of the World.* Toronto: Viking Canada.

———. 2008. *A Fair Country: Telling Truths about Canada.* Toronto: Viking Canada.

Saul, Stephanie. 2011. "Profits and Questions at Online Charter Schools. Parents Get to Choose, but Standards Slip and Scores Suffer." *New York Times,* December 13, 2011, A1, A18–A19.

Savran, David. 1998. *Taking It a Like a Man: White Masculinity, Masochism, and Contemporary American Culture.* Princeton, NJ: Princeton University Press.

Scanlon, Michael J. 2005. "Arendt's Augustine." In Caputo and Scanlon, *Augustine and Postmodernism,* 159–72.

Schmidt, Larry, ed. 1978a. *George Grant in Process: Essays and Conversations.* Toronto: Anansi.

———. 1978b. "George Grant and the Problem of History." In Schmidt, *George Grant in Process,* 130–38.

Schwab, J. 1983. "The practical 4: Something for curriculum professors to do." *Curriculum Inquiry* 13, no. 3: 239–65.

Schwartz, John. 2015. Greenpeace Subterfuge Tests Climate Research. *New York Times,* December 9, 2015, A26.

Scott, A. O. 2017. "Personal and Political Passions." *New York Times,* October 20, 2017, C5.

Seixas, Peter. 2011. "Assessment of Historical Thinking." In *New Possibilities for the Past*: *Shaping History Education in Canada*, edited by Penney Clark, 139–53. Vancouver: University of British Columbia Press.

Sekyi-Otu, Ato 1996. *Fanon's Dialectic of Experience*. Cambridge, MA: Harvard University Press.

Shatz, Adam. 2018. "The Mythologies of R.B." *New York Review of Books*, June 7, 10, 12, 14.

Shipps, Dorothy. 2000. "Echoes of Corporate Influence: Managing Away Urban School Troubles." In *Reconstructing the Common Good in Education: Coping with Intractable Dilemmas*, edited by Larry Cuban and Dorothy Shipps, 82–105. Stanford, CA: Stanford University Press.

Shaw, Francine Shuchat. 1980. "The Meanings of Congruence." *JCT* 2, no. 1: 178–202.

Sibley, Robert C. 2006. "Grant, Hegel, and the 'Impossibility of Canada.'" In Angus, Dart, and Peters, *Athens and Jerusalem*, 93–107.

———. 2008. *Northern Spirits: John Watson, George Grant, and Charles Taylor – Appropriations of Hegelian Political Thought*. Montreal: McGill-Queen's University Press.

Signatories. 2013. "Our Collective Support..." (advertisement). *New York Times*, February 12, 2013, A7.

Sikka, Sonya. 1997. *Forms of Transcendence: Heidegger and Medieval Mystical Theology*. Albany: State University of New York Press.

Silverman, Kaja. 2009. *Flesh of My Flesh*. Stanford, CA: Stanford University Press.

Simon, Roger I. 2005. *The Touch of the Past. Remembrance, Learning, and Ethics*. New York: Palgrave Macmillan.

Singer, Natasha. 2018. "On Campus, Computer Science Departments Find a Blind Spot: Ethics." *New York Times*, February 13, 2018, B4.

Singer, Natasha, and Mike Isaac. 2016. "Learning System Expands to Nearly 120 Schools." *New York Times*, August 10, 2016, B5.

Sisario, Ben. 2017. "Streaming Services Struggle to Root Out Music That Incites Hatred." *New York Times*, August 18, 2017, B5.

Smith, David Geoffrey. 2014. "Wisdom Responses to Globalization." In Pinar, *International Handbook of Curriculum Research*, 45–59.

Smith, Wilfred Cantwell. 1983. "Responsibility." In Combs, *Modernity and Responsibility*, 74–84.

Spring, Joel. 1972. *Education and the Rise of the Corporate State*. Boston, MA: Beacon Press.

———. 1976. *The Sorting Machine*. New York: David McKay.

———. 2006. *Pedagogies of Globalization: The Rise of the Educational Security State*. Mahwah, NJ: Lawrence Erlbaum.

———. 2012. *Education Networks: Power, Wealth, Cyberspace, and the Digital Mind*. New York: Routledge.

Stamps, Judith. 1995. *Unthinking Modernity: Innis, McLuhan, and the Frankfurt School*. Montreal: McGill-Queen's University Press.

Steimatsky, Noa. 1998. "Pasolini on *Terra Sancta*: Towards a Theology of Film." *Yale Journal of Criticism* 11, no. 1: 239–58.

———. 2003. "Pasolini on *Terra Sancta*: Towards a Theology of Film." In *Rites of Realism: Essays on Corporeal Cinema*, edited by Ivone Margulies, 245–69. Durham, NC: Duke University Press.

———. 2008. *Italian Locations: Reinhabiting the Past in Postwar Cinema*. Minneapolis: University of Minnesota Press.

Stewart, Jeffrey C. 2018. *The New Negro: The Life of Alain Locke*. New York: Oxford University Press.

Strange, Susan. 1996. *The Retreat of the State: The Diffusion of Power in the World Economy*. Cambridge: Cambridge University Press.

Streitfeld, David. 2017. "Changing the World, but Not Quite the Way They Had Imagined." *New York Times*, October 13, 2017, A1, A11.

Strong-Wilson, Teresa. 2008. *Bringing Memory Forward*. New York: Peter Lang.

Sullivan, Andrew. 2015. "Democracies End When They Are Too Democratic. And Right Now, America is a Breeding Ground for Tyranny." *New York Magazine*, May 2–15, 30–4, 36, 101–3.

Summit, Jennifer, and Blakey Vermeule. 2018. *Actions Versus Contemplation: Why An Ancient Debate Still Matters*. Chicago: University of Chicago Press.

Sunstein, Cass R. 2018. "It Can Happen Here." *New York Review of Books*, June 28, 64–5.

Sztajn, Paola, Jere Confrey, P. Holt Wilson, and Cynthia Edgington. 2012. "Learning Trajectory Based Instruction: Toward a Theory of Teaching." *Educational Researcher* 41, no. 5: 147–56.

Taba, Hilda. 1932. *The Dynamics of Education: A Methodology of Progressive Educational Thought*. With a foreword by William Heard Kilpatrick. New York: Harcourt, Brace and Company.

———. 1945. "General Techniques of Curriculum Planning." In *American Education in the Post War Period: Curriculum Reconstruction*, the forty-fourth yearbook, part 1 (1945), of the National Society for the Study of Education, ch. 5, 12, 267.

———. 1962. *Curriculum Development: Theory and Practice*. New York: Harcourt, Brace & World, Inc.

Taubman, Peter M. 1990. "Achieving the Right Distance." *Educational Theory* 40, no. 1: 121–33.

———. 2009. *Teaching by Numbers: Deconstructing the Discourse of Standards and Accountability in Education*. New York: Routledge.

———. 2011. *Disavowed Knowledge*. New York: Routledge.

Taylor, Charles. (1982) 2006. *Radical Tories: The Conservative Tradition in Canada*. Afterword by Rudyard Griffiths. Toronto: Anansi.

Thibon, Gustave. (1947) 2002. Introduction to Weil, *Gravity and Grace*, vii–xl.

Thirty Schools. 1943. *Thirty Schools Tell Their Story: Each School Writes of Its Participation in the Eight-Year Study*. New York: Harper & Brothers.

Toews, John. 2004. *Becoming Historical: Cultural Reformation and Public Memory in Early Nineteenth-Century Berlin*. New York: Cambridge University Press.

Tomkins, George S. 1986. *A Common Countenance: Stability and Change in the Canadian Curriculum*. Scarborough, ON: Prentice-Hall. Reissued in 2008 by Pacific Educational Press (Vancouver).

———. (1986) 2008. *A Common Countenance: Stability and Change in the Canadian Curriculum*. Vancouver, CANADA: Pacific Educational Press.

Tradigo, Alfredo. 2006. *Icons and Saints of the Eastern Orthodox Church*. Translated by Stephen Sartarelli. Los Angeles: The J. Paul Getty Museum.

Trilling, Lionel. 1972. *Sincerity and Authenticity*. Cambridge, MA: Harvard University Press.

Tröhler, Daniel. 2011. *Languages of Education: Protestant Legacies, National Identities, and Global Aspirations*. New York: Routledge.

———. 2016. "Educationalization of Social Problems and the Educationalization of the Modern World." *Encyclopedia of Educational Philosophy and Theory*, edited by Michael A. Peters, 1–10. Singapore: Springer.

Trudel, Marcel. 2013. *Canada's Forgotten Slaves: Two Hundred Years of Bondage*. With the collaboration of Micheline D'Allaire. Translated by George Tombs. Montreal: Véhicule Press.

Trueit, Donna, ed. 2012. *Pragmatism, Postmodernism, Complexity Theory: The Fascinating Imaginative Realm of William E. Doll, Jr*. New York: Routledge.

Tyler, Ralph W. 1949. *Basic Principles of Curriculum and Instruction*. Chicago, IL: University of Chicago Press.

Umar, Yusuf K. 1992. "The Philosophical Context of George Grant's Political Thought." In Umar and Cooper, *George Grant and the Future of Canada*, 1–16.

Umar, Yusuf K., and Barry Cooper, ed. 1992. *George Grant and the Future of Canada*. Calgary, AB: University of Calgary Press.

Viano, Maurizio. 1993. *A Certain Realism: Making Use of Pasolini's Film Theory and Practice*. Berkeley: University of California Press.

Vries, Hent de. 2005. "Instances." In Caputo and Scanlon, *Augustine and Postmodernism*, 68–94.

Walsh, Declan, Ihsanullah Tipu Mehsud, and Ismail Khan. 2016. "Taliban Attack on Pakistan School, Renewing Fears." *New York Times*, January 21, 2016, A1, A10.

Walsh, Susan, Barbara Bickel, and Carl Leggo, ed. 2014. *Arts-based and Contemplative Practices in Research and Teaching: Honoring Presence*. New York: Routledge.

Wang, Hongyu. 2004. *The Call from the Stranger on a Journey Home: Curriculum in a Third Space*. New York: Peter Lang.

———. 2014. "A Nonviolent Perspective on Internationalizing Curriculum Studies." In Pinar, *International Handbook of Curriculum Research*, 67–76.

Wapner, Paul. 2010. *Living Through the End of Nature: The Future of American Environmentalism*. Cambridge, MA: MIT Press.

Ward, Bruce. 1990. "George Grant and the Problem of Theodicy in Western Christianity." In Whillier, *Two Theological Languages by George Grant and Other Essays in Honour of His Work*, 94–104.

Ware, Kallistos. 2012. Foreword to *Ponder These Things: Praying with Icons of the Virgin* by Rowan Williams, ix–xi. Brewster, MA: Paraclete Press.

Warren, David. 1990. "On George Grant's Nationalism." In Emberley, *By Loving Our Own*, 59–73.

Watson, Alexander John. 2007. *Marginal Man: The Dark Vision of Harold Innis*. Toronto: University of Toronto Press.

Weaver, John A. 2010. "The Posthuman Condition: A Complicated Conversation." In *Curriculum Studies Handbook: The Next Moment*, edited by Erik Malewski, 190–200. New York: Routledge.

Webster's New Collegiate Dictionary. 1975. Springfield, MA: G. & C. Merriam Company.

Weeks, I. G. 1990. "Two Uses Of Secrecy: Leo Strauss and George Grant." In Whillier, *Two Theological Languages by George Grant and Other Essays in Honour of His Work*, 82–93.

Weil, Simone. (1947) 2002. *Gravity and Grace*. With an introduction and postscript by Gustave Thibon. Translated by Emma Crawford and Mario van der Ruhr. London and New York: Routledge.

Weintraub, Karl Joachim. 1978. *The Value of the Individual: Self and Circumstance in Autobiography*. Chicago: University of Chicago Press.

Weitz, Eric D. 2007. *Weimar Germany: Promise and Tragedy*. Princeton, NJ: Princeton University Press.

Welchman, Alistair. 2016. "Eternity in Kant and Post-Kantian European Thought." In Melamed, *Eternity*, 179–225.

Westbrook, Robert. 1991. *John Dewey and American Philosophy*. Ithaca, NY: Cornell University Press.

Wexler, Philip. 1996. *Holy Sparks*. New York: St. Martin's.

———. 2013. *Mystical Sociology: Toward Cosmic Social Theory*. New York: Peter Lang.

Wexler, Philip, and Yotam Hotam, ed. 2015. *New Social Foundations for Education: Education in "Post-Secular" Society*. New York: Peter Lang.

Whillier, Wayne. 1990a. Introduction to *Two Theological Languages by George Grant and Other Essays in Honour of His Work*, edited by Wayne Whillier, iii–vi. Queenston, ON: Edwin Mellen Press.

———. 1990b. "George Grant and Leo Strauss: A Parting of the Way." In Whillier, *Two Theological Languages by George Grant and Other Essays in Honour of His Work*, 63–81.

Wilberding, James G. 2016. "Eternity in Ancient Philosophy." In Melamed, *Eternity*, 14–55.

Williams, Rowan. 2012. *Ponder These Things: Praying with Icons of the Virgin*. Brewster, MA: Paraclete Press.

Williamson, Ben. 2013. *The Future of the Curriculum: School Knowledge in the Digital Age*. Cambridge, MA: MIT Press.

Williamson, Elizabeth. 2018. "Sandy Hook Suits Target Fabulist And Online 'Post-Truth' Culture." *New York Times*, May 24, 2018, A1, A16.

Willinsky, John. 2006. *The Access Principle: The Case for Open Access to Research and Scholarship*. Cambridge, MA: MIT Press.

Wingfield, Rick. 2016. "Seattle, Vancouver Eye Tech Ambitions Without Borders." *Bellingham Herald*, October 3, 2016. 1A–2A.

Wiskus, Jessica. 2013. *The Rhythm of Thought: Art, Literature, and Music after Merleau-Ponty*. Chicago: University of Chicago Press.

Zaretsky, Eli. 2004. *Secrets of the Soul: A Social and Cultural History of Psychoanalysis*. New York: Alfred A. Knopf.

Zernike, Kate. 2016. "How Trump's Choice for Education Shaped Schools in Detroit." *New York Times*, December 13, 2016, A12, A21.

Zhang, Hua, and William F. Pinar, ed. 2015. *Autobiography and Teacher Development in China: Subjectivity and Culture in Curriculum Reform*. New York: Palgrave Macmillan.

Ziarek, Ewa Plonowska. 2001. *An Ethics of Dissensus: Postmodernity, Feminism, and the Politics of Radical Democracy*. Stanford, CA: Stanford University Press.

Zimmerman, Jonathan. 2002. *Whose America? Culture Wars in the Public Schools*. Cambridge, MA: Harvard University Press.

Zylstra, Bernard. 1978. "Philosophy, Revelation and Modernity: Crossroads in the Thought of George Grant." In Schmidt, *George Grant in Process*, 148–56.

Earlier versions and permissions to quote

Earlier and abbreviated versions of chapters 2 and 4 appeared as follows:

"The First Task of Thought in Our Time," *Critical Literacy: Theories and Practices* 7, no. 1 (2013): 1–16. Reprinted in William F Pinar, *Educational Experience as Lived*, New York: Routledge, 2015.

"Modernity, Technology, Nationality," Critical Literacy: Theories and Practices 7, no. 2 (2013): 3–19.

"George Grant's Cosmopolitan Critique of Education," *Encounters/ Encuentros/Rencontres on Education* 14 (2013): 49–69.

"On the Teachings of George Grant," *Critical Studies in Education* 55, no. 1 (2014): 8–17.

Index

Education

Series editors: Nicholas Ng-A-Fook and Carole Fleuret

Our educational series seeks to advance thought-provoking research within the broader field of education. Scholarly works in this series examine educational research from a multidisciplinary perspective and address a variety of issues in the field including curriculum studies, arts-based education, educational philosophy, life writing, foundations in education, teacher education, evaluation, and counselling.

Previous titles in this collection

For a complete list of our titles in this series, see:
press.uottawa.ca/series/contemporary-society/education.html

www.ingramcontent.com/pod-product-compliance
Lightning Source LLC
Chambersburg PA
CBHW081401090726
47908CB00012B/2748